IP Solutions for Windows® 2000

ISBN 0-13-091170-4

90000

9 780130 911704

PRENTICE HALL PTR MICROSOFT® TECHNOLOGIES SERIES

NETWORKING

- IP Solutions for Windows 2000
  Ammann
- Microsoft Technology: Networking, Concepts, Tools
  Woodard, Gattuccio, Brain
- NT Network Programming Toolkit
  Murphy
- Building COM Applications with Internet Explorer
  Loveman
- Understanding DCOM
  Rubin, Brain
- Web Database Development for Windows Platforms
  Gutierrez

PROGRAMMING

- Windows 2000 Kernel Debugging
  McDowell
- Windows Script Host
  Aitken
- The Windows 2000 Device Driver Book, Second Edition
  Baker, Lozano
- Win32 System Services: The Heart of Windows 98 and Windows 2000, Third Edition
  Brain, Reeves
- Programming the WIN32 API and UNIX System Services
  Merusi
- Windows CE 3.0: Application Programming
  Grattan, Brain
- The Visual Basic Style Guide
  Patrick
- Windows Shell Programming
  Seely
- Windows Installer Complete
  Easter
- Windows 2000 Web Applications Developer's Guide
  Yager
- Developing Windows Solutions with Office 2000 Components and VBA
  Aitken
- Multithreaded Programming with Win32
  Pham, Garg
- Developing Professional Applications for Windows 98 and NT Using MFC, Third Edition
  Brain, Lovette
- Introduction to Windows 98 Programming
  Murray, Pappas
- The COM and COM+ Programming Primer
  Gordon
- Understanding and Programming COM+: A Practical Guide to Windows 2000 DNA
  Oberg
- Distributed COM Application Development Using Visual C++ 6.0
  Maloney
- The Essence of COM, Third Edition
  Platt
- COM-CORBA Interoperability
  Geraghty, Joyce, Moriarty, Noone
- MFC Programming in C++ with the Standard Template Libraries
  Murray, Pappas
- Introduction to MFC Programming with Visual C++
  Jones
- Visual C++ Templates
  Murray, Pappas
- Visual Basic Object and Component Handbook
  Vogel
- Visual Basic 6: Error Coding and Layering
  Gill
- ADO Programming in Visual Basic 6
  Holzner
- Visual Basic 6: Design, Specification, and Objects
  Hollis
- ASP/MTS/ADSI Web Security
  Harrison

BACKOFFICE

- Microsoft SQL Server 2000 Optimization Guide
  Fields
- BizTalk: Implementing Business-To-Business E-Commerce
  Kobielus
- Designing Enterprise Solutions with Microsoft Technologies
  Kemp, Kemp, Goncalves
- Microsoft Site Server 3.0 Commerce Edition
  Libertone, Scoppa
- Building Microsoft SQL Server 7 Web Sites
  Byrne
- Optimizing SQL Server 7
  Schneider, Goncalves

ADMINISTRATION

- Tuning and Sizing Windows 2000 for Maximum Performance
  Aubley
- Windows 2000 Cluster Server Guidebook
  Libertone
- Windows 2000 Hardware and Disk Management
  Simmons
- Windows 2000 Server: Management and Control, Third Edition
  Spencer, Goncalves
- Creating Active Directory Infrastructures
  Simmons
- Windows 2000 Registry
  Sanna
- Configuring Windows 2000 Server
  Simmons
- Supporting Windows NT and 2000 Workstation and Server
  Mohr
- Zero Administration Kit for Windows
  McInerney
- Windows NT 4.0 Server Security Guide
  Goncalves
- Windows NT Security
  McInerney

CERTIFICATION

- Core MCSE: Windows 2000 Edition
  Dell
- Core MCSE: Designing a Windows 2000 Directory Services Infrastructure
  Simmons
- MCSE: Implementing and Supporting Windows 98
  Dell
- Core MCSE
  Dell
- Core MCSE: Networking Essentials
  Keogh
- MCSE: Administering Microsoft SQL Server 7
  Byrne
- MCSE: Implementing and Supporting Microsoft Exchange Server 5.5
  Goncalves
- MCSE: Internetworking with Microsoft TCP/IP
  Ryvkin, Houde, Hoffman
- MCSE: Implementing and Supporting Microsoft Proxy Server 2.0
  Ryvkin, Hoffman
- MCSE: Implementing and Supporting Microsoft SNA Server 4.0
  Mariscal
- MCSE: Implementing and Supporting Microsoft Internet Information Server 4
  Dell
- MCSE: Implementing and Supporting Web Sites Using Microsoft Site Server 3
  Goncalves
- MCSE: Microsoft System Management Server 2
  Jewett
- MCSE: Implementing and Supporting Internet Explorer 5
  Dell
- Core MCSD: Designing and Implementing Desktop Applications with Microsoft Visual Basic 6
  Holzner
- MCSD: Planning and Implementing SQL Server 7
  Vacca
- MCSD: Designing and Implementing Web Sites with Microsoft FrontPage 98
  Karlins

PRENTICE HALL PTR MICROSOFT® TECHNOLOGIES SERIES

IP Solutions for Windows® 2000

Paul T. Ammann

PH PTR

Prentice Hall PTR, Upper Saddle River, NJ 07458
www.phptr.com

Library of Congress Cataloging-in-Publication Data

Ammann, Paul T.
IP solutions for windows 2000 / Paul Ammann.
p. cm. –
Includes bibliographical references and index.
ISBN 0-13-091170-4
1. TCP/IP (Computer network protocol) 2. Computer networks–Management. I. Title.

TK5105.585 .A45 2001
005.7'1376–dc21 00-066541

Editorial/Production Supervision: *Jan H. Schwartz*
Acquisitions Editor: *Jill Pisoni*
Marketing Manager: *Dan DePasquale*
Buyer: *Maura Zaldivar*
Cover Design Direction: *Jerry Votta*
Cover Design: *Nina Scuderi*
Art Director: *Gail Cocker-Bogusz*
Interior Series Design: *Meg VanArsdale*
Editorial Assistant: *Justin Somma*
Composition: *PreTeX, Inc.*

Prentice-Hall, Inc.
Upper Saddle River, NJ 07458

Prentice Hall books are widely used by corporations and government agencies for training, marketing, and resale.

The publisher offers discounts on this book when ordered in bulk quantities. For more information, contact Corporate Sales Department, phone: 800-382-3419; fax: 201-236-7141; email: corpsales@prenhall.com or write Corporate Sales Department, Prentice Hall PTR, One Lake Street, Upper Saddle River, NJ 07458.

Printed in the United States of America

10 9 8 7 6 5 4 3 2 1

ISBN 0-13-091170-4

Prentice-Hall International (UK) Limited, *London*
Prentice-Hall of Australia Pty. Limited, *Sydney*
Prentice-Hall Canada Inc., *Toronto*
Prentice-Hall Hispanoamericana, S.A., *Mexico*
Prentice-Hall of India Private Limited, *New Delhi*
Prentice-Hall of Japan, Inc., *Tokyo*
Pearson Education Asia Pte. Ltd.
Editora Prentice-Hall do Brasil, Ltda., *Rio de Janeiro*

This book is dedicated to my wife Eve, who is the sunshine of my life.

CONTENTS

PREFACE

TCP/IP is available as a standard protocol included with all Windows operating systems and is installed by default in Windows 2000. IP Solutions for Windows 2000 focuses on Microsoft's implementation of TCP/IP, DHCP, WINS, and DNS in Windows 2000. It discusses guidelines for planning, testing, and implementing substantial changes such as the setup or migration of a Windows 2000 TCP/IP network. This is the one book that focuses on the tools and techniques for implementing and working with Windows 2000 TCP/IP connectivity.

As the community of administrators using Microsoft TCP/IP matures, your need for reliable, technically focused information will increase. This publication provides real-world implementation advice using the latest TCP/IP advances, approaching these topics from the perspective of the true networking professional. *IP Solutions for Windows 2000* cuts through the complexities and provides the most informative and complex reference book on Windows-based TCP/IP topics. This book is a tutorial-reference hybrid, focusing on how Microsoft TCP/IP works, using practical examples. Concepts essential to TCP/IP administration will be explained thoroughly, then related to the practical use of Microsoft TCP/IP in a serious network environment. This book begins with coverage of TCP/IP architecture and advanced installation and configuration issues, then moves on to cover routing with TCP/IP, DHCP management, WINS/DNS name resolution, and dynamic DNS.

It is the main intention of the author, however, to provide in-depth information on the most current protocols, technologies, and implementations of TCP/IP under Windows 2000 that are actually used and deployed throughout the Internet as well as in private TCP/IP networks. This material has been compiled as both an overview and a technical reference for advanced TCP/IP users and experts in this area who want to broaden their scope of knowledge.

How This Book Is Laid Out

This book covers four main areas of Windows 2000: TCP/IP, DHCP, WINS, and DNS. The discussion focuses on what's new with each of these applications under Windows 2000 and how this difference may vary from Windows NT 4.0 and from the Internet Engineering Task Force (IETF) standards.

From there, the focus is be on planning, configuring, managing, supporting clients, setting up options, modifying server defaults, monitoring, optimizing, and interoperability issues, depending on the application. Practical examples are used throughout these discussions.

Finally, a review of the majority of menu options under the MMC for each application is presented. These sections, like the rest of the book, have been cross-referenced to provide you with a thorough understanding of Microsoft TCP/IP.

ACKNOWLEDGMENTS

I would like to extend a warm thank you to Jill Pisoni and to everyone at Prentice Hall for all their hard work in making this book possible.

I would also like to thank Thomas A. Maufer for doing the technical review and playing devil's advocate to help ensure the accuracy of the information presented to you in this book.

ONE

TCP/IP Overview

TCP/IP for Windows 2000

Transmission Control Protocol/Internet Protocol (TCP/IP) for Windows 2000 is:

- Networking software based on industry-standard networking protocols.
- A scalable, enterprise networking protocol that supports the connection of your Windows-based computer to both LAN and WAN environments.
- Core technologies and utilities for enabling your Windows-based computer to connect to and share information with dissimilar systems.
- A foundation for gaining access to global Internet services, such as the World Wide Web and File Transfer Protocol (FTP) servers.
- A robust, scalable, cross-platform, client/server framework.

Because most modern operating systems support the TCP/IP protocol suite, you can use TCP/IP to share information with a wide variety of systems and resources, as shown in the Figure 1-1.

TCP/IP for Windows 2000 provides basic TCP/IP utilities that enable a computer running Windows 2000 to connect and share information with other Microsoft and non-Microsoft systems, including:

- Internet hosts
- Apple Macintosh OS systems
- IBM mainframes
- UNIX systems
- Open VMS systems

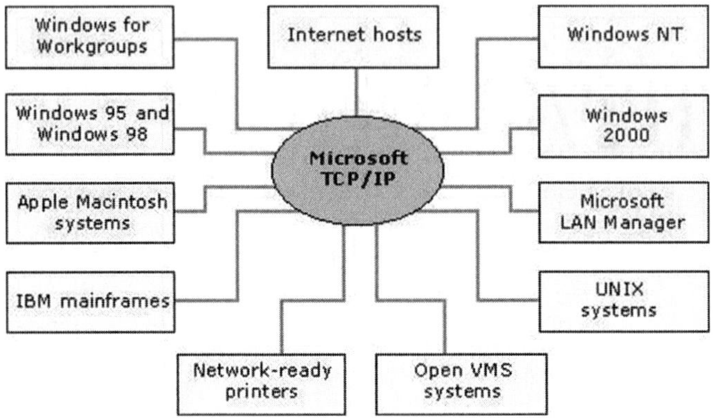

FIGURE 1–1 *How TCP/IP supports open system use*

- Microsoft Windows NT and Windows 2000
- Microsoft Windows 98
- Microsoft Windows 95
- Microsoft Windows for Workgroups
- Microsoft LAN Manager
- Network-ready printers, such as HP LaserJet series printers that use HP JetDirect cards

TCP/IP Background

TCP/IP is an industry-standard suite of protocols designed for large-scale internetworks that span LAN and WAN environments.

As the timeline in Figure 1-2 shows, the origins of TCP/IP began in 1969, when the U.S. Department of Defense (DoD) commissioned the Advanced Research Projects Agency Network (ARPANET).

The ARPANET was the result of a resource-sharing experiment. The purpose was to provide high-speed network communication links between various supercomputers located at various regional sites within the United States.

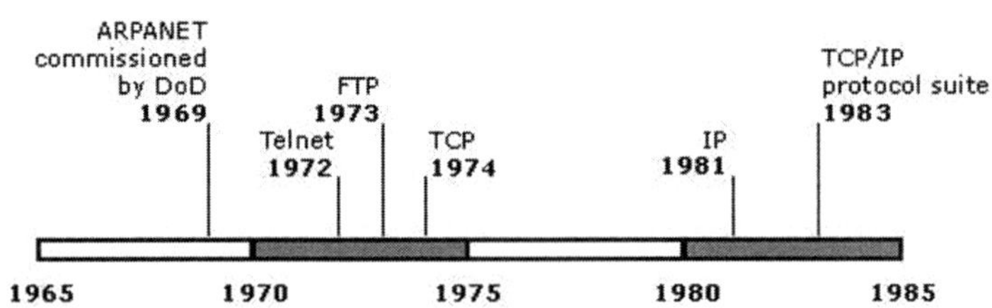

FIGURE 1–2 *Timeline for TCP/IP*

Early protocols such as Telnet (for virtual terminal emulation) and the FTP were first developed to specify basic utilities needed for sharing information across the ARPANET. As the ARPANET grew in size and scope, two other important protocols appeared:

- In 1974, the Transmission Control Protocol (TCP) was introduced as a draft specification that described how to build a reliable, host-to-host data transfer service over a network.
- In 1981, the Internet Protocol (IP) was introduced in draft form and described how to implement an addressing standard and route packets between interconnected networks.

On January 1, 1983, ARPANET began to require standard use of the TCP and IP protocols for all network traffic and essential communication. From this date forward, ARPANET started to become more widely known as the *Internet,* and its required protocols started to become more widely known as the *TCP/IP protocol suite.*

The TCP/IP protocol suite is implemented in a variety of TCP/IP software offerings available for use with many computing platforms. Today, TCP/IP software remains widely in use on the Internet and is used often for building large, routed, private internetworks.

The TCP/IP Model

TCP/IP is based on a four-layer reference model. All protocols that belong to the TCP/IP protocol suite are located in the top three layers of this model.

As shown in Figure 1-3, each layer of the TCP/IP model corresponds to one or more layers of the seven-layer Open Systems Interconnection (OSI) reference model proposed by the International Standards Organization (ISO).

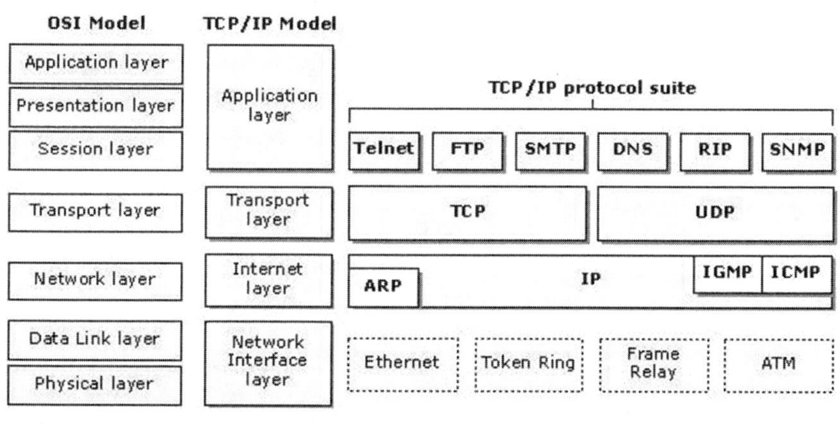

FIGURE 1–3 *OSI layer model and TCP/IP model*

The types of services performed and protocols used at each layer within the TCP/IP model are described in more detail in Table 1.1.

TABLE 1.1 *Services and Protocols in the TCP/IP Model*

Layer	Description	Protocols
Application	Defines TCP/IP application protocols and how host programs interface with transport layer services to use the network.	HTTP, Telnet, FTP, TFTP, SNMP, DNS, SMTP, X Windows, other application protocols
Transport	Provides communication session management between host computers. Defines the level of service and status of the connection used when transporting data.	TCP, UDP, RTP
Internet	Packages data into IP datagrams, which contain source and destination address information that is used to forward the datagrams between hosts and across networks. Performs routing of IP datagrams.	IP, ICMP, ARP, RARP
Network interface	Specifies details of how data is physically sent through the network, including how bits are electrically signaled by hardware devices that interface directly with a network medium, such as coaxial cable, optical fiber, or twisted-pair copper wire.	Ethernet, Token Ring, FDDI, X.25, Frame Relay, RS-232, v.35

For more information about Address Resolution Protocol (ARP), Internet Control Message Protocol (ICMP), Internet Group Management Protocol (IGMP), User Datagram Protocol (UDP), IP, and TCP, see "Understanding TCP/IP" in this chapter.

Note The OSI Reference Model (OSI RM) is not specific to TCP/IP. Beginning in the late 1970s, the ISO developed it as a generic framework describing all aspects of communication protocols. The OSI RM is a widely known and accepted reference model in the data communications field and is used here only for comparison purposes.

TCP/IP Utilities

Windows 2000 includes three types of TCP/IP-based utilities:

- Connectivity utilities that you can use to interact with and use resources on a variety of Microsoft and non-Microsoft hosts, such as UNIX systems.
- Diagnostic utilities that you can use to detect and resolve networking problems.
- TCP/IP server software that provides printing and publishing services to TCP/IP-based clients on Windows 2000.

Tables 1.2, 1.3, and 1.4 briefly describe both familiar and some new TCP/IP-based utilities in Windows 2000. For more information on using these utilities and their syntax, refer to Appendix E, "TCP/IP Utilities."

TABLE 1.2 *Connectivity Utilities*

Utility	Description
FTP	Transfers files of any size between Windows 2000 and any computer running FTP server software.
LPR	Sends print jobs to remote UNIX printers managed by Line Printer Daemon (LPD) print server software.
RCP	Copies files between Windows 2000 and computers running Remote Copy Protocol (RCP) server software.
REXEC	Executes processes on remote computers.
RSH	Runs commands on a computer running Remote Shell (RSH) server software.
TELNET	Uses terminal-based login to remotely access network devices that are running Telnet server software.
TFTP	Transfers small files between Windows 2000 and computers running Trivial File Transfer Protocol (TFTP) server software.

TABLE 1.3 *Diagnostic Utilities*

Utility	Description
ARP	Displays and modifies the ARP cache. This cache is a local table used by Windows 2000 to resolve IP addresses to media access control addresses used on the local network.
Hostname	Returns the host name of the local computer.
IPCONFIG	Displays the current TCP/IP configuration. Also used to manually release and renew TCP/IP configurations assigned by a DHCP server.
LPQ	Obtains print queue status information from computers running LPD print server software.
NBSTAT	Displays the local NetBIOS name table, a table of NetBIOS names registered by local applications, and the NetBIOS name cache, a local cache listing of NetBIOS computer names that have been resolved to IP addresses.
Netstat	Displays TCP/IP protocol session information.
NSLOOKUP	Checks records, domain host aliases, domain host services, and operating system information by querying Domain Name System (DNS) servers.
PING	Verifies configurations and tests IP connectivity.
ROUTE	Displays or modifies the local routing table.
TRACERT	Traces the route a packet takes to a destination.
PATHPING	Traces the route a packet takes to a destination and displays information on packet losses for each router in the path. Pathping can also be used to troubleshoot Quality of Service (QoS) connectivity.

TABLE 1.4 *Server-based Software*

Server software	Description
TCP/IP Printing service	The TCP/IP Printing service offers an LPD printing service for computers running Windows 2000. This service allows UNIX computers to send print jobs to computers running Windows 2000 by using the Line Printer Remote (LPR) utility for printing.
Internet Information Services	Internet Information Services (IIS) offers Web, Gopher, and FTP server software for providing TCP/IP-based publishing services. IIS is provided with Windows 2000 Server to offer an enterprise-ready Web server to use with an unlimited number of simultaneous connections.
Peer Web Services	Peer Web Services is supplied with Windows 2000 Professional to provide Web publishing services similar to those offered by IIS for serving fewer than 10 simultaneous connections.

New TCP/IP Features for Windows 2000

TCP/IP for Windows 2000 has been updated to include several features that simplify configuration on a single subnet and optimize TCP performance in a wider variety of network environments.

These new features include support for:

- Automatic private address configuration (pre-standard).
- Large TCP windows (RFC 1323).
- TCP selective acknowledgments ("sack") (RFC 2018).
- Better TCP round trip time (RTT) estimation (RFC 1323).
- ICMP Router Discovery Protocol (RFC 1256).
- DNS caching.
- Disabling NetBIOS over TCP/IP.

Automatic Private Address Configuration

Automatic Private IP Addressing (APIPA) is used to allocate addresses within subnetworks that either do not have a local DHCP server or do not have a routed path to a DHCP server on another subnetwork.

By default, a computer running Windows 2000 first tries to contact a DHCP server to obtain an IP address and related configuration information for each installed network connection:

- If a DHCP server is reached and the leased configuration is successful, TCP/IP configuration is completed.
- If a DHCP server is not reached, the computer instead uses APIPA to automatically configure TCP/IP. When you use APIPA, Windows 2000

determines an address in the reserved IP address range from 169.254.1.1 through 169.254.254.254. This address is used as a temporary IP address configuration until a DHCP server is located. The subnet mask is set to 255.255.0.0.

The APIPA range of IP addresses (169.254.0.0/16) has been set aside for use in IP address autoconfiguration by the Internet Assigned Numbers Authority (IANA; *www.iana.org/*). Any IP addresses within this range are not usable on the Internet.

APIPA eliminates IP address configuration for single-network small office or home office networks that are not connected to the Internet.

Large TCP Windows

Window size reflects the maximum number of packets that can be sent without waiting for positive acknowledgment. Large TCP windows improve TCP/IP performance by allowing large amounts of data to be in transit between the sender and receiver. In typical TCP-based communication, the maximum window size is usually fixed at the onset of connection and is often statically limited to 64 kilobytes (65,536 bytes).

With large window support, the TCP connection endpoints can dynamically recalculate and optimize the actual window size by using a TCP option as needed during longer sessions. With this option, more data packets are in transit on the network at one time, which increases throughput by reducing or eliminating the time that either TCP endpoint spends waiting for new data after it has acknowledged what it has already received.

For more information about large TCP windows, see RFC 1323, "TCP Extensions for High Performance."

Selective Acknowledgments

In typical TCP-based communication, acknowledgments are cumulative. TCP only acknowledges segments received that are contiguous with previously acknowledged segments. Noncontiguous segments—segments received out of sequence—are not explicitly acknowledged. TCP requires that segments are received and acknowledged within a brief time period, or the missing segment, and all subsequent segments that follow it, must be retransmitted.

Selective acknowledgments are a recent TCP option that allow the receiver to selectively notify and request that a sender resend only data that is actually missing. This results in smaller amounts of data that require retransmission and better use of network bandwidth, provided that both TCP endpoints support this option.

For more information about selective acknowledgments, see RFC 2018, "TCP Selective Acknowledgment Options."

Better RTT Estimation

Round trip time (RTA) is used by TCP to estimate the amount of time that is needed for round trip communication between a sender and a receiver. Windows 2000 supports the use of the TCP Round Trip Time Measurement option to improve how RTT is estimated. By calculating more accurate RTT information more often, TCP uses better estimates for setting retransmission timers, which helps improve overall TCP speed and performance.

Improvements in estimating RTT help significantly when TCP connections include long-delay network links, such as long-distance or intercontinental WAN links, or wireless or satellite links.

For more information about TCP round trip time measurement, see RFC 1323.

ICMP Router Discovery

Internet Control Message Protocol Router Discovery messages are used to discover the default gateway on a network segment when a default gateway is either not manually configured or was not specified by DHCP. ICMP Router Discovery is implemented by use of two ICMP message types: the router solicitation and the router advertisement. A router solicitation packet is sent by a host when it needs to discover the routers on the network. Routers send router advertisement packets either on demand (i.e., in response to a router solicitation) or periodically (to notify hosts on the network that it is available). ICMP Router Discovery operates by default (as necessary) on TCP/IP for Windows 2000 hosts.

When a Windows 2000 Server computer (running the Routing and Remote Access service) is operating as a router, it can be configured to support the ICMP Router Discovery protocol as a router (e.g., it will send router advertisement messages when appropriate).

ICMP Router Discovery is described in RFC 1256, "ICMP Router Discovery Messages."

DNS Caching

The Windows 2000 DNS name resolver caches DNS name queries, and the cache can be viewed with the *ipconfig* utility. For specific information on the ipconfig command, refer to Appendix E.

Disabling NetBIOS over TCP/IP

With Windows 2000, you can disable NetBIOS over TCP/IP (NetBT) for each network connection. This feature is intended for computers that use only DNS name registration and resolution techniques and that communicate by using the Client for Microsoft Networks and the File and Print Sharing for Microsoft Networks components with other computers where NetBT is disabled. Examples of disabling NetBT include computers in specialized or secured roles for your network, such as an edge proxy server or bastion host in a firewall environment, where NetBT support is not required or desired.

The following are considerations for disabling NetBT on computers running Windows 2000:

- The computer no longer listens for traffic to the NetBIOS datagram service at UDP port 138, the NetBIOS name service at UDP port 137, and the NetBIOS session service at TCP port 139.
- TCP/IP-based connections that use the Client for Microsoft Networks and the File and Print Sharing for Microsoft Networks components are possible only to other computers that have NetBT disabled. This affects the ability to see computers on the network and connect to file shares and network printers.
- NetBIOS name resolution techniques, such as Windows Internet Name Service (WINS), local subnet broadcasts, and the LAN Manager Hosts (Lmhosts) file, are no longer used. All name resolution occurs through DNS queries and the Hosts file.
- If the computer needs to participate in WINS as a client, it must have NetBT enabled on at least one network connection.
- If a Windows 2000 Server computer needs to run the WINS service, it must have NetBT enabled on at least one network connection.

A good example of disabling NetBT is for a server computer that has a connection to a private network and a connection to an external network, such as the Internet. In this case, NetBT is not required for the Internet connection. By disabling NetBT on only the Internet connection, the dual-homed computer continues to function as either a WINS server or client for the internal network, and WINS clients are still serviced for connections made by using other physical network adapters installed on the computer.

What Is A Dual-Homed System? The dual-homed system is a computer that includes at least two network interface cards. Windows 2000 supports this configuration, and you can enable or disable routing between the cards, depending on your requirements. Routing is disabled between the network interface cards in the dual-homed system so that the application-level software can control how traffic is handled between networks.

There is one other use for this type of configuration. Assume that the dual-homed host runs an HTTP Web service. If routing is disabled, then the host on either network can still access the Web services, but packets cannot be exchanged between the networks. For example, if several departments in an organization need to share the same Web server but you don't want to create a routable link between the departments, you could use this configuration.

You can disable NetBT on the **WINS** tab in the properties of the TCP/IP protocol. For information about configuring TCP/IP to use WINS, see Chapter 2, "Installing, Managing, and Diagnosing TCP/IP." A vendor-specific DHCP option has been defined by Microsoft that allows NetBT to be enabled or disabled by the DHCP server.

Additional Feature Information

For additional information about TCP/IP performance enhancements and features in Windows 2000, see the RFC documents previously listed. For information about obtaining RFC documents, see Appendix A, "TCP/IP Resources."

Security Features of TCP/IP for Windows 2000

TCP/IP for Windows 2000 incorporates security features that provide protection of the TCP/IP data as it is sent on the network and configuration of the types of local host traffic that are processed.

Internet Protocol Security

Internet Protocol security (IPSec) is a set of Internet standards employing cryptographic algorithms to provide the following:

- *Confidentiality*. IPSec traffic may be encrypted. Such traffic, when captured by a third party, is unintelligible without knowledge of the mutually determined *key* that each endpoint used to encrypt the traffic.
- *Authentication*. IPSec traffic may be digitally signed with a mutually determined authentication key so that either IPSec peer can verify that every authenticated packet was sent by the other IPSec peer. Packets can be authenticated without being encrypted.
- *Data integrity*. IPSec traffic contains a cryptographic checksum that incorporates the encryption key. The receiver can verify that the packet was not modified in transit.

For information about configuring IPSec policies for TCP/IP, see Chapter 2.

TCP/IP Filtering

With TCP/IP filtering, a feature known as TCP/IP Security in Windows NT version 4.0, you can specify exactly which types of incoming TCP/IP traffic are processed for each IP interface. This feature is designed to isolate the traffic that is processed by Internet or intranet servers in the absence of other TCP/

IP filtering provided by the Routing and Remote Access service or other TCP/IP applications or services. TCP/IP filtering is disabled by default. This service effectively allows a limited "firewall" capability to be placed *inside* the TCP/IP stack.

TCP/IP filtering is a set of filters for inbound local host TCP/IP traffic. Local host traffic is traffic that is processed by the host because the destination IP address of inbound TCP/IP traffic is addressed to an assigned interface address, an appropriate subnet broadcast address, or a multicast group address that this end-station has joined. TCP/IP filtering does not apply to routed traffic that is forwarded between interfaces (this only matters for systems with multiple interfaces that run the Routing and Remote Access service and have been configured to act as routers).

With TCP/IP filtering, the local host's inbound TCP/IP traffic can be selectively permitted or denied based on each packet's:

- Destination TCP port
- Destination UDP port
- IP protocol

For information about configuring TCP/IP filtering, see Chapter 2.

Core Protocols of TCP/IP

This section covers

- Address Resolution Protocol
- Internet Protocol
- Internet Control Message Protocol
- Internet Group Management Protocol
- User Datagram Protocol
- Transmission Control Protocol

Address Resolution Protocol

Address Resolution Protocol is a TCP/IP standard defined in RFC 826, "Address Resolution Protocol (ARP)." ARP resolves IP addresses used by TCP/IP-based software to media access control (MAC) layer addresses used by LAN hardware. ARP provides the following protocol services to hosts located on the same physical network:

- MAC addresses are obtained by using a subnetwork broadcast request in the form of the question, What is the MAC address for a device that is currently using the enclosed IP address?
- When an ARP request is answered, both the sender of the ARP reply and the original ARP requester record each other's IP address and

media access control address as an entry in a local table called the ARP cache for future reference. Often, systems that hear the original ARP request also record that system's MAC and IP addresses, so that if they need to communicate with that IP address in the future, they will not need to send an ARP request before doing so.

HARDWARE ADDRESSING

Hardware built for use on LANs must contain a unique address programmed into the device by the manufacturer. For Ethernet and Token Ring LAN hardware, this address is known as a MAC address.

Each MAC address identifies the device within its own local physical subnetwork. The MAC address takes the form of a 6-byte number programmed into the read-only memory (ROM) of each physical hardware device, such as an Ethernet or Token Ring network adapter. MAC addresses are typically displayed in hexadecimal notation (for example, 00-AA-00-3F-89-4A).

Registration of MAC addresses is overseen under the authority of the Institute of Electrical and Electronics Engineers (IEEE). Currently, the IEEE registers and assigns unique numbers for the first three bytes of the media access control address to individual manufacturers. Each manufacturer can then assign the last three bytes of the media access control address to individual network adapters.

HOW ARP RESOLVES MAC ADDRESSES FOR LOCAL TRAFFIC

Figure 1-4 shows how ARP resolves IP addresses to MAC addresses for hosts on the same local subnetwork.

In this example, two TCP/IP hosts, Hosts A and B, are both located on the same physical network. Host A is assigned the IP address of 10.0.0.99 and Host B is assigned the IP address of 10.0.0.100.

When Host A tries to communicate with Host B, the following steps resolve Host B's software-assigned address (10.0.0.100) to Host B's hardware-assigned MAC address:

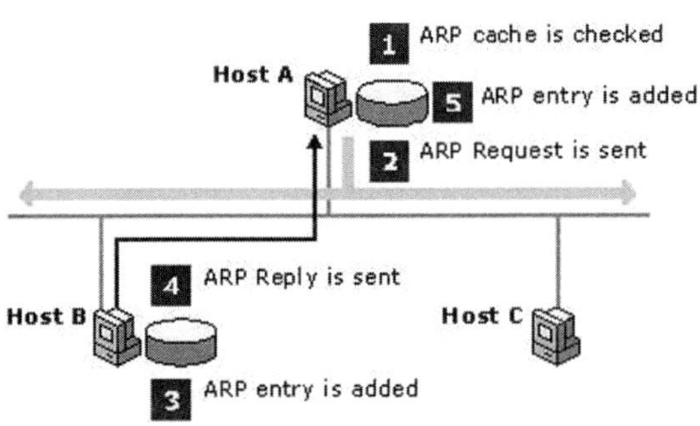

FIGURE 1–4 *How ARP resolves media access control addresses for local traffic*

1. Based on the contents of the routing table on Host A, IP determines that the forwarding IP address to be used to reach Host B is 10.0.0.100. Host A then checks its own local ARP cache for a MAC address matching Host B's IP address.
2. If Host A finds no mapping in the cache, it broadcasts an ARP request frame to all hosts on the local network with the question, What is the MAC address for 10.0.0.100? Both MAC and IP addresses for the source, Host A, are included in its ARP request.

   Each host on the local network receives the ARP request and checks for a match to its own IP address. If a host does not find a match, it discards the ARP request.
3. Host B determines that the IP address in the ARP request matches its own IP address and adds a MAC/IP address mapping for Host A to its local ARP cache.
4. Host B sends an ARP reply message containing its own MAC address directly back to Host A.
5. When Host A receives the ARP reply message from Host B, it updates its ARP cache with a MAC/IP address mapping for Host B.

Once the MAC address for Host B has been determined, Host A can send IP traffic to Host B by encapsulating the IP packets destined for Host B in MAC-layer frames destined for Host B's MAC address.

HOW ARP RESOLVES MAC ADDRESSES FOR REMOTE TRAFFIC

ARP is also used to forward IP datagrams to local routers for destinations that are not on the local subnetwork. In this situation, ARP resolves the MAC address of a router interface on the local network, usually the host's *default gateway*, which is either manually defined or learned by DHCP.

Figure 1-5 shows how ARP resolves IP addresses to MAC addresses for two hosts on different physical subnetworks connected by a common router.

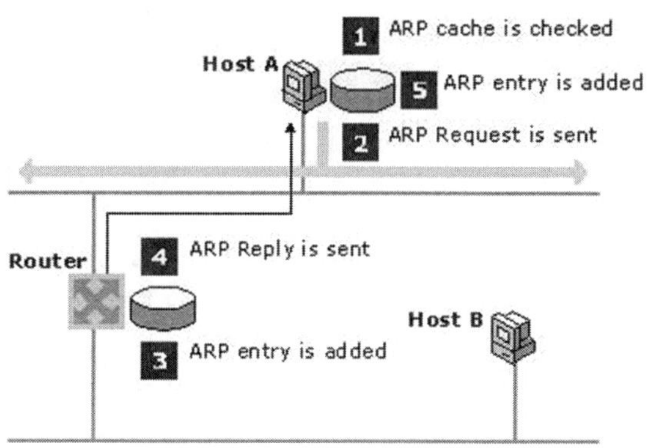

FIGURE 1–5 *How ARP resolves media access control addresses for remote traffic*

In this example, Host A is assigned an IP address of 10.0.0.99 and Host B uses an IP address of 192.168.0.99. Router interface 1 is on the same physical network as Host A and uses the IP address 10.0.0.1. Router interface 2 is on the same physical network as Host B and uses the IP address 192.168.0.1.

When Host A tries to communicate with Host B, the following steps resolve Router interface 1's software-assigned address (10.0.0.1) to its hardware-assigned MAC address:

1. Based on the contents of the routing table on Host A, IP determines that the forwarding IP address to be used to reach Host B is 10.0.0.1, the IP address of its default gateway. Host A then checks its own local ARP cache for a matching hardware address for 10.0.0.1.
2. If Host A finds no mapping in the cache, it broadcasts an ARP request frame to all hosts on the local network with the question, What is the MAC address for 10.0.0.1? Both MAC and IP addresses for the source, Host A, are included in the ARP request.

   Each host on the local network receives the ARP request and checks for a match to its own IP address. If a host does not find a match, it discards the ARP request.
3. The router determines that the IP address in the ARP request matches its own IP address and adds a MAC/IP address mapping for Host A to its local ARP cache.
4. The router then sends an ARP reply message containing its MAC address directly back to Host A.
5. When Host A receives the ARP reply message from the router, it updates its ARP cache with a MAC/IP address mapping for 10.0.0.1.

Once the MAC address for Router interface 1 has been determined, Host A can send IP traffic to Router interface 1 by encapsulating it in a frame destined for Router interface 1's MAC address. The router then forwards the traffic to Host B through the same ARP process as discussed in the previous section, "How ARP Resolves MAC Addresses for Local Traffic."

THE ARP CACHE

To minimize the number of broadcasts, ARP maintains a cache of IP address-to-MAC address mappings for future use. The ARP cache can contain both dynamic and static entries. Dynamic entries are added and removed automatically over time. Static entries remain in the cache until the computer is restarted.

Each dynamic ARP cache entry has a potential lifetime of 10 minutes. New entries added to the cache are time stamped. If an entry is not reused within two minutes of being added, it expires and is removed from the ARP cache. If an entry is used, it receives two more minutes of lifetime. If an entry keeps getting used, it receives an additional two minutes of lifetime up to a maximum lifetime of 10 minutes.

Author's Note That a dynamic ARP cache entry has a potential lifetime of 10 minutes is OS-specific. The ARP specification does not mandate a cache lifetime. The fact that Windows 2000 does this is just silly.

You can view the ARP cache by using the **arp** command. To view the ARP cache on a computer running Windows 2000, type *arp -a* at a Windows 2000 command prompt. To view **arp** command-line options, type *arp /?* at a command prompt.

Note There is a separate ARP cache for each network adapter on a computer running Windows 2000.

Internet Protocol

IP is a TCP/IP standard defined in RFC 791, "Internet Protocol (IP)." IP is a connectionless datagram protocol primarily responsible for addressing and routing packets between hosts.

Connectionless means that packets can be sent into the network without requiring a per-destination setup procedure. Unreliable means that delivery is not guaranteed, yet IP always makes a best-effort attempt to deliver a packet. An IP packet might be lost, delivered out of sequence, duplicated, or delayed. IP does not attempt to recover from these types of errors. The acknowledgment of packets delivered and the recovery of lost packets is the responsibility of a higher-layer protocol, such as TCP.

An IP packet, also known as an *IP datagram*, consists of an IP header and an IP payload, as shown in Figure 1-6.

Table 1.5 lists the fields for addressing and routing contained in the IP header.

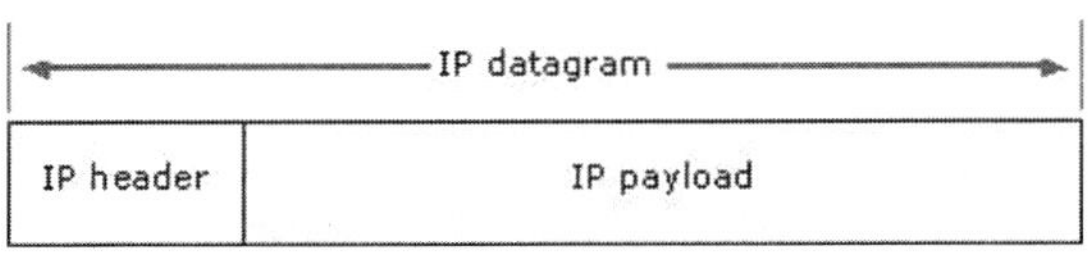

FIGURE 1–6 An IP datagram

TABLE 1.5 *IP Header Fields*

IP header field	Function
Source IP address	The IP address of the original source of the IP datagram.
Destination IP address	The IP address of the final destination of the IP datagram.
Time-to-Live (TTL)	Designates the number of network segments on which the datagram is allowed to travel before being discarded by a router. The TTL is set by the sending host and is used to prevent packets from endlessly circulating on an IP internetwork. When forwarding an IP packet, routers are required to decrease the TTL by at least 1.

Internet Control Message Protocol

Internet Control Message Protocol is a TCP/IP standard defined in RFC 792, "Internet Control Message Protocol (ICMP)." With ICMP, hosts and routers that use IP communication can report errors and exchange limited control and status information.

ICMP messages are usually sent automatically in one of the following situations:

- An IP datagram cannot reach its destination.
- An IP router (gateway) cannot forward datagrams at the current rate of transmission.
- An IP router redirects the sending host to use a better route to the destination.

ICMP messages are encapsulated within IP datagrams, as shown in Figure 1-7.

Different types of ICMP messages are identified in the ICMP header. Because ICMP messages are carried in IP datagrams, they are unreliable.

The most common ICMP messages are listed and described in Table 1.6.

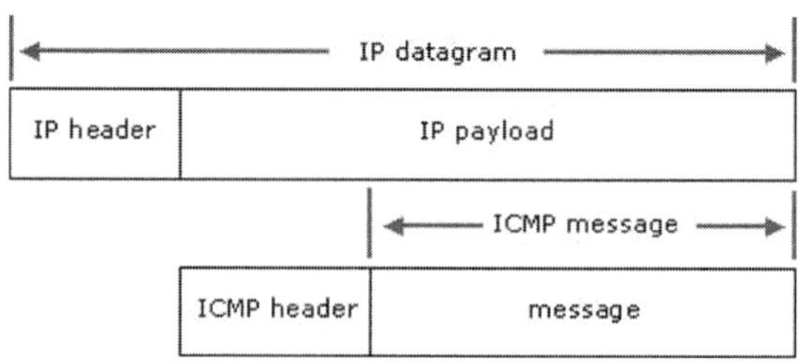

FIGURE 1–7 *ICMP encapsulation in an IP datagram*

TABLE 1.6 *ICMP Messages*

ICMP message	Description
Echo request	Determines whether an IP node (a host or a router) is available on the network.
Echo reply	Replies to an ICMP echo request.
Destination unreachable	Informs the host that a datagram cannot be delivered.
Redirect	Informs the host of a preferred route.
Time exceeded	Indicates that the TTL of an IP datagram has expired.

You can use the **ping** command to send ICMP echo request messages and record the receipt of ICMP echo reply messages. With these messages, you can detect network or host communication failures and troubleshoot common TCP/IP connectivity problems.

For more information about ICMP, see RFC 792. For more information about obtaining RFCs, see Appendix A.

Internet Group Management Protocol

The use of IP multicasting in TCP/IP networks is defined as a TCP/IP standard in RFC 1112, "Internet Group Management Protocol (IGMP)." In addition to defining address and host extensions for how IP hosts support multicasting, this RFC also defines the Internet Group Management Protocol version 1. RFC 2236, "Internet Group Management Protocol (IGMP), version 2" defines IGMP version 2. Both versions of IGMP provide a protocol to exchange and update information about host membership in specific multicast groups.

WHAT IS IP MULTICASTING?

Multicast IP traffic is sent to a single address but is processed by multiple hosts. IP multicasting is similar to a newsletter subscription. Just as only subscribers receive the newsletter when it is published, only host computers belonging to the multicast group receive and process IP traffic sent to the group's selected IP address. The set of hosts listening on a specific IP multicast address is called a *multicast group*.

Other important aspects of IP multicasting include the following:

- Group membership is dynamic, allowing hosts to join and leave the group at any time.
- The ability of hosts to join multicast groups is performed through the sending of IGMP messages.
- Groups are not limited by size and members can be spread out across multiple IP subnetworks (if a connected set of intervening routers support the propagation of IP multicast traffic).

- Any host can send IP traffic to any group's IP address without being a member of the corresponding group.

MULTICAST ADDRESSING

IP multicast addresses are reserved and assigned from within the Class D address range from 224.0.0.0 through 239.255.255.255. Table 1.7 is a partial list of well-known Class D addresses used by Windows 2000 components that are reserved for IP multicasting and registered with IANA.

TABLE 1.7 *Class D Addresses Used by Windows 2000*

IP multicast address	Description
224.0.0.0	Base address (reserved).
224.0.0.1	The All Hosts multicast group that contains all systems on the same network segment.
224.0.0.2	The All Routers multicast group that contains all routers on the same network segment.
224.0.0.5	The Open Shortest Path First (OSPF) AllSPFRouters address. Used to send OSPF routing information to all OSPF routers on a broadcast-capable subnetwork segment.
224.0.0.6	The OSPF AllDRouters address. Used to send OSPF routing information to OSPF designated routers on a broadcast-capable subnetwork segment.
224.0.0.9	The Routing Information Protocol (RIP) version 2 group address. Used to send RIP routing information to all RIP v2 routers on a network segment.
224.0.1.24	WINS server group address. Used to support autodiscovery and dynamic configuration of replication for WINS servers. For more information, see "WINS Replication" in Chapter 6, "WINS Overview."

A single IP address within the Class D reserved range identifies each multicast group. Each group's reserved IP address is shared by all host members of the group who listen and receive any IP messages sent to the group's IP address.

Author's Note Except for 224.0.1.24, none of these addresses are joined by hosts. And although, strictly speaking, it is illegal, the 224.0.0.x (where x is not 1) addresses are usually not joined by IGMP reports, even though RFC 1112 says they should be explicitly joined.

IP multicast addresses are mapped to a reserved set of media access control multicast addresses.

IP multicast is an open, IETF (Internet Engineering Task Force) standard for distributing data to multiple recipients. The multicast recipient group can change dynamically. A host may decide to join or leave a group at any time and a host may be a member of more than one multicast group. In addition, any host can be a multicast source by simply sending packets addressed to a particular multicast group.

Routers in this scheme must be multicast enabled. When a multicast source transmits a multicast datagram, the local router forwards the packets to other routers with attached networks that include members of the multicast group.

IP multicast uses class D addressing, which is a special form of the IP address designed for multicasting. All hosts connected to the Internet have an IP address that is either part of the class A, class B, or class C scheme. A host can also have one or more class D multicast addresses, depending on the multicast groups it wants to belong to. A class D address is 32 bits long. The first 4 bits are used to identify it as a class D address. The remaining 28 bits identify multicast groups.

A class D address can be compared to the channel number of a TV station. When you tune in to a particular class D address, you receive packets that are being multicast by other systems that multicast on the address.

An industry consortium called the IPMI (IP Multicast Initiative) is dedicated to advancing the deployment of IP multicast and making information about it available. The IPMI Web site is at *www.ipmulticast.com*.

Note Web addresses can change, so you might be unable to connect to the Web site or sites mentioned here.

IGMP MESSAGES

IGMP allows IP routers to learn which of their directly attached subnetworks contain active group members at any given point in time. Membership in a multicast group is reported by at least one member host per subnetwork, in response to group membership solicitations (i.e., IGMP queries) that are periodically issued by multicast routers.

IGMP message types are described in Table 1.8.

TABLE 1.8 *IGMP Message Types*

IGMP message type	Description
Host membership report	When a host joins a multicast group, it sends an IGMP host membership report message, declaring its membership in a specific host group. IGMP host membership report messages are also sent in response to IGMP host membership query messages that are periodically sent by a router.
Host membership query	Used by a multicast router to periodically poll a network for group members.
Leave group	Sent by a host when it leaves a host group. If the host pays attention, it may decide to not send this message unless it can tell that it is the only group member present on its subnetwork.

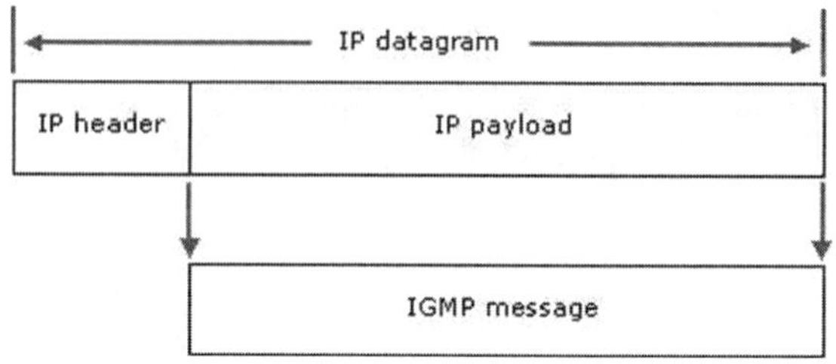

FIGURE 1–8 GMP encapsulation in an IP datagram

IGMP messages are encapsulated and sent within IP datagrams, as shown in Figure 1-8.

User Datagram Protocol

The User Datagram Protocol is a TCP/IP standard defined in RFC 768, "User Datagram Protocol (UDP)." UDP is used when applications require only the most basic transport-layer services. UDP functions mainly to allow multiple programs using different UDP ports to coexist on the same host. DNS, TFTP, Simple Network Management Protocol (SNMP), and Real-Time Protocol (RTP) are the principal uses of UDP.

UDP provides a connectionless datagram service that offers best-effort delivery, which means that UDP does not guarantee delivery or proper sequencing for any datagrams. A source host that needs reliable communication must use either TCP or an alternative transport protocol that provides its own sequencing and acknowledgment services.

UDP messages are encapsulated and sent within IP datagrams, as shown in Figure 1-9.

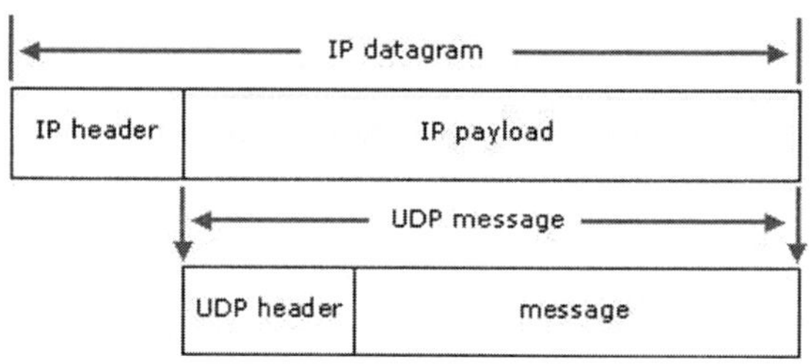

FIGURE 1–9 UDP encapsulation in an IP datagram

UDP PORTS

UDP ports provide a location for sending and receiving UDP messages. A UDP port functions as a single message queue for receiving all datagrams intended for the program specified by each protocol port number. This means UDP-based programs can receive more than one message at a time.

The server side of each program that uses UDP listens for messages arriving on its well-known port number. All UDP server port numbers less than 1,024 (and some higher numbers) are reserved and registered by IANA.

A well-known, or reserved, port number identifies every UDP-based program. Table 1.9 shows a partial list of well-known UDP server port numbers that are used by standard UDP-based programs.

TABLE 1.9 *UDP Server Port Numbers Used by Standard UDP-based Programs*

UDP port number	Description
53	DNS name queries
69	Trivial File Transfer Protocol
137	NetBIOS name service
138	NetBIOS datagram service
161	Simple Network Management Protocol
520	Routing Information Protocol (RIP)

UDP AND TCP

In general, differences in how UDP and TCP deliver data are similar to the differences between a telephone call and a postcard. TCP works like a telephone call by verifying that the destination is available and ready to communicate. UDP works like a postcard—messages are small and delivery is likely, but not always assured.

UDP is typically used when programs only need to transmit small amounts of data at a time, or by programs that have real-time requirements. In these situations, UDP's low overhead and multicasting potential (for example, one datagram, many recipients) may be a better match for certain applications than is TCP.

UDP contrasts directly with the services and features provided by TCP. Table 1.10 compares differences in how TCP/IP communication is handled depending on whether UDP or TCP is used for transporting data.

TABLE 1.10 *Differences in TCP/IP Communications Handling*

UDP	TCP
Connectionless service; no session is established between hosts.	Connection-oriented service; a session is established between hosts.
UDP does not guarantee or acknowledge delivery, or sequence data.	TCP guarantees delivery through the use of acknowledgments and sequenced delivery of data.
Programs that use UDP are responsible for providing any reliability needed to transport data.	Programs that use TCP are provided assurance of reliable data transport.
UDP is fast, has low overhead requirements, and can support point-to-point and point-to-multipoint communication.	TCP is slower, has higher overhead requirements, and only supports point-to-point communication.

Author's Note I am not propagating the falsehood that TCP is slower than UDP. This is simply not true. TCP can be just as fast as UDP. NFS was originally written with UDP, due to its perceived speed, but then NFS had to rather inelegantly reinvent a lot of the services that TCP does very efficiently. The author of NFS, years later, wished he had used TCP in the first place.

Both UDP and TCP use ports to identify communications for each TCP/IP program.

Transmission Control Protocol

Transmission Control Protocol is a TCP/IP standard defined in RFC 793, "Transmission Control Protocol (TCP)," that provides a reliable, connection-oriented packet delivery service. The Transmission Control Protocol:

- Guarantees delivery of IP datagrams.
- Performs segmentation and reassembly of large blocks of data sent by programs.
- Ensures proper sequencing and ordered delivery of segmented data.
- Performs checks on the integrity of transmitted data by using checksum calculations.
- Sends positive messages depending on whether data was received successfully. When using the optional selective acknowledgment extensions, negative acknowledgments for data not received may also be sent.
- Offers a preferred method of transport for programs that must use reliable session-based data transmission, such as client/server database and e-mail programs.

HOW TCP WORKS

TCP is based on point-to-point communication between two network hosts. TCP receives data from programs and processes this data as a stream of bytes. Bytes are grouped into segments that TCP then numbers and sequences for delivery.

Before two TCP hosts can exchange data, they must first establish a session with each other. A TCP session is initialized through a process known as a three-way handshake. This process synchronizes sequence numbers and provides control information that is needed to establish a virtual connection between both hosts.

Once the initial three-way handshake completes, segments are sent and acknowledged in a sequential manner between both the sending and receiving hosts. A similar handshake process is used by TCP before closing a connection to verify that both hosts are finished exchanging data.

TCP segments are encapsulated and sent within IP datagrams, as shown in Figure 1-10.

TCP PORTS

TCP ports use a specific program port for delivery of data sent by using Transmission Control Protocol. TCP ports are more complex and operate differently from UDP ports.

While a UDP port operates as a single message queue and the network endpoint for UDP-based communication, the final endpoint for all TCP communication is a unique connection. Each TCP connection is uniquely identified by dual endpoints.

Each single TCP server port is capable of offering shared access to multiple connections because all TCP connections are uniquely identified by two pairs of IP address and TCP ports (one address/port pairing for each connected host).

TCP programs use reserved or well-known port numbers, as shown in Figure 1-11.

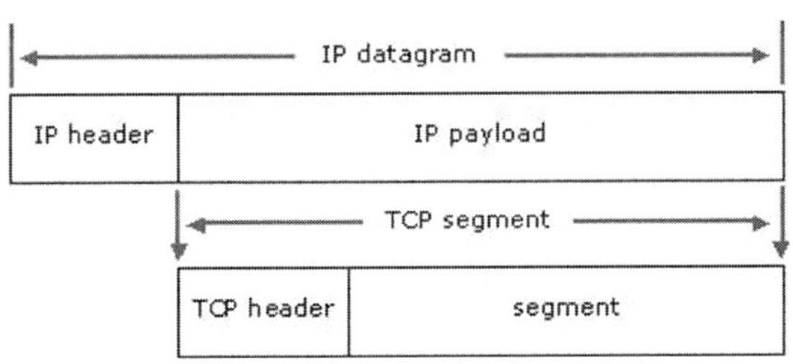

FIGURE 1–10 *TCP encapsulation in an IP datagram*

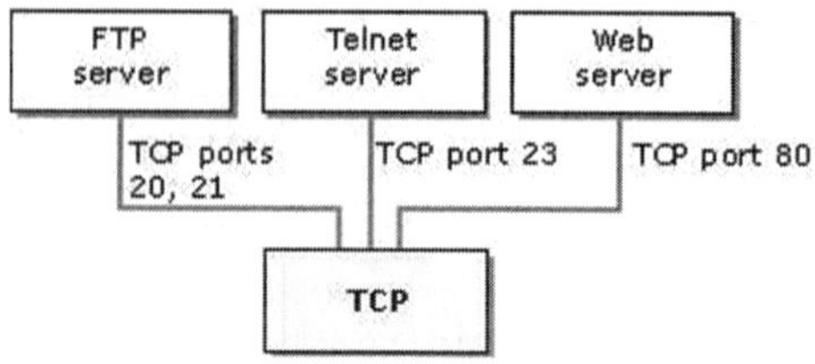

FIGURE 1–11 *TCP ports as used by programs*

The server side of each program that uses TCP ports listens for messages arriving on its well-known TCP port number. All TCP server port numbers less than 1,024 (and some higher numbers) are reserved and registered by IANA.

Table 1.11 is a partial list of some well-known TCP server ports used by standard TCP-based programs.

TABLE 1.11 *TCP Server Ports Used by Standard TCP-based Programs*

TCP port number	Description
20	FTP server (data channel)
21	FTP server (control channel)
23	Telnet server
25	Simple Mail Transport Protocol (SMTP)
53	Domain Name System zone transfers
80	Web server (HTTP)
139	NetBIOS session service

IP Addressing and Routing

This section covers:

- IP addressing
- Subnet masks
- IP routing
- The Windows 2000 IP routing table

Author's Note This section provides a general and brief overview of IP addressing and routing. For readers interested in learning more about this topic, especially beginners, I highly recommend IP Fundamentals: What Everyone Needs to Know About Addressing & Routing by Thomas A. Maufer.

Tom strikes a commendable balance between thoroughness and practicality. He makes sure—through liberal use of examples—that you understand everything necessary to complete your job. But he also goes to extraordinary lengths to bolster your grasp of the IP suite; his chapters conclude with fact-rich endnotes, plus references to journal articles and standards documents. In this way, IP Fundamentals helps you surpass mere technical competence to become an IP addressing and routing expert.

IP Addressing

Each TCP/IP host is identified by a logical IP address. This address is unique for each host that communicates by using TCP/IP. Each 32-bit IP address identifies a location of a host system on the network in the same way that a street address identifies a house on a city street.

Just as a street address has a standard two-part format (a street name and a house number), each IP address is separated internally into two parts—a network ID and a host ID:

- The network ID, also known as a network address, identifies a single network segment within a larger TCP/IP internetwork (a network of networks). All the systems that attach and share access to the same network have a common network ID within their full IP address. This ID is also used to uniquely identify each network within the larger internetwork.
- The host ID, also known as a host address, identifies a TCP/IP node (a workstation, server, router, or other TCP/IP device) within each network. The host ID for each device identifies a single system uniquely within its own network.

Here is an example of a 32-bit IP address:

```
10000011 01101011 00010000 11001000
```

To make IP addressing easier, IP addresses are expressed in dotted decimal notation. The 32-bit IP address is segmented into four 8-bit octets. The octets are converted to decimal (base-10 numbering system) and separated by periods. Therefore, the previous IP address example is 131.107.16.200 when converted to dotted decimal notation.

For more information about dotted decimal notation and the conversion of numbers from binary to decimal, see Appendix A.

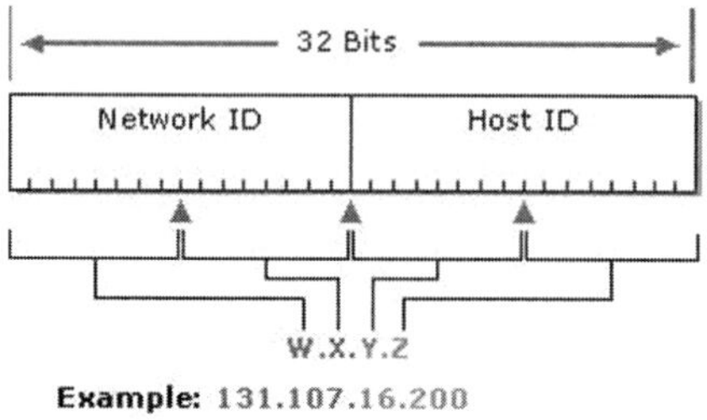

FIGURE 1–12 *The IP address: network ID and host ID*

Figure 1-12 shows a sample view of an IP address (131.107.16.200) as it is divided into network and host ID sections. The network ID portion (131.107) is indicated by the first two numbers of the IP address. The host ID portion (16.200) is indicated by the last two numbers of the IP address.

Note Because IP addresses identify devices on a network, a unique IP address must be assigned to each device on the network.

In general, most computers have only a single network adapter installed and therefore require only a single IP address. If a computer has multiple network adapters installed, each adapter needs its own IP address.

IP ADDRESS CLASSES

The Internet community has defined five address classes. Class A, B, and C addresses are used for assignment to TCP/IP nodes.

The class of address defines which bits are used for the network and host ID parts of each address. The address class also defines how many networks and hosts per network can be supported.

Table 1.12 uses *w.x.y.z* to designate the four octet values in any given IP address. The table is used to show:

- How the value of the first octet (*w*) of any given IP address effectively indicates the class of address.
- How the octets in an address are divided into network ID and host ID.
- The number of possible networks and hosts per network available for each class.

TABLE 1.12 *Octet Values in an IP Address*

Class	Value of w	Network ID	Host ID	Number of networks	Maximum hosts per network
A	1-126	w	x.y.z	126	16,777,214
B	128-191	w.x	y.z	16,384	65,534
C	192-223	w.x.y	z	2,097,152	254
D	224-239	Reserved for multicast addressing	N/A	N/A	N/A
E	240-254	Reserved for experimental use	N/A	N/A	N/A

Subnet Masks

Network IDs and host IDs within an IP address are distinguished by using a subnet mask. Each subnet mask is a 32-bit number that uses consecutive bit groups of all ones (1) to identify the network ID and all zeros (0) to identify the host ID portions of an IP address.

For example, the subnet mask normally used with the IP address 131.107.16.200 is the following 32-bit binary number:

```
11111111 11111111 00000000 00000000
```

This subnet mask number is 16 one-bits followed by 16 zero-bits, indicating that the network ID and host ID sections of this IP address are both 16 bits in length. Normally, this subnet mask is displayed in dotted decimal notation as 255.255.0.0.

Table 1.13 displays subnet masks for the Internet address classes.

TABLE 1.13 *Subnet Masks for the Internet Address Classes*

Address class	Bits for subnet mask	Subnet mask
Class A	11111111 00000000 00000000 00000000	255.0.0.0
Class B	11111111 11111111 00000000 00000000	255.255.0.0
Class C	11111111 11111111 11111111 00000000	255.255.255.0

Typically, default subnet mask values (as shown in Table 1.13) are acceptable for most networks with no special requirements and where each IP network segment corresponds to a single physical network.

In some cases, you can use customized subnet masks to implement IP subnetting. With IP subnetting, you can subdivide the default host ID portion of an IP address to specify subnets, which are subdivisions of the original class-based network ID.

By customizing the subnet mask length, you can reduce the number of bits that are used for the actual host ID.

Important To prevent addressing and routing problems, you should make sure all TCP/IP computers on any network segment use the same subnet mask.

IP Routing

In general terms, routing is the process of forwarding packets between connected networks. For TCP/IP-based networks, routing is part of the Internet Protocol and is used in combination with other network protocol services to provide forwarding capabilities between hosts that are located on separate network segments within a larger TCP/IP-based network.

IP is the mailroom of the TCP/IP protocol, where IP data sorting and delivery take place. Each incoming or outgoing packet is called an *IP datagram*. An IP datagram contains two IP addresses: the source address of the sending host and the destination address of the receiving host. Unlike hardware addresses, the IP addresses within a datagram remain the same as it travels across a TCP/IP network.

Routing is the primary function of IP. IP datagrams are exchanged and processed on each host by using IP at the Internet layer.

Above the IP layer, transport services on the source host pass data in the form of TCP segments or UDP messages to the IP layer. The IP layer assembles IP datagrams with source and destination address information that is used to route the data through the network. The IP layer then passes datagrams down to the network interface layer. At this layer, data-link services convert IP datagrams into frames for transmission over network-specific media on a physical network. This process happens in reverse order on the destination host.

Each IP datagram contains a source and destination IP address. IP layer services on each host examine the destination address of each datagram, compare this address to a locally maintained routing table, and then decide what further forwarding action to take. IP routers are attached to two or more IP network segments and are enabled to forward packets between them. The following sections discuss IP routers and the use of routing tables in further detail.

IP ROUTERS

TCP/IP network segments are interconnected by IP routers. Routers are sometimes referred to as *gateways,* though that term is no longer in common use, except for the term *default gateway*, which you may have seen in your PC's IP configuration. Routers are devices that pass IP datagrams from one network or subnetwork to another. This process is known as IP routing and is shown in Figure 1-13.

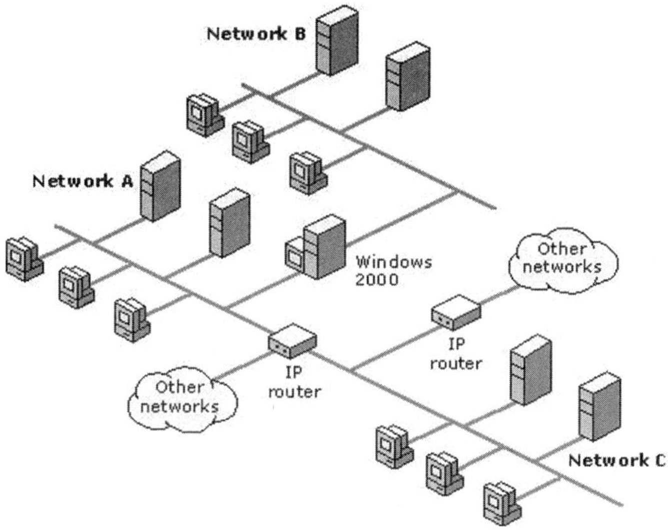

FIGURE 1–13 *IP routing*

IP routers provide the primary means of joining together two or more physically separated IP network segments. All IP routers share two essential characteristics:

- *IP routers are multihomed hosts.* A multihomed host is a network host that uses two or more network connection interfaces to connect to each physically separated network segment.
- *IP routers provide packet forwarding for other TCP/IP hosts.* IP routers are distinct from other hosts that use multihoming in one important way: an IP router must be able to forward IP-based communication between networks for other IP network hosts.

You can implement IP routers by using a variety of possible hardware and software products. Box-based routers—dedicated hardware devices that run specialized software—are common. In addition, you can use routing solutions that are based on software, such as the Routing and Remote Access service, which runs on a computer running Windows 2000 Server.

Regardless of the type of IP routers that you use, all IP routing relies on the use of a routing table to facilitate communication between network segments.

ROUTING TABLES

TCP/IP hosts use a routing table to maintain knowledge about other IP networks and IP hosts. Most hosts, such as the typical PC, have a very simple routing table, usually containing two entries. One of the entries represents the

PC's local subnetwork, while the other represents all other nonlocal networks. The latter entry is usually referred to as a *default route*. In certain circumstances, hosts may have more than just these two entries. Routers have more entries in their routing tables, including entries for the router's directly attached subnetworks, as well as all the destination subnetworks that the router has learned of. Each network or subnetwork and host is identified by an IP address and an associated subnet mask. In addition, routing tables are important because they provide needed information to each local host regarding how to communicate with remote networks and hosts.

For each computer on an IP network, you can maintain a routing table with an entry for every other computer or network that communicates with the local computer. In general, this is not practical, and a default gateway (IP router) is used instead.

When a computer prepares to send an IP datagram, it inserts its own source IP address and the destination IP address of the recipient into the IP header. The computer then examines the destination IP address, compares it to a locally maintained IP routing table, and takes appropriate action based on what it finds. The computer does one of three things:

- It passes the datagram up to a protocol layer above IP on the local host.
- It forwards the datagram through one of its attached network interfaces.
- It discards the datagram.

IP searches the routing table for the route that is the closest match to the destination IP address. The most specific to the least specific route is in the following order:

- A route that exactly matches the destination IP address (host route).
- A route that matches the network ID of the destination IP address (network route).
- The default route.

If a matching route is not found, IP discards the datagram.

The Windows 2000 IP Routing Table

Every computer that runs TCP/IP makes routing decisions. These decisions are controlled by the IP routing table. To display the IP routing table on a computer that is running Windows 2000, you can type *route print* at a command prompt.

Table 1.14 shows an example of an IP routing table. This example is for a computer running Windows 2000 with one network adapter and the following configuration:

- IP address: 10.0.0.169
- Subnet mask: 255.0.0.0
- Default gateway: 10.0.0.1

TABLE 1.14 *IP Routing Table Example*

Description	Network destination	Netmask	Gateway	Interface	Metric
Default route	0.0.0.0	0.0.0.0	10.0.0.1	10.0.0.169	1
Loopback network	127.0.0.0	255.0.0.0	127.0.0.1	127.0.0.1	1
Local network	10.0.0.0	255.0.0.0	10.0.0.169	10.0.0.169	1
Local IP address	10.0.0.169	255.255.255.255	127.0.0.1	127.0.0.1	1
Multicast addresses	224.0.0.0	240.0.0.0	10.0.0.169	10.0.0.169	1
Limited broadcast address	255.255.255.255	255.255.255.255	10.0.0.169	10.0.0.169	1

Note The descriptions in the first column of Table 1.14 are not actually displayed in the output of the route print command.

The routing table is built automatically, based on the current TCP/IP configuration of your computer. Each route occupies a single line in the displayed table. The routing table is searched by your computer for an entry that is the most specific match to the destination IP address. The most specific matching routing table entry is the entry with the most leading bits in common with the destination IP address.

Your computer uses the default route if no other host or network route matches the destination address included in an IP datagram. The default route typically forwards an IP datagram (for which there is no matching or explicit local route) to a default gateway address for a router on the local subnet. In the previous example, the default route forwards the datagram to a router whose address is 10.0.0.1.

The default gateway contains information about the network IDs of the other IP subnets within the larger TCP/IP internetwork. It uses this information to forward the datagram to the next-hop gateway en route to the destination. The packet may need to cross many routers in order to reach its ultimate destination.

The following sections describe each of the columns displayed in the IP routing table: network destination, netmask, gateway, interface, and metric.

NETWORK DESTINATION

The network destination is used with the netmask to match the destination IP address. The network destination can range from 0.0.0.0 for the default route through 255.255.255.255 for the limited broadcast, which is a special broadcast address encompassing all hosts on the same network segment.

NETMASK

The netmask is the subnet mask that is applied to the destination IP address when matching to the value in the network destination. When netmask is written in binary, a "1" must match and a "0" need not match. For example, a 0.0.0.0 netmask is used for the default route, which means that none of the bits must match. For host routes, a route that represents just a single IP address, a netmask of 255.255.255.255 is used.

GATEWAY

The gateway address is the IP address that the local host uses to forward IP datagrams to other IP networks. This is either the IP address of a local network adapter or the IP address of an IP router (such as a default gateway router) on the local network segment.

INTERFACE

The interface is the IP address that is configured on the local computer for the local network adapter that is used when an IP datagram is forwarded on the network.

METRIC

A metric indicates the cost of using a route, which may equate to the number of hops to the IP destination. Whatever the "cost" represents, larger numbers generally mean that the associated network is further away. Anything on the local subnet is one hop, and each router crossed after that is an additional hop. If there are multiple routes to the same destination with different metrics, the route with the lowest metric is selected.

For information about adding and deleting routes in the IP routing table, see Chapter 2.

MULTIHOMED WINDOWS 2000 HOSTS

Table 1.15 shows the default routing table for a multihomed Windows 2000 host with this configuration:

- Network adapter 1
  - IP address: 10.0.0.169
  - Subnet mask: 255.0.0.0
  - Default gateway: 10.0.0.1
- Network adapter 2
  - IP address: 192.168.0.200
  - Subnet mask: 255.255.0.0
  - Default gateway: 192.168.0.1

TABLE 1.15 *Default Routing Table for a Multihomed Windows 2000 Host*

Network destination	Netmask	Gateway	Interface	Metric
0.0.0.0	0.0.0.0	10.0.0.1	10.0.0.169	1
0.0.0.0	0.0.0.0	192.168.0.1	192.168.0.200	1
127.0.0.0	255.0.0.0	127.0.0.1	127.0.0.1	1
10.0.0.0	255.0.0.0	10.0.0.169	10.0.0.169	1
10.0.0.169	255.255.255.255	127.0.0.1	127.0.0.1	1
192.168.0.0	255.255.0.0	192.168.0.200	192.168.0.200	1
192.168.0.200	255.255.255.255	127.0.0.1	127.0.0.1	1
192.168.0.255	255.255.255.255	192.168.0.200	192.168.0.200	1
224.0.0.0	240.0.0.0	10.0.0.169	10.0.0.169	1
224.0.0.0	240.0.0.0	192.168.0.200	192.168.0.200	1
255.255.255.255	255.255.255.255	10.0.0.169	10.0.0.169	1
255.255.255.255	255.255.255.255	192.168.0.200	192.168.0.200	1

For information about enabling IP forwarding on a multihomed computer running Windows 2000, see Chapter 2.

Note When you configure a default gateway to each network adapter, you create a 0.0.0.0 route for each network adapter. However, only one default route is actually used. In the previous example, the 10.0.0.169 IP address is the first network adapter in the TCP/IP bindings, and therefore the default route for Network adapter 1 is used. Because only one default gateway is used, you only need to configure one network adapter with a default gateway. This reduces confusion and assures the results you intended.

If the IP router is a Windows 2000 router and does not have an interface on a given network, it needs a route to get there. You can add static routes or use routing protocols that are provided by the Routing and Remote Access service.

Name Resolution

As we have seen, IP is designed to work with the 32-bit IP addresses of the source and the destination hosts. Computers are used by people who are not very good at using and remembering the IP addresses of the computers with which they want to communicate. People are much better at using and remembering names rather than IP addresses.

If a name is used as an alias for an IP address, you need to ensure that the name is unique and that it resolves to the correct IP address.

In Windows 2000, there are two types of names to resolve:

- *Host names*. Programs that use the Windows Sockets programming interface, such as Web browsers, use host names. For information, see Appendix D, "DNS Resources and Troubleshooting."
- *NetBIOS names*. NetBIOS names are used by network programs or services that use the NetBIOS programming interface, such as Client for Microsoft Networks and File and Printer Sharing for Microsoft Networks. For more information, see Appendix C, "WINS Resources and Troubleshooting."

TCP/IP Configuration Items

For Windows 2000 TCP/IP to function properly, you need to configure the following:

- IP address
- Subnet mask
- Default gateway
- DNS server
- WINS server

IP Address

Each interface on each TCP/IP node (host or router) must be configured with a unique IP address that is correct for the attached network segment. The IP address is a required configuration item.

For more information, see "IP Addressing" in this chapter.

Subnet Mask

Each interface on each TCP/IP node (host or router) must be configured with a subnet mask that, when combined with the IP address, yields the network ID. All IP interfaces on the same network segment must use the same network ID. Therefore, all IP interfaces on the same network segment must use the same subnet mask. The subnet mask is a required configuration item.

For more information, see "Subnet Masks" in this chapter.

Default Gateway

To communicate with TCP/IP nodes on other network segments, you must configure at least one interface with the IP address of a default gateway (a local router that forwards remote TCP/IP traffic to its destination).

You do not need to configure a default gateway for a network that consists of a single network segment.

For more information, see "IP Routing" in this chapter.

DNS Server

A DNS server can resolve domain names to IP addresses. When a TCP/IP host is configured with the IP address of a DNS server, the TCP/IP host sends DNS name queries to the DNS server for resolution. Computers running Active Directory-based Windows 2000 require that a DNS server be present.

You do not need to configure a DNS server for a network that consists of a single network segment.

A computer running Windows 2000 Server can be a DNS server. This is covered later in the book.

WINS Server

A WINS server can store and resolve NetBIOS names to IP addresses. When a TCP/IP host is configured with the IP address of a WINS server, the TCP/IP host registers its own NetBIOS names with the WINS server and sends NetBIOS name queries to the WINS server for resolution. A WINS server is highly recommended when there is more than one network segment in your network and when you have computers that are not based on Active Directory (for example, computers running Windows NT 4.0, Windows 95, and Windows 98).

You do not need to configure a WINS server for a network that consists of a single network segment.

A computer running Windows 2000 Server can be a WINS server. This is covered later in the book.

TCP/IP Configuration Methods

You can configure TCP/IP in Windows 2000 by using the following methods: automatic configuration, dynamic configuration, and manual configuration.

If you are using either a dynamic or manual configuration, find out more about developing an effective TCP/IP network numbering plan in "Numbering Your Network" in this chapter.

Automatic Configuration

By using the new Automatic Private IP Addressing feature (also known as DHCP Autoconfiguration), Windows 2000 provides default automatic configuration of the IP address within the range reserved for APIPA that runs from 169.254.0.1 through 169.254.255.254 and uses an associated subnet mask of 255.255.0.0. There is no automatic configuration of a default gateway, DNS server, or WINS server. APIPA is designed for networks that consist of a single network segment that are not connected to the Internet. Therefore, you do not need to configure the default gateway, DNS server, and WINS server.

For information about configuring TCP/IP for automatic addressing, see Chapter 2.

Dynamic Configuration

By using DHCP, TCP/IP configuration is done dynamically and automatically when the computer is started. Dynamic configuration requires the configuration of a DHCP server. By default, computers running Windows 2000 are DHCP clients. By properly configuring the DHCP server, TCP/IP hosts can obtain IP address, subnet mask, default gateway, DNS server, NetBIOS node type, and WINS server configuration information. Dynamic configuration (using DHCP) is recommended for medium-to-large TCP/IP networks.

For information about configuring TCP/IP for dynamic addressing, see Chapter 2.

Manual Configuration

By manually configuring the properties of the TCP/IP protocol through the properties of a network connection (in Network and Dial-up Connections), you can assign an IP address, subnet mask, default gateway, DNS server, and WINS server. Manual configuration is required in a network with multiple network segments when no DHCP server is present.

For information about configuring TCP/IP for static addressing, see Chapter 2.

Installing TCP/IP

Before you install Microsoft TCP/IP on a computer running Windows 2000, you need to know:

- Whether your network supports a *dynamic* TCP/IP configuration, which uses the Dynamic Host Configuration Protocol (DHCP). A dynamic configuration is the simplest to complete and can be used if another computer on your network is installed as a DHCP server. The DHCP server provides IP address, subnet mask, default gateway (IP router), DNS domain name, DNS server, and WINS server configuration information.

- Whether your network requires a *manual* TCP/IP configuration. Some existing networks either do not use DHCP or require that TCP/IP configuration is performed manually for each computer.

For more information about configuration methods, see "TCP/IP Configuration Methods" in this chapter.

If you do not use DHCP to configure TCP/IP dynamically, obtain the following information from your network administrator to configure TCP/IP manually:

- The IP address and subnet mask for each network adapter that is installed on the computer.
- The IP address for the default local gateway (IP router).
- The name of your DNS domain and the IP addresses of the DNS servers on the network.

  For Active Directory deployment, the primary DNS suffix of a computer, also known as the computer's primary domain name, is by default the name of the Active Directory domain that the computer has joined. If you want your computer's primary DNS suffix to be different from the name of the Active Directory domain that the computer has joined, you must consult "To Change the DNS Suffix of Your Computer" in this chapter.
- The IP addresses for the WINS servers, if WINS services are available on your network.

For more information about configuration items, see "TCP/IP Configuration Items" in this chapter. For instructions about installing and configuring TCP/IP, see Chapter 2.

To Change the DNS Suffix of Your Computer

To change the DNS suffix of your computer, you must be logged on as an administrator to the local computer to change the DNS suffix:

1. Open System in Control Panel.

   To open a Control Panel item, click **Start**, point to **Settings**, click **Control Panel**, and then double-click the appropriate icon.
2. On the **Network Identification** tab, click **Properties**, and then click **More**.
3. Under **Primary DNS suffix of this computer**, type the DNS suffix you want to use.

The default setting for the local primary DNS suffix is the same as the Active Directory domain name. Changing the DNS suffix will not affect your domain membership, but it could prevent other users from finding your computer on the network. If you make the primary DNS suffix of the computer different from the Active Directory domain name, the domain administrator must enable registration of the new full computer name in the Active Directory domain.

A DNS suffix may contain up to 155 characters, including hyphens and periods.

4. If you want your computer to automatically update the DNS suffix if you become a member of a different Windows 2000 domain, select the **Change primary DNS suffix when domain membership changes** check box.

If you switch to a new Windows 2000 secure domain and select the **Change primary DNS suffix when domain membership changes** check box, the DNS suffix is updated to show a new DNS suffix that matches the new Windows 2000 secure domain you are joining. For example, if you create a DNS suffix called *MyMachine* for membership in your current domain and join a new Windows 2000 secure domain called *example.microsoft.com*, then the new DNS suffix (*example.microsoft.com*) is displayed under **Primary DNS suffix of this computer**. This new DNS suffix replaces the previous name *(MyMachine)* you created for membership under your old domain.

If this computer belongs to a group with a group policy enabled on **Primary DNS suffix of this computer**, the string specified in the group policy is used as the primary DNS suffix. The local setting is used only if a group policy is disabled or unspecified.

Numbering Your Network

For private TCP/IP networks that are indirectly connected to the Internet by using a network address translator (NAT) or an application layer gateway such as a proxy server, IANA recommends that you use the private IP addresses shown in Table 1.16.

TABLE 1.16 *Recommended Private IP Addresses*

Private network ID	Subnet mask	Range of IP addresses
10.0.0.0	255.0.0.0	10.0.0.1 - 10.255.255.254
172.16.0.0	255.240.0.0	172.16.0.1 - 172.31.255.254
192.168.0.0	255.255.0.0	192.168.0.1 - 192.168.255.254

Numbers in these ranges are reserved by IANA for private use on TCP/IP networks and are not used on the Internet.

For security reasons, it is unlikely that you would need to connect more than a few TCP/IP systems within your network directly to the Internet. For any host systems on your network that connect to the Internet, you must obtain the use of registered IP addresses from your Internet service provider (ISP).

Note If your ISP cannot provide sufficient public addresses to accommodate your needs and you are located in the United States, you can apply directly to the American Registry for Internet Numbers (ARIN) to obtain an IANA-assigned IP network address. For more information about registering a public address, see the ARIN Web site (www.arin.net/intro.html).

Web addresses can change, so you might be unable to connect to the Web site or sites mentioned here.

For more information about private IP address numbering for private networks, see RFC 1918, "Address Allocation for Private Internets."

Default Gateways

Default gateways serve an important role in TCP/IP networking. They provide a default route for TCP/IP hosts to use when communicating with other hosts on remote networks.

Figure 1-14 shows the roles played by the default gateways (IP routers) for two networks: Network 1 and Network 2.

In order for Host A on Network 1 to communicate with Host B on Network 2, Host A first checks its routing table to see if a specific route to Host B exists. If there is no specific route to Host B, Host A forwards its TCP/IP traffic for Host B to its own default gateway, IP Router 1.

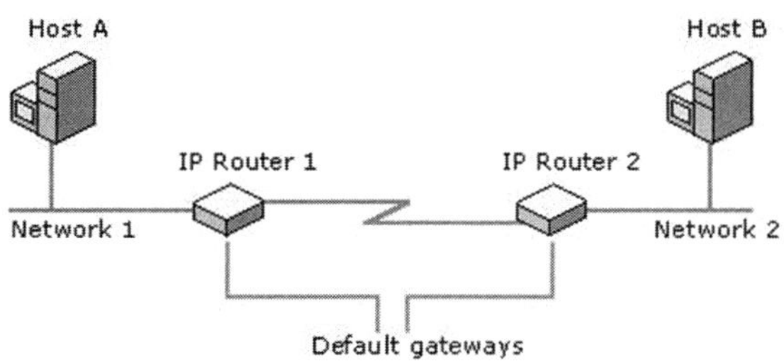

FIGURE 1–14 *Role of default gateways*

The same principle applies if Host B is sending to Host A. Without a specific route to Host A, Host B forwards any TCP/IP traffic destined for Host A to its own default gateway, IP Router 2.

Why Gateways Work

Default gateways are important to make IP routing work efficiently. In most cases, the router that acts as the default gateway for TCP/IP hosts—either a dedicated router or a computer that connects two or more network segments—maintains knowledge of other networks in the larger network and how to reach them.

TCP/IP hosts rely on default gateways for most of their communication needs with hosts on remote network segments. In this way, individual hosts are freed of the burden of having to maintain extensive and continuously updated knowledge about individual remote IP network segments. Only the router that acts as the default gateway needs to maintain this level of routing knowledge to reach other remote network segments in the larger internetwork.

If the default gateway fails, communication beyond the local network segment may be impaired. To prevent this, you can use the **Advanced TCP/IP Settings** dialog box (in Network and Dial-up Connections) for each connection to specify multiple default gateways. You can also use the **route** command to manually add routes to the routing table for heavily used hosts or networks.

Using Multiple Gateways

When configuring TCP/IP for Windows 2000, you can add more default gateways for each network adapter. When a computer is configured for multiple default gateways, all remote TCP/IP traffic that does not match an entry in the routing table is passed to the first default gateway defined for the first network adapter.

Because only one default gateway (the one defined for the first network adapter) is used, you should configure only one network adapter to have default gateways. This practice reduces confusion and assures the results you intended. For example, if you have two network adapters and configure a default gateway for each, the default gateway of the first network adapter is used. The default gateway for the second is used if the first is unavailable.

Author's Note The "multiple default gateways" feature is proprietary to Microsoft dead gateway detection and only works for TCP-based applications.

Advanced Configuration

Beyond the configuration of an IP address, subnet mask, default gateway, DNS server, and WINS server, you can configure Windows 2000 TCP/IP for:

- Advanced IP settings
- Advanced DNS settings
- Advanced WINS settings
- Advanced options

Advanced IP Settings

Advanced IP settings include:

- *Multiple IP addresses.* You can use multiple IP addresses per network adapter to allow for implementation of multiple IP numbering schemes, such as public addresses used for the Internet and private addresses, and for multiple logical IP networks on the same physical network segment.
- *Multiple default gateways.* You can use TCP/IP for Windows 2000 to detect downed routers by using a feature called *dead gateway detection.* If multiple default gateways are configured, a failing TCP connection updates the IP routing table with the next default gateway in the list.

For more information about configuring advanced IP settings, see Chapter 2.

Advanced DNS Settings

Advanced DNS settings include:

- *Multiple DNS servers.* If multiple DNS servers are configured and TCP/IP fails to receive any response from the current DNS server, TCP/IP switches to the next DNS server.
- *Unqualified name resolution.* For unqualified names, you can configure TCP/IP to either
  - Append the primary and connection-specific DNS suffixes to the unqualified name for DNS queries. For example, when looking up the machine named elvis, Windows 2000 completes the rest of the domain name by adding graceland.com for a fully-qualified name of elvis.graceland.com. Any unqualified name would have graceland.com appended to it.

- Append a series of configured DNS suffixes to the unqualified name for DNS queries. If the DNS resolver is presented with an unqualified domain name, it will try to add each configured domain extension and see if there is a match. For instance, if the system is looking up the domain name *corp-acctg,* the resolver will try appending *graceland.com* and look up *corp-acctg.graceland.com*. If that name does not exist, the system will then try appending *memphis.com* to see if *corp-acctg.memphis.com* exists, and if not, then it would try the next extension. If there were no matches, then the system would return an error indicating that the name does not exist. In that case, the user could try to be more specific and type the entire, fully qualified domain name (if they know it).

- *Connection-specific DNS suffixes*. You can configure each connection in Network and Dial-up Connections to have its own DNS suffix in addition to the primary DNS suffix that is configured for the computer on the **Network Identification** tab (available in System in Control Panel).

  Again, an example would be very helpful here. For instance, you could show how a computer that has a dial-up connection at home might also have an Ethernet connection at work. The DNS configuration for the corporate network would clearly need to be different than that of the dialup ISP.

- *DNS dynamic update behavior*. If you have DNS servers that support DNS dynamic update (such as the Windows 2000 DNS service), you can enable the DNS dynamic update of the domain name and IP addresses for the computer. If you configure a connection-specific DNS suffix, you can also enable the DNS dynamic update of the domain name and IP addresses for the connection.

For more information about configuring advanced DNS settings, see Chapter 2.

Advanced WINS Settings

Advanced WINS settings include:

- *Multiple WINS servers*. If multiple WINS servers are configured and TCP/IP fails to receive any response from the current WINS server, TCP/IP switches to the next WINS server.
- *Enabling and disabling the use of the Lmhosts file*. If the Lmhosts file is enabled, TCP/IP parses the Lmhosts file found in the *systemroot\System32\Drivers\Etc* folder during NetBIOS name resolution. By default, the use of the Lmhosts file is enabled. For more information, see Appendix A.

- *Enabling and disabling the use of NetBIOS over TCP/IP.* You can enable or disable the use of NetBIOS over TCP/IP. If the use of NetBIOS over TCP/IP is disabled, NetBIOS programs cannot run over TCP/IP. Therefore, you may not be able to connect to computers that are running an operating system other than Windows 2000. By default, the use of NetBIOS over TCP/IP is specified by the settings obtained from a DHCP server.

For more information about configuring advanced WINS settings, see Chapter 2.

Note You can no longer configure the NetBIOS scope ID on the WINS tab. To configure the NetBIOS scope ID, set the following registry value to the name of the scope ID that you want to use:

HKEY_LOCAL_MACHINE\SYSTEM\CurrentControlSet\Services\NetBT\Parameters\ScopeID

Advanced Options

Advanced options include:

- *Enabling Internet Protocol security and specifying an IPSec security policy.* If IPSec is configured, secure end-to-end communication of IP-based traffic on a private network or the Internet is used. By default, IPSec is disabled. For more information, see Chapter 2.
- *Enabling TCP/IP filtering and specifying TCP/IP traffic.* If TCP/IP filtering is enabled, you can specify what types of TCP/IP traffic are processed. For more information, see Chapter 2.

T W O

Installing, Managing, and Diagnosing TCP/IP

Install TCP/IP

To install TCP/IP, you must be logged on as an administrator or a member of the Administrators group:

1. To open Network and Dial-up Connections, click **Start**, point to **Settings**, and then click **Network and Dial-up Connections**. (See Figure 2-1.)

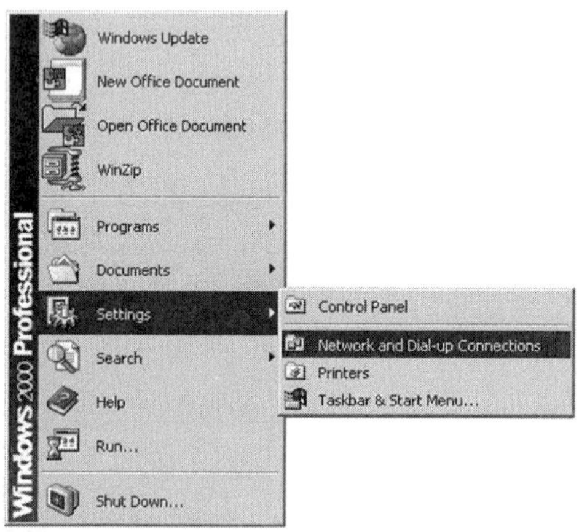

FIGURE 2-1 *Accessing Network and Dial-up Connections through Start | Settings menu*

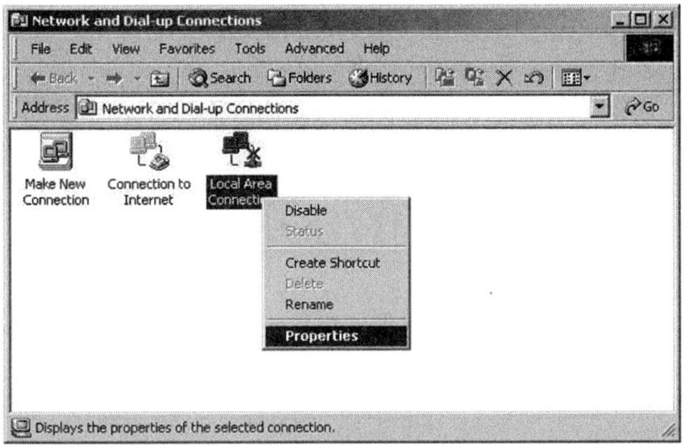

FIGURE 2–2 *Select Properties from the short-cut menu*

2. Right-click the network connection for which you want to install and enable TCP/IP, and then click **Properties**. (See Figure 2-2.)
3. On the **General** tab (for a local area connection, shown in Figure 2-3) or the **Networking** tab (for all other connections, also shown in Figure 2-3), if Internet Protocol (TCP/IP) is not in the list of installed components, then do the following:

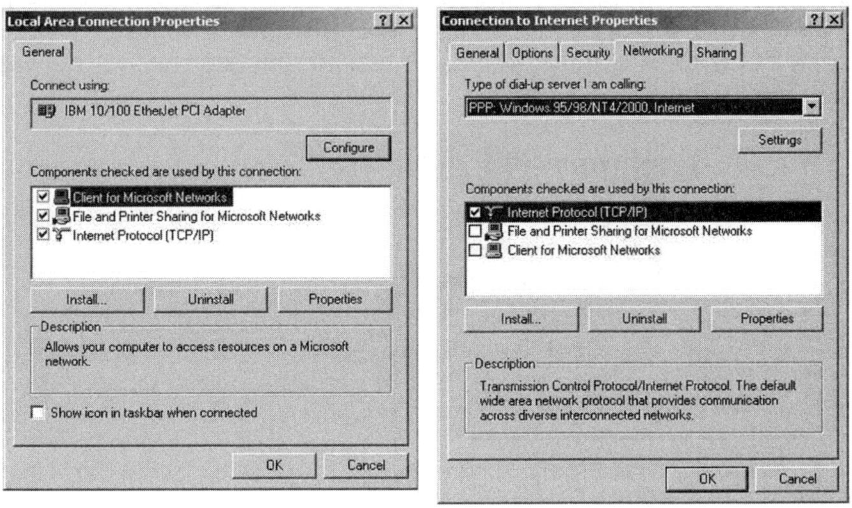

FIGURE 2–3 *General tab for LAN connections and Networking tab for all others*

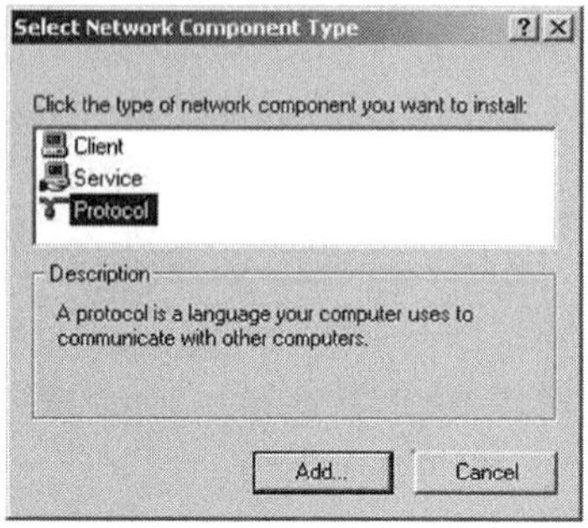

FIGURE 2–4 *Select the Protocol your computer will use to communicate with other computers*

a. Click **Install**.
b. Click **Protocol**, and then click **Add**. (See Figure 2-4.)
c. In the Select Network Protocol dialog box, click **Internet Protocol (TCP/IP)**, and then click **OK**.

4. Verify that the **Internet Protocol (TCP/IP)** check box is selected, and then click **OK**.

TCP/IP is installed as the default network protocol if network adapter hardware was detected during Windows 2000 Setup. You only need to follow these instructions if the TCP/IP default selection was overridden during Setup.

Configure TCP/IP

This section covers:

- Configuring TCP/IP for dynamic addressing.
- Configuring TCP/IP for automatic addressing.
- Disabling automatic address configuration.
- Configuring TCP/IP for static addressing.
- Configuring TCP/IP to use DNS.
- Configuring TCP/IP to use WINS.
- Configuring TCP/IP to use an IPSec policy.
- Configuring TCP/IP to use TCP/IP filtering.

Configure TCP/IP for Dynamic Addressing

To configure TCP/IP for dynamic addressing, you must be logged on as an administrator or a member of the Administrators group.

1. To open Network and Dial-up Connections, click **Start**, point to **Settings**, and then click **Network and Dial-up Connections**.
2. Right-click the network connection that you want to configure, and then click **Properties**.
3. On the **General** tab (for a local area connection) or the **Networking** tab for all other connections), click **Internet Protocol (TCP/IP)**, and then click **Properties**.
4. Click **Obtain an IP address automatically**, and then click **OK**. (See Figure 2-5.)

These instructions are only required if a static TCP/IP configuration was previously used. By default, Windows 2000 attempts to obtain the TCP/IP configuration from a DHCP server on your network.

Configure TCP/IP for Automatic Addressing

You must be logged on as an administrator or a member of the Administrators group in order to complete this procedure:

1. To open Network and Dial-up Connections, click **Start**, point to **Settings**, and then click **Network and Dial-up Connections**.
2. Right-click the network connection that you want to configure, and then click **Properties**.

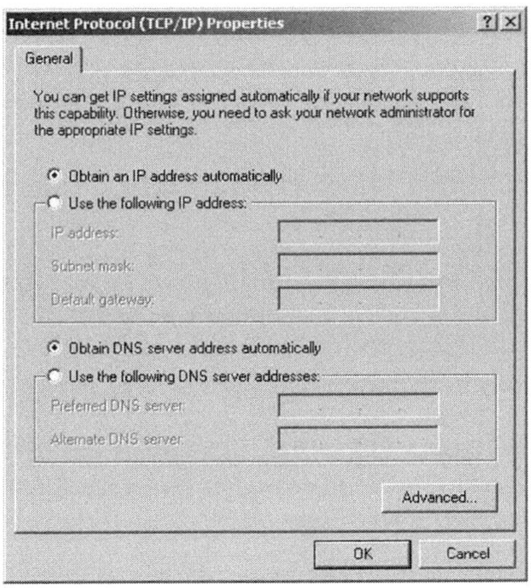

FIGURE 2–5 *Click Obtain an IP address automatically for dynamic addressing*

3. On the **General** tab (for a local area connection) or the **Networking** tab (for all other connections), click **Internet Protocol (TCP/IP)**, and then click **Properties**.
4. Click **Obtain an IP address automatically**, and then click **OK** (see Figure 2-5).

Windows 2000 uses Automatic Private IP Addressing (APIPA) to automate Internet Protocol (IP) configuration of network connections.

By default, the computer first tries to contact a DHCP server on the network and dynamically obtain configuration for each installed network connection, as follows:

- If a DHCP server is reached and leased configuration is successful, TCP/IP configuration is completed.
- If a DHCP server is not reached or if leased configuration fails, the computer uses APIPA to automatically configure TCP/IP. When APIPA is used, Windows 2000 determines an address in the Microsoft-reserved IP addressing range from 169.254.0.1 through 169.254.255.254. This address is used until a DHCP server is located. The subnet mask is set to 255.255.0.0.

The range of IP addresses (from 169.254.0.1 through 169.254.255.254) used for APIPA is reserved by the Internet Assigned Numbers Authority (IANA). Any IP addresses within this range are not used on the Internet.

Author's Note I would like to note that any machines on a network that are using APIPA-assigned addresses will only be able to communicate with each other, and will not be able to communicate with any hosts beyond that subnetwork (even hosts on other subnetworks that are also using APIPA-assigned addresses).

Disable Automatic Address Configuration

To disable automatic address configuration, you must be logged on as an administrator or a member of the Administrators group:

1. To open Registry Editor, click **Start**, click **Run**, type *regedt32*, and then click **OK**. (See Figure 2-6.)

Caution Incorrectly editing the registry may severely damage your system. Before making changes to the registry, you should back up any valued data on the computer. You can also use the Last Known Good Configuration startup option if problems are encountered after manual changes have been applied.

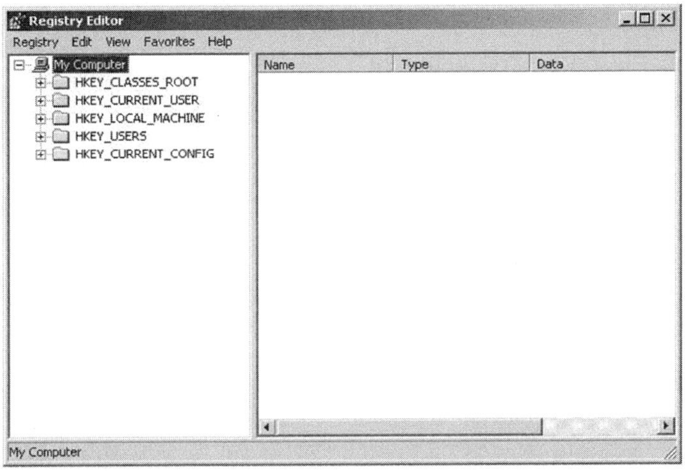

FIGURE 2–6 *You should back up any valued data on the computer before opening the Registry Editor*

2. In **Registry Editor**, navigate to the following registry key (see Figure 2-7):

HKEY_LOCAL_MACHINE\SYSTEM\CurrentControlSet\Services\Tcpip \Parameters\Interfaces\adapter_name

3. Create the following entry:

IPAutoconfigurationEnabled: REG_DWORD

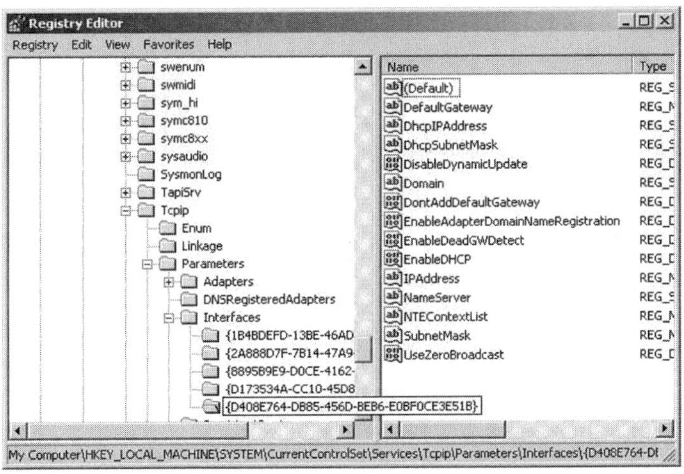

FIGURE 2–7 *Select the adapter you want to edit in the Registry*

4. Assign a value of **0** to disable APIPA support for the selected network adapter.
5. Close Registry Editor.

If the **IPAutoconfigurationEnabled** entry is not present, a default value of 1 is assumed, which indicates that APIPA is used when necessary (i.e., when normal DHCP operation fails).

If multiple adapters are installed, you can disable APIPA for all installed adapters by setting the **IPAutoconfigurationEnabled** entry to **0** at the following registry key:

HKEY_LOCAL_MACHINE\SYSTEM\CurrentControlSet\Services\Tcpip\Parameters

Configure TCP/IP for Static Addressing

To configure TCP/IP for static addressing, you must be logged on as an administrator or a member of the Administrators group:

1. To open Network and Dial-up Connections, click **Start**, point to **Settings**, and then click **Network and Dial-up Connections**.
2. Right-click the network connection you want to configure, and then click **Properties**.
3. On the **General** tab (for a local area connection) or the **Networking** tab (for all other connections), click **Internet Protocol (TCP/IP)**, and then click **Properties**.
4. Click **Use the following IP address** (see Figure 2-8), and do one of the following:

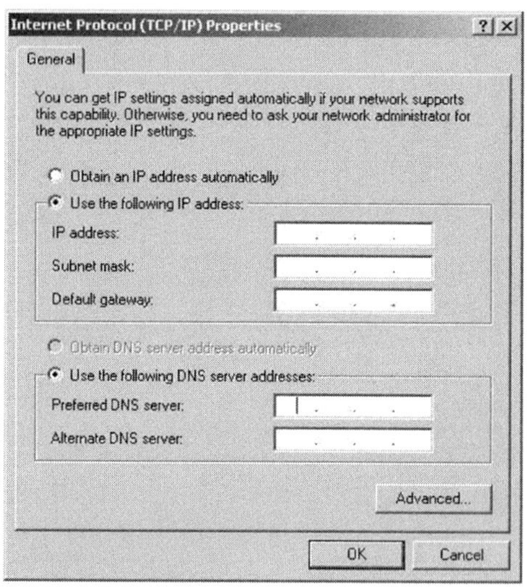

FIGURE 2-8 *Ask your network administrator for the appropriate IP settings*

- For a local area connection, in **IP address**, **Subnet mask**, and **Default gateway**, type the IP address, subnet mask, and default gateway addresses.
- For all other connections, in **IP address**, type the IP address.

5. Click **Use the following DNS server addresses**.
6. In **Preferred DNS server** and **Alternate DNS server**, type the primary and secondary DNS server addresses.
7. To configure advanced settings, click **Advanced**, and do one or more of the following:

   - To configure additional IP addresses,
     a. On the **IP Settings** tab, in **IP addresses**, click **Add**.
     b. In **IP Address** and **Subnet mask**, type an IP address and subnet mask, and then click **Add**.
     c. Repeat step 1 for each IP address you want to add, and then click **OK**.
   - To configure additional default gateways,
     a. On the **IP Settings** tab, in **Default gateways**, click **Add**.
     b. In **Gateway** and **Metric**, type the IP address of the default gateway and the metric, and then click **Add**.
     c. Repeat step 1 for each default gateway you want to add, and then click **OK**.
   - To configure a custom metric for this connection, type a metric value in **Interface metric**.

Configure TCP/IP to Use DNS

To configure TCP/IP to use DNS, you must be logged on as an administrator or a member of the Administrators group:

1. To open Network and Dial-up Connections, click **Start**, point to **Settings**, and then click **Network and Dial-up Connections**.
2. Right-click the network connection you want to configure, and then click **Properties**.
3. On the **General** tab (for a local area connection) or the **Networking** tab (for all other connections), click **Internet Protocol (TCP/IP)**, and then click **Properties**.
4. If you want to obtain DNS server addresses from a DHCP server, click **Obtain DNS server address automatically** (see Figure 2-8).
5. If you want to manually configure DNS server addresses, click **Use the following DNS server addresses**, and in **Preferred DNS server** and **Alternate DNS server**, type the preferred DNS server and alternate DNS server IP addresses.
6. To configure advanced DNS properties, click **Advanced**, click the **DNS** tab, and do one or more of the following (see Figure 2-9):

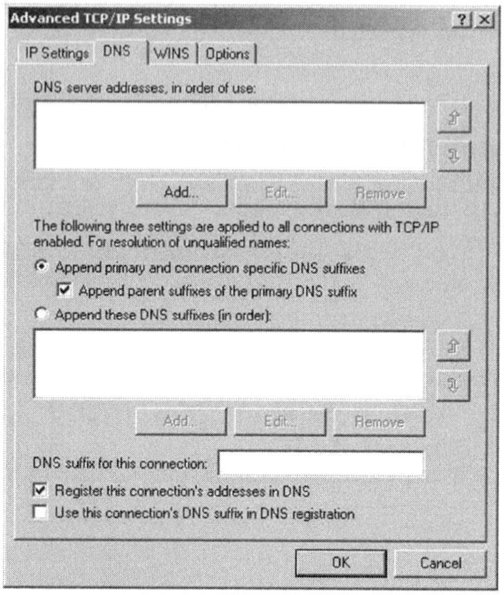

FIGURE 2–9 *To configure advanced DNS properties, click Advanced, then click the DNS tab*

- To configure an additional DNS server IP address,
  a. Under DN server addresses, in order of use, click **Add**.
  b. In **DNS server**, type the IP address of the DNS server, and then click **Add**.
- To modify the resolution behavior for unqualified DNS names, do the following:
  - To resolve an unqualified name by appending the primary DNS suffix and the DNS suffix of each connection (if configured), click **Append primary and connection specific DNS suffixes**. If you also want to search the parent suffixes of the primary DNS suffix up to the second level domain, select the **Append parent suffixes of the primary DNS suffix** check box.
  - To resolve an unqualified name by appending the suffixes from a list of configured suffixes, click **Append these DNS suffixes (in order)**, and then click **Add** to add suffixes to the list.
- To configure a connection-specific DNS suffix (local area connection only), type the DNS suffix in **DNS suffix for this connection**.
- To modify DNS dynamic update behavior (local area connection only), do the following:

- To use a DNS dynamic update to register the IP addresses of this connection and the primary domain name of the computer, select the **Register this connection's addresses in DNS** check box. This option is enabled by default. The primary domain name of the computer is the primary DNS suffix appended to the computer name and can be viewed as the full computer name on the **Network Identification** tab (available in System in Control Panel).
- To use a DNS dynamic update to register the IP addresses and the connection-specific domain name of this connection, select the **Use this connection's DNS suffix in DNS registration** check box. This option is disabled by default. The connection-specific domain name of this connection is the DNS suffix for this connection appended to the computer name.

To completely disable DNS dynamic update for all names on the computer, clear the **Register this connection's addresses in DNS** and **Use this connection's DNS suffix in DNS registration** check boxes for all connections in Network and Dial-up Connections.

Configure TCP/IP to Use WINS

To configure TCP/IP to use WINS, you must be logged on as an administrator or a member of the Administrators group:

1. To open Network and Dial-up Connections, click **Start**, point to **Settings**, and then click **Network and Dial-up Connections**.
2. Right-click the network connection you want to configure, and then click **Properties**.
3. On the **General** tab (for a local area connection) or the **Networking** tab (all other connections), click **Internet Protocol (TCP/IP)**, and then click **Properties**.
4. Click **Advanced**, click the **WINS** tab, and then click **Add**. (See Figure 2-10.)
5. In **TCP/IP WINS server**, type the IP address of the WINS server, and then click **Add**.
6. Repeat steps 4 and 5 for each WINS server IP address you want to add, and then click **OK**.
7. To enable the use of the lmhosts file to resolve remote NetBIOS names, select the **Enable LMHOSTS lookup** check box. This option is enabled by default.
8. To specify the location of the file that you want to import into the lmhosts file, click **Import LMHOSTS** and select the file in the **Open** dialog box.
9. To modify the behavior of NetBIOS over TCP/IP behavior, do the following:

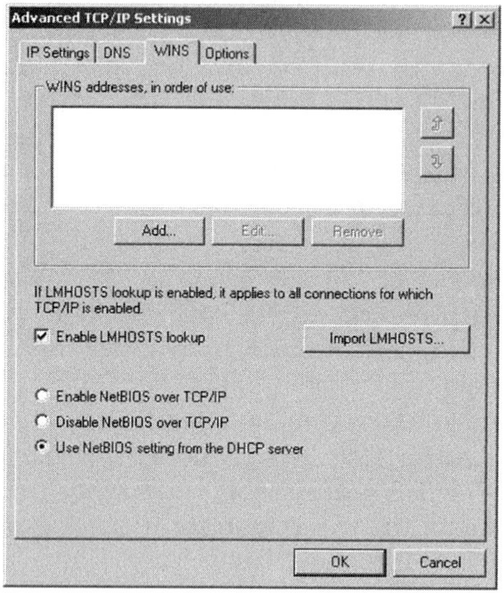

FIGURE 2–10 *You may configure advanced WINS properties by clicking Advanced, click the WINS tab*

- To enable the use of NetBIOS over TCP/IP, click **Enable NetBIOS over TCP/IP**.
- To disable the use of NetBIOS over TCP/IP, click **Disable NetBIOS over TCP/IP**.
- To have the DHCP server determine the NetBIOS behavior, click **Use NetBIOS setting from the DHCP server**.

If you are using a DHCP server to allocate WINS server IP addresses, you do not need to add WINS server addresses.

If you disable NetBIOS over TCP/IP, you may not be able to connect to computers that are running operating systems other than Windows 2000.

You can no longer configure the NetBIOS scope ID on the **WINS** tab. To configure the NetBIOS scope ID, set the following registry value to the name of the scope ID that you want to use:

HKEY_LOCAL_MACHINE\SYSTEM\CurrentControlSet\Services\NetBT\Parameters \ScopeID

Configure TCP/IP to Use an IPSec Policy

To configure TCP/IP to use an IPSec policy, you must be logged on as an administrator or a member of the Administrators group.

1. To open Network and Dial-up Connections, click **Start**, point to **Settings**, and then click **Network and Dial-up Connections**.
2. Right-click the network connection that you want to configure, and then click **Properties**.
3. On the **General** tab (for a local area connection) or the **Networking** tab (for all other connections), click **Internet Protocol (TCP/IP)**, and then click **Properties**.
4. Click **Advanced**.
5. On the **Options** tab, click **IP security**, and then click **Properties**. (See Figure 2-11.)
6. To enable IP security, click **Use this IP security policy**, and then click the name of a policy.

   To disable IP security, click **Do not use IPSEC**.

Author's Note Since IP Security is beyond the scope of this book and is only briefly mentioned, I recommend that you check out the following references for more information.

"IP Security in Windows 2000: Get Ready to Secure Your IP Network with IPSec" by Tao Zhou, Windows 2000 Magazine, March 2000. This article can be accessed from the Internet at *www.winntmag.com*.

Microsoft's "IP Security for MS Windows 2000 Server" whitepaper may be referenced at *www.microsoft.com/technet/*win2000/win2ksrv/technote/ipsecure.asp.

Microsoft's "Windows 2000 IP Security Interop" page may be referenced at http://w2kipsec-pub.rte.microsoft.com/htm/Clear.asp.

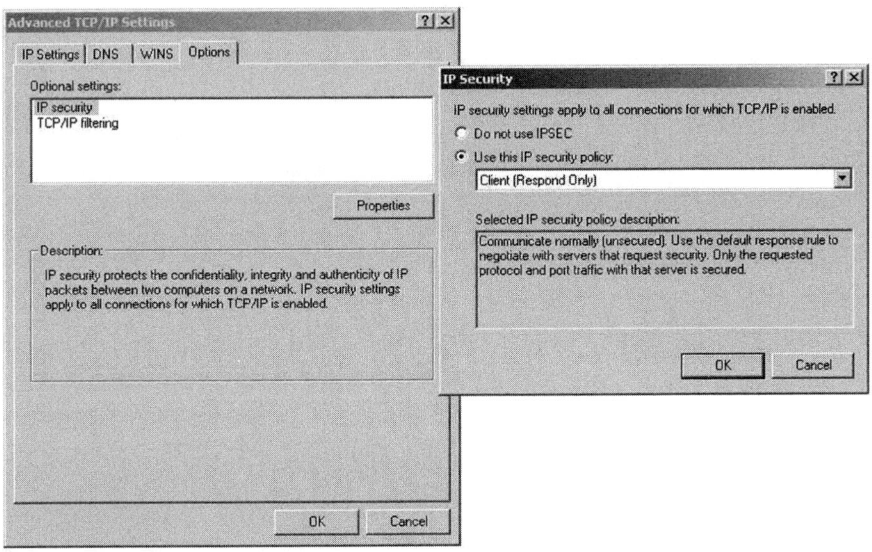

FIGURE 2–11 *Configuring TCP/IP to use an IPSec policy*

Configure TCP/IP to Use TCP/IP Filtering

To configure TCP/IP to use TCP/IP filtering:

1. To open Network and Dial-up Connections, click **Start**, point to **Settings**, and then click **Network and Dial-up Connections**.
2. Right-click the network connection you want to configure, and then click **Properties**.
3. On the **General** tab (for a local area connection) or the **Networking** tab (for all other connections), click **Internet Protocol (TCP/IP)**, and then click **Properties**.
4. Click **Advanced**.
5. Click **Options**, click **TCP/IP filtering**, and then click **Properties**. (See Figure 2-12.)
6. Do one of the following:
   - To enable TCP/IP filtering for all adapters, select the **Enable TCP/IP Filtering (All adapters)** check box.
   - To disable TCP/IP filtering for all adapters, clear the **Enable TCP/IP Filtering (All adapters)** check box.
7. Based on your requirements for TCP/IP filtering, configure TCP ports, UDP ports, or IP protocols for the allowed traffic.

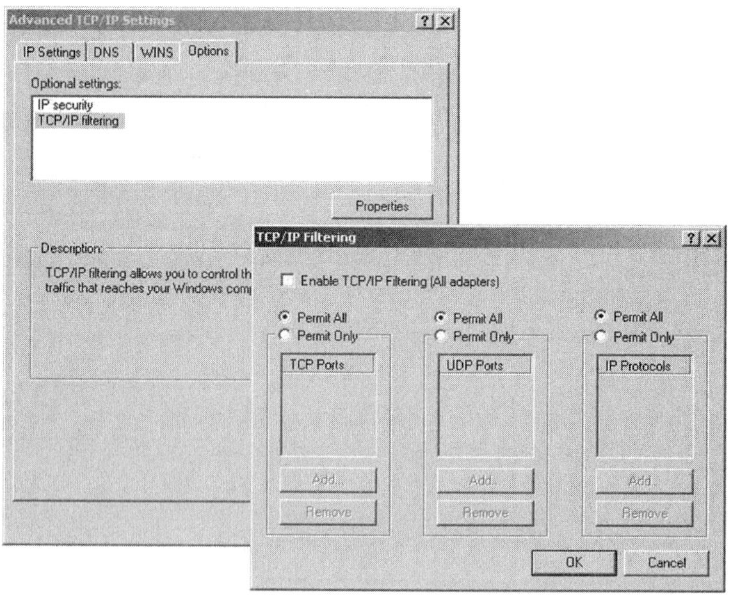

FIGURE 2–12 *Configuring TCP/IP to use TCP/IP filtering*

Install Simple TCP/IP Services

To install Simple TCP/IP Services, you must be logged on as an administrator or a member of the Administrators group:

1. To open Add/Remove Programs, click **Start**, point to **Settings**, click **Control Panel**, and then double-click **Add/Remove Programs**.
2. Click **Add/Remove Windows Components**. (See Figure 2-13.)
3. In the Windows Components Wizard, click **Next**.
4. In **Components**, click **Networking Services**, and then click **Details**. (See Figure 2-14.)

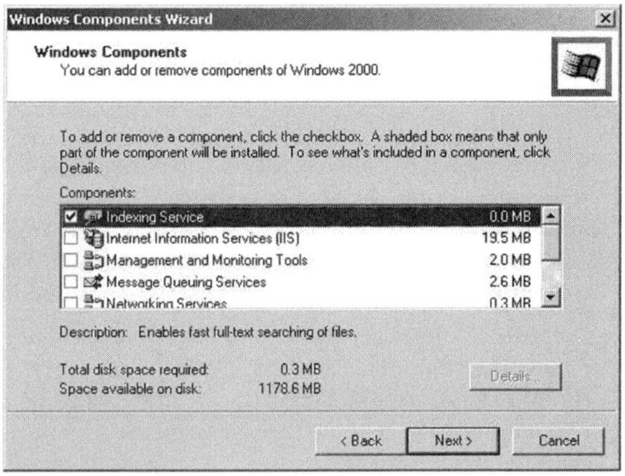

FIGURE 2–13 *Add or remove components through the Windows Components Wizard*

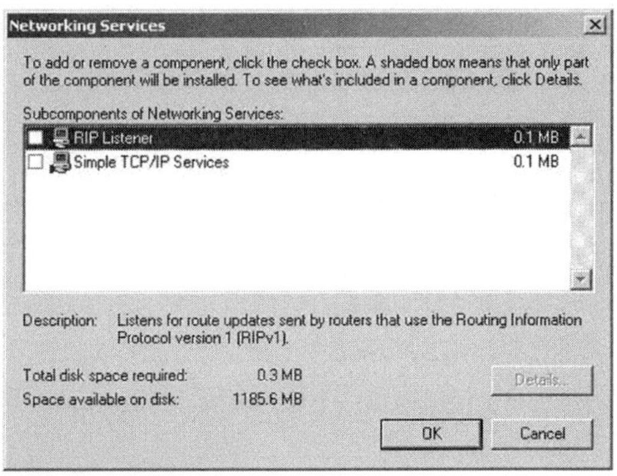

FIGURE 2–14 *Additional components that may be installed through the Networking Services*

5. In **Subcomponents of Networking Services**, click **Simple TCP/IP Services**, and then click **OK**.
6. Click **Next**.
7. If prompted, type the path where the Windows 2000 distribution files are located, and then click **OK**.
8. Complete any remaining screens in the wizard, and then click **Finish**.

Simple TCP/IP Services includes Windows 2000 utility software that provides support for the optional TCP/IP protocol services listed in Table 2.1.

TABLE 2.1 *Subcomponents of Networking Services under Simple TCP/IP Services*

Protocol	Description	RFC
Character Generator (CHARGEN)	Sends data made up of the set of 95 printable ASCII characters. Useful as a debugging tool for testing or troubleshooting line printers.	864
Daytime	Returns messages containing the day of the week, month, day, year, current time (in *hh:mm:ss* format), and time-zone information. Some programs can use the output from this service for debugging or monitoring variations in system clock time or on a different host, or to reset system time.	867
Discard	Discards all messages received on this port without response or acknowledgment. Can serve as a null port for receiving and routing TCP/IP test messages during network setup and configuration or, in some cases, can be used by programs as a message discard function.	863
Echo	Echoes back data from any messages it receives on this server port. Can be useful as a network debugging and monitoring tool.	862
Quote of the Day (QUOTE)	Returns a quotation as one or more lines of text in a message. Quotations are taken at random from the following file: *systemroot\System32\Drivers\Etc\Quotes*. A sample quote file is installed with the Simple TCP/IP Services. If this file is missing, the quote service fails.	865

All of these protocol services are classified as elective Internet standards and are defined and described in the specified Request for Comments (RFC) document listed in the table. For more information on these protocol services, see the RFCs.

Do not install Simple TCP/IP Services unless you specifically need this computer to support communication with other systems that use these protocol services.

Remove TCP/IP

To remove TCP/IP, you must be logged on as an administrator or a member of the Administrators group.

1. To open Network and Dial-up Connections, click **Start**, point to **Settings**, and then click **Network and Dial-up Connections**.
2. Right-click any network connection, and then click **Properties**.
3. On the **General** tab (for a local area connection) or the **Networking** tab (for all other connections), click **Internet Protocol (TCP/IP)**, and then click **Uninstall**.
4. In the **Uninstall Internet Protocol (TCP/IP)** dialog box, click **Yes**.

If Uninstall is dimmed, there are no other protocols installed. You cannot uninstall TCP/IP if no other protocols are available.

If you remove TCP/IP, you lose IPSec, the Active Directory, the Point-to-Point Tunneling Protocol (PPTP), and the Layer-2 Tunneling Protocol (L2TP).

View the IP Routing Table

To view the IP routing table:

1. To open Command Prompt, click **Start**, point to **Programs**, point to **Accessories**, and then click **Command Prompt**.
2. At the command prompt, type: *route print*. (See Figure 2-15.)

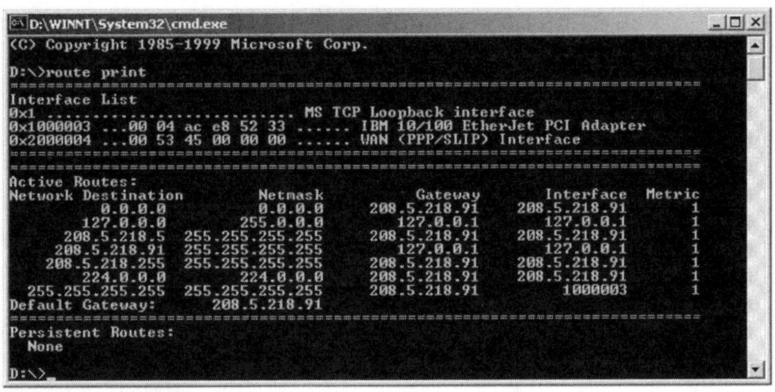

FIGURE 2–15 *An example of using the route print command to display active routes*

Add a Static IP Route

To add a static IP route:

1. To open Command Prompt, click **Start**, point to **Programs**, point to **Accessories**, and then click **Command Prompt**.
2. At the command prompt, type:

route add *destination* **mask** *subnetmask gateway* **metric** *costmetric* **if** *interface*

where:

destination	Specifies either an IP address or host name for the network or host.
subnetmask	Specifies a subnet mask to be associated with this route entry. If subnetmask is not specified, 255.255.255.255 is used.
gateway	Specifies either an IP address or host name for the gateway or router to use when forwarding.
costmetric	Assigns an integer cost metric (ranging from 1 through 9,999) to be used in calculating the fastest, most reliable, and/or least expensive routes. If costmetric is not specified, 1 is used.
interface	Specifies the interface to be used for the route that uses the interface number. If an interface is not specified, the interface to be used for the route is determined from the gateway IP address.

For example, to add a static route to the 10.0.0.0 network that uses a subnet mask of 255.0.0.0, a *gateway* of 192.168.0.1, and a cost metric of 2, you type the following at a command prompt:

route add 10.0.0.0 mask 255.0.0.0 gateway 192.168.0.1 metric 2

To make a static route persistent, you can either enter **route add** commands in a batch file that is run during system startup or use the **-p** option when adding routes.

Routes added by using the **-p** option are stored in the Windows 2000 registry under the following key:

HKEY_LOCAL_MACHINE\SYSTEM\CurrentControlSet\Services\Tcpip\Parameters \PersistentRoutes

All symbolic names used for *destination* or *gateway* are looked up in the network and in computer name database files (Networks and Hosts) which are stored in the local *systemroot\System32\Drivers\Etc* folder.

If a route addition fails, you can use the **tracert** command to verify that the gateway specified is directly reachable from the same subnet as this computer.

Remove a Static IP Route

To remove a static IP route:

1. To open Command Prompt, click **Start**, point to **Programs**, point to **Accessories**, and then click **Command Prompt**.
2. At the command prompt, type:

   route delete *destination*

   where

   destination Specifies either an IP address or network name for the remote TCP/IP host computer or network.

   For example, to delete a static route to the 10.0.0.0 network, you type the following at a command prompt:

   route delete 10.0.0.0

All symbolic names used for *destination* are looked up in the network database file Networks, which is stored in the local *systemroot\System32\Drivers\Etc* folder.

Enable IP Forwarding

To enable IP forwarding, you must be logged on as an administrator or a member of the Administrators group.

1. To open Registry Editor, click **Start**, click **Run**, type *regedt32*, and then click **OK**. (See Figure 2-16.)
2. In Registry Editor, navigate to the following registry key (see Figure 2-17):

HKEY_LOCAL_MACHINE\SYSTEM\CurrentControlSet\Services\Tcpip\Parameters

3. Select the following entry:

IPEnableRouter: REG_DWORD: 0x0

4. To enable IP forwarding for all network connections installed and used by this computer, assign a value of **1**.
5. Close Registry Editor.

By default, IP forwarding is disabled.

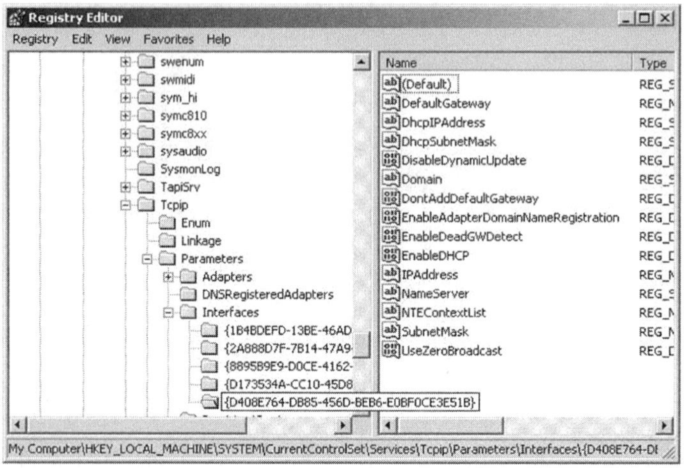

FIGURE 2–16 *Select the adapter you want to edit in the Registry*

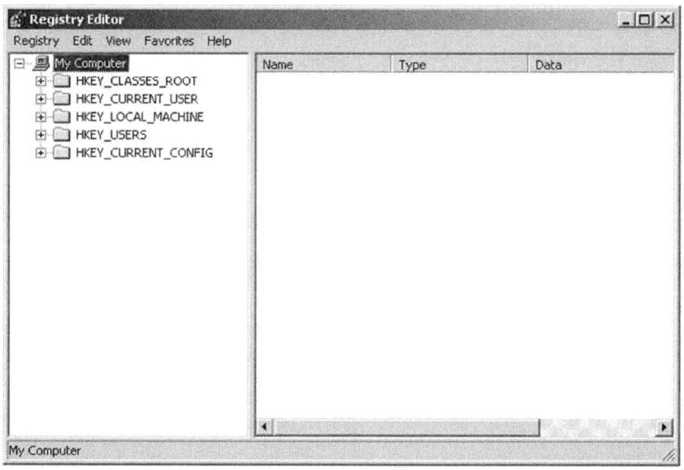

FIGURE 2–17 *You should back up any valued data on the computer before opening the Registry Editor*

Caution Incorrectly editing the registry may severely damage your system. Before making changes to the registry, you should back up any valued data on the computer. You can also use the Last Known Good Configuration startup option if you encounter problems after manual changes have been applied.

Test a TCP/IP Configuration by Using the Ping Command

To test a TCP/IP configuration by using the **ping** command,

1. Open Command Prompt, and then type *ipconfig*.
   To open Command Prompt, click **Start**, point to **Programs**, point to **Accessories**, and then click **Command Prompt**. (See Figure 2-18.)
2. At the command prompt, "ping" the loopback address by typing *ping 127.0.0.1*. (See Figure 2-19.)

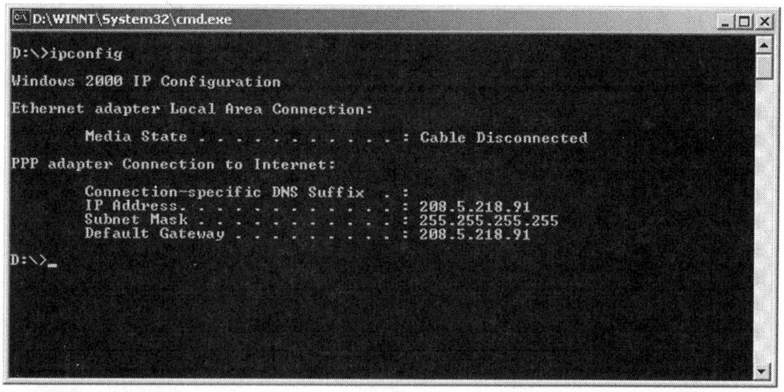

FIGURE 2-18 *An example of the ipconfig command and its output*

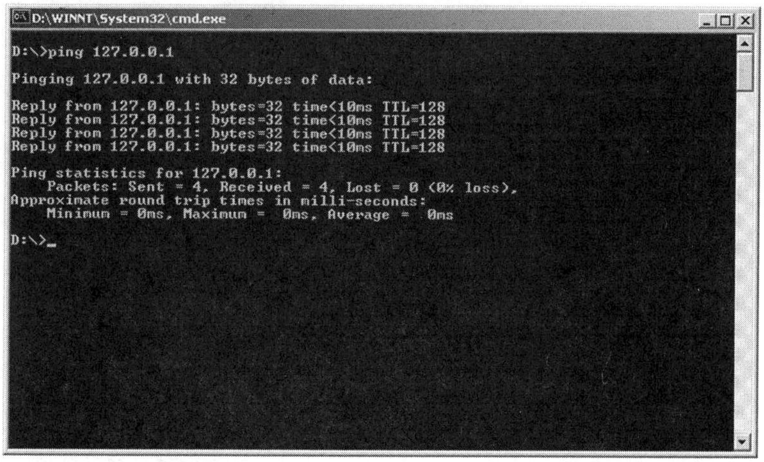

FIGURE 2-19 *Output generated by pinging the loopback address*

If the **ping** command fails, verify that the computer was restarted after TCP/IP was installed and configured.

3. Ping the IP address of the computer. (See Figure 2-20.)

   If the **ping** command fails, verify that the computer was restarted after TCP/IP was installed and configured.

4. Ping the IP address of the default gateway.

   If the **ping** command fails, verify that the default gateway IP address is correct and that the gateway (router) is operational.

5. Ping the IP address of a remote host (a host that is on a different subnet).

   If the **ping** command fails, verify that the remote host IP address is correct, that the remote host is operational, and that all the gateways (routers) between this computer and the remote host are operational.

6. Ping the IP address of the DNS server.

   If the **ping** command fails, verify that the DNS server IP address is correct, that the DNS server is operational, and that all the gateways (routers) between this computer and the DNS server are operational. (See Figure 2-21.)

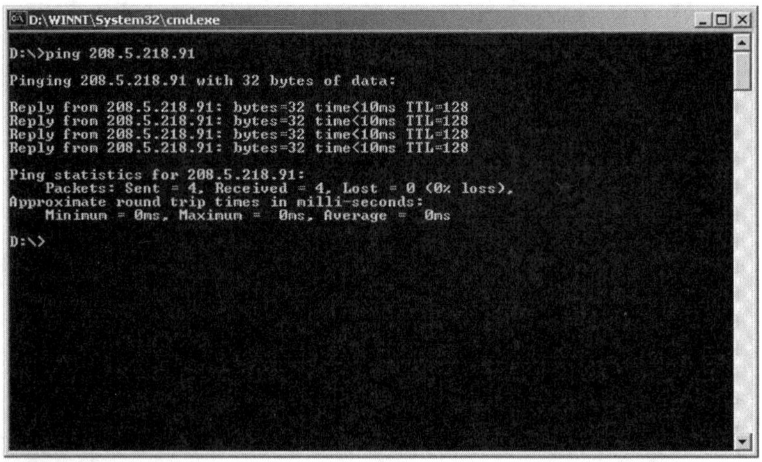

FIGURE 2–20 *Output generated by pinging the IP address of the computer*

Author's Note In the above procedures, when testing a TCP/IP configuration by using the ping command, I made the assumption that the user has administrative access to all the routers along the path, and the even bigger assumption that the user knows which routers those are.

It is recommended to always try traceroute (tracert under Windows 2000) if ping fails, so you at least know how far your packets got, and also so you can start troubleshooting at the point where the tracert failed.

Even if you don't have administrative access to the network, at least then end users can call the network manager and tell him or her, "When I try to send packets to destination x from my address, they stop at router Q."

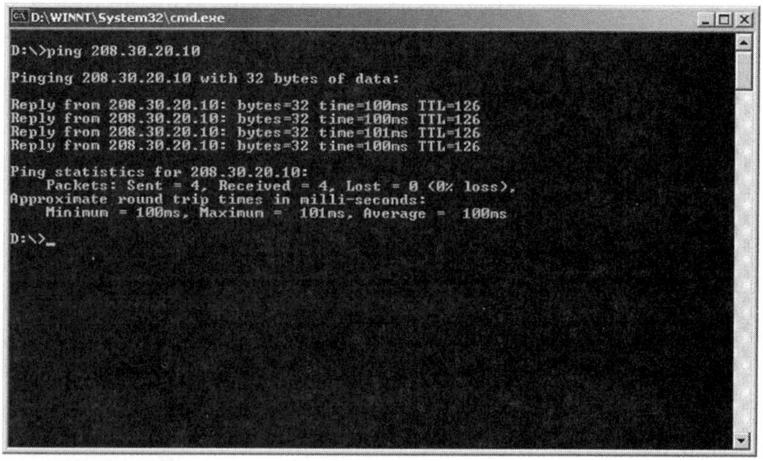

FIGURE 2–21 *Output from pinging a DNS server*

If the **ping** command is not found or the command fails, you can use Event Viewer to check the System Log and look for problems reported by Setup or the Internet Protocol (TCP/IP) service.

Test TCP/IP Connections by Using the Ping and Net View Commands

To test TCP/IP connections by using the **ping** and **net view** commands:

1. Open the **Command Prompt**, and then ping the desired host using its IP address.

   If the **ping** command fails with a "Request timed out" message, verify that the host IP address is correct, that the host is operational, and that all the gateways (routers) between this computer and the host are operational.
2. Ping the desired host using its host name.

   If the **ping** command fails with an "Unknown Host" message, verify that the host name is correct and that your DNS server should be able to resolve the host name.

3. To test TCP/IP connectivity by using the **netview** command, open Command Prompt, and then type *net view\\computername*. The **net view** command lists the file and print shares of a computer running Windows 2000 by establishing a temporary NetBIOS connection. If there are no file or print shares on the specified computer, the **net view** command displays a "There are no entries in the list" message.

   If the **net view** command fails with a "System error 53 has occurred" message, verify that *computername* is correct, that the computer running Windows 2000 is operational, and that all the gateways (routers) between this computer and the computer running Windows 2000 are operational. Again, see earlier comment about tracert, in cases where the user doesn't have administrative access to all the routers, or does not even know what the routed path should be.

   To further troubleshoot this connectivity problem, do the following:

   - Use the **ping** command to ping *computername*.
   - If the **ping** command fails with an "Unknown host" message, then *computername* cannot be resolved to its IP address.
   - Use the **net view** command and the IP address of the computer running Windows 2000, as follows:

   net view*IP address*

   If the **net view** command succeeds then *computername* is being resolved to the wrong IP address.

   If the **net view** command fails with a "System error 53 has occurred" message, the computer running Windows 2000 is not running the File and Printer Sharing for MicrosoftNetworks service.

See Author's Note on using **tracert** in the section "Test a TCP/IP Configuration by Using the Ping Command."

If the **ping** command is not found or the command fails, you can use Event Viewer to check the System Log and look for problems reported by Setup or the Internet Protocol (TCP/IP) service.

Trace a Path by Using the Tracert Command

To trace a path by using the **tracert** command:

Open **Command Prompt**, and type the following:

tracert host_name

Or, type:

tracert ip_address

where *host_name* or *ip_address* is the host name or IP address, respectively, of the remote computer.

For example, to trace a connection route from this computer to *www.microsoft.com,* type the following at a command prompt (see Figure 2-22):

tracert www.microsoft.com

Tracert sends a packet to the requested destination with its IP TTL set to 1. The first router the packet encounters will send back an error message using the "ICMP Time Exceeded" message (not echo request or reply). Upon receiving this message, the system will send a packet to the destination with a TTL of 2, which will cause the second router along the path to send back an "ICMP Time Exceeded" error message. These error messages serve to identify the routers along the path without the sending station needing to know anything more than its own default gateway. The process continues, each iteration incrementing the packet's TTL and causing the next router to send an "ICMP Time Exceeded" error message back to the original host. When the packet reaches its final destination, the UDP destination port is examined and no local service is running on that port, so the destination host returns an "ICMP Port Unreachable" error message, completing the traceroute procedure.

If **tracert** is unsuccessful, you can use the command output to help determine at which intermediate router forwarding failed. **Tracert** may also be used to pinpoint links between routers that are experiencing excessive delay, enabling the user to alert the network administrator that there may be a problem with those routers or the link(s) between them.

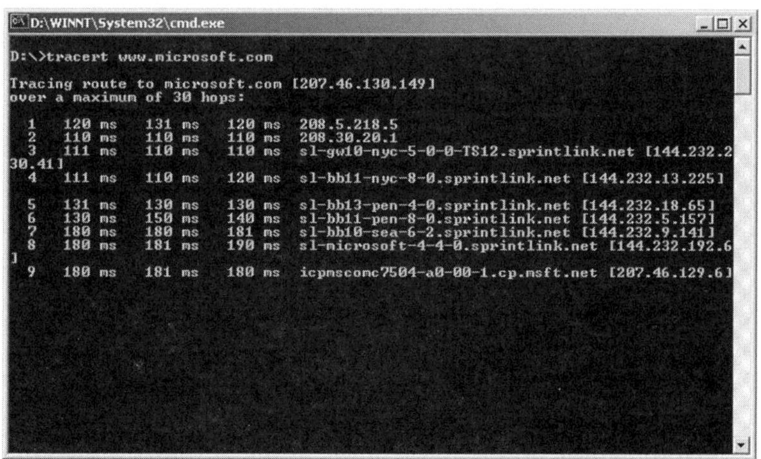

FIGURE 2–22 *A sample output from doing a trace route on www.microsoft.com*

View the NetBIOS Name Table by Using the nbtstat Command

To view the NetBIOS name table by using the **nbtstat** command:

1. Click **Start**, point to **Programs**, point to **Accessories**, and then click **Command Prompt**.
2. At the command prompt, type:

nbtstat -n

The NetBIOS local name table for this computer is displayed as command-line output. The name type is listed to indicate whether each name is a unique name or a group name. Also, the status for each name is given, indicating whether the name is registered or unregistered with the network.

The **nbtstat** command displays statistics and names information used by NetBIOS over TCP/IP (NetBT) connections. The **-n** option is used to list only local NetBIOS names for this computer. You can also use **nbtstat** to:

- List the NetBIOS name table of a remote computer.
- Display the contents of the NetBIOS names cache on this computer or another remote computer.
- Manually load or reload the NetBIOS names cache by using entries in the lmhosts file with a **#PRE** option.
- List NetBIOS over TCP/IP sessions statistics.
- Release and refresh NetBIOS names in WINS.

Release and Refresh NetBIOS Names by Using the nbtstat Command

To release and refresh NetBIOS names by using the **nbtstat** command,

1. Click **Start**, point to **Programs**, point to **Accessories**, and then click **Command Prompt**.
2. At the command prompt, type:

nbtstat -RR

The progress of the release and refresh process is displayed as command-line output. This information indicates if all local NetBIOS names currently registered in WINS for this computer have released and renewed their registration with a WINS server.

NetBIOS names are registered with WINS and are normally released when the computer shuts down properly. If the computer did not properly shut down or could not contact a WINS server during shutdown and release its names, you can use this command to force a refresh and update in WINS of the local names for this computer. This is useful for mobile or portable computers that are moved between different locations on a network.

You can also use the **nbtstat** command to:

- List the NetBIOS names registered to this computer or another remote computer.
- Display the contents of the NetBIOS names cache on this computer or another remote computer.
- Manually load or reload the NetBIOS names cache by using entries in the lmhosts file with a **#PRE** option.
- List statistics for NetBIOS over TCP/IP sessions.

View the Address Resolution Protocol Cache

To view the Address Resolution Protocol (ARP) cache:

1. Click **Start**, point to **Programs**, point to **Accessories**, and then click **Command Prompt**.
2. At the command prompt, type *arp -a*. (See Figure 2-23.)

For example, if you recently used the **ping** command to test and verify connectivity from this computer to a host computer at IP address 10.0.0.99,

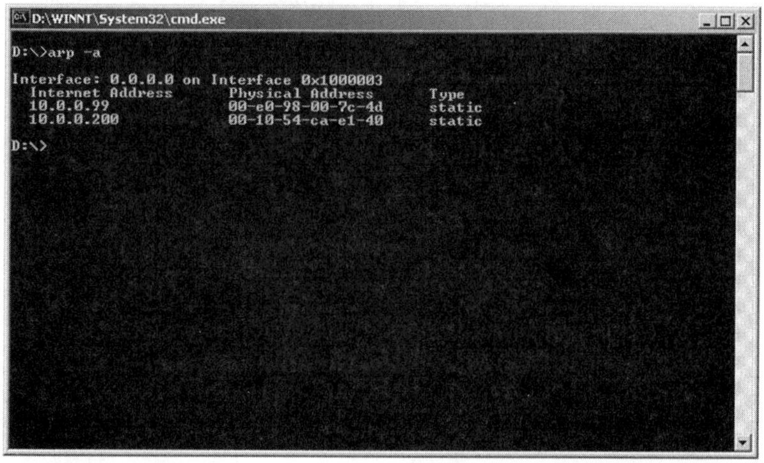

FIGURE 2–23 *Use arp -a to view the ARP cache*

the ARP cache displays the following entry (presuming that this computer and 10.0.0.99 are on the same subnetwork):

```
Interface: 10.0.0.1 on Interface 0x1
Internet Address        Physical Address       Type
10.0.0.99               00-e0-98-00-7c-dc      dynamic
```

In this example, the cache entry indicates that the remote host computer at 10.0.0.99 resolved to a media access control address of 00-e0-98-00-7c-dc assigned in the network adapter hardware of the remote computer. The media access control address is the address that your computer used to physically communicate with this remote TCP/IP host on your network.

To minimize ARP broadcast traffic on your network, Windows 2000 maintains a cache of MAC-to-IP address mappings for future use. This cache contains the following two types of entries:

- *Dynamic ARP cache entries*. These entries are added and deleted automatically during normal use of TCP/IP sessions with remote computers. Dynamic entries age and expire from the cache if not reused within two minutes. If a dynamic entry is reused within two minutes, it may remain in the cache and age up to a maximum cache life of 10 minutes before being removed or requiring cache renewal by using the ARP broadcast process.
- *Static ARP cache entries*. These entries are added manually by using the **arp** command with the **-s** option. Static entries remain in the ARP cache until the computer is restarted.

Author's Note I would like to note that the ARP specification does not have rules for ARP cache management, and that other operating systems (even other versions of Windows) may not behave like Windows 2000.

Add a Static ARP Cache Entry

Static ARP entries may be used to optimize communication with hosts that are frequently used. To add a static ARP cache entry:

1. Click **Start**, point to **Programs**, point to **Accessories**, and then click **Command Prompt**.
2. At the command prompt, type:

arp -s ip_address mac_address

where:

ip_address	Specifies the IP address of a local (on the same subnet) TCP/IP node.
mac_address	Specifies the media access control address for a network adapter installed and used on the local TCP/IP node.

For example, to add a static ARP entry for a local TCP/IP node with an IP address of 10.0.0.200 that resolves to a media access control address of 00-10-54-CA-E1-40, you type the following at a command prompt:

arp -s 10.0.0.200 00-10-54-CA-E1-40

Static entries are valid only until Windows 2000 is restarted. To make static ARP cache entries persistent, you can add **arp** commands to a batch file that is run at system startup.

View Current TCP/IP Protocol and Connection Statistics

To view current TCP/IP protocol and connection statistics:

1. Click **Start**, point to **Programs**, point to **Accessories**, and then click **Command Prompt**.
2. At the command prompt, type:

netstat

To view **netstat** command-line options, type *netstat /?*

For more information on **netstat**, refer to Appendix E, "TCP/IP Utilities."

T H R E E

DHCP Overview

DHCP Defined

Dynamic Host Configuration Protocol (DHCP) is a TCP/IP draft-standard for centralizing management of host IP configuration. The DHCP protocol provides for the use of DHCP servers as a way to centrally and dynamically manage allocation of IP addresses and other related configuration details to DHCP-enabled clients on your network.

Every computer on a TCP/IP network must have a unique computer name and IP address. The IP address (together with its related subnet mask) identifies both the host computer and the subnet to which it is attached. When you move a computer to a different subnet, the IP address must be changed. DHCP allows you to dynamically assign an IP address to a client from a DHCP server IP address database on your local network, as shown in Figure 3-1.

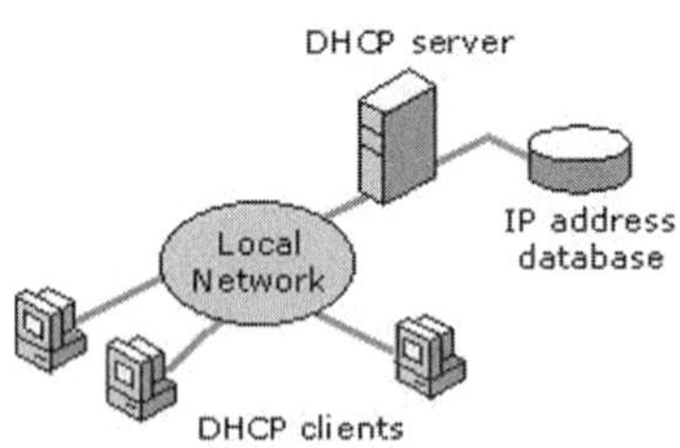

FIGURE 3–1 *Simple DHCP network*

For TCP/IP-based networks, DHCP reduces the complexity and amount of administrator work involved in reconfiguring computers.

Windows 2000 Server provides an RFC-compliant DHCP service you can use to centrally manage IP client configuration and automate IP address assignment on your network. For more information on the DHCP standard specifications, see Appendix B, "DHCP Resources and Troubleshooting."

Benefits of Using DHCP

DHCP provides the following benefits for administering your TCP/IP-based network:

- *Safe and reliable configuration.* DHCP avoids configuration errors caused by the need to manually type in values at each computer. Also, DHCP helps prevent address conflicts caused by a previously assigned IP address being reused to configure a new computer on the network.
- *Reduces configuration management.* Using DHCP servers can greatly decrease time spent configuring and reconfiguring computers on your network. Servers can be configured to supply a full range of additional configuration values when assigning address leases. These values are assigned using DHCP options.

  Also, the DHCP lease renewal process helps assure that where client configurations need to be updated often (such as for users with mobile or portable computers who change locations frequently), these changes can be made efficiently and automatically by clients communicating directly with DHCP servers.

How DHCP Works

DHCP uses a client-server model. The network administrator establishes one or more DHCP servers that maintain TCP/IP configuration information and provide it to clients. The server database includes the following:

- Valid configuration parameters for all clients on the network.
- Valid IP addresses maintained in a pool for assignment to clients, plus reserved addresses for manual assignment.
- Duration of a lease offered by the server. The lease defines the length of time for which the assigned IP address can be used.

With a DHCP server installed and configured on your network, DHCP-enabled clients can obtain their IP address and related configuration parameters dynamically each time they start and join your network. DHCP servers provide this configuration in the form of an address-lease offer to requesting clients.

This may sound like the client gets a different address each time it boots. In fact, a design goal of DHCP was to provide dynamic assignment, but to keep track of which IP addresses were assigned to which media access control (MAC) addresses in the past. As long as there are adequate IP addresses in the pool, the DHCP server will always give the same IP address to the same MAC address, once it has been initially assigned. It will get the same address even if the lease expired long ago—as long as the address pool didn't run dry while the station's lease was expired. *Only if the pool is dry* will the client not be able to obtain the same IP address. In that case, once the network administrator has expanded the pool, subdivided the network, or otherwise solved the problem, the end-station won't get the same address again, since it will have by then been assigned to another station.

DHCP Terminology

Table 3.1 defines some of the common DHCP terminology.

DHCP Tools

The primary tool that you use to manage DHCP servers is the DHCP console, which is added to the Administrative Tools folder in Control Panel when you install a DHCP server for Windows 2000 Server. The DHCP console appears as a Microsoft Management Console (MMC) snap-in to further integrate DHCP administration into your total network management.

After you install a DHCP server, you can use the DHCP console to perform these basic administrative server tasks:

- Create scopes.
- Add and configure superscopes and multicast scopes.
- View and modify scope properties for scopes, such as setting additional exclusion ranges.
- Activate scopes or superscopes.
- Monitor each scope's leasing activity occasionally by reviewing the Active Leases for each scope.
- Create reservations in scopes as needed for DHCP clients that require a permanent IP address for leased use.

TABLE 3.1 *DHCP Terminology*

Term	Description
address pool	After you define a DHCP scope and apply exclusion ranges, the remaining addresses form the available address pool within the scope. Pooled addresses are eligible for dynamic assignment by the server to DHCP clients on your network.
exclusion range	An exclusion range is a limited sequence of IP addresses within a scope, excluded from DHCP service offerings. Addresses in these exclusion ranges are not offered by the server to DHCP clients on your network.
lease	A lease is a length of time that a DHCP server specifies, during which a client computer can use ann assigned IP address. When a lease is made to a client, the lease is active. Before the lease expires, the client typically needs to renew its address lease assignment with the server. A lease becomes inactive when it expires or is deleted at the server. The duration for a lease determines when it will expire and how often the client needs to renew it with the server.
option types	Option types are other client configuration parameters a DHCP server can assign when serving leases to DHCP clients. For example, some commonly used options include IP addresses for default gateways (routers), WINS servers, and DNS servers. Typically, these option types are enabled and configured for each scope. The DHCP console also permits you to configure default option types that are used by all scopes added and configured at the server. Most options are predefined through RFC2132, but you can use the DHCP console to define and add custom option types if needed.
options class	An options class is a way for the server to further manage option types provided to clients. When an options class is added to the server, clients of that class can be provided class-specific option types for their configuration. For Windows 2000, client computers can also specify a class ID when communicating with the server. For earlier DHCP clients that do not support the class ID process, the server can be configured with default classes to use instead when placing clients in a class. Options classes can be of two types: vendor classes and user classes.
reservations	You use a reservation to create a permanent address lease assignment by the DHCP server. Reservations assure that a specified hardware device on the subnet can always use the same IP address. In effect, these IP addresses have an infinite lease.
scope	A scope is the full consecutive range of possible IP addresses for a network. Scopes typically define a single physical subnet on your network to which DHCP services are offered. Scopes also provide the primary way for the server to manage distribution and assignment of IP addresses and any related configuration parameters to clients on the network.
superscope	A superscope is an administrative grouping of scopes that can be used to support multiple logical IP subnets on the same physical subnet. Superscopes only contain a list of member scopes or child scopes that can be activated together. Superscopes are not used to configure other details about scope usage. For configuring most properties used within a superscope, you need to configure member scope properties individually.

In addition, you can use the DHCP console to perform the following optional or advanced setup tasks:

- Add new cstom default option types.
- Add and configure any user or vendor-defined option classes.
- Further configure other server properties, such as audit logging or BOOTP (Bootstrap Protocol) tables.

Let's take a moment to discuss BOOTP. BOOTP is an Internet protocol that can provide network configuration information to diskless workstations or other workstations if necessary on a local network. When a workstation boots, it broadcasts a BOOTP message on the network. A BOOTP server receives this message, obtains the configuration information for the designated computer, and returns it to the computer. Note that the booting system does not have an IP address when it sends out a BOOTP message. Instead, the hardware address of this NIC (network interface card) is placed in the message and the BOOTP server returns its reply to this address.

Information returned by the BOOTP server to the booting computer includes its IP address, the IP address of the server, the host name of the server, and the IP address of a default router. It also specifies the location of a boot image that the booting computer can obtain in order to complete its startup operation. Diskless workstations need to obtain a boot image from a disk on the network because they do not have their own disks from which to obtain this information. The boot image provides all the files required to start the operating system on the computer.

Note that administrators must manually configure the information on a BOOTP server. An IP address must be matched to the MAC addresses of computers on the network. To minimize this configuration requirement, DHCP was developed to automatically allocate IP addresses to clients.

In addition, this version of the DHCP console also contains new features and enhancements, many of which were suggested by network managers. These include enhanced server performance monitoring, more predefined DHCP option types, dynamic update support for clients running earlier versions of Windows, and detection of unauthorized DHCP servers on your network.

Note For Windows 2000 Server, DHCP administration can also be performed using command-line based tools. For information about netshell commands for DHCP, see Appendix B or Chapter 5, "Installation and Administration of DHCP Servers & Clients."

New Features

DHCP in Windows 2000 Server provides the following new features:

- *New local groups for providing limited server and console access to DHCP administrators and users.* Two new local administrative groups are created when a DHCP server is installed on a server computer: the DHCP Users and DHCP Administrators groups. The DHCP Users group can be used to provide read-only console access to the server. Where used, this group grants members the ability to view, but not modify, server data.

The DHCP Administrators group provides a higher level of administrative access. Members added to this group can fully manage and modify any data at the DHCP server, but are not provided full unlimited administrative access, such as if the local Administrators group were used instead to provide administrative access to the applicable DHCP server.

- *Automatic assignment of IP addresses.* For Windows 2000 (and Windows 98), DHCP-enabled clients can now configure themselves to use a temporary IP configuration if a DHCP server is unavailable to provide a lease when they start on a network. For DHCP clients running these versions of Windows, the client tries to contact a DHCP server in the background every five minutes to eventually obtain its valid IP address lease.

  Automatic assignment is always transparent to users, who are not prompted if the client fails to obtain a lease from a DHCP server. Addresses are self-assigned from a network address range that is reserved for private TCP/IP usage and not used on the Internet. For more information, see "Automatic Client Configuration" in this chapter.

Author's Note This is not to say that APIPA is transparent to users. If the machine gets an APIPA address, then it can't access DNS servers, so the user will have to know the IP address for any machine he or she wishes to access. The remote machine will only be accessible if it is on the user's same subnetwork and if that machine also has an APIPA address and if the user knows which APIPA address corresponds to the machine he or she is interested in.

- *Enhanced performance monitoring and server reporting capabilities.* DHCP is critical to the success of your network infrastructure. Without working DHCP servers, IP clients can lose some or all of their ability to access or use your network. Because many experienced network administrators realize the importance of close monitoring of DHCP servers, several changes have been made to assist in this area.

  New performance monitoring counters have been added to Windows 2000 Server to help you monitor DHCP server performance on your network. For information about monitoring server performance, see Chapter 4.
- *Expanded scope support for multicast scopes and superscopes.* Microsoft DHCP server now supports additional scopes that you

can use to streamline your ongoing administration of IP address configurations.

New multicast scopes make it possible for DHCP-enabled clients to lease Class D-type IP addresses (224.0.0.0 to 239.255.255.255) for participation in multicast groups. For information about using multicast scopes, see Chapter 4.

Author's Note What I am referring here to is Multicast Address Dynamic Client Allocation Protocol (MADCAP), i.e., RFC 2730. This protocol was derived from DHCP and it allows servers to obtain addresses for their streaming content. Clients learn mappings from content names to class-D addresses by means of a Web page or a service announcement protocol of some sort. Though I am referring to MADCAP here, please understand that it's not part of DHCP, even if the OS blurs the distinction.

Superscopes (a late addition to Windows NT Server 4.0) are useful for creating an administrative grouping of member scopes. Superscopes can be helpful when you want to renumber or expand the IP address space on your network without disturbing currently active scopes. For information about using superscopes, see Chapter 4.

- *Support for user-specified and vendor-specified option classes.* You can use this feature to separate and distribute appropriate options for clients with similar or special configuration needs.

  For example, you might assign all DHCP-enabled clients on the same floor of your building to the same option class. You could use this class (configured with the same DHCP Class ID value) to distribute other options data during the lease process, overriding any scope or global default options. In this way, options appropriate to a set of class-member clients in the same network location (such as a specific default gateway or parent domain name) are applied as class-specific options. For information about using option classes, see Chapter 4.
- *Integration of DHCP with DNS.* With Windows 2000, a DHCP server can enable dynamic updates in the DNS namespace for any of its clients that support these updates. Scope clients can then use DNS dynamic update protocol to update their host name-to-address mapping information (which is stored in *zones* on the DNS server) whenever changes occur to their DHCP-assigned address. For information about using DNS servers with DHCP, see Chapter 4.
- *Detection of unauthorized DHCP servers through the use of Active Directory integration.* When a DHCP server is started on a network unintentionally, it can disturb normal TCP/IP network operations. This is because DHCP clients use broadcasts to the network to discover a DHCP server when started. To prevent unintended problems,

Windows 2000 Server provides a method of authorizing a DHCP server as well as a means to detect and shut down unauthorized servers.

When a Windows 2000 DHCP server attempts to start on the network, Active Directory is queried and the server computer's IP address is compared to the list of authorized DHCP servers. If a match is found, the server computer is authorized as a DHCP server. If a match is not found, the server is not authorized and is identified as an unauthorized server. In this case, the DHCP Server service installed and running on the unauthorized server is automatically shut down before it can disturb the network.

For these features to be used, you must also deploy and use Active Directory with Windows 2000 DHCP servers. DHCP servers from other vendors do not necessarily support this feature. Server detection is performed using a *DHCP server object* created in Active Directory. This object lists the IP addresses of the servers authorized to provide DHCP service to clients on the network. For information about authorizing DHCP servers, see Chapter 4.

- Dynamic support for BOOTP clients. The DHCP service provides additional support for BOOTP clients in large enterprise networks through the addition of dynamic BOOTP.

  Dynamic BOOTP is an extension of the BOOTP protocol that permits the DHCP server to configure BOOTP clients without having to use explicit fixed address configuration. This feature provides easier administration of large BOOTP networks by allowing automatic distribution of IP addresses (much the same way that DHCP does) without having to change client-side behavior. For more information on using dynamic BOOTP with your DHCP servers, see Chapter 4.

DHCP in IPv6

Although IPv6 introduces stateless address autoconfiguration, DHCPv6 retains its importance as the stateful alternative for those sites that wish to have more control over their addressing scheme. Used together with stateless autoconfiguration, DHCP provides a means of passing additional configuration options to nodes once they have obtained their addresses.

There is currently no RFC covering DHCP in IPv6, although there is work in progress described in two Internet drafts, *Dynamic Host Configuration Protocol for IPv6 (DHCPv6)* and *Extensions for the Dynamic Host Configuration Protocol for IPv6*.

Differences Between DHCPv6 and DHCPv4

DHCPv6 has some significant differences to DHCPv4, as it takes advantage of some of the inherent enhancements of the IPv6 protocol. Some of the principal differences are as follows:

- As soon as a client boots, it already has a link-local IP address, which it can use to communicate with a DHCP server or a relay agent.
- The client uses multicast addresses, rather than broadcasts, to contact the server.
- IPv6 allows the use of multiple IP addresses per interface, and DHCPv6 can provide more than one address when requested.
- Some DHCP options are now unnecessary. Default routers, for example, are now obtained by a client using IPv6 neighbor discovery.
- DHCP messages (including address allocations) appear in IPv6 message extensions, rather than in the IP header as in IPv4.
- There is no requirement for BOOTP compatibility.
- There is a new reconfigure message, which is used by the server to send configuration changes to clients (for example, the reduction in an address lifetime). Clients must continue to listen for reconfigure messages once they have received their initial configuration.

DHCP Servers

Configuring DHCP servers for a network provides the following benefits:

- The administrator can assign and specify global and subnet-specific TCP/IP parameters centrally for use throughout the entire network.
- Client computers do not require manual TCP/IP configuration.
- When a client computer moves between subnets, its old IP address is freed for reuse. The client reconfigures its TCP/IP settings automatically when the computer is restarted in its new location.
- When properly configured, most routers can forward DHCP and BOOTP configuration requests, so DHCP servers are not required on every subnet in the network.

How Clients Use Servers

A computer running Windows 2000 becomes a DHCP client if **Obtain an IP address** is selected in its TCP/IP properties. When a client computer is set to use DHCP, it accepts a lease offer and can receive from the server the following:

- Temporary use of an IP address known to be valid for the network it is joining.

- Additional TCP/IP configuration parameters for the client to use in the form of *options* data.

Also, if conflict detection is configured, the DHCP server attempts to ping each available address in the scope prior to presenting the address in a lease offer to a client. This ensures that each IP address offered to clients is not already in use by another non-DHCP computer that uses manual TCP/IP configuration.

Author's Note I would like to clarify that the clients don't detect conflicts. Microsoft's DHCP server does. The *normal* DHCP procedure is that the client broadcasts a DHCPDISCOVER, then awaits DHCPOFFERS, sends in a DHCPREQUEST, and awaits the server's DHCPACK, after which the server considers the address to be in use. After sending the DHCPREQUEST, the client will send an ARP for the IP address that it has been presented with. If it detects a machine that is already using that address, it will respond to the server's DHCPACK with a DHCPDECLINE message, thereby refusing the offered IP address. The DHCP protocol has built-in distributed mechanisms to ensure that clients get usable addresses. So there is no need for the server to ping all the available addresses before assigning one. If it gets a DHCPDECLINE, then it knows that an address has been "stolen" from its pool.

This isn't the first time that Microsoft "embraced and extended" something, but in this case, I would like to stress that this is not part of DHCP's functionality.

How Servers Provide Optional Data

In addition to an IP address, DHCP servers can be configured to provide optional data to fully configure TCP/IP for clients. Some of the most common DHCP option types configured and distributed by the DHCP server during leases include:

- Default gateways (routers), which are used to connect a network segment to other network segments.
- Other optional configuration parameters to assign to DHCP clients, such as IP addresses for the DNS servers or WINS servers that the client can use in resolving network host names.

For more information, see "DHCP options" in this chapter.

DHCP Clients

This section covers:

- Client overview
- Microsoft DHCP clients
- Automatic client configuration
- How clients obtain configuration

Client Overview

DHCP clients can be any Microsoft Windows-based clients or other clients that support and comply with client behavior described in the updated DHCP standards document, RFC 2132, published by the Internet Engineering Task Force (IETF).

In most cases, no additional steps are needed to enable Windows-based clients to use DHCP configuration. If a Windows-based client computer is not configured to use DHCP (that is, it is currently configured statically for its IP address), it can be enabled to with a simple configuration change. For information about configuring TCP/IP for dynamic addressing, see Chapter 2, "Installing, Managing, and Diagnosing TCP/IP."

Microsoft DHCP Clients

DHCP client support is provided for computers running under any of these Microsoft operating systems:

- Windows 2000 (all released versions)
- Windows NT (all released versions)
- Windows 98
- Windows 95
- Windows for Workgroups version 3.11 (with the Microsoft 32-bit TCP/IP VxD installed)
- Microsoft-Network Client version 3.0 for MS-DOS (with the real-mode TCP/IP driver installed)
- LAN Manager version 2.2c

SUPPORTED OPTIONS FOR MICROSOFT DHCP CLIENTS

By default, Microsoft-based DHCP clients can recognize and use option types in two categories:

1. *Information options.* You can use the DHCP console to *explicitly* configure these option types and any associated values provided to clients. These options are not required and can be assigned at your discretion.
2. *Protocol options.* You *implicitly* configure values for these options based on **Properties** configured at either the applicable server or one of its scopes. These options are always included in DHCP client/server messages as they are a required part of protocol design.

INFORMATION OPTIONS • All Microsoft DHCP clients support a common set of DHCP standard options. This support is provided for all clients running released versions of Windows and MS-DOS operating systems. For Windows 2000 DHCP clients only, some additional DHCP standard and Microsoft-specific options are also supported.

A client can request options by tag type in its DHCPREQUEST. If a client receives options, it is not required to accept them.

Table 3.2 lists DHCP standard options that all Microsoft DHCP clients, regardless of operating system version, are able to support and use, if provided by the DHCP server during the lease process.

TABLE 3.2 *DHCP Standard Options*

Code	Description
3	Router
6	DNS server
15	DNS domain name
44	WINS server
46	NetBIOS node type

Table 3.3 lists additional DHCP standard options that are limited to use by Windows 2000 DHCP clients, provided that the DHCP server has been properly configured to provide these options during the IP address leasing process.

TABLE 3.3 *DHCP Standard Options Limited to Windows 2000 Clients*

Code	Description
31	Perform router discovery
33	Static route

When a DHCP server actively provides these options, clients receive and use the associated values in their local TCP/IP configurations for the period of leased configuration.

In addition to these standard options, you can also use or assign other Microsoft vendor-specific options when using Microsoft predefined user and vendor classes. For more information about Microsoft options, see Appendix B.

PROTOCOL OPTIONS • Table 3.4 shows internal option types that Microsoft DHCP clients use when communicating with a DHCP server to obtain or renew their leased configurations.

In most cases, the actual values provided with these protocol options are provided to clients based on **Properties** set at the applicable DHCP server where the client obtains its address lease. You can also use the DHCP console to configure or tune these options individually for defined scopes, identifying members of a specified user or vendor class, or for a single reserved client. For more information about DHCP options, see Appendix B.

TABLE 3.4 *Internal Option Types for Microsoft DHCP Clients*

Code	Description
1	Subnet mask
51	IP address lease time
53	DHCP message type
54	Server identifier
58	Lease renewal time
59	Lease rebinding time

Automatic Client Configuration

For Windows 2000, DHCP clients automatically configure an IP address and subnet mask when started if a DHCP server is unavailable. This feature—referred to as *IP autoconfiguration*—can be useful for clients on small private networks, such as a small business office or home network environment.

If clients are configured to use a DHCP server (instead of being manually configured with an IP address and other parameters), then the DHCP client service engages each time the computer starts. For Windows 2000, the DHCP client service uses a three-step process to configure the client with an IP address and other configuration information:

1. The DHCP client attempts to locate a DHCP server and obtain a configuration from it.
2. If a DHCP server cannot be found, the DHCP client autoconfigures its IP address and subnet mask using a selected address from the Microsoft-reserved class B network, 169.254.0.0, with the subnet mask 255.255.0.0.

   The DHCP client will test for an address conflict by using a gratuitous ARP to make sure that the IP address it has chosen is not already in use on the network. If a conflict is found, the client selects another IP address to try and use. For each address conflict, the client will retry autoconfiguration for up to 10 addresses.
3. Once the DHCP client succeeds in selecting an address in the 169.254.0.0 network range not in use, it will configure the interface with this address.

   In the background, the client continues to check for a DHCP server every five minutes. When a DHCP server is found, the client abandons its autoconfigured information as soon as it has received a proper IP address (and any other provided DHCP options information) from the newly discovered DHCP server.

In the case where the DHCP client has previously obtained a lease from a DHCP server, the following modified sequence of events occurs:

1. If the client lease is still valid (not expired) at boot time, the client will try to renew its lease with the DHCP server.
2. If during the renewal attempt the client fails to locate any DHCP server, it will attempt to ping the default gateway that is listed in the lease. Depending on whether the ping fails or succeeds, the DHCP client proceeds as follows:

   a. If a ping of the default gateway *succeeds*, the DHCP client assumes that it is still located on the same network where it obtained its current lease, and continue to use the lease. By default, the client next attempts to renew its lease in the background when 50 percent of its assigned lease time has expired.
   b. If a ping request of the default gateway *fails*, the client assumes that it has been moved to a network where DHCP services are not available, such as a home network. The client then autoconfigures its IP address as described previously. Once the client is autoconfigured, it continues to try to locate a DHCP server every five minutes in the background until it eventually obtains a lease.

How Clients Obtain Configuration

DHCP clients use two different processes to communicate with DHCP servers and obtain a configuration. The lease process varies depending on whether the client is initializing or renewing its lease.

The initialization process occurs when a client computer first starts and attempts to join the network. The renewal process occurs after a client has an expired lease, meaning that the client needs to renew that lease with the server.

INITIAL LEASE PROCESS

When a DHCP-enabled client first starts, it automatically follows an initialization process to obtain a lease from a DHCP server. The steps for this process are:

1. The DHCP client broadcasts a DHCPDISCOVER message onto the local subnet.
2. A DHCP server can respond with a DHCP offer message (DHCPOFFER) that contains an offered IP address for lease to the client.
3. If no DHCP servers respond to the client discovery request, the client can proceed in either of two ways:
   a. If the client is running under Windows 2000 and IP autoconfiguration *has not been* disabled, the client self-configures an IP address for use with automatic client configuration.

b. If the client is not running under Windows 2000 (or IP autoconfiguration *has been* disabled), the client fails to initialize. Instead, if left running, it continues to resend DHCPDISCOVER messages in the background (four times every five minutes) until it receives a DHCPOFFER message from a server.

4. As soon as a DHCPOFFER message is received, the client selects the offered address by replying to the server with a DHCPREQUEST.
5. Typically, the offering server sends a DHCP acknowledgment message (DHCPACK), approving the lease. Also, other DHCP options information is included in the DHCPACK.
6. Once the client receives acknowledgment, it checks to make sure that its new address isn't already in use. If so, the client sends a DHCPDECLINE message to the server. Otherwise, if the address appears to be available, the client then configures its TCP/IP properties using the information in the DHCPOFFER and DHCPACK, and joins the network.

Figure 3-2 shows the lease process between the DHCP server and client.

Note In rare cases, a DHCP server can alternately return a DHCP negative acknowledgment message (DHCPNAK) to the client for step 5. This can happen when a client requests an invalid or duplicate address for the network. If a client receives a negative acknowledgment, the current initialization process fails. In this case, the client starts over at step 1, repeating the process as outlined above

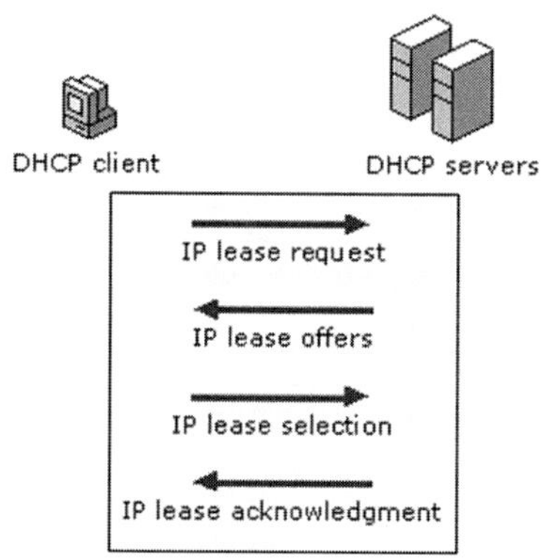

FIGURE 3-2 *Initial DHCP lease process between server and client*

LEASE RENEWAL PROCESS

When a DHCP client shuts down and restarts (on the same subnet), it typically obtains a lease for the same IP address it had prior to the shutdown.

After 50 percent of the client lease time elapses, the client tries to renew its lease with the DHCP server as follows:

1. The client sends a DHCPREQUEST message directly to the server that originated the lease, to renew and extend its current address lease.
2. If the server is reachable, it typically replies with a DHCPACK message to the client, which renews the current lease. Also, as in the initial lease process, other DHCP options information is included in this reply. If any options information has changed since the client first obtained its lease, the client updates its configuration accordingly.
3. If the client is unable to communicate with its original DHCP server, the client waits until it reaches a rebinding state. When the client reaches this state, it attempts to renew its current lease with any available DHCP server.
4. If a server responds with a DHCPOFFER message to update the current client lease, the client can renew its lease based on the offering server and continue operation.
5. If the lease expires and no server has been contacted, the client must immediately discontinue using its leased IP address.
6. The client then follows the same process used during its initial startup operation to obtain a new IP address lease.

DHCP/BOOTP Relay Agents

This section covers:

- Understanding relay agents
- Relay agent configurations
- Relay agent design issues

Understanding Relay Agents

A relay agent is a small program that relays DHCP/BOOTP messages between clients and servers on different subnets. DHCP/BOOTP relay agents are part of the DHCP and BOOTP standards and function according to DHCP's and BOOTP's Requests for Comments (RFCs), documents that describe protocol design and related behavior. For more information about DHCP RFCs, see Appendix B.

DHCP/BOOTP ROUTER SUPPORT

In TCP/IP networking, routers are used to interconnect hardware and software used on different physical network segments, called *subnets,* and to forward IP packets between each of the subnets. To support and use DHCP service across multiple subnets, routers connecting each subnet should comply with DHCP/BOOTP relay agent capabilities described in RFC 1542.

To be compliant with RFC 1542 and provide relay agent support, each router must be able to recognize BOOTP and DHCP protocol messages and process (relay) them appropriately. Because routers interpret DHCP messages as BOOTP messages (such as a User Datagram Protocol (UDP) message sent through the same UDP port number and containing a common message structure), a router with BOOTP-relay agent capability typically relays DHCP packets and any BOOTP packets sent on the network.

If a router cannot function as a DHCP/BOOTP relay agent, each subnet must have either its own DHCP server or another computer that can function as a relay agent on that subnet. In cases where it is impractical or impossible to configure routers to support DHCP/BOOTP relay, you can configure a computer running Windows NT Server 4.0 or later to act as a relay agent by installing the DHCP Relay Agent service.

In most cases, routers support DHCP/BOOTP relay. If your routers do not, contact your router manufacturer or supplier to find out if a software or firmware upgrade is available to support this feature.

HOW RELAY AGENTS WORK

A relay agent relays DHCP/BOOTP messages that are broadcast on one of its connected physical interfaces, such as a network adapter, to other remote subnets to which it is connected by other physical interfaces. Figure 3-3 shows how client C on Subnet 2 obtains a DHCP address lease from DHCP server 1 on Subnet 1.

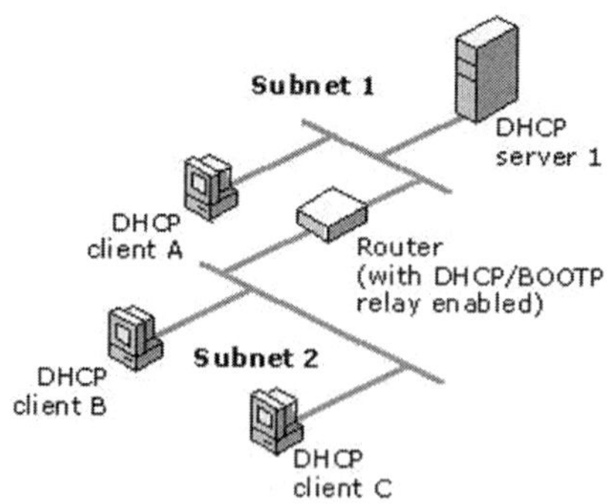

FIGURE 3–3 *DHCP/BOOTP relay agent*

1. DHCP client C broadcasts a DHCP/BOOTP discover message (DHCPDISCOVER) on Subnet 2, as a UDP datagram using the well-known UDP server port of 67 (the port number reserved and shared for BOOTP and DHCP server communication). The UDP packet is encapsulated in an IP packet whose destination address is typically the limited broadcast address (255.255.255.25), and the IP packet is transmitted onto the LAN to the MAC-layer broadcast address 0xFF-FF-FF-FF-FF-FF. Because the packet is broadcast, all stations, including the router, should receive it. The router would normally discard the packet because the packet is not addressed specifically to the router; however, because the router is configured as a DHCP/BOOTP relay, it checks every broadcast packet that it receives to see if it is a UDP packet destined for UDP port 67.
2. The relay agent, in this case a DHCP/BOOTP relay-enabled router, examines the gateway IP address (giaddr) field in the DHCP/BOOTP message header. If the field has an IP address of 0.0.0.0, the agent fills it with the relay agent or router's IP address. In particular, the giaddr field is filled in with the IP address of the router interface on which the UDP broadcast packet was received. (This is how the DHCP server knows which subnet the requesting client is located on.) The DHCP relay then forwards the message to the remote Subnet 1 where the DHCP server is located.
3. When DHCP server 1 on remote Subnet 1 receives the message, it examines the giaddr field for a DHCP scope that can be used by the DHCP server to supply an IP address lease.
4. If DHCP server 1 has multiple DHCP scopes, the address in the giaddr field identifies the DHCP scope from which to offer an IP address lease.

   For example, if the giaddr field has an IP address of 10.0.0.2, the DHCP server checks its available set of address scopes for a scope range of addresses that matches the class A IP network that includes the gateway address as a host. In this case, the DHCP server would make a check for a scope of addresses between 10.0.0.1 and 10.0.0.254. If a matching scope exists, the DHCP server selects an available address from the matched scope to use in an IP address lease offer response to the client.
5. When DHCP server 1 receives the DHCPDISCOVER message, it processes and sends an IP address lease offer (DHCPOFFER) directly to the relay agent identified in the giaddr field.
6. The router then relays the address lease offer (DHCPOFFER) to the DHCP client. The client still does not know its IP address, so the DHCPOFFER has to be broadcast on the local subnet. Similarly, a DHCPREQUEST message is relayed from client to server, and a DHCPACK message is relayed from server to client, according to RFC 1542.

Note Some IP stacks can receive packets addressed to the station's MAC address and its newly assigned IP address. Such stations can clear the "broadcast" bit in the flags field of the DHCPDISCOVER, which then allows the relay to respond with a packet directly addressed to the station that sent the DHCPDISCOVER in the first place. This has the advantage of not bothering all the other stations that would have had to receive the packet had it been broadcast back to the originating station. For more information, see "Relay Agent Design Issues" in this chapter.

Relay Agent Configurations

There are several relay agent configuration options available if you plan to incorporate a relay agent into your DHCP/BOOTP-enabled network. These include using other routers, Windows 2000 Routing and Remote Access service, and the DHCP Relay Agent component provided in Windows NT Server 4.0.

THIRD PARTY ROUTER

Figure 3-4 shows a third party router configuration. The router is running a relay agent, forwarding DHCP requests between Subnet A and Subnet B. Typically, the relay agent on the router must be configured with the IP Helper Address of the DHCP server.

WINDOWS 2000 SERVER ROUTING AND REMOTE ACCESS SERVICE

Figure 3-5 shows the Windows 2000 Server Routing and Remote Access configuration. The DHCP Relay Agent on Windows 2000 Server must be configured with the IP address of the DHCP server to relay DHCP requests between Subnet A and Subnet B.

WINDOWS NT SERVER 4.0

Figure 3-6 shows how a standard IP router can be used with Windows NT Server 4.0 to relay DHCP requests between Subnet A and Subnet B.

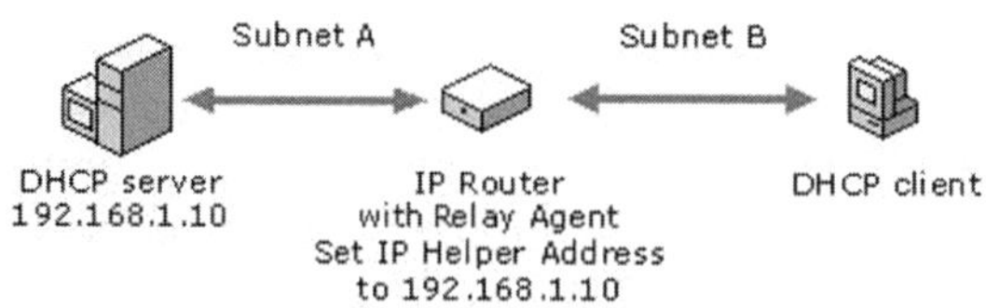

FIGURE 3–4 *Third party router*

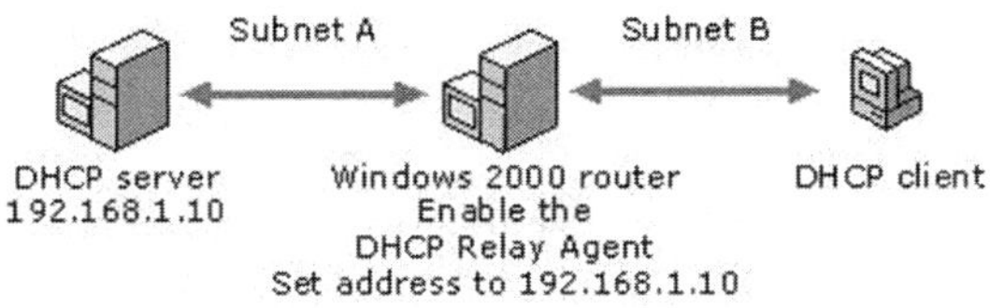

FIGURE 3–5 *Windows 2000 Routing and Remote Access*

Relay Agent Design Issues

There are important design issues to consider before you set up relay agents on your network.

When you have multiple DHCP servers, Microsoft recommends that you place your DHCP servers on different subnets to achieve a degree of fault tolerance, rather than having all of them on one subnet. The servers should not have common IP addresses in their scopes (each server should have a unique pool of addresses).

If the DHCP server on the local subnet shuts down, requests are relayed to a remote subnet. The DHCP server at that location can respond to DHCP requests if it maintains a scope of IP addresses for the requesting subnet. If the remote server has no scope defined for the requesting subnet, it cannot provide IP addresses even if it has available addresses for other scopes. If each DHCP server has a pool of addresses for each subnet, then it can provide IP addresses for remote clients whose own DHCP server is offline.

RECOMMENDED

The relay agent implementation shown in Figure 3-7 is recommended for best routed DHCP network performance. It uses two DHCP servers that are attached to two different subnets. The relay agents operating on each of the routers used to connect the subnets have varied delay intervals (one is set to 4 seconds, the other uses no delay). This eliminates the risk of undesirable floods of DHCP packets through randomly selected network paths.

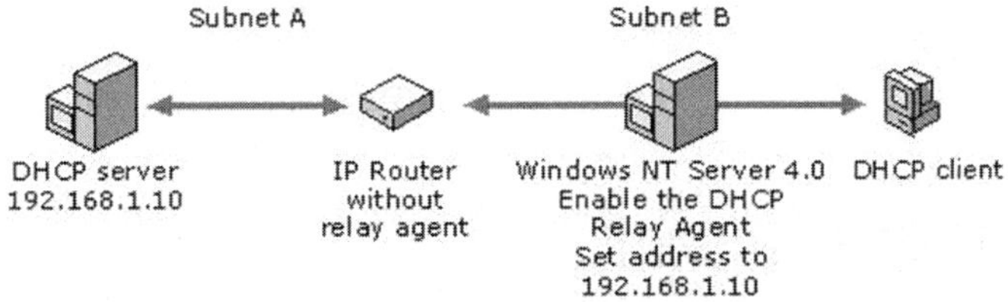

FIGURE 3–6 *Standard IP router used with Windows NT 4.0*

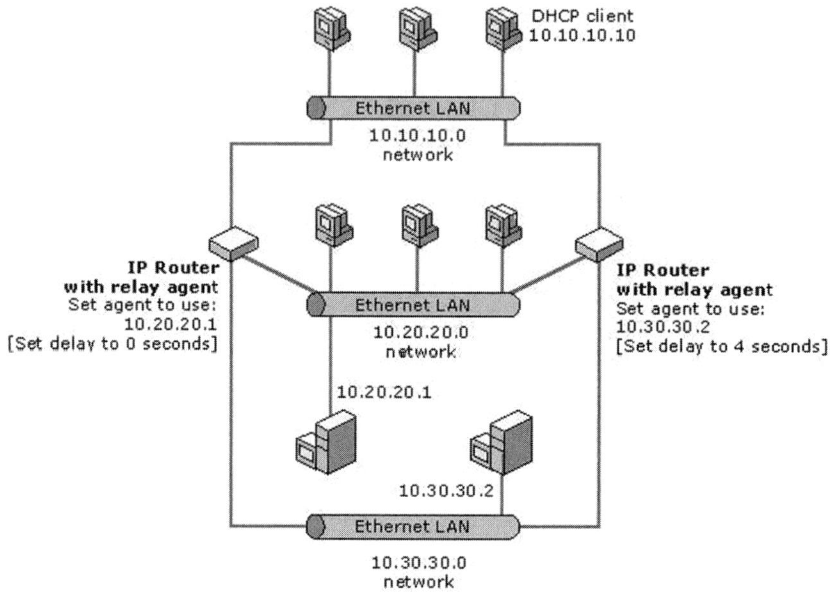

FIGURE 3–7 *Recommended DHCP/BOOTP relay agent configuration*

NOT RECOMMENDED

The relay agent implementation shown in Figure 3-8 is not recommended. It has the same number of DHCP servers and subnets as in the previous example, but less caution has been used. The risk of DHCP discovery messages (DHCPDISCOVERs), which are broadcasted by the DHCP clients at startup, being randomly forwarded or duplicated when destined for the other subnets is much higher. Moreover, the relay agents do not use any delay interval. This increases the likelihood that both relay agents (routers) duplicate any client-broadcasted messages, which could potentially flood the remote subnets.

DHCP in Windows 2000

This section covers:

- Audit logging
- Multicast address allocation

Audit Logging

Windows 2000 DHCP servers include several new logging features and server parameters that provide enhanced auditing capabilities. You can now specify the following features:

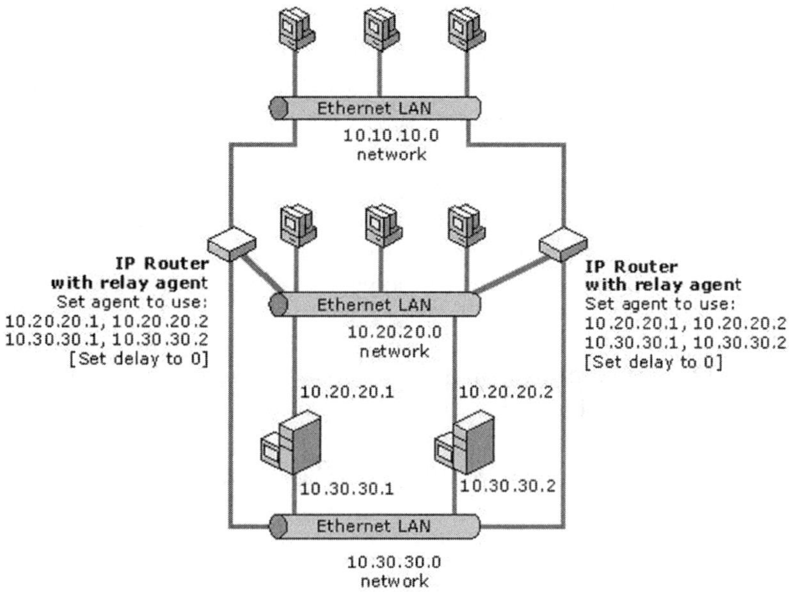

FIGURE 3–8 *DHCP/BOOTP relay agent configuration not recommended*

- The directory path in which the DHCP server stores audit log files.
- A maximum size restriction (in megabytes) for the total amount of disk space available for all audit log files created and stored by the DHCP service.
- An interval for disk checking that is used to determine how many times the DHCP server writes audit log events to the log file before checking for available disk space on the server.
- A minimum size requirement (in megabytes) for server disk space that is used during disk checking to determine if sufficient space exists for the server to continue audit logging.

Note You can selectively enable or disable the audit-logging feature at each DHCP server. For more information, see Chapter 5, "Installation and Administration of DHCP Servers and Clients."

Only the directory path in which the DHCP server stores audit log files can be modified using the DHCP console. To do so, first select the applicable DHCP server in the console tree. On the Action menu, click Properties. Next, click the Advanced tab and edit Audit log file path as necessary.

Other audit logging parameters described above are adjusted through registry-based configuration changes. For more information on the Windows 2000 DHCP server registry, see the Windows 2000 Server Resource Kit.

HOW AUDIT LOGGING WORKS

The audit logging behavior discussed in this section applies only to the DHCP Server service provided with Windows 2000 Server. It replaces the previous DHCP logging behavior used in earlier versions of Windows NT Server, which do not perform audit checks and use only a single log file named *Dhcpsrv.log* for logging service events.

The formatted structure of DHCP server logs and the level of reporting maintained for audited logging are the same as in earlier DHCP server versions provided with Windows NT Server. For information about analyzing server log files, see Chapter 4.

NAMING AUDIT LOG FILES • The DHCP Server service bases the name of the audit log file on the current day of the week, as determined by checking the current date and time at the server.

For example, when the DHCP server starts, if the current date and time is:

Wednesday, March 5, 1998, 04:56:42 P.M.,

then the server audit log file is named

DhcpSrvLog.Wed.

STARTING A DAILY AUDIT LOG • When a DHCP server starts or a new week day begins (when the local time on the computer is 12:00 A.M.), the server writes a header message in the audit log file, indicating that logging has started. Then, depending on whether the audit log file is a new or existing file, the following actions occur:

- If the file already existed without modification for more than a day, it is overwritten.
- If the file already existed but was modified within the previous 24 hours, the file is not overwritten. Instead, new logging activity is appended to the end of the existing file.

DISK CHECKS • After audit logging starts, the DHCP server performs disk checks at regular intervals to ensure both the ongoing availability of server disk space and that the current audit log file does not become too large or that log-file growth is not occurring too rapidly.

The DHCP server performs a full disk check whenever either of the following conditions occurs:

- A set number of server events are logged.
- The date changes on the server computer.

By default, the DHCP server performs a periodic disk space check for every 50 events it writes to the audit log. The DHCP server can also detect a date change when the server computer reaches 12:00 A.M. on its locally set Date/Time clock.

Each time a disk check is completed, the server determines whether disk space is filled. The disk is considered full if either of the following conditions is true:

- *Disk space on the server computer is lower than the required minimum amount for DHCP audit logging.* By default, if the amount of disk space remaining on the server disk reaches less than 20 megabytes, audit logging is halted.
- *The current audit log file is larger than one-seventh (1/7) of the maximum allotted space or size for the combined total of all audit logs currently stored on the server.* At the time of the disk check, the DHCP server compares the exact size (in megabytes) of the current audit log file with a value obtained by dividing the current value for the maximum number of log files the server permits to be stored simultaneously before overwriting and discarding of older log files. By default, seven is the maximum number of log files the server permits to be stored, one for each day of the week. Assuming the default is set, the largest size that the current audit log file can reach is one megabyte.

In either case, if the disk is full, the DHCP server closes the current file and ignores further requests to log audit events until either 12:00 A.M. or until disk status is improved and the disk is no longer full.

Even if audit logged events are ignored because of a disk-full condition, the DHCP server continues disk checking every 50 events (or the currently set interval) to determine whether disk conditions have improved. If subsequent disk checks determine that the required amount of server disk space is available, the DHCP server reopens the current log file and resumes logging.

ENDING A DAILY AUDIT LOG • At 12:00 A.M. local time on the server computer, the DHCP server closes the existing log and moves to the log file for the next day of the week. For example, if the day of the week changes at 12:00 A.M. from Wednesday to Thursday, the log file named DhcpSrvLog.Wed is closed and the file named DhcpSrvLog.Thu is opened and used for logging events.

MULTICAST ADDRESS ALLOCATION

Windows 2000 DHCP servers have been extended to allow the assignment of multicast addresses, in addition to assignment of unicast addresses.

A proposed IETF standard defines a client/server protocol, the Multicast Address Dynamic Client Allocation Protocol, for defining multicast address allocation between supporting servers and clients. The primary benefit of the proposed MADCAP standard is that you can use it to leverage your existing network infrastructure for assigning multicast addresses similar to the way that other IP addresses are currently assigned, using DHCP.

Typical applications for multicast are conferencing and audio, which usually require users to specially configure multicast addresses. Unlike IP broadcasts, which must be received by all computers on the network, a multicast address is a group of computers, using the concept of a group membership to identify those to which the message is to be sent.

The multicast address allocation feature has two parts:

1. *A MADCAP server,* which distributes multicast addresses. To use this feature, the administrator first configures multicast scopes and the corresponding multicast IP ranges on the MADCAP server through the DHCP console. Once these scopes are administratively set and activated, the Windows 2000 DHCP Server service can provide multicast addresses in the same way it normally provides unicast IP addresses, where DHCP scopes are used.
2. *Client-side application programming interfaces (APIs),* which MADCAP clients can use to request, renew, or release multicast addresses. Applications that implement MADCAP client support can call these APIs to request a multicast address from a given multicast scope at the MADCAP server. The underlying MADCAP implementation uses protocol messages (inspired by the DHCP message format) to negotiate the multicast address lease between the MADCAP client and server.

For information about using multicast scopes, see Chapter 4.

Note The standards for multicast address allocation are currently under review and are managed by the Multicast address-allocation (MALLOC) working group of the IETF. You can obtain RFCs from the Request for Comments Web site at *www.rfc-editor.org/*.

Members of the Information Sciences Institute (ISI), which publishes a classified listing of all RFCs, currently maintain this Web site. Nonstandards-track RFCs are classified as one of the following: Internet best current practices (BCP), or For Your Information (FYI) documents. Standards-track RFCs are classified as approved Internet standard, draft Internet standard, or proposed Internet standard. Standards-track RFCs proceed from "proposed" status to "draft" before becoming full Internet "standards." It is important to remember that while all Internet standards are RFCs, not all RFCs are standards.

DHCP Options

DHCP provides an internal framework for passing configuration information on to clients on your network. Configuration parameters and other control information are carried as tagged data items stored within protocol messages exchanged between the DHCP server and its clients. These data items are called *options*.

Most standard DHCP options are currently defined in RFCs published by IETF. The full set of core DHCP options are described specifically in RFC 2132, "DHCP Options and BOOTP Vendor Extensions."

All DHCP options mentioned in RFC 2132 are predefined for you to configure and use at any Windows 2000 DHCP server. If needed, you can also use the DHCP console to define new DHCP options at each server.

Even though most DHCP servers can assign many options, most DHCP clients are typically designed to request or support only a subset of the full RFC-specified standard options set.

For more information, see "DHCP RFCs" and "DHCP Options Reference" in Appendix B.

How Options Are Applied

Options can be managed using different levels assigned for each managed DHCP server, including:

- *Server options*. These options are applied for all scopes defined at a DHCP server.
- *Scope options*. These options are applied specifically to all clients that obtain a lease within a particular scope.
- *Class options*. These options are applied only to clients that are identified as members of a specified user or vendor class when obtaining a lease.
- *Client options*. These options apply only for a single reserved client computer and require a reservation to be used in an active scope.

For information about setting up options, see Chapter 4.

Understanding User and Vendor Classes

There are significant differences in the way in which vendor and user classes are available for use by DHCP clients and servers. Table 3.5 compares and contrasts the features of these classes.

Table 3.5 *Comparison of Vendor and User Classes for DHCP Clients and Servers*

User classes	Vendor classes
Part of proposed DHCP standard drafts. For updated information, obtain the latest draft from the RFC Web site at *http://www.rfc-editor.org/*.	Part of current DHCP specifications (RFC 2131, 2132). For more information, see "DHCP RFCs" in Appendix B.
Clients identify user class membership with User class information.	Clients identify vendor class membership by using the vendor class identifier option.
User class IDs can be set and viewed at Windows 2000 DHCP clients using the **ipconfig** command. For information about setting and showing DHCP class ID information, see Chapter 5.	Vendor class IDs are configured internally by DHCP client system vendors, such as Microsoft and other vendors. When adding a vendor class at the server, you need to specify class data at the server that matches identically the class ID used by same-vendor clients. For more information, contact the applicable vendor.
Once you create a user class, you can selectively assign options to be provided to identifying members of it.	Once you create a vendor class, you need to add and define options to make it useful to either all or some clients of the DHCP server.
With user classes, you can take advantage of predefined classes that can be used to support specialized groups of clients, such as BOOTP or Routing and Remote Access clients. For more information, see Microsoft predefined user classes.	With vendor classes, Microsoft has implemented vendor classes to the provided classification of its DHCP clients by Windows 2000, Windows 98, or Microsoft DHCP clients, which share the use of the Microsoft-reserved vendor prefix ("MSFT") in any class-related data used. For more information, see Microsoft vendor classes.
User classes are typically created for administrative reasons, such as to identify all DHCP clients in a specific site or location. For example, all computers and printers located on the same floor in an office building might be assigned or configured as part of the same user class.	Vendor classes are typically created for the enhancement of vendor-specific DHCP functionality. For example, Microsoft provides several additional vendor-specific options, such as the ability to disable NetBIOS over TCP/IP at Windows 2000 DHCP clients. For more information, see Microsoft vendor-specific options.
User classes are most helpful to users for managing DHCP option assignments based on their needs. If your DHCP network is large enough to benefit from user classes, you can freely customize your DHCP environments with them. In most cases, the user class provides a way to assign and override standard DHCP option values set at the server, scope, or reserved client level.	Vendor classes are most helpful to vendors for managing DHCP option assignments based on vendor-specific needs, without disturbing other non-vendor DHCP clients. With a vendor class, options are passed to clients using the Vendor specific information option, which encapsulates the options it sends. This helps non-vendor clients to recognize the information as vendor-specific and ignore and discard it as needed.

For information about using option classes, see Chapter 4. For information about creating a new user or vendor class, see Chapter 5.

BOOTP and DHCP

The Bootstrap Protocol (BOOTP) is a host configuration protocol developed before DHCP. DHCP improves on BOOTP and resolves specific limitations BOOTP had as a host configuration service. RFC 951 defines BOOTP.

BOOTP and DHCP Similarities

Because of the relationship between BOOTP and DHCP, both protocols share some defining characteristics. The common elements include:

- *The packet format structure each uses to exchange messages between the server and clients.* BOOTP and DHCP use nearly identical request messages (sent by clients) and reply messages (sent by servers). Messages in either of these protocols use a single UDP datagram of 576 bytes to enclose each protocol message. Message headers are the same for both BOOTP and DHCP with one exception: the final message header field used to carry optional data. For BOOTP, this optional field is called the vendor-specific area and is limited to 64 octets. For DHCP, this area is called the options field and can carry up to 312 octets of DHCP options information.
- *Use of well-known UDP ports for client/server communication.* Both BOOTP and DHCP use the same reserved protocol ports for sending and receiving messages between servers and clients. Both BOOTP and DHCP servers use UDP port 67 to listen for and receive client request messages. BOOTP and DHCP clients typically reserve UDP port 68 for accepting message replies from either a BOOTP server or DHCP server.

  Because DHCP and BOOTP messages use nearly identical format types and packet structures, and typically use the same well-known service ports, BOOTP or DHCP relay agent programs usually treat BOOTP and DHCP messages as essentially the same message type, without differentiating between them.
- *IP address distribution as an integral part of configuration service.* Although both BOOTP and DHCP allocate IP addresses to clients during startup, they use different methods of allocation. BOOTP typically provides fixed allocation of a single IP address for each client, permanently reserving this address in the BOOTP server database. DHCP additionally provides dynamic, leased allocation of available IP addresses, reserving each DHCP client address temporarily in the DHCP server database.

BOOTP and DHCP Differences

There are significant differences in the way in which BOOTP and DHCP perform host configuration. Table 3.6 compares and contrasts the features of the two protocols that vary.

TABLE 3.6 *Differences in BOOTP and DHCP Host Configuration*

BOOTP	DHCP
Designed prior to DHCP.	Extension of BOOTP.
Intended to configure diskless workstations with limited boot capabilities.	Intended to configure frequently relocated networked computers (such as portables) that have local hard drives and full boot capabilities.
Supports a limited number of client configuration parameters, called vendor extensions.	Supports a larger and extensible set of client configuration parameters, called options.
Describes a two-phase bootstrap configuration process. First, clients contact BOOTP servers to perform address determination and boot file name selection. Then, clients contact Trivial File Transfer Protocol (TFTP) servers to perform file transfer of their boot image.	Describes a single-phase boot configuration process whereby a DHCP client negotiates with a DHCP server to determine its IP address and obtain any other initial configuration details it needs for network operation.
BOOTP clients do not rebind or renew configuration with the BOOTP server except when the system restarts.	DHCP clients do not require a system restart to rebind or renew configuration with the DHCP server. Instead, clients automatically enter a rebinding state at set, timed intervals to renew their leased address allocation with the DHCP server. This process occurs in the background and is transparent to the user.

The DHCP Database

The DHCP database in Windows 2000 Server uses the performance-enhanced Exchange Server Storage engine version 4.0.

There is no built-in limit to the number of records that a DHCP server can store. The size of the database depends upon the number of DHCP clients on the network. The DHCP database grows over time as a result of clients starting and stopping on the network.

The size of the DHCP database is not directly proportional to the number of active client lease entries. Over time, as some DHCP client entries become obsolete and are deleted, there remains some unused space.

Author's Note DHCP's design calls for the server to remember all assignments it has made, even if the leases have expired, so that clients get consistent IP addresses, if at all possible. Therefore, the database should grow to the maximum size that would match all the scopes being full. If you remove information, then the DHCP service becomes less predictable. Only when there are no addresses left in a scope and there are expired leases in the scope, will the DHCP server map an IP address to a different MAC address.

Again, this isn't the first time that Microsoft took liberties with an implementation. I would like to point out that this is where Microsoft's DHCP deviates from the IETF's DHCP.

To recover the unused space, the DHCP database must be compacted. Starting with Windows NT Server 4.0, dynamic database compaction occurs on DHCP servers as an automatic background process during idle time after a database update.

Although dynamic compacting greatly reduces the need for doing offline compaction, it does not fully eliminate the need for offline compacting. Offline compaction more effectively reclaims the space and should be performed about once a month for very large and busy networks with 1,000 or more DHCP clients. For smaller networks, manual compaction can be useful when performed every few months.

Because dynamic database compaction occurs while the database is in use, stopping the DHCP server is not necessary for it to occur. However, for manual compacting, a DHCP server must be stopped and compacting performed offline.

Note When using or upgrading DHCP databases used with earlier versions of Windows NT Server, the DHCP database requires conversion. For Windows 2000 Server, if a previous copy of the DHCP server database is detected during an upgrade, it is automatically converted to the current database version and format. For larger databases, this process can increase the time needed to complete the installation.

For more information on manual compaction of the DHCP server database using Jetpack.exe, see Chapter 4. For more information on the files used to support the server database, see Appendix B.

F O U R

Using DHCP

Planning DHCP Networks

This topic covers the following DHCP network planning issues:

- How many DHCP servers to use
- How to support DHCP clients on additional subnets
- Planning for routed DHCP networks
- Other planning considerations for enterprise networks

How Many DHCP Servers to Use

When deciding how many DHCP servers you need, consider the location of routers on the network and whether you want a DHCP server in each subnet. When extending use of a DHCP server across more than one network, you often need to configure additional DHCP relay agents and, in some cases, use superscopes as well.

Transmission speed between the segments for which DHCP service is provided is another important factor. If you have slower WAN links or dial-up links, you typically need a DHCP server on both sides of these links to service clients locally.

There is no fixed limit to the maximum number of clients that a single DHCP server can serve. However, your network can have practical constraints based on the IP address class selected for use and other server configuration details.

When you are examining factors that could enhance DHCP server performance, consider the following:

1. *The primary contributing factor to improving DHCP server performance is the speed of the server disk drives.* For this reason, you should carefully evaluate disk access time and average times for disk read/write operations when sizing and planning for your DHCP server hardware specifications. In many instances, this is more important than other server requirements, such as memory and processor.
2. *As a general recommendation, limit each DHCP server to having no more than 1,000 scopes defined for use.* When adding a large number of scopes to the server, be aware that each scope creates a corresponding need for additional incremental increases to the amount of disk space used for the DHCP server registry and for the server paging file.
3. *For the best possible DHCP server design in most networks, it is recommended that you have, at most, 10,000 clients per server.* This recommended per-server maximum reflects suggested baseline DHCP server performance monitoring and provides for unusual burst traffic conditions, such as after a large-scale power outage when many DHCP client computers might restart simultaneously. In addition to observing recommended server capacity baselines, split each of your scopes (such as by applying an 80/20 rule) between two to three servers for fault tolerance. For more information, see "Configuring Scopes" in this chapter.

For example, if you were to define 1,000 scopes for a DHCP server, each of the scopes should provide addresses actively to an average of no more than 10 clients. In any event, you need to allocate additional disk space to store the added scope information and likely would also need to change the default server registry and paging file size settings to permit increased growth when accommodating a large number of scopes and clients.

Windows 2000 Server provides added performance monitoring tools that you can use to test and monitor your servers. Also, you might want to review DHCP server performance test results that were generated by the Windows 2000 development team during product development. For more information, see "Monitoring Server Performance" in this chapter.

A DHCP PLANNING ALTERNATIVE: CONFIGURING STANDBY SERVERS

Most networks need one primary online DHCP server and one other DHCP server acting as a secondary or backup server. If you choose not to implement two DHCP servers using the 80/20 rule for balancing scopes but want to continue to provide a measure of potential fault tolerance, you might consider implementing a backup or hot standby DHCP server as an alternative.

In the hot standby configuration, the standby DHCP server is another server computer that is installed and configured identically to your primary DHCP server. In the case of the standby, the only difference is that the standby server and its scopes are not activated for use under normal conditions. Duplicate scopes are configured but not activated except when critically needed, such as to substitute for the primary DHCP server because it has stopped or been taken offline for an extended period of time.

Because the hot standby solution requires special attention to its configuration and also manual administration for ensuring fall-over transition for DHCP clients to use it, it is less recommended as a planning alternative than the use of two to three DHCP servers that balance active scope use.

Supporting Additional Subnets

For DHCP service to support additional subnets on your network, you must first determine whether the routers used to connect adjoining subnets can support relaying of Bootstrap Protocol (BOOTP) and DHCP messages. If routers cannot be used for DHCP and BOOTP relay, you can set up either of the following for each subnet:

- *A computer running either Windows 2000 Server or Windows NT Server 4.0 configured to use the DHCP Relay Agent component.* This computer simply forwards messages back and forth between clients on the local subnet and a remote DHCP server, using the IP address of the remote server. The DHCP Relay Agent service is available only on computers running Windows 2000 Server or Windows NT Server 4.0.
- *A computer running Windows 2000 Server configured as a DHCP server for the local subnet.* This server computer must contain and manage scope and other address-configurable information for the local subnet it serves.

For information about relay agent configurations, see Chapter 3, "DHCP Overview."

Planning for Routed DHCP Networks

In routed networks that use subnets to divide network segments, planning options for DHCP services must observe some specific requirements for a full implementation of DHCP services to function. These requirements include:

- One DHCP server must be located on at least one subnet in the routed network.
- For a DHCP server to support clients on other remote subnets separated by routers, a router or remote computer must be used as a DHCP and BOOTP relay agent to support forwarding of DHCP traffic between subnets.

Figure 4-1 shows a simple routed network with DHCP implemented.

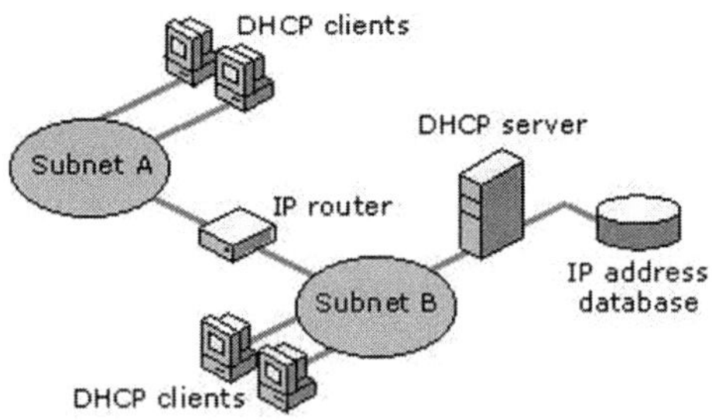

FIGURE 4–1 *Example of a routed DHCP network*

Enterprise Planning Considerations

For an enterprise DHCP network, you should:

- *Plan the physical subnets of the network and relative placement of DHCP servers.* This includes planning for placement of DHCP (and WINS) servers in subnets in a way that reduces b-node broadcasts across routers. A b-node is a broadcast message used to resolve names.
- *Specify the DHCP option types and their values to be predefined per scope for the DHCP clients.* This can include planning for scopes based on the needs of particular groups of users. For example, for a unit that frequently moves computers to different locations, like a marketing group that uses portable computers docked at different stations, shorter lease durations can be defined for the related scopes. This approach collects IP addresses that are changed frequently and disposed of and returns them to the pool of available addresses that can be used for new lease offerings.
- *Recognize the impact that slower links have on your WAN environment.* Place DHCP, WINS, and DNS servers to maximize response time and minimize low-speed traffic.

Managing DHCP Servers

This section cover:

- Authorizing DHCP servers
- Monitoring server performance
- Restoring server data
- Moving a DHCP database to another server
- Analyzing server log files
- Clustering support for DHCP servers

Authorizing DHCP Servers

Windows 2000 Server provides integrated security support for networks that use Active Directory. This support adds and uses a class of objects that is part of the base directory schema, providing the following enhancements:

- A list of IP addresses available for the computers that you authorize to operate as DHCP servers on your network.
- Detection of unauthorized DHCP servers and prevention of their starting or running on your network.

The following sections discuss:

- Background information about the detection of unauthorized DHCP servers.
- How computers are authorized in Active Directory to provide DHCP service.
- How an unauthorized server is detected and prevented from providing DHCP service.
- Notes and limitations for implementing DHCP service, depending on whether Active Directory service is available.

BACKGROUND ON UNAUTHORIZED DHCP SERVERS

When configured correctly and authorized for use on a network, DHCP servers provide a useful and intended administrative service. However, when a misconfigured or unauthorized DHCP server is introduced into a network, it can cause problems. For example, if an unauthorized DHCP server starts, it might begin either leasing incorrect IP addresses to clients or negatively acknowledging DHCP clients attempting to renew current address leases.

Either of these configurations can produce further problems for DHCP-enabled clients. For example, clients that obtain a configuration lease from the unauthorized server can fail to locate valid domain controllers, preventing clients from successfully logging on to the network.

To avoid these problems in Windows 2000, servers are verified as legal in the network before they can service clients. This avoids most of the accidental damage caused by running DHCP servers with incorrect configurations or correct configurations on the wrong network.

HOW DHCP SERVERS ARE AUTHORIZED

The authorization process for DHCP server computers in Active Directory depends on the installed role of the server on your network. For Windows 2000 Server (as in earlier versions), there are three roles or server types for which each server computer can be installed:

- *Domain controller.* The computer keeps and maintains a copy of the Active Directory service database and provides secure account management for domain member users and computers.
- *Member server.* The computer is not operating as a domain controller but has joined a domain in which it has a membership account in the Active Directory service database.
- *Standalone Server.* The computer is not operating as a domain controller or a member server in a domain. Instead, the server computer is made known to the network through a specified workgroup name, which can be shared by other computers, but is used only for browsing purposes and not to provide secured logon access to shared domain resources.

If you deploy Active Directory, all computers operating as DHCP servers must be either domain controllers or domain member servers before they can be authorized in the directory service and provide DHCP service to clients.

To authorize a computer as a DHCP server, the following process can be used:

1. Log on to the network using either an account that has enterprise administrative privileges or one that has been delegated authority to authorize DHCP servers for your enterprise. In most cases, it is simplest to log on to the network from the computer where you want to authorize the new DHCP server. This ensures that other TCP/IP configuration of the authorized computer has been set up correctly prior to authorization. Typically, you can use an account that has membership in the Enterprise Administrators group. The account you use must allow you to have Full Control rights to the NetServices container object, as it is stored in the enterprise root of the Active Directory service.
2. Install the DHCP service on this computer. For more information, see Chapter 5, "Installation and Administration of DHCP Servers and Clients."
3. Start the DHCP console and select the computer operating as a DHCP server that you want to have added as an authorized server in the directory service database. If the local computer is to be authorized, select **Local computer** for connection when starting the DHCP console. If another computer on your network is to be authorized, select **Remote computer**. For information about opening the DHCP console and about authorizing a DHCP server in Active Directory, see Chapter 5.

When a DHCP server is authorized, the server computer is added to the list of authorized DHCP servers maintained in the directory service database. You can verify that a server has been added by checking the properties, using the Active Directory Sites and Services console. These properties appear under **Configuration**, which is a global container maintained at the following folder location relative to the enterprise root:

\Configuration\Services\NetServices

In some cases, you might choose to delegate the ability for nonenterprise administrators to have appropriate security access to this object type to create and modify the list of authorized DHCP servers. This can be useful in cases where the DHCP server is set up and prepared at another location before being shipped to a remote site for installation and authorization for service on the network.

For information about delegating the ability to authorize DHCP servers to a nonenterprise administrator, see Chapter 5.

HOW UNAUTHORIZED SERVERS ARE DETECTED

Windows 2000 DHCP servers provide detection of both authorized and unauthorized servers, using the following specific enhancements for the DHCP standard:

- The use of information messaging between DHCP servers using DHCP informational messages.
- The addition of several new vendor-specific option types for communicating information about the root domain.

The Windows 2000 DHCP server uses the following process to detect other DHCP servers currently running on the same network and determine if they are authorized to provide service.

When the DHCP service starts, it sends a DHCP informational message (DHCPINFORM) request to the reachable network, using the local limited broadcast address (255.255.255.255), to locate the root domain on which other DHCP servers are installed and configured. This message includes several vendor-specific option types that are known and supported by other DHCP servers running Windows 2000 Server. When received by other DHCP servers, these option types enable the query and retrieval of information about the root domain.

When queried, other DHCP servers reply with DHCP acknowledgment messages (DHCPACK) to both acknowledge and answer with root domain information. In this way, the initializing DHCP server collects and compiles a list of all currently active DHCP servers on the reachable network, along with the root (of the root domain) used by each server.

Typically, only one single enterprise root is detected, and it is the same for all DHCP servers that are reachable and that respond to acknowledge the initializing server. However, if additional enterprise roots are detected, each root is queried to determine whether the computer is authorized for DHCP service for those other enterprises discovered during this phase.

After a list of all DHCP servers running on the network is built, the next step in the detection process depends on whether a directory service is found to be available from the local computer. If the directory service is not available (such as where the initializing DHCP server is installed in a confined network environment used for testing), the initializing server can start if no other

DHCP servers that are part of any enterprise are discovered on the network. Where this condition is met, the server successfully initializes and begins serving DHCP clients.

However, the server continues every five minutes to collect information about other DHCP servers running on the network, using DHCPINFORM as it did at startup. Each time, it checks whether the directory service is available. If a directory service is found, the server ensures that it is authorized by following the procedure, depending on whether it is a member server or a standalone server:

- *For member servers* (a server joined to a domain that is part of the enterprise), the DHCP server queries the directory service for the DHCP server list of addresses that have been authorized. If the server finds its IP address in the authorized list, it initializes and starts providing DHCP service to clients. If it does not find itself in the authorized list, it does not initialize and stops providing DHCP services.
- *For standalone servers* (a server not joined to any domain or part of an existing enterprise), the DHCP server queries the directory service with the root of the enterprise returned by each of the other DHCP servers to see if it can find itself on the authorized list with any of the reported enterprises. The server initializes and starts providing DHCP services to clients *only if* the server finds its IP address in the authorized list for each of the enterprise roots reported by other DHCP servers. If it does not find itself in the authorized list for each of the reported enterprise roots, it does not initialize and the DHCP service is stopped.

Note The process of authorizing DHCP servers is only useful for DHCP servers running Windows 2000 Server. Authorization does not apply if DHCP servers are running (a) Windows NT Server 4.0 and earlier versions, or (b) other DHCP server software.

For the directory authorization process to work properly, it is necessary that the first DHCP server introduced onto your network participate in Active Directory. This requires that the server be installed as either a domain controller or a member server. When planning or deploying Active Directory with Windows 2000 DHCP, it is important that you do not select to install your first DHCP server computer as a standalone server.

Most commonly, there will be only one enterprise root and therefore only a single point for directory authorization of the DHCP servers. However, there is no restriction on authorizing DHCP servers for more than one enterprise root.

Monitoring Server Performance

Because DHCP servers are of critical importance in most environments, monitoring their performance can help in troubleshooting cases where server performance has been degraded.

Windows 2000 Server provides a set of DHCP server performance counters that can be used to measure and monitor various aspects of server activity, such as the following:

- All types of DHCP messages sent and received by the DHCP service.
- The average amount of processing time spent by the DHCP server per message packet sent and received.
- The number of message packets dropped because of internal delays at a DHCP server computer.

For information about DHCP performance monitoring, see Appendix B, "DHCP Resources and Troubleshooting."

SAMPLE DHCP SERVER PERFORMANCE TEST RESULTS

The DHCP development and testing team compiled the following statistics as a profile of DHCP server performance during preliminary testing of Windows 2000 Server.

DHCP SERVER PERFORMANCE MEASUREMENTS • For this test, the DHCP server and client computers used for testing were configured as follows:

- Four client computers were positioned on a routed network to simulate DHCP client activity. Two of the computers were located locally on the same subnet as the server and two were located on a remote subnet reachable through a router.
- All client computers were configured to run a client stress application recreating the simulated effect of 10 actual DHCP client computers simultaneously sending DHCP messages on the network to the server.
- The client computers were set up to perform sending of DHCP discovery messages (DHCPDISCOVERs) 20 percent of the time, such as occurs in the case of a computer newly added and started on the network and obtaining a new IP address lease. For the remaining 80 percent of the time, the client computers sent DHCP request messages (DHCPREQUESTs), such as are typically generated when clients renew a current IP address lease.

For the clients to perform sending of DHCP discovery messages (DHCPDISCOVERs), each of the client computers generated and included a new media access control (MAC) address in its request. To the DHCP server, the unique MAC address implies that the client is new, and the server leases it accordingly.

Server performance was measured each hour for the first 12 hours of testing and the results are noted in Table 4.1.

TABLE 4.1 *DHCP Server Performance in Discovery Message Handling*

Hours of client stress completed	Total leases provided by server
1 hour	489,867
2 hours	379,319
3 hours	378,223
4 hours	383,694
5 hours	352,832
6 hours	338,830
7 hours	340,378
8 hours	320,391
9 hours	301,145
10 hours	312,588
11 hours	317,580
12 hours	314,683

DHCP SCOPE PERFORMANCE MEASUREMENTS • The same test was performed four times, with each iteration increasing the number of configured scopes at the DHCP server. The client activity was re-created using a single client computer configured to run the client stress application operating as described for the previous sample tests.

Scope performance was measured at the server for response times for each set of 25,000 DHCP acknowledgment messages (DHCPACKs) the server returned when leasing clients. Time was measured for both initializing and renewing clients. (For more information about how clients obtain configuration, see Appendix B.)

Prior to performing these tests, the server registry size was increased to 100 megabytes (MB) and the server paging file size was increased to one gigabyte (GB).

The results of each of these four tests are listed in Table 4.2.

Caution Based on these test results, it is generally not recommended to have more than 1,000 scopes on a DHCP server.

TABLE 4.2 *DHCP Server Performance in Initializing and Renewing Clients*

Number of scopes	Initial lease offer time (milliseconds)	Lease renewal time (milliseconds)
100	87	87
1,000	78	80
10,000	90	92
250,000	212	197

BACKGROUND INFORMATION ON SAMPLE DHCP SERVER TESTS • Table 4.3 lists the specific hardware that the Windows 2000 DHCP development and test team used for the server computer.

TABLE 4.3 *Hardware Used for DHCP Server Tests*

Hardware components	Sizing
Number of processors	two
Processor speed	400 MHz Xeon
Amount of RAM	2 GB
Hard disk drive space	70 GB
Hard disk type	SCSI-2 RAID 0 controller
Number of disk drives in array	17

These measurements were based on the server computer running a DHCP server and with no other additional services in use. Where other hardware specifications or software configurations are made when deploying Windows 2000 DHCP servers, your performance results are likely to vary from those documented here.

For more information on determining how to perform DHCP server capacity planning, see "How Many DHCP Servers to Use" in this chapter.

Restoring Server Data

Restoring the DHCP server database can be useful in situations where the database has been either corrupted or lost. Where DHCP database corruption or loss occurs, Windows 2000 Server provides a progressive set of recovery and repair options for restoration of DHCP data on the server computer.

In troubleshooting data corruption problems, use the following general process steps to detect corruption and restore DHCP service:

- First, confirm the source of data loss or corruption at the DHCP server. To do so, you can use *JetPack.exe* to perform a preliminary diagnosis or useful repairs, such as offline database compaction. Additionally, verify that corruption is not related to other problems or conditions with hardware or software changes. Where data loss occurs, verify that the server computer disk drives are operating properly.

  In most cases, database corruption first appears in the form of Jet database error messages in the System event log. For more information on how to use *Jetpack.exe* to manually repair or compact the DHCP database, see Chapter 5 and also refer to "Detecting DHCP Jet data corruption" in this chapter.
- Second, when repair through *Jetpack.exe* compaction fails, you can perform a quick recovery of the DHCP server based on your available options for server backup. One option is to manually make an offline backup of the DHCP server database files and then copy the server database back during restoration from your archived source, such as from a recent tape backup of the server computer disk drives.

  Another option is to use the Netshell **set databaserestore flag** command to set the restore flag, which permits the DHCP Server service to load a copy of the DHCP database in its default backup directory when reinitialized. For more information about Netshell commands for DHCP, see Appendix B.

  When backing up the server computer, you can use either Windows 2000 backup and restore options or other backup and restoration software.
- Third, where other server data recovery options are not available or are tried but unsuccessful, you can use advanced DHCP recovery options. For more information, see "Additional Recovery Options" in this chapter.

DETECTING DHCP JET DATA CORRUPTION

The DHCP service messages listed in Table 4.4 can appear in the System event log when the DHCP server database becomes corrupted.

TABLE 4.4 *Service Messages for Corrupted DHCP Server Database*

Event ID	Source	Description
1014	DhcpServer	The JET database returned the following Error: -510.
1014	DhcpServer	The JET database returned the following Error: -1022.
1014	DhcpServer	The JET database returned the following Error: -1850.

Typically, Jet errors can be resolved by manual offline compaction of the database using the Jetpack utility. In cases where *Jetpack.exe* fails to repair the database, restoration of the DHCP server database, as described in the previous section, might be sufficient.

ADDITIONAL RECOVERY OPTIONS

To recover a corrupted DHCP database, you can use the following options for restoring the database:

- *Simple recovery*. Restore the database from a backup copy of the database file, *Dhcp.mdb*. This is recommended as the preferred method of recovery because it involves less risk of losing information previously configured and stored by the DHCP server and is much simpler to perform. For more information, see "Reconciling Scopes" in this chapter.
- *Advanced recovery*. Generate a new database file using the DHCP Configuration registry key. This can be useful as an additional method to use for data recovery where simple restoration of the database is not possible. For more information, see "Moving a DHCP Database to Another Server" in this chapter.

In some cases of apparent DHCP database corruption, you might also want to determine whether the server has run out of disk space, which could prevent the DHCP server from continuing to service clients on the network until there is room to continue growth and expansion of the DHCP database.

Moving a DHCP Database to Another Server

Windows 2000 provides the DHCP console, which allows you to manage DHCP servers installed and running on a single DHCP server computer. However, the DHCP console does not allow you to move a database from one installed DHCP server to another server computer.

This topic provides details of how to move a database from one server computer to another server computer, assuming the DHCP database and its backup directories are on default drive and path locations.

BACKING UP THE DHCP SERVER DATABASE AT THE SOURCE SERVER

Complete the following procedures at the server computer being used as the source for the DHCP database (steps 6 and 7 are optional):

1. Stop the DHCP server.
2. Disable the DHCP Server service in the list of services. This prevents the DHCP server from starting after the database has been transferred. To perform this task, use Computer Management and select the **DHCP Server** service from the list for it to be disabled.

3. Copy the DHCP server directory tree *systemroot\System32\Dhcp* to a temporary location on the new (destination) DHCP server. For example, copy the directory tree to *C:\Temp\System32\Dhcp*.
4. Start the Registry Editor *(Regedt32.exe)* and go to the following subkey:

   HKEY_LOCAL_MACHINE\SYSTEM\CurrentControlSet\Services\DHCPServer

5. Save the specified key to a text file.
6. Delete the DHCP server database folder *%SystemRoot%\System32\Dhcp* at the source server.
7. Uninstall the DHCP server to remove it from this server.

For information about stopping a DHCP server and about uninstalling DHCP, see Chapter 5.

RESTORING THE DHCP SERVER DATABASE AT THE DESTINATION SERVER

Complete the following procedures at the server computer being used as the destination for the DHCP database:

1. If you have not already installed the DHCP server software, install it and then restart the server computer.
2. Stop the DHCP Server service.
3. Rename the *System.mdb* file to *System.src* in the temporary folder, such as the *C:\Temp\System32\Dhcp directory*.
4. Copy the DHCP server directory tree from the temporary folder to *systemroot\System32\Dhcp* to replace the existing DHCP server directory.
5. Start Registry Editor *(Regedt32.exe)* and go to the following subkey:

   HKEY_LOCAL_MACHINE\SYSTEM\CurrentControlSet\Services\DHCPServer

6. Select the **DHCPServer** key (located under the Services key).
7. Restore the registry hive information from the file you saved in Step 5 of the previous section.
8. In **Restore Key**, for **File name** specify the following:

   systemroot\System32\Dhcp\Backup\Dhcpcfg

9. When prompted, click **Yes**.

   After clicking **Yes** to the prompt to overwrite the existing registry entries, if you have problems completing the restore operation, retry the previous step. Be sure that you are not attempting the restore using Registry Editor from a remote computer. Also, verify that this error was not caused by clicking **Save Subtree As** instead of **Save Key**, as indicated in Step 5 in the previous section when saving registry information at the source server.
10. Exit Registry Editor.
11. Start the DHCP Server service.
12. Open the DHCP console and use **Reconcile All Scopes** to reconcile the DHCP server database to the restored information now merged into the Windows 2000 registry.

For information about installing a DHCP server, stopping a DHCP server, and reconciling the DHCP database, see Chapter 5. Also see Appendix B for information about DHCP database files.

Analyzing Server Log Files

Windows 2000 DHCP server log files are designed to use Audit logging to permit log files to remain enabled for use without requiring added monitoring or administering to manage log file growth or conserve disk resources.

The following section outlines the format of these log files and how they can be used to gather more information about DHCP Server service operations on the network.

DHCP SERVER LOG FILE FORMAT

DHCP server logs are comma-delimited text files with each log entry representing a single line of text. The following are the fields (and the order in which they appear) in a log file entry:

ID, Date, Time, Description, IP Address, Host Name, MAC Address

Each of these fields is described in detail in Table 4.5.

TABLE 4.5 *DHCP Server Log File Fields*

Field	Description
ID	A DHCP server event ID code.
Date	The date on which this entry was logged on the DHCP server.
Time	The time at which this entry was logged on the DHCP server.
Description	A description of this DHCP server event.
IP Address	The IP address of the DHCP client.
Host Name	The host name of the DHCP client.
MAC Address	The media access control address used by the network adapter hardware of the client.

DHCP SERVER LOG: COMMON EVENT CODES

DHCP server audit log files use reserved event ID codes to provide information about the type of server event or activity logged. Table 4.6 describes these event ID codes in more detail. These events apply for both Windows 2000 DHCP servers and for servers running earlier versions of Windows.

TABLE 4.6 *DHCP Server Log Event ID Codes*

EventID	Description
00	The log was started.
01	The log was stopped.
02	The log was temporarily paused due to low disk space.
10	A new IP address was leased to a client.
11	A client renewed a lease.
12	A client released a lease.
13	An IP address was found in use on the network.
14	A lease request could not be satisfied because the address pool of the scope was exhausted.
15	A lease was denied.
20	A BOOTP address was leased to a client.

DHCP SERVER LOGS: SERVER AUTHORIZATION EVENTS

Table 4.7 lists additional server log event ID codes and descriptions. These events can appear in logs made by Windows 2000 DHCP servers. They pertain to the applicable DHCP server and its authorization status when deployed in Active Directory environments.

TABLE 4.7 *DHCP Server Authorization Events*

EventID	Description
50	*Unreachable domain.* The DHCP server could not locate the applicable domain for its configured Active Directory installation.
51	*Authorization succeeded.* The DHCP server was authorized to start on the network.
52	*Upgraded to Windows 2000.* The DHCP server was recently upgraded to Windows 2000 Server and therefore the unauthorized DHCP server detection feature (used to determine whether the server has been authorized in Active Directory) was disabled.
53	*Cached Authorization.* The DHCP server was authorized to start using previously cached information. Active Directory was not currently visible at the time the server was started on the network.
54	*Authorization failed.* The DHCP server was not authorized to start on the network. When this event occurs, the server being stopped likely follows it.
55	*Authorization (servicing).* The DHCP server was successfully authorized to start on the network.
56	*Authorization failure, stopped servicing.* The DHCP server was not authorized to start on the network and was shut down by Windows 2000 Server. You must first authorize the server in the directory before starting it again. For more information, see "To Authorize a DHCP Server in Active Directory" in this chapter.

(continued)

TABLE 4.7 *DHCP Server Authorization Events (Continued)*

EventID	Description
57	*Server found in domain.* Another DHCP server using the same IP address or DNS name already exists and is authorized for service in the same Active Directory domain.
58	*Server could not find domain.* The DHCP server could not locate the specified Active Directory domain.
59	*Network failure.* A network-related failure prevented the server from determining if it is authorized.
60	*No DC is DS-enabled.* No Windows 2000 domain controller (DC) was located. For detecting whether the server is authorized, a DC that is enabled for Active Directory is needed.
61	*Server found that belongs to DS domain.* Another DHCP server was found on the network that belongs to the Active Directory domain.
62	*Another server found.* Another DHCP server was found on the network.
63	*Restarting rogue detection.* The DHCP server is trying again to determine whether it is authorized to start and provide service on the network.
64	*No DHCP-enabled interfaces.* The DHCP server has its service bindings or network connections configured so that it is not enabled to provide service. This usually means one of the following: • The network connections of the server are either not installed or not actively connected to a network. • The server has not been configured with at least one static IP address for one of its installed and active network connections. (See "Configure TCP/IP for Static Addressing" in Chapter 2, "Installing, Managing, and Diagnosing TCP/IP.") • All of the statically configured network connections for the server are disabled. (See "Multihomed DHCP servers" in this chapter.)

EXAMPLE: EXCERPT FROM A SAMPLE DHCP SERVER AUDIT LOG

The following is a brief excerpt of sample log activity from an audit log generated by the DHCP Server service:

```
ID Date,Time,Description,IP Address,Host Name,MAC Address
00,00/19/99,12:43:06,Started,,,
60,04/19/99,12:43:21,No DC is DS Enabled,,MYDOMAIN,
63,04/19/99,12:43:28,Restarting rogue detection,,,
01,04/19/99,13:11:13,Stopped,,,
00,04/19/99,12:43:06,Started,,,
55,04/19/99,12:43:54,Authorized(servicing),,MYDOMAIN,
```

In this sample, the DHCP server could not be authorized when initially started and is subsequently stopped. Once authorized in Active Directory, the server is then able to start and service clients. For information about audit logging, see Chapter 3.

Clustering Support for DHCP Servers

The Windows 2000 DHCP Server service is a cluster-aware application You can implement additional DHCP—or Multicast Address Dynamic Client Allocation Protocol (MADCAP)—server reliability by deploying a DHCP server cluster using the Cluster service provided with Windows 2000 Advanced Server.

By using clustering support for DHCP, you can implement a local method of DHCP server failover, achieving greater fault tolerance. You can also enhance fault tolerance by combining DHCP server clustering with a remote failover configuration, such as by using a split scope configuration.

REQUIREMENTS FOR SETTING UP A DHCP CLUSTERED RESOURCE

The DHCP Server service, when used in a server cluster, requires the following resource types: a disk resource, an IP address resource, and a name resource.

In this type of configuration, a virtual IP address is defined for the IP address resource using the Cluster Administrator tool. This address must be a static IP address, not one obtained from another DHCP server.

The DHCP Server service then binds to this virtual IP address. This IP address must then be the one used to authorize the DHCP Server service in Active Directory so it can function correctly and service clients on the network.

Once the virtual IP is set using cluster configuration, each network adapter installed on each node (that is, a server in the cluster) needs an IP address configuration. Because the DHCP Server service does not bind to adapter IP addresses, you can either provide them through DHCP or configure them statically. If you use static configuration, the IP addresses for each linked pair of network adapters (linked node-to-node) should be from the same subnet.

Addresses that are statically configured using TCP/IP properties from the Network and Dial-up Connections folder can also be viewed through server bindings properties in the DHCP console. However, for a DHCP server cluster, the bindings information that appears in these views does not correspond to the virtual IP address used for the server cluster. Therefore, these settings do not apply.

When a scope is created for a DHCP clustered server, the virtual IP addresses used in the cluster context must be excluded so that they are not distributed to clients. Additionally, you should configure the database path, audit log file path, and the database backup path using the Cluster Administrator tool on the shared disk.

OTHER OPTIONS FOR DHCP FAILOVER

Another way to implement DHCP remote failover is to deploy two DHCP servers in the same network that share a split scope configuration based on the 80/20 rule. For more information, see "Using the 80/20 Rule for Scopes" in this chapter.

Note If you need only to remotely manage DHCP server clusters deployed on other remote computers running Windows 2000 Advanced Server, you can use Cluster Administrator to do this. Additional information on configuring DHCP clustering is available in the Windows 2000 Resource Kit.

Setting Up Scopes

This section covers:

- Removing scopes
- Managing leases
- Using client reservations
- Reconciling scopes

Configuring Scopes

A scope is an administrative grouping of computers for a subnet that uses DHCP service. The administrator first creates a scope for each physical subnet and then uses the scope to define the parameters used by clients. A scope has the following properties:

- A range of IP addresses from which to include or exclude addresses used for DHCP service lease offerings.
- A unique subnet mask, which determines the subnet for a given IP address.
- A scope name assigned when it is created.
- Lease duration values, which are assigned to DHCP clients that receive dynamically allocated IP addresses.

BEFORE ADDING SCOPES

A DHCP scope consists of a pool of IP addresses on a given subnet, such as 192.168.0.1 to 192.168.0.254, that the DHCP server can lease to clients.

Each subnet can have only a single DHCP scope with a single continuous range of IP addresses. To use several address ranges within a single scope or subnet for DHCP service, you must first define the scope and then set any needed exclusion ranges.

- *Defining the scope.* Use the entire range of consecutive IP addresses that make up the local IP subnet for which you are enabling DHCP service.
- *Setting exclusion ranges.* You should set exclusion ranges for any IP addresses within the scope that you do not want the DHCP server to offer or use for DHCP assignment. For example, you can exclude the first 10 addresses in the previous example scope by creating an "exclusion" for 192.168.0.1 to 192.168.0.10. By excluding these addresses, you specify that DHCP clients are never offered these addresses when they request leased configuration from the server. Excluded IP addresses can be active on your network, but only by manually configuring these addresses at hosts that do not use DHCP to obtain an address.

CREATING SCOPES

When you create a DHCP scope, you use the DHCP console to enter the following required information:

- A scope name, assigned by you or the administrator who created the scope.
- A unique subnet mask used to identify the subnet to which an IP address belongs.
- A range of IP addresses contained within the scope.
- A time interval (known as the *lease duration*). The lease duration specifies how long a DHCP client can use an assigned IP address before it must renew its configuration.

USING THE 80/20 RULE FOR SCOPES • For balancing DHCP server usage, a good practice is to use the *80/20 rule* to divide the scope addresses between the two DHCP servers. If DHCP server 1 is configured to make available most (approximately 80 percent) of the addresses, then DHCP server two can be configured to make the other addresses (approximately 20 percent) available to clients. Figure 4-2 is an example of the 80/20 rule.

Note When creating a new scope, the IP address used to create it should not include addresses of existing statically configured computers. Either these static addresses should be outside the range for the scope or they should be immediately excluded from the range.

Because Windows 2000 Server requires that a computer running the DHCP service have its IP address statically configured, be sure that the server computer has its IP address either outside of, or excluded from, the range of the scope.

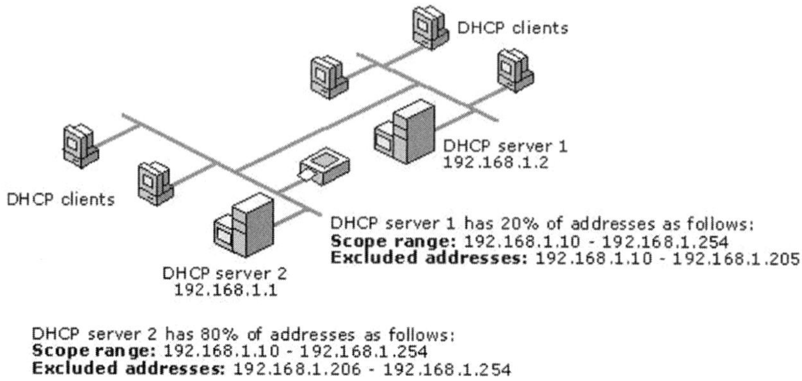

FIGURE 4–2 *80/20 rule*

AFTER SCOPES ARE ADDED

After you define a scope, you can additionally configure the scope by performing the following tasks:

- *Set additional exclusion ranges.* You can exclude any other IP addresses that must not be leased to DHCP clients. You should use exclusions for all devices that must be statically configured. The excluded ranges should include all IP addresses that you assigned manually to other DHCP servers, non-DHCP clients, diskless workstations, or Routing and Remote Access and PPP clients.
- *Create reservations.* You can choose to reserve some IP addresses for permanent lease assignment to specified computers or devices on your network. You should make reservations only for devices that are DHCP-enabled and that must be reserved for specific purposes on your network (such as print servers).
- *Adjust the length of lease durations.* You can modify the lease duration to be used for assigning IP address leases. The default lease duration is eight days. For most LANs, the default value is acceptable but can be further increased if computers seldom move or change locations. Also, infinite lease times can be set but should be used with caution. For information about circumstances under which modifying this setting is most useful, see "Managing Leases" in this chapter.
- *Configure options and classes to be used with the scope.* To provide full configuration for clients, DHCP options need to be configured and enabled for the scope. For more information, see "Setting Up Options" in this chapter.

For more advanced discrete management of scope clients, you can add or enable user or vendor-defined option classes. For more information, see "Using Option Classes" in this chapter.

Note After you define and configure a scope, the scope must be activated before the DHCP server begins providing service to clients. However, you should not activate a new scope until you have specified the DHCP options for it. For information on how to activate a scope, see Chapter 5.

After you activate a scope, you should not change the range of scope addresses.

Using Superscopes

A superscope is an administrative feature of Windows 2000 DHCP servers that you can create and manage through the DHCP console. Using a superscope, you can group multiple scopes as a single administrative entity. With this feature, a DHCP server can:

- Support DHCP clients on a single physical network segment (such as a single Ethernet LAN segment) where multiple logical IP networks are used. When more than one logical IP network is used on each physical subnet or network, such configurations are often called *multinets*.
- Support remote DHCP clients located on the far side of DHCP and BOOTP relay agents (where the network on the far side of the relay agent uses multinets).

In multinet configurations, you can use DHCP superscopes to group and activate individual scope ranges of IP addresses used on your network. In this way, the DHCP server computer can activate and provide leases from more than one scope to clients on a single physical network.

Superscopes can resolve certain types of DHCP deployment issues for multinets, including situations in which:

- The available address pool for a currently active scope is nearly depleted, and more computers need to be added to the network. The original scope includes the full addressable range for a single IP network of a specified address class. You need to use another IP network range of addresses to extend the address space for the same physical network segment.
- Clients must be migrated over time to a new scope (such as to renumber the current IP network from an address range used in an existing active scope to a new scope that contains another IP network range of addresses).
- You want to use two DHCP servers on the same physical network segment to manage separate logical IP networks.

SUPERSCOPE CONFIGURATIONS FOR MULTINETS

The following section shows how a simple DHCP network, consisting originally of one physical network segment and one DHCP server, can be extended to use superscopes for support of multinet configurations:

EXAMPLE 1: NON-ROUTED DHCP SERVER BEFORE SUPERSCOPE • In this preliminary instance, a small LAN with one DHCP server supports a single physical subnet, Subnet A. The DHCP server in this configuration is limited to leasing addresses to clients on this same physical subnet.

Figure 4-3 shows this example network in its original state. At this point, no superscopes have been added and a single scope, Scope 1, is used to service all DHCP clients on Subnet A.

EXAMPLE 2: SUPERSCOPE FOR NON-ROUTED DHCP SERVER SUPPORTING LOCAL MULTINETS • To include multinets implemented for client computers on Subnet A, the same network segment where the DHCP server is located, you can configure a superscope that includes as members the original scope (Scope 1) and additional scopes for the logical multinets for which you need to add support (Scope 2, Scope 3).

Figure 4-4 shows the scope and superscope configuration to support the multinets on the same physical network (Subnet A) as the DHCP server.

EXAMPLE 3: SUPERSCOPE FOR ROUTED DHCP SERVER WITH RELAY AGENT SUPPORTING REMOTE MULTINETS • To include multinets implemented for client computers on Subnet B, the remote network segment located across a router from the DHCP server on Subnet A, you can configure a superscope that includes as members the additional scopes for the logical multinets for which you need to add remote support (Scope 2, Scope 3).

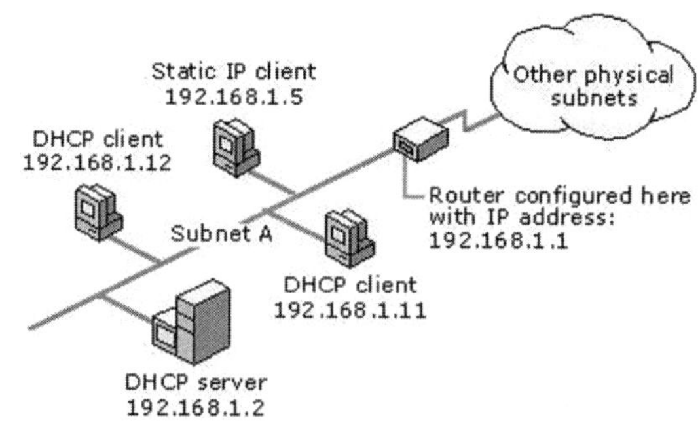

FIGURE 4–3 *Non-routed DHCP server before superscope*

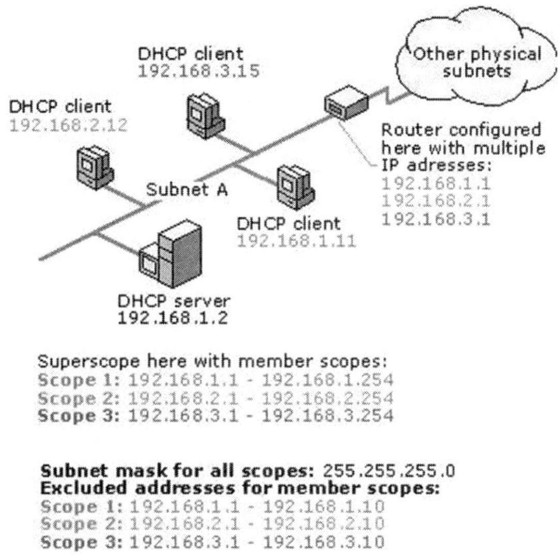

FIGURE 4–4 *Example 2: Superscope for non-routed DHCP server supporting local multinets*

Note that since the multinets are for the remote network (Subnet B), the original scope (Scope 1) does not need to be part of the added superscope.

Figure 4-5 shows the scope and superscope configuration to support the multinets on the remote physical network (Subnet B) away from the DHCP server.

Note A DHCP relay agent is used for DHCP servers to support clients on remote subnets, as shown in Example 3. For more information about relay agents, see Chapter 3.

Using Multicast Scopes

Multicast scopes are supported through the use of Multicast Address Dynamic Client Allocation Protocol, a new proposed standard protocol for performing multicast address allocation. The MADCAP protocol describes how multicast address allocation servers (MADCAP servers) can dynamically provide IP addresses to other computers (MADCAP clients) on your network.

Typically, a MADCAP client might also be a multicast server (MCS) used to support IP multicasting. An MCS, such as a server computer running the Site Server Internet Location Server (ILS) service, manages the shared or

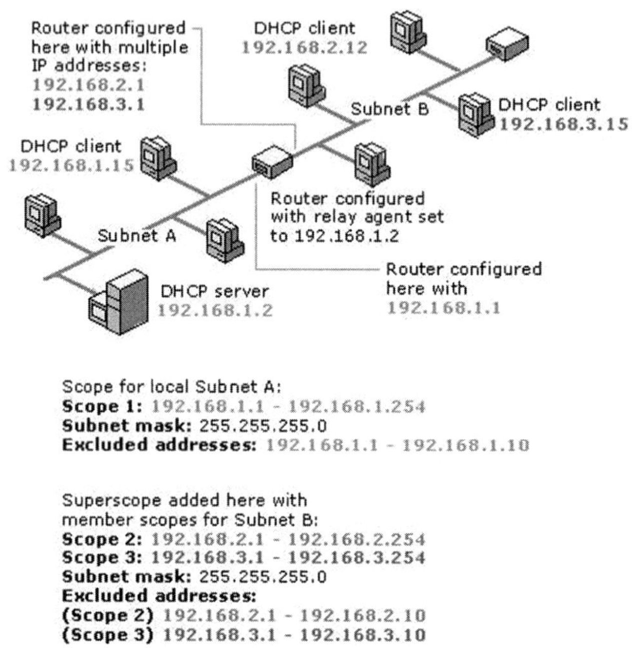

FIGURE 4–5 *Example 3: Superscope for routed DHCP server with relay agent supporting remote multinets*

group use of the allocated multicast IP address and streams data traffic to members that share the use of the specified group address.

Once an MCS is configured and has allocated an IP group address to use, any multicast clients that have registered their membership with the MCS can receive streams sent to this address. By registering with the MCS, clients can participate efficiently in the stream process, such as for real-time video or audio network transmissions. The MCS also manages the multicast group list, updating its membership and status so that all current members receive multicast traffic.

BACKGROUND ON MULTICAST ADDRESSES

Ordinarily, you use DHCP scopes to provide client configurations by allocating ranges of IP addresses from the standard address classes, Class A, B, or C. By using DHCP scopes, you can assign IP addresses from the ranges provided by these addresses for your DHCP clients to be configured to use unicast (or point-to-point) directed communication between other TCP/IP networked computers.

The multicast address range uses an additional address class, Class D, covering IP addresses that range from 224.0.0.0 to 239.255.255.255. Addresses in this class are used for multicasting only and not for regular DHCP scopes.

In all TCP/IP networks, each host is required to first be configured with its own IP address, taken from one of the standard address classes. You must assign this required unicast IP address to one of its interfaces before you can configure a host to support and use other IP addresses, such as a multicast IP address.

Another difference between unicast and multicast addresses is that a group of TCP/IP host computers is intended to be able to share the use of a multicast IP address. This is not normally the case with unicast IP addresses, which are intended to be assigned individually to only one configured host and generally not shared with other hosts.

When the destination address for an IP datagram is an IP multicast address, the datagram is forwarded to all members of the corresponding *multicast group*, which is a set of zero or more hosts identified by the address. The membership of a multicast group is dynamic, in that individual hosts can join or leave the group at any time.

Membership and use of multicast groups is unrestricted and can be compared to membership and use of a group e-mail address: group membership can be any size, and hosts can be members of many multicast groups.

Some of the multicast addresses that you use may be so-called "permanent" group addresses that have been registered with the Internet Assigned Numbers Authority (IANA).

Most multicast IP addresses in use have not been permanently reserved with IANA. All unreserved Class D addresses are typically dynamically assigned as needed to serve temporary multicast groups. These temporary groups can exist as long as one or more hosts on the network are configured with the group address and actively share its use. Remember that even if there are several hosts that have joined a group, the group doesn't really exist unless some server is actually sending IP packets with the group's address in the header's Destination Address field.

For more information about Internet Group Management Protocol (IGMP), see Chapter 1, "TCP/IP Overview."

DETERMINING THE RANGES TO USE FOR MULTICAST SCOPES

When deciding the IP address ranges to use for multicast scopes on your MADCAP server, there are two overall best practices recommended by the IETF's Multicast Allocation (MALLOC) working group. These practices include administrative scoping and global scoping.

Administrative scoping is most useful when you are using multicast IP addresses privately in your own network. It is similar to private IP addressing, as used currently in the unicast IP address spaces (such as the use of the 10.0.0.0 network address space). It is fully discussed in RFC 2365, "Administratively Scoped IP Multicast." Multicast addresses selected from the administratively scoped range are restricted to use within a single administrative domain.

With administratively scoped multicast IP, the range most recommended that you begin with is the 239.192.0.0 range. This range is known as the IPv4 Organization Local Scope and has an associated subnet mask of 255.252.0.0 (14 bits in length). It is intended for use by an entire organization, setting multicast scopes privately for its own internal or organizational use. Starting with this address, you can create a considerable number of addresses—up to 2^{18}, or 262,144 group addresses—for use across all subnets within your organization's network.

For more information, refer directly to the RFC, which can be obtained at the Request for Comments Web site *(www.rfc-editor.org/)*.

Global scoping is most useful when multicast group IP addresses are being used in a public network, notably the Internet. In these situations, the group's members may be located in various different administrative domains.

Author's Note Global scoping is highly experimental and for that reason is briefly mentioned here. It only applies to ISPs/Content-Providers that have an Autonomous System (AS) number. This does not apply to your average, everyday corporate network.

MADCAP AND DHCP

The Windows 2000 DHCP Server service supports both the DHCP and MADCAP protocols. These protocols function separately and are independent of each other. For example, a DHCP client might or might not be a MADCAP client and a MADCAP client might or might not be a DHCP client.

It's also worth mentioning that the DHCP Server service can be used to deploy MADCAP servers independent of how DHCP servers are used on your network. For example, to install Windows 2000 DHCP for MADCAP service only:

1. Create multicast scopes.
2. Do not create other scopes or superscopes.

Only where other scopes or superscopes are configured does the server computer also function as a DHCP server. For more information about MADCAP, see Chapter 3.

Important Multicast scopes and MADCAP only provide a mechanism for dynamically allocating IP address configuration for multicast-ranged IP addresses. Other network configuration details are normally required to enable multicasting for your deployment needs.

Note Multicast scopes do not require or support the use of DHCP options, but can be configured with a finite lifetime, enabling the multicast scope to expire and be removed by the server.

Removing Scopes

When a subnet is no longer in use, or any other time you want to remove an existing scope, you can remove it at the DHCP console. In most cases, scopes are removed only when you need to renumber your network to use a different IP address range.

To retire a current scope and renumber your network to use a different scope, be sure to do the following first:

1. Create the new scope using a different range of addresses.
2. Configure options for the new scope.
3. Activate the new scope and deactivate the old scope.
4. When all clients are no longer using the old scope, remove the old scope.

Before you remove a scope, you must first deactivate it for a period of time. Deactivating a scope starts lease recall on the selected scope.

Before deactivating a scope, a replacement scope should be active on the subnet. The replacement scope can be on a different DHCP server from the deactivated scope as long as the replacement scope is on the same subnet.

You must deactivate a scope before removing it. This enables clients using the scope to renew their lease in a different scope. Otherwise, clients lose their leases. If any IP address in the scope is still leased or in use, you must keep the scope active until either the client lease expires or the client lease renewal request is denied.

After a scope is deactivated, it does not acknowledge lease or renewal requests, so existing clients lose their leases at renewal time and reconfigure with another available DHCP server. To ensure that all clients migrate smoothly to a new scope, you should deactivate the old scope for at least half of the lease time, or until you have manually renewed all clients to move them off of the inactive scope.

To move a Windows 2000-based client manually, type either *ipconfig/ release or ipconfig /renew* at the command prompt of the client computer. For other cases, restarting the client computer might be necessary.

Managing Leases

The DHCP server leases IP addresses to its clients. Each lease has an expiration date, which the client must renew if it is going to continue to use that address.

Leases are retained in the DHCP server database approximately one day after expiration. This grace period protects a client lease in case the client and server are in different time zones, the individual computer clocks are not synchronized, or the client computer is off the network when the lease expires. Expired leases are included in the list of active leases but are distinguished by a dimmed icon.

You can delete the lease of any DHCP client in the scope. The main reason for doing so is to remove a lease that conflicts with an IP address exclusion or a client reservation that you want to add. Deleting a lease has the same effect as if the client lease expired: When the client computer next starts, it must reenter the initialization state and obtain new IP configuration information from a DHCP server. There is nothing, however, to prevent the client from obtaining a new lease for the same IP address. You must make the address unavailable before the client requests another lease.

Delete only entries for clients that are no longer using the assigned DHCP lease or that are to be moved immediately to a new address. Deleting an active client could result in duplicate IP addresses on the network, because deleted addresses will be assigned to new active clients. After you delete the lease of the client and set a reservation or exclusion, you should always use *ipconfig/release* on the client computer to force the client to free its IP address.

Note You can view lease information for individual clients by first selecting the Active Leases folder for a scope in the DHCP console. When Active Leases for a scope is selected as the console view, the list of currently active client leases for the scope appears in the details pane.

MODIFYING DEFAULT LEASE DURATIONS FOR A SCOPE

When a scope is created, the default lease duration is set to eight days. In most cases, this value is sufficient. However, because lease renewal is an ongoing process that can affect the performance of DHCP clients and your network, it is sometimes useful to change the lease duration. Use the following guidelines to decide how to best modify lease duration settings for improving DHCP performance on your network:

- If you have are a large number of IP addresses available and configurations that rarely change on your network, increase the lease duration to reduce the frequency of lease renewal queries between clients and the DHCP server. This reduces some network traffic caused by clients renewing their leases.
- If you have a limited number of IP addresses available and if client configurations change or clients move often on your network, reduce the lease duration to promote scavenging of old IP addresses by the

DHCP server. This increases the rate at which addresses are returned to the available address pool for reassignment to new clients.

Note You can also set a separate lease time, different from the default scope lease time used by your DHCP clients; for example, alternate lease times for supporting other types of clients, such as BOOTP or Routing and Remote Access clients.

Using Client Reservations

With client reservations, you can reserve a specific IP address for permanent use by a DHCP client. Typically, you will need to do this if the client uses an IP address that was assigned using another method for TCP/IP configuration.

If multiple DHCP servers are configured with a scope that covers the range of the reserved IP address, the client reservation must be made and duplicated at each of these DHCP servers. Otherwise, the reserved client computer can receive a different IP address, depending on the responding DHCP server.

If you want to change a reserved IP address for a current client, you have to remove the existing address reservation of the client, and then add a new reservation. You can change any other information about a reserved client while keeping the reserved IP address.

If you are reserving an IP address for a new client, or an address that is different from its current one, you should verify that the DHCP server has not already leased the address. Reserving an IP address in a scope does not automatically force a client currently using that address to stop using it.

If the address is already in use, the client using the address must first release it by issuing a DHCP release message (DHCPRELEASE). To make this happen, at the command prompt of a client computer running under Windows 2000, type *ipconfig /release*.

Reserving an IP address at the DHCP server also does not force the new client for which the reservation is made to immediately move to that address. In this case, too, the client must first issue a DHCP request message (DHCPREQUEST). To make this happen, at the command prompt of a client computer running under Windows 2000, type *ipconfig /renew*.

For clients using Windows 95 or Windows 98, you can use the *Winipcfg.exe* program to cause release or renewal of the reserved IP address in DHCP. For clients using MS-DOS, and some clients using other operating systems, a computer must be restarted for the change to take effect.

Once these changes are made, the reserved client is leased the IP address now reserved for its permanent use each time it renews its lease with the DHCP server.

Note Reserved clients can have DHCP options configured specifically for their use. When options are configured for a reserved client, these values override any option type parameters distributed via server-based, scope-based, or class-based options assignment.

You can also use the **ipconfig** command on computers running earlier versions of Windows NT to release and renew DHCP leases. However, not all other **ipconfig** command options are available when executed at clients running under these earlier versions.

Reconciling Scopes

Reconciling scopes can fix inconsistencies, such as incorrect or missing information for client IP addresses that are stored in scope lease information. When inconsistencies are found, the DHCP server can use duplicate scope address lease information recorded in the Windows 2000 registry to detect any lease entries not currently reflected in the DHCP server database.

To correct and repair these inconsistencies, you need to reconcile any scope inconsistencies found when performing this operation. Once you select and reconcile scope inconsistencies, the DHCP console either restores those IP addresses to the original owner or creates a temporary reservation for those addresses. These reservations are valid for the lease time assigned to the scope. When the lease time expires, the addresses are recovered for future use.

RESTORING SCOPES USING RECONCILE OPTIONS

The **Reconcile** feature can also be used to restore DHCP scope data in the event of server recovery. Before using this feature to fully recover DHCP scopes, complete the following preliminary tasks on the server:

1. Obtain and verify that you have a backup copy of the DHCP database, including all of its required files and subdirectories.
2. Stop the DHCP server (see Chapter 5).
3. Delete all files in the currently set **Database path**, which can be viewed or set from the **Advanced** tab in **Properties** at the applicable DHCP server.
4. All DHCP server registry keys must either be restored or exist and remain intact from previous service operation on the server computer. If you are not sure how to make a copy of the DHCP server registry keys, refer to the procedures for using Registry Editor (Regedt32.exe) in "Moving a DHCP Database to Another Server" in this chapter.
5. Regenerate a fresh version of the DHCP server database file in the current **Database path**, such as the *SystemRoot\System32\Dhcp* folder, on the server computer. A fresh copy of the DHCP server database can be generated by:

   a. Stopping the DHCP server.

b. Deleting all of the DHCP database files in the current **Database path** folder.

c. Restarting the DHCP server.

   When deleting server database files, it is not necessary to delete the *\backup* subfolder as well, unless you are deliberately choosing to not have the server restore from one its previous backup copies archived there.

When the DHCP server registry information and DHCP database files have been either restored or regenerated at the server and the server restarted, you might notice that upon opening the DHCP console, scope information is present but no active leases or other information for scopes is displayed.

To regain your active leases for each scope, you must use either the **Reconcile** feature to recover each scope or the **Reconcile All Scopes** feature at the applicable server. For information about reconciling the DHCP database and reconciling a scope, see Chapter 5.

If the reconcile scope option is used, the procedure needs to be repeated for each scope defined and used at the server. After reconciliation is completed, scope client lease and reservation information is added back into the **Active Leases** for each scope, based on DHCP scope registry information previously stored at the server computer.

After using the **Reconcile** feature, you might notice that when viewing properties for individual clients shown in **Active Leases**, client information is displayed incorrectly. This information is corrected and updated in the console as scope clients renew their leases.

Note After using the recovery methods discussed here, you can enable address conflict detection on the server for a period of time. For more information, see Chapter 5.

Although the Reconcile feature can be used to recover scope information in the event of DHCP server disaster recovery, it is not intended to be a replacement for other traditional backup measures. It is recommended that you implement other methods (such as using backup to a tape drive) to provide offline storage and duplicate archives of your DHCP database. For information, see "Restoring Server Data" in this chapter.

Supporting Clients

This section covers:

- Supporting DHCP clients
- Supporting Routing and Remote Access clients
- Supporting BOOTP clients

Supporting DHCP Clients

When installing a DHCP server to support a combination of DHCP clients provided by Windows and other operating systems on your network, consider some of the following issues:

- Windows 2000 DHCP servers can assign any of the predefined options that are part of the DHCP standard set of options described in RFC 2132. Servers can also be modified to provide additional custom options as needed and requested by DHCP clients that have support for and have requested such options.
- Microsoft DHCP clients (including those running Windows 2000) only support and request a small number of the full standard set of DHCP options in their default configuration. This subset of supported options contrasts with the larger set of options that are predefined for assigned use within the DHCP console when managing Windows DHCP servers. For more information about Microsoft DHCP clients, see Chapter 3.
- Other DHCP clients provided in systems supplied from other software vendors (such as UNIX or Linux clients) can request and recognize different DHCP options than those commonly supported by default for all released Microsoft DHCP clients. For these other DHCP clients, you can assign options at the server that are recognized by and configured for the supporting clients.

    Typically, if DHCP clients are unable to recognize or support an assigned DHCP option provided by the server during leasing, they silently ignore it. Another method to control options assignment is to use vendor-defined or user-defined classes. In this arrangement, you can assign options for distribution only to identified members of the applicable class at the DHCP server. For more information, see "Using Option Classes" in this chapter.
- In some advanced deployment cases, you can tune or customize your Windows applications for Windows 2000 clients to leverage current DHCP client application programming interfaces (APIs), which are documented as part of the Microsoft Platform SDK available through the Microsoft Developers Network (MSDN).

    These published DHCP client APIs can enable you to customize DHCP client behavior, such as to enable other DHCP options to be requested and used at a Windows 2000 DHCP client. For more information on using these APIs, see the Microsoft Web site.

Supporting Routing and Remote Access Clients

Windows 2000 DHCP servers provide support for Routing and Remote Access clients in two primary ways:

- A reserved user class, the **Default Remote Access class**, is predefined at each server. When used, this class can provide configured options that are specific only to Windows Routing and Remote Access clients.
- Special DHCP client configuration behavior occurs on the part of Routing and Remote Access servers, which perform proxy DHCP service for their clients that use DHCP to obtain a lease.

Optionally, you can use the **Default Remote Access class** to assign options specific to your remote access clients. In any instance where these clients use DHCP to obtain an IP address, they obtain a proxy IP address lease from the Routing and Remote Access server, which gathers IP addresses from the DHCP server for its distribution needs. In this process, the server provides optional values according to its own methods to its DHCP clients that use proxy leases.

For example, using either *Winipcfg.exe* (for Windows 95 or Windows 98) or *Ipconfig.exe* (for Windows 2000, earlier versions of Windows NT, or Windows 98) you can display the following information about the DHCP lease for a Routing and Remote Access client computer:

```
Lease Obtained:    Tue Jan 1 80 12:00:00 AM
Lease Expires:     Tue Jan 1 80 12:00:00 AM
```

When a Routing and Remote Access server assigns an IP address to one of its clients, either from its own static address pool or from its cached DHCP address pool, there is no effective lease time for the IP address, since it is released when the client disconnects.

However, remote access clients can still receive additional TCP/IP configuration information from the Routing and Remote Access server. For example, WINS and DNS server assignments can be delegated to the client when it connects.

Again, this information is not taken from the options given in the DHCP lease. Instead, these are taken directly from the Routing and Remote Access server settings. If a Routing and Remote Access server has WINS or DNS servers as configured entries in its dial-up connection properties, these settings are passed on to its clients.

Table 4.8 lists the options that Windows-based DHCP clients support and how each of these options has its values assigned to clients that use DHCP through connection to the Routing and Remote Access server:

TABLE 4.8 *Windows-based DHCP Client Options*

Option	Description
IP address	The Routing and Remote Access server proactively obtains IP addresses from the DHCP server and builds a cached pool of DHCP leased addresses. It then distributes these cached IP addresses upon demand to dial-up clients and manages each lease accordingly. This is the only information from the DHCP server that the Routing and Remote Access client receives.
WINS server	Values provided with this option are taken from the dial-up connection properties of the Routing and Remote Access server if it is configured with WINS server addresses. The client acquires the list of WINS servers that are configured on the Routing and Remote Access server.
DNS server	Values provided with this option are taken from the dial-up connection properties of the Routing and Remote Access server if it is configured with DNS server addresses. The client acquires the first DNS server address listed in the search list.
Subnet mask	The subnet mask corresponds to the default subnet mask associated with the standard address class type (Class A, Class B, or Class C) of the given IP address.
NetBIOS scope ID	NetBIOS scope ID information is not passed to the client. If you need to modify this setting, you must change it directly on the client.
Node type	Node type is not taken from the DHCP lease but can change on the Routing and Remote Access client, depending upon WINS information. If the Routing and Remote Access server has no locally defined WINS servers, a b-node Routing and Remote Access client remains a b-node client. If the Routing and Remote Access server has locally defined WINS servers, a b-node Routing and Remote Access client switches to h-node for the duration of the connection.

Supporting BOOTP Clients

The Bootstrap protocol is an established TCP/IP standard for host configuration that precedes DHCP.

BOOTP was originally designed to enable boot configuration for diskless workstations on older systems. This protocol approach was necessary because clients of this type have limited ability to store configurable information required during their respective boot processes used to start and participate in a network.

Windows 2000 DHCP servers respond to both BOOTP and DHCP requests. The initialization process for BOOTP clients is different from the lease process used for DHCP clients.

For BOOTP, clients obtain their configuration in a two-phase process, as follows:

1. The BOOTP client requests an IP address and other relevant information. This information might typically include IP addresses for a router (default gateway) address or a DNS server. For information about standard DHCP and BOOTP options, see Appendix B.

2. The BOOTP client also requests additional information. This information is needed for the client to locate a Trivial File Transfer Protocol (TFTP) server that serves its platform-specific boot image file. This file is needed by the client to complete its boot configuration.

Once all of the information requested by the BOOTP client is fulfilled by the BOOTP (or Windows 2000 DHCP) server, the client can make the separate request to its TFTP server to complete the second phase of its boot process.

The following sections cover how to configure Windows 2000 DHCP servers to support BOOTP clients during both of these phases of the BOOTP configuration process.

BOOTP CLIENTS REQUESTING IP ADDRESS INFORMATION ONLY

Previously, BOOTP client support through the DHCP server always required an explicit client reservation to be made for each BOOTP client.

With new support for *dynamic BOOTP*, a pool of addresses can be designated—similar to how a scope is used for DHCP clients—to dynamically manage IP address assignment for BOOTP clients. The DHCP Server service can later reclaim addresses used in the dynamic BOOTP address pool, after first verifying a specified lease time has elapsed and that each address is not still in use by the BOOTP client.

To configure your DHCP server to assign and distribute IP address information to BOOTP clients, you must first configure a BOOTP address pool within a DHCP scope on the server. For information about how to add BOOTP address pools, see Chapter 5.

Another option to the dynamic BOOTP address pool is to add a client reservation for each non-dynamic BOOTP client within your DHCP scopes. A reservation builds an association between the BOOTP client's MAC address (i.e., the address encoded in its physical interface hardware) and its leased IP address.

When a reserved client requests an IP address, the DHCP Server service returns the appropriate reserved IP address in the lease response based on the MAC address of the client included in the BOOTP request message.

Important When configuring client reservations for use with BOOTP clients, note that DHCP options can apply equally to DHCP and BOOTP clients. Therefore, correct scope configuration is imperative.

BOOTP CLIENTS REQUESTING BOOT FILE INFORMATION

To configure Windows 2000 DHCP servers to provide boot file information to your BOOTP clients, complete the following:

1. Add a client reservation for each BOOTP client within an active DHCP scope.
2. Add BOOTP entries for each client-specific platform in the BOOTP table on the DHCP server.

For information about adding a client reservation and adding an entry to the BOOTP table, see Chapter 5.

BOOTP clients use information stored in the BOOTP table to complete the second phase of their boot process. This information is returned to any requesting BOOTP client on the network that broadcasts a BOOTP request message.

If at least one BOOTP entry has been added to the BOOTP table, a Windows 2000 DHCP server replies to BOOTP client requests. If no BOOTP entries are configured, the server ignores BOOTP request messages.

CONFIGURING THE BOOTP TABLE

Each record in the BOOTP table contains the three fields that contain the information returned to the BOOTP client:

- *Boot image file name.* Identifies the generic file name (such as *unix*) of the requested boot file, based on the BOOTP client hardware type.
- *Full server path to boot image.* Identifies the full path of the boot file (such as */etc/vmunix*) returned to the client by the BOOTP server, using TFTP.
- *TFTP file server.* Identifies the name of the TFTP server used to source the boot file.

To add these entries into the BOOTP table, use the DHCP console.

ADDITIONAL BOOTP CONFIGURATION DETAILS

For your Windows 2000 DHCP servers to supply boot image file and TFTP server information to BOOTP clients, some DHCP options are used by the server for the purpose of fulfilling information stored in configured BOOTP table entries.

Table 4.9 lists these options, which are used to complete BOOTP messages returned to clients during their initial bootstrap sequence.

TABLE 4.9 *DHCP Options for Completing BOOTP Messages*

Code	Description
66	TFTP server name
67	Boot file name

Once you add BOOTP entries to the BOOTP table at a Windows 2000 DHCP server, you are also configuring the previous options for use in supporting your BOOTP clients. You do not need to further configure DHCP options at the server for these options to be provided and used as part of its BOOTP support.

Note Windows 2000 DHCP servers provide a predefined user class, the **Default BOOTP class**, for assigning options specific to BOOTP clients.

Setting Up Options

This section covers:

- Assigning options
- Using option classes

Assigning Options

You can manage DHCP options at four distinct levels:

- *Predefined options.* At this level, you control which types of options are predefined for the DHCP server to expose as available options for assigning from any of the option configuration dialog boxes (such as **Server Options**, **Scope Options**, or **Client Options**) available through the DHCP console. You can add or remove options to and from the predefined list of standard options as needed. Although options are made available in this way, they are not assigned values until administratively configured at the server, scope, or client.
- *Server options.* Assign values here (using the **General** tab) for options that should apply to or be inherited by all scopes and clients of the DHCP server as defaults. Options configured here can have their values overridden by different values if those values are set at a scope, options class, or reserved client level.
- *Scope options.* Assign values here (using the **General** tab) for options that should apply only to clients of an applicable scope selected in the DHCP console tree. Options configured here can have their values overridden by different values if those values are set at either an options class or reserved client level.
- *Client options.* Assign values here (using the **General** tab) for options that should apply only to a specific reserved DHCP client. To use this level of assignment, you must first add a reservation for the applicable client to the applicable DHCP server and scope where the client

is to obtain its IP address. These options are set for an individual DHCP client configured with an address reservation in a scope. Only properties manually configured at the client computer can override options assigned at this level.

- *Class options*. When using any of the option configuration dialog boxes (**Server Options**, **Scope Options** or **Client Options**) you can click the **Advanced** tab of the applicable dialog box to configure and enable options for assignment to identifying member clients of a specified user or vendor class. Depending on the context, only those DHCP clients that identify themselves according to the selected class are distributed options data that you have configured specifically for that class. For example, if a class-assigned option is set at a scope, only clients of that scope that indicate class membership during leasing activity are configured with class-assigned option values. Other nonmember clients are configured using scope option values set from the **General** tab.

  Options configured here can override values assigned and set at the same context (e.g., server, scope, or client options) or values inherited from options configured at a higher context. However, the ability of the client to indicate membership in a specific options class is typically the decisive criteria for using this level of options assignment.

GUIDELINES FOR ASSIGNING OPTIONS

The following guidelines can help you determine what level to assign the options you use for clients on your network:

- Add or define new custom option types only if you have new software or applications that require a nonstandard DHCP option.
- If your DHCP server manages many scopes for a large network, be selective when assigning **Server Options**. These options apply by default to *all* clients of a DHCP server computer, unless otherwise overridden.
- Use **Scope Options** for assigning most options that clients use. In most networks, this level is typically preferred for assigning and enabling the use of DHCP options.
- Use **Class Options** if you have a mixture of DHCP clients with diverse needs that are able to identify a specific class on the DHCP server when obtaining a lease. For example, if you have a limited number of client computers running Windows 2000 DHCP clients, these clients can be configured to receive vendor-specific options that other clients do not use.
- Use **Client Options** for individual DHCP clients in your network that have special configuration requirements.

For any hosts (that is, computers or other networked devices) that do not support DHCP or are not recommended to use it, you can also consider excluding IP addresses for those computers and devices and manually setting the IP address configuration directly at the applicable host.

COMMONLY USED OPTIONS

After you set basic TCP/IP configuration settings (such as IP address, subnet mask, and default gateway) for clients, most clients also need the DHCP server to provide other information through DHCP options. The most common of these include the following:

- *Routers.* A preferred list of IP addresses for routers on the same subnet as DHCP clients. The client can then contact these routers as needed to forward IP packets destined for remote hosts.
- *DNS servers.* IP addresses for DNS name servers that DHCP clients can use to resolve a domain host name query.
- *DNS domain.* Specifies the domain name that DHCP clients should use when resolving unqualified names during DNS domain name resolution.
- *WINS node type.* A preferred NetBIOS name resolution method for the DHCP client to use (such as b-node for broadcast only or h-node for a hybrid of point-to-point and broadcast methods).
- *WINS server.* IP addresses of primary and secondary WINS servers for the DHCP client to use.

For information about Microsoft DHCP clients, see Chapter 3, and for information about DHCP options, see Appendix B.

Using Option Classes

Option classes offer an additional method for grouping DHCP-provided configuration details for clients within a scope. For Windows 2000 Server, there are two types of option classes that can be used for submanaging options.

- *User classes,* for assigning options to clients identified as sharing a common need for similar DHCP options configuration.
- *Vendor classes,* for assigning vendor-specific options to clients identified as sharing a commonly defined vendor type.

For information about user and vendor classes, see Chapter 3.

HOW USER CLASSES WORK

User classes allow DHCP clients to differentiate themselves from each other by specifying a User Class option. When available for client use, this option includes a user-determined class ID that can help to group clients of similar configuration needs within a scope. For example, you might support users and computers with mobile computing needs by configuring a user class at the DHCP server and setting the related class ID at the client computers. Note that in order to access user class-specific information, the DHCP client must be configured in advance with the user class ID. In other words, a DHCP client must have some configuration in order to access information based on its user class.

A user class is useful when you need to keep separate options that cover the special needs of identifying client computers, such as providing a shorter lease time for portable computers that either move frequently or use remote access often. In such cases, you could configure the DHCP server to distribute different option values that are specific to the needs of certain clients.

For instance, shorter leases could be assigned to mobile clients. For information about changing the lease time for remote access clients, see Chapter 5.

The user class feature gives you greater flexibility in configuring DHCP clients on your network, but is not required for standard DHCP use. If user-defined option classes are not configured, options are provided through the applicable server, scope, or client option settings instead. For more information, see "Assigning options" in this chapter.

Windows 2000 DHCP servers support recognition of user class IDs and perform the following added steps to lease clients identifying themselves according to this process:

1. The server determines whether the user class identified by the client in its lease request is a recognized class, previously defined on the server. If predefined user classes exist at the server and are configured, class-based assignment is enabled. For other user classes, you must first add and configure them at the server before they are available for use.
2. If the user class is recognized, the server determines whether any additional DHCP options are configured for this class in the active lease context (either the scope or a client reservation) where the server is leasing the client.
3. If the scope or reserved client options are configured to provide options for the user-defined class of the client, the server returns those options to the client as part of its DHCP acknowledgment message (DHCPACK), which is sent to confirm the lease.

ADDITIONAL USER CLASS EXAMPLES • For Windows 2000 computers, you can define specific user class identifiers to convey information about client software configuration, its physical location in a building, or about its user preferences. For example, an identifier can specify that DHCP clients are members of a user-defined class called "2nd floor, West," which has need for a special set of router, DNS, and WINS server settings.

You can also use the Microsoft predefined user classes for isolating configuration details specific for clients with special needs, such as BOOTP or Routing and Remote Access service. For information about assigning advanced class-based options, see Chapter 5.

Note

In addition to configuring or adding user classes at the DHCP server, in Windows 2000 you can set a DHCP user class ID at the client computer with the **ipconfig/setclassid** command. For more information, see Chapter 5.

When you configure user classes at the DHCP server, be certain that the class identifying data you set at both the DHCP server and member client computers is identically matching binary or ASCII data. For information aboutcreating a new user or vendor class, see Chapter 5.

The user class option permits only one class ID to be used for identifying clients. Each client computer can only be identified as a member of a single user class at the DHCP server. You can use additional user classes and make new hybrids from your other user classes, as needed.

HOW VENDOR CLASSES WORK

DHCP clients that are configured to optionally identify themselves to the DHCP server by their vendor type can use vendor-defined option classes when obtaining a lease. For a client to identify its membership in a vendor class, the client provides a value in the **Vendor class identifier** option when it requests or selects a lease from the server.

The vendor class identifier information is a string of character data interpreted by a DHCP server. Microsoft supports vendor class identification for its DHCP clients running Windows 2000 or Windows 98.

Most vendor types are derived from standard reserved hardware and operating system type abbreviation codes listed in Request for Comments (RFC) 1700. For more information about TCP/IP RFCs, see Appendix A, "TCP/IP Resources."

Other vendors might choose to define their own specific vendor class IDs for either conveying vendor-specific information or handling special needs for their DHCP clients.

Windows 2000 DHCP servers support recognition of vendor class IDs and perform the following additional steps to lease the clients that identify themselves according to this process:

1. The server determines whether the vendor class identified by the client in its lease request is a recognized class, previously defined on the server. Only Microsoft vendor classes are predefined at the server. For other vendor classes, you must manually add and configure these options at your Windows 2000 DHCP servers before they are available for use.

2. If the vendor class is a recognized one, the server determines whether any additional DHCP options are configured for this class in the active lease context (either the scope or a client reservation) where the server is leasing the client.
3. If the scope or reserved client options are configured to provide options for the vendor-defined class of the client, the server returns them using the **Vendor-specific information** option as part of its DHCP acknowledgment message (DHCPACK), which is sent to confirm the lease.

Vendor classes permit other system vendors to support custom applications for DHCP in mixed vendor environments. Vendor-specific options, when provided, are used in addition to any of the standard DHCP options assigned or required for DHCP.

For more information on vendor classes, see "DHCP RFCs" in Appendix B or refer directly to RFC 2132.

Note In most cases, the default (or unspecified) vendor class, DHCP standard options, can provide a useful default for grouping any DHCP clients that do not specify or recognize vendor class IDs. When you add new vendor classes at the DHCP server, be sure that the vendor class ID data you set at the server matches the actual vendor class ID used by clients from the other vendor. For more information, contact the appropriate vendor.

Interoperability Issues

The following section covers issues that affect the use of the Windows 2000 DHCP server with other services or network configurations on your network:

- Using DNS servers with DHCP
- Using Routing and Remote Access servers with DHCP
- Multihomed DHCP servers

Using DNS Servers with DHCP

When installing a Windows 2000 DHCP server, you can configure the server to perform updates on behalf of its DHCP clients to any Domain Name System (DNS) servers that support dynamic updates.

HOW DHCP AND DNS UPDATE INTERACTION WORKS

The DHCP server can be used to register and update the pointer (PTR) and host (A) resource records on behalf of its DHCP-enabled clients.

This process requires the use of an additional DHCP option, the Client FQDN option (option 81). This option permits the client to provide its fully qualified domain name (FQDN) as well as instructions to the DHCP server on how it would like the server to process DNS dynamic updates (if any) on its behalf.

When this option is issued by a qualified DHCP client, such as a DHCP-enabled computer running Windows 2000, it is processed and interpreted by Windows 2000 DHCP servers to determine how the server initiates updates on behalf of the client.

For example, the server might be configured in one of the following ways to process client requests:

- The DHCP server registers and updates client information with its configured DNS servers *according to the client request.* Once a new DHCP server is installed, this is the default configuration for Windows 2000 DHCP servers and clients. In this mode, any Windows 2000 DHCP client can request the way in which the DHCP server performs updates of its host (A) and PTR resource records. If possible, the DHCP server accommodates the client request for handling updates to its name and IP address information in DNS. This can be set at the applicable DHCP server by configuring the **Update DNS only if DHCP client requests** option located in **Properties** on the **DNS** tab.
- The DHCP server *always* registers and updates client information with its configured DNS servers. This is a modified configuration supported for Windows 2000 DHCP servers and clients. In this mode, the DHCP server always performs updates of the client's FQDN and leased IP address information, both its host (A) and pointer (PTR) resource records, regardless of whether the client has requested to perform its own updates. This can be set at the applicable DHCP server by configuring the **Always update DNS** option located in **Properties** on the **DNS** tab.
- The DHCP server *never* registers and updates client information with its configured DNS servers. To set this behavior, the DHCP server must be configured to disable performance of DHCP/DNS proxy updates. By disabling this feature, no client host (A) or PTR resource records are updated in DNS for DHCP clients. If necessary, this change in setting can be made at Windows 2000 DHCP servers by clearing the **Automatically update DHCP client information in DNS** check box, which is located in **Properties** on the **DNS** tab on the applicable DHCP server or one of its scopes. By default, updates are always performed for newly installed Windows 2000 DHCP servers and any new scopes created for them.

ADDITIONAL ADVANCED DHCP/DNS SERVER CONFIGURATION OPTIONS • In addition to these standard DHCP/DNS interactions, the Windows 2000 DHCP server can be configured to perform these optional update tasks:

1. The server can selectively be configured to *not* send updates for discarding the client host (A) resource record when the client lease expires. When the DHCP server is enabled to perform DNS updates, it always sends updates to discard the client PTR resource records when the lease expires. Whether the server does this also with client host (A) resource records when the client's lease expires (by default, the server discards these) is a configurable option. To modify this at the applicable DHCP server, clear the **Discard forward (name-to-address) lookups when lease** check box in **Properties** on the **DNS** tab.
2. The server can be selectively configured to *not* send updates for clients unable to use the Client FQDN option (option 81) to request the way that updates are handled. By default, the DHCP server sends updates for clients that do not support option 81. This allows the server to perform proxy updates in DNS for all of its DHCP clients that are running earlier versions of Windows operating systems. To modify this at the applicable DHCP server, clear or select the **Enable updates for DNS clients that do not support dynamic updates** check box in **Properties** on the **DNS** tab.

Important For the DHCP/DNS interaction described in the following sections to be in effect:

1. Be certain that you are using DHCP and DNS servers running Windows 2000 Server.

2. Make any configuration changes needed to enable the use of dynamic updates at your DHCP and DNS servers, as described in the DNS dynamic update protocol.

WINDOWS DHCP CLIENTS AND DNS DYNAMIC UPDATE PROTOCOL

DHCP clients running Windows 2000 and earlier versions of Windows interact differently when performing the DHCP and DNS interactions previously described. The following examples and graphics show how this process varies in different cases:

EXAMPLE 1: DHCP AND DNS UPDATE INTERACTION FOR WINDOWS 2000 DHCP CLIENTS • Windows 2000 DHCP clients interact with DNS dynamic update protocol as follows (see Figure 4-6):

1. The client initiates a DHCP request message (DHCPREQUEST) to the server.
2. The server returns a DHCP acknowledgment message (DHCPACK) to the client, granting an IP address lease.
3. By default, the client sends a DNS update request to the DNS server for its own forward lookup record, a host (A) resource record. Alternately, the server can perform this update to the DNS server on behalf of the client if both the client and its configuration are modified accordingly.

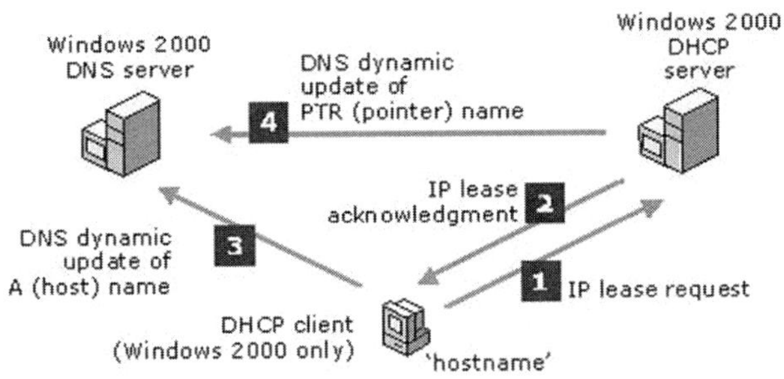

FIGURE 4–6 DHCP and DNS update interaction for Windows 2000 DHCP clients

4. The server sends updates for the DHCP client's reverse lookup record—a PTR resource record—using the process defined by the DNS dynamic update protocol.

EXAMPLE 2: DHCP AND DNS UPDATE INTERACTION FOR EARLIER WINDOWS DHCP CLIENTS • Earlier versions of Windows DHCP clients (prior to Windows 2000) do not support the DNS dynamic update process directly, and therefore can not directly interact with the DNS server. For these DHCP clients, updates are typically handled as follows (see Figure 4-7):

1. The client initiates a DHCP request message (DHCPREQUEST) to the server.
2. The server returns a DHCP acknowledgment message (DHCPACK) to the client, granting an IP address lease.
3. The server then sends updates to the DNS server for the client's forward lookup record, which is a host (A) resource record.
4. The server also sends updates for the client's reverse lookup record, which is a PTR resource record.

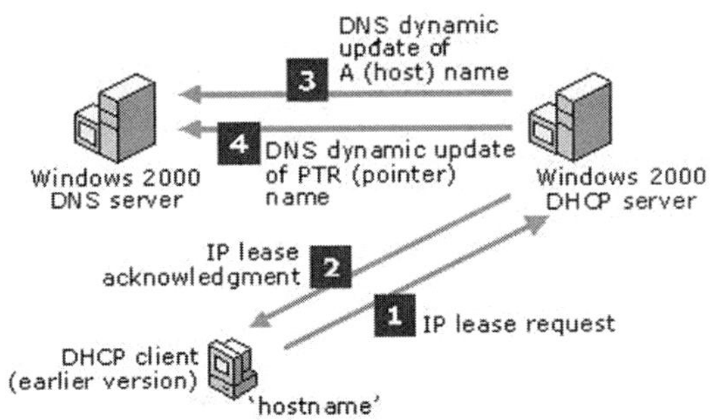

FIGURE 4–7 DHCP and DNS update interaction for earlier Windows DHCP clients (prior to Windows 2000)

USING THE DNSUPDATEPROXY SECURITY GROUP

As previously described, you can configure a Windows 2000 DHCP server so that it dynamically registers host (A) and PTR resource records on behalf of DHCP clients. In this configuration, the use of secure dynamic update with Windows 2000 DNS servers might cause stale resource records.

For example, suppose the following sequence of events occurs:

1. A Windows 2000 DHCP server (DHCP1) performs a secure dynamic update on behalf of one of its clients for a specific DNS domain name.
2. Because the DHCP server successfully created the name, it becomes the owner of the name.
3. Once the DHCP server becomes the owner of the client name, only that DHCP server can update the name.

In some circumstances, this might cause problems. For instance, suppose that DHCP1 later fails. If a backup DHCP server comes online, it cannot update the client name because it is not the owner of the name.

In a similar example, suppose DHCP1 registered in DNS on behalf of its client the name *host.example.microsoft.com,* and then the administrator upgraded that computer from an earlier version of Windows to Windows 2000. Since the DHCP server (DHCP1) is the owner of this name, the client cannot update its DNS records once the computer is upgraded to Windows 2000.

To solve this problem, a new built-in security group called *DnsUpdateProxy* is provided. Any object created by the members of this group has no security and the first user (that is not a member of the DnsUpdateProxy group) to modify the set of records associated with a client becomes its owner. Thus, if every DHCP server registering resource records for older clients is a member of this group, the problems discussed earlier are eliminated.

ADDING MEMBERS TO THE DNSUPDATEPROXY GROUP • You can configure the DnsUpdateProxy security group through Active Directory Users and Computers.

Important If you are using multiple DHCP servers for fault tolerance and also securing dynamic updates, add each of the computers operating a Windows 2000 DHCP server as members of the DnsUpdateProxy global security group.

SECURITY CONCERNS WHEN USING THE DNSUPDATEPROXY GROUP • Although adding all DHCP servers as members to this special built-in group helps to resolve some DNS update concerns about maintaining secure updates, this solution also introduces some additional security concerns.

For example, any DNS domain names registered by the computer running the DHCP server are not secure. The DHCP server's own host resource record is an example of such a record. This issue is more significant if the DHCP server (that is a member of the DnsUpdateProxy group) is installed on a domain controller. To protect against issue, you can manually specify a different owner for any DNS records associated with the DHCP server itself.

In this case, all service location (SRV), host (A), or alias (CNAME) resource records registered by the Netlogon service for the domain controller are not secure. To minimize the problem, it is recommended that you do not install a DHCP server on a domain controller.

Another strong argument against running a Windows 2000 DHCP server on a Windows 2000 domain controller is that the DHCP server has full control over all DNS objects stored in Active Directory, because the DHCP server is running under the computer (in this case, the domain controller) account.

ADDITIONAL RESOURCES ON DHCP AND DNS INTERACTION

Because of the close integration of DHCP and DNS described in this section, you might want to investigate or review these additional topics as resources for your deployment issues related to this feature.

For more information On the DNS dynamic update protocol and considerations for securing dynamic updates when using Active Directory, see "Dynamic Update" in Chapter 8, "DNS Overview."

On how to configure Windows 2000 DNS servers to enable some or all updates for specific zones, see "Allow Dynamic Updates" and "Allow Only Secure Dynamic Updates" in Chapter 10, "Installing and Maintaining DNS Servers."

On how to enable Windows 2000 DHCP servers to initiate updates on behalf of its clients for specific scopes (or all scopes), see "Enable DNS Dynamic Updates for Clients" in Chapter 5.

On how you can modify or set Windows 2000 computers to initiate dynamic updates on their own behalf, see "Configure TCP/IP to Use DNS" in Chapter 2.

Caution For Windows 2000, the use of secure dynamic updates can be compromised by running a DHCP server on a domain controller when Windows 2000 DHCP server is configured to perform registration of DNS records on behalf of its clients. To avoid this issue, deploy DHCP servers and domain controllers on separate computers. If you are not concerned about security of reverse lookup (PTR) records, this precaution is only advisable if the DHCP server is configured to perform registration of host records on behalf of its clients (which is not a default behavior).

Note Microsoft supports the DHCP/DNS update interaction currently under final review as a proposed Internet standard RFC document by the IETF. This interactive process is fully described in the applicable draft, "Interaction Between DHCP and DNS."To obtain the current or final version of this draft, see the Request for Comments Web site (http://www.rfc-editor.org/).

If you are using legacy DNS servers that do not support dynamic updates, you can implement the following changes for dynamically updating and registering names and addresses for your DHCP clients:

1. If you are also using WINS and legacy Windows DNS servers (that is, DNS servers running Windows NT Server 4.0), you might be able to use the information provided in Chapter 8 in the section "WINS Lookup Integration" to support resolution of client names and addresses on your network that are not updated dynamically in DNS.
2. Upgrade or replace your older DNS servers with Windows 2000 DNS servers.

Using Routing and Remote Access Servers with DHCP

The DHCP Server service can be deployed along with the Routing and Remote Access service to provide remote access clients with a dynamically assigned IP address during connection. When these services are used together on the same server computer, the information provided during dynamic configuration is provided differently than in the case of typical DHCP configuration for LAN-based clients.

In LAN environments, DHCP clients negotiate and receive the following configuration information, based entirely on settings configured in the DHCP console for the DHCP server:

- A leased IP address provided from the available address pool of an active scope on the DHCP server. The DHCP server directly manages and distributes the address to the LAN-based DHCP client.
- Additional parameters and other configuration information provided through assigned DHCP options in the address lease. The values and list of options used correspond to option types configured and assigned on the DHCP server.

When a Routing and Remote Access server provides dynamic configuration for dial-up clients, it first performs the following steps:

- When the Routing and Remote Access server starts with the **Use DHCP to assign remote TCP/IP addresses** option, it makes advance requests to the DHCP server to obtain DHCP client addresses for dial-up clients, caching these addresses.
- The number of client addresses that are requested in advance is equal to the number of Routing and Remote Access ports set to receive calls and one additional address.

For example, if the server has two analog modem ports and two ISDN adapter ports that are set to receive calls, it requests a total of five IP addresses from the DHCP server. The first four are for assigning to clients that dial in to the analog and ISDN server ports. The fifth address is reserved for the server itself, so it can configure and use its own IP address when processing connections for dial-up clients.

When the Routing and Remote Access server uses this type of proactive caching of DHCP address leases for dial-up clients, it records the following information for each lease response it obtains from the DHCP server:

- The IP address of the DHCP server
- The client leased IP address (for later distribution to the Routing and Remote Access client)
- The time at which the lease was obtained
- The time at which the lease expires
- The duration of the lease

All other DHCP options information returned by the DHCP server (such as server, scope, or reserved client options) are discarded. When the client dials into the server and requests an IP address (that is, when **Server Assigned IP Address** is selected), it uses one of these cached DHCP leases to provide the dial-up client dynamic IP address configuration.

When the IP address is provided to the dial-up client, the client is unaware that the IP address has been obtained through this intermediate process between the DHCP server and the Routing and Remote Access server. The Routing and Remote Access server maintains the lease on behalf of the client. Therefore, the only information that the client receives from the DHCP server is the IP address lease.

In dial-up environments, DHCP clients negotiate and receive dynamic configuration using the following modified behavior:

- A leased IP address from the Routing and Remote Access server cache of DHCP scope addresses. The Routing and Remote Access server obtains and renews its cached address pool with the DHCP server.
- If additional parameters and other configuration information provided through assigned DHCP options in the address lease is normally provided by the DHCP server, this information is returned to the Routing and Remote Access client based on TCP/IP properties configured on the Routing and Remote Access server.

For more information, see "Supporting Routing and Remote Access Clients" in this chapter.

Note For Windows 2000, DHCP servers provide a predefined user class, the **Default remote access class**, for assigning options that are specific and provided only to Routing and Remote Access clients.

Multihomed DHCP Servers

A multihomed DHCP server is a computer running Windows 2000 Server that uses the DHCP service for more than a single network connection. For a server computer to be multihomed, each network connection must attach the computer to more than a single physical network. This requires that additional hardware (in the form of multiple installed network adapters) be used on the computer.

A server running Windows 2000 Server can perform as a multihomed DHCP server. For multihomed servers, the DHCP service binds to the first IP address configured on the first network connection in use. Typically, this is the first physical network adapter interface on the server computer and appears as "Local Area Connection" in the Network and Dial-up Connections folder.

By default, the service bindings depend on whether the first network connection is configured dynamically or statically for TCP/IP. Based on the method of configuration it uses, reflected by its current settings in **Internet Protocol (TCP/IP)** properties, the DHCP Server service performs default service bindings as follows:

- If the first network connection uses a manually specified IP address, the connection is enabled in server bindings. For this to occur, a value for **IP address** must be configured and the **Use the following IP address** option selected in Internet Protocol (TCP/IP) properties. In this mode, the DHCP server listens for and provides service to DHCP clients.
- If the first network connection uses an IP address configured dynamically, the connection is disabled in server bindings. This occurs when the **Obtain an IP address automatically** option is selected in Internet Protocol (TCP/IP) properties. For Windows 2000, this is the typical default setting. In this mode, the DHCP server does not listen for and provide service to DHCP clients until a static IP address is configured.

Note

By design, DHCP server bindings are enabled and disabled on a per-connection, not per-address, basis. All bindings are based on the first configured IP address for each connection appearing in the Network and Dial-up Connections folder. Additional static IP addresses (for example, as set in Advanced TCP/IP properties) are never used by Windows 2000 DHCP servers and are inconsequential for server bindings.

Windows 2000 DHCP servers never bind to any of the Network Driver Interface Specification, Wide Area Network (NDISWAN) or DHCP-enabled interfaces used on the server. These interfaces are not displayed in the DHCP console under the current server bindings list because they are never used for DHCP service. Only additional network connections that have a primary static IP address configured can appear in the server bindings list (or be selectively enabled or disabled there).

For information about selectively setting DHCP server bindings for network connections, see Chapter 5.

EXAMPLE: CONFIGURING A MULTIHOMED DHCP SERVER

Figure 4-8 is an example of a multihomed DHCP server with three network adapters installed. Each adapter is configured to lease addresses on separate physical subnets.

Note that in the graphic, the multihomed DHCP server has three adapters installed and configured statically with a single IP address for each. Because the IP addressing for the DHCP server also uses an adjusted or custom subnet mask value (255.255.255.224), that value is applied for all IP addresses that are configured at the server and for other computers in use on the same example private IP network. In this network example, a Class C range of IP addresses, 192.168.200.1 to 192.168.200.254, is used.

In this example, each of the three adapters connects the server to three different physical subnets (Subnets A, B, and C). To achieve the intended result of having the DHCP provide leased configuration service to all clients in each of the respective subnets, two configuration details are essential and must be verified during deployment plans:

1. The server must use a statically configured IP address within the same range of valid IP addresses for the physical network on which it is servicing clients.
2. The server must have each of its valid subnet IP addresses excluded from the scope used to offer leases to clients.

For example, if no special subnetting is used in this environment, the selection of DHCP server IP addresses is not as critical because the IP network and IP subnet are the same. When the default subnet mask value

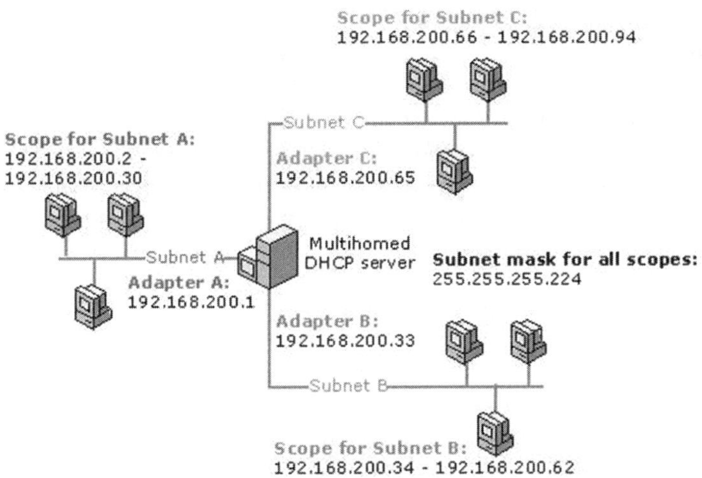

FIGURE 4–8 *Multihomed DHCP server*

(255.255.255.0) is used, all 254 possible host IDs are considered to be part of one single unified subnet.

In the case of this example, however, if a custom subnet mask of 255.255.255.224 is applied, the network ID and subnet ID are not the same. Whenever the subnet ID is not the same as the network ID, care and attention must be taken so that the DHCP server is provided IP address assignment within the same subnet it is intended to service.

For instance, with the mask set to 255.255.255.224 at all hosts, the first three-bit places of the least significant octet (224) are taken from the full eight-bit places that would normally comprise the full host ID section. These bits are used for physical subnet identification. This leaves the remaining five-bit places to be used as the actual or reduced host ID field.

In the example network shown above, the three subnets in use can have a maximum of eight (or 2^3) potentially different subnet IDs. Likewise, each of these subnets can in turn, only support up to 32 (or 2^5) potential host IDs.

Because of the use of subnetting, in this example Subnet A consists of the first 32 address values in the network, from 0 to 31. Host ID may not consist of the "all zeros" or "all ones" bit patterns in the host ID field. Therefore, the useful range of available IP addresses for each subnet drops from a total of 32 to a total of 30—the addresses 1 through 30 in this example.

Of these remaining 30 addresses, the DHCP server just needs to use one. The remaining 29 can be configured in a regular DHCP scope and used for assigning leases to clients. The choice of which address to use for the DHCP server is preferential, as well as the decision to include the statically assigned IP address of the DHCP server within the scope defined for use in each subnet.

In this example, the IP addresses (192.169.200.1, 192.168.200.33, and 192.168.200.65) of the multihomed server are configured using the first IP address available for each of the three subnets. In the configuration shown, these addresses are excluded from the defined boundaries of each of the scopes created for these subnets.

Alternatively, you could set up your scopes so as to include these addresses within the defined boundaries of the scope. If you do, you need to create address exclusions to exclude these server IP addresses from each of the respective scopes.

FIVE

Installation and Administration of DHCP Servers and Clients

Install a DHCP Server

To install a DHCP server,

1. To open the Windows Component wizard, from the desktop, click **Start**, point to **Settings**, and click **Control Panel**. (See Figure 5-1.)

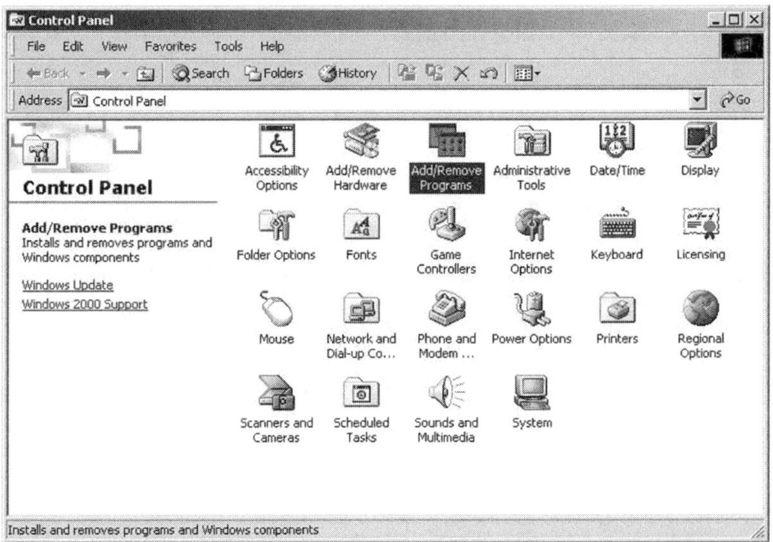

FIGURE 5-1 *Windows 2000 Control Panel*

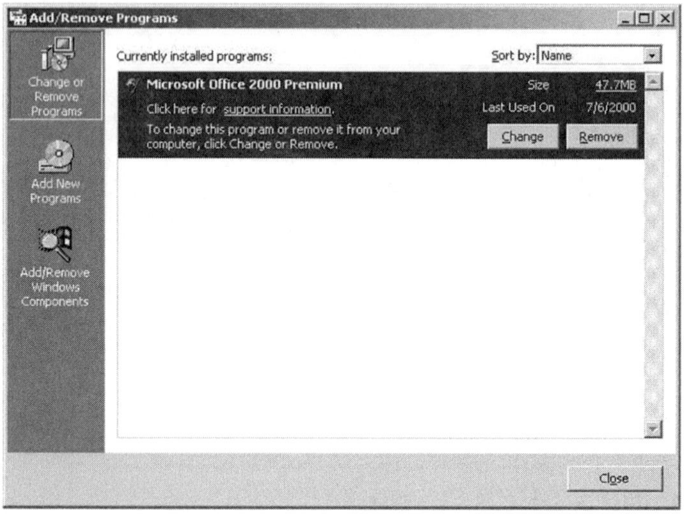

FIGURE 5–2 *Add/Remove Programs window*

2. On the left panel, click **Add/Remove Windows Components**, since it gathers all Windows 2000 features and Microsoft extensions. (See Figure 5-2.)
3. Under **Components**, scroll to and click **Networking Services**. (See Figure 5-3.)
4. Click **Details**. (See Figure 5-4.)

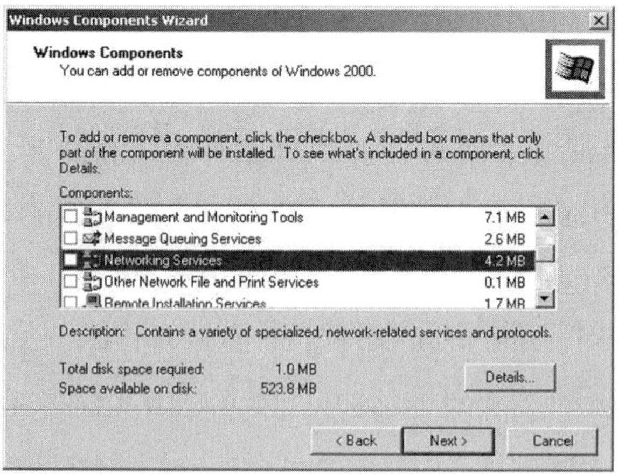

FIGURE 5–3 *Windows Components window*

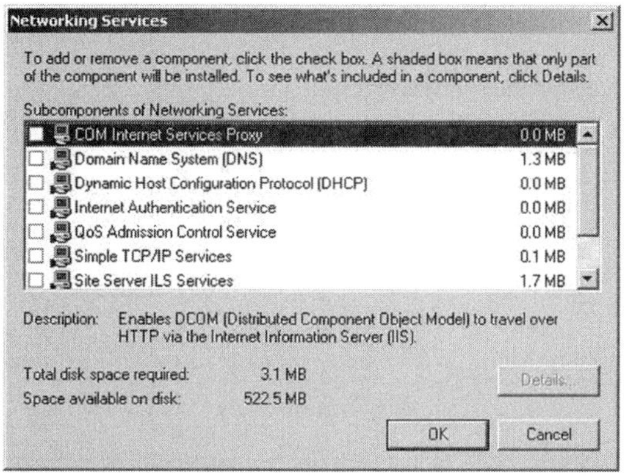

FIGURE 5–4 *Displaying available networking services*

5. Under **Subcomponents of Networking Services**, click **Dynamic Host Configuration Protocol (DHCP)**, and then click **OK** twice.
6. If prompted, type the full path to the Windows 2000 distribution files and click **Continue**.

   Required files are copied to your hard disk. Server software can be used after restarting the system.

   Keep in mind that a DHCP server requires a static IP configuration. Should the server computer be configured as a DHCP client, you will get a warning (see Figure 5-5), after which you can define a static address.
7. When DHCP server is installed, you will see a window similar to Figure 5-6.
8. This installation differs from Windows NT 4.0, where restarting the system is not necessary. Instead, you can immediately begin to configure. Click **Finish**.

When Control Panel opens, double-click **Add/Remove Programs** and then click **Add/Remove Windows Components**.

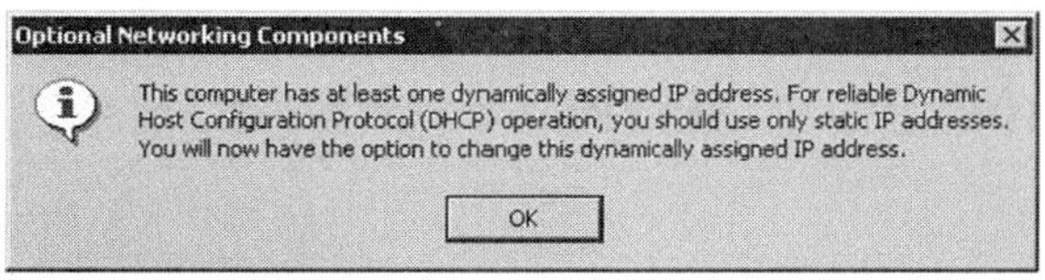

FIGURE 5–5 *Warning notice*

FIGURE 5–6 *Installation completion*

Certain Windows components require configuration before they can be used. If you installed one or more of these components, but did not configure them, when you click **Add/Remove Windows Components**, a list of components that need to be configured is displayed. To start the Windows Components wizard, click **Components**.

It is strongly recommended that you manually configure the computer to use a static IP address.

Open the DHCP Console

To open the DHCP console,

1. Open DHCP, click **Start**, point to **Programs**, point to **Administrative Tools**, and then click **DHCP**.
2. The DHCP console (see Figure 5-7) is an administrative tool for managing DHCP servers.

Connect to a DHCP Server

To connect to a DHCP server,

1. To open DHCP, click **Start**, point to **Programs**, point to **Administrative Tools**, and then click **DHCP**.
2. In the console tree, click **DHCP**.

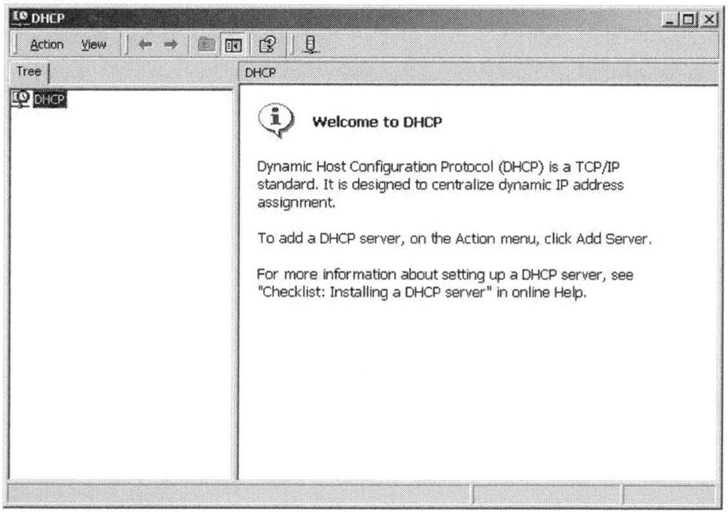

FIGURE 5–7 *DHCP console*

3. On the **Action** menu, click **Add Server**.
4. Select either this server or another authorized DHCP server to which to connect. For more information on specific items in this dialog box, click **What's This?**, and then click the item.

If you are operating DHCP in an Active Directory environment and are connecting to a server for the first time, you need to first authorize the new DHCP server in the directory service.

If DHCP is installed and running on this computer, you do not need to make a manual connection using the wizard. In most cases, the local DHCP server automatically appears in the list of servers when the DHCP console starts, and you connect to the server by clicking it in the console tree.

Only users belonging to the DHCP Users, DHCP Administrators, or Administrators groups can connect to a DHCP server. Only users in the DHCP Administrators or Administrators groups can modify the DHCP server configuration.

Disconnect From a DHCP Server

To disconnect from a DHCP server,

1. To open DHCP, click **Start**, point to **Programs**, point to **Administrative Tools**, and then click **DHCP**.

2. In the console tree, click the applicable DHCP server (console tree | DHCP | *applicable DHCP server*).
3. On the **Action** menu, click **Delete**.
4. When prompted to confirm removing the server, click **Yes**.

Start or Stop a DHCP Server

To start or stop a DHCP server,

1. To open DHCP, click **Start**, point to **Programs**, point to **Administrative Tools**, and then click **DHCP**.
2. In the console tree, click the applicable DHCP server (console tree | DHCP | *applicable DHCP server*).
3. On the **Action** menu, point to **All Tasks** and then click one of the following:
    a. To start the service, click **Start**.
    b. To stop the service, click **Stop**.
    c. To interrupt the service, click **Pause**.
    d. To stop and then automatically restart the service, click **Restart**.

After you pause or stop the server, the **Resume** option appears and can be clicked to immediately resume service.

You can also perform most of these tasks at a command prompt by using the following commands:

net start dhcpserver
net stop dhcpserver
net pause dhcpserver
net continue dhcpserver

Reconcile the DHCP Database

To reconcile the DHCP database,

1. To open DHCP, click **Start**, point to **Programs**, point to **Administrative Tools**, and then click **DHCP**.
2. In the console tree, click the applicable DHCP server (console tree | DHCP | *applicable DHCP server*).
3. On the **Action** menu, click **Reconcile All Scopes**.
4. In the **Reconcile Database** dialog box, click **Verify**.
   Inconsistencies found are reported in the status window.

5. If the database is found to be consistent, click **OK**. If the database is not consistent, select the displayed addresses that need to be reconciled, and click **Reconcile** to repair inconsistencies.

Manually Compact or Repair the DHCP Database

To manually compact or repair the DHCP database,

1. At a DHCP server computer, open a command prompt.
2. Use the *Jetpack.exe* command-line utility to perform offline compaction. The correct syntax for *Jetpack.exe* is:

jetpack database_name temporary_database_name

These are example commands to compact the DHCP database:

```
cd %systemroot%\system32\dhcp
net stop dhcpserver
jetpack dhcp.mdb tmp.mdb
net start dhcpserver
```

In the examples above, *Tmp.mdb* is a temporary database that is used by *Jetpack.exe*. *Dhcp.mdb* is the DHCP database file. *Jetpack.exe* compacts the DHCP database by doing the following:

1. Copying database information to a temporary database file called *Tmp.mdb*.
2. Deleting the original DHCP database file, *Dhcp.mdb*.
3. Renaming the temporary database file to the original file name.

Windows 2000 Server includes the *Jetpack.exe* utility so that it can be used to compact the DHCP and other Jet databases (such as WINS) when those databases are offline.

It is recommended that you use *Jetpack.exe* to compact a Jet database periodically whenever the database grows beyond 30 megabytes in size. For Windows 2000 Server, the DHCP Server service performs dynamic Jet compaction of the DHCP database while the server is online. This reduces the need to use *Jetpack.exe* for offline compaction. Therefore, this procedure is most useful for DHCP and WINS servers running under earlier versions of Windows NT Server.

Remove or Uninstall DHCP

To remove or uninstall DHCP,

1. If necessary, stop the DHCP server on this computer.
2. To open Add/Remove Programs, click **Start**, point to **Settings**, click **Control Panel**, and then double-click the appropriate icon.
3. Click **Add/Remove Windows Components**.
4. In **Components**, select **Networking Services** from the list of components, and then click **Details**.
5. In **Subcomponents of Networking Services**, scroll to **Dynamic Host Configuration Protocol (DHCP)** and clear the check box.

When you remove DHCP, all DHCP files are deleted from the server except program files that are in use. When the system is restarted, these files are removed as well.

If you do not stop the DHCP Server service in step 1, this procedure only deletes the DHCP server registry entries.

Certain Windows components require configuration before they can be used. If you installed one or more of these components, but did not configure them, when you click **Add/Remove Windows Components**, a list of components that need to be configured is displayed. To start the Windows Components wizard, click **Components**.

Authorize a DHCP Server in Active Directory

To authorize a DHCP server in Active Directory,

1. To open DHCP, click **Start**, point to **Programs**, point to **Administrative Tools**, and then click **DHCP**.
2. In the console tree, click **DHCP**.
3. On the Action menu, click Manage authorized servers. The Manage Authorized Servers dialog box appears.
4. Click **Authorize**.
5. When prompted, type the name or IP address of the DHCP server to be authorized, and then click **OK**.

For a DHCP server to be authorized in an Active Directory domain environment, you must first be logged on as a member of the Enterprise Administrators group for the enterprise where the server is being added.

This procedure is usually only needed if you are running a DHCP server on a member server. In most cases, if you are installing a DHCP server on a computer also running as a domain controller, the server is automatically authorized the first time you add the server to the DHCP console.

Delegate Ability to Authorize DHCP Servers to a Nonenterprise Administrator

To delegate ability to authorize DHCP servers to a nonenterprise administrator,

1. Open Active Directory Sites and Services while logged on as an enterprise administrator. To open Active Directory Sites and Services, click **Start**, point to **Programs**, point to **Administrative Tools**, and then click **Active Directory Sites and Services**. To be logged on as an enterprise administrator, you must log on using a member account in the Enterprise Administrators group. By default, this can typically be done by logging on as local Administrator at the first domain controller created in your enterprise.
2. On the **View** menu, click **Show Services Node**.
3. In the console tree, click **NetServices** (console tree | Active Directory Sites and Services | Services | NetServices).
4. On the **Action** menu, click **Delegate Control**. The Delegation of Control wizard appears.
5. Click **Next**, then for Users and Groups, click **Add**.
6. In **Select Users**, **Computers**, or **Groups**, locate and select the user or group account you want to permit access to the **NetServices** object for authorizing DHCP servers. For example, you might select the DHCP Administrators group for a specific domain, such as the EXAMPLE domain.
7. Click **Add**, and then click **OK**.
8. For **Tasks to Delegate**, select **Create a custom task to delegate**, and then click **Next**.
9. For **Delegate control of**, select **This folder**, **existing objects in this folder**, and **creation of new objects in this folder**, and then click **Next**. For **Permissions**, click **Full Control**, and then click **Next**.

   This enables access control rights to the user or group account specifically delegated in this procedure for it to add, modify, or delete new objects of DHCP class type in the NetServices folder.

To be logged on as an enterprise administrator, you must log on using a member account in the Enterprise Administrators group. By default, this can typically be done by logging on as local Administrator at the first domain controller created in your enterprise.

Selectively Set DHCP Server Bindings for Network Connections

To selectively set DHCP server bindings for network connections,

1. To open DHCP, click **Start**, point to **Programs**, point to **Administrative Tools**, and then click **DHCP**.
2. In the console tree, click the applicable DHCP server (console tree | DHCP | *applicable DHCP server*).
3. On the **Action** menu, click **Properties**.
4. Click the **Advanced** tab.
5. Click **Bindings**.
6. In the **Bindings** dialog box, for the list of **Connections and server bindings**, select or clear check boxes for any statically configured network connections that should be enabled or disabled for use at the applicable DHCP server.
7. Click **Apply**.

If a network connection has more than one IP address configured, only the first configured IP address is used or affected by the DHCP server bindings. Any additional configured IP addresses are not used or configurable for bindings and are never used to service clients.

The DHCP Server service never binds to any WAN or DHCP-enabled network connections on a server computer. For this reason, these connections do not appear in the **Bindings** dialog box.

Add a User or Group as a DHCP User at a Member Server

To add a user or group as a DHCP user at a member server,

1. Open Computer Management if the DHCP server is installed as a domain member server (or a standalone workgroup server). To open Computer Management, click **Start**, point to **Settings**, and then click **Control Panel.** Double-click **Administrative Tools**, and then double-click **Computer Management**.
2. In the console tree, click **Local Users and Groups** (console tree | Computer Management (Local) | System Tools | Local Users and Groups).
3. In the details pane, click **DHCP Users**.
4. On the **Action** menu, click **Properties**.

5. Click the **Members** tab, and then click **Add**.
6. Click **Look in** to display a list of domains from which users and computers can be added to the group, and then click the domain containing the users and computers you want to add.
7. Click the users and computers to be added, and then click **Add**.

The DHCP Users group provides a way to grant read-only console access to the DHCP server. Other users or groups added as members of this group are granted the right to view, but not modify, data for the applicable server in the DHCP console.

Add a User or Group as a DHCP User at a Domain Controller

To add a user or group as a DHCP user at a domain controller,

1. Open Active Directory Users and Computers if the DHCP server is installed at a domain controller. To open Active Directory Users and Computers, click **Start**, point to **Programs**, point to **Administrative Tools**, and then click **Active Directory Users and Computers**.
2. In the console tree, click **Users** (console tree | Active Directory Users and Computers | *applicable domain* | Users).
3. In the details pane, click **DHCP Users**.
4. On the **Action** menu, click **Properties**.
5. Click the **Members** tab, and then click **Add**.
6. Click **Look in** to display a list of domains from which users and computers can be added to the group, and then click the domain containing the users and computers you want to add.
7. Click the users and computers to be added, and then click **Add**.

The DHCP Users group provides a way to grant read-only console access to the DHCP server. Other users or groups added as members of this group are granted the right to view, but not modify, data for the applicable server in the DHCP console.

To add users and computers to a group, you can also select the users and computers to be added, click the **Add selected objects** button on the toolbar, and then click the group to which they will be added.

Add a User or Group as a DHCP Administrator at a Member Server

To add a user or group as a DHCP administrator at a member server,

1. Open Computer Management if the DHCP server is installed as a domain member server (or a stand-alone workgroup server).To open Computer Management, click **Start**, point to **Settings**, and then click **Control Panel**. Double-click **Administrative Tools**, and then double-click **Computer Management**.
2. In the console tree, click **Local Users and Groups** (console tree | System Tools | Local Users and Groups).
3. In the details pane, click **DHCP Administrators**.
4. On the **Action** menu, click **Properties**.
5. Click the **Members** tab, and then click **Add**.
6. Click **Look in** to display a list of domains from which users and computers can be added to the group, and then click the domain containing the users and computers you want to add.
7. Click the users and computers to be added, and then click **Add**.

The DHCP Administrators group provides a way to grant limited administrative access to the DHCP server only, while not providing full access to the server computer. Other users or groups added as members of this group are granted the right to fully administer the applicable server in the DHCP console, but are not able to perform other administrative actions on the server computer.

To add users and computers to a group, you can also select the users and computers to be added, click the **Add selected objects** button on the toolbar, and then click the group to which they will be added.

Add a User or Group as a DHCP Administrator at a Domain Controller

To add a user or group as a DHCP administrator at a domain controller,

1. Open Active Directory Users and Computers if the DHCP server is installed at a domain controller. To open Active Directory Users and Computers, click **Start**, point to **Programs**, point to **Administrative Tools**, and then click **Active Directory Users and Computers**.
2. In the console tree, click **Users** (console tree | Active Directory Users and Computers | *applicable domain* | Users).

3. In the details pane, click **DHCP Administrators**.
4. On the **Action** menu, click **Properties**.
5. Click the **Members** tab, and then click **Add**.
6. Click **Look in** to display a list of domains from which users and computers can be added to the group, and then click the domain containing the users and computers you want to add.
7. Click the users and computers to be added, and then click **Add**.

The DHCP Administrators group provides a way to grant limited administrative access to the DHCP server only, while not providing full access to the server computer. Other users or groups added as members of this group are granted the right to fully administer the applicable server in the DHCP console, but are not able to perform other administrative actions on the server computer.

To add users and computers to a group, you can also select the users and computers to be added, click the **Add selected objects** button on the toolbar, and then click the group to which they will be added.

Enable Server Statistics to Automatically Refresh

To enable server statistics to automatically refresh,

1. To open DHCP, click **Start**, point to **Programs**, point to **Administrative Tools**, and then click **DHCP**.
2. In the console tree, click the applicable DHCP server (console tree | DHCP | *applicable DHCP server*).
3. On the **Action** menu, click **Properties**.
4. On the **General** tab, for **Automatically update statistics every**, specify the number of hours and minutes to use as a refresh interval, and then click **OK**.

Enable DHCP Server Logging

To enable DHCP server logging,

1. To open DHCP, click **Start**, point to **Programs**, point to **Administrative Tools**, and then click **DHCP**.
2. In the console tree, click the applicable DHCP server (console tree | DHCP | *applicable DHCP server*).
3. On the **Action** menu, click **Properties**.
4. On the **General** tab, select **Enable DHCP audit logging**, and then click **OK**.

Enable Address Conflict Detection

To enable address conflict detection,

1. To open DHCP, click **Start**, point to **Programs**, point to **Administrative Tools**, and then click **DHCP**.
2. In the console tree, click the applicable DHCP server (console tree | DHCP | *applicable DHCP server*).
3. On the **Action** menu, click **Properties**.
4. Click the **Advanced** tab.
5. For **Conflict detection attempts**, type a number greater than 0 (zero), and then click **OK**. The number you type determines how many times the DHCP server tests an IP address before leasing it to a client.

When conflict detection attempts are set, the DHCP server uses the Packet Internet Groper (ping) process to test available scope IP addresses before including these addresses in DHCP lease offers to clients.

A successful ping means the IP address is in use on the network. Therefore, the DHCP server does not offer to lease the address to a client. If the ping request fails and times out, the IP address is not in use on the network. In this case, the DHCP server offers to lease the address to a client.

Each additional conflict detection attempt delays the DHCP server response by a second while waiting for the ping request to time out. This increases the load on the server. A value of no greater than two (2) for ping attempts is recommended.

Enable DNS Dynamic Updates for Clients

To enable DNS dynamic updates for clients,

1. To open DHCP, click **Start**, point to **Programs**, point to **Administrative Tools**, and then click **DHCP**.
2. In the console tree, click the applicable DHCP server (console tree | DHCP | *applicable DHCP server*).
3. On the **Action** menu, click **Properties**.
4. Click the **DNS** tab.
5. Select the **Automatically update DHCP client information in DNS** check box.
6. If needed, modify other DNS update settings. To view a description of a dialog box item, right-click the item, and then click **What's This?**.

Manually Refresh Server Statistics

To manually refresh server statistics,

1. To open DHCP, click **Start**, point to **Programs**, point to **Administrative Tools**, and then click **DHCP**.
2. In the console tree, click the applicable DHCP server (console tree | DHCP | *applicable DHCP server*).
3. On the **Action** menu, click **Display Statistics**.
4. In the **Server Statistics** dialog box, click **Refresh**.

View DHCP Server Statistics

To view DHCP server statistics,

1. To open DHCP, click **Start**, point to **Programs**, point to **Administrative Tools**, and then click **DHCP**.
2. In the console tree, click the applicable DHCP server (console tree | DHCP | *applicable DHCP server*).
3. On the **Action** menu, click **Display Statistics**.

View DHCP Server Properties

To view DHCP server properties,

1. To open DHCP, click **Start**, point to **Programs**, point to **Administrative Tools**, and then click **DHCP.**
2. In the console tree, click the applicable DHCP server (console tree | DHCP | *applicable DHCP server*).
3. On the **Action** menu, click **Properties**.
4. View or modify server properties as needed. To view a description of a dialog box item, right-click the item, and then click **What's This?**.

Create a New Scope

To create a new scope,

1. To open DHCP, click **Start**, point to **Programs**, point to **Administrative Tools**, and then click **DHCP**.
2. In the console tree, click the applicable DHCP server (console tree | DHCP | *applicable DHCP server*).

FIGURE 5–8 *Creating a new scope*

3. On the **Action** menu, click **New Scope**. (See Figure 5-8.)
4. Click **Next**. You will see a window similar to Figure 5-9.
5. Define a name for the new scope and provide a description. In our example, we used the name NewDHCPonWin2000 and a description, New Address Range. If you need several scopes, you should name them explicitly. Click **Next** to continue. You will see a window similar to Figure 5-10.

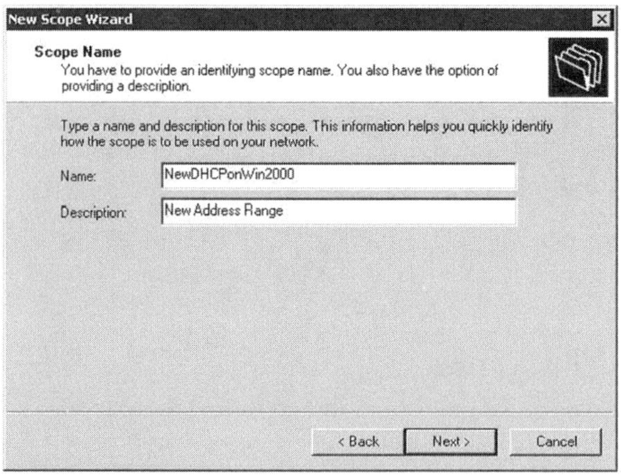

FIGURE 5–9 *Naming the scope*

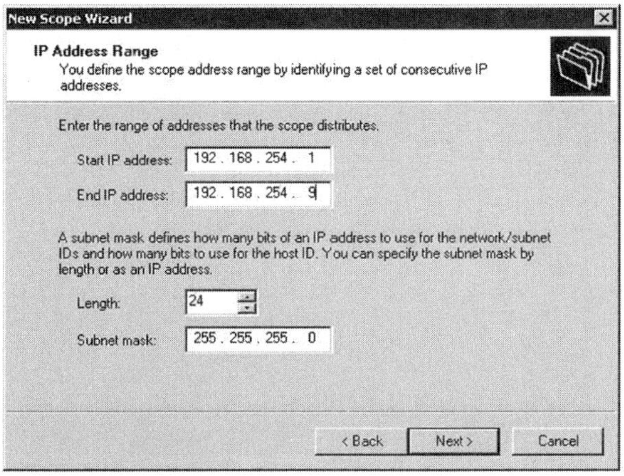

FIGURE 5–10 *Defining an address range*

6. In the **Start IP address** field and the **End IP address** field, enter the IP range that should be managed by DHCP. Only use valid addresses and make sure you don't define them twice, especially if your company or organization uses dynamic and static addresses.
7. Click **Next** to continue. The New Scope Wizard (Figure 5-11) allows you to enter exclusions, if necessary. This feature enables you to define a contiguous address pool and reserve one or more addresses out of the pool to specific machines that are configured as static.

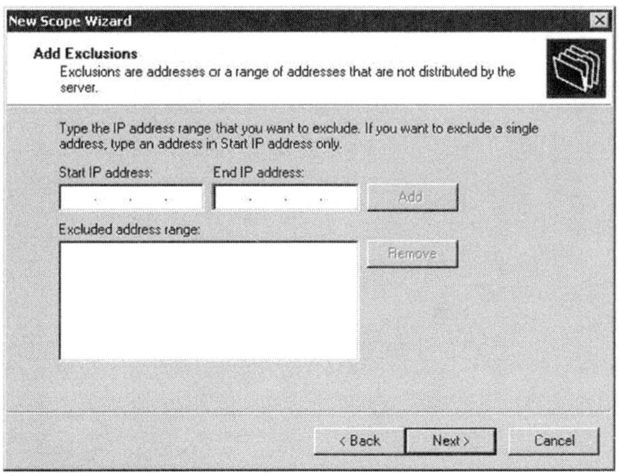

FIGURE 5–11 *Adding exclusions*

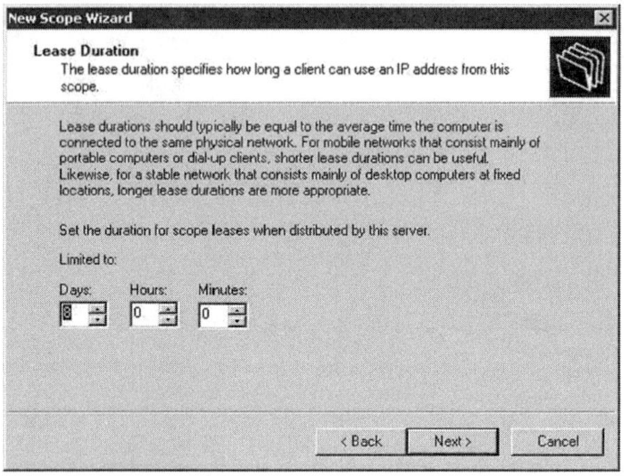

FIGURE 5–12 *Defining lease duration*

8. If you have no exclusions, leave the fields blank and click **Next**. You will see a window similar to Figure 5-12.
9. Define the lease duration. In our example, we set the duration for scope leases to eight days. Click **Next** to continue. You will see a window similar to Figure 5-13.
10. Configure your options. Select **Yes, I want to configure these options now**. Click **Next** to configure the WINS server immediately. You will see a window a similar to Figure 5-14.

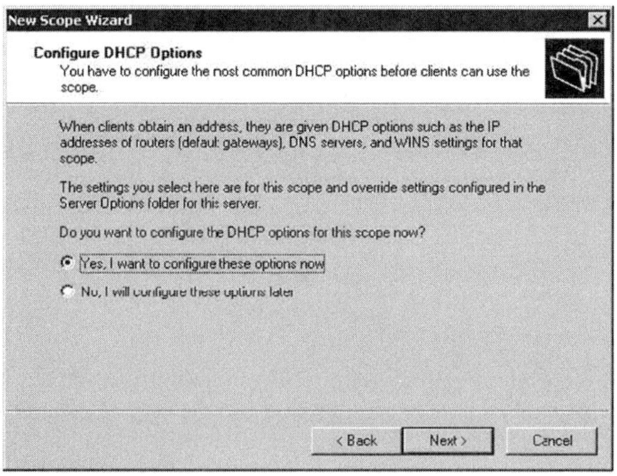

FIGURE 5–13 *Configure DHCP Options*

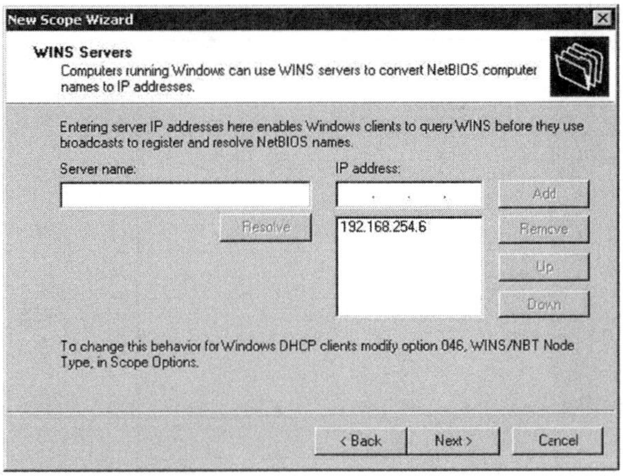

FIGURE 5–14 *Defining WINS servers for lookup*

11. Add the server IP address and click **Next**. You will see a window similar to Figure 5-15.
12. Select **Yes, I want to activate this scope now.** Click **Next** to continue. You will see a window similar to Figure 5-16.
13. Click **Finish**.

Before you create the scope, determine starting and ending IP addresses to be used within it.

Depending on the starting and ending IP addresses for your scope, the DHCP console suggests a default subnet mask useful for most networks. If

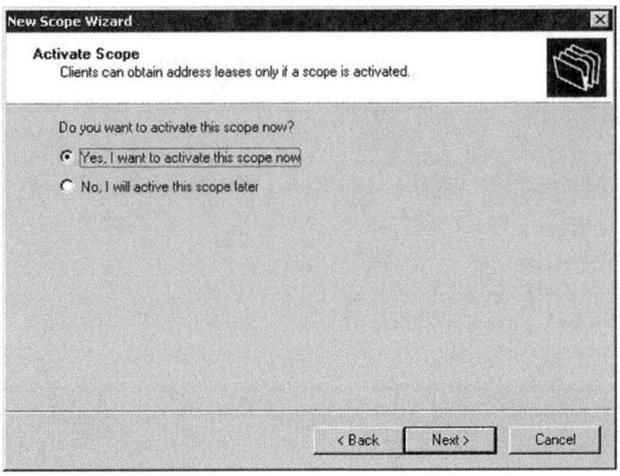

FIGURE 5–15 *New scopes must be activated*

FIGURE 5–16 *Wizard completes*

you know a different subnet mask is required for your network, you can modify the value as needed.

When you finish creating a new scope, you might need to complete additional tasks, such as activating the scope for use or assigning scope options.

Remove a Scope

To remove a scope,

1. To open DHCP, click **Start**, point to **Programs**, point to **Administrative Tools**, and then click **DHCP**.
2. In the console tree, click the applicable scope (console tree | DHCP | *applicable DHCP server* | *applicable superscope, if used* | *applicable scope*).
3. On the **Action** menu, click **Delete**.
4. When prompted, click **Yes** to delete the scope.

Important Before removing a scope, be sure to have deactivated the scope long enough to migrate clients to a different scope. To migrate clients, either wait for 50 percent of the configured scope lease time to elapse or manually renew clients in another active scope. Once all clients have been moved or forced to seek leases in another scope, you can safely remove the inactive scope.

Exclude an Address From a Scope

To exclude an address from a scope,

1. To open DHCP, click **Start**, point to **Programs**, point to **Administrative Tools**, and then click **DHCP**.
2. In the console tree, click **Address Pool** (console tree | DHCP | *applicable DHCP server* | *applicable superscope, if used* | *applicable scope* | Address Pool).
3. On the **Action** menu, click **New Exclusion Range**.
4. In the **Add Exclusion** dialog box, type the **Start IP address** that you want to exclude from this scope. To exclude a range of more than one IP address, type an **End IP address**.
5. Click **Add**.

Addresses that are excluded from the scope are not offered by the DHCP server to clients obtaining leases from this scope.

You cannot exclude a range of addresses that includes an active lease. You must first delete the active lease and then retry the exclusion.

Activate a Scope

To activate a scope,

1. To open DHCP, click **Start**, point to **Programs**, point to **Administrative Tools**, and then click **DHCP**.
2. In the console tree, click the applicable scope (console tree | DHCP | *applicable DHCP server* | *applicable superscope, if used* | *applicable scope*).
3. On the **Action** menu, click **Activate**.

Activating a scope is needed only for new scopes to start lease distribution. You must activate a scope to make it available for DHCP clients.

Do not activate a scope until you specify the options you want.

The **Action** menu command changes to **Deactivate** when the selected scope is currently activated. Do not deactivate a scope unless you are retiring it permanently from use on your network.

Deactivate a Scope

To deactivate a scope,

1. To open DHCP, click **Start**, point to **Programs**, point to **Administrative Tools**, and then click **DHCP**.

2. In the console tree, click the applicable scope (console tree | DHCP | *applicable DHCP server* | *applicable superscope, if used* | *applicable scope*).
3. On the **Action** menu, click **Deactivate**.

Important Do not use **Deactivate** to pause a scope. Instead, adjust the available scope address range by setting exclusions for scope addresses.

The **Action** menu command name changes to **Activate** when the selected scope is currently deactivated.

Because deactivation begins recall of scope addresses, it is recommended that you avoid reactivating scopes. Typically, this command is used when you want to retire a scope and remove it from the server.

Change or View Scope Properties

To change or view scope properties,

1. To open DHCP, click **Start**, point to **Programs**, point to **Administrative Tools**, and then click **DHCP**.
2. In the console tree, click the applicable scope (console tree | DHCP | *applicable DHCP server* | *applicable superscope, if used* | *applicable scope*).
3. On the **Action** menu, click **Properties**.
4. View or modify scope properties as needed. To view a description of a dialog box item, right-click the item, and then click **What's This?**.

The subnet identifiers and address pool (defined by the Start and End IP addresses used to create the scope) make up the basic properties of a scope. You can only change some properties of an existing scope, such as the exclusion ranges, client reservations, configured scope option type values, or the time set for leasing scope addresses to clients.

You cannot exclude a range of addresses that includes an active lease. You must first delete the active lease, and then retry the exclusion.

You can extend the address range of the scope, but you cannot reduce it. However, you can at any time selectively exclude any unwanted addresses from the full scope range of addresses.

Reconcile a Scope

To reconcile a scope,

1. To open DHCP, click **Start**, point to **Programs**, point to **Administrative Tools**, and then click **DHCP**.

2. In the console tree, click the applicable scope (console tree | DHCP | *applicable DHCP server* | *applicable superscope, if used* | *applicable scope*).
3. On the **Action** menu, click **Reconcile**.
4. In the **Reconcile** dialog box, click **Verify**.

   Inconsistencies found are reported in the status window.
5. If the scope is found to be consistent, click **OK**. If the scope is not consistent, select the displayed addresses that need to be reconciled, and click **Reconcile** to repair inconsistencies.

Create a Superscope

To create a superscope,

1. To open DHCP, click **Start**, point to **Programs**, point to **Administrative Tools**, and then click **DHCP**.
2. In the console tree, click the applicable DHCP server (console tree | DHCP | *applicable DHCP server*).
3. On the **Action** menu, click **New Superscope**.
4. This menu option appears only if at least one scope that is not currently part of a superscope has been created at the server.
5. Follow the instructions in the New Superscope wizard.

A superscope can have scopes added to it, either during or after its creation.

Scopes that are contained within superscopes are sometimes called *child scopes* or *member scopes*.

Remove a Superscope

To remove a superscope,

1. To open DHCP, click **Start**, point to **Programs**, point to **Administrative Tools**, and then click **DHCP**.
2. In the console tree, click the applicable superscope (console tree | DHCP | *applicable DHCP server* | *applicable superscope*).
3. On the **Action** menu, click **Delete**.
4. When prompted, click **Yes** to delete the superscope.

Removing a superscope does not remove any of the scopes included in it.

Add a Scope to a Superscope

To add a scope to a superscope,

1. To open DHCP, click **Start**, point to **Programs**, point to **Administrative Tools**, and then click **DHCP**.
2. In the console tree, click the applicable superscope (console tree | DHCP | *applicable DHCP server* | *applicable superscope*).
3. On the **Action** menu, click **Add To Superscope**.
4. In the **Available superscopes** list, click the superscope to which you want to add this scope.

In order to complete this procedure, at least one superscope must already exist at the applicable DHCP server.

Activate a Superscope

To activate a superscope,

1. To open DHCP, click **Start**, point to **Programs**, point to **Administrative Tools**, and then click **DHCP**.
2. In the console tree, locate the applicable superscope (console tree | DHCP | *applicable DHCP server* | *applicable superscope*).
3. On the **Action** menu, click **Activate**.

Activating a superscope is needed only for new superscopes. When you activate a superscope, it activates all of its member scopes on your network. You must activate a superscope to make IP addresses for all of its member scopes available for use by DHCP clients.

Do not activate a superscope until you specify the options you want for each of its member scopes.

The **Action** menu command changes to **Deactivate** when the selected scope is currently activated. Do not deactivate a superscope unless you intend to permanently retire all of its member scopes from use on your network.

Deactivate a Superscope

To deactivate a superscope,

1. To open DHCP, click **Start**, point to **Programs**, point to **Administrative Tools**, and then click **DHCP**.

2. In the console tree, click the applicable superscope (console tree | DHCP | *applicable DHCP server* | *applicable superscope*).
3. On the **Action** menu, click **Deactivate**.

Important Do not use **Deactivate** to pause a superscope. Instead, you can adjust the superscope membership by adding or removing from the list of member scopes.

Because deactivation begins recall of member scope addresses, use this command only when you intend to retire all member scopes and remove the superscope from the server.

The **Action** menu command name changes to **Activate** when the selected superscope is currently deactivated. Avoid reactivating a superscope once you deactivate it.

Create a Multicast Scope

To create a multicast scope,

1. To open DHCP, click **Start**, point to **Programs**, point to **Administrative Tools**, and then click **DHCP**.
2. In the console tree, click the applicable DHCP server (console tree | DHCP | *applicable DHCP server*).
3. On the **Action** menu, click **New Multicast Scope**.
4. Follow the instructions in the New Multicast Scope wizard.

Remove a Multicast Scope

To remove a multicast scope,

1. To open DHCP, click **Start**, point to **Programs**, point to **Administrative Tools**, and then click **DHCP**.
2. In the console tree, click the applicable multicast scope (console tree | DHCP | *applicable DHCP server* | *applicable multicast scope*).
3. On the **Action** menu, click **Delete**.
4. When prompted, click **Yes** to remove the multicast scope.

Removing a multicast scope does not necessarily stop the use of multicast groups associated with scope addresses on your network. If computers on your network are configured by means other than DHCP to use these same addresses, the multicast group might still be used even after this procedure is complete.

Set the Multicast Scope Time-to-Live Value

To set the multicast scope Time-to-Live (TTL) value,

1. To open DHCP, click **Start**, point to **Programs**, point to **Administrative Tools**, and then click **DHCP**.
2. In the console tree, click the applicable multicast scope (console tree | DHCP | *applicable DHCP server* | *applicable multicast scope*).
3. On the **Action** menu, click **Properties**.
4. In **Time to live**, specify a new value.

The multicast TTL value specifies the number of routers (hops) that multicast traffic is permitted to pass through before expiring on the network. For each hop, the original specified TTL is decremented by one (1). When its TTL reaches a value of zero (0), each multicast datagram expires and is no longer forwarded through the network to other subnets.

Specify a Finite Lifetime for a Multicast Scope

To specify a finite lifetime for a multicast scope,

1. To open DHCP, click **Start**, point to **Programs**, point to **Administrative Tools**, and then click **DHCP**.
2. In the console tree, click the applicable multicast scope (console tree | DHCP | *applicable DHCP server* | *applicable multicast scope*).
3. On the **Action** menu, click **Properties**.
4. Click the **Lifetime** tab.
5. For **Multicast scope lifetime**, click **Multicast scope expires on**.
6. Using the controls, specify a date and time when the multicast scope is to be expired and removed from the applicable DHCP server.

By default, multicast scopes do not expire. When created, they exist until they are manually removed. This procedure, however, can be used to provide a means of having the DHCP server automatically remove the multicast scope at an appointed future date and time.

Assign a Server-based Option

To assign a server-based option,

1. To open DHCP, click **Start**, point to **Programs**, point to **Administrative Tools**, and then click **DHCP**.

2. In the console tree, click **Server Options** (console tree | DHCP | *applicable DHCP server* | Server Options).
3. On the **Action** menu, click **Configure Options**.
4. In list of **Available Options**, select the check box for the first option you want to configure.
5. Under **Data entry**, type the information required for this option.
6. Repeat steps 4 and 5 for any other server options you want to specify, and then click **OK**.
7. In addition, you can click the **Advanced** tab and specify additional server options to be applied only for members of select user or vendor classes. Options assigned at this level are only provided to clients identified as members of the classes specified at this tab.

Server options are inherited as default values for all scopes created at the applicable DHCP server. Option values you configure here are overridden by any scope-based or client-based values assigned for the same options.

Assign a Scope-based Option

To assign a scope-based option,

1. To open DHCP, click **Start**, point to **Programs**, point to **Administrative Tools**, and then click **DHCP**.
2. In the console tree, click **Scope Options** (console tree | DHCP | *applicable DHCP server* | *applicable superscope, if used* | *applicable scope* | Server Options).
3. On the **Action** menu, click **Configure Options**.
4. In list of **Available Options**, select the check box for the first option you want to configure.
5. Under **Data entry**, type the information required for this option.
6. Repeat the two previous steps for any other server options you want to specify, and then click **OK**.
7. In addition, you can click the **Advanced** tab and specify additional scope options to be applied only for members of select user or vendor classes.

   Options assigned at this level are only provided to clients identified as members of the classes specified at this tab.

Scope options are inherited as default values for all clients of the applicable scope. Option values you configure here are overridden by any reserved client-based values assigned for the same options.

Assign an Advanced (Class-Based) Option

To assign an advanced (class-based) option,

1. To open DHCP, click **Start**, point to **Programs**, point to **Administrative Tools**, and then click **DHCP**.
2. In the console tree, choose one of the following:
   a. Click **Server Options** if you want to assign advanced options for use by all new scopes at the DHCP server (console tree | DHCP | *applicable DHCP server* | Server Options).
   b. Click **Scope Options** if you want to assign advanced options for use by a specific scope at the DHCP server (console tree | DHCP | *applicable DHCP server* | *applicable superscope, if used* | *applicable scope* | Server Options).
3. Right-click the folder, and click **Configure Options**.
4. Click the **Advanced** tab.
5. Select from the following:
   a. For **Vendor class**, scroll to select the defined vendor class at the DHCP server (or use the default, **DHCP Standard Options**) for assigning options for the server or scope.
   b. For **User class**, scroll to select the defined user class at the DHCP server (or use the default, **Default User Class**) for assigning options for the server or scope.
6. In the list of **Available Options**, select the check box for the first option you want to configure.
7. Under **Data entry**, type the information required for this option.
8. Repeat steps 6 and 7 for any other options you want to specify, and then click **OK**.

If a class-based option is assigned, it only applies to DHCP clients that are identified as members of the specified user or vendor class.

Create a New User or Vendor Class

To create a new user or vendor class,

1. To open DHCP, click **Start**, point to **Programs**, point to **Administrative Tools**, and then click **DHCP**.
2. In the console tree, click the applicable DHCP server (console tree | DHCP | *applicable DHCP server*).
3. On the **Action** menu, choose one of the following:

  a. To create a new user class, click **Define User Classes**.
  b. To create a new vendor class, click **Define Vendor Classes**.

4. Click **Add**.
5. In **New Class**, type the required information. To view a description of a dialog box item, right-click the item, and then click **What's This?**.

In the **DHCP User Classes** and **DHCP Vendor Classes** dialogs, you can also click either **Edit** or **Remove** to modify or delete option classes.

In the **New Class** dialog box, for **ID**, set the same binary or ASCII string that matches the DHCP class ID string, which is either implemented or set at member clients.

For Windows 2000 DHCP client computers, the *ipconfig /setclassid* command can be used to set the specified DHCP class ID string.

Define a New Option

To define a new option,

1. To open DHCP, click **Start**, point to **Programs**, point to **Administrative Tools**, and then click **DHCP**.
2. In the console tree, click the applicable DHCP server (console tree | DHCP | *applicable DHCP server*).
3. On the **Action** menu, click **Set Predefined Options**.
4. In **Predefined Options and Values**, click **Add**.
5. In **Option Type**, type the required information to define the new option, and then click **OK**. To view a description of a dialog box item, right-click the item, and then click **What's This?**.

By default, standard DHCP options and BOOTP extensions as described in RFC 2132 are predefined for use at Windows 2000 DHCP servers.

Modify an Option

To modify an option,

1. To open DHCP, click **Start**, point to **Programs**, point to **Administrative Tools**, and then click **DHCP**.
2. In the console tree, click the applicable DHCP server (console tree | DHCP | *applicable DHCP server*).
3. On the **Action** menu, click **Set Predefined Options**.
4. In **Predefined Options and Values**, select the following:

   a. For **Option class**, select the class where the option to be modified is used.
   b. For **Option name**, scroll to select the option you want to modify.

5. Click **Edit**.
6. Modify the **Name** and **Description** fields for the option as needed.

For options already defined, only the **Name** and **Description** fields can be modified using this procedure. To change other fields (such as **Data type**, **Code**, or the applicable class where the option is used), the existing option must be removed and a new option defined.

By default, standard DHCP options and BOOTP extensions as described in RFC 2132 are predefined for use at Windows 2000 DHCP servers.

Remove an Option

To remove an option,

1. To open DHCP, click **Start**, point to **Programs**, point to **Administrative Tools**, and then click **DHCP**.
2. In the console tree, click the applicable DHCP server (console tree | DHCP | *applicable DHCP server*).
3. On the **Action** menu, click **Set Predefined Options**.
4. In **Predefined Options and Values**, select the following:
   a. For **Option class**, select the class where the option to be removed is used.
   b. For **Option name**, scroll to select the user-defined option you want to remove.
5. Click **Delete**.

By default, standard DHCP options and BOOTP extensions as described in RFC 2132 are predefined at Windows 2000 DHCP servers for use and cannot be removed using this procedure.

View Client Lease Information

To view client lease information,

1. To open DHCP, click **Start**, point to **Programs**, point to **Administrative Tools**, and then click **DHCP**.

2. In the console tree, click **Address Leases** (console tree | DHCP | *applicable DHCP server* | *applicable superscope, if used* | *applicable scope* | Address Leases).
3. In the details pane, locate the client lease for which you want to view information.

For most clients displayed in the DHCP console, you cannot edit the displayed lease information. Only reserved scope clients permit some of this information to be edited.

Delete a Client Lease

To delete a client lease,

1. To open DHCP, click **Start**, point to **Programs**, point to **Administrative Tools**, and then click **DHCP**.
2. In the console tree, click **Address Leases** (console tree | DHCP | *applicable DHCP server* | *applicable superscope, if used* | *applicable scope* | Address Leases).
3. In the details pane, click the IP address of the client you want to delete.
4. On the **Action** menu, click **Delete**.
5. Make a reservation with the IP address, or exclude it from the range.
6. Force the client with the existing lease to give it up. At the command prompt on the client computer, type *ipconfig /release*.
7. If needed, give the client a new IP address. At the command prompt on the client computer, type *ipconfig /renew*.

If you want, you can cancel leases for all clients in the scope. To cancel all current leases, select all of the clients in **Address Leases**, right-click, and then click **Delete**.

Deleting a client lease does not prevent the server from offering that IP address again in a future client lease. It also does not prevent the client from requesting the address again, unless steps 5 to 7 are followed.

For Windows 95 and Windows 98 clients, you can use *Winipcfg.exe* to release or renew a computer address lease.

View, Release, or Renew a Client Address Lease

To verify, release, or renew a client address lease,

1. At a DHCP-enabled client computer running Windows, open a command prompt.

2. Use the **Ipconfig** command-line utility to verify, release, or renew the lease of the client with a DHCP server, as follows:
   a. To verify a DHCP client lease, type **ipconfig** to view lease-status information. Or, type *ipconfig/all.*
   b. To release a DHCP client lease, type **ipconfig /release**.
   c. To renew a DHCP client lease, type **ipconfig /renew**.

The **Ipconfig** utility is also supported for use in Windows NT. For Windows 95 and Windows 98 clients, use **Winipcfg**, the Windows IP configuration program, to perform these same tasks.

To run **Winipcfg** on supporting clients, type *winipcfg* at either an MS-DOS command prompt or in the **Run** command window (click **Start**, and then click **Run**). When using **Winipcfg** to release or renew leases, click **Release** or **Renew** to perform these respective tasks.

Set DHCP Class ID Information at a Client Computer

To set DHCP class ID information at a client computer,

1. At a DHCP-enabled client computer running Windows 2000, open a command prompt.
2. Use the **Ipconfig** command-line utility to set the DHCP class ID the client uses when obtaining its lease from the DHCP server.

You can type the **ipconfig /setclassid** command as demonstrated in the following example command, which sets an ASCII string (MyNewClassId) as the DHCP class ID string for the local area network connection in use at the client computer.

```
C:\>ipconfig /setclassid "Local Area Connection" MyNewClassId
Windows 2000 IP Configuration
DHCP ClassId successfully modified for adapter "Local Area Connection"
```

For a DHCP options class to be in effect between the DHCP server and its clients, both must be configured with a matching DHCP class ID string that identifies the client as a member of a specific user or vendor options class when it obtains its address lease from the server.

Show DHCP Class ID Information at a Client Computer

To show DHCP class ID information at a client computer,

1. At a DHCP-enabled client computer running Windows 2000, open a command prompt.

2. Use the **Ipconfig** command-line utility to show the DHCP class ID that the client uses when obtaining its lease from the DHCP server.

You can type the **ipconfig /showclassid** command as demonstrated in the following example command. This example shows an ASCII string (MyNewClassId) that is currently set as the DHCP class ID for the local area network connection at the client computer.

```
C:\>ipconfig /showclassid "Local Area Connection"

Windows 2000 IP Configuration

DHCP Class ID for Adapter "Local Area Connection":
        DHCP ClassID Name . . . . . . . . . : Default BOOTP Class
        DHCP ClassID Description  . . . . : User class for BOOTP
clients
        DHCP ClassID Name . . . . . . . . . : Default Remote Access Class
        DHCP ClassID Description  . . . . : User class for remote
access clients

        Host Name . . . . . . . . . . . . . : HOSTA
        Primary DNS Suffix  . . . . . . . : example.microsoft.com
        Node Type . . . . . . . . . . . . . : Hybrid
        IP Routing Enabled. . . . . . . . . : No
        WINS Proxy Enabled. . . . . . . . . : No

Ethernet adapter Local Area Connection:

        Connection-specific DNS Suffix  . :
        Description . . . . . . . . . . . . : Combo PCMCIA EthernetCard
        Physical Address. . . . . . . . . . : 00-00-00-00-7C-DC
        DHCP Enabled. . . . . . . . . . . . : Yes
        Autoconfiguration Enabled . . . . : Yes
        IP Address. . . . . . . . . . . . . : 10.0.0.51
        Subnet Mask . . . . . . . . . . . . : 255.255.255.0
        Default Gateway . . . . . . . . . . : 10.0.0.1
        DHCP Class ID . . . . . . . . . . . : MyNewClassId
        DNS servers . . . . . . . . . . . . : 10.0.0.3
        Primary WINS server . . . . . . . : 10.0.0.5
```

For a DHCP options class to be in effect between the DHCP server and its clients, both must be configured with a matching DHCP class ID string that identifies the client as a member of a specific user or vendor options class when it obtains its address lease from the server.

Add a Client Reservation

To add a client reservation,

1. To open DHCP, click **Start**, point to **Programs**, point to **Administrative Tools**, and then click **DHCP**.
2. In the console tree, click **Reservations** (console tree | DHCP | *applicable DHCP server* | *applicable superscope, if used* | *applicable scope* | Reservations).
3. On the **Action** menu, click **New Reservation**.
4. In **New Reservation**, type the information required to complete the client reservation. To view a description of a dialog box item, right-click the item, and then click **What's This?**.
5. To add the client reservation to the scope, click **Add**.
6. Repeat steps 4 and 5 for any other client reservations you want to add, and then click **Close**.

When adding a reservation, the DHCP server checks for the address you enter in the database to make sure it is not currently in use by another client.

Reservations are applied on the basis of the DHCP client Media Access Control (MAC) address for the applicable network connection.

To locate this address, at the client computer, type *ipconfig /all* at a command prompt and view the Physical Address for the connection. Alternately, you can right-click the connection in the Network and Dial-up Connections folder and select **Properties** to view this information.

Change Information for a Reserved Client

To change information for a reserved client,

1. To open DHCP, click **Start**, point to **Programs**, point to **Administrative Tools**, and then click **DHCP**.
2. In the console tree, click **Reservations** (console tree | DHCP | *applicable DHCP server* | *applicable superscope, if used* | *applicable scope* | Reservations).
3. In the details pane, click the reserved client for which you want to change information. Note any information currently used for the reservation that you want to preserve.
4. On the **Action** menu, click **Delete**.
5. Add a new reservation, merging any of the reserved client information you want to keep, or modify as needed.

Reservations, once made, cannot be modified. To change information for an existing client reservation, you must delete and recreate it.

Assign an Option to a Reserved Client

To assign an option to a reserved client,

1. To open DHCP, click **Start**, point to **Programs**, point to **Administrative Tools**, and then click **DHCP**.
2. In the console tree, click **Reservations** (console tree | DHCP | *applicable DHCP server* | *applicable superscope, if used* | *applicable scope* | Reservations).
3. In the details pane, click the reserved client for which you want to assign options.
4. On the **Action** menu, click **Configure Options**.
5. In the list of **Available Options**, select the check box for the first option you want to configure.
6. Under **Data entry**, type the information required for this option.
7. Repeat steps 5 and 6 for any other reserved client options you want to specify, and then click **OK**.

Reserved client options configured here override option values assigned at either the server or scope levels of configuration.

Configure Advanced (Class-Based) Options for a Reserved Client

To configure advanced (class-based) options for a reserved client,

1. To open DHCP, click **Start**, point to **Programs**, point to **Administrative Tools**, and then click **DHCP**.
2. In the console tree, click **Reservations** (console tree | DHCP | *applicable DHCP server* | *applicable superscope, if used* | *applicable scope* | Reservations).
3. In the details pane, click the reserved client for which you want to assign options.
4. On the **Action** menu, click **Configure Options**.
5. Click the **Advanced** tab.
6. Select from the following:
   a. For **Vendor class**, scroll to select the defined vendor class at the DHCP server (or use the default, **DHCP Standard Options**) for assigning options to the reserved client.
   b. For **User class**, scroll to select the defined user class at the DHCP server (or use the default, **Default User Class**) for assigning options to the reserved client.

7. In the list of **Available Options**, select the check box for the first option you want to configure.
8. Under **Data entry**, type the information required for this option.
9. Repeat steps 7 and 8 for any other options you want to specify, and then click **OK**.

If a class-based option is assigned, it only applies if the reserved client is identified as a member of the specified user or vendor classes.

Change the Reserved IP Address for a Client

To change the reserved IP address for a client,

1. To open DHCP, click **Start**, point to **Programs**, point to **Administrative Tools**, and then click **DHCP**.
2. In the console tree, click **Reservations** (console tree | DHCP | *applicable DHCP server* | *applicable superscope, if used* | *applicable scope* | Reservations).
3. In the details pane, select the reserved client for which you want to change the IP address.
4. To delete the current reservation, on the **Action** menu, click **Delete**.
5. Add a new reservation in DHCP that uses the new IP address for the client.

The IP address in an existing client reservation cannot be modified directly. To achieve similar results, the existing reservation must be deleted and a new reservation added.

View the BOOTP Table

To view the BOOTP table,

1. To open DHCP, click **Start**, point to **Programs**, point to **Administrative Tools**, and then click **DHCP**.
2. In the console tree, click the applicable DHCP server (console tree | DHCP | *applicable DHCP server*).
3. On the **Action** menu, click **Properties**.
4. Verify that the **Show the BOOTP table folder** check box is selected.
5. In the console tree, click **BOOTP Table** (console tree | DHCP | *applicable DHCP server* | BOOTP Table).

By default, the BOOTP table is empty.

Add an Entry to the BOOTP Table

To add an entry to the BOOTP table,

1. To open DHCP, click **Start**, point to **Programs**, point to **Administrative Tools**, and then click **DHCP**.
2. In the console tree, click **BOOTP Table** (console tree | DHCP | *applicable DHCP server* | BOOTP Table).
3. On the **Action** menu, click **New Boot Image**.
4. In the **Add BOOTP Entry** dialog box, enter the required information. To view a description of a dialog box item, right-click the item, and then click **What's This?**.
5. Click **Add**.
6. Repeat steps 4 and 5 for each additional BOOTP entry you want to add, and then click **Close**.

Add Dynamic BOOTP Client Support to a Scope

To add dynamic BOOTP client support to a scope,

1. To open DHCP, click **Start**, point to **Programs**, point to **Administrative Tools**, and then click **DHCP**.
2. In the console tree, click the applicable scope (console tree | DHCP | *applicable DHCP server* | *Applicable superscope, if used* | *applicable scope*).
3. On the **Action** menu, click **Properties**.
4. Click the **Advanced** tab.
5. For **Assign IP addresses dynamically to clients of**, click either **Both** or **BOOTP only**.
6. If needed, in **Lease duration for BOOTP clients**, adjust the default lease length.

The lease length is used by the DHCP server to determine how long to preserve leases made dynamically for BOOTP clients of the applicable scope. Unlike DHCP, where clients can initiate a protocol message to release or renew their address lease, BOOTP clients can only obtain or negotiate their IP address lease at boot time. For this reason, it is recommended that you select a lease length for BOOTP clients that exceeds the time between when BOOTP clients are restarted on the network.

Change the Lease Time for Remote Access Clients

To change the lease time for remote access clients,

1. To open DHCP, click **Start**, point to **Programs**, point to **Administrative Tools**, and then click **DHCP**.
2. In the console tree, click **Scope Options** (console tree | DHCP | *applicable DHCP server* | *applicable superscope, if used* | *applicable scope*).
3. Right-click **Scope Options** and click **Configure Options**.
4. Click **Advanced**.
5. In **User class**, select **Default remote access class**.
6. In **Available Options**, click the check box for **051 Lease**.
7. In **Long**, type the lease value in seconds. For example, if you want the lease time to be one hour, type *0x3600*.

Optimize the Command Prompt for Use with Command-line Tools

To optimize the command prompt for use with command-line tools,

1. To open Command Prompt, click **Start**, point to **Programs**, and then click **Command Prompt**.
2. Click the upper left corner of the command prompt window, and then click **Properties**.
3. Click the **Options** tab.
4. Modify command prompt options.
5. For command history, increase **Buffer Size** to 500 and **Number of Buffers** to 5. Under edit options, click **Quick Edit Mode** and **Insert Mode**.
6. Click the **Layout** tab.
7. Increase **Screen Buffer Size** to 2500.
8. Click **OK** to apply changes. When prompted, select **Modify shortcut that started this window**.

As a keyboard option for step 2, access the Command Prompt Properties dialog box by doing the following: press the ALT key and the spacebar at the same time, then press *P* to select **Properties**.

By optimizing the command prompt window using this procedure, you can use Windows Explorer features, such as scrolling, and can quickly mark, copy, and paste to and from the command prompt window. By increasing the screen buffer size, you can scroll back to previous command output and more easily view command-line help text.

Use DHCP Commands Interactively at the Command Prompt

To use DHCP commands interactively at the command prompt,

1. To open Command Prompt, click **Start**, point to **Programs**, and then click **Command Prompt**.
2. Type: *netsh*
3. At the **netsh>** (Netshell) command prompt, type: *dhcp*
4. At the **dhcp>** (DHCP helper) command prompt, type either *server \\servername or server ip_address* for the server you want to manage.

   Once a server that you have rights to manage has been successfully reached, you should see "You have Read and Write access to the server *servername*."
5. Once connected, you can use any supported Netshell command for DHCP. Type */?* or *help* to display the immediate DHCP subcommand menu or as an option, type **list** to list all Netshell subcommands available for use with DHCP.

The **\\servername** parameter is optional and can be left unspecified if you are performing commands locally at the DHCP server located on the same computer as the command is executed. If the server being managed is remote, this parameter is required and the name of the server must be specified.

In order to manage a DHCP server using the Netshell command-line, you must be logged on as a member of either the local Administrators group or (for Windows 2000 Server only) the local DHCP Administrators group on the applicable server computer.

Use DHCP Commands Noninteractively or in Scripts

To use DHCP commands noninteractively or in scripts,

1. To open Command Prompt, click **Start**, point to **Programs**, and then click **Command Prompt**.
2. At the command prompt or in scripted usage, you can use Netshell commands for DHCP noninteractively by using the following fully qualified command syntax:

netsh dhcp server [*servername*] *subcommand*

The ***servername*** parameter is optional and can be left unspecified if you are performing commands locally at the DHCP server located on the same computer as the command is executed. If the server being managed is remote, this parameter is required and the name of the server must be specified.

In order to manage a DHCP server using the Netshell command-line, you must be logged on as a member of either the local Administrators group or (for Windows 2000 Server only) the local DHCP Administrators group on the applicable server computer.

S I X

WINS Overview

WINS Defined

Windows Internet Name Service (WINS) provides a distributed database for registering and querying dynamic mappings of NetBIOS names for computers and groups used on your network. WINS maps NetBIOS names to IP addresses and was designed to solve the problems arising from NetBIOS name resolution in routed environments. WINS is the best choice for NetBIOS name resolution in routed networks that use NetBIOS over TCP/IP.

NetBIOS names are used by earlier versions of Microsoft operating systems to identify and locate computers and other shared or grouped resources needed to register or resolve names for use on the network.

NetBIOS names are a requirement for establishing networking services in earlier versions of Microsoft operating systems. Although the NetBIOS naming protocol can be used with network protocols other than TCP/IP (such as NetBEUI or IPX/SPX), WINS was designed specifically to support NetBIOS over TCP/IP (NetBT).

WINS simplifies managing the NetBIOS namespace in TCP/IP-based networks. Figure 6-1 shows a typical series of events involving WINS clients and servers.

In this example, the following occurs:

1. A WINS client, HOST-A, registers any of its local NetBIOS names with WINS-A, its configured WINS server.
2. Another WINS client, HOST-B, queries WINS-A to locate the IP address for HOST-A on the network.
3. WINS-A replies with the IP address for HOST-A, 192.168.1.20.

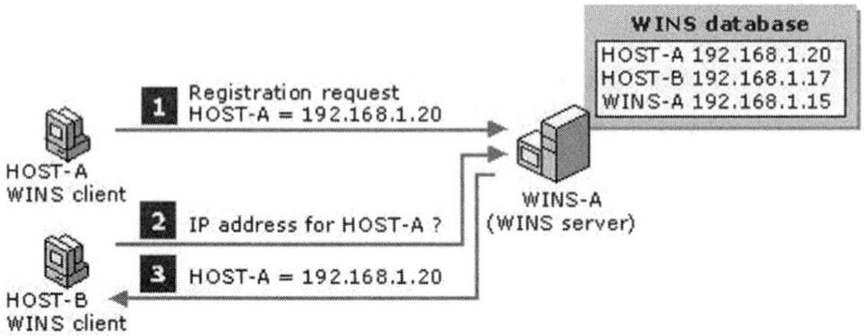

FIGURE 6–1 *WINS exemplified*

WINS reduces the use of local IP broadcasts for NetBIOS name resolution and enables users to locate systems on remote networks easily. Because WINS registrations are done automatically each time clients start and join the network, the WINS database is automatically updated when dynamic address configuration changes are made. For example, when a DHCP server issues a new or changed IP address to a WINS-enabled client computer, WINS information for the client is updated. This requires no manual changes to be made by either a user or network administrator.

The WINS protocol is based on and is compatible with the protocols defined for NetBIOS name service specified in RFCs 1001 and 1002, so it is interoperable with any other implementations of these RFCs. For more information about WINS RFCs, see Appendix C, “WINS Resources and Troubleshooting.”

In order to more fully unnerstand WINS, knowledge of the history and need for NetBIOS naming is helpful. For more general background information, see “NetBIOS Over TCP/IP Concepts” in this chapter.

Replication of NetBIOS names data in WINS is Microsoft proprietary technology and is not interoperable with other NetBIOS name servers.

Benefits of Using WINS

WINS provides the following benefits for administering your TCP/IP-based network:

- A dynamic name-to-address database that maintains support for computer name registration and resolution.
- Centralized management of the name-to-address database, alleviating the need for managing lmhosts files.

- Reduction of NetBIOS-based broadcast traffic on subnets, by permitting clients to query WINS servers to directly locate remote systems.
- Support for earlier Windows and NetBIOS-based clients on your network, permitting these types of clients to browse lists for remote Windows domains without requiring a local domain controller to be present on each subnet.
- Support for DNS-based clients by enabling those clients to locate NetBIOS resources when WINS lookup integration is implemented. See Chapter 7, "Using WINS," for more information.

When to Use WINS

For networks with servers running Windows 2000 Server and all other computers running Windows 2000 Professional, NetBIOS is no longer required for TCP/IP-based networking. Because of this change, WINS is needed for most networks but might not be required in some instances. When deciding whether you need to use WINS, you should first consider the following questions:

- *Do I have any legacy computers on my network that require the use of NetBIOS names?* Remember that all networked computers that run under any previously released Microsoft operating system, such as versions of MS-DOS, Windows, or Windows NT, require NetBIOS names support. Windows 2000 is the first Microsoft operating system that no longer requires NetBIOS naming. Therefore, NetBIOS names can still be required on your network to provide basic file and print services and support for many legacy applications used.
- *Are all computers on my network configured and able to support the use of another type of network naming, such as DNS?* Network naming is still a vital service for locating computers and resources throughout your network, even when NetBIOS names are not required. Before you decide to eliminate WINS or NetBIOS names support, be sure that all computers and programs on your network are able to function using another naming service, such as DNS. In general, Windows operating systems support two major methods of performing network name resolution:
    - *Host name resolution.* This is Windows sockets-based name resolution, which implements the gethostbyname () API to search for a host IP address based on a queried host name. This method relies on either a Hosts file or querying DNS to perform resolution of the name.

- *NetBIOS name resolution.* This is name resolution that uses the NetBIOS redirector to search for an address based on a queried NetBIOS name. This method relies on either an lmhosts file or querying WINS to perform resolution of the name.

  WINS clients running under Windows 2000 are configured by default to first use DNS to resolve names that are longer than 15 characters or that make use of periods (.) within the name. For names that are less than 15 characters and do not use periods, DNS is also used again as a final option after a WINS query fails if the client is configured to use a DNS server.

  If you are running either a pure Windows 2000 environment, review that DNS is currently configured and can be used by all client computers on your network to resolve names. If you run a mixed environment of computers running under Windows 2000 and other platforms (such as UNIX), confirm that these other hosts can rely on using only DNS for host name resolution.
- *Is your network a single subnet or routed with multiple subnets?* If your entire network is made up of a single small LAN that occupies one physical network segment and has less than 50 clients, you can probably do without a WINS server. All computers that run under Windows 2000—and most earlier Microsoft-based WINS clients—are configured as hybrid node (h-node) type clients and can use either of the following methods to handle NetBIOS requests to resolve or register names:
  - Direct (point-to-point) contact with a WINS server, if one is configured.
  - Broadcast of the NetBIOS request to the local subnet.

For small networks, the latter option is typically an effective and simple solution for providing NetBIOS name service to a small number of LAN-based clients.

To provide for the full use of DNS query as it is described in this section and used in the NetBIOS name resolution process for Windows 2000, you can selectively enable the **Enable DNS For WINS Resolution** for some earlier Windows-based clients, such as Windows 95 or Windows NT 4.0 client computers that support this option as a configurable TCP/IP property setting.

How WINS Works

By default, when a computer running Windows 20000is configured with WINS server addresses (either manually or through DHCP) for its name resolution, it adheres to using h-node as its node type for NetBIOS name registration unless another NetBIOS node type is configured. For NetBIOS name query and resolution, it also adheres to h-node behavior, but with a few differences.

For NetBIOS name resolution, a WINS client typically performs the following general sequence of steps to resolve a name:

1. Client checks to see if the name queried is its local NetBIOS computer name, which it owns.
2. Client checks its local NetBIOS name cache of remote names. Any name resolved for a remote client is placed in this cache, where it remains for 10 minutes.
3. Client forwards the NetBIOS query to its configured primary WINS server. If the primary WINS server fails to answer the query—either because it is not available or because it does not have an entry for the name—the client will try to contact other configured WINS servers in the order they are listed and configured for its use.
4. Client broadcasts the NetBIOS query to the local subnet.
5. Client checks the lmhosts file for a match to the query, if it is configured to use the lmhosts file.
6. Client tries the Hosts file and then a DNS server, if it is configured for one.

For a more detailed description of the default NetBIOS name resolution process as it is performed by computers running Windows 2000, see "Resolving Names" in this chapter.

WINS Tools

The primary tool that you use to manage WINS servers is the WINS console, which is added to the Administrative Tools when you install WINS. For Windows 2000 Server, the WINS console works within the Microsoft Management Console (MMC) to further integrate WINS administration into your total network management.

After you install a WINS server, you can use the WINS console to perform these basic server administrative tasks:

1. View and filter NetBIOS name registrations stored at the WINS server for client names used on your network.
2. Add and configure replication partners for the WINS server.
3. Perform maintenance-related tasks, including backup, restoration, compaction, and scavenging, on the WINS server database.

In addition, you can also use the WINS console to perform the following optional or advanced setup tasks:

- View and modify WINS properties, such as the **Renew Interval** and other intervals that are used when registering, renewing, and verifying name records stored in the server database.
- Add and configure static WINS mappings, if they are needed for use on your network.
- Delete or tombstone WINS records that appear in WINS server data used throughout your network.

For Windows 2000 Server, WINS administration can also be performed using command-line based tools. For information about Netshell commands for WINS and using WINS command-line tools, see Chapter 7.

New Features

For Windows 2000, WINS provides the following feature enhancements:

- *Persistent connections*. You can now configure each WINS server to maintain a persistent connection with one or more replication partners. This increases the speed of replication and eliminates the overhead of opening and terminating connections. For more information, see "Persistent Connections" in this chapter.
- *Manual tombstoning*. You can manually mark a record for eventual deletion, or *tombstoning*. The tombstone state of the record replicates to other WINS servers, preventing any replicated copies of the deleted records from re-appearing at the same server where they were originally deleted. For more information, see "Deleting and Tombstoning Records" in this chapter.
- *Improved management utility*. The WINS console is fully integrated with the MMC, a powerful and more user-friendly environment you can customize for your efficiency. Because all server administrative utilities included for your use in Windows 2000 Server are part of MMC, new MMC-based utilities are easier to use, as they operate more predictably and follow a common design.
- *Improved ease of use for both using and managing advanced WINS features*. Several useful WINS features from earlier versions of Windows NT Server that were only configurable through the registry are now more directly usable. These include the ability to block records by a specific owner or WINS replication partner (formerly known as *Persona Non Grata*), or allow override of static mappings (formerly known as *Migrate On/Off*). For more information, see "Blocking Rep-

lication Partners" in this chapter; for information about using static mappings, see Chapter 7.

- *Enhanced filtering and record searching.* Improved filtering and new search functions help you locate records by showing only those records that fit the criteria you specify. These functions are particularly useful in analyzing very large WINS databases.
- *Dynamic record deletion and multi-select.* These features help you more easily manage the WINS database. With the WINS snap-in, you can simply point, click, and delete either one or more WINS static or dynamic-type entries. Previously, this functionality was only available when using command-based utilities, such as *Winscl.exe,* designed for earlier versions of WINS. It is also possible now to delete records that use names based on non-alphanumeric characters.
- *Record verification and version number validation.* These features quickly check the consistency of names stored and replicated on your WINS servers. Record verification compares the IP addresses returned by a NetBIOS name query of different WINS servers. Version number validation examines the owner address-to-version number mapping tables. For information about checking the WINS database for consistency, see Chapter 7.
- *Export function.* When you *export,* you place WINS data in a comma-delimited text file. You can export this file to Microsoft Excel, reporting tools, scripting programs, or similar programs for analysis and reporting. For more information about exporting WINS console data to a text file, see Chapter 7.
- *Increased fault tolerance for clients.* Clients running Windows 2000 or Windows 98 can specify more than two WINS servers (up to a maximum of 12 addresses) per interface. The extra WINS server addresses are used only if the primary and secondary WINS servers fail to respond. WINS clients also benefit from the use of burst handling, which is enabled by default. For more information, see "Primary and Secondary WINS Servers" and "Burst Handling" in this chapter.
- *Dynamic reinsertion of client names.* WINS clients no longer have to be restarted after they use WINS to force reinsertion and update of local NetBIOS names. The Nbstat command includes a new option, resource record, which provides this functionality. If WINS clients are running Windows NT 4.0, updated to Service Pack 4 or later, the resource record option can also be used with those clients. For information about verifying WINS registration of client NetBIOS names, see Chapter 7.
- *Read-only console access to the WINS console.* This feature provides a special purpose local users group, the WINS Users group, which is automatically added when WINS is installed. By adding mem-

bers to this group, you can provide read-only access in the WINS console to WINS-related information on this server computer for users that are not administrators. You can allow a user in this group to view, but not modify, information and properties stored at a specific WINS server.
- *Command-line administration of WINS servers.* In addition to a full graphical user interface for managing WINS servers, Windows 2000 Server provides a fully equivalent WINS command-line based tool. For information about Netshell commands for WINS, see Appendix C.
- *Improved database engine.* WINS uses the same performance-enhanced database engine technology that is used in Active Directory.

NetBIOS Over TCP/IP Concepts

This section covers,

- Background on NetBIOS
- NetBIOS names
- Disabling NetBIOS over TCP/IP
- Lmhosts files

Background on NetBIOS

In 1983, Sytek, Inc. (currently part of Hughes LAN Systems) first developed the NetBIOS interface for the International Business Machines Corporation (IBM). It operated over proprietary Sytek protocols on IBM's PC Network, an early form of broadband LAN technology that accommodated up to a maximum of 72 connected devices. It is important to emphasize that from its early origins, NetBIOS was never originally designed to scale and grow into use in large networks.

At Microsoft, NetBIOS started as a high-level programming language interface for MS-DOS programs used to network IBM PC-compatible microcomputers introduced during the late 1980s. To build LANs based on the networking hardware and software available for those computers, Microsoft and other vendors standardized the use of the NetBIOS interface to design their networking system components and programs. This interface uses single-part names, which are limited to 16 characters in length to identify each network resource.

The NetBIOS namespace is flat, meaning that names can be used only once within a network. These names are dynamically registered when computers start up, services start, or users log on. NetBIOS names can be registered as unique or as group names. Unique names have one address associated with a name. Group names have more than one address mapped to a name.

Prior to Windows 2000, all MS-DOS and Windows-based operating systems required the NetBIOS naming interface to support network capabilities. With the release of Windows 2000, support for the NetBIOS naming interface is no longer required for networking computers. For example, an environment consisting of host computers and programs that support the use of the Domain Name System (DNS) could be built to run using Windows 2000 and other operating systems not requiring NetBIOS names, such as some versions of UNIX. However, most networks still need to integrate legacy operating systems that require NetBIOS network names with computers running Windows 2000.

For this reason, Microsoft has continued with Windows 2000 to provide default support for NetBIOS names to ease interoperability with legacy operating systems that require their use. This support is provided mainly in two ways.

- By default, all Windows 2000 computers that use TCP/IP are enabled to provide client-side support for registering and resolving NetBIOS names. This support is provided through NetBT and can, if desired, be manually disabled. For information about disabling NetBIOS over TCP/IP, see Chapter 1, "TCP/IP Overview."
- Windows 2000 Server continues to provide server-side support through WINS, which can be used to effectively manage NetBT-based networks.

NetBIOS Names

A NetBIOS name contains 16 bytes. The first 15 bytes of each name are user-specified indicating either,

- a unique name identifying a resource associated with a single user or computer on the network, or
- a group name identifying a resource associated with a group or collection of users or computers on the network.

The 16th character in each NetBIOS name is used by Microsoft NetBIOS clients as a name suffix to identify the name and indicate information about the resource that the name is being used to register on the network. Each NetBIOS name is configured as either a unique (exclusive) or group (nonexclusive) name.

Unique names are typically used to send network communications to a specific process on a computer. Group names are used to simultaneously send information to multiple computers.

HOW A NETBIOS NAME IS USED

For example, the Server service uses a NetBIOS name. When the server computer starts, this service registers a unique NetBIOS name, based on its configured NetBIOS computer name—SERVER1, in this example—on the network. The exact name registered is a combination of the characters SERVER1, assigned for the NetBIOS computer name, plus a 16th character that contains the hexadecimal byte value of 20 (or [20h], as it appears when viewing records in the WINS console).

When other computers on the network use the net use command to attempt to connect to SERVER1, a name-query request searches for this NetBIOS name. The query uses direct contact with a WINS server or a broadcast to the local network to process the query. When the matching named server process is found—for example, a NetBIOS name entry of SERVER1 with a name suffix value of 20 for the 16th character—the IP address contained in this name record is returned to the requesting computer. Communications can then be established using underlying network transport protocol services.

NETBIOS BEFORE WINDOWS 2000

In earlier versions of Windows NT, all network services were registered using only NetBIOS names. For Windows 2000, the Netlogon service, and potentially other network services, will register in DNS instead. Also, legacy network command-line applications (such as the various **net** commands) use NetBIOS names to access these services.

NetBIOS names are also used by other NetBIOS-based computers, such as Windows for Workgroups, LAN Manager, and LAN Manager for UNIX hosts. For more information on NetBIOS names and how they are used to register and indicate named types of service on the network, see Appendix C, "WINS Resources and Troubleshooting."

INSIDE NETBIOS

NetBIOS defines two components.

- *A session-level interface.* The NetBIOS interface is a standard API that applications can use. These applications submit network input and output and control directives to underlying network protocol software for transfer through the network. You can run any application program using the NetBIOS API for network communication on any protocol software that supports the NetBIOS interface.
- *A protocol for session management and data transport.* The protocol used here can be any networking protocol and its related software used to perform the actual transport and communication of the NetBIOS interface command set. Two examples are TCP/IP and NetBEUI protocol software, both of which are generally provided with earlier versions of Windows operating systems.

Disabling NetBIOS Over TCP/IP

Windows 2000 provides for the ability to disable NetBT for select clients where it is useful to do so. If you require, or would prefer to only use DNS to provide name registration and resolution on a specified computer used in a specialized or secured role for your network (such as an edge proxy server or bastion host in a firewall environment), you can select to disable NetBT services for one or all installed network adapter interfaces on that computer.

When NetBT is disabled, the following considerations are to be noted for computers running Windows 2000:

- The computer no longer listens for traffic to the NetBIOS datagram service at User Datagram Protocol (UDP) port 138, the NetBIOS name service at UDP port 137, or the NetBIOS session service at Transmission Control Protocol (TCP) port 139.
- If WINS is installed on the computer, the computer can no longer function as a WINS server to service WINS clients over this connection unless NetBT is reenabled.
- If the computer needs to participate in WINS as a client, it must be physically multihomed (that is, it must have other physical network connections active and available for its use) for it to continue communicating with and using a WINS server.
- For computers operating as WINS clients, any WINS servers configured in TCP/IP properties for the disabled network adapter do not apply for other installed network adapters. For those adapters to use WINS, you must either manually configure a list of WINS servers on the NetBT-enabled connections or provide such a list to these connections from a DHCP server.

One possible use for this configuration setting is a case where a server computer is dual-homed on an internal private network and an exposed external network, such as the Internet. In this example, disabling NetBT for the installed external network connection makes sense. This allows the dual-homed computer to continue to function as either a WINS server or client for the internal network, and WINS clients can still be serviced for connections made using other physical network adapter installed on the computer.

For any Windows 2000 computers, NetBIOS can be disabled through manual configuration of TCP/IP settings. For information about disabling WINS/NetBT name resolution, see Chapter 7.

If you are using Windows 2000 DHCP servers, you can use DHCP options to dynamically update and disable NetBT at any Windows 2000 DHCP clients located on your network. Microsoft provides a vendor-specific option for performing this configuration.

Lmhosts Files

The lmhosts file is a static file that assists with remote NetBIOS name resolution on computers that cannot respond to NetBIOS name-query broadcasts. It contains NetBIOS name-to-IP addresses mappings. Its function is similar to that of the Hosts file; the difference is that the Hosts file can be used to map DNS domain names for host computers to their IP addresses.

Computers in a Microsoft-based network can resolve NetBIOS names in several ways. If one method fails, they try the next method, in a fixed order. In a broadcast-based network, the computer first checks its NetBIOS name cache. Normally, the cache contains the name only if it was used recently, but names can be preloaded from an lmhosts file into the cache.

If static name-to-address mappings are entered in the lmhosts file using the #pre notation, then these names are considered to be preloaded into the NetBIOS names cache and are used first to resolve name query, before a NetBIOS subnet broadcast or WINS query are used.

After checking the local cache, WINS servers are contacted (if they are configured and reachable) first before the name query is broadcast locally on the client subnet to further attempt resolution of the name. If these methods fail, the client (if enabled to do so) can later refer to an lmhosts file again to further search for and obtain the name-to-IP address mapping; for example, to resolve a name used by another computer located on another subnet located across a router from the client.

LIMITATIONS OF LMHOSTS FILES

Despite the many uses of the lmhosts file, there are some limitations to its design. Its greatest limitation is that it is a static file. Because of this, entries must be updated if the name or the IP address of the computer changes.

An IP address for a client might change for several reasons, such as

- It changes (physically moves) to another subnet within your routed LAN.
- The computer is a portable and changes to another site location, such as a remote dial-up user dialing in from home through remote access to your network.
- The DHCP server leases the client a different IP address after its lease expires.

When such changes occur, they must also be propagated to all the computers that need access to the resource with the changed name-to-IP-address mapping. A centrally maintained lmhosts file can reduce some of the manual administration needed to propagate new or revised mappings to the required computers. However, entering and changing the mappings is still a manual, labor-intensive process. While maintaining an lmhosts file centrally is certainly preferable to keeping an lmhosts file on each computer, this solution can only be feasible for an organization with a small number of servers and clients. On larger networks, it becomes too complicated to maintain and is not a viable or recommended solution.

The WINS console supports the ability to import static mappings from an lmhosts file into a WINS server database, creating static type WINS entries. For information about importing a file containing static mapping entries, see Chapter 7.

Locating Network Services

This section covers,

- Browsing overview
- Browsing WANs with TCP/IP
- Browsing WANs using WINS
- Locating domain controllers using NetBT

Browsing Overview

The information in this topic is provided to explain how browsing a network is done for domains in routed WAN networks that use NetBT. Domains used in this type of environment are likely to be controlled by computers running earlier versions of Windows NT operating systems. In this environment, the use of WINS is needed to provide effective browsing of shared resources located in remote domains on other physical networks.

Windows-based computers operating on each subnet use the Computer Browser service. Computers designated as browsers maintain the browse lists, which contain all shared resources used on the network. Browsing is required by some network applications provided in earlier versions of Windows, such as My Network Places, the NET VIEW command, and Windows NT Explorer.

For example, when a user at a computer running Windows 95 opens My Network Places, the displayed list of domains and computers is generated. This is done by the computer obtaining a copy of the browse list from a browser computer functioning in that role on the same subnet.

Most computers on the network operate as non-browsers, but computers running the Computer Browser service can become potential browsers for each subnet. For computers active as browsers on the network and maintaining copies of the browse list, Windows NT assigns special roles.

Table 6.1 describes the various roles computers operating this service can perform for the purpose of network browsing.

TABLE 6.1 *Computer Browser Service Functions*

Browser role	Description
Domain master browser	Used only in domain environments. By default, the Primary Domain Controller for a domain operates in this role. Collects and maintains the master browse list of available servers for its domain, as well as any names for other domains and workgroups used in the network. Distributes and synchronizes the master browse list for master browsers on other subnets that have computers belonging to the same domain.
Master browser	Collects and maintains the list of available network servers in its subnet. Fully replicates its listed information with the domain master browser to obtain a complete browse list for the network. Distributes its completed list to backup browsers located on the same subnet.
Backup browser	Receives a copy of the browse list from the master browser for its subnet. Distributes the browse list to other computers upon request.
Potential browser	Under normal conditions, operates similarly to a non-browser. Capable of becoming a backup browser if instructed to by the master browser for the subnet.
Non-browser	Does not maintain a browse list. Can operate as a browse client, requesting browse lists from other computers operating as browsers on the same subnet. Configured so it cannot become a browser.

Under some conditions, such as failure or shutdown of a computer designated a specified browser role, browsers (or potential browsers) may change to a different role of operation. This is typically performed through a process known as a *browser election*.

Browsing services in earlier versions of Windows operating systems can be understood in terms of three key processes:

- *Collection of browsing information*. Browse lists are made up of computers that share resources through the use of the Server service. Periodically, every computer running this service broadcasts a host announcement message for its configured domain or workgroup name to the local subnet. These announcements are collected and processed on an ongoing basis by the master browser for each subnet.

  When the master browser on a subnet receives a host announcement, it compares the name of the sending computer to its current browse list. If the name already appears, it is refreshed in the list. If the name does not appear, it is added to the list.
- *Distribution of browsing information*. Browse lists are distributed to backup browsers by the master browser for the subnet. Periodically, the master browser must broadcast an announcement message for its

configured domain or workgroup name to the local subnet. This message confirms the master browser's presence on the network. If the master browser fails to announce itself for a period of time, a browser election can occur.

Once a master browser is either present or (in the event of a failure) replaced, other backup browsers periodically contact it to obtain an updated copy of the browse list that it maintains for the subnet.

- *Servicing of browse requests from clients.* When a browse client computer starts on a subnet, it broadcasts a request to the master browser for a list of the backup browsers on the subnet. The master browser responds to this request and provides the client a list of three backup browsers. The browse client then randomly selects one of the backup browsers from the list and contacts it for a copy of the browse list.

  For subsequent browse list requests, the client continues to use the list of backup browsers provided by the master browser during its startup and does not repeat the broadcast. The success of this process depends first upon the client getting a response from its master browser and second, on its ability to resolve the names of backup browsers it selects from the list.

HOW BROWSING WORKS

Figure 6-2 illustrates these processes for an example domain called MIS.

In this example, the MIS domain has three master browser computers—PDC-MIS, A-MB1, and C-MB1—present on subnets A, B, and C. In addition, PDC-MIS, has special significance as the domain master browser for the domain, as well as acting as the subnet master browser for subnet B.

As the master browsers on each subnet, these three computers perform the following to create and manage the update and distribution of the MIS domain browse list across all three subnets:

- Process browser announcements that are broadcast by any servers on each of their respective local subnets.
- Replicate their local subnet browse lists with one another. This eventually builds and replicates a complete browse list for the domain that can be distributed and used on each of the three subnets that have computers participating in the domain.
- Replicate their current browse list to backup browsers on each of their respective subnets for fault tolerance and load balancing.
- As clients request the browse list, the master browsers for each subnet answer their local clients with the list of backup browsers to use in contacting and obtaining the browse list. Clients then use this list to contact the backup browsers and obtain copies of the actual browse list.

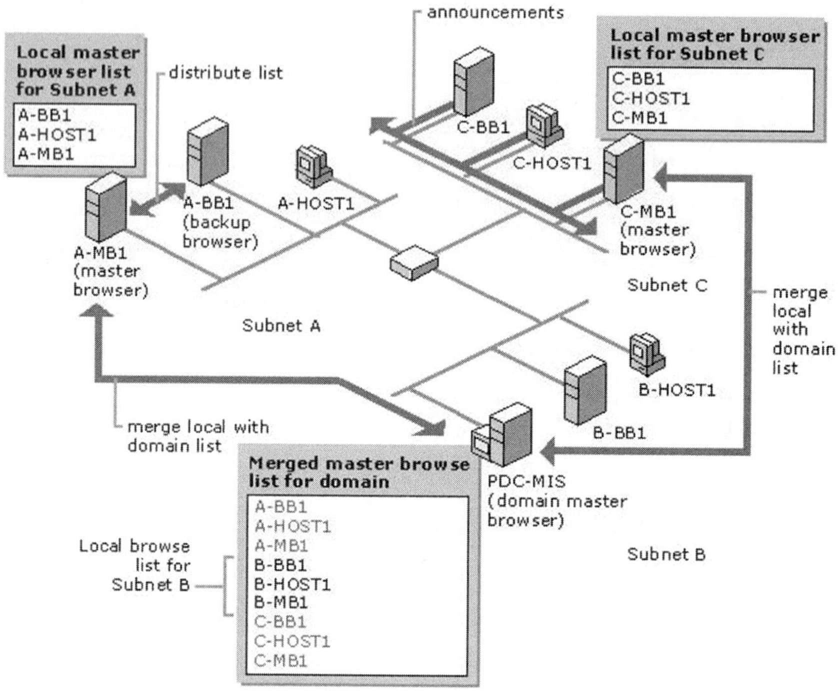

FIGURE 6–2 *How browsing works to collect, distribute, and merge lists*

Browsing WANs With TCP/IP

The Computer Browser service relies almost entirely on using broadcast communication on each subnet in a network. In a WAN that uses TCP/IP, where domains can be separated by routers, special problems for browsing can occur. Most IP routers are not configured to forward broadcasts.

For browsing in these environments, there are two issues to consider.

- How browsers separated by a router perform browser functions, such as updating and maintaining a complete browse list of all network servers, domains, and workgroups.
- How local browse clients on each subnet browse remote domains not present on the same subnet.

These issues can be addressed in three possible ways: using WINS, maintaining an lmhosts file for each subnet master browser, or enabling NetBIOS broadcasts through IP routers.

The last option, enabling broadcasts across IP routers, is not recommended for most routed TCP/IP networks. The second option, using lmhosts files, offers a partial solution to these issues by providing a way to maintain browse lists for all master browsers in a single domain. Only the first option, the use of WINS, offers a preferred solution to both issues and permits browsing of remote domain resources by browse clients.

BROWSING DOMAINS IN A ROUTED IP NETWORK

As shown in Figure 6-3, PDC-MASTER is the computer name of a Primary Domain Controller (PDC) running an earlier version of Windows NT Server for a domain named MIS that spans two subnets, Subnets 1 and 2. PDC-MASTER acts as the domain master browser for the MIS domain and also functions as a master browser for Subnet 2. On Subnet 1, a computer named BROWSER1 acts as the master browser for that subnet and is configured to use the same LAN group (the MIS domain) as PDC-MASTER.

In this example, BROWSER1—which could be any Windows-based computer on Subnet 1 able to operate as a browser—periodically contacts PDC-MASTER on Subnet 2 to exchange information contained in their respective browse lists. Because the router that separates Subnets 1 and 2 does not forward NetBT broadcasts, BROWSER1 must use direct communication to contact PDC-MASTER.

If BROWSER1 is WINS-enabled, it can directly query a WINS server for the <MIS> [1B] name. This name maps the IP address for the computer (PDC-MASTER) that is performing in this role for the MIS domain. Otherwise, it must preload a mapped entry for this computer from its lmhosts file to make direct contact possible across subnets.

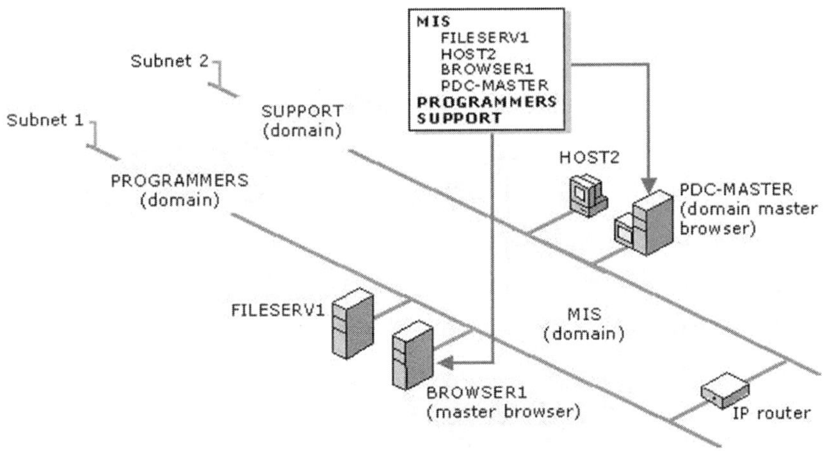

FIGURE 6–3 *Browsing domains in a routed IP network*

For example, if the domain master browser (PDC-MASTER) has an IP address of 192.168.5.8, the entry in the lmhosts file at BROWSER1 (if it is running Windows NT) would need to be

```
192.168.5.8      PDC-MASTER      #PRE      #DOM:MIS
```

If BROWSER1 is running under another Windows platform that supports browsing services, such as Windows 95 or Windows for Workgroups, the entry would be:

```
192.168.5.8   "MIS               \0x1B"  #PRE
```

WAN BROWSING CONSIDERATIONS

The following are additional considerations to keep in mind when planning browsing services across a routed TCP/IP-based network:

- Computers running earlier versions of Windows operating systems (Windows NT Workstation, Windows NT Server, Windows for Workgroups, Windows 95, and Windows 98), can perform the master browser and backup browser roles.
- Only computers running an earlier version of Windows NT Server and operating as the PDC for a domain typically perform the domain master browser role.
- Only domains can span multiple subnets. Workgroups cannot span multiple subnets and can only view other workgroups on the same subnet.

Browsing WANs Using WINS

WINS acts as a directory service for NetBIOS names and IP addresses. The use of WINS can improve browsing for wide area networks through the following enhancements:

- WINS-enabled clients can directly query their configured WINS server for NetBIOS names used to implement browsing and domain services.
- If a domain master browser is a WINS-enabled client, it queries WINS periodically (every 12 to 15 minutes) to obtain a list of all domains stored in the WINS database.

These enhancements make it possible for WINS to assist in fully browsing the entire network and resources shared in remote domains. The process of implementing this enhanced browsing involves the use of WINS in two ways.

- Names for remote domains are registered in WINS and replicated to all WINS servers used in the network.

- WINS-enabled clients use a modified process of WINS query and directed communication with computers in the remote domain to obtain browse list information about servers and shared resources in these remote domains.

HOW REMOTE DOMAINS REGISTER IN WINS

For example, as shown in Figure 6-4, three PDCs for three separate domains (ADMIN, FINANCE, MIS) are operating as domain master browsers for their respective domains. All of these computers are WINS-aware computers running as WINS clients.

When each of the PDC computers starts for its domain, it registers the [1B] name for the domain with its preferred WINS server. For example, in the ADMIN domain, the computer PDC-ADMIN registers its IP address (192.168.1.2) as the domain master browser. These [1B] names then appear at other WINS servers as WINS database replication occurs in the routed network.

Because each of the four PDC computers operating as the domain master browser for their respective domains are configured to use WINS, they query WINS every 15 minutes to update their respective browse lists to include all

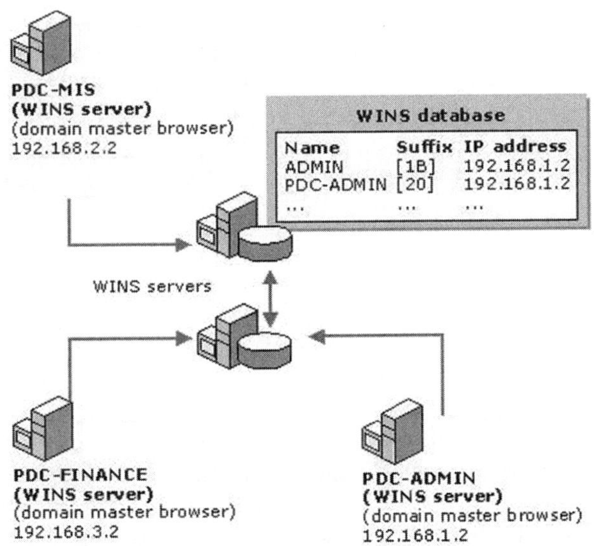

FIGURE 6–4 *How domain master browser information is shared and replicated through WINS*

other domains used in the network. Once all domains are registered in WINS, domain master browsers operating locally for each domain can use a two-part process to query the WINS server and discover remote domains:

1. The local domain master browser does a wildcard query of WINS for domain names ending with a name suffix of [1B]. Note that the result of this query—a list of domain names—contains only the names and a single IP address corresponding to the domain master browser (or PDC computer) for the domain. It does not contain all of the names of master browsers for each domain, as would normally be obtained if the remote domains had member computers located on the same subnet. For domains active on the local subnet, this information is normally obtained through master browser announcements that are broadcast to the local subnet.
2. To obtain a master browser for one of the remote domains, the local domain master browser does a reverse query based on the IP address returned for each remote <domain> [1B] name collected in step 1. The reverse query is used to learn the name of the computer that registered the remote domain name. In this way, the local domain master browser completes its list of remote domain names and their corresponding domain master browsers.

Only WINS-aware domain master browsers (those in Windows NT Server 3.5 or later) register their <domain> [1B] names with the WINS server and perform enhanced WINS queries for learning about remote domains. Domain master browsers running Windows NT Server 3.1 do not use WINS.

This information describes browsing enhancements for server and client computers that are WINS-aware. For more information about specific differences in browsing service for different versions of Windows operating systems, see Microsoft Support Online, *support.microsoft.com*.

BROWSING REMOTE DOMAINS WITH WINS CLIENTS

In wide area networks, the use of a replicated WINS database that contains reference information about each of the domains can assist WINS-enabled clients in browsing remote domains.

As described earlier, NetBT clients can use broadcasts to their local subnets for <domain> [1D] names. When this happens and the domain is located at a remote subnet or site, the query fails. Under these circumstances, browsing is not possible unless special configurations are made and maintained. Without WINS, each domain master browser would need static information entered in an lmhosts file to further process a client request. This requires careful administration to maintain and update static lmhosts files at each domain master browser in the enterprise.

With WINS, clients can leverage the replicated names database more effectively and administrators can eliminate reliance on lmhosts management. The process used by WINS clients to resolve a browser request for a remote domain name is different from the process used by non-WINS (NetBIOS broadcast-only) computers or to obtain information about local domains that are present on the same subnet.

HOW WINS CLIENTS OBTAIN REMOTE DOMAIN BROWSE LISTS

Figure 6-5 shows how a WINS client located in Sydney, SYD-PC-2, is able to obtain browse list information about the remote SEA domain located in Seattle.

1. After the WINS client (SYD-PC-2) fails to locate a master browser for SEA domain using a broadcast for the [1D] name, it queries its configured WINS server (SYD-WINS1) for the <SEA> [1B] name. The [1B] query is used to learn the IP address of the domain master browser (the PDC) for the remote domain. If all PDCs are configured to use WINS, as described in the earlier section of this chapter, "How Remote Domains Register in WINS," the queried names should be present in the replicated WINS database.
2. The WINS server resolves the request for <SEA> [1B] and returns the answer to the client. The WINS response includes the IP address of SEA-PDC, the domain master browser for the remote SEA domain to the client.

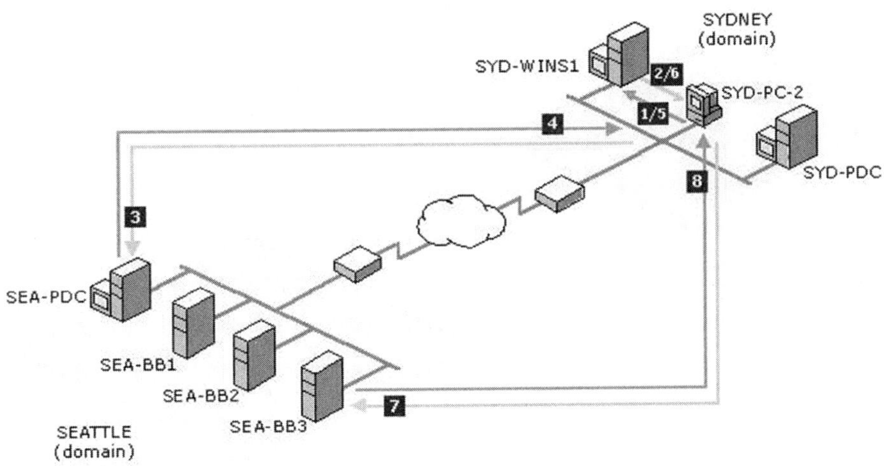

FIGURE 6–5 *Browsing remote domains in a wide area network using WINS*

3. The client then uses the IP address to send a direct request to SEA-PDC to obtain a list of backup browsers for the requested domain.
4. The remote domain master browser (SEA-PDC) responds with a list of up to three backup browsers for the requested SEA domain to the client. For this example, the list of backup browsers returned by SEA-PDC includes the computer names of SEA-BB1, SEA-BB2, and SEA-BB3.
5. The WINS client then randomly selects one of the backup browsers from the list and queries WINS again. For instance, if the client randomly selects SEA-BB3, it then attempts to have WINS resolve the name <SEA-BB3> [20] to get the IP address of this computer.
6. The WINS server resolves the request for SEA-BB3 [20] and returns the answer to the client. The WINS response includes the IP address of SEA-BB3, the selected backup browser for the remote SEA domain to the client.
7. The client then sends a request directly to the backup browser, SEA-BB3, located within the remote domain in Seattle, requesting a copy of the browse list for the SEA domain.
8. The remote backup browser then returns the browse list for the remote domain to the client.

IF WINS QUERY FOR THE REMOTE DOMAIN FAILS

In some instances, the WINS client can receive a negative name response from the WINS server during step 2 of the previous process, changing how the client attempts to request and obtain browse list information for the remote domain.

Some reasons for a negative response from a WINS server include

- The remote [1B] name queried was found to be for a workgroup, not a domain.
- The PDC for the remote domain is not a WINS client.
- The PDC for the remote domain is a WINS client, but the PDC and the browsing client are not sharing a common WINS database (replication is not occurring).

In this case, the WINS client does the following:

1. It makes a connection with its local master browser (on the same subnet as the client) and requests the name of the master browser of the desired domain or workgroup.
2. The local master browser returns the name of the master browser that advertised the domain or workgroup.
3. The client resolves the unique name of the <*master_browser*> [20] that advertised the domain or workgroup.
4. The client then makes a connection with that master browser to request a list of servers in the domain or workgroup.
5. The list of servers in the domain or workgroup is returned to the client.

Locating Domain Controllers Using NetBT

A domain is a logical grouping of network servers and other computers that share common security and user account information. In a domain-based network, Windows NT computers are configured as members of a specified domain.

When domain computers require access, such as network logon or access to a shared resource in the domain, authentication of the user in the domain security database is needed to control access. Domain controllers are computers running Windows NT Server that perform the specialized function of controlling this access. If a domain controller for the domain cannot be located, the user is denied access. For this reason, it is critical that member computers in each domain be able to locate domain controllers.

For environments with domains running Windows NT Server 4.0 and earlier versions, the process of locating domain controllers involves the resolution of the <domain> [1C] name. This name is registered for use by the domain controllers within each domain and can contain up to 25 IP addresses.

The first IP address is always for the PDC. The additional (up to 24) IP addresses are for Backup Domain Controllers (BDCs). Because this name is treated as a domain group by WINS, each member of the group (a domain controller) must renew its name individually in WINS, or its IP address entry in the list is released and can be eventually overwritten.

Each time a domain controller starts, it registers its <domain>[1Ch] name. This record can then be updated dynamically in the WINS database and replicated to other WINS servers located throughout the network.

In addition to locating domain controllers, some domain functions are reserved for handling only by the domain master browser or PDC. Because the PDC or domain master browser is a single server computer, locating it involves resolution of a special record type, the <domain> [1B] name. This record can be registered by the PDC in WINS and is used to map the domain name to a single IP address of the server computer performing in this domain role.

Note For Windows 2000 Server, domains are established with Active Directory, which uses a method based on DNS query to locate Windows 2000 domain controllers.

HOW <DOMAIN> [1B] NAMES ARE USED

Queries for <domain> [1B] names are made by,

- *Domain-based password changes.* When a user in a Windows NT domain attempts to change their password at a domain member computer, a WINS query is used to locate the configured <domain>[1B] name of the domain master browser (typically, also the PDC) to authenticate the current password and process the request to update the password in domain data.

- *Obtaining browse list information for remote domains.* The <domain>[1B] names are used to assist in obtaining browse list information for remote Windows NT domains on your network. For more information, see "Browsing WANs Using WINS" in this chapter.

HOW <DOMAIN> [1C] NAMES ARE USED

Queries for <domain> [1C] names are made by,

- *Users logging on to a domain.* When a computer that participates in a domain starts on the network, it queries for its configured <domain> [1C] name to locate a domain controller that can authenticate the logon request.
- *Domain controllers replicating the domain user account database.* A broadcast is sent from the PDC to the BDCs in the domain, instructing them to request replication of the new changes to the domain accounts database.

Since these broadcasts do not cross IP routers, directed traffic must be used to accomplish these tasks. When a broadcast is sent to the domain for these tasks, the message is also sent directly to remote domain controllers. Either WINS or entries in the lmhosts file can determine the list of computers receiving the direct message.

- *WINS clients.* These clients contact WINS and ask for the list of domain controllers in the domain. WINS replies with a list of up to 25 domain controllers. The client then sends the domain message directly to these domain controllers.
- *Non-WINS clients.* The client broadcasts the message directly to the domain and also looks for any #DOM entries in the lmhosts file with a matching domain name. If it finds a matching entry, it sends the same message directly to the computer listed.

It is recommended to add remote domain controller #DOM entries to each client. This way, if the local domain controllers are offline, the user is still able to log on. If there are no local domain controllers, a #DOM entry is required if the user wants to log on.

A Non-WINS PDC must have #DOM entries for all BDCs. All of the BDCs must have an entry for the PDC. One recommended practice here is for all domain controllers to use #DOM entries for each other, as well. This way, if a BDC is later promoted to a PDC, all of the remaining BDCs still have a #DOM mapping to the new PDC.

HOW WINS CLIENTS LOCATE DOMAIN CONTROLLERS

When a WINS-enabled client is configured to use a WINS server, it queries the WINS server for its <domain>[1C] name if it needs to locate a domain controller.

When a WINS server receives a <domain> [1C] name query from a WINS client, either a domain controller or a computer logging on to the domain, it replies with up to 25 IP addresses of domain controllers for the queried domain name.

In the reply, IP addresses for any domain controllers that registered with the queried WINS server are returned first, sorted by registration date and time. The response list is ordered so the first entry in list is the IP address that matches the mapped address for the <domain> [1B] name registered with the queried WINS server. After locally owned entries are listed in the response, any IP addresses of domain controllers for the domain that are owned by WINS servers (other than the one queried) are included.

WINS INTERACTION FOR STATIC <DOMAIN> [1C] NAMES

WINS applies the following handling for static <domain>[1C] names when they are found in database changes:

- If a static <domain>[1C] name is added at the local WINS server and a dynamic mapping for the same already exists, the listed entries from both are merged and a union of the two mappings is formed.
- When a static <domain>[1C] name is replicated and it clashes with a dynamically registered version of the <domain>[1C] name, the static mapping overwrites the dynamic mapping.
- If the <domain>[1C] name in use at a WINS server is static, the members of the list do not have to renew their IP addresses.

When used in WINS, static <domain>[1C] names can eventually cause other problems in your network. For example, if an IP address for a domain controller changes, or if a domain controller is retired or removed from the network, the static <domain>[1C] record might list stale members. This can cause failures for clients if they then query WINS and use the stale members provided there when attempting to locate domain services.

WINS Components

This section covers,

- WINS servers
- WINS clients
- WINS proxies
- The WINS database

WINS Servers

WINS consists of two main components, the WINS server and WINS clients.

The WINS server handles name registration requests from WINS clients, registers their names and IP addresses, and responds to NetBIOS name queries submitted by clients, returning the IP address of a queried name if it is listed in the server database.

Also, as Figure 6-6 shows, WINS servers can replicate the contents of their databases (which contain NetBIOS computer name mappings to IP addresses) to other WINS servers. When a WINS-enabled client computer (such as a workstation computer on either Subnet 1 or Subnet 2) starts on the network, its computer name and IP address are sent in a registration request directly to its configured primary WINS server, WINS-A. Because WINS-A is the server that registers these clients, it is said to be the *owner* for the records of the clients in WINS.

In this example, server WINS-A has clients registering with it that are both local (that is, clients on Subnet 2 where it resides) and remote (clients located across a router on Subnet 1). A second WINS server, WINS-B, is located on Subnet 3 and only owns mappings for local clients registering from its same subnet. WINS-A and WINS-B can later complete replication of their databases so that records for clients on all three subnets are in the WINS database at both servers. For more information, see "WINS Replication" in this chapter.

PRIMARY AND SECONDARY WINS SERVERS

WINS servers are used by clients in one of two ways: either as a primary or secondary WINS server.

The difference between primary and secondary WINS servers is not based in any way on the servers (which for all functional purposes are the same in

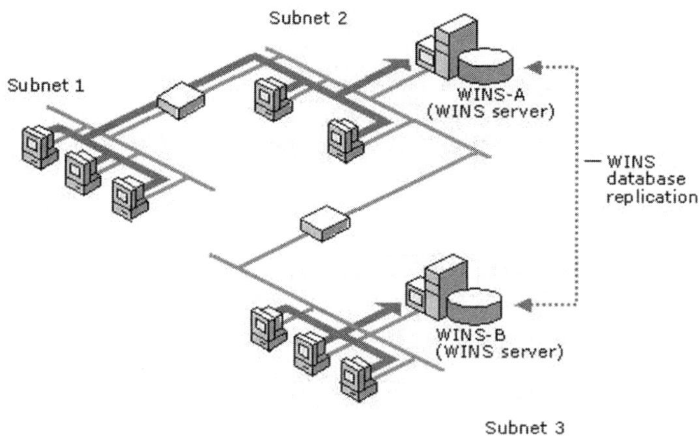

FIGURE 6–6 *WINS servers*

WINS). The difference occurs at the client, which differentiates and orders the list of WINS servers when provided more than one WINS server to use.

For most cases, the client contacts the primary WINS server for all of its NetBIOS name service functions (name registration, name renewal, name release, and name query and resolution). The only case where secondary WINS servers are ever used is when the primary WINS server is either not available on the network when the service request is made or unable to resolve a name for the client (in the case of a name query).

In the case of a failure by the primary WINS server, the client requests the same service function from its secondary WINS servers. If more than two WINS servers are configured at the client, the additional WINS servers are tried until the list is exhausted or one of the secondary WINS servers succeeds in processing and responding to the request. After a secondary WINS server is used, a client periodically tries to switch back to its primary WINS server for future service requests.

For most recent WINS clients (Windows 2000 and Windows 98), a list of up to 12 secondary WINS servers can be configured (either manually through TCP/IP properties or dynamically by a DHCP server providing a list using DHCP option type 44). This feature is useful in an environment where there are a large number of mobile clients and NetBIOS-based resources and services are used often. Because in these types of environments, the WINS database may not be consistent throughout the network of WINS servers due to convergence issues, it can be helpful for clients to be able to query more than two WINS servers.

However, this option should not be overused needlessly, as it produces a tradeoff in terms of the actual benefit for adding fault tolerance by listing additional WINS servers. The benefit of this feature must be weighed against the fact that for each additional WINS server listed, the time to process a query request fully in WINS takes incrementally longer to achieve. For example, if a WINS client tries three or more WINS servers before failing, it can substantially delay the processing of the name query before alternative methods for resolution are tried, such as searching of a local Hosts file or querying a DNS server.

WINS Clients

WINS clients attempt to register their names with a WINS server when they start or join the network. Clients thereafter query the WINS server to resolve remote names as needed.

WINS-enabled clients are computers that can be configured to make direct use of a WINS server. Most WINS clients typically have more than one NetBIOS name that they must register for use with the network. These names are used to publish various types of network service, such as the Messenger or Workstation service, that each computer can use in various ways to communicate with other computers on the network.

Microsoft supports WINS clients running on the following platforms:

- Windows 2000 Server
- Windows 2000 Professional
- Windows NT Server
- Windows NT Workstation
- Windows 98
- Windows 95
- Windows for Workgroups
- Microsoft LAN Manager
- MS-DOS clients
- OS/2 clients
- Linux and UNIX clients (with Samba installed)

WINS-enabled clients communicate with the WINS server to

- Register client names in the WINS database.
- Renew client names with the WINS database.
- Release client names from the WINS database.
- Resolve names by obtaining mappings from the WINS database for user names, NetBIOS names, DNS names, and IP addresses.

Clients that are not WINS-enabled can participate in these processes in a limited way by using WINS proxies.

WINS Proxies

A WINS proxy is a WINS client computer configured to act on behalf of other host computers that cannot directly use WINS. WINS proxies help resolve NetBIOS name queries for computers located on routed TCP/IP networks.

By default, most computers not able to use WINS use broadcasts to resolve NetBIOS name queries and register their NetBIOS names on the network. You can configure a WINS proxy to listen on behalf of these computers and to query WINS for names not resolved by broadcast.

WINS proxies are only useful or necessary on networks that include NetBIOS broadcast-only (or b-node) clients. For most networks, WINS-enabled clients are common and WINS proxies are typically not needed.

WINS proxies are WINS-enabled computers that listen for b-node NetBIOS name service functions (name registration, name release, and name query) and can respond for those names that are remote and not used on the local network. Proxies communicate directly with a WINS server to retrieve the information necessary to respond to these local broadcasts.

WINS proxies are used in the following ways:

- When a b-node client registers its name, the proxy checks the name against the WINS server database. If the name exists in the WINS database, the proxy might send a negative registration response back to the b-node client attempting to register the name.
- When a b-node client releases its name, the proxy deletes the client name from its remote name cache.

- When a b-node client sends a name query, the proxy attempts to resolve the name, using information either locally contained in its cache of remote names or through the use of information it obtains from the WINS server.

HOW WINS PROXIES RESOLVE NAMES

Figure 6-7 illustrates the use of a WINS proxy, HOST-B, for a subnet containing a b-node client, HOST-A.

In this example, the WINS proxy resolves names for the b-node computer using the following steps:

1. HOST-A broadcasts a NetBIOS name query to the local subnet.
2. HOST-B accepts the broadcast and checks its cache for the appropriate NetBIOS computer name-to-IP address mapping.
3. HOST-B processes the request. If HOST-B has a name-to-IP address mapping cached that matches the one HOST-A requested, it returns this information to HOST-A. If not, HOST-B queries a WINS server for the mapping requested by HOST-A.
4. When HOST-B receives the requested name-to-IP address mapping from its configured WINS server (in this example, WINS-A), it briefly caches this information. By default, WINS proxies cache remote name mappings that it queries in WINS for 6 minutes, but this value is configurable with a minimum value of 1 minute.
5. HOST-B can then use this mapping information to respond to subsequent NetBIOS name queries broadcast from either HOST-A or other b-node computers on the subnet.

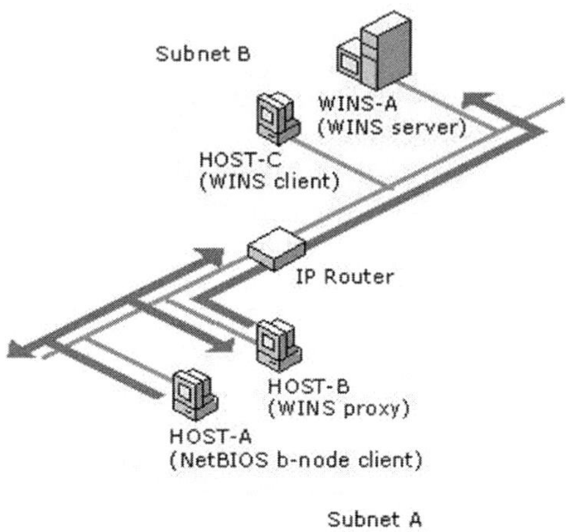

FIGURE 6-7 *Example of WINS proxy*

Because WINS servers do not respond to broadcasts, you should configure a computer as a WINS proxy on each subnet that contains non-WINS computers that must use broadcasts to resolve NetBIOS names.

When a WINS proxy is used to answer a query for a multihomed client or a group record containing a list of IP addresses, only the first listed address is returned to the b-node client.

The WINS Database

The WINS database stores and replicates the NetBIOS name-to-IP address mappings for your network. In Windows 2000 Server, the WINS database uses the performance-enhanced Exchange Server storage engine.

COMPACTING THE DATABASE

There is no built-in limit to the number of records that a WINS server can replicate or store. The size of the database depends on the number of WINS clients on the network. The WINS database changes over time as clients log on and log off the network.

However, the size of the WINS database is not directly proportional to the number of active client entries. Over time, as some WINS client entries become obsolete and are deleted, the size of the WINS database grows larger than the actual space currently in use by the database. This is because the server does not automatically reclaim the space used to store obsolete records once the space is freed and no longer in use.

Compacting the WINS database recovers the unused space. Dynamic database compaction occurs on WINS servers as an automatic background process during idle time after a database update. Compaction can also be done manually offline. Windows 2000 Server and Windows NT Server 4.0 support both dynamic and manual compaction. Windows NT Server 3.51 (or earlier) supports only manual compacting of the WINS server database.

Although dynamic compacting greatly reduces the need for offline compaction, offline compaction reclaims the space better and should be done periodically. How frequently you manually compact the WINS database depends on your network. For large, busy networks with 1,000 or more WINS clients, you should compact offline each month. Smaller networks usually require less frequent manual compaction.

Because the dynamic database compaction occurs while the database is in use, you do not need to stop the WINS server during this process. However, for manual compacting, you must stop the WINS server and take it offline.

BACKING UP THE WINS DATABASE

The WINS console provides the tools you need to maintain, view, back up, and restore the WINS server database. You should back up the database whenever you back up other files on the WINS server.

WINS DATABASE FILES

WINS uses the Jet database format for storing its data. Jet produces *J<n>.log* and other files in the *systemroot\System32\Wins* folder to increase the speed and efficiency of data storage.

Table 6.2 describes the files that are created and used by the Jet database in each WINS server.

TABLE 6.2 *Files Created and Used by the Jet Database*

File	Description
J50.log and J50#####.log	A log of all transactions done with the WINS database. This file is used by WINS to recover data if necessary. To increase speed and efficiency of data storage, the Jet database writes current transactions to log files rather than directly to the database. Therefore, the most current view of the data includes both the database and any transactions in the log files. Both of these files are used for recovery if the WINS service abruptly or unexpectedly stops. If the service stops in an unexpected manner, the log files are automatically used to re-create the correct state of the WINS database. Log files maintain a specific size; however, they can grow quickly on a busy WINS server. Inevitably, WINS writes more transactions to a log than the log size can accommodate. When a log file is filled, it is renamed, indicating that it is an older log and not in use. A new transaction log is created with the *J<n>.log* file name, where *<n>* is a decimal number, such as *J50.log*. The naming format of the previous log file is *JetXXXXX.log*, where each *X* denotes a hexadecimal number from 0 to F. Previous log files are maintained in the same folder as the current log files. The log files are processed (all entries written to the database) and deleted when a successful backup occurs or when the WINS server is shut down properly. If many *J<n>.log* files accumulate, you should schedule frequent backups to maintain the logs. After the entries are processed, you can manually delete the log files; however, this prevents a successful recovery of the database if it should be needed. For this important reason, do not manually delete or remove the log files from the system until a backup has been performed.
J50.chk	A checkpoint file that indicates the location of the last information successfully written from the transaction logs to the database. In a data recovery scenario, the checkpoint file indicates where the recovery or replaying of data should begin. This checkpoint file is updated every time data is written to the database file *(Wins.mdb)*.
Wins.mdb	The WINS server database file, which contains two tables: the IP address-to-Owner ID mapping table and the Name-to-IP address mapping table.
Winstmp.mdb	A temporary file that is created by the WINS server service. This file functions as a swap file during index maintenance operations and can remain in the *systemroot\System32\Wins* directory after a system failure.
Res#.log	These are reserved log files, which function in emergencies when the server runs out of disk space. If a server attempts to create another transaction log file and there is insufficient disk space, the server flushes any outstanding transactions into these reserved log files. The service then shuts down and logs an event to Event Viewer.

Important The J50.log, J50#####.log, Wins.mdb, Winstmp.mdb, and Res#.log files should not be removed or altered.

WINS Replication

This section covers,

- Replication overview
- Pull partners
- Push partners

Replication Overview

Where multiple WINS servers are used on your network, they can be configured to replicate records in their databases to other servers. This process is shown in Figure 6-8. Two WINS servers, WINS-A and WINS-B, are configured to fully replicate their records with each other.

By using replication between these WINS servers, a consistent set of WINS information is maintained and distributed throughout the network. For example, in Figure 6-8, a WINS client (HOST-1) on Subnet 1 registers its name with its primary WINS server, WINS-A. Another WINS client (HOST-2) on Subnet 3

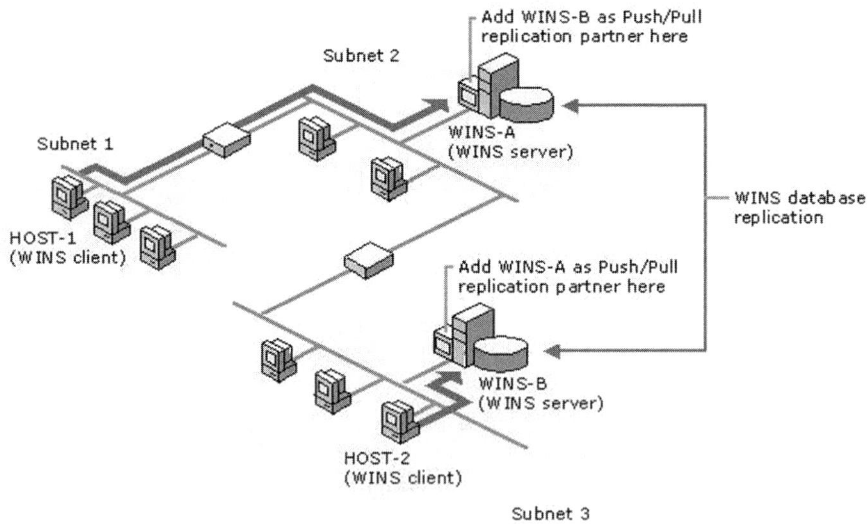

FIGURE 6–8 *WINS replication overview*

registers its name with its primary WINS server, WINS-B. If either of these hosts later attempts to locate the other host using WINS—for example, HOST-1 queries to find an IP address for HOST-2—replication between the WINS servers (WINS-A and WINS-B) makes resolving this query possible.

For replication to work, each WINS server must be configured with at least one other WINS server as its replication partner. This ensures that a name registered with one WINS server is eventually replicated to all other WINS servers in the network. A replication partner can be added and configured as either a pull partner or a push partner, or to use both types of replication as a push/pull partner. The push/pull partner type is the default configuration and is the type recommended for use in most cases.

When WINS servers replicate, a latency period exists before a client name-to-address mapping from any given server is propagated to all other WINS servers in the network. This latency is known as the *convergence time* for the entire WINS system. For example, a name release request by a client will not propagate as fast as a name registration request. This is intended by design because it is common for client names to be released and then reused with the same mapping as computers are restarted or periodically shut down. Replicating each of these name releases would unnecessarily increase the network load of replication.

Also, when a WINS client computer is shut down improperly, as in the case of an unexpected power outage, the registered names of the computer are not released as they normally would be by sending a name release request to the WINS server. Therefore, the presence of a name-to-address record in the WINS database does not necessarily mean that a client computer is still using the name or its associated IP address. It only means that at some recent time in the past, a computer by the registered name claimed the mapped IP address for its use.

Note The primary and secondary WINS servers of any client should typically have a push and pull relationship with each other. However, a direct push/pull configuration is not required as long as similar results can be indirectly achieved during a normal replication cycle.

WINS replication is always incremental, meaning that only changes in the database, not the entire database, are replicated each time replication occurs.

Pull Partners

A pull partner is a WINS server that pulls or requests replication of updated WINS database entries from other WINS servers (those configured to use it as a push partner) at a configured interval. Requesting entries with a higher version ID than the last entry received from its configured partner accomplishes this.

You can enable WINS to pull (request) a replication with its configured partners when one of the following events occurs:

- When the WINS server starts.
- When a set amount of time has elapsed.

The amount of time between pull replications is indicated in the **Replication interval**, which can be specified either globally for all pull partners or individually for specific partners. When the time has elapsed for each interval, WINS sends a pull replication trigger to its pull partners. The partners can then respond with incremental changes, if any have been made since the last time replication occurred.

To configure which of these options WINS uses, you need to configure pull parameters, either the default parameters that the server uses for all pull partners or the parameters in effect for a specific partner. For information about modify pull partner properties, see Chapter 7.

Additionally, you have the administrative option of manually sending a pull replication trigger to another pull partner of the selected WINS server. For information about sending a replication trigger to a selected partner, see Chapter 7.

HOW WINS DETERMINES WHICH ENTRIES TO PULL REPLICATE

Because push-based replication uses notification, it does not transfer any records until the notified partner has returned a subsequent pull trigger. For this reason, pull replication can be viewed as the single process used to replicate WINS data between servers.

All WINS servers maintain an internal mapping table—an owner-version mapping table—which is used to complete the replication process. This table is built dynamically at startup by the server and is held in memory.

The owner-version mapping table contains the following:

1. An owner ID that maps to the IP address for each WINS server that appears in the database as an owner for records currently stored there. For practical purposes, WINS automatically assigns and increments an integer value for the owner ID and then maps that value to a corresponding server IP address. However, when you examine this information in the WINS console, only the owner IP address is actually displayed.
2. When replication occurs with another WINS server, the version ID field for all records currently in the database is scanned for the highest version ID associated with each identified distinct owner.

A sample Owner/Version ID table for WINS-A when it is started might look like Table 6.3, if viewed using **View Records** in the WINS console.

The owner-version mappings are used by WINS to determine the state of the database at any point in time before or after replication. The following section provides more detailed information about how WINS manages replication.

TABLE 6.3 *Sample Owner/Version ID Table*

Owner ID (not displayed)	Owner	Name	Highest ID
(0)	192.168.1.5	WINS-A	1F
(1)	192.168.2.5	WINS-H	125
(2)	192.168.3.5	WINS-B	31
(3)	192.168.4.5	WINS-C	100
(4)	192.168.5.5	WINS-D	200

HOW PULL REPLICATION WORKS

Figure 6-9 demonstrates how four WINS servers—WINS-A, WINS-B, WINS-C, and WINS-D—are all configured to be spokes (push/pull partners) of a central hub server, WINS-H.

Before replication with WINS-H, the owner-version mapping table at WINS-A contains a set of highest version IDs for all owners in its database. For the purpose of this example, assume these values are the same as those shown in the sample table provided in the previous section.

In reality, pull replication might be occurring dynamically between all four spokes at various times with WINS-H, so this table might not remain static for long. For a basic understanding of the details of an individual pull

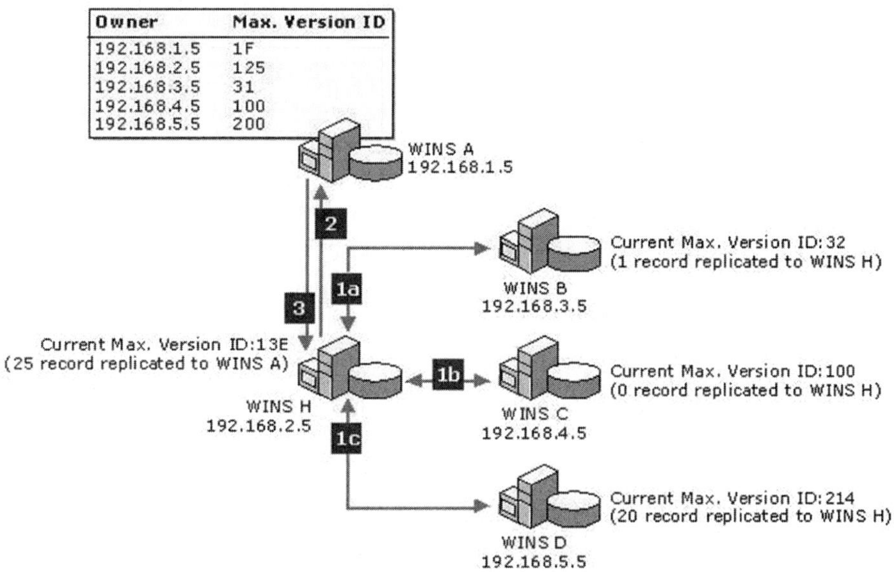

FIGURE 6–9 *How pull replication works*

replication cycle, however, it is easier to focus on what might happen when just one of the spokes—for example, WINS-A—replicates its database with WINS-H.

In Figure 6-9, the following changes in the replicated WINS network occur:

1. The three other spokes (WINS-B, WINS-C and WINS-D) each replicate with WINS-H, based on the highest version ID.
   a. WINS-B has added or updated one new record since its last replication cycle, which WINS-H replicates and adds to its database.
   b. WINS-C has the same version ID and does not have any new records to be replicated at WINS-H.
   c. WINS-D has updated a total of 20 records since its last replication cycle, which WINS-H replicates and adds to its database.
2. WINS-H sends a trigger to WINS-A initiating replication. The updated owner-version mapping table information is provided as part of the trigger.
3. WINS-A responds by pulling entries from WINS-H. WINS-A determines which owner servers to pull from based on the difference between its locally held highest version ID for each owner and the corresponding updated highest version IDs provided by WINS-H. WINS-A specifies the range of records to be pulled and replicated by comparing versions.

In the case where another pull replication to the same partner is already queued, WINS sees the subsequent request as further down in the queue and discards it in favor of keeping the one with a higher placement in the service process queue.

In addition to modifying settings for pull replication properties, WINS also provides the option to enable the use of persistent connections with either a specified pull partner or all pull partners of a WINS server.

For more information, see “Persistent Connections” in this chapter. For information about enabling the use of persistent connections with a partner server, see Chapter 7.

Push Partners

A push partner is a WINS server that pushes or notifies other WINS servers (those configured to use it as a pull partner) of the need to replicate their database entries at a configured interval. To configure a WINS server to use push replication, you can choose from several WINS console configurable options. For example, you can enable WINS to push notify configured partners when one of the following events occurs:

- When the WINS server starts.
- Whenever an IP address change occurs for a name-to-address mapping in the WINS server database.

- When a value for **Number of changes in version ID before replication** is specified—either globally for all push partners or individually for specific push partners. WINS can use this value as a threshold for determining how many incremental changes must be made to the database before it starts push replication to its partners.

To configure any of these options for WINS use, you need to configure push parameters, either the default parameters that the server uses for all push partners or the parameters in effect for a specific partner. For information about modifying push partner properties, see Chapter 7.

Additionally, you can manually start push replication to other WINS servers. For information about sending a replication trigger to a selected partner or to any specified WINS server, see Chapter 7.

HOW UPDATES AND WINS SETTINGS AFFECT PUSH REPLICATION

By default, WINS does not perform push replication unless other related settings are also configured on the **Push Replication** tab in **Replication Partners Properties**. For example, WINS uses an *update count* value of 0. This is set using **Number of changes in version ID before replication**.

Push replication only occurs at configured replication intervals, unless other push replication settings are configured as well, such as,

- For **Start push replication**, selected events such as the **At service startup** or the **When address changes** check boxes are selected.
- The **Use persistent connections for push replication partners** check box is selected, which can affect how the value of **Number of changes in version ID before replication** is handled by WINS.

By default, persistent connections are not used and replication with partners does not occur except at configured intervals. This default can be changed, but a specified minimum number of update changes to WINS must be set first. Without the use of persistent connections, a minimum value of 20 for **Number of changes in version ID before replication** is required.

With persistent connections enabled for push replication, the default value of 0 causes the local WINS server to send a push trigger and notify its push partners each time an update occurs. An update is defined as an incremental increase to the highest version ID in the local WINS database for records the server owns. This can occur when a new name record is registered and added locally or if an IP address change occurs for an existing record.

With persistent connections, you can reduce the update frequency for push notifications by specifying a nonzero value instead. If a value greater than zero is used, WINS only starts push replication when the highest ID for records it owns has increased an equal number of times.

For example, the current highest version ID for an example server, WINS-A, is currently 1C4 (which is 452 in converted decimal notation). WINS-A also has its **Number of changes in version ID before replication** set to 2 for either all or some of its push partners.

Suppose that the following four distinct sets of database changes are then made to the WINS server database at WINS-A:

1. HOST-A refreshes its previously registered name record, though it does not change its IP address.
2. HOST-B registers a name record, creating a new dynamic name-to-address mapping to the database.
3. HOST-C registers a previously released name record and, in the process, reports an updated change of IP address for this record.
4. A pull replication occurs at a specified interval with another WINS server.

Once these changes are entered into the database, the newly revised highest version ID for WINS-A is 1C6 (454 decimal). This is because the changes made to WINS server data that were caused by items 2 and 3 (either a client registering a new mapping or updating the IP address used with a previous mapping) each caused the version ID at that server to increment.

For items 1 and 4 in the previous list of changes, the highest version ID at the WINS server does not increase.

After these changes occur, any or all partners of WINS-A that are configured with a **Number of changes in version ID before replication** of 2 would then be push notified by WINS sending a replication trigger to those servers.

HOW PUSH WITH PROPAGATION WORKS

Figure 6-10 shows an example of the use of push partners in a replicated WINS network of four servers. In this example, two of the servers—WINS-A and WINS-B—are located at regional data center locations.

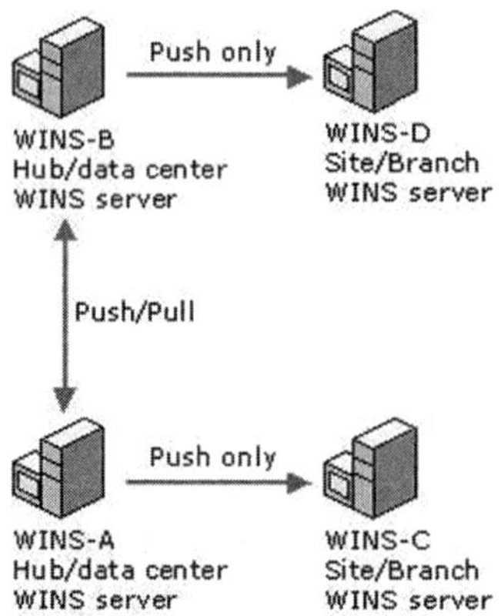

FIGURE 6–10 *WINS push with propagation in a push replication design*

These servers are both central hub servers in a multiple hub-and-spoke enterprise WINS replication design. In order to ensure frequent convergence of names data between the separate regional hubs, both WINS-A and WINS-B maintain a full push/pull relationship with each other.

WINS-C and WINS-D are site or branch-level spoke servers used on the same replicated WINS network. Respectively, they are both configured as push-only partners of WINS-A and WINS-B.

If updates occur at one hub WINS-A, it is unlikely a remote spoke operating as a push-only partner (WINS-D) would receive those updates in a timely or predictable manner. Although replication between the hubs might occur frequently enough to pose no significant issues, setting the update count to an arbitrarily high value at WINS-B might delay convergence at WINS-D until more than one replication cycle has been completed.

To administratively correct this delay, you can initiate a push replication trigger at WINS-A to be sent to WINS-B, which would queue a replication immediately between the hubs. In doing so, if you also chose the **Propagate to all partners** when manually starting push replication, then WINS-B would propagate the push replication trigger to WINS-D. This would result in an early notification to WINS-D of the need to use a pull replication to WINS-B, obtaining any interim updates from WINS-A.

In addition to modifying settings for push replication properties, WINS also provides you the option to enable the use of persistent connections with either a specified push partner or all push partners of a WINS server.

For more information, see "Persistent connections" in this chapter. For information about enabling the use of persistent connections with a partner server, see Chapter 7.

WINS Resolution

This section covers,

- Resolution overview
- Registering names
- Releasing names
- Renewing names
- Resolving names

Resolution Overview

WINS is used to resolve NetBIOS names, but in order for name resolution to be effective, clients need to be able to dynamically add, remove, or update their names in WINS. The following sections provide a functional description of each of these processes, specifically how names are registered, renewed, released, and resolved for clients on a WINS-based network.

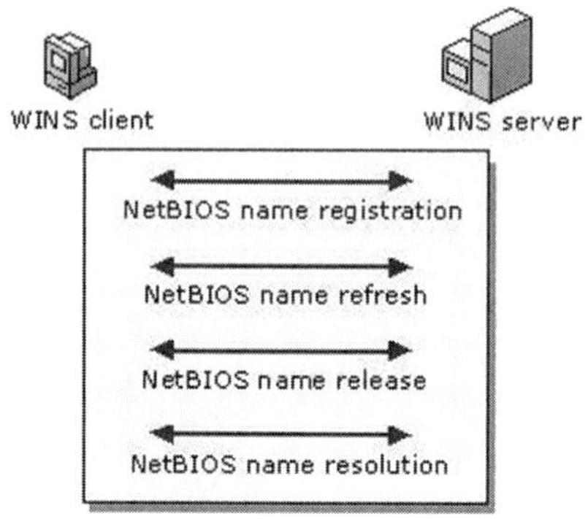

FIGURE 6–11 *WINS resolution overview*

This process of WINS client/server communications is outlined in Figure 6-11.

In a WINS system, all names are registered with a WINS server. The names are stored in a database on the WINS server, which answers requests for name-to-IP address resolution based on the entries in this database.

Redundancy and load balancing are maintained with more than one WINS server in the network. Periodically, servers replicate their database entries among one another in order to maintain a consistent view of the NetBIOS namespace.

Each name has an entry in the database. It is owned by the WINS server it registered with and is a replica on all other WINS servers. Each entry has a state associated with it—the entry can be in the active, released, or extinct (also known as tombstone) state. Entries are also assigned a version ID. This number is used in the replication process and is discussed in more detail in "WINS Replication" in this chapter. For more information, see "Push Partners," also in this chapter.

WINS also allows the registration of static names. This enables the administrator to register names for servers running operating systems that are not capable of dynamic name registration. WINS distinguishes between dynamic and static entries. Static names are treated somewhat differently than dynamic names. For information about using static mappings, see Chapter 7.

Registering Names

Name registration is a WINS client requesting the use of a NetBIOS name on the network. The request may be for a unique (exclusive) or a group (shared) name. NetBIOS applications can also register one or more names.

As illustrated in Figure 6-12, a WINS client (HOST-C) sends a Name Registration Request directly to its configured WINS server, WINS-A.

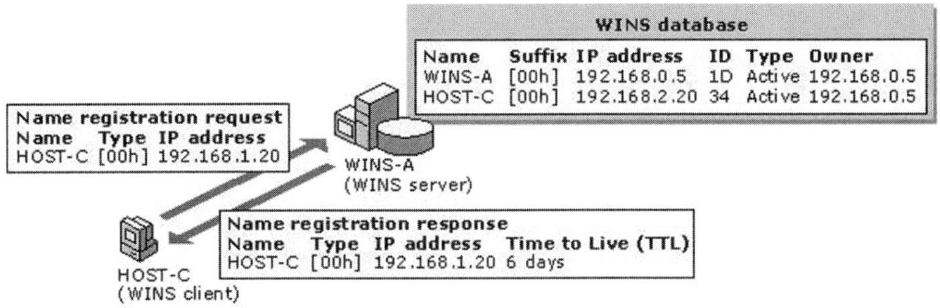

FIGURE 6–12 *How clients register with WINS*

WINS-A can accept or reject the name registration request by issuing either a positive or negative name registration response to HOST-C. The action taken by WINS-A depends on several factors:

- Whether the name already exists in the server database at WINS-A.
- If a record of the name exists, the state in the server database of the record at WINS-A might make a difference. Also, if the recorded IP address for the name is the same or different from the IP address of the requesting client, HOST-C.
- Whether the request is for a unique or group name entry.

If the name does not exist in the database, it is accepted as a new registration and the following steps occur:

1. The name for HOST-C is entered with a new version ID, given a time stamp, and marked with the owner ID of the WINS server. The time stamp is calculated based on adding the value of the **Renew interval** (which by default is 6 days) set on the WINS server to the current date and time of the server.
2. A positive registration response is sent back to HOST-C with a Time-to-Live (TTL) value equal to the time stamp recorded for the name at WINS-A.

NAME REGISTERED FOR SAME IP ADDRESS

If the name HOST-C is already entered in the database with the same IP address as that being requested, the action taken depends on the state and ownership of the existing name.

1. If the entry is marked as *active* and the entry is owned by the server (WINS-A), the server updates the time stamp for the record and returns a positive response back to the client.
2. If the entry is marked as being either *released* or *tombstoned*, or if another WINS server owns the entry, the registration is treated as a new registration. Time stamp, version ID, and ownership are all updated and a positive response is returned.

NAME REGISTERED FOR DIFFERENT IP ADDRESS

In the case where the name exists in the WINS database but with a different IP address than that being requested, the WINS server is expected to avoid duplicate names. If the database entry is in the released or tombstone state, the WINS server is free to assign that name.

If, however, the entry is in the active state, the node holding the name is challenged to determine if it still exists on the network. In this case, the WINS server (WINS-A) could perform a challenge of the name and do the following:

1. WINS-A sends a Wait for Acknowledgment (WACK) response to the requesting client (HOST-C), specifying a time in the TTL field that the client should be prepared to wait for a response.
2. WINS-A then issues a name query request to the node currently registered for this name in the server database.
3. If the node still exists, it sends a positive response back to WINS-A.
4. WINS-A, in turn, sends a negative name registration response back to the requesting client (HOST-C), rejecting the name registration.
5. If a positive response is not received back from the first challenge query made by WINS-A, two subsequent name query requests are made. After three attempts with no response, the challenge process is complete and a positive registration response is returned to the requesting client (HOST-C) and the name updated in the server database for the new client registration.

Unlike WINS-enabled clients, which can directly contact a WINS server, non-WINS clients (such as NetBT b-node clients) must register and then continuously defend their names by sending and replying to broadcast name queries within the local network.

NetBIOS names are registered with WINS and are normally released when the computer is properly shutdown. If the computer was not properly shutdown, or the computer was not able to contact a WINS server during shutdown, the nbtstat command can be used to refresh in WINS the local names for this computer. This can be useful for mobile or portable computers that are moved between different locations on a network.

For information about verifying WINS registration of client NetBIOS names, see Chapter 7.

Releasing Names

Name release occurs when a WINS client computer finishes using a particular name, when a proper shutdown occurs. In releasing its name, a WINS client notifies its WINS server (or potentially other computers on the network) that it is no longer using its registered name.

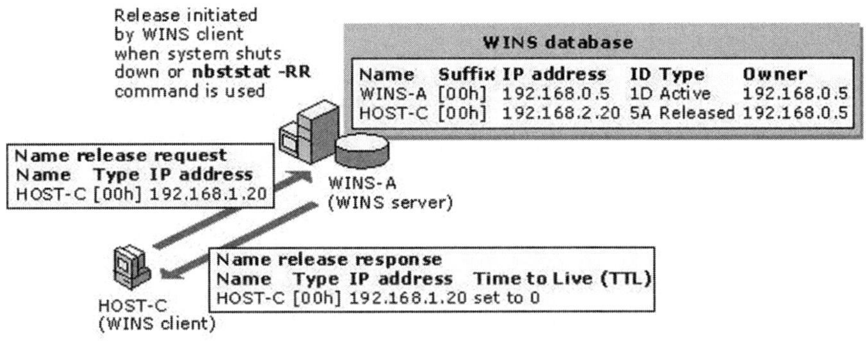

FIGURE 6–13 *How clients release names in WINS*

As shown in Figure 6-13, when a WINS-enabled client (HOST-C) releases its name, the following steps occur:

1. The computer named HOST-C either shuts down properly or a user enters the **nbtstat -RR** command, initiating a name release request to be sent to the WINS server, WINS-A.
2. WINS-A marks the related database entry for HOST-C as *released*. If the entry remains released for a period of time, WINS-A marks the entry as *tombstoned*, updates the version ID for the entry, and notifies other WINS servers of the change.
3. WINS-A returns a release confirmation message to the WINS client, HOST-C.

If a name entry is marked as released, the WINS server can immediately update or revise a marked name entry when a new registration request arrives from a WINS client with the same name but with a different IP address. This is possible because the WINS database shows that the WINS client at the old IP address is no longer using that name. For example, this can happen when a DHCP-enabled laptop changes subnets.

Name release is most often used to simplify WINS registration for clients that shut down and restart on the network. If a computer released its name during a normal shutdown, the WINS server does not challenge the name when the computer reconnects. If a proper shutdown did not occur, the name registration with a new IP address causes the WINS server to challenge the previous registration. When the challenge fails (because the client computer is no longer using the old IP address), the registration succeeds.

In some cases, a client is not able to release its name by contacting the WINS server, so broadcasts must be used to release a name. This can happen when a WINS-enabled client shuts down without receiving confirmation of its name release by the WINS server.

Renewing Names

Periodic name renewal is required for WINS client computers to renew their NetBIOS name registrations with the WINS server. The WINS server treats name renewal requests similarly to new name registrations.

When a client computer first registers with a WINS server, the WINS server returns a message with a TTL value that indicates when the client registration expires or needs to be renewed. If renewal does not occur by that time, the name registration expires on the WINS server and the name entry is eventually removed from the WINS database. However, static WINS name entries do not expire, and therefore do not need to be renewed in the WINS server database. For information about using static mappings, see Chapter 7.

The default **Renew interval** for entries in the WINS database is six days. Renewal occurs every three days for most WINS clients because WINS clients attempt to renew their registrations when 50 percent of the TTL value has elapsed.

A name must be refreshed before this interval ends, or it will be released. Names are refreshed by sending a name refresh request to the WINS server, as shown in Figure 6-14.

It is the responsibility of the client (HOST-C) to refresh its name before the Renew interval expires. If the WINS server, WINS-A, does not respond to the refresh request, the client, HOST-C, can increase the rate at which it attempts to refresh its name.

Important In most cases, the default value is the appropriate Renew interval. You should always set the same Renew interval for all server replication partners whenever multiple WINS servers are used.

Incorrectly adjusting the Renew interval can adversely affect system and network performance.

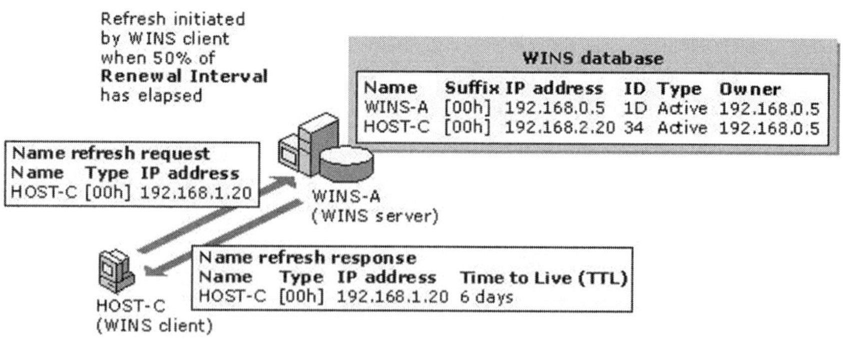

FIGURE 6–14 *How clients refresh names in WINS*

Resolving Names

Name resolution for WINS clients is an extension of the same name resolution process used by all Microsoft NetBT clients to resolve NetBIOS name queries on your network. The actual method of name resolution is transparent to the user.

For Windows 2000, WINS clients use the following sequential flow of options for resolving a name once the query has been made by using net use or a similar NetBIOS-based application.

1. Determine if the name is longer than 15 characters or if it contains periods (.). If so, query DNS for the name.
2. Determine if the name is stored in the remote name cache at the client.
3. Contact and try configured WINS servers to attempt to resolve the name using WINS.
4. Use local IP broadcasts to the subnet.
5. Check an lmhosts file if **Enable LMHOSTS Lookup** is enabled in the **Internet Protocol (TCP/IP)** properties for the connection.
6. Check a Hosts file.
7. Query a DNS server.

WINS Features

This section covers,

- Persistent connections
- Burst handling
- Deleting and tombstoning records
- Blocking replication partners

Persistent Connections

For Windows 2000 Server, WINS introduces persistent connections between WINS server replication partners. This feature is helpful because typically WINS servers disconnect from their replication partners each time replication is completed. In many cases, where WINS servers are interconnected through high speed LAN links, it is preferable to keep connections open instead of closing them after replication is completed.

For earlier versions of WINS, servers had to establish new WINS-server connections each time replication was performed. Each connection required a modest number of processor cycles. For efficiency, network managers often configured systems to accumulate a larger number of changes before connecting for replication. These reconnections sometimes caused delays (perhaps as long as several minutes) in the replication process, which meant that inconsistencies in server data commonly existed when WINS was updated.

Persistent connections increase the speed of replication because a server can immediately send records to its partners without incurring the cost of establishing temporary connections each time. Every record is immediately updated across the network upon registration in WINS, making replication more consistent. The bandwidth used by persistent connections is minimal because the connection is usually idle.

Burst Handling

WINS servers can now support handling of high-volume *(burst)* server loads. Bursts occur when a large number of WINS clients actively and simultaneously try to register their local names in WINS, such as when a power failure occurs. When power is later restored, many users start and register their names simultaneously on the network, which creates high levels of WINS traffic. With burst-mode support, a WINS server can respond positively to these client requests, even before it processes and physically enters those updates in the WINS server database.

HOW BURST HANDLING WORKS

Burst mode uses a burst-queue size as a threshold value. This value determines how many name registration and name refresh requests sent by WINS clients are processed normally before burst-mode handling is started. By default, the value is 500. A WINS server initiates burst handling whenever the number of WINS client registration requests exceeds the burst queue size.

In burst handling, the WINS server immediately answers additional client requests with a positive response. The response also includes a varied TTL to clients, which helps regulate the client registration load and distribute processing of the requests over time. This slows the refresh and retry rate for new WINS clients and regulates the burst of WINS client traffic.

For example, if the burst queue size is 500 entries, and more than 500 requests are active, the WINS server replies immediately to the next 100 WINS client registration requests by sending early success responses with a starting TTL value of 5 minutes. For each additional round of 100 client requests, 5 minutes more are added to the TTL, up to a maximum of 50 minutes. If WINS client traffic still arrives at burst levels, the next round of 100 client requests are answered with the initial TTL value of 5 minutes, and the entire process for incrementing the response TTL is repeated.

This behavior continues until the WINS server reaches its maximum intake level of 25,000 name registration and refresh queries. At this point, the WINS server begins dropping queries.

Using the WINS console, you can choose to configure the level of burst handling used by the server, which modifies the size of the burst queue to accommodate either a low, medium, or large burst situation.

Note Any WINS server running either Windows 2000 Server or Windows NT Server 4.0 (with Service Pack 3 or later installed) can use burst handling.

Deleting and Tombstoning Records

WINS now provides improved database management through support for the following deletion operations:

- Simple deletion, for deleting WINS database records stored on a single server database.
- Tombstoned deletion, for deleting WINS database records replicated to databases on other WINS servers.
- Multiple-group selection of displayed database records, for either simple or tombstoned deletion.

The WINS console also provides a simple and convenient utility for administratively removing records of any type, regardless of whether they are statically or dynamically added. In previous releases of Windows NT Server, other available WINS management tools could only administratively delete entries (such as static mappings) that were added in the same way.

HOW SIMPLE DELETION WORKS

Simple deletion removes the records that are selected in the WINS console only from the local WINS server you are currently managing. If the WINS records deleted in this way exist in WINS data replicated to other WINS servers on your network, these additional records are not fully removed. Also, records that are simply deleted on only one server can reappear after replication between the WINS server where simple deletion was used and any of its replication partners.

HOW TOMBSTONING WORKS

Tombstoning marks the selected records as *tombstoned,* that is, marked locally as *extinct* and immediately released from active use by the local WINS server. This method allows the tombstoned records to remain present in the server database for purposes of subsequent replication of these records to other servers.

When the tombstoned records are replicated, the tombstone status is updated and applied by other WINS servers that store replicated copies of these records. Each replicating WINS server then updates and tombstones these records. When all WINS servers complete replication of these records and a specified length of time (determined by the Verification Interval for each WINS server) elapses, then the records are automatically removed from WINS.

In most cases, WINS records should be tombstoned at the WINS server that originally owned them, to prevent deleted records from reappearing in WINS after subsequent replication with other servers.

The owner of a given WINS server record is typically the first server contacted by the WINS client during the registration process and the server first actually used to register the local names of the client in WINS. In most cases, the WINS server that owns a client name record in WINS corresponds to the primary WINS server configured on the WINS client computer. If the configured primary WINS server is not available during client registration, a configured secondary WINS server can perform the actual registration of the client name and become the owner.

TOMBSTONED DELETION IN REPLICATED WINS • Where tombstoned deletion is used at an owner WINS server in a replicated WINS network, the following sequence of events occurs to effect full removal of the selected records from all WINS servers that replicate the selected records.

1. The owner WINS server marks and changes the status of the selected WINS records in its local WINS server database from active to tombstoned. WINS then treats the records as inactive and released from use. When these records are tombstoned locally, the owner WINS server does not respond to or resolve NetBIOS name queries for these names unless the WINS client registers the records again.
2. The owner WINS server replicates the selected records as tombstoned at subsequent replication cycles. The records are not forcibly and immediately removed from WINS, but are flagged, or marked, for eventual deletion. The exact replication cycle interval is configured by the server Intervals properties, which you set in the WINS console. Records are not removed from WINS data until the time specified in the Extinction Interval has elapsed. This allows other WINS servers to be notified that these records are no longer in use, update their replicated mappings for these records, and further replicate this updated WINS data to other servers.
3. Records become extinct on all replicated WINS servers and are eventually removed physically from all WINS servers. After all WINS servers that participate in replication complete a full replication cycle and arrive at a consistent state, the tombstoned records expire and are removed from the WINS database of each server at the next database scavenging operation. After scavenging occurs on all servers, the records no longer appear in the WINS console and are no longer physically stored in the WINS database.

Even if records are manually tombstoned (or otherwise marked as released by WINS), released records remain in the WINS database for some time before being completely removed during subsequent scavenging operations. Typically, the period before records extinction is the sum of the following settings:

- Extinction interval
- Extinction time-out
- Verification interval

You can view and configure these settings on the **Intervals** tab, located in the **WINS <*Server name*> Properties** dialog box. By default, the sum of these settings is 36 days.

Blocking Replication Partners

After a WINS server is removed from a network, records it owns often continue to be distributed to other servers in a replicated WINS environment. In some cases, WINS either does not delete entries owned by servers no longer active on the network or, by default, preserves stale mappings for an extended period of time. The reasons for this can include:

- Static mappings originally made at the inactive WINS server replicate indefinitely among the other active WINS servers in the network, unless manually deleted or tombstoned. By default, WINS servers preserve static name-to-address mappings whenever such mappings are challenged. This can occur when a WINS client attempts to register or update a static mapping with a dynamic-type mapping of the same name. This behavior, however, can be modified. For information about using static mappings, see Chapter 7.
- Dynamic mappings originally registered at the inactive WINS server are not immediately removed from the WINS database. In the case of dynamic entries, WINS must check with an owner server before entries are deleted. If a WINS server is no longer in use, other WINS servers conservatively retain records they cannot verify as expired on an owner server. For example, even if an owner is deleted in the WINS console for a particular server, these unwanted or stale names can continue to be replicated throughout the WINS network from other servers storing replica entries of these names.

  WINS processes removal of dynamic-type records according to the **Intervals** tab settings for **WINS Server Properties**, which can be configured at each server. In most default cases, a typical extinction period of 36 days passes before a record is fully removed from the database through the scavenging process.

For Windows 2000 Server, the Block records for these owners feature provides a way to block further replication of entries owned by inactive servers. It allows you to specify the IP addresses of inactive WINS servers that own records you want to assure are removed from WINS in a timely manner.

Because it can prevent any further replication of unwanted or stale mappings between active WINS servers remaining on the network, this feature is most useful when you need to remove WINS servers from your network.

BLOCKING RECORDS OWNED BY A WINS SERVER

Figure 6-15 shows a typical WINS replication design based on the recommended hub-and-spoke WINS replication design model.

In the example, replicated WINS network, WINS-D, is an inactive spoke server in the process of being removed from the network. Because WINS-A is the hub in this design, it must be configured to block records for WINS-D in order to prevent replica entries for WINS-D that are present at other spokes from replicating back to WINS-A and reappearing throughout the network.

When WINS-D server is given blocked partner status, it can be deleted as an owner in the WINS console at WINS-A, and its entries will not be replicated back from other spoke servers, such as WINS-B, WINS-C, or WINS-E. For information about deleting an owner from the WINS database, see Chapter 7.

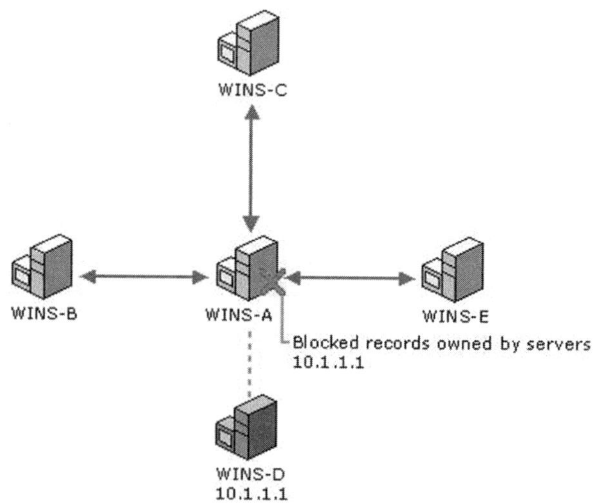

FIGURE 6–15 *Blocking WINS replication in a hub-and-spoke configuration*

Note

If you are not using a hub-and-spoke WINS replication model, it might be necessary to enforce blocking at other servers in your network. If this is the case, you might need to list the blocked partner by blocking records owned by servers or for WINS running on earlier versions, and add and configure the PersonaNonGrata registry parameter at each server. These steps can help achieve the intended results of full replication for records owned by the partner to other WINS servers in the network.

After adding IP addresses to the list of blocked partners at a WINS server, it is recommended to stop and restart WINS to ensure that the change is in effect the next time replication at that WINS server occurs. For information about starting and stopping a WINS server, see Chapter 7.

SEVEN

Using WINS

Planning WINS Networks

Before you install WINS servers on your network, plan the following tasks:

1. *Determine the number of WINS servers that you need.* One WINS server can handle NetBIOS name resolution requests for a large number of computers. However, consider the location of routers on your network and the distribution of clients in each subnet when you decide how many WINS servers are actually required. For more information, see the next section, "Planning How Many WINS Servers to Use."
2. *Plan the replication partnerships.* Determine whether to configure WINS servers as either pull or push partners, and set partner preferences for each server. For more information, see "Configuring WINS Replication" in this chapter.
3. *Assess the impact of WINS communication traffic on slower links.* Although WINS is designed to help reduce broadcast traffic within local subnets, it does create some traffic between servers and clients. This can be particularly important if you use WINS on routed TCP/IP networks.

   Also consider the effects of slower speed links (such as those typically used for wide area networks) on both replication traffic between WINS servers and NetBIOS registration and renewal traffic required for WINS clients. For more information, see "Planning for Network Performance" in this chapter.
4. *Assess the level of fault tolerance within your network for WINS.* Consider how shutting down a WINS server (even temporarily) affects your network. Use additional WINS servers for disaster recovery, backup, and

redundancy. For more information on planning a fault-tolerant WINS installation, see "Planning for Fault Tolerance" in this chapter.

5. *Test and revise your planned WINS installation.* By testing the performance of your network installation of WINS, you can better identify potential problems before they occur. Use WINS server performance counters, which are available through the use of System Monitor. For information about WINS performance monitoring, see Appendix C, "WINS Resources and Troubleshooting."

Planning How Many WINS Servers to Use

On a smaller network, a single WINS server can adequately service up to 10,000 clients for NetBIOS name resolution requests. To provide additional fault tolerance, you can configure a second computer running Windows 2000 Server as a secondary (or backup) WINS server for clients. If you use only two WINS servers, you can easily set them up as replication partners of each other. For simple replication between two servers, one server should be set as a pull partner and the other as a push partner. Replication can be either manual or automatic, which you can configure by selecting the **Enable automatic partner configuration** check box on the **Advanced** tab of the **Replication Partner Properties** dialog box.

A larger network sometimes requires more WINS servers for several reasons including, most importantly, the number of client connections per server. The number of users that each WINS server can support varies with usage patterns, data storage, and the processing capabilities of the WINS server computer. Some enterprise network environments require more robust hardware to handle WINS activity, so you might benefit from upgrading the server computer.

When planning your servers, remember that each WINS server can simultaneously handle hundreds of registrations and queries per second. The WINS development and testing team compiled the following statistics as a profile of WINS performance during preliminary testing of Windows 2000 Server:

- Average registrations/second 300
- Average queries/second 350

These measurements were based on a server computer running WINS with no other additional services running and installed on currently available hardware. The list of specific hardware used includes a single Intel Pentium II 350 MHz processor, 128 MB of RAM, and a standard IDE hard drive, which was used to store the WINS database. As a point of reference, WINS records data exchanged between servers and clients is typically small. On average, WINS records are about 40 bytes in size.

A conservative recommendation for large networks is to install one WINS server and a backup server for every 10,000 computers on the network. This reflects the previously suggested baseline performance and provides for large-scale power outages that could cause many WINS computers to restart simultaneously. Capacity is dependent upon server and network resources. Processor speed, available RAM, database storage space, and network resources can have a significant impact.

Two factors can enhance WINS server performance,

- Using two installed processors on the computer running WINS. This can increase performance by almost 25 percent.
- Using a dedicated high-performance disk drive, separate from the system drive, for WINS replication.

After you establish WINS servers on your intranet, you can adjust the **Renew interval**, which is the time between a WINS client name registration and name renewal. By using this setting to reduce the numbers of registrations, you can tune server response time. The **Renew interval** is set in the **WINS server properties** dialog box.

Planning for Fault Tolerance

To ensure you are planning a fault-tolerant WINS design, ask the following question for each server on your network: *What happens to WINS if this server shuts down or if clients cannot reach it?*

To help answer the question, consider the two common scenarios in which a WINS server could fail to perform in its role on a network:

1. Hardware or power failures that require downtime for server repair or maintenance.
2. A network link or router failure that isolates a WINS server from clients.

To plan for these, determine the maximum length of time any given WINS server could be out of service on your network, factoring in the length of both planned and unplanned outages.

Also consider what happens to your WINS clients if their primary WINS server is shut down. By maintaining and assigning secondary WINS servers for clients, you can reduce the effects of a single WINS server being offline.

Planning for Network Performance

Begin planning by estimating the amount of network traffic between WINS clients and WINS servers under normal conditions. You should predict and monitor the following:

- NetBIOS names commonly registered by WINS clients.
- WINS registration and renewal caused by daily startup of clients.

- Roving users and their effect when moving within a routed network.
- WAN links and their effect on replication performance and convergence.

When planning for WINS network performance, its important to understand the types of traffic that WINS clients typically generate on a network, as listed below:

- Name registration
- Name refresh
- Name release
- Name query

DAILY STARTUP OF WINS CLIENTS

When a WINS-enabled client starts on the network, it sends a name registration request for the computer name, user name, domain name, and any additional Windows NT network client services running on the computer.

A WINS client running Windows 2000 (or earlier versions of Windows NT) usually registers more NetBIOS names than other WINS-enabled clients. The name registration requests generated by a computer running under these versions of Windows can include File Server, Domain, Replicator service, Messenger service, Computer Browser service, and additional network service names.

An active WINS client name registration in a WINS server database replicates to all pull partners configured on that WINS server. Eventually, the active name registration replicates to all WINS servers on the network.

When a WINS client is shut down at the end of a workday, it releases the name. When the computer is restarted at the beginning of next workday, the WINS client registers the name again with the WINS server and receives a new version ID. This new, active name registration entry replicates to the pull partners of the WINS server.

Assuming that this cycle occurs each day for each computer, the number of name registration entries replicated each day is approximately the number of computers that start each day multiplied by the number of NetBIOS names registered at each computer.

On large networks (50,000 or more computers), the biggest traffic load represents the name registration requests generated when WINS clients start on the network.

PLANNING CONSIDERATIONS FOR ROUTED WINS NETWORKS

When planning for WINS client traffic on large routed networks, consider the effect of name query, registration, and response traffic routed between subnets. Name requests and responses that occur at the daily startup of computers must pass through the traffic queues on the routers, and can cause delays at peak times.

Roving or mobile users also present challenges for planning WINS in routed networks. When a user stops a computer and then moves it to another location—starting the computer on a different subnet with a different primary WINS server—the resulting changes can generate name-challenge traffic for WINS.

Typically, the name registration request is answered with a brief "Wait for Acknowledgment" message. Assuming the name being registered was previously replicated to the new server, it challenges the IP address currently in its database for this name with a brief query. When, as expected, there is no reply, the WINS server retries the challenge two more times for a total of three attempts. If all three attempts fail, the challenge is successful and the new WINS server updates the name registration entry in its database with the new IP address, incrementing the version ID. The new version ID indicates that the entry must be replicated from its new owner—the new WINS server—to other WINS servers on the network.

You can estimate WINS client traffic based on the behavior of the WINS clients, as described in the preceding sections. However, when estimating WINS client traffic, also consider the network topology and the design or configuration of the network routers. In some cases, it is not possible to predict the traffic load on a specific network router because the routers are configured to autonomously route traffic based on factors other than traffic load.

Configuring WINS Replication

Before configuring replication, you should first carefully design and review your WINS replication topology. For WANs, this planning can be critical to the success of your deployment and use of WINS. In general, WINS offers you the following options when you are configuring replication:

- You can manually configure WINS replication for a WAN environment.
- For some larger campus networks, you might also configure WINS to replicate within a LAN environment.
- In smaller or bounded LAN installations, you might consider enabling and using WINS automatic partner configuration for simplified setup of WINS replication.
- In some larger or more global installations, you might have to configure WINS across untrusted Windows NT domains.

Replication Across Wide Area Networks

When configuring WINS replication, the two most important planning issues are,

- Whether your WINS replication occurs over slower WAN links.

- The length of time required for all replicated changes in the WINS database to converge and achieve consistency on the network.

The frequency of WINS database replication between WINS servers is a major planning issue. The WINS server database should be replicated frequently enough to prevent the downtime of a single WINS server from affecting the reliability of the mapping information in other WINS servers. However, the time interval between replications should not be so small that it interferes with network throughput.

Network topology can influence your decision on replication frequency. For example, if your network has multiple hubs connected by relatively slow WAN links, you can configure WINS database replication between WINS servers on the slow links to occur less frequently than replication on the local area network or on fast WAN links. This reduces traffic across the slow link and reduces contention between replication traffic and WINS client name queries.

For example, as shown in Figure 7-1, the intervals used for configuring pull replication for WINS servers could be set according to proximity between servers and the likelihood of a high-speed link connecting servers configured as replication partners of each other.

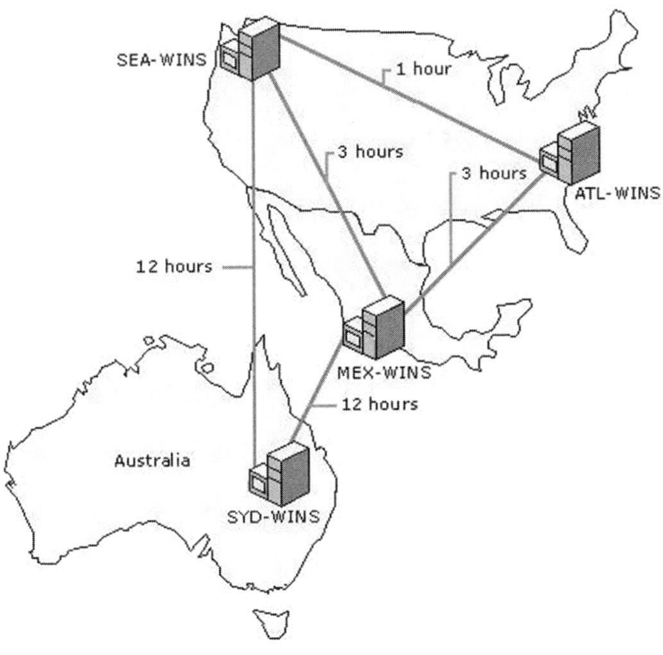

FIGURE 7–1 *WINS convergence in a wide area network*

In this example, two WINS servers—SEA-WINS and ATL-WINS—are located in Seattle and Atlanta. Another two servers—MEX-WINS and SYD-WINS—are located outside the United States in Mexico City and Sydney. Because SEA-WINS and ATL-WINS are located across a higher-speed WAN link, they are configured to replicate once every hour. For the servers outside the United States, replication intervals might be set higher, such as at either 3 or 12 hours, because lower-speed links are associated with these connections.

PLANNING THE CONVERGENCE TIME

Convergence time is the time needed to replicate a new entry in a WINS database from the WINS server that owns the entry to all other WINS servers on the network. When planning for WINS servers, you must decide what is acceptable as the convergence time for your network.

Using Figure 7-1, if a WINS client in Seattle registers its name with the WINS server SEA- other WINS clients in remote locations might query for the client name and not find it in WINS. In some cases, if the address of the client has been changed, the remote locations would only have a mapping for the previous IP address of the client in their local server databases.

WINS clients that query any of the other WINS servers in the figure (that is, ATL-WINS, MEX-WINS, SYD-WINS) receive a positive and correct response only when the new or updated mapping for the client has been fully replicated from the owning WINS server, SEA-WINS, to all of the other servers. Replications from SEA-WINS could be triggered in one of two ways,

1. A push replication trigger is sent based on the frequency of updates made at SEA-WINS.
2. A pull replication trigger is sent to other WINS servers based on the configured **Replication interval** set in Replication Partners Properties at SEA-WINS.

Given this configuration, a new or updated entry at SEA-WINS is replicated only when the pull **replication interval** expires, but queries at remote sites for the new name mapping might not succeed until later. This is because the time interval for replication to ATL-WINS is 1 hour; it is three hours for MEX-WINS; and it is 12 hours for SYD-WINS. In this case, WINS convergence time is calculated as

```
12 hours + 2 * (1 hour) = 14 hours
```

In reality, name query requests can succeed before the convergence time elapses. This happens when the entries replicate over a shorter path than the worst-case path. It also happens when the number of changes in version ID before replication threshold in push replication settings passes before the **Replication Interval** expires in pull replication settings. This results in earlier replication of the new entry. The longer the replication path, the longer the convergence time.

Note After each administrator configures the respective WINS server, you can use **Replicate Now** (in the WINS console) to start immediate replication between the configured WINS servers.

When replication occurs, you can use **Find by Owner** to view records for the remote WINS server database. However, to make changes to the remote WINS database, you must be logged on under an account with required permissions in the respective domains for both servers involved.

Replication can also occur between two separate, standalone servers that participate in a workgroup.

Replication Across Local Area Networks

When configuring WINS replication for LANs, the issues are similar to those that occur in WAN environments, although less critical.

Because the speed of the underlying network links for LANs is much greater than for WANs, it might be acceptable to increase the frequency of WINS database replication by optimizing push and pull parameters for LAN-based replication partners. For push/pull partners, you can do this by decreasing the **Number of changes in version ID before replication** and **Replication interval** settings accordingly, from what you would use for WAN-based partners on slower links.

For example, between LAN-based replication partners it often works to enable WINS to use a persistent connection between the servers. If a persistent connection were not used, the normal update count threshold would default to a minimum of 20. With persistence, a smaller update count value can be specified.

Next, you could specify a much smaller number, such as a value of 1 to 3 in **Number of changes in version ID before replication**, before WINS sends a push replication trigger to the other partner. For pull partners, you might also consider setting the **Replication interval** to a value in minutes, instead of in hours.

As in WAN replication planning, the WINS server database should be replicated frequently enough to prevent the downtime of a single WINS server from affecting the reliability of the mapping information in other WINS servers. However, the time interval between replications should not be so small that it interferes with network throughput.

For network-intensive environments, it is a good idea to use a network-monitoring tool such as Network Monitor to help measure and determine how to optimize your WINS replication strategy.

Automatic Partner Configuration

You can configure a WINS server to automatically configure other WINS server computers as its replication partners. With this automatic partner configuration, other WINS servers are discovered when they join the network and are added as replication partners.

Automatic configuration is possible because each WINS server announces its presence on the network through periodic multicasts. These announcements are sent as IGMP messages for the multicast group address of 224.0.1.24 (the well-known multicast IP address reserved for WINS server use).

Automatic replication configuration monitors multicast announcements from other WINS servers and automatically performs the following configuration steps:

- Adds the IP addresses for the discovered servers to its list of replication partner servers.
- Configures the discovered servers as both push and pull partners.
- Configures pull replication at two-hour intervals with the discovered servers.

If a remote server is discovered and added as a partner through multicasting, it is removed as a replication partner when WINS shuts down properly. To have automatic partner information persist when WINS restarts, you must manually configure the partners.

To manually configure replication with other WINS servers, use the WINS console to specify roles for each partner and any related information.

Note Automatic partner configuration is typically useful in small networks, such as single subnet LAN environments. It can, however, be used in routed networks. For WINS multicast support in routed networks, the forwarding of multicast traffic is made possible by configuring routers for each subnet to forward multicast traffic for the reserved WINS server multicast group. The destination IP address for this group is 224.0.1.24 between routed subnets.

Because periodic multicast announcements between WINS servers can add traffic to your network, automatic partner configuration is recommended only if you have a small number of installed WINS servers (typically, three or fewer) on the reachable network.

Replication Between Untrusted Domains

It is possible to set up WINS replication between one or more WINS servers in domains that do not have a trust relationship. You can do this without a valid user account in the untrusting domain. To configure replication, an administrator for each WINS server must use the WINS console to manually configure that server to permit this replication.

Using Static Mappings

Mapped name-to-address entries can be added to WINS in either of two ways:

- Dynamically, by WINS-enabled clients directly contacting a WINS server to register, release, or renew their NetBIOS names in the server database.
- Manually, by an administrator using the WINS console or command-line tools to add or delete statically mapped entries in the server database.

Static entries are only useful when you need to add a name-to-address mapping to the server database for a computer that does not directly use WINS. For example, in some networks, servers running other operating systems cannot register a NetBIOS name directly with a WINS server. Although these names might be added to and resolved from an lmhosts file or by querying a DNS server, you might consider using a static WINS mapping instead.

Migrating Static Mappings to Dynamic Mappings

Unlike dynamic mappings, which can age and be automatically removed from WINS over time, static mappings can remain in WINS indefinitely unless administrative action is taken.

By default, if during an update process WINS is presented with both a static and dynamic-type entry for the same name, it preserves the static-type entry. You can, however, use the **Overwrite unique static mappings at this server (migrate on)** feature provided with WINS to change this behavior.

For example, Figure 7-2 shows the default migration behavior for a WINS server, WINS-A, when presented with a registration request by a WINS client, Host C, that challenges a static mapping already in the server database.

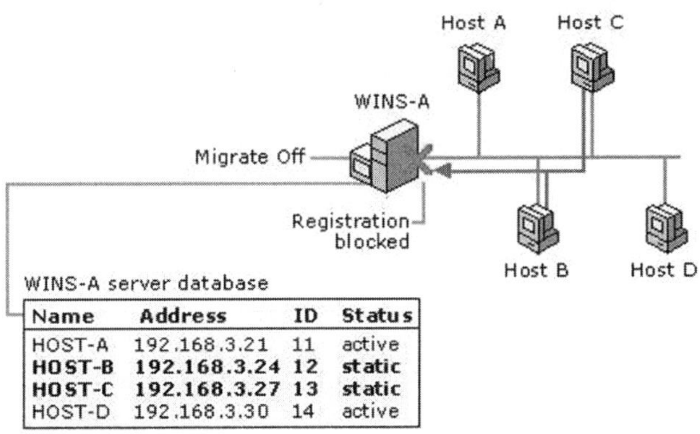

FIGURE 7–2 *Migrate off*

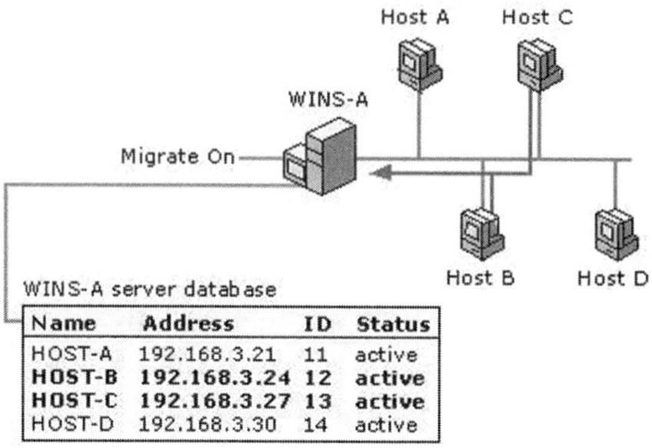

FIGURE 7–3 *Migrate on*

In this example, WINS-A prevents the client from registering and updating the statically mapped information for Host C. In Figure 7-3, the same situation is repeated but in this example, the Migrate feature has been turned on at WINS-A.

As shown in the revised graphic, enabling the Migrate feature at WINS-A permits previously entered static mappings for Host B and C to be overwritten by WINS client computers that attempt to register dynamically and update entries for these same names. This feature is useful in simplifying the update of legacy NetBIOS b-node (broadcast-only) type clients that are later upgraded to support WINS.

Important Never add static mappings for computers that can directly use WINS. Doing so can cause undesirable problems, such as demanding additional work to migrate, delete, or tombstone these mappings in a replicated WINS environment

You can add static entries either interactively, using the WINS console or command-based tools, or by importing an lmhosts file.

The Overwrite unique static mappings at this server (migrate on) feature was designed primarily to migrate records for older non-WINS clients that do not dynamically register themselves in WINS. Some special group names, such as <domain> [1Ch] names, are not affected by this setting00.

Modifying Server Defaults

WINS uses several default server configuration parameters that determine how NetBIOS name records are managed in the WINS server database. These parameters affect the default settings applied by each WINS server for any records stored locally.

The following sections describe the default, minimum, and maximum settings that can be applied for database records. Included is the examination of behavior differences in servers running under each of the released versions of WINS. In most cases, default values are acceptable. In some cases, you might choose to modify the defaults to accommodate special circumstances, such as when a host name change must be made or when you renumber your network so that hosts use different IP addresses.

All of these settings are configured on the **Intervals** tab of the **WINS** ***<Server name>*** **Properties** dialog box.

Renew Interval

The WINS Renew interval setting specifies how often a client renews registration of its names. Table 7.1 shows the supported range of values for Renew interval.

TABLE 7.1 *WINS Renew Interval Settings*

Settings	Range of values
Default	5 hours (Windows NT Server 3.5) 4 days, or 96 hours (Windows NT Server 3.51) 6 days, or 144 hours (Windows 2000 Server and Windows NT Server 4.0)
Maximum	999 hours (Windows NT Server 3.5, 3.51, and 4.0) 365 days (Windows 2000 Server)
Minimum	40 minutes (Windows 2000 Server and all versions of Windows NT Server)

When adjusting this value from its service default, consider the guide0lines in Table 7.2.

TABLE 7.2 *Guidelines for Adjusting Renew Interval Settings*

Increasing the renew interval	Decreasing the renew interval
Causes client names to be renewed with WINS less often.	Causes client names to be renewed with WINS more often.
Reduces client registration activity and performance loads on the WINS server.	Increases client registration activity and performance loads on the WINS server.
Allows WINS data to become less consistent with the current state of the network (when WINS names are changed or modified, changes are reflected less quickly in the WINS database).	Allows WINS data to become more consistent with the current state of the network (when WINS names are changed or modified, changes are reflected more quickly in the WINS database).

Important Any changes made to the WINS renew interval also directly affect the extinction interval and extinction time-out values, which are dependent on this setting.

Extinction Interval

The WINS extinction interval specifies the time interval between when an entry is marked as released and when it is marked as extinct in the WINS database. The default value is dependent on the renew interval and, if the WINS server has replication partners, on the maximum replication time interval. Table 7.3 shows the supported range of values for **Extinction interval**.

TABLE 7.3 *WINS Extinction Interval Settings*

Settings	Range of Values
Default	Dependent on renew interval
Maximum	999 hours (Windows NT Server 3.5, 3.51, and 4.0) 365 days (Windows 2000 Server)
Minimum	40 minutes (Windows NT Server 3.5, 3.51, and Windows 2000 Server) 1 hour (Windows NT Server 4.0)

Extinction Timeout

The WINS Extinction timeout specifies the interval between when an entry is marked extinct and when the entry is scavenged from the database. The default value is dependent on the renew interval and, if the WINS server has replication partners, on the maximum replication time interval. Table 7.4 shows the supported range of values for Extinction time-out.

TABLE 7.4 *Extinction Time-out Settings*

Settings	Range of Values
Default	Dependent on renew interval
Maximum	999 hours (Windows NT Server 3.5, 3.51, and 4.0) 365 days (Windows 2000 Server)
Minimum	24 hours (Windows 2000 Server and all versions of Windows NT Server)

Verification Interval

The WINS Verification interval specifies the time after which the WINS server must verify that old names that it does not own are still active. The default is dependent on the extinction interval. Table 7.5 shows the supported range of values for Verification interval.

TABLE 7.5 *Verification Interval Settings*

Settings	Range of Values
Default	Dependent on Renew interval
Maximum	9999 hours (Windows NT Server 3.5, 3.51, and 4.0) 365 days (Windows 2000 Server)
Minimum	24 days (Windows 2000 Server and all versions of Windows NT Server)

WINS Database Management

This section covers,

- WINS database management
- Finding and viewing WINS records
- Maintaining the WINS database
- Checking the WINS database for consistency

Finding and Viewing WINS Records

The WINS console provides two primary methods for displaying WINS database records,

- **Find by Name** is used to query and filter displayed results to a limited number of NetBIOS name records that start with a specified set of one or more characters.
- **Find by Owner** is used to display WINS server data for one or more owners (WINS servers). This feature also supports additional filtering of the displayed results to show only records of selected NetBIOS name record suffix types.

FINDING RECORDS BY NAME

Find by Name locates records through either a full NetBIOS name or a specified set of matching characters. When typing characters in **Find by Name**, you can enter some or all of the characters in the name.

For WINS to include a targeted name in the results of a find operation, the name must begin with and contain all of the characters selected in **Find names beginning with**. However, names that match the search criteria can contain additional characters that follow the string specified.

For example, if the following are all name records that begin with the letter A in the WINS database,

A, AB, AXB

then entering *A* as the search string finds all three records. If you enter *AB* as the search string, only the record *AB* (which matches both of the specified characters) is found. If you enter "ABC" as the search string, none of the three example records would be found or returned in your search results.

When finding records by name, you can control whether WINS uses case-sensitive searching when it checks for specified search string matches in the server database. By default, WINS searches for all records by name that match the specified search string and does not perform case-sensitive searches. Names that have a mixture of uppercase and lowercase letters are viewed as being equal. If the **Match case** option is used, case-sensitive searches occur instead.

For example, the following are all name records in the WINS database:

ABC, Abcd, aBcE

If you were to enter *Ab* as the search string, WINS performs the search depending upon whether **Match case** is selected. If selected, only the *Abcd* record is found. If cleared, all three example records are found.

Find by Name is ideal for either targeting a known name or similar names located on a specific WINS server. For example, it can be used to troubleshoot WINS name resolution problems in a wide area network by verifying that a known NetBIOS name exists in data stored at any of your remote WINS servers. This command typically generates minimal network traffic and can be used routinely for locating the source of "name not found" errors that result from NetBIOS name resolution.

VIEWING RECORDS BY OWNER

Find by Owner is ideal for doing full display searches and obtaining either a full or filtered view of the WINS database for one or more servers that own records registered in the database.

Because this type of viewing potentially requires WINS to pull data from one or more servers, its use should be handled carefully in WINS networks where either a large amount of data is stored and replicated or a large number of WINS servers are involved. However, for in-depth troubleshooting and close viewing of local WINS databases (either local viewing on the same WINS server computer or viewing a WINS server on the same local area network), this feature should not present an overly demanding load for either the WINS server or the local area network involved.

However, if for display records for either All owners or a remote owner (such as another WINS server located on a WAN) is selected when using This owner, this command might generate a substantial or undesirable increase in network traffic. For this reason, it should be used either sparingly or during off-peak hours.

When viewing records by owner, you can additionally filter WINS data to be included in the view by selecting and using NetBIOS name suffix types as criteria.

For example, to isolate browsing problems associated with the Computer Browser service when WINS clients are using browsing on a WAN, you can filter WINS data by including only those records that use the [1Bh] suffix type, which maps the domain master browser record for each primary domain controller (PDC) in a Windows NT domain environment. For more information on browsing and WINS, see Chapter 6, "WINS Overview."

The WINS console provides you with the ability to add, edit, and remove your own NetBIOS name suffix filter types. It also provides a predefined list that is sufficient for typical use.

Maintaining the WINS Database

The WINS console provides tools for maintaining the WINS server database. For example, you can use the WINS console to backup and restore WINS server database files. This should be done periodically in a way that is similar to other backup operations that are planned and used for saving files on a server computer.

Scavenging and compaction are additional maintenance operations that can be used selectively to help reduce database size and reclaim disk space that is no longer used by the database. For Windows 2000 Server, dynamic compaction is performed automatically by WINS at periodic intervals and manual compaction is not generally necessary.

BACKING UP THE DATABASE

The WINS console provides its own backup feature for backing up the WINS server database during normal operation. After you specify a backup directory for the database, WINS performs complete database backups every three hours, by default.

You should also periodically back up the registry entries for the WINS server.

SCAVENGING THE DATABASE

Scavenging the WINS server database is the process of deleting and removing obsolete information that remains after changes occur. Like any database, the WINS server database of address mappings needs to be periodically scavenged and backed up.

The local WINS server database sometimes retains both released and old entries that were registered at another WINS server (and replicated to the local WINS server). Automatic scavenging takes place at intervals defined by the relationship between the renewal and extinct intervals you define. You can also manually clean the database.

Table 7.6 describes the results of scavenging the WINS database for a WINS server. The first column shows the record criteria and state of any database entries before scavenging is started. The second column indicates the state of the same entries after the scavenging process.

TABLE 7.6 *Scavenging WINS Database for a WINS Server*

Entry state before scavenging	Entry state after scavenging
Active names owned by this WINS server for which the renew interval has expired	Marked as released.
Released names owned by this WINS server for which the extinction interval has expired	Marked as tombstoned.
Tombstoned names for which the extinction timeout has expired	Deleted and removed from the database.
Tombstoned names, replicated from other servers for which the extinction timeout has expired	Deleted and removed from the database.
Active names replicated from other servers for which the verification interval has expired	Revalidated.
Tombstoned or deleted names replicated from other servers	Removed from the database.

Checking the WINS Database for Consistency

Consistency checking helps maintain database integrity among WINS servers in a large network. When you initiate consistency checking at the WINS console, all records are pulled from each owner listed in the current server database, including other WINS servers that are indirect (not directly configured) replication partners.

All records pulled from remote databases are compared to records in the local database, using the following checks for consistency:

- If the record in the local database is identical to the record pulled from the owner database, its time stamp is updated.
- If the record in the local database has a lower version ID than the record pulled from the owner database, the pulled record is added to the local database, and the original local record is marked for deletion

VERIFYING REGISTERED NAME RECORDS ON WINS SERVERS

The WINS console provides a Check Registered Names command that enables you to perform the following verification process among WINS servers on your networks:

- A NetBIOS name records list that can be specified either manually or within a stored file called *Names.txt* that contains names to be used for testing and verification.
- A WINS server list that can be specified either manually or within a stored file called *Servers.txt* that contains a list of WINS servers to be used in verifying NetBIOS names you specify for testing and verification checking.

WINS uses a NetBIOS names list (such as *Names.txt*) to build a query and test for those records with any matched records currently registered and stored in local databases at other WINS servers. The list of WINS servers used for checking the specified names is determined by the IP addresses of WINS servers included in a server list (such as *Servers.txt*), which is the list of WINS servers to query.

Once initiated, WINS completes the name verification check as follows:

1. The names list is used to build a name query list.
2. Names are verified by query for the first listed name, starting with the WINS server specified in the server list.
3. For each name in the names list, WINS queries each server to verify that the name is registered. If a failure is encountered, WINS can retry the query up to three times at the same server.
4. Once the first listed name has been queried and checked at all servers, WINS proceeds to the next name in the list.

The process is repeated until all listed names have been checked at all listed servers. The results and outcome of each name/server query are displayed in **Checking Name Registrations**.

Typical results are listed in Table 7.7.

TABLE 7.7 *Typical Results of a Name/Server Query*

Status	Description
ok	Indicates both that the query was successfully completed and that the specified name was verified at the current WINS server.
no response	Indicates that the current WINS server did not respond to the NetBIOS name query.
name not found	Indicates that the current WINS server responded to the NetBIOS name query but could not resolve the specified name.

When all specified names have been queried at all specified servers, a summary is provided, which includes the following information:

- Any specified NetBIOS names that were verified to their mapped IP address.

- Specified NetBIOS names for which not all WINS servers resolved to the same IP address, indicating that the name is stored and used inconsistently in WINS.
- WINS servers that generated an incomplete response, indicating that they did not have all of the names specified for verification.
- WINS servers that did not respond.
- Specified names for which an IP address could not be verified.

If a WINS database is extremely large, the consistency checking process can be highly resource intensive, affecting network, disk, and processor usage. For this reason, consider doing this during off-peak hours when other network traffic loads and usage are minimal.

If the **Verify name records with all partners of each selected server** check box is cleared, listed names are only verified at each of the specified servers. When this option is selected, replication partners of each listed server are additionally queried for any specified names.

For Windows 2000 Server, use the WINS console to perform consistency checking. For earlier versions, consistency checking must be enabled either through changes to the Windows NT registry or triggered through use of the WINSCL utility, provided as part of the Windows NT 4.0 Server Resource Kit.

Interoperability Issues

Using DHCP with WINS

When using DHCP and WINS together on your network, consider the following options for interoperation:

- *Use additional DHCP scope options.* Specifically, use DHCP options to assign WINS node types (option type 46) and to identify WINS servers for use by DHCP clients (option type 44). In some cases, this can involve adjusting these option types for each physical subnet in which DHCP and WINS are implemented.
- Assign a length of time for DHCP lease durations comparable to the time WINS uses for renew intervals, when both services are deployed. By default, DHCP leases are three days in length and the WINS renew interval is six days. If lease lengths for DHCP widely differ from WINS renew intervals, the effect on your network can be an increase in lease-management traffic and might cause a WINS registration for both services. If you shorten or lengthen the DHCP lease time for clients, then modify the WINS renew interval accordingly.

Using DNS with WINS

When using DNS and WINS together, consider the following options for their interoperation:

- *If a large percentage of clients use NetBIOS and you are using DNS, consider using WINS lookup on your DNS servers.* If WINS lookup is enabled on Microsoft DNS Service, WINS is used for final resolution of any names that are not found using DNS resolution. The WINS forward lookup and WINS-R reverse lookup records are supported only by DNS. If you use servers on your network that do not support DNS, use DNS Manager to ensure that these WINS records are not propagated to DNS servers that do not support WINS lookup.
- *If you have a large percentage of computers running Windows 2000 on your network, consider creating a pure DNS environment.* This involves developing a migration plan to upgrade legacy WINS clients to Windows 2000. Support issues involving network name service are simplified by using a single naming and resource locator service (such as WINS and DNS) on your network. For more information, see "Migrating from WINS to DNS" in this chapter.

Multihomed WINS Servers

For multihomed WINS servers, where more than one local network connection appears in the Network and Dial-up Connections folder, Windows 2000 does not guarantee the binding order for NetBIOS when more than one connection is present and active. Therefore, for a multihomed WINS server to function properly, all installed connections should be configured as routable interfaces.

All multihomed WINS servers should have their primary IP addresses assigned to each network connection, configured as push and pull replication partners at other servers that can be reached through each of the respective connections. When configuring replication partners, you can specify an IP address for the remote multihomed server you are adding at a WINS server, which ensures that a specific network connection is used.

Otherwise, when replication partners are specified and resolved by a name entered in the WINS console, it is possible that a packet generated by WINS could use any of the installed interfaces and their respective IP addresses. This seemingly random behavior results from WINS referring to its local IP routing table, which contains all of the installed IP interfaces, before it sends packets to the remote server.

Migrating from WINS to DNS

For pure Windows 2000 Server environments, it is not possible to reduce or even eliminate WINS on your network. The process of removing installed WINS servers from your network is called *decommissioning*. Before you decide to decommission WINS on your network, consider the following issues:

- Whether there are Windows-based computers on your network running earlier versions of Windows or Windows NT.
- Whether client computers in your enterprise run legacy MS-DOS or Windows-based programs that still require NetBIOS name service, such as NET command-line utilities.

If either of these issues describe your network, you must keep WINS active on your network to provide compatibility with legacy clients and programs. If not, you might proceed with decommissioning WINS servers used on your network.

For example, NetBIOS naming is still required for some BackOffice applications, such as client/server mail configurations that use Microsoft Exchange Server. For more information, search for the title "Microsoft applications that do not require NetBIOS" when using the Business Support Center located at the Microsoft Web site.

When redesigning or preparing your network for eventual WINS decommissioning, you must first complete a full implementation of DNS as your primary naming service for all Windows-based computers installed and active on your network. For more information on planning and designing your DNS network, see Chapter 9, "Using DNS."

Once DNS is implemented, the process of decommissioning WINS follows this general sequence.

1. Reconfigure client computers not to use WINS. You must reconfigure your WINS clients to stop the registering and renewing of their names with the WINS servers you want to remove. Clients are configured to use WINS based on their TCP/IP configuration. This is done in one of two ways.
   a. For clients that are manually configured to use TCP/IP, remove IP addresses for either primary WINS or secondary WINS servers from configured TCP/IP properties for each network connection used by the client computer.
   b. For clients that are dynamically configured by a DHCP server for TCP/IP usage, reconfigure options at your DHCP server (including any server, scope, or client-configured options) to no longer provide distribution of option code 44 to clients. This option type is used to provide a list of WINS server IP addresses to clients.

You can also reconfigure your WINS clients to disable NetBIOS over TCP/IP, though this step is not a required procedure for migrating from WINS to DNS. For information about disabling NetBIOS over TCP/IP, see Chapter 1, "TCP/IP Overview."

2. While reconfiguring clients, verify that DNS is configured and functioning for them. When reconfiguring WINS clients to stop registration of their names and use of WINS servers, verify that DNS is fully configured for all clients before removing WINS servers from your network. Clients register in DNS on the basis of their being configured for TCP/IP. This reconfiguration is done in one of the two following ways:
   a. For clients that are manually configured to use TCP/IP, add IP addresses for either Primary DNS or Secondary DNS servers in the configured TCP/IP properties for each network connection used by the client computer.
   b. For clients that are dynamically configured by a DHCP server to use TCP/IP, reconfigure options at your DHCP server (including any server, scope, or client-configured options) to provide distribution of option code 6 to clients. This option type provides a list of DNS server IP addresses to clients.

3. Turn off WINS servers and remove them from your network. After you reconfigure clients to use DNS and stop using WINS for name service, you can begin eliminating WINS servers. For more information, see "Decommission a WINS Server" in this chapter.

When removing a WINS server, it is important that, whenever possible, any records owned by the server are tombstoned at the server. You can use the **Delete Owner** command to select the local server from the list of owners and then select **Replicate deletion to other servers (tombstone)** to accomplish this within a single command operation at the WINS console.

If owner or record deletion was performed at another WINS server, consider using the **Block records for these owners** feature in **Replication Partner Properties** to prevent the deleted owner or its records from replicating back to the non-owner server used to decommission another server.

Even when WINS remains a requirement in your environment, many sites can still benefit from implementation of the DNS and DHCP capabilities provided by Windows 2000. For example, you can use DNS dynamic updates and DHCP-DNS integration for proxy update of host (A) and pointer (PTR) resource records registration for earlier non-dynamic clients. In many cases, this helps reduce NetBIOS and WINS traffic.

For information about dynamic update, see Chapter 8, "DNS Overview." For information on using DNS servers with DHCP, see Chapter 9.

Install a WINS Server

To install a WINS server,

1. To open the Windows Component wizard, from the desktop, click **Start**, point to **Settings**, and then click **Control Panel**. When Control Panel opens, double-click **Add/Remove Programs**, and then click **Add/Remove Windows Components**.
2. Under **Components**, scroll to and click **Networking Services**.
3. Click **Details**.
4. Under **Subcomponents of Networking Services**, click **Windows Internet Name Service (WINS)**, and then click **OK**.
5. If prompted, type the full path to the Windows 2000 distribution files and click **Continue**. Required files are copied to your hard disk, and server software can be used after restarting the system.

It is strongly recommended that you manually configure the computer to use a static IP address.

Certain Windows components require configuration before they can be used. If you installed one or more of these components, but did not configure them, when you click **Add/Remove Windows Components**, a list of components that need to be configured is displayed. To start the Windows Components wizard, click **Components**.

Open the WINS Console

To open the WINS console, click **Start**, point to **Programs**, point to **Administrative Tools**, and then click **WINS**.

The WINS console is an administrative tool for managing WINS servers.

Add a WINS Server to the Console

To add a WINS server to the console,

1. Click **Start**, point to **Programs**, point to **Administrative Tools**, and then click **WINS**.
2. In the console tree, click **WINS**.
3. On the **Action** menu, click **Add Server**.

4. In **Add Server**, for **WINS Server** type the appropriate server information. Optionally, click **Browse** to locate the WINS server computer by name on your network.

To configure a WINS server, you must be logged on as a member of the Administrators group for the server.

If WINS is locally installed on a server, the local WINS server is added to the console automatically. For remote WINS servers, you must add them to the console and then save the file.

Remove a WINS Server from the Console

To remove a WINS server from the console,

1. Click **Start**, point to **Programs**, point to **Administrative Tools**, and then click **WINS**.
2. Click the WINS server that you want to remove.
3. On the **Action** menu, click **Delete**.
4. When prompted "Are you sure you want to remove WINS server *servername* from this list?" click **Yes**.

This procedure affects only the management console at which you are working, not the WINS server itself that continues to provide service and registration on the network.

Start or Stop a WINS Server

To start or stop a WINS server,

1. Click **Start**, point to **Programs**, point to **Administrative Tools**, and then click **WINS**.
2. In the console tree, click the applicable WINS server (console tree | WINS | *applicable WINS server*).
3. On the **Action** menu, point to **All Tasks** and then click one of the following:
    a. To start the service, click **Start**.
    b. To stop the service, click **Stop**.
    c. To interrupt the service, click **Pause**.
    d. To stop and then automatically restart the service, click **Restart**.

After you pause or stop the service, the **Resume** option appears and can be clicked to immediately resume WINS service.

You can also perform most of these tasks at a command prompt by using the following commands:

- **net start wins**
- **net stop wins**
- **net pause wins**
- **net continue wins**

Decommission a WINS Server

To decommission a WINS server,

1. Before decommissioning a WINS server, make sure that any computers previously configured to be WINS clients of this server are reconfigured to point to other servers as their primary or secondary WINS servers. Reconfiguration is necessary only if these clients are to continue using WINS to register and resolve network names.
2. To open WINS, click **Start**, point to **Programs**, point to **Administrative Tools**, and then click **WINS**.
3. In the console tree, click **Active Registrations** (console tree | WINS | *applicable WINS server* | Active Registrations).
4. On the **Action** menu, click **Delete Owner**.
5. In **Delete Owner**, for **Delete this owner**, click the IP address for the WINS server you want to decommission. If the WINS server is not running locally on this computer, it might take awhile to load the records for the selected server.
6. For Use this operation to delete the selected owner and its records, click **Replicate deletion to other WINS servers (tombstone)**, and then click **OK**. When prompted to confirm tombstoning, click **Yes**.
7. In the console tree, click **Replication Partners**.
8. On the **Action** menu, click **Replicate Now**.
9. Once you have verified that records tombstoned in step 6 have been replicated to other partner servers, stop and remove WINS on the decommissioned server.

If the WINS server you want to decommission does not appear in the console tree, you can add it.

Tombstoning ensures that the WINS servers that are replication partners with the decommissioned WINS server are updated properly so that they release the records. If tombstone status is not properly replicated, you can manually delete the records at each WINS server on which tombstone replication failed.

WINS supports remote record deletion for servers running Windows NT Server 4.0, if updated to Service Pack 4 (SP4) or later. For further information, see these sections in this chapter: "View WINS Server Statistics," "Add a WINS Server to the Console," "Remove a WINS Server From the Console," "Remove or Uninstall WINS," and "Migrating From WINS to DNS."

Remove or Uninstall WINS

To remove or uninstall WINS,

1. Stop the WINS service on this computer.
2. To open Add/Remove Programs, click **Start**, point to **Settings**, click **Control Panel**, and then double-click the appropriate icon.
3. Click **Add/Remove Windows Components**.
4. In **Windows 2000 Components, select Networking Services** from the list of components, and then click **Details**.
5. In **Subcomponents of Networking Services**, scroll to **Windows Internet Name Service (WINS)** and clear the check box.

When you remove WINS, all WINS files are deleted from the server except program files that are in use. When the system is restarted, these files are removed as well.

If you do not stop the WINS service in step 1, this procedure deletes only the WINS server registry entries.

Certain Windows components require configuration before they can be used. If you installed one or more of these components, but did not configure them, when you click **Add/Remove Windows Components**, a list of components that need to be configured is displayed. To start the Windows Components wizard, click **Components**.

Modify Backup Settings

To modify backup settings,

1. To open WINS, click **Start**, point to **Programs**, point to **Administrative Tools**, and then click **WINS**.
2. In the console tree, click the applicable WINS server (console tree | WINS | *applicable WINS server*).
3. On the **Action** menu, click **Properties**.

4. On the **General** tab, under **Database backup**, modify default backup settings as needed. To view a dialog box item's description, right-click the item, and then click **What's This?**.

Modify Name Record Settings

To modify name record settings,

1. To open WINS, click **Start**, point to **Programs**, point to **Administrative Tools**, and then click **WINS**.
2. In the console tree, click the applicable WINS server (console tree | WINS | *applicable WINS server*).
3. On the **Action** menu, click **Properties**.
4. Click the **Intervals** tab.
5. Modify default settings as needed. To view a dialog box item's description, right-click the item, and then click **What's This?**.

For most networks, the default interval settings for Renew interval, Extinction interval, Extinction timeout, and Verification interval are acceptable and do not require modification. As an option, you can click **Restore Default** to restore WINS default intervals used for registering, renewing, and verifying name records in the database.

Modify WINS Logging Properties

To modify WINS logging properties,

1. To open WINS, click **Start**, point to **Programs**, point to **Administrative Tools**, and then click **WINS**.
2. In the console tree, click the applicable WINS server (console tree | WINS | *applicable WINS server*).
3. On the **Action** menu, click **Properties**.
4. Click the **Advanced** tab.
5. Select the **Log detailed events to Windows event log** check box.

When Log detailed events to Windows event log is checked, WINS logs additional detailed information to the system event log, which can be viewed by using Event Viewer. Because this feature can degrade system performance when enabled, it is turned off by default.

Modify Burst Handling Properties

To modify burst handling properties,

1. To open WINS, click **Start**, point to **Programs**, point to **Administrative Tools**, and then click **WINS**.
2. In the console tree, click the applicable WINS server (console tree | WINS | *applicable WINS server*).
3. On the **Action** menu, click **Properties**.
4. Click the **Advanced** tab.
5. In **Enable burst handling**, modify default settings as needed. To view a dialog box item's description, right-click the item, and then click **What's This?**.

By default, burst handling is enabled and the burst queue sized to medium.

Set the WINS Database Path

To set the WINS database path,

1. To open WINS, click **Start**, point to **Programs**, point to **Administrative Tools**, and then click **WINS**.
2. In the console tree, click the applicable WINS server (console tree | WINS | *applicable WINS server*).
3. On the **Action** menu, click **Properties**.
4. Click the **Advanced** tab.
5. In **Database path**, modify the database path as needed. To view a dialog box item's description, right-click the item, and then click **What's This?**.

Important This setting affects WINS backup and restore operations. If you change the path used here, be sure to run WINS backup again to archive the database with the updated path information. Otherwise, WINS cannot restore previously archived copies of the database where another path was specified, for either the WINS database path or the WINS database backup path.

This procedure describes how to set the path used by WINS to store the database on the applicable server. It does not specify the path that WINS uses when backing up the database.

Increase the Starting Version Count

To increase the starting version count,

1. To open WINS, click **Start**, point to **Programs**, point to **Administrative Tools**, and then click **WINS**.
2. In the console tree, click the applicable WINS server (console tree | WINS | *applicable WINS server*).
3. On the **Action** menu, click **Properties**.
4. Click the **Advanced** tab.
5. For **Starting version ID (hexadecimal)**, enter a new number to be used by WINS as the new starting version ID when WINS is next restarted.

Because a higher version ID is used by WINS during replication to determine between two servers storing the same record which version is more recent, increasing the starting version ID count can be useful in some cases where you are attempting to effect a forced update and replication of names between servers.

If you enter a number that is less than the actual value of the highest version ID currently in use by the selected server, WINS might increase the actual number used for its start version count when service is restarted.

Disable LAN Manager Compatibility

To disable LAN Manager compatibility,

1. To open WINS, click **Start**, point to **Programs**, point to **Administrative Tools**, and then click **WINS**.
2. In the console tree, click the applicable WINS server (console tree | WINS | *applicable WINS server*).
3. On the **Action** menu, click **Properties**.
4. Click **Advanced**.
5. Clear the **Use computer names that are compatible with LAN Manager** check box.

View WINS Server Statistics

To view WINS server statistics,

1. To open WINS, click **Start**, point to **Programs**, point to **Administrative Tools**, and then click **WINS**.

2. In the console tree, click the applicable WINS server (console tree | WINS | *applicable WINS server*).
3. On the **Action** menu, click **Show Server Statistics**.

   To update the display while viewing WINS statistics, click **Refresh**.

Reset WINS Server Statistics

To reset WINS server statistics,

1. To open WINS, click **Start**, point to **Programs**, point to **Administrative Tools**, and then click **WINS**.
2. In the console tree, click the applicable WINS server (console tree | WINS | *applicable WINS server*).
3. On the **Action** menu, click **Show Server Statistics**.
4. Click **Reset**.

   To update the display while viewing WINS statistics, click **Refresh**.

Modify Auto-Refresh of WINS Statistics

To modify auto-refresh of WINS statistics,

1. To open WINS, click **Start**, point to **Programs**, point to **Administrative Tools**, and then click **WINS**.
2. In the console tree, click the applicable WINS server (console tree | WINS | *applicable WINS server*).
3. On the **Action** menu, click **Properties**.
4. Under the **Automatically update statistics every** check box, modify as needed the refresh interval in hours, minutes, or seconds.

By default, statistics automatically refresh every 10 minutes. As an option, you can also disable this feature by clearing the **Automatically update statistics every** check box.

Export WINS Console Data to a Text File

To export WINS console data to a text file,

1. To open WINS, click **Start**, point to **Programs**, point to **Administrative Tools**, and then click **WINS**.

2. In the console tree, click the node item for which you want to export all currently displayed console data. For example, if you want to export all console data about a specific WINS server, click this server in the console tree.
3. On the **Action** menu, click **Export List**.
4. Enter a name for the text *(*.txt)* file to be used to export the output of this operation.

For the **Active Registrations** node, you need to use either **Find by Name** or **Find by Owner** to load and display records for the applicable server in the console prior to performing this procedure.

Modify the WINS Console View

To modify the WINS console view,

1. To open WINS, click **Start**, point to **Programs**, point to **Administrative Tools**, and then click **WINS**.
2. In the console tree, click **WINS**.
3. On the **Action** menu, click **Properties**.
4. Modify console defaults to specify how WINS servers added to the console are displayed. To view a description of a dialog box item, right-click the item, and then click **What's This?**.

By default, the WINS console orders servers by name and uses only short (host-only) DNS names when displaying WINS servers that are added to the console. In addition, WINS does not validate its cache of WINS servers, which can prolong the length of time needed to load the WINS console when started.

Configure WINS for Non-DHCP Clients

To configure WINS for non-DHCP clients, WINS servers must be manually added for each network connection that does not use DHCP.

If you manually configure a list of WINS servers for the connection, which later leases and obtains its IP address using DHCP, the list you configure supercedes any WINS servers returned in an options list provided by the DHCP server.

Configure WINS for DHCP-enabled Clients

To configure WINS for DHCP-enabled clients, Windows 2000 clients are configured by default to use a DHCP server to obtain an IP address. No further client-side configuration is needed. Instead, configure your DHCP server to assign WINS-related option types needed to enable DHCP-enabled clients on your network to use WINS.

In most cases, WINS clients only need to be provided the following NetBIOS over TCP/IP (NetBT) option types for basic WINS configuration: 44 (WINS servers) and 46 (WINS node type). These options must be configured at the DHCP server providing each client its dynamically leased IP address.

Disable WINS/NetBT Name Resolution

To disable WINS/NetBT name resolution,

1. To open Network and Dial-up Connections, click **Start**, point to **Settings**, and then click **Network and Dial-up Connections**.
2. Click the Local Area Connection to be statically configured and then, from the **File** menu, click **Properties**.
3. In the list of components, click **Internet Protocol (TCP/IP)**, and then click **Properties**.
4. Click **Advanced**.
5. Click the **WINS** tab.
6. Click **Disable NetBIOS over TCP/IP**. Optionally, you can select **Use NetBIOS setting from the DHCP server** if you are using a DHCP server that can selectively enable and disable NetBIOS configuration through DHCP option types.

NetBIOS over TCP/IP can also be disabled for computers running Windows 2000 using DHCP option types supported by the Windows 2000 DHCP Server service.

Verify WINS Registration of Client NetBIOS Names

To verify WINS registration of client NetBIOS names,

1. On the WINS client computer, at the command prompt, type: *nbtstat -n*

The local NetBIOS names table for the WINS client computer is listed. Verify that each name indicates Registered in the Status column, such as shown in the sample command output:

```
Node IpAddress: [10.0.0.1] Scope Id: []

            NetBIOS Local Name Table

   Name                 Type          Status
-------------------------------------------
BRADMA8           <20>  UNIQUE       Registered
BRADMA8           <00>  UNIQUE       Registered
WORKGROUP         <00>  GROUP        Registered
INet~Services     <1C>  GROUP        Registered
IS~BRADMA8.....<00>  UNIQUE       Registered
BRADMA8           <03>  UNIQUE       Registered
ADMINISTRATOR     <03>  UNIQUE       Registered
WORKGROUP         <1E>  GROUP        Registered
WORKGROUP         <1D>  UNIQUE       Registered
..__MYBROWSE__.<01>  GROUP        Registered
```

2. The Status column should indicate a status of either Registered, Registering, or Conflict. For cases where the name is shown to be either Registered or Registering, you can type *nbtstat -RR* to release and refresh registration of the local NetBIOS names of the client with WINS.

   For cases where the Status column indicates a conflict for the name, try either of the following to resolve the conflicted name state at the client computer:

   a. For Windows 2000 WINS clients, you can selectively disconnect and reconnect the network connection in the Network and Dial-up Connections folder to force release and refresh of all client NetBIOS names in WINS.

   b. For other earlier versions of Windows, shut down and restart the system to achieve similar results.

3. After the release/refresh process is completed, repeat **nbtstat -n** to verify that all local names have a status of Registered in WINS.

For name conflicts, you may only need to perform step 2 if the name in conflict is critically necessary for the WINS client to maintain visibility or locate other computers on the network. Names that fit this description might include the [00h] and [20h] type names, if they match the client NetBIOS computer name. The need to resolve a name conflict for other types of names might be less critical to support needs.

The nbtstat command can also be used to perform other useful procedures related to WINS client support.

Search for Names That Begin with a Specified Set of Characters

To search for names that begin with a specified set of characters,

1. To open WINS, click **Start**, point to **Programs**, point to **Administrative Tools**, and then click **WINS**.
2. In the console tree, click **Active Registrations** (console tree | WINS | *applicable WINS server* | Active Registrations).
3. On the **Action** menu, click **Find by Name**.
4. In **Find names beginning with**, type or select a set of specific characters to be used in the search.
5. Click **Find Now** to begin the search.

WINS searches the server database and displays any names that begin with the specified characters. As an option, you can click **Match case** to enable a case-sensitive search.

Show All Records in the WINS Database

To show all records in the WINS database,

1. To open WINS, click **Start**, point to **Programs**, point to **Administrative Tools**, and then click **WINS**.
2. In the console tree, click **Active Registrations** (console tree | WINS | *applicable WINS server* | Active Registrations).
3. On the **Action** menu, click **Find by Owner**.
4. For **Display records for**, click **All owners**, and then click **OK**. The entire WINS database appears in the details pane.

Loading and displaying all records for all owners in the WINS database can take a long time.

View Properties for a Selected WINS Record

To view properties for a selected WINS record,

1. To open WINS, click **Start**, point to **Programs**, point to **Administrative Tools**, and then click **WINS**.

2. In the console tree, click **Active Registrations** (console tree | WINS | *applicable WINS server* | Active Registrations).
3. On the **Action** menu, click either **Find by Name** or **Find by Owner** to display WINS records in the details pane.
   a. For **Find by Name**, specify the leading characters for the name or names you want to view, then click **Find Now**.
   b. For **Find by Owner**, click either **All owners** or **This owner** to use in displaying WINS database records, and then click **OK**.
4. In the details pane, click the record that you want to view.
5. On the **Action** menu, click **Properties**.

View or Download the WINS Database by Owner

To view or download the WINS database by owner,

1. To open WINS, click **Start**, point to **Programs**, point to **Administrative Tools**, and then click **WINS**.
2. In the console tree, click **Active Registrations** (console tree | WINS | *applicable WINS server* | Active Registrations).
3. On the **Action** menu, click **Find by Owner**.
4. Under **Display records for**, click **This owner**, and then click a selected owner from the list. After you click **OK**, the filtered WINS database appears in the details pane, showing only those records which are registered to the selected owner.

   If the selected owner is a remote computer, a brief delay might occur.

Filter the WINS Database View

To filter the WINS database view,

1. To open WINS, click **Start**, point to **Programs**, point to **Administrative Tools**, and then click **WINS**.
2. In the console tree, click **Active Registrations** (console tree | WINS | *applicable WINS server* | Active Registrations).
3. On the **Action** menu, click **Find by Owner**.
4. Click the **Record Types** tab.
5. Clear the check box for any name record types you want excluded from filtered viewing of the WINS database. When you click **OK**, the filtered WINS database appears in the details pane.

By default, all predefined NetBIOS name type filters are included in the filter mask. To clear all filters, click **Clear all**. To restore the default settings, click **Select all**.

A brief delay might occur while WINS searches the database to sort and load only the records that match the selected filter criteria.

Clear All WINS Data Filters

To clear all WINS data filters,

1. To open WINS, click **Start**, point to **Programs**, point to **Administrative Tools**, and then click **WINS**.
2. In the console tree, click **Active Registrations** (console tree | WINS | *applicable WINS server* | Active Registrations).
3. On the **Action** menu, click **Find by Owner**.
4. Click the **Record Types** tab.
5. Click **Clear all**.

By default, all predefined NetBIOS name type filters are included in the filter mask. To restore the default settings, click **Select all**.

Add, Modify, or Remove a Filter Type

To add, modify, or remove a filter type,

1. To open WINS, click **Start**, point to **Programs**, point to **Administrative Tools**, and then click **WINS**.
2. In the console tree, click **Active Registrations** (console tree | WINS | *applicable WINS server* | Active Registrations).
3. On the **Action** menu, click **Find by Owner**.
4. Click the **Record Types** tab.
5. Click either **Add**, **Edit**, or **Delete** to add, modify, or remove name type filters.
6. When adding a new filter type, click **Add** and complete the following for **Add Record Type**:

   a. For **ID (hexadecimal)**, specify a unique 2-digit hexadecimal number that can be used to identify a distinct set of records in the WINS database.
   b. For **Description**, enter descriptive text that indicates how the new filter type is to be used.

Only user-defined filters can be modified or deleted. Predefined filters provided for default use by WINS cannot be modified or deleted.

Scavenge the WINS Database

To scavenge the WINS database,

1. To open WINS, click **Start**, point to **Programs**, point to **Administrative Tools**, and then click **WINS**.
2. In the console tree, click the applicable WINS server (console tree | WINS | *applicable WINS server* | Active Registrations).
3. On the **Action** menu, click **Scavenge Database**.

Like other databases, you must periodically maintain the WINS database to remove outdated information. This process is called *scavenging,* which removes old and released entries that were registered at another WINS server and replicated to the server being maintained.

WINS automatically scavenges the server database at intervals you specify in server properties.

Backup the WINS Database

To backup the WINS database,

1. To open WINS, click **Start**, point to **Programs**, point to **Administrative Tools**, and then click **WINS**.
2. In the console tree, click the applicable WINS server (console tree | WINS | *applicable WINS server*).
3. On the **Action** menu, click **Backup Database**.
4. When prompted to confirm, click **Yes**. After backup is completed, click **OK**.

Important Do not specify a network drive as the backup location. In addition, if you change the WINS backup or database path in server properties, perform new backups to ensure successful future restorations of the WINS database.

The WINS console provides backup tools so that you can back up and restore the WINS database. After you specify a backup folder for the database, WINS performs complete database backups every three hours, using the specified folder.

WINS can also be configured to back up the database automatically when the service is stopped or the server computer shut down.

When WINS backs up the server database, it creates a *\Wins_bak\New* folder under the backup folder you have specified for **Default backup path** in *server* **Properties**. Actual backups of the WINS database *(Wins.mdb)* are stored in this folder. By default, the backup path is the root folder on your system partition, such as *C:*.

Restore the WINS Database

To restore the WINS database,

1. To open WINS, click **Start**, point to **Programs**, point to **Administrative Tools**, and then click **WINS**.
2. Stop WINS.

   In this step, wait for WINS to completely stop before proceeding. A busy server might require several minutes before it can stop WINS and you can proceed with restoring the database.
3. Delete all files in the folder path on the WINS server computer where you are restoring the database.
4. Open WINS.
5. In the console tree, click the applicable WINS server (console tree | WINS | *applicable WINS server*).
6. On the **Action** menu, click **Restore Database**.
7. In the **Browse for Folder** dialog box, click the same folder (such as *C:*) that was used previously to back up the local WINS database, and then click **OK**.

When restoring the database, WINS requires that the backup path used for restoration match the path that was originally specified in *server* **Properties** as the **Backup path**. By default, this path is the root folder on the system partition. If you specify a different path, be sure to use that same path in step 7.

WINS does not permit you to restore the server databases remotely from another computer.

The restore option is only available when viewing a computer on which WINS is stopped. In some cases, you might need to refresh the WINS console to activate the restore option. If necessary, click **Refresh** from the **Action** menu to refresh the server node so that the WINS console detects that WINS is stopped on the server.

In case of database corruption, the WINS database can be restored from the backup. You can sometimes repair WINS database corruption by incrementing the starting version count for the WINS server and restarting the server.

Delete or Tombstone an Entry in the WINS Database

To delete or tombstone an entry in the WINS database,

1. To open WINS, click **Start**, point to **Programs**, point to **Administrative Tools**, and then click **WINS**.
2. In the console tree, click **Active Registrations** (console tree | WINS | *applicable WINS server* | Active Registrations).
3. On the **Action** menu, click either **Find by Name** or **Find by Owner** to display the names you want to delete from the database.
4. In the details pane, click the entry you want to delete. You can hold down the CTRL or SHIFT keys to select multiple entries.
5. On the **Action** menu, click **Delete**.
6. In the **Delete Record** dialog box, click one of the following options for deleting the selected records:

    a. **Delete the record only from this server.**
    b. **Replicate deletion of the record to other servers (tombstone).**

Tombstoning marks records as inactive for a period of time. When the WINS database on this server replicates these records to other WINS servers, the other servers preserve the tombstone state and can eventually remove these entries from a replicated WINS network of server databases.

In step 6, if you click **Delete the record only from this server** and another WINS server owns the records, then deleted records can reappear after WINS replication occurs with other partner servers. To avoid this, click **Replicate deletion of the record to other servers (tombstone)**.

Once an entry has been tombstoned and its status is replicated to other servers, the tombstoned entries can be removed from WINS, in either of two ways.

1. Automatically, using the **Extinction Interval**, which is set from the **Intervals** tab in WINS server properties.
2. Manually, by performing a scavenging operation.

Delete an Owner from the WINS Database

To delete an owner from the WINS database,

1. To open WINS, click **Start**, point to **Programs**, point to **Administrative Tools**, and then click **WINS**.
2. In the console tree, click **Active Registrations** (console tree | WINS | *applicable WINS server* | Active Registrations).

3. On the **Action** menu, click **Delete Owner**.
4. In **Delete Owner**, click the owner you want to delete.
5. Select from the following options for deleting records in the WINS database associated with the owner you are deleting:

    a. To delete the owner and all of its records from this WINS server only, click **Delete from this server only**.
    b. To replicate deletion of the selected owner and all its records at this and other WINS servers, click **Replicate deletion to other servers (tombstone)**.

Tombstoning marks records as inactive for a period of time. When the WINS database on this server replicates these records to other WINS servers, the other servers preserve the tombstone state and can eventually remove these entries from a replicated WINS network of server databases.

In step 5, if you click **Delete from this server only**, records first introduced by the deleted owner can reappear after WINS replication with other partner servers that have replicated these records. To avoid this, click **Replicate deletion to other servers (tombstone)**.

Once an entry has been tombstoned and its status is replicated to other servers, the tombstoned entries can be removed from WINS, in either of two ways.

1. Automatically, using the **Extinction Interval**, which is set from the **Intervals** tab in WINS server properties.
2. Manually, by performing a scavenging operation.

Enable Periodic Consistency Checking of the WINS Database

To enable periodic consistency checking of the WINS database,

1. To open WINS, click **Start**, point to **Programs**, point to **Administrative Tools**, and then click **WINS**.
2. In the console tree, click the applicable WINS server (console tree | WINS | *applicable WINS server*).
3. On the **Action** menu, click **Properties**.
4. Click the **Database Verification** tab.
5. In Database Verification settings, select the **Verify database consistency every [number of hours] hours** check box.
6. If necessary, modify default settings to be used when consistency checks are performed. To view a dialog box item's description, right-click the item, and then click **What's This?**.

Because consistency checking might affect WINS server performance, this feature is not enabled by default.

When enabled, the default settings for this feature provide for up to 30,000 records in the WINS server database to be checked on a daily basis, beginning at 2:00 A.M. each night. During each of these scheduled consistency checks, the selected WINS server compares local copies of records it stores with the same record as stored at the WINS server listed as the owner for each record.

Manually Check Database Consistency

To manually check database consistency,

1. To open WINS, click **Start**, point to **Programs**, point to **Administrative Tools**, and then click **WINS**.
2. In the console tree, click the applicable WINS server (console tree | WINS | *applicable WINS server*).
3. On the **Action** menu, click **Check Database Consistency**.
4. When prompted if you want to continue, click **Yes** to start consistency checking.

Checking consistency can be resource-intensive when there is a large number of names to be checked or a large number of WINS servers involved. You might want to perform this only during off-peak hours to minimize the impact on your WINS servers and network.

Consistency checking can also be scheduled through server properties.

Check Version Number Consistency Between Servers

To check version number consistency between servers,

1. To open WINS, click **Start**, point to **Programs**, point to **Administrative Tools**, and then click **WINS**.
2. In the console tree, click the applicable WINS server (console tree | WINS | *applicable WINS server*).
3. On the **Action** menu, click **Check Version Number Consistency**.
4. When prompted if you want to continue, click **Yes** to start this operation.

This operation gets the Owner-to-Highest-Version-ID mappings from different WINS servers. It checks the consistency of the WINS databases at all tested servers by ensuring that each server always has the highest version ID among the network of WINS servers for any records that it owns.

Checking version ID number consistency can be resource-intensive when there are a large number of WINS servers tested.

Add a Replication Partner

To add a replication partner,

1. To open WINS, click **Start**, point to **Programs**, point to **Administrative Tools**, and then click **WINS**.
2. In the console tree, click **Replication Partners** (console tree | WINS | *applicable WINS server* | Replication Partners).
3. On the **Action** menu, click **New Replication Partner**.
4. In **New Replication Partner**, type the name or IP address of the WINS server to add as a replication partner.

You must be logged on as an administrator or a member of the Administrators group in order to complete this procedure. If your computer is connected to a network, network policy settings may also prevent you from completing this procedure.

By default, replication partners are configured as push/pull type partners. Once you have added a partner, however, you can change it to be a push-only or pull-only type partner.

Delete a Replication Partner

To delete a replication partner,

1. To open WINS, click **Start**, point to **Programs**, point to **Administrative Tools**, and then click **WINS**.
2. In the console tree, click **Replication Partners** (console tree | WINS | *applicable WINS server* | Replication Partners).
3. In the details pane, click the replication partner you want to remove.
4. On the **Action** menu, click **Delete**.
5. When prompted, click **Yes** to confirm that you want to delete the partner.

Enable Replication with Non-Partner WINS Servers

To enable replication with non-partner WINS servers,

1. To open WINS, click **Start**, point to **Programs**, point to **Administrative Tools**, and then click **WINS**.
2. In the console tree, click **Replication Partners** (console tree | WINS | *applicable WINS server* | Replication Partners).
3. On the **Action** menu, click **Properties**.
4. Clear the **Replicate only with partners** check box, and then click **Apply**.

By default, WINS only replicates with other WINS servers configured as replication partners.

Modify Push Partner Properties

To modify push partner properties,

1. To open WINS, click **Start**, point to **Programs**, point to **Administrative Tools**, and then click **WINS**.
2. In the console tree, click **Replication Partners** (console tree | WINS | *applicable WINS server* | Replication Partners).
3. On the **Action** menu, click **Properties**.
4. Click the **Push Replication** tab.
5. As needed, reconfigure push partner defaults to be used by this server when it performs replication with any of its newly added push partners. To view a dialog box item's description, right-click the item, and then click **What's This?**.

Modify Pull Partner Properties

To modify pull partner properties,

1. To open WINS, click **Start**, point to **Programs**, point to **Administrative Tools**, and then click **WINS**.
2. In the console tree, click **Replication Partners** (console tree | WINS | *applicable WINS server* | Replication Partners).
3. On the **Action** menu, click **Properties**.
4. Click the **Pull Replication** tab.

5. As needed, reconfigure pull partner defaults to be used by this server when it performs replication with any of its newly added pull partners. To view a dialog box item's description, right-click the item, and then click **What's This?**.

Enable Automatic Partner Configuration

To enable automatic partner configuration,

1. To open WINS, click **Start**, point to **Programs**, point to **Administrative Tools**, and then click **WINS**.
2. In the console tree, click **Replication Partners** (console tree | WINS | *applicable WINS server* | Replication Partners).
3. On the **Action** menu, click **Properties**.
4. Click the **Advanced** tab.
5. Select the **Enable automatic partner configuration** check box.
6. If necessary, modify the multicast interval and multicast Time-to-Live (TTL) parameters to be used by this server when automatic partner configuration is enabled for use by WINS. To view a dialog box item's description, right-click the item, and then click **What's This?**.

Start Replication Immediately

To start replication immediately,

1. To open WINS, click **Start**, point to **Programs**, point to **Administrative Tools**, and then click **WINS**.
2. In the console tree, click **Replication Partners** (console tree | WINS | *applicable WINS server* | Replication Partners).
3. On the **Action** menu, click **Replicate Now**.
4. When prompted, click **Yes** to start replication immediately.

This operation queues replication requests for triggering replication with any of its push and pull partner servers. For this operation to have any effect, replication partners must already be added at this server.

Using Event Viewer, you can monitor the system event log at this server for more information about the status of when actual replication is completed between this server and its partner servers.

Send a Replication Trigger to a Selected Partner

To send a replication trigger to a selected partner,

1. To open WINS, click **Start**, point to **Programs**, point to **Administrative Tools**, and then click **WINS**.
2. In the console tree, click **Replication Partners** (console tree | WINS | *applicable WINS server* | Replication Partners).
3. In the details pane, click the partner that you want to start replication with.
4. On the **Action** menu, click either **Start Push Replication** or **Start Pull Replication**, depending on whether you want to start push or pull replication to the selected partner.
5. Confirm starting of either push or pull replication to the selected partner:

    a. If using pull replication, in **Start Pull Replication**, click **Yes** to confirm.

    b. If using push replication, in **Start Push Replication**, choose a push replication method, and then click **OK**:

    - Click **Start for this partner only** to start push replication for the selected partner only.
    - Click **Propagate to all partners** to request that the selected partner in turn propagate a push replication request to its configured partners.

When this procedure is completed, replication with the partner server might not start immediately. Actual replication depends on server activity and the priority of other requests queued at the selected partner.

By default, WINS only enables replication between configured replication partners.

When a push replication is started using this procedure, actual replication requires the selected partner to complete a subsequent pull replication. This occurs because WINS replication is essentially a pull operation.

Send a Replication Trigger to Any Specified WINS Server

To send a replication trigger to any specified WINS server,

1. To open WINS, click **Start**, point to **Programs**, point to **Administrative Tools**, and then click **WINS**.
2. In the console tree, click the applicable WINS server (console tree | WINS | *applicable WINS server* | Replication Partners).

3. On the **Action** menu, click either **Start Push Replication** or **Start Pull Replication**.
4. In Start Replication for WINS server, type or browse for the specified WINS server with which you want to start replication, and then click **OK**.
5. Confirm starting of either push or pull replication:

    a. If using pull replication, in **Start Pull Replication**, click **Yes** to confirm.

    b. If using push replication, in **Start Push Replication**, choose a push replication method, and then click **OK**:

    - Click **Start for this partner only** to start push replication for the selected server only.
    - Click **Propagate to all partners** to request that the selected server in turn propagate a push replication request to its configured partners.

By default, WINS only enables replication between configured replication partners. To use this procedure, first configure the server to enable it to replicate with non-partners.

When this procedure is completed, replication with the specified server might not start immediately. Actual replication depends on server activity and the priority of other requests queued at the server.

When a push replication request is started using this procedure, actual replication requires the specified WINS server to complete a subsequent pull replication. This occurs because WINS replication is essentially a pull operation.

Block Replication of Records Owned by a Specified Server

To block replication of records owned by a specified server,

1. To open WINS, click **Start**, point to **Programs**, point to **Administrative Tools**, and then click **WINS**.
2. In the console tree, click **Replication Partners** (console tree | WINS | *applicable WINS server* | Replication Partners).
3. On the **Action** menu, click **Properties**.
4. Click the **Advanced** tab.
5. Click **Add**.
6. In **Add Server**, enter the NetBIOS name or IP address of the owner (a WINS server) that you want to block any of its records from being replicated to this server.

Once a server has been added to the list of blocked partners, any records shown to be owned by the listed servers are not entered into the local database of this server during subsequent replication cycles with other partner servers.

This feature was previously implemented as a registry-only configuration in Windows NT Server, using the PersonaNonGrata registry parameter.

Change a Replication Partner Type

To change a replication partner type,

1. To open WINS, click **Start**, point to **Programs**, point to **Administrative Tools**, and then click **WINS**.
2. In the console tree, click **Replication Partners** (console tree | WINS | *applicable WINS server* | Replication Partners).
3. In the details pane, click the partner at which you want to change the type of replication it uses with the applicable WINS server.
4. On the **Action** menu, click **Properties**.
5. Click the **Advanced** tab.
6. For **Replication partner type**, select a new type, such as **Push**, **Pull**, or **Push/Pull**.

Enable the Use of Persistent Connections with a Partner Server

To enable the use of persistent connections with a partner server,

1. To open WINS, click **Start**, point to **Programs**, point to **Administrative Tools**, and then click **WINS**.
2. In the console tree, click **Replication Partners** (console tree | WINS | *applicable WINS server* | Replication Partners).
3. In the details pane, click the partner server for which you want to enable the use of persistent connections for replication purposes.
4. On the **Action** menu, click **Properties**.
5. Click the **Advanced** tab.
6. Select the appropriate **Use persistent connection for replication** check box, depending on whether the partner server is a **Push**, **Pull**, or **Push/Pull** partner of this server.

In step 6, if the partner is configured as a Push/Pull partner of this server, you can select both **Use persistent connection for replication** check boxes.

Enable the Use of Persistent Connections with Pull Partners

To enable the use of persistent connections with pull partners,

1. To open WINS, click **Start**, point to **Programs**, point to **Administrative Tools**, and then click **WINS**.
2. In the console tree, click **Replication Partners** (console tree | WINS | *applicable WINS server* | Replication Partners).
3. On the **Action** menu, click **Properties**.
4. Click the **Pull Replication** tab.
5. Select the **Use persistent connections for pull replication partners** check box.

Enable the Use of Persistent Connections with Push Partners

To enable the use of persistent connections with push partners,

1. To open WINS, click **Start**, point to **Programs**, point to **Administrative Tools**, and then click **WINS**
2. In the console tree, click **Replication Partners** (console tree | WINS | *applicable WINS server* | Replication Partners).
3. On the **Action** menu, click **Properties**.
4. Click the **Push Replication** tab.
5. Select the **Use persistent connections for push replication partners** check box.

Add a Static Mapping Entry

To add a static mapping entry,

1. To open WINS, click **Start**, point to **Programs**, point to **Administrative Tools**, and then click **WINS**.

2. In the console tree, click **Active Registrations** (console tree | WINS | *applicable WINS server* | Active Registrations).
3. On the **Action** menu, click **New Static Mapping**.
4. Enter the following information to complete the static mapping:
   a. In **Computer name**, type the NetBIOS name of the computer.
   b. In **NetBIOS scope (optional)**, you can type a NetBIOS scope identifier, if one is used, for the computer. Otherwise, leave this field blank.
   c. In **Type**, click one of the supported types to indicate whether this entry is a **Unique**, **Group**, **Domain Name**, **Internet**, or **Multihomed** type entry.
   d. In **IP address**, type the address for the computer.
5. Click **Apply** to add the static mapping entry to the database.

Or, you can add additional static mapping entries. Click **Apply** each time you complete an entry, and then click **Cancel** to close when you finish adding static mapping entries.

Important Because each static mapping is added to the database when you click Add, you cannot cancel work in the dialog box. If you make a mistake when entering a name or address for a mapping, delete the erroneous mapping and add a new one, using the correct information.

In general, only use static WINS mappings for computer names (not group names) that do not directly use WINS to register their names. Static mappings can overwrite dynamic mappings at other WINS servers and can be increasingly difficult to remove from all servers once they are introduced into a replicated WINS environment.

Edit a Static Mapping Entry

To edit a static mapping entry,

1. To open WINS, click **Start**, point to **Programs**, point to **Administrative Tools**, and then click **WINS**.
2. In the console tree, click **Active Registrations** (console tree | WINS | *applicable WINS server* | Replication Partners).
3. In the details pane, double-click the static mapping you want to edit.
4. Edit the information for the existing static mapping, as needed. For **IP Address**, you can change the address, or for supported types, you can add or remove addresses from the address list and change the order of addresses.

Only the IP address for an entry can be edited. To change other properties for an entry, you must delete the existing entry and add a new entry.

Import a File Containing Static Mapping Entries

To import a file containing static mapping entries,

1. To open WINS, click **Start**, point to **Programs**, point to **Administrative Tools**, and then click **WINS**.
2. In the console tree, click **Active Registrations** (console tree | WINS | *applicable WINS server* | Replication Partners).
3. On the **Action** menu, click **Import LMHOSTS File**.
4. In the **Open** dialog box, locate and click the lmhosts-formatted file that you want to use to import static mappings, and then click **Open**.

WINS immediately begins importing the file into the server database. Wait for WINS to finish this before you click **OK**. Typically, the lmhosts file is stored in the *systemroot\System32\Drivers\Etc* folder.

Enable Static Mappings to be Overwritten During Replication

To enable static mappings to be overwritten during replication,

1. To open WINS, click **Start**, point to **Programs**, point to **Administrative Tools**, and then click **WINS**.
2. In the console tree, click **Replication Partners** (console tree | WINS | *applicable WINS server* | Replication Partners).
3. On the **Action** menu, click **Properties**.
4. If needed, click the **General** tab.
5. Select the **Overwrite unique static mappings at this server (migrate on)** check box, and then click **Apply**.

Optimize the Command Prompt for Use with Command-Line Tools

To optimize the command prompt for use with command-line tools,

1. To open Command Prompt, click **Start**, point to **Programs**, and then click **Command Prompt**.

2. Click the upper left corner of the command prompt window, and then click **Properties**.
3. Click the **Options** tab.
4. Modify command prompt options. For command history, increase **Buffer Size** to 500 and **Number of Buffers** to 5. Under **edit options**, click **Quick Edit Mode** and **Insert Mode**.
5. Click the **Layout** tab.
6. Increase **Screen Buffer Size** to 2500.
7. Click **OK** to apply changes. When prompted, select **Modify shortcut that started this window**.

As a keyboard option for step 2, access **Command Prompt Properties** by doing the following: press the ALT key and the spacebar at the same time, then press *P* to select **Properties**.

By optimizing the command prompt window using this procedure, you can use Windows Explorer features, such as scrolling, and quickly mark, copy, and paste to and from the command prompt window. By increasing the screen buffer size, you can scroll back to previous command output and more easily view command-line help text.

Use WINS Commands Interactively at the Command Prompt

To use WINS commands interactively at the command prompt,

1. To open Command Prompt, click **Start**, point to **Programs**, and then click **Command Prompt**.
2. Type: *netsh*
3. At the **netsh>** (Net Shell) command prompt , type: *wins*
4. At the **wins>** (WINS helper) command prompt, type either *server \\servername* or *server ip_address* for the server you want to manage.

   Once a server that you have rights to manage has been successfully contacted, you should see "You have Read and Write access to the server *servername*."
5. Once you are connected to this WINS server, you can use any supported command.

Type */?* or *help* to display the immediate WINS subcommand menu. Or, type *list* to display all NetShell subcommands available for use with WINS.

In order to have administrative rights to manage a WINS server, you must be logged on with a user account that has membership in the local WINS Users group. For Windows NT Server, you must belong to the local Administrator group on the server.

Use WINS Commands Noninteractively or in Scripts

To use WINS commands noninteractively or in scripts,

1. To open Command Prompt, click **Start**, point to **Programs**, and then click **Command Prompt**.
2. At the command prompt or in scripted form, you can use NetShell commands for WINS noninteractively by using the following fully-qualified command syntax:

netsh wins server [\\servername] subcommand

The *servername* parameter is optional when performing WINS commands locally on the same computer where the command is executed. If the WINS server being managed is on a remote computer, this parameter is required and the remote server name must be used.

In order to have administrative rights to manage a WINS server, you must be logged on with a user account that has membership in the local WINS Users group. For Windows NT Server, you must belong to the local Administrator group on that server.

E I G H T

DNS Overview

DNS Defined

DNS is an abbreviation for Domain Name System, a system for naming computers and network services that is organized into a hierarchy of domains. DNS naming is used in TCP/IP networks, such as the Internet, to locate computers and services through user-friendly names. When a user enters a DNS name in an application, DNS services can resolve the name to other information associated with the name, such as an IP address.

For example, most users prefer a friendly name such as *example.microsoft.com* to locate a computer such as a mail or Web server on a network. A friendly name can be easier to learn and remember. However, computers communicate over a network by using numeric addresses. To make use of network resources easier, name services such as DNS provide a way to map the user-friendly name for a computer or service to its numeric address. If you have ever used a Web browser, you have used DNS.

Figure 8-1 shows a basic use of DNS, which is finding the IP address of a computer based on its name.

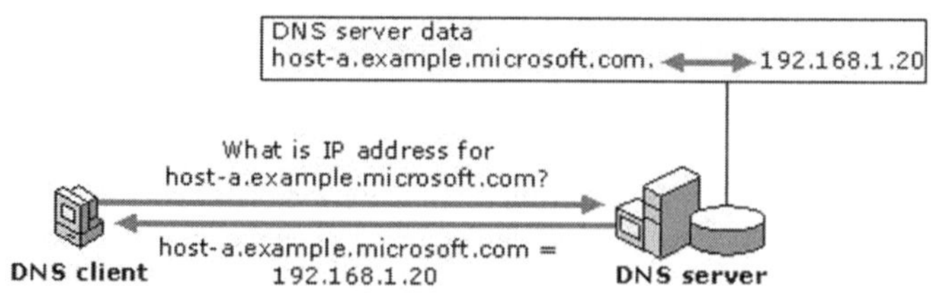

FIGURE 8–1 *Example of DNS forward lookup*

In this example, a client computer queries a server, asking for the IP address of a computer configured to use *host-a.example.microsoft.com* as its DNS domain name. Because the server is able to answer the query based on its local database, it replies with an answer containing the requested information, which is a host (A) resource record that contains the IP address information for *host-a.example.microsoft.com*.

The example shows a simple DNS query between a single client and server. In practice, DNS queries can be more involved than this and include additional steps, which are reviewed in "How DNS Query Works" in this chapter.

DNS Tools

Windows 2000 provides a number of utilities for administering, monitoring, and troubleshooting both DNS servers and clients. These utilities include:

- The DNS console, which is part of Administrative Tools.
- Command-line utilities, such as Nslookup, which can be used to troubleshoot DNS problems.
- Logging features, such as the DNS server log, which can be viewed using Event Viewer. File-based logs can also be used temporarily as an advanced debugging option to log and trace selected service events.
- Performance monitoring utilities, such as statistical counters to measure and monitor DNS server activity with System Monitor.

The DNS Console

The primary tool that you use to manage Windows 2000 DNS servers is the DNS console, which is provided in the Administrative Tools folder in Control Panel. The DNS console appears as a Microsoft Management Console (MMC) snap-in to further integrate DNS administration into your total network management.

After you install a DNS server, you can use the DNS console to perform these basic administrative server tasks:

1. Performing initial configuration of a new DNS server.
2. Connecting to and managing a local DNS server on the same computer, or remote DNS servers on other computers.
3. Adding and removing forward and reverse lookup zones as needed.
4. Adding, removing, and updating resource records in zones.
5. Modifying how zones are stored and replicated between servers.
6. Modifying how servers process queries and handle dynamic updates.
7. Modifying security for specific zones or resource records.

In addition, you can also use the DNS console to perform the following tasks:

- Perform maintenance on the server. You can start, stop, pause, or resume the server, or manually update server data files.
- Monitor the contents of the server cache and, as needed, clear it.
- Tune advanced server options.
- Configure and perform aging and scavenging of stale resource records stored by the server.

In addition, you can operate the DNS console from a non-server computer to remotely administer Windows 2000 DNS servers (provided you have first installed the DNS Server service on them).

Important The DNS console can only be used to manage Windows 2000 DNS servers.

The DNS console provides new ways to perform familiar DNS administrative tasks previously performed in Windows NT Server 4.0 using DNS Manager.

For Windows 2000 Server, the DNS console appears after a DNS server is installed. To use the DNS console from another non-server computer, such as one running Windows 2000 Professional, you must install the Administrative Tools pack.

Command-line Utilities

Windows 2000 provides several command-line utilities. You can use them to manage and troubleshoot DNS servers and clients. Table 8.1 describes each of these utilities, which can be run either by typing them at a command prompt or by entering them in batch files for scripted use.

TABLE 8.1 *Command-Line Utilities*

Command	Description
Nslookup	Used to perform query testing of the DNS domain namespace. For more information, see Chapter 10, "Installing and Maintaining DNS Servers."
Dnscmd	A command-line interface for managing DNS servers. This utility is useful in scripting batch files to help automate routine DNS management tasks or to perform simple unattended setup and configuration of new DNS servers on your network. For more information, see Appendix D, "DNS Resources and Troubleshooting."
Ipconfig	This command is used to view and modify IP configuration details used by the computer. For Windows 2000, additional command-line options are included with this utility to provide help in troubleshooting and supporting DNS clients. For more information, see Chapter 10.

Event Monitoring Utilities

Windows 2000 Server includes two options for monitoring DNS servers,

- *Default logging of DNS server event messages to the DNS server log.* For Windows 2000 Server, server event messages are separated and kept in their own system event log, the DNS server log, which can be viewed using Event Viewer.

  The DNS server log contains basic events logged by the DNS Server service. For example, when the DNS server starts or stops, a corresponding event message is written to this log. Some additional critical DNS service events are also logged here, such as when the server starts but cannot locate initializing data, such as zones or boot information stored in the Windows 2000 registry or (in some cases) Active Directory.

  The event types logged by Windows 2000 DNS servers are predetermined. For more information, see Appendix D.

  You can also use Event Viewer to view and monitor client-related DNS events. These appear in the System log and are written by the DNS Client service at any computers running Windows 2000 (all versions).
- *Optional debug options for trace logging to a text file on the DNS server computer.* You can also use the DNS console to selectively enable additional debug logging options for temporary trace logging to a text-based file of DNS server activity. The file created and used for this feature, *Dns.log,* is stored in the *systemroot\System32\Dns* folder. For information about using server debug logging options, see Chapter 9, "Using DNS."

Performance Monitoring Utilities

Performance monitoring for Windows 2000 DNS servers can be done using additional service-specific counters that measure DNS server performance. These counters are accessible through System Monitor, which is provided in the Performance console.

When using System Monitor, you can create charts and graphs of server performance trends over time for any of your Windows 2000 DNS servers. These can be further studied and analyzed to determine if additional server tuning is needed.

By measuring and reviewing server metrics over a period of time, it is possible to determine performance benchmarks and decide if further adjustments can be made to optimize the system. For information about monitoring server performance, see Chapter 4, "Using DHCP."

If you have previously used Windows DNS servers, the DNS console replaces DNS Manager, which was used in Windows NT Server 4.0.

Server Features

The DNS service running in Windows 2000 Server provides the following:

- *An RFC-compliant DNS name server. DNS is an open protocol and is standardized by a set of Requests for Comments (RFCs).* Microsoft supports and complies with these standard specifications. For more information, see Appendix D.
- *Interoperability with other DNS server implementations.* Because the DNS service is RFC-compliant and can use standard DNS data file and resource records formats, it can successfully work with most other DNS server implementations, such as those that use the Berkeley Internet Name Domain (BIND) software. For information about interoperability, see Chapter 9.
- *Support for Active Directory. DNS is required for support of Active Directory.* If you install Active Directory on a server computer, Windows 2000 Server can automatically install and configure a DNS server if one cannot be located based on the current configuration of the server computer.

  First, in the Active Directory installation wizard, you specify the DNS name of the Active Directory domain for which you are promoting the server to become a domain controller. Later in the installation process, the wizard tests for the following:

1. Based on its TCP/IP client configuration, it checks to see whether a preferred DNS server is configured for its use.
2. If a preferred DNS server is available, it queries to find the primary authoritative server for the DNS domain you specified earlier in the wizard.
3. It then tests to see whether the authoritative primary server can support and accept dynamic updates as described in the DNS dynamic update protocol.
4. If, at this point in the process, a supporting DNS server cannot be located to accept updates for the specified DNS domain name you are using with Active Directory, you are provided with the option to install one that uses the DNS Server service.

In general, the use of the Windows 2000 DNS Server service is strongly recommended for the best possible integration and support of Active Directory and enhanced DNS server features. You can, however, use another type of DNS server to support Active Directory deployment.

When using other DNS servers, consider additional issues related to DNS interoperability. For more information, see Chapter 9.

- *Integration with other Microsoft networking services.* The DNS service offers integration with other Windows 2000 services and contains features beyond those specified in the RFCs. These include integration with Active Directory, WINS, and DHCP services. For more information, see "Windows 2000 DNS Implementation" in this chapter.
- *Improved ease of administration.* The DNS snap-in offers an improved graphical user interface for managing the DNS service. Also, Windows 2000 Server provides several new configuration wizards for performing common server administration tasks. In addition to the DNS snap-in, other tools are provided to help you better manage and support DNS servers and clients on your network. For more information, see "DNS Tools" in this chapter.
- *RFC-compliant dynamic update protocol support.* The DNS service allows clients to dynamically update resource records, based on the DNS dynamic update protocol (RFC 2136). This improves DNS administration by reducing the time needed to manually manage these records. Computers running Windows 2000 can dynamically register their DNS names and IP addresses. For more information, see "Dynamic Update" in this chapter.
- *Support for incremental zone transfer between servers.* Zone transfers are used between DNS servers to replicate information about a portion of the DNS namespace. Incremental zone transfer is used to replicate only the changed portions of a zone, conserving network bandwidth. For more information, see "Understanding Zones and Zone Transfer" in this chapter.
- *Support for new resource record types.* The DNS service includes support for several new resource record types. These types, which include the service location (SRV) and ATM address (ATMA) resource records, expand the possibilities for using DNS as a names database service. For more information, see Appendix D.

Client Features

The DNS Client service running in Windows 2000 is used to resolve DNS domain names and implements the following features:

- *System-wide caching.* Resource records from query responses are added to the client cache as applications query DNS servers. This information is then cached for a set Time-to-Live (TTL) and can be used again to answer subsequent queries.

- *RFC-compliant negative caching support.* In addition to caching positive query responses from DNS servers (which contain resource record information in the answered reply), the DNS Client service also caches negative query responses. A negative response results when a resource record for the queried name does not exist.

  Negative caching prevents the repeating of additional queries for names that do not exist, which can adversely affect client system performance. Any query information negatively cached is kept for a shorter period of time than is used for positive query responses; by default, no more than 5 minutes. This avoids continued negative caching of stale information if the records later become available. Negative caching is a new DNS standard specification defined in RFC 2308. For more information, refer to this RFC. For more information on obtaining RFCs, see Appendix A, "TCP/IP Resources."
- *Avoidance of unresponsive DNS servers.* The DNS Client service uses a server search list, ordered by preference. This list includes all preferred and alternate DNS servers configured for each of the active network connections on the system. Windows 2000 rearranges these lists based on the following criteria:

  1. Preferred DNS servers are given first priority.
  2. If no preferred DNS servers are available, then alternate DNS servers are used.
  3. Unresponsive servers are removed temporarily from these lists.

Important In Windows 2000, the DHCP Client service initiates dynamic registration for client DNS names. For more information, see "Dynamic Update" in this chapter, or refer to Chapter 4.

DNS Domain Names

The Domain Name System was originally defined in RFCs 1034 and 1035. These documents specify elements common to all implementations of DNS-related software, including,

- A DNS domain namespace, which specifies a structured hierarchy of domains used to organize names.
- Resource records, which map DNS domain names to a specific type of resource information for use when the name is registered or resolved in the namespace.
- DNS servers that store and answer name queries for resource records.

- DNS clients, also known as resolvers, which query servers to look up and resolve names to a type of resource record specified in the query.

Understanding the DNS Domain Namespace

The DNS domain namespace, as shown in Figure 8-2, is based on the concept of a tree of named domains. Each level of the tree can represent either a branch or a leaf of the tree. A branch is a level where more than one name is used to identify a collection of named resources. A leaf represents a single name used once at that level to indicate a specific resource.

Figure 8-2 shows how Microsoft is assigned authority by the Internet root servers for its own part of the DNS domain namespace tree on the Internet. DNS clients and servers use queries as the fundamental method of resolving names in the tree to specific types of resource information. This information is provided by DNS servers in query responses to DNS clients, who then extract the information and pass it to a requesting program for resolving the queried name.

In the process of resolving a name, keep in mind that DNS servers often function as DNS clients, querying other servers in order to fully resolve a queried name. For more information, see "How DNS Query Works" in this chapter.

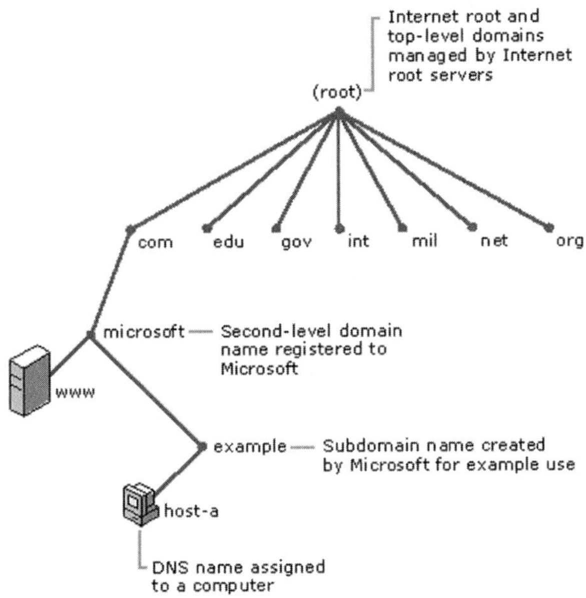

FIGURE 8-2 *DNS Domain namespace*

How the DNS Domain Namespace Is Organized

Any DNS domain name used in the tree is technically a domain. Most DNS discussions, however, identify names in one of five ways, based on the level and the way a name is commonly used. For example, the DNS domain name registered to Microsoft *(microsoft.com.)* is known as a second-level domain. This is because the name has two parts (known as labels) that indicate it is located two levels below the root or top of the tree. Most DNS domain names have two or more labels, each of which indicates a new level in the tree. Periods are used in names to separate labels.

In addition to second-level domains, other terms used to describe DNS domain names by their function in the namespace are described in Table 8.2.

TABLE 8.2 *DNS Domain Names by Function*

Name type	Description	Example
The domain root	This is the top of the tree, representing an unnamed level; it is sometimes shown as two empty quotation marks (""), indicating a null value. When used in a DNS domain name, it is stated by a trailing period to designate that the name is located at the root or highest level of the domain hierarchy. In this instance, the DNS domain name is considered to be complete and points to an exact location in the tree of names. Names stated this way are called fully qualified domain names (FQDNs).	A single period (.) or a period used at the end of a name, such as *example.microsoft.com.*
Top-level domain	A name of two or three letters used to indicate a country/region or the type of organization using a name.	*.com,* which indicates a name registered to a business for commercial use on the Internet
Second-level domain	Variable-length names registered to an individual or organization for use on the Internet. These names are always based upon an appropriate top-level domain, depending on the type of organization or geographic location where a name is used.	*microsoft.com.,* which is the second-level domain name registered to Microsoft by the Internet DNS domain name registrar.
Subdomain	Additional names that an organization can create that are derived from the registered second-level domain name. These include names added to grow the DNS tree of names in an organization and divide it into departments or geographic locations.	*example.microsoft.com.,* which is a fictitious subdomain assigned by Microsoft for use in documentation example names.
Host or resource name	Names that represent a leaf in the DNS tree of names and identify a specific resource. Typically, the leftmost label of a DNS domain name identifies a specific computer on the network. For example, if a name at this level is used in a host resource record, it is used to look up the IP address of computer based on its host name.	*host-a.example.microsoft.com.,* where the first label (host-a) is the DNS host name for a specific computer on the network.

Interpreting a DNS Domain Name

DNS has a method of noting and interpreting the fully qualified path to a DNS domain name similar to the way full paths to files or directories are noted or displayed at a command prompt.

For example, a directory tree path helps point to the exact location of a file stored on your computer. For Windows computers, the backslash (\) indicates each new directory that leads to the exact location of a file. For DNS, the equivalent is a period (.) indicating each new domain level used in a name.

For example, for a file called Services, the full path to this file, as displayed at a Windows command prompt would be:

C:\Winnt\System32\Drivers\Etc\Services

To interpret the full path of the file, the name is read in a left-to-right direction from the highest or most general piece of information (drive C, the drive where the file is stored) to its most specific information, the file name *Services*. This example shows five separate levels of hierarchy that lead toward the location of the *Services* file on drive C.

1. The root folder for drive C *(C:\)*.
2. The system root folder where Windows is installed *(Winnt)*.
3. A system folder where system components are stored *(System32)*.
4. A subfolder where system device drivers are stored *(Drivers)*.
5. A subfolder where miscellaneous files used by system and network device drivers are stored *(Etc)*.

For DNS, an example of a domain name with multiple levels is the following, a fully qualified domain name (FQDN):

host-a.example.microsoft.com.

Unlike the file name example, a DNS FQDN, when read from left to right, moves from its most specific information (the DNS name for a computer called host-a) to its highest or most general piece of information (the trailing period that indicates the root of the DNS name tree). This example shows the four separate DNS domain levels that lead away from the specific host location of *host-a*.

1. The *example* domain, which corresponds to a subdomain where the computer name *host-a* is registered for use.
2. The *microsoft* domain, which corresponds to the parent domain that roots the *example* subdomain.
3. The *com* domain, which corresponds to the top-level domain designated for use by business or commercial organizations that roots the *microsoft* domain.

4. The trailing period (.), which is a standard separator character used to qualify the full DNS domain name to the root level of the DNS namespace tree.

Background on DNS and the Internet

The Domain Name System was developed because of the need to provide a name-to-address mapping service for computers on the Internet. Before DNS was introduced in 1987, the practice of mapping friendly computer names to IP addresses was done mainly through the use of a shared static file, known as a Hosts file.

Originally, the Internet was small enough to use one centrally administered file that was published and downloaded using FTP for Internet-connected sites. Periodically, each Internet site would update its copy of the Hosts file, and updated versions of the Hosts file were posted to reflect network changes.

As the number of computers on the Internet grew, it became unworkable to have one centralized authority managing a single Hosts file for all Internet hosts. The file became increasingly larger, which made it harder to maintain and distribute to all sites in a current and updated form.

The DNS standard was developed to provide an alternative to Hosts files. RFCs 1034 and 1035 specify most of the core protocols and have been added to and updated by additional RFCs submitted to the Internet Engineering Task Force (IETF). The IETF reviews and approves new drafts continuously, so the standards for DNS evolve and change as needed.

DNS domain names are required to be unique at each level, but individual name labels can be reused in other domains. For example, the name *mailserver* can be used one time only in both the *example.microsoft.com* and *microsoft.com* domains.

For more information on the use of labels, FQDNs, and other DNS host naming requirements, see Chapter 9.

For Windows 2000, Hosts files are supported as a local static file method of mapping DNS domain names for host computers to their IP addresses. In addition to this basic and traditional function, Windows 2000 preloads any mapped entries added to this file into the local DNS names cache on each computer when the DNS Client service is started.

The Hosts file is provided in the *systemroot\System32\Drivers\Etc* folder. To view or modify this file, you can use Notepad or another text-based editor. For more information on creating or editing the Hosts file, refer to the comments and examples in the file.

How DNS Query Works

When a DNS client needs to look up a name used in a program, it queries DNS servers to resolve the name. Each query message the client sends contains three pieces of information, specifying a question for the server to answer:

- A specified DNS domain name, stated as an FQDN.
- A specified query type, which can either specify a resource record by type or by a specialized type of query operation.
- A specified class for the DNS domain name. For Windows DNS servers, this should always be specified as the Internet (IN) class.

For example, the name specified could be the FQDN for a computer, such as *host-a.example.microsoft.com.*, and the query type specified to look for an address resource record by that name. Think of a DNS query as a client asking a server a two-part question, such as "Do you have any A record records for a computer named *hostname.example.microsoft.com.*?" When the client receives an answer from the server, it reads and interprets the answered A resource record, learning the IP address for the computer it asked for by name.

DNS queries resolve in a number of different ways. A client can sometimes answer a query locally, using cached information obtained from a previous query. The DNS server can use its own cache of resource record information to answer a query. A DNS server can also query or contact other DNS servers on behalf of the requesting client to fully resolve the name, and then send an answer back to the client. This process is known as *recursion*.

In addition, the client itself can attempt to contact additional DNS servers to resolve a name. When a client does so, it uses separate and additional queries based on referral answers from servers. This process is known as *iteration*.

In general, the DNS query process occurs in two parts:

- A name query begins at a client computer and is passed to a resolver, the DNS Client service, for resolution.
- When the query cannot be resolved locally, DNS servers can be queried as needed to resolve the name.

Both of these processes are explained in more detail in the following sections.

Part 1: The Local Resolver

Figure 8-3 shows an overview of the complete DNS query process.

As shown in the initial steps of the query process, a DNS domain name is used in a program on the local computer. The request is then passed to

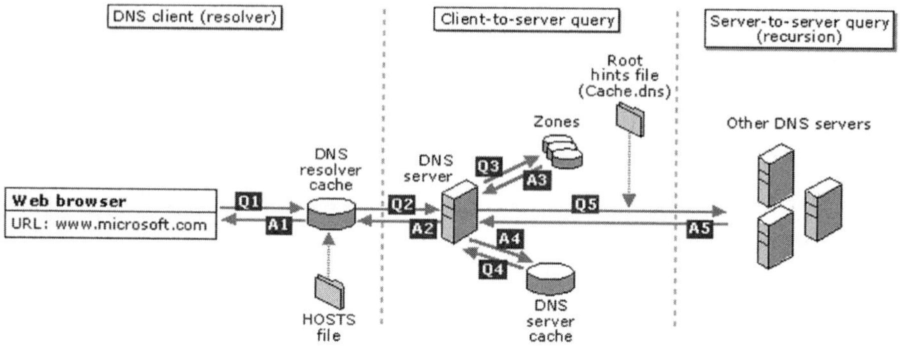

FIGURE 8–3 *How a DNS query works*

the DNS Client service for resolution, using locally cached information. If the queried name can be resolved, the query is answered and the process is completed.

The local resolver cache can include name information obtained from two possible sources:

- If a Hosts file is configured locally, any host name-to-address mappings from that file are preloaded into the cache when the DNS Client service is started.
- Resource records obtained in answered responses from previous DNS queries are added to the cache and kept for a period of time.

If the query does not match an entry in the cache, the resolution process continues, with the client querying a DNS server to resolve the name.

Part 2: Querying a DNS Server

As indicated in the previous graphic, the client queries a preferred DNS server. The actual server used during the initial client/server query part of the process is selected from a global list. For more information on how this global list is compiled and updated by Windows 2000, see "Client Features" in this chapter.

When the DNS server receives a query, it first checks to see if it can answer the query authoritatively, based on resource record information contained in a locally configured zone on the server. If the queried name matches a corresponding resource record in local zone information, the server answers authoritatively, using this information to resolve the queried name.

If no zone information exists for the queried name, the server then checks to see if it can resolve the name using locally cached information from previous queries. If a match is found here, the server answers with this information. Again, if the preferred server can answer with a positive matched response from its cache to the requesting client, the query is completed.

If the queried name does not find a matched answer at its preferred server—either from its cache or zone information—the query process can continue, using recursion to fully resolve the name. This involves assistance from other DNS servers to help resolve the name. By default, the DNS Client service asks the server to use a process of recursion to fully resolve names on behalf of the client before returning an answer. In most cases, the DNS server is configured, by default, to support the recursion process, as shown in Figure 8-4.

In order for the DNS server to do recursion properly, it first needs some helpful contact information about other DNS servers in the DNS domain namespace. This information is provided in the form of *root hints,* a list of preliminary resource records that can be used by the DNS service to locate other DNS servers that are authoritative for the root of the DNS domain namespace tree. Root servers are authoritative for the domain root and top-level domains in the DNS domain namespace tree. For more information, see Chapter 9.

By using root hints to find root servers, a DNS server is able to complete the use of recursion. In theory, this process enables any DNS server to locate the servers that are authoritative for any other DNS domain name used at any level in the namespace tree.

For example, consider the use of the recursion process to locate the name *host-b.example.microsoft.com.* when the client queries a single DNS server. The process occurs when a DNS server and client are first started and have no locally cached information available to help resolve a name query. It assumes that the name queried by the client is for a domain name of which the server has no local knowledge, based on its configured zones.

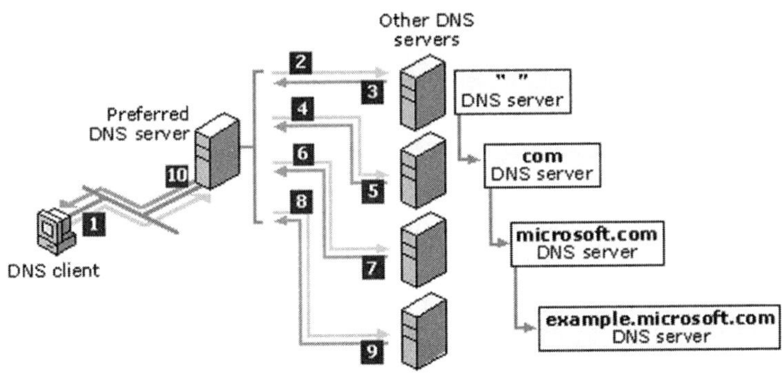

FIGURE 8–4 *How recursion works*

First, the preferred server parses the full name and determines that it needs the location of the server that is authoritative for the top-level domain, *com*. It then uses an iterative query to the *com* DNS server to obtain a referral to the *microsoft.com* server. Next, a referral answer comes from the *microsoft.com* server to the DNS server for *example.microsoft.com*.

Finally, the *example.microsoft.com.* server is contacted. Because this server contains the queried name as part of its configured zones, it responds authoritatively back to the original server that initiated recursion. When the original server receives the response indicating that an authoritative answer was obtained to the requested query, it forwards this answer back to the requesting client and the recursive query process is completed.

Although the recursive query process can be resource-intensive when performed as described above, it has some performance advantages for the DNS server. For example, during the recursion process, the DNS server performing the recursive lookup obtains information about the DNS domain namespace. This information is cached by the server and can be used again to help speed the answering of subsequent queries that use or match it. Over time, this cached information can grow to occupy a significant portion of server memory resources, although it is cleared whenever the DNS service is cycled on and off.

Alternate Query Responses

The previous discussion of DNS queries assumes that the process ends with a positive response returned to the client. However, queries can return other answers as well. These are the most common:

- An authoritative answer
- A positive answer
- A referral answer
- A negative answer

An authoritative answer is a positive answer returned to the client and delivered with the authority bit set in the DNS message to indicate the answer was obtained from a server with direct authority for the queried name.

A positive response can consist of the queried resource record or a list of resource records (also known as a resource record set) that fits the queried DNS domain name and record type specified in the query message.

A referral answer contains additional resource records not specified by name or type in the query. This type of answer is returned to the client if the recursion process is not supported. The records are meant to act as helpful reference answers that the client can use to continue the query using iteration.

A referral answer contains additional data such as resource records that are other than the type queried. For example, if the queried host name was *www* and no A resource records for this name were found in this zone, but a

CNAME resource record for *www* was found instead, the DNS server can include that information when responding to the client.

If the client is able to use iteration, it can make additional queries using the referral information in an attempt to fully resolve the name. For more information, see "How Iteration Works" in this chapter.

A negative response from the server can indicate that one of two possible results was encountered while the server attempted to process and recursively resolve the query fully and authoritatively.

- An authoritative server reported that the queried name does not exist in the DNS namespace.
- An authoritative server reported that the queried name exists but no records of the specified type exist for that name.

The resolver passes the results of the query, in the form of either a positive or negative response, back to the requesting program and caches the response.

If the resultant answer to a query is too long to be sent and resolved in a single UDP message packet, the DNS server can initiate a failover response over TCP port 53 to answer the client fully in a TCP connected session.

Disabling the use of recursion on a DNS server is generally done when DNS clients are being limited to resolving names to a specific DNS server, such as one located on your intranet. Recursion might also be disabled when the DNS server is incapable of resolving external DNS names, and clients are expected to failover to another DNS server for resolution of these names.

For Windows 2000 Server, you can disable the use of recursion for DNS servers as needed by configuring in Advanced properties in the DNS console on the applicable server. For more information, see Chapter 10.

By default, Windows 2000 DNS servers use several default timings when performing a recursive query and contacting other DNS servers. These are,

- A recursion retry interval of 3 seconds. This is the length of time the DNS service waits before retrying a query made during a recursive lookup.
- A recursion time-out interval of 15 seconds. This is the length of time the DNS service waits before failing a recursive lookup that has been retried.

Under most circumstances, these parameters do not need adjustment. However, if you are using recursive lookups over a slow-speed WAN link, you might be able to improve server performance and query completion by making slight adjustments to the settings. For information about tuning advanced server parameters, see Chapter 9.

How Iteration Works

Iteration is the type of name resolution used between DNS clients and servers when the following conditions are in effect:

- The client requests the use of recursion, but recursion is disabled on the DNS server.
- The client does not request the use of recursion when querying the DNS server.

An iterative request from a client tells the DNS server that the client expects the best answer the DNS server can provide immediately, without contacting other DNS servers.

When iteration is used, a DNS server answers a client based on its own specific knowledge about the namespace with regard to the names data being queried. For example, if a DNS server on your intranet receives a query from a local client for *www.microsoft.com,* it might return an answer from its names cache. If the queried name is not currently stored in the names cache of the server, the server might respond by providing a referral—that is, a list of NS and A resource records for other DNS servers that are closer to the name queried by the client.

When a referral is made, the DNS client assumes responsibility to continue making iterative queries to other configured DNS servers to resolve the name. For example, in the most involved case, the DNS client might expand its search as far as the root domain servers on the Internet in an effort to locate the DNS servers that are authoritative for the *com* domain. Once it contacts the Internet root servers, it can be given further iterative responses from these DNS servers that point to actual Internet DNS servers for the *microsoft.com* domain. When the client is provided records for these DNS servers, it can send another iterative query to the external Microsoft DNS servers on the Internet, which can respond with a definitive and authoritative answer.

When iteration is used, a DNS server can further assist in a name query resolution beyond giving its own best answer back to the client. For most iterative queries, a client uses its locally configured list of DNS servers to contact other name servers throughout the DNS namespace if its primary DNS server cannot resolve the query.

How Caching Works

As DNS servers process client queries using recursion or iteration, they discover and acquire a significant store of information about the DNS namespace. The server then caches this information.

Caching provides a way to speed the performance of DNS resolution for subsequent queries of popular names, while substantially reducing DNS-related query traffic on the network.

As DNS servers make recursive queries on behalf of clients, they temporarily cache resource records. Cached resource records contain information obtained from DNS servers that are authoritative for DNS domain names learned while making iterative queries to search and fully answer a recursive query performed on behalf of a client. Later, when other clients place new queries that request resource record information matching cached resource records, the DNS server can use the cached resource record information to answer them.

When information is cached, a TTL value applies to all cached resource records. As long as the TTL for a cached resource record does not expire, a DNS server can continue to cache and use the resource record again when answering queries by its clients that match these resource records. Caching TTL values used by resource records in most zone configurations are assigned the *Minimum (default) TTL,* which is set using the zone's start of authority (SOA) resource record. By default, the minimum TTL is 3,600 seconds (1 hour) but can be adjusted or, if needed, individual caching TTLs can be set at each resource record.

You can install a Windows 2000 DNS server to operate as a caching-only server (without any configured zones). For information about using caching-only servers, see Chapter 9.

By default, Windows 2000 DNS servers use a root hints file, *Cache.dns,* that is stored in the *%SystemRoot%\System32\Dns* folder on the server computer. The contents of this file are preloaded into server memory when the service is started and contain pointer information to root servers for the DNS namespace where you are operating DNS servers. For more information on this file or how it is used, see Appendix D.

Understanding Zones and Zone Transfer

The Domain Name System allows a DNS namespace to be divided up into zones, which store name information about one or more DNS domains. For each DNS domain name included in a zone, the zone becomes the authoritative source for information about that domain.

Understanding the Difference Between Zones and Domains

A zone starts as a storage database for a single DNS domain name. If other domains are added below the domain used to create the zone, these domains can either be part of the same zone or belong to another zone. Once a subdomain is added, it can then either be,

- Managed and included as part of the original zone records, or
- Delegated away to another zone created to support the subdomain.

For example, Figure 8-5 shows the *microsoft.com* domain, which contains domain names for Microsoft. When the *microsoft.com* domain is first created at a single server, it is configured as a single zone for all of the Microsoft DNS namespace. If, however, the *microsoft.com* domain needs to use subdomains, those subdomains must be included in the zone or delegated away to another zone.

In this example, the *example.microsoft.com* domain shows a new subdomain—the *example.microsoft.com* domain—delegated away from the *microsoft.com* zone and managed in its own zone. However, the *microsoft.com* zone needs to contain a few resource records to provide the delegation information that references the DNS servers that are authoritative for the delegated *example.microsoft.com* subdomain.

If the *microsoft.com* zone does not use delegation for a subdomain, any data for the subdomain remains part of the *microsoft.com* zone. For example, the subdomain *dev.microsoft.com* is not delegated away but is managed by the *microsoft.com* zone.

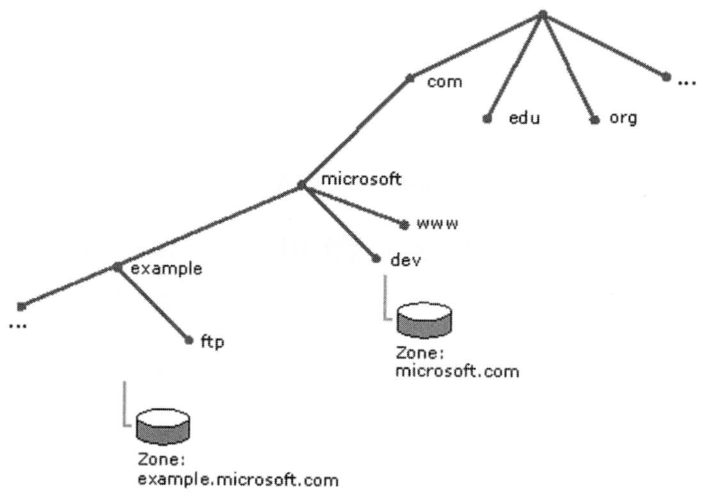

FIGURE 8–5 *Difference between a zone and a domain*

Why Zone Replication and Zone Transfers Are Needed

Because of the important role that zones play in DNS, it is intended that they be available from more than one DNS server on the network to provide availability and fault tolerance when resolving name queries. Otherwise, if a single server is used and that server is not responding, queries for names in the zone can fail. For additional servers to host a zone, zone transfers are required to replicate and synchronize all copies of the zone used at each server configured to host the zone.

When a new DNS server is added to the network and is configured as a new secondary server for an existing zone, it performs a full initial transfer of the zone to obtain and replicate a full copy of resource records for the zone. For many earlier DNS server implementations, this same method of full transfer for a zone is also used when the zone requires updating after changes are made to the zone. For Windows 2000 Server, the DNS service supports *incremental zone transfer,* a revised DNS zone transfer process for intermediate changes.

Incremental Zone Transfers

Incremental zone transfers are described in RFC 1995 as an additional DNS standard for replicating DNS zones. When incremental transfers are supported by both a DNS server acting as the source for a zone and any servers that copy the zone from it, it provides a more efficient method of propagating zone changes and updates.

In earlier DNS implementations, any request for an update of zone data required a full transfer of the entire zone database using an all zone transfer (AXFR) query. With incremental transfer, an alternate query type, the incremental zone transfer (IXFR), can be used instead. This allows the secondary server to pull only those zone changes it needs to synchronize its copy of the zone with its source, either a primary or secondary copy of the zone maintained by another DNS server.

With IXFR zone transfers, differences between the source and replicated versions of the zone are first determined. If the zones are identified to be the same version—as indicated by the serial number field in the SOA resource record of each zone—no transfer is made.

If the serial number for the zone at the source is greater than at the requesting secondary server, a transfer is made of only those changes to resource records for each incremental version of the zone. For an IXFR query to succeed and changes to be sent, the source DNS server for the zone must keep a history of incremental zone changes to use when answering these queries. The incremental transfer process requires substantially less traffic on a network and zone transfers are completed much faster.

HOW ZONE TRANSFER WORKS

A zone transfer might occur during any of the following scenarios:

- When the refresh interval expires for the zone.
- When a secondary server is notified of zone changes by its master server.
- When the DNS Server service is started at a secondary server for the zone.
- When the DNS console is used at a secondary server for the zone to manually initiate a transfer from its master server.

Zone transfers are always initiated at the secondary server for a zone and sent to their configured master servers that act as their source for the zone. Master servers can be any other DNS server that loads the zone, such as either the primary server for the zone or another secondary server. When the master server receives the request for the zone, it can reply with either a partial or full transfer of the zone to the secondary server.

As shown in Figure 8-6, zone transfers between servers follow an ordered process. This process varies, depending on whether a zone has been previously replicated or if initial replication of a new zone is being performed.

In this example, the following sequence is performed for a requesting secondary server—the destination server—for a zone and its source server, another DNS server that hosts the zone.

1. During new configuration, the destination server sends an initial AXFR request to the master DNS server configured as its source for the zone.
2. The master (source) server responds and fully transfers the zone to the secondary (destination) server. The zone is delivered to the destination server requesting the transfer, with its version established by use of a Serial number field in the properties for the SOA resource record. The SOA resource record also contains a stated refresh interval in seconds (by default, 900 seconds or 15 minutes) to indicate when the destination server should next request to renew the zone with the source server.

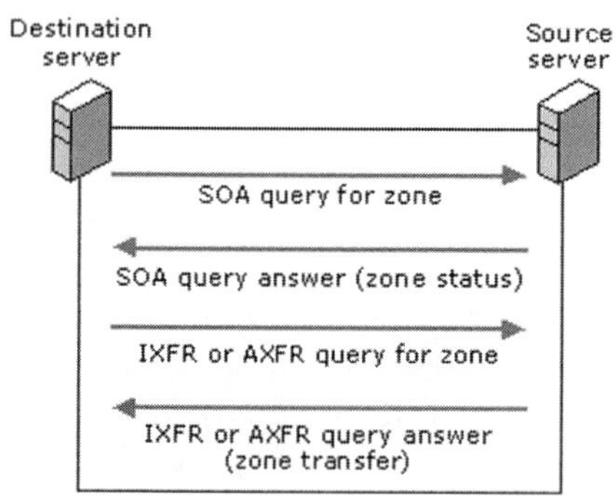

FIGURE 8–6 Zone transfer

3. When the refresh interval expires, the destination server requests renewal of the zone from the source server by using an SOA query.
4. The source server answers the query for its SOA record. This response contains the serial number for the zone in its current state at the source server.
5. The destination server checks the serial number of the SOA record in the response and determines how to renew the zone. If the value of the serial number in the SOA response is equal to its current local serial number, it concludes that the zone is the same at both servers and that a zone transfer is not needed. The destination server then renews the zone by resetting its refresh interval based on the value of this field in the SOA response from its source server. If the value of the serial number in the SOA response is higher than its current local serial number, it concludes that the zone has been updated and that a transfer is needed.
6. If the destination server concludes that the zone has changed, it sends an IXFR query to the source server, containing its current local value for the serial number in the SOA record for the zone.
7. The source server responds with either an incremental or full transfer of the zone. If the source server supports incremental transfer by maintaining a history of recent incremental zone changes for modified resource records, it can answer with an IXFR of the zone. If the source server does not support incremental transfer, or does not have a history of zone changes, it can answer with a full AXFR transfer of the zone instead.

For Windows 2000 Server, incremental zone transfer through IXFR query is supported. For earlier versions of the DNS service running on Windows NT Server 4.0 and for many other DNS server implementations, IXFR is not available and only AXFR queries and transfers are used to replicate zones.

DNS Notify

Windows DNS servers support DNS Notify, an update to the original DNS protocol specification that permits a means of initiating notification to secondary servers when zone changes occur (RFC 1996). DNS notification implements a push mechanism for notifying a select set of secondary servers for a zone when it is updated. Servers that are notified can then initiate a zone transfer as described above to pull zone changes from their master servers and update their local replicas of the zone.

For secondaries to be notified by the DNS server acting as their configured source for a zone, each secondary server must first have its IP address in the notify list of the source server. When using the DNS console to manage zones loaded at Windows 2000 DNS servers, this list is maintained in the **Notify** dialog box, which is accessible from the **Zone Transfer** tab located in *zone* **Properties**.

In addition to notifying the listed servers, the DNS console permits you to use the contents of the notify list as a means to restrict or limit zone transfer access to only those secondary servers specified in the list. This can help prevent an undesired attempt by an unknown or unapproved DNS server to pull, or request, zone updates. For information about creating and managing a notify list for a primary zone, see Chapter 10.

The following is a brief summary of the typical DNS notification process for zone updates:

1. The local zone at a DNS server acting as a master server, a source for the zone to other servers, is updated. When the zone is updated at the master or source server, the serial number field in the SOA resource record is also updated, indicating a new local version of the zone.
2. The master server sends a DNS notify message to other servers that are part of its configured notify list.
3. All secondary servers that receive the notify message can then respond by initiating a zone transfer request back to the notifying master server.

The normal zone transfer process can then continue as described in the previous section.

Important Use DNS notification only to notify servers operating as secondary servers for a zone. For replication of directory-integrated zones, DNS notification is not needed. This is because any DNS servers that load a zone from Active Directory automatically poll the directory (approximately once every 15 minutes) to update and refresh the zone. In these cases, configuring a notify list can actually degrade system performance by causing unnecessary additional transfer requests for the updated zone.

Reverse Lookup

In most DNS lookups, clients typically perform a forward lookup, which is a search based on the DNS name of another computer as stored in an address resource record. This type of query expects an IP address as the resource data for the answered response.

DNS also provides a reverse lookup process, enabling clients to use a known IP address during a name query and look up a computer name based on its address. A reverse lookup takes the form of a question, such as "Can you tell me the DNS name of the computer that uses the IP address 192.168.1.20?"

DNS was not originally designed to support this type of query. One problem for supporting the reverse query process is the difference in how the DNS namespace organizes and indexes names and how IP addresses are assigned. If the only method to answer the previous question was to search in all domains in the DNS namespace, a reverse query would take too long and require too much processing to be useful.

To solve this problem, a special domain, the *in-addr.arpa* domain, was defined in the DNS standards and reserved in the Internet DNS namespace to provide a practical and reliable way to perform reverse queries. To create the reverse namespace, subdomains within the *in-addr.arpa* domain are formed using the reverse ordering of the numbers in the dotted-decimal notation of IP addresses.

This reversed ordering of the domains for each octet value is needed because, unlike DNS names, when IP addresses are read from left to right, they are interpreted in the opposite manner. When an IP address is read from left to right, it is viewed from its most generalized information (an IP network address) in the first part of the address to the more specific information (an IP host address) contained in the last octets.

For this reason, the order of IP address octets must be reversed when building the *in-addr.arpa* domain tree. With this arrangement, administering lower limbs of the DNS *in-addr.arpa* tree can be given to companies as they are assigned a specific or limited set of IP addresses within the Internet-defined address classes.

Finally, the *in-addr.arpa* domain tree, as built into DNS, requires that an additional resource record type—the PTR resource record—be defined. This resource record is used to create a mapping in the reverse lookup zone that typically corresponds to a host (A) named resource record for the DNS computer name of a host in its forward lookup zone.

The *in-addr.arpa* domain applies for use in all TCP/IP networks that are based on Internet Protocol version 4 (IPv4) addressing. The New Zone wizard automatically assumes that you are using this domain when creating a new reverse lookup zone.

If you are installing DNS and configuring reverse lookup zones for an Internet Protocol version 6 (IPv6) network, you can specify an exact name in the New Zone wizard. This will permit you to create reverse lookup zones in the DNS console that can be used to support IPv6 networks, which uses a different special domain name, the *ip6.int* domain.

Additional information is available on IPv6 and DNS, including examples of how to create and use *ip6.int* domain names in RFC 1886, "DNS Extensions to support IP version 6." For more information, refer directly to this RFC, which can be obtained from *www.rfc-editor.org/*.

REVERSE QUERY FOR IPV4 NETWORKS

Figure 8-7 shows an example of a reverse query initiated by a DNS client (host-b) to learn the name of another host (host-a) based on its IP address, 192.168.1.20.

The reverse query process as shown in Figure 8-7 occurs in the following steps:

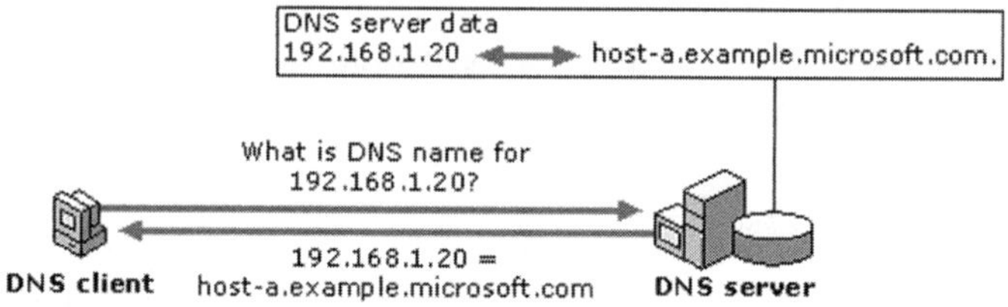

FIGURE 8–7 DNS reverse lookup

1. The client, host-b, queries the DNS server for a PTR resource record that maps to the IP address of 192.168.1.20 for host-a. Because the query is for PTR records, the resolver reverses the address and appends the *in-addr.arpa* domain to the end of the reverse address. This forms the fully qualified domain name *20.1.168.192.in-addr.arpa.,* for which to be searched in a reverse lookup zone.
2. Once located, the authoritative DNS server for *20.1.168.192.in-addr.arpa* can respond with the PTR record information. This includes the DNS domain name for host-a, completing the reverse lookup process.

Keep in mind that if the queried reverse name is not answerable from the DNS server, normal DNS resolution (either recursion or iteration) can be used to locate a DNS server that is authoritative for the reverse lookup zone and that contains the queried name. In this sense, the name resolution process used in a reverse lookup is identical to that of a forward lookup.

For Windows 2000 Server, the DNS snap-in provides a means for you to configure a subnetted reverse lookup "classless" zone when the **Advanced** view is selected. This allows you to configure a zone in the *in-addr.arpa* domain for a limited set of assigned IP addresses, where a nondefault IP subnet mask is used with those addresses. For information about managing reverse lookup zones, see Chapter 9.

Inverse Queries

Inverse queries are an outdated practice, originally proposed as part of the DNS standard to look up a host name based on its IP address. They use a nonstandard DNS query operation, and their use is limited to some of the earlier versions of Nslookup, a command-line utility for troubleshooting and testing DNS service.

For Windows 2000 Server, DNS service recognizes and accepts inverse query messages, answering them with a fake inverse query response. For DNS servers running in Windows NT Server 4.0, this support is available by default if the server computer has been updated to Service Pack 4 or later.

The configuration of PTR resource records and reverse lookup zones for identifying hosts by reverse query is strictly an optional part of the DNS standard implementation. You are not required to use reverse lookup zones, although for some networked applications, they are used to perform security checks.

Dynamic Update

Dynamic update enables DNS client computers to register and dynamically update their resource records with a DNS server whenever changes occur. This reduces the need for manual administration of zone records, especially for clients that frequently move or change locations and use DHCP to obtain an IP address.

Windows 2000 provides client and server support for the use of dynamic updates, as described in RFC 2136. For DNS servers, the DNS service allows dynamic update to be enabled or disabled on a per-zone basis at each server configured to load either a standard primary or directory-integrated zone. By default, client computers running under any version of Windows 2000 dynamically update their host resource records in DNS when configured for TCP/IP.

How Windows 2000 Computers Update Their DNS Names

By default, computers that run Windows 2000 and are statically configured for TCP/IP attempt to dynamically register host and PTR resource records for IP addresses configured and used by their installed network connections. By default, all computers register records based on their Full computer name.

For Windows 2000 computers, the primary Full computer name, an FQDN, is based on the following system settings: the **Primary DNS suffix of this computer** appended to the **Computer name**.

Both of these settings are displayed or configured from the **Network Identification** tab in **System properties**. For information about configuring the primary DNS suffix for a client computer, see Chapter 10.

Dynamic updates can be sent for any of the following reasons or events:

- An IP address is added, removed, or modified in the TCP/IP properties configuration for any one of the installed network connections.
- An IP address lease changes or renews with the DHCP server any one of the installed network connections. For example, when the computer is started or if the ipconfig /renew command is used.
- The ipconfig /registerdns command is used to manually force a refresh of the client name registration in DNS.
- At startup time, when the computer is turned on.

When one of the previous events triggers a dynamic update, the DHCP Client service (not the DNS Client service) sends updates. This is designed so that if a change to the IP address information occurs because of DHCP, corresponding updates in DNS are performed to synchronize name-to-address mappings for the computer. The DHCP Client service performs this function for all network connections used on the system, including connections not configured to use DHCP.

The process of how dynamic updates are performed for Windows 2000 computers that use DHCP to obtain their IP address is different than is described in this section. For more information, see Chapter 4.

The update process described in this section assumes Windows 2000 installation defaults are in effect. Specific names and update behavior is tunable where advanced TCP/IP properties are configured to use nondefault DNS settings.

In addition to the full computer name (or primary name) of the computer, additional connection-specific DNS names can be configured and optionally registered or updated in DNS. For more information, see both Chapter 9 and Chapter 2, "Installing, Managing, and Diagnosing TCP/IP."

HOW DYNAMIC UPDATE WORKS

For Windows 2000, dynamic updates are typically requested when either a DNS name or IP address changes on the computer. For example, suppose a client named *oldhost* is first configured in System properties with the following names:

Computer name	*oldhost*
DNS domain name of computer	*example.microsoft.com*
Full computer name	*oldhost.example.microsoft.com*

In this example, no connection-specific DNS domain names are configured for the computer. Later, the computer is renamed from *oldhost* to *newhost*, resulting in the following name changes on the system:

Computer name	*newhost*
DNS domain name of computer	*example.microsoft.com*
Full computer name	*newhost.example.microsoft.com*

Once the name change is applied in System properties, Windows 2000 prompts you to restart the computer. When the computer restarts Windows, the DHCP Client service performs the following sequence to update DNS:

1. The DHCP Client service sends an SOA-type query, using the DNS domain name of the computer. The client computer uses the currently

configured FQDN of the computer (such as *newhost.example.microsoft.com*) as the name specified in this query.

2. The authoritative DNS server for the zone containing the client FQDN responds to the SOA-type query. For standard primary zones, the primary server (owner) returned in the SOA query response is fixed and static. It always matches the exact DNS name as it appears in the SOA resource record stored with the zone. If, however, the zone being updated is directory-integrated, any DNS server loading the zone can respond and dynamically insert its own name as the primary server (owner) of the zone in the SOA query response.
3. The DHCP Client service then attempts to contact the primary DNS server. The client processes the SOA query response for its name to determine the IP address of the DNS server authorized as the primary server for accepting its name. It then proceeds to perform the following sequence of steps as needed to contact and dynamically update its primary server:
   a. It sends a dynamic update request to the primary server determined in the SOA query response. If the update succeeds, no further action is taken.
   b. If this update fails, the client next sends an NS-type query for the zone name specified in the SOA record.
   c. When it receives a response to this query, it sends an SOA query to the first DNS server listed in the response.
   d. After the SOA query is resolved, the client sends a dynamic update to the server specified in the returned SOA record. If the update succeeds, no further action is taken.
   e. If this update fails, then the client repeats the SOA query process by sending to the next DNS server listed in the response.
4. Once the primary server that can perform the update is contacted, the client sends the update request and the server processes it. The contents of the update request include instructions to add A (and possibly PTR) resource records for *newhost.example.microsoft.com* and remove these same record types for *oldhost.example.microsoft.com,* the name that was previously registered.

   The server also checks to ensure that updates are permitted for the client request. For standard primary zones, dynamic updates are not secured, so any client attempt to update succeeds. For Active Directory-integrated zones, updates are secured and performed using directory-based security settings.

Dynamic updates are sent or refreshed periodically. By default, Windows 2000 sends a refresh once every 24 hours. If the update results in no changes to zone data, the zone remains at its current version and no changes are written. Updates result in actual zone changes or increased zone transfer only if names or addresses actually change.

Note that names are not removed from DNS zones if they become inactive or are not updated within the refresh interval (24 hours). DNS does not use a mechanism to release or tombstone names, although DNS clients do attempt to delete or update old name records when a new name or address change is applied.

When the DHCP Client service registers A and PTR resource records for a Windows 2000 computer, it uses a default caching TTL of 15 minutes for host records. This determines how long other DNS servers and clients cache a computer's records when they are included in a query response.

Secure Dynamic Update

For Windows 2000, DNS update security is available only for zones that are integrated into Active Directory. Once you directory-integrate a zone, access control list (ACL) editing features are available in the DNS console so you can add or remove users or groups from the ACL for a specified zone or resource record. For information about modifying security for a resource record and for a directory integrated zone, see Chapter 10.

By default, dynamic update security for Windows 2000 DNS servers and clients can be handled as follows:

- Windows 2000 DNS clients attempt to use unsecured dynamic update first. If an unsecured update is refused, clients try to use secure update. Also, clients use a default update policy that permits them to attempt to overwrite a previously registered resource record, unless they are specifically blocked by update security.
- Once a zone becomes Active Directory-integrated, Windows 2000 DNS servers default to allowing only secure dynamic updates. When using standard zone storage, the default for the DNS Server service is to not allow dynamic updates on its zones. For zones that are either directory-integrated or use standard file-based storage, you can change the zone to allow all dynamic updates, which permits all updates to be accepted, by passing the use of secure updates.

Important For Windows 2000 Server, the DHCP Server service can perform proxy registration and update of DNS records for legacy clients that do not support dynamic updates.

If you use multiple Windows 2000 DHCP servers on your network and also configure your zones to allow secure dynamic updates only, you need to use Active Directory Users and Computers to add your DHCP server computers to the built-in DnsUpdateProxyGroup. This will permit all of your DHCP servers the secure rights to perform proxy updates for any of your DHCP clients. For information, see Chapter 4.

Caution For Windows 2000, the use of secure dynamic updates can be compromised by running a DHCP server on a domain controller when Windows 2000 DHCP server is configured to perform registration of DNS records on behalf of its clients. To avoid this issue, deploy DHCP servers and domain controllers on separate computers. If you are not concerned about security of reverse lookup (PTR) records, this precaution is only advisable if the DHCP server is configured to perform registration of host (A) records on behalf of its clients (which is not a default behavior). For more information, see Chapter 4.

Windows 2000 DNS Implementation

This section covers,

- Active Directory integration
- Understanding aging and scavenging
- Unicode character support
- WINS lookup integration

Active Directory Integration

For Windows 2000 Server, the DNS Server service has been carefully integrated into the design and implementation of Active Directory, the next-generation directory service designed by Microsoft for networks using Windows NT technologies. Active Directory provides an enterprise-level tool for organizing, managing, and locating resources in a network.

There are two significant changes when deploying Windows 2000 DNS servers together with Active Directory:

- DNS is required for locating Windows 2000 domain controllers. The Netlogon service uses new DNS server support to provide registration of domain controllers in your DNS domain namespace.
- Windows 2000 DNS servers can use Active Directory for storing and replicating your zones. By directory-integrating your zones, you can take advantage of additional Windows 2000 DNS features, such as secure dynamic updates and record aging/scavenging features.

For more information, see "Secure Dynamic Update" and "Understanding Aging and Scavenging" in this chapter.

HOW DNS INTEGRATES WITH ACTIVE DIRECTORY

When you install Active Directory on a server computer, you promote the server to the role of a domain controller (DC) for a specified domain. When completing this process, you are prompted to specify a DNS domain name for the Active Directory domain for which you are joining and promoting the server.

If during this process, a DNS server authoritative for the domain that you specified either cannot be located on the network or does not support the DNS dynamic update protocol, you are prompted with the option to install a Windows 2000 DNS server. This option is provided because a DNS server is required to support the use of Active Directory and for Windows 2000 computers to locate this server or other domain controllers for the domain.

Once you have installed Active Directory, you have two options for storing and replicating your zones when operating the DNS server at the new domain controller:

- *Standard zone storage, using a text-based file.* Zones stored this way are located in *.Dns* files that are stored in the *%SystemRoot%\System32\Dns* folder on each computer operating a DNS server. Zone file names correspond to the name you choose for the zone when creating it, such as *Example.microsoft.com.dns* if the zone name was *example.microsoft.com*.
- *Directory-integrated zone storage, using the Active Directory database.* Zones stored this way are located in the Active Directory tree under the domain object container. Each directory-integrated zone is stored in a *dnsZone* container object identified by the name you choose for the zone when creating it.

BENEFITS OF ACTIVE DIRECTORY INTEGRATION

For networks deploying DNS to support Active Directory, directory-integrated primary zones are strongly recommended and provide the following benefits:

- *Multimaster update and enhanced security based on the capabilities of Active Directory.* In a standard zone storage model, DNS updates are conducted based upon a single-master update model. In this model, a single authoritative DNS server for a zone is designated as the primary source for the zone. This server maintains the master copy of the zone in a local file. With this model, the primary server for the zone represents a single fixed point of failure. If this server is not available, update requests from DNS clients are not processed for the zone.

  With directory-integrated storage, dynamic updates to DNS are conducted based upon a multimaster update model. In this model, any authoritative DNS server, such as a DC running the Windows 2000 DNS Server service, is designated as a primary source for the zone. Because the master copy of the zone is maintained in the Active Directory database, which is fully replicated to all DCs, the DNS servers operating at any of the domain's DCs can update the zone.

  With the multimaster update model of Active Directory, any of the primary servers for the directory-integrated zone can process requests from DNS clients to update the zone, as long as a DC is available and reachable on the network.

Also, when using directory-integrated zones, you can use ACL editing to secure a *dnsZone* object container in the directory tree. This feature provides granulated access to either the zone or a specified resource record in the zone. For example, an ACL for a zone resource record can be restricted so that dynamic updates are only allowed for a specified client computer or a secure group such as a domain administrators group. This security feature is not available with standard primary zones.

Note that when you change the zone type to be directory-integrated, the default for updating the zone changes to allow only secure updates.

- *Zones are replicated and synchronized to new DCs automatically whenever a new one is added to an Active Directory domain.* Although DNS service can be selectively removed from a DC, directory-integrated zones are already stored at each DC, so zone storage and management is not an additional resource. Also, the methods used to synchronize directory-stored information offer performance improvement over standard zone update methods, which can potentially require transfer of the entire zone.
- *By integrating storage of your DNS zone databases in Active Directory, you can streamline database replication planning for your network.* When your DNS and Active Directory namespaces are stored and replicated separately, you need to plan and potentially administer each namespace separately. For example, when using standard DNS zone storage and Active Directory together, you would need to design, implement, test, and maintain two different database replication topologies. For instance, one replication topology is needed for replicating directory data between DCs, and another topology would be needed for replicating zone databases between DNS servers.

  This can create additional administrative complexity for planning and designing your network and allowing for its eventual growth. By integrating DNS storage, you unify storage management and replication issues for both DNS and Active Directory, merging and viewing them together as a single administrative entity.
- *Directory replication is faster and more efficient than standard DNS replication.* Because Active Directory replication processing is performed on a per-property basis, only relevant changes are propagated. This allows less data to be used and submitted in updates for directory-stored zones.

Only primary zones can be stored in the directory. A DNS server cannot store secondary zones in the directory. It must store them in standard text files.

The Windows 2000 DNS server includes an option to initialize a DNS server running on a DC and to load all DNS zones and related configuration details stored in the Active Directory for the Active Directory domain. For information about modifying server defaults, see Chapter 9.

Understanding Aging and Scavenging

Windows 2000 DNS servers support aging and scavenging features. These features are provided as a mechanism for performing cleanup and removal of stale resource records, which can accumulate in zone data over time.

With dynamic update, resource records are automatically added to zones when computers start on the network. However, in some cases, they are not automatically removed when computers leave the network. For example, if a computer registers its own host resource record at startup and is later improperly disconnected from the network, its host resource record might not be deleted. If your network has mobile users and computers, this situation can occur frequently.

If left unmanaged, the presence of stale resource records in zone data might cause some problems. The following are examples:

- If a large number of stale resource records remain in server zones, they can eventually take up server disk space and cause unnecessarily long zone transfers.
- DNS servers loading zones with stale resource records might use outdated information to answer client queries, potentially causing the clients to experience name resolution problems on the network.
- The accumulation of stale resource records at the DNS server can degrade its performance and responsiveness.
- In some cases, the presence of a stale resource record in a zone could prevent a DNS domain name from being used by another computer or host device.

To solve these problems, the DNS Server service has the following features:

- *Time stamping, based on the current date and time set at the server computer, for any resource records added dynamically to primary-type zones.* In addition, time stamps are recorded in standard primary zones where aging and scavenging are enabled.

  For resource records that you add manually, a time stamp value of zero is used, indicating that they are not affected by the aging process and can remain without limitation in zone data unless you otherwise change their time stamp or delete them.
- *Aging of resource records in local data, based on a specified refresh time period, for any eligible zones.* Only primary type zones that are loaded by the DNS Server service are eligible to participate in this process.

- *Scavenging for any resource records that persist beyond the specified refresh period.* When a Windows 2000 DNS server performs a scavenging operation, it can determine that resource records have aged to the point of becoming stale and remove them from zone data. Servers can be configured to perform recurring scavenging operations automatically, or you can initiate an immediate scavenging operation at the server. For information about enabling automatic scavenging of stale resource records and starting immediate scavenging of stale resource records, see Chapter 10.

Caution By default, the aging and scavenging mechanism is disabled at Windows 2000 DNS servers. It should be enabled only when all parameters are fully understood. Otherwise, the server could be accidentally configured to delete records that should not be deleted. If a record is accidentally deleted, not only will users fail to resolve queries for that record, but also any user can create the record and take ownership of it, even on zones configured for secure dynamic update.

The server uses the contents of each resource record-specific time stamp, along with other aging and scavenging properties that you can adjust or configure, to determine when it scavenges records.

PREREQUISITES FOR AGING AND SCAVENGING

Before the aging and scavenging features of Windows 2000 DNS can be used, these conditions must be met:

1. Scavenging and aging must be enabled both at the DNS server and on the zone. By default, aging and scavenging of resource records is disabled.
2. Resource records must either be dynamically added to zones or manually modified to be used in aging and scavenging operations. Typically, only those resource records added dynamically using the DNS dynamic update protocol are subject to aging and scavenging (see "Dynamic Update" in this chapter). You can, however, enable scavenging for other resource records added through non-dynamic means. For records added to zones in this way, either by loading a text-based zone file from another DNS server or by manually adding them to a zone, a time stamp of zero is set. This makes these records ineligible for use in aging and scavenging operations.

   In order to change this default, you can administer these records individually, to reset and permit them to use a current (non-zero) time stamp value. This enables these records to become aged and scavenged. For information about resetting scavenging and aging properties for a specified resource record, see Chapter 10.

In the case of changing a zone from standard primary to Active Directory-integrated, you might want to enable scavenging of all existing resource records in the zone. To enable aging for all existing resource records in a zone, you can use the AgeAllRecords command, which is available through the dnscmd command-line tool. For more information about automating server administration using dnscmd, see Chapter 9.

AGING AND SCAVENGING TERMINOLOGY

The aging and scavenging process is a new feature in Windows 2000 Server. Table 8.3 indicates new or revised terms that have been introduced to help specifically when discussing these features.

TABLE 8.3 *Aging and Scavenging Terminology*

Term	Description
Resource record time stamp	A date and time value used by the DNS server to determine removal of the resource record when it performs aging and scavenging operations.
Current server time	The current date and time on the DNS server. This number can be expressed as an exact numeric value at any point in time.
No-refresh interval	An interval of time, determined for each zone, as bounded by the following two events: ● The date and time when the record was last refreshed and its time stamp set. ● The date and time when the record next becomes eligible to be refreshed and have its time stamp reset. This value is needed to decrease the number of write operations to the Active Directory database. By default, this interval is set to 7 days. It should not be increased to an unreasonably high level, because the benefits of the aging and scavenging feature might either be lost or diminished.
Refresh interval	An interval of time, determined for each zone, as bounded by the following two distinct events: ● The earliest date and time when the record becomes eligible to be refreshed and have its time stamp reset. ● The earliest date and time when the record becomes eligible to be scavenged and removed from the zone database. This value should be large enough to allow all clients to refresh their records. By default, this interval is set to 7 days. It should not be increased to an unreasonably high level, because the benefits of the aging and scavenging feature might either be lost or diminished.
Start scavenging time	A specific time, expressed as a number. The server uses this time to determine when a zone has become available for scavenging. For more information, see "When Scavenging Can Start" in this chapter.
Scavenging period	When automatic scavenging is enabled at the server, this period represents the time between repetitions of the automated scavenging process. The default value for this is 7 days. To prevent deterioration of DNS server performance, the minimum allowed value for this is 1 hour.

TABLE 8.3 *Aging and Scavenging Terminology (Continued)*

Term	Description
Record refresh	When a DNS dynamic update is processed for a resource record when only the resource record time stamp, and no other characteristics of the record, are revised. Refreshes generally occur for the following reasons: • When a computer is restarted on the network and, if at startup, its name and IP address information are consistent with the same name and address information it used prior to being shut down, it sends a refresh to renew its associated resource records for this information. • The computer sends a periodic refresh while it is running. For Windows 2000, all computers renew DNS registration of their associated resource records every 24 hours. When this renewal attempt occurs, if the same DNS name and IP address mappings information are in effect, the resulting update request is considered to be a refresh and not a resource record update. • Other network services make refresh attempts, such as DHCP servers, which renew client address leases; cluster servers, which register and update records for a cluster; and the Net Logon service, which can register and update resource records used by Active Directory domain controllers.
Record update	When a DNS dynamic update is processed for a resource record where other characteristics of the record in addition to its time stamp are revised. Updates generally occur for the following reasons: • When a new computer is added to the network and, at startup, it sends an update to register its resource records for the first time with its configured zone. • When a computer with existing records in the zone has a change in IP address, causing updates to be sent for its revised name-to-address mappings in DNS zone data. • When the Net Logon service registers a new Active Directory domain controller.
Scavenging servers	An optional advanced zone parameter that enables you to specify a restricted list of IP addresses for DNS servers that are enabled to perform scavenging of the zone. By default, if this parameter is not specified, all Windows 2000 DNS servers enabled to use scavenging that load a directory-integrated zone (also enabled for scavenging) attempt to perform scavenging of the zone. In some cases, this parameter can be useful if it is preferable that scavenging only be performed at some servers loading the directory-integrated zone. To set this parameter, you must specify the list of IP addresses for the servers enabled to scavenge the zone in the ScavengingServers parameter for the zone. This can be done using the **dnscmd** command, a command-line based tool for administering Windows DNS servers. For more information, see Chapter 9.

WHEN SCAVENGING CAN START

Once all prerequisites for enabling the use of scavenging are met, it can start for a server zone when the current server time is greater than the value of the start scavenging time for the zone.

The server sets the time value to start scavenging on a per-zone basis whenever one of the following events occurs:

- Dynamic updates are enabled for the zone.
- A change in the state of the **Scavenge stale resource records** check box is applied. You can use the DNS console to modify this setting at either an applicable DNS server or one of its primary zones.
- The DNS server loads a primary zone enabled to use scavenging.
- When a zone resumes service after having been paused.

When the previous events occur, the DNS server sets the value of start scavenging time by calculating the following sum:

Current server time + Refresh interval = Start scavenging time

This value is used as a basis of comparison during scavenging operations.

AGING AND SCAVENGING PROCESS FOR A SAMPLE RECORD

To understand the process of aging and scavenging at the server, consider the lifespan and successive stages of a single resource record as it is added to a server and zone where this process is in effect and then aged and removed from the database.

1. A sample DNS host, *host-a.example.microsoft.com*, registers its host resource record at the DNS server for a zone where aging and scavenging is enabled for use.
2. When registering the record, the DNS server places a time stamp on this record based on current server time. After the record time stamp is written, the DNS server does not accept refreshes for this record for the duration of the zone no-refresh interval. It can, however, accept updates prior to that time. For example, if the IP address for *host-a.example.microsoft.com* changes, the DNS server can accept the update. In this case, the server also updates (resets) the record time stamp.
3. Upon expiration of the no-refresh period, the server begins to accept attempts to refresh this record. Once the initial no-refresh period ends, the refresh period immediately begins for the record. During this time, the server does not suppress attempts to refresh the record for its remaining life span.
4. During and after the refresh period, if the server receives a refresh for the record, it processes it. This resets the time stamp for the record based on the method described in step 2.
5. When the server for the *example.microsoft.com* zone subsequently performs scavenging, the record (and all other zone records) are examined by the server. Each record is compared to current server time on the basis of the following sum to determine whether the record should be removed:

Record time stamp + **No-refresh interval** *for zone +* **Refresh interval** *for zone*

If the value of this sum is greater than current server time, no action is taken and the record continues to age in the zone. If value of this sum is less than current server time, the record is deleted both from any zone data currently loaded in server memory and also from the applicable DnsZone object store in Active Directory for the directory-integrated *example.microsoft.com* zone.

For more information about managing the aging and scavenging of server data, see Chapter 9.

Unicode Character Support

Originally, Internet host names were restricted to the character set specified in RFCs 952 and 1123. These restrictions include limiting names to using uppercase and lowercase letters (A–Z, a–z), numbers (0–9) and hyphens (-). In addition, the first character of the DNS name can be a number and names must be encoded and represented using US-ASCII-based characters.

These requirements were maintained when DNS was introduced as part of RFC 1035, one of the core DNS standards specifications. For use of DNS in international settings, this requirement has significant limitations where extended character sets are used for local naming standards.

In order to remove these limitations, Microsoft has provided the ability with Windows 2000 Server to expand DNS character support beyond the RFC 1035 specification. For this release, DNS service now provides enhanced default support for UTF-8, a Unicode transformation format.

WHAT IS UTF-8?

UTF-8 is the recommended character set for protocols evolving beyond the use of ASCII. The UTF-8 protocol provides for support of extended ASCII characters and translation of UCS-2, a 16-bit Unicode character set that encompasses most of the world's writing systems. UTF-8 enables a far greater range of names than can be achieved using ASCII or extended ASCII encoding for character data.

Beginning with Windows 2000 Server, the DNS service is UTF-8 aware. This means that when UTF-8 encoded characters are received or used as data by the server, the server can load and store this data in its zones. Although DNS servers running in Windows 2000 Server are UTF-8 aware, they remain compatible with other DNS servers that use traditional US-ASCII data encoding and current DNS standards.

HOW THE DNS SERVICE IMPLEMENTS UTF-8

To provide standards compatibility and interoperability with other DNS implementations, the DNS service uses uniform downcasing of any received character data. In this process, the DNS service converts all uppercase characters used in standard US-ASCII data to lowercase equivalent data for the following reasons:

- To maintain compatibility with current and existing DNS standards.
- To provide interoperability with DNS server implementations that don't recognize or support UTF-8 encoding.

To understand why uniform downcasing was chosen, several related points must first be considered from the current revised Internet standards for DNS. Several key points in the standards pertain directly to how character data is to be handled between DNS servers and other servers and clients. These include the following:

- Any binary string can be used in a DNS name. (RFC 2181)
- DNS servers must be able to compare names in a case-insensitive way. (RFC 1035)
- The original case for character data should be preserved whenever possible as the data is entered into the system. (RFC 1035)

Because case insensitivity is a required part of the core DNS standard and case preservation is an optional recommendation, uniform downcasing was chosen to provide an effective standards-compliant solution. By downcasing UTF-8 encoded names before transmission, other DNS servers (which are not UTF-8 aware) are able to receive and perform successful binary comparisons of the data and obtain the desired results.

CONSIDERATIONS FOR INTEROPERABILITY WITH UTF-8

For Windows 2000 Server, the DNS service can be configured to allow or disallow the use of UTF-8 characters on a per-server basis. Although other DNS server implementations that are not UTF-8 aware might be able to accept the transfer of a zone containing UTF-8 encoded names, these servers might not be able to write back those names to a zone file or reload those names from a zone file. Administrators should exercise caution when transferring a zone containing UTF-8 names to a DNS server that is not UTF-8-aware.

Some protocols place restrictions on the characters allowed in a name. In addition, names that are intended to be globally visible (RFC 1958) should contain ASCII-only characters, as recommended in RFC 1123.

The use of UTF-8 for transformation of Unicode characters is not noticeable for general users. Only where Network Monitor or another similar tool is used to analyze DNS-related traffic over the physical network are UTF-8 encoded characters observable.

In addition to DNS server support for the UTF-8 encoding format, the Windows 2000 Server client resolver defaults to using the UTF-8 character-encoding format. Names encoded in UTF-8 format must not exceed the size limits clarified in RFC 2181, which specifies a maximum of 63 octets per label and 255 octets per name. Character count is insufficient to determine size because some UTF-8 characters exceed one octet in length.

The UTF-8 encoding protocol adapts to use with existing DNS protocol implementations that expect US-ASCII characters because representation of US-ASCII characters in UTF-8 is identical, byte for byte, to the US-ASCII representation. DNS clients in earlier Windows NT DNS or other DNS server implementations that do not recognize UTF-8 characters always encode names in the US-ASCII format. Those names are always correctly interpreted by the DNS service running in Windows 2000 Server.

The DNS service provides the ability to configure name checking to allow or restrict the use of UTF-8 characters in DNS data. This option can be configured on a per-server or per-zone basis. For information about changing the name-checking method used by the DNS server, see Chapter 10.

By default, multibyte UTF-8 name checking is used, allowing the greatest tolerance when the DNS service processes characters. This is the preferred name-checking method for most privately operated DNS servers that are not providing name service for Internet hosts.

WINS Lookup Integration

Support for using Windows Internet Name Service (WINS) is provided to look up DNS names that cannot be resolved by querying the DNS domain namespace. To accomplish WINS lookup, two specific resource record types are used and can be enabled for any zones loaded by the DNS service:

- The WINS resource record, which can be enabled to integrate WINS lookup into forward lookup zones.
- The WINS-R resource record, which can be enabled to integrate WINS reverse lookup for reverse lookup zones.

THE WINS RESOURCE RECORD

The WINS and DNS services are used to provide name resolution for the NetBIOS namespace and the DNS domain namespace, respectively. Although both DNS and WINS can provide a separate and useful name service to clients, WINS is mainly needed to provide support for older clients and programs that require support for NetBIOS naming.

However, the DNS service can work with WINS to provide combined name searches in both namespaces when resolving a DNS domain name not found in zone information. To provide this interoperability, a new record (the WINS record) was defined as part of the zone database file.

The WINS resource record is specific to Windows 2000 Server and earlier versions of Windows NT Server, and can be attached only to the domain of origin for a zone. The presence of a WINS resource record can instruct the DNS service to use WINS to look up any forward queries for host names or names that are not found in the zone database. This functionality is particularly useful for name resolution required by clients that are not WINS-aware (for example, UNIX) for the names of computers not registered with DNS, such as Windows 95 or Windows 98 computers.

HOW WINS LOOKUP WORKS

Figure 8-8 is an example of a DNS client, *host-b,* querying its DNS server in an attempt to look up the address for another computer named *host-a.example.microsoft.com.*

In step 1, the client queries its preferred DNS server. In steps 2 through 8, the normal process of recursion proceeds as the preferred DNS server queries other DNS servers in succession on behalf of the client. This process concludes at step 8, when the DNS server for the *example.microsoft.com* zone is located through the previous chain of referral answers. At this point in the process, the server contacted is a Windows DNS server either running Windows NT Server 4.0 or Windows 2000 Server.

When the Windows DNS server for the *example.microsoft.com* zone receives the query for *host-a,* it looks in its configured zone to see if a matching address resource record can be found. If no A record is found and the zone is enabled to use WINS lookup, the server does the following:

- The DNS server separates the host part of the name, *host-a,* from the FQDN contained in the DNS query.
- The server then sends a NetBIOS name request to the WINS server using the host name, *host-a.*
- If the WINS server can resolve the name, it returns the IP address to the DNS server.

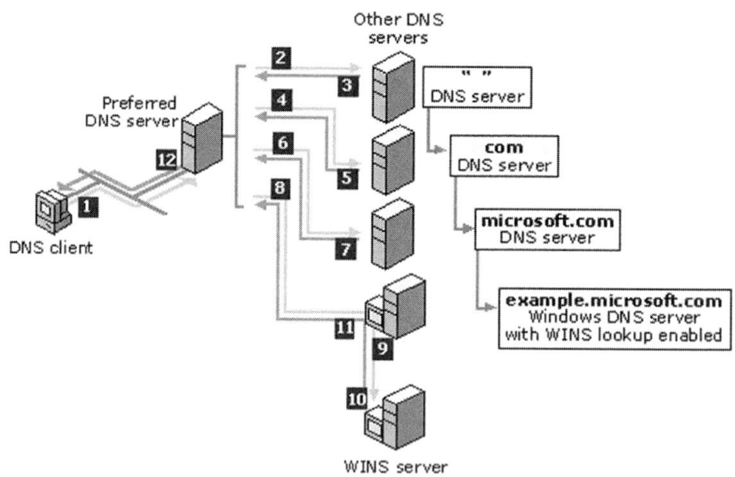

FIGURE 8–8 Example of WINS lookup integration with DNS

- The Windows DNS server then returns this IP address information to the original preferred DNS server that was queried by the requesting client, *host-b*.
- The preferred DNS server then passes the query answer back to the requesting client

HOW WINS REVERSE LOOKUP WORKS

There is also a WINS-R record or WINS reverse lookup entry that can be enabled and added to reverse lookup zones. However, because the WINS database is not indexed by IP address, the DNS service cannot send a reverse name lookup to WINS to get the name of a computer, given its IP address.

Because WINS does not provide reverse lookup capability, the DNS service instead sends a *node adapter status request* directly to the IP address implied in the DNS reverse query. When the DNS server gets the NetBIOS name from the node status response, it appends the DNS domain name back onto the NetBIOS name provided in the node status response and forwards the result to the requesting client.

The WINS and WINS-R resource records are proprietary to the DNS service provided by Windows 2000 Server and earlier versions of Windows NT Server. You can prevent these resource records from being included in zone transfers to other DNS server implementations. For more information about using WINS lookup, see Chapter 9.

N I N E

Using DNS

Planning Issues

This section covers,

- Namespace planning for DNS
- Zone planning for DNS
- Server planning for DNS
- Migrating servers
- Interoperability issues

Namespace Planning for DNS

Before you begin using DNS on your network, decide on a plan for your DNS domain namespace. Coming up with a namespace plan involves making some decisions about how you intend to use DNS naming and what goals you are trying to accomplish in using DNS. Some questions you might have at this stage include the following:

- Have you previously chosen and registered a DNS domain name for use on the Internet?
- Are you going to set up DNS servers on a private network or the Internet?
- Are you going to use DNS to support your use of Active Directory?
- What naming requirements do you need to follow when choosing DNS domain names for computers?

Each of these questions is further discussed in the following sections.

CHOOSING YOUR FIRST DNS DOMAIN NAME

When setting up DNS servers, it is recommended that you first choose and register a unique parent DNS domain name that can be used for hosting your organization on the Internet, for example, *microsoft.com*. This name is a second-level domain within one of the top-level domains used on the Internet. For a list and description of the most common top-level domains used on the Internet, see in Appendix D, "DNS Resources and Troubleshooting."

Once you have chosen your parent domain name, you can combine this name with a location or organizational name used within your organization to form other subdomain names. For example, if a subdomain were added, such as the *itg.example.microsoft.com* domain tree (for resources used by the information technology group at your organization), additional subdomain names could be formed using this name. For instance, a group of programmers working on electronic data interchange (EDI) in this division could have a subdomain named *edi.itg.example.microsoft.com*. Likewise, another group of workers providing support in this division might use *support.itg.example.microsoft.com*.

Before you decide on a parent DNS domain name for your organization to use on the Internet, perform a search to see if the name is already registered to another organization or person. The Internet DNS namespace is currently managed by the Internet Network Information Center (InterNIC). In the future, other domain name registrars might also be available. For more information, see "Using DNS on the Internet" in this chapter.

DNS NAMESPACE PLANNING FOR ACTIVE DIRECTORY

If you are using Active Directory, you need to first establish a namespace plan. Before a DNS domain namespace can be properly implemented in Windows 2000, the Active Directory structure needs to be available. Therefore, begin with the Active Directory design and support it with the appropriate DNS namespace. Upon review, if you detect unforeseen or undesirable consequences for either of your plans, make revisions as needed.

In Windows 2000, Active Directory domains are named with DNS names. When choosing DNS names to use for your Active Directory domains, start with the registered DNS domain name suffix that your organization has reserved for use on the Internet, such as *microsoft.com,* and combine this name with either geographical or divisional names used in your organization to form full names for your Active Directory domains.

For example, the Windows test group at Microsoft might call their domain *wintest.example.microsoft.com*. This method of naming ensures that each Active Directory domain name is globally unique. And, once employed, this naming method also makes it easy to use existing names as parents for creating additional subdomains and further grow the namespace to accommodate new departments within your organization.

For a small organization using only a single domain or a small multidomain model, planning can be straightforward and follow an approach similar to the previous examples. For a larger organization using a more complex domain model, refer to additional Microsoft resources such as the *Windows 2000 Server Resource Kit Deployment Planning Guide*, which provides more advanced planning information for Active Directory namespace design.

Caution When planning your DNS and Active Directory namespace, it is recommended that you use a differing set of distinguished names that do not overlap as the basis for your internal and external DNS use. As an example, assuming your organization's parent domain name is example.microsoft.com,

- For internal DNS names usage, you could use a name such as *internal.example.microsoft.com*.
- For external DNS names usage, you could use a name such as *external.example.microsoft.com*.

By keeping your internal and external namespaces separate and distinct in this way, you enable simplified maintenance of configurations such as domain name filter or exclusion lists.

CHOOSING NAMES

It is strongly recommended that you use only characters in your names that are part of the Internet standard character set permitted for use in DNS host naming. Allowed characters are defined in RFC 1123 as follows: all uppercase letters (A–Z), lowercase letters (a–z), numbers (0–9), and the hyphen (-).

For organizations with a prior investment in Microsoft NetBIOS technology, existing computer names might conform to the NetBIOS naming standard. If this is the case, consider revising the names of your computers to the Internet DNS standard.

The process of adjusting your naming conventions might prove to be time consuming. To ease the transition from Windows NT 4.0 NetBIOS names to Windows 2000 DNS domain names, the DNS service includes support for extended ASCII and Unicode characters. However, this additional character support can only be used in a pure Windows 2000 network environment. This is because most other DNS resolver client software is based on RFC 1123, the specification that standardizes Internet host naming requirements. If a nonstandard DNS domain name is entered during Windows 2000 setup, a warning message appears recommending that a standard DNS name be used instead.

In Windows NT 4.0 and earlier versions, the name used to identify a Windows computer on the network was a NetBIOS name. In Windows 2000, a computer can be identified in any of the following ways:

- A NetBIOS computer name, which is optional and is used for interoperability with earlier Windows systems.
- The Full computer name, which is a fully qualified domain name (FQDN) for the computer and is its primary (or default) name.

In addition to these, a computer might also be identified by the FQDN comprised of the computer (or host) name and a connection-specific domain name, where one is configured and applied for a specific network connection on the computer.

The full computer name is a combination of both the computer name and the DNS domain name for the computer. The DNS domain name for the computer is part of the System properties for the computer and is not related to any specifically installed networking components. However, computers running Windows 2000 that do not use either networking or TCP/IP do not have a DNS domain name.

Table 9.1 is a comparison of NetBIOS and DNS computer names.

TABLE 9.1 *NetBIOS and DNS Computer Names*

	NetBIOS computer name	DNS computer name
Type	Flat	Hierarchical
Character restrictions	Unicode characters, numbers, white space. Symbols: ! @ # $ % ^ & ') (. - _ { } ~	Same as for NetBIOS except no white space permitted. Period (.) has special reserved meaning.
Maximum length	15 character bytes	63 octets per label 255 octets per FQDN
Name service	Windows Internet Name Service (WINS) NetBIOS broadcast	Domain Name System (DNS) service

To ensure interoperability between NetBIOS and DNS naming in Windows 2000, a new naming parameter called the NetBIOS computer name was introduced. The value of this parameter, which is not required in a pure Windows 2000 environment, is derived from the first 15 octets of the DNS full computer name.

When the full computer name is a combination of the computer name and the DNS domain name for the computer, the impact of renaming and making the transition from a NetBIOS namespace to a DNS namespace can be minimal. Users continue to focus on the short computer name. If this name is 15 characters or less, it can be made identical to the NetBIOS computer name. The administrator can then also assign a DNS domain name for each computer. This can be done using remote administration tools.

In this way, the System properties page can have the following settings on the **Network Identification** tab (or its related dialog boxes):

Computer name:	longer-than-15characters-name
NetBIOS computer name:	longer-than-15c
Primary DNS suffix for this computer:	*example.microsoft.com*

In addition to the primary DNS domain name for a computer, Windows 2000 provides connection-specific DNS naming as well. For more information, see "Configuring Multiple Names" in this chapter.

INTEGRATION PLANNING: SUPPORTING MULTIPLE NAMESPACES

In addition to support for the internal DNS namespace used by Windows 2000 and Active Directory, many networks require support for resolving external DNS names, such as those used on the Internet. The DNS service provides ways to integrate and manage disjointed namespaces where both external and internal DNS names are resolved on your network.

In deciding how to integrate namespaces, determine which of the following scenarios most closely resembles your situation and proposed use of DNS:

- An internal DNS namespace, used only on your own network.
- An internal DNS namespace with referral and access to an external namespace, such as referral or forwarding to a DNS server on the Internet.
- An external DNS namespace, used only on a public network such as the Internet.

If you decide to limit the use of DNS for name service within your private namespace, there are no restrictions on how it is designed or implemented. For example, you can choose any DNS naming standard, configure DNS servers to be valid root servers for your network's DNS distributed design, or form an entirely self-contained DNS domain tree structure and hierarchy.

When you start providing either referral to an external DNS namespace or full DNS service on the Internet, you need to consider compatibility between your private and external namespaces. Additionally, Internet service requires the registration of parent domain names for your organization.

For more information on planning secure integration of Internet DNS names referral through your secured private network (such as one supported by Microsoft Proxy Server or another firewall product), refer to additional Microsoft information resources on Windows DNS planning available from the Microsoft Web site.

When you add and connect to a Windows 2000 DNS server for the first time using the DNS console, the root hints file *Cache.dns* is automatically primed for use on your network. This occurs transparently and does not require that you take any further action for this to be done.

Depending on how you use DNS, you can update this file in one of the following ways:

- If you are connected to the Internet, you can either edit or update this file when the root hints file, *Named.root,* is updated and released. For a current copy of this file, you can use anonymous FTP to *ftp://rs.internic.net/domain/named.root*.

- If you are not connected to the Internet, you can remove the default resource records contained in this file and replace them with NS and A resource records for the DNS authoritative servers at the root domain of your site. For root domain servers on your private network, you can safely remove this file entirely because servers operating at this domain level do not require or use a cache of root hints.

If you delete the *Cache.dns* file for a private root domain server when you have configured the DNS service using the **Boot From File** method, as opposed to the default **Boot From Registry** option, you also need to remove the **cache** directive from the server boot file before restarting the DNS service.

Zone Planning for DNS

When first partitioning your namespace into zones, review traffic patterns in your current or proposed network. Although DNS is designed to help reduce broadcast traffic between local subnets, it does create some traffic between servers and clients that should be reviewed. This is particularly true in cases where DNS is used on routed networks.

To review DNS traffic, you can use DNS server statistics or the DNS performance counters provided with System Monitor. For more information, see "Verifying Server Configuration" and "Monitoring Server Performance" in this chapter.

In addition to routing traffic, consider the impact of the following common types of DNS-related communication, especially when you are operating across slow-speed links on a wide area network:

- Server-to-server traffic caused both by zone transfers with other DNS servers and by DNS interoperability with other servers (for example, when WINS lookup is enabled).
- Client-to-server traffic caused by both query loads and dynamic updates sent by DNS client computers or Windows 2000 DHCP servers providing dynamic updating for earlier-version DNS clients that do not support dynamic updates.

For small, flat namespaces, you might use full replication of all DNS zones to all DNS servers in your network. For large, vertical namespaces, this is neither possible nor recommended. In larger networks, it is often necessary to study, test, analyze, and revise your zone plans based on observed or estimated traffic patterns. After careful analysis, you can partition and delegate your DNS zones based on what is required for providing efficient and fault-tolerant name service to each location or site.

When creating zones, if you intend to use the DNS snap-in to manage your zones, note the following recommended limits when adding new zones or extending your current zones:

- Do not attempt to add more than 65,553 resource records to a zone.
- Do not attempt to add or load more than 1,000 zones on any DNS server.

These recommended limits are stated based on current Windows 2000 DNS implementation. For more information or updates to these limits when working with zones, see Appendix D.

If you are using a mixture of Windows DNS servers, be aware that zone transfers can sometimes be slow between the DNS service and some other DNS server implementations. For more information, see "Zone Transfer with BIND and Other DNS Server Implementations" in this chapter.

For Windows 2000 Server, the DNS service supports incremental zone transfers between servers replicating a standard zone. This feature can reduce DNS replication traffic considerations and should be reviewed in zone planning. For more information, see Chapter 8, "DNS Overview."

Although it is useful to plan zones, you might also want to explore the use of caching-only DNS servers, which do not host DNS zones. Caching-only servers are a good option at small remote sites that have a stable and minimal use for DNS name service but are located across a WAN where the transfer of a large zone over a slower link can be resource-intensive. For more information, see "Using Caching-only Servers" in this chapter.

Server Planning for DNS

When planning for your DNS servers, it is important to make the following considered choices:

- Perform capacity planning and review server hardware requirements.
- Determine how many DNS servers you need and their role in your network. When deciding the number of DNS servers to use, decide which servers will host primary and secondary copies of zones. Also, if you are using Active Directory, determine whether the server computer will perform as a domain controller or a member server for the domain.
- Decide where you are going to place DNS servers on your network for traffic loads, replication, and fault tolerance.
- Decide whether to use only Windows 2000 DNS servers for all your DNS servers or if you are operating a mixture of Windows and other DNS server implementations.

For more information on migration and interoperability of the DNS service with other DNS server implementations, see "Migrating Servers" and "Interoperability Issues" in this chapter.

SERVER CAPACITY PLANNING

Planning and deploying DNS servers on your network involves examining several aspects of your network and the capacity requirements for any DNS servers you intend to use in it. Some questions to consider when planning include the following:

- How many zones is the DNS server expected to load and host?
- For each zone the server is loading for service, how large is the zone (based on the size of the zone file or the number of resource records used in the zone)?
- For a multihomed DNS server, how many interfaces are to be enabled for listening to and servicing DNS clients on each of the server's connected subnets?
- How many total or overall DNS query requests from all of its clients is a DNS server expected to receive and service?

In many cases, adding more RAM to a DNS server can provide the most noticeable improvements in performance. This is because the DNS Server service fully loads all of its configured zones into memory at startup. If your server is operating and loading a large number of zones, and dynamic updates occur frequently for zone clients, additional memory can be helpful.

Keep in mind that for typical usage, the DNS server consumes system memory as follows:

- Approximately 4 MB of RAM is used when the DNS server is started without any zones.
- For each addition of zones or resource records to the server, the DNS server consumes additional server memory.
- It is estimated that for the addition of every resource record to a server zone, an average of approximately 100 bytes of server memory is used. For example, if a zone containing 1000 resource records is added to a server, it would require approximately 100 KB of server memory.

In determining your server plans, you can start by reviewing sample DNS server performance test results collected by the Windows 2000 DNS development and testing teams. In addition, you can use DNS server related counters provided for use with Windows 2000 monitoring tools to obtain your own performance measurements for Windows 2000 DNS servers you deploy on your network. For more information, see "Monitoring Server Performance."

Important The previous recommendations are not intended to indicate maximum performance or limitations for Windows 2000 DNS servers.

These numbers are approximate and can be influenced by the type of the resource records entered in zones, the number of resource records with the same owner name, and the number of zones in use at a specific DNS server.

WHERE TO PLACE DNS SERVERS

In general, place your DNS servers at a location on your network that is centrally accessible to your clients. It is often most practical to use a DNS server on each subnet. There are several factors to consider when deciding where a DNS server is needed.

- If you are deploying DNS to support Active Directory, is the DNS server computer also a domain controller or likely to be promoted to one in the future?
- If the DNS server stops responding, are its local clients able to gain access to an alternate DNS server?
- If the DNS server is located on a subnet that is remote to some of its clients, what other DNS servers or name resolution options are available if the routed connection stops responding?

For DNS server installations where the use of Active Directory is an issue, review special interoperability issues and installation details. For more information, see "DNS Considerations for Active Directory" in this chapter.

For all DNS server installations, including those in which the use of Active Directory is not an issue, the following server placement and planning guidelines can be usefully applied.

For example, if you have a routed local area network (LAN) and high-speed links that are fairly reliable, you might be able to use one DNS server for a larger, multiple subnetted network area. If you have a high number of client nodes on a single subnet design, you might want to add more than one DNS server to the subnet to provide backup and failover if the preferred DNS server stops responding.

When determining the number of DNS servers you need to use, assess the effect of zone transfers and DNS query traffic on slower links in your network. Although DNS is designed to help reduce broadcast traffic between local subnets, it does create some traffic between servers and clients that should be reviewed, particularly when used in complexly routed LAN or WAN environments.

Consider the effects of zone transfer over slower speed links, like those typically used for a wide area network (WAN) connection. Although the DNS service supports incremental zone transfers and Windows 2000 DNS clients and servers can cache recently used names, traffic considerations are sometimes still an issue, particularly when DHCP leases are shortened and, as a result, dynamic updates in DNS are performed more frequently. One option for dealing with remote locations on WAN links is to set up a DNS server at these locations to provide caching-only DNS service.

With most installations, you should have at least two server computers hosting each of your DNS zones for fault tolerance. DNS was designed to have two servers for each zone, one as a primary server and the other as a backup or secondary server. When making any final determinations about the number of servers to use, first assess the level of fault tolerance you need for your network.

When only a single Windows 2000 Server is used on a small LAN in a single-subnet environment, you can configure the single server to simulate both the primary and secondary servers for a zone.

For best results and simplified DNS administration, you can consider using the DNS service supplied with Windows 2000 Server for all of your DNS servers.

When administering zone files created by the DNS service, it is recommended that you use the DNS console tool to make changes. As an alternate option, it is possible to administer all of your DNS zone files manually using any application that supports file saving in text mode. Whether you decide to edit zone files manually in a text editor or use the DNS console to modify them, select one method for updating zones and use it consistently. This helps prevent having zone edits overwritten or rejected, which might happen if you change from one method to another.

Migrating Servers

For Windows 2000 Server, DNS migration can occur in one of the following ways:

1. Upgrading a computer running the version of DNS included in Windows NT Server 4.0 to Windows 2000 Server.
2. Moving zone files from an existing DNS server running another DNS server implementation, such as server running a version of the Berkeley Internet Name Domain (BIND) software.
3. Migrating zones using master-secondary zone transfer from BIND servers to Windows 2000 DNS servers.

UPGRADING DNS SERVERS FROM WINDOWS NT SERVER 4.0

For this scenario—upgrading an existing DNS server running under Windows NT Server 4.0 to Windows 2000 Server—there are no known issues. Any zones or server configuration files and parameters created and stored using the Windows NT Server 4.0 version of the DNS service are stored in the same system folder locations. There is no conversion of data required during the upgrade process.

MOVING BIND-BASED FILES

When moving from a BIND DNS server to DNS service, however, you need to copy and rename any BIND-created zone or boot files that you intend to use with the DNS service. Also, if you continue to use a BIND boot file to provide the initial configuration settings used by the DNS service when it is started, you need to change the boot method used by the DNS service. For information about changing the boot method used by the DNS server, see Chapter 10, "Installing and Maintaining DNS Servers."

Keep in mind that any zone files created and stored on UNIX DNS servers that use BIND need to be manually copied from those servers to the *systemroot\System32\Dns* folder on the computer running Windows 2000 Server and appropriately renamed. BIND zone files have a different naming convention from that used by DNS servers running under the DNS service provided in Windows operating systems.

Table 9.2 shows examples of how BIND server files are renamed for use with the DNS service provided in Windows 2000 Server.

TABLE 9.2 *BIND Server Files Renamed for DNS Server Use*

Description	UNIX file name	Windows 2000 file name
Boot file	named.boot	Boot
Forward lookup zone file	db.*domain_name*	*domain_name*.dns
Reverse lookup zone file	db.*IP_network_forward_notation*	*IP_network_reverse_notation*.dns

For a reverse lookup zone, BIND uses a convention of noting reverse domain names as a forward notation of mapped IP network, such as db.192.1.168 for a reverse lookup zone created for an example IP network address of 192.168.1.0. Windows 2000 DNS servers, however, use the FQDN for the zone, which includes the *in-addr.arpa* domain, to complete the file name. In this example, the correct name to use for the same zone in Windows 2000 Server is *168.1.192.in-addr.arpa.dns* when copying and renaming the file.

If you are using the BIND boot file with the DNS service after migration, there are other limitations that apply to the use of this file by the DNS service. For example, some BIND boot directives are not supported—in particular, xfrnets and other directives provided with versions of BIND, such as version 8.1.1 or later.

If you are accustomed to manually editing DNS zone files, be aware that the DNS service uses RFC-compliant notation for its supported resource records. In most cases, the DNS service interprets and loads resource records from zone files originally created for BIND DNS servers without any need for file changes. If, however, you have used non-standard record formatting, the DNS service can detect these edits and interpret them as bad or erroneous zone data.

MIGRATING FROM BIND SERVERS USING ZONE TRANSFER

Another possible scenario for server migration is using zone transfer to migrate BIND-based server zones to Windows 2000 DNS servers. To accomplish this, you can take the following steps:

1. At your Windows 2000 server computer, install a DNS server.

2. Using the DNS console, at the new server add secondary zones for all of your existing zones hosted at the BIND-based DNS servers. Configure the BIND servers as the master servers for each of the secondary zones you need to create.
3. Initiate zone transfer at your Windows 2000 DNS servers to transfer the zones from the BIND servers.
4. After completing the zone transfers, convert any of the secondary zones to primary zones that were obtained from primary zones at the BIND servers.
5. For the other secondary zones that remain, update the master servers for those zones to use the new primary servers running Windows 2000 Server.

For more information about performing these procedures, see Chapter 10.

If you choose to continue to use your BIND DNS servers as secondary servers for zones for which your DNS server running Windows 2000 Server is the primary server, you should review interoperability issues related to zone transfer for this configuration. For more information, see "Zone Transfer with BIND and Other DNS Server Implementations" in this chapter.

Interoperability Issues

The DNS service supports and implements some Request for Comment (RFC) draft specifications used to define DNS usage for the Internet. In general, the DNS service adds design support for most approved RFCs (that is, those classified as "required") that form the current or ongoing DNS protocol standard. This design feature provides clear benefits for operating Windows DNS servers in mixed or heterogeneous environments.

The primary benefits for interoperability in these environments include:

- Full interoperability with other DNS server implementations that implement RFC-compliant behavior for DNS name service.
- Use of Windows DNS servers to provide DNS service on the Internet.

For interoperability testing, the Windows 2000 development team has tested the Windows 2000 DNS Server service with the following versions of the Berkeley Internet Name Domain (BIND) DNS server implementation:

- BIND 4.9.7
- BIND 8.1.2
- BIND 8.2

Interoperability and configuration issues related to using Windows 2000 DNS with other various environments, or when using DNS servers on the Internet, are covered in the following sections.

DNS CONSIDERATIONS FOR ACTIVE DIRECTORY

For Active Directory, DNS is required. Therefore, you can elect to set up DNS servers as part of the process of installing Active Directory and promoting the server computer to the role of a domain controller.

When a Windows 2000 server computer is promoted to domain controller, you have the option to install a DNS server and add new zones automatically as part of Active Directory installation. Separately installing a DNS server at the server computer is only necessary if it is not currently a domain controller or expected to be promoted to one in the future.

When you select the option to install and configure a DNS server during the Active Directory Installation wizard, zones are created based on the DNS name you have specified during the process of promoting the server to a domain controller. Other tasks might also be useful once the first server in the domain is promoted to a domain controller, such as changing the zone type from **Standard primary** to **Active Directory-integrated** and changing the update policy for the zone to **Allow Only Secure Updates**.

If you are deploying DNS to support Active Directory, a simple method for redundancy and fault tolerance planning is to have a DNS server running on each domain controller. For each subnet, a good rule to follow is to have two Windows 2000 Server computers configured as domain controllers that are also running as DNS servers that load and store only Active Directory-integrated zones.

By observing these guidelines for simplified DNS and Active Directory configuration, you can enable your DNS servers to fully leverage the enhanced benefits of using Active Directory and Windows 2000 DNS servers, such as integrated storage, merged replication of Active Directory and DNS data, and secure authentication when allowing dynamic updates.

ZONE TRANSFER WITH BIND AND OTHER DNS SERVER IMPLEMENTATIONS

When transferring a zone between two Windows DNS servers, the DNS Server service always uses a fast transfer method that uses compression. This method includes multiple resource records in each message sent to complete the transfer of the zone between servers. For Windows 2000 DNS servers, this is the default method used when initiating transfer with other DNS server implementations.

If necessary, Windows 2000 DNS servers can be configured to transfer a zone using the slower uncompressed transfer format. This enables successful zone transfers to be made with DNS servers that do not support the faster transfer method, such as BIND servers prior to version 4.9.4.

When the **Bind Secondaries** option in advanced server properties is checked, no fast transfers are made. By default, the check box is cleared to enable fast transfers. For more information, see Chapter 10.

SUPPORTING ACTIVE DIRECTORY WITH OTHER DNS SERVER IMPLEMENTATIONS

In many large organizations, DNS is already implemented using other solutions, such as UNIX DNS servers that run legacy versions of BIND software. In some cases, these DNS servers are not equipped to support the DNS requirements for deploying Active Directory. This issue can be addressed in one of two ways:

- Upgrade any BIND DNS servers to version 8.1.2 or later of the BIND software to meet the DNS requirements for Active Directory support.
- Use the DNS service provided with Windows 2000 Server, if possible, when migrating any of your current DNS zones to Windows 2000 DNS servers.

Although the DNS service is recommended to support Active Directory, you can use other DNS server implementations for this purpose. These other implementations should, however, support the following standard specifications:

- The service location (SRV) resource record, as described in the Internet draft, "A DNS RR for specifying the location of services (DNS SRV)."
- Dynamic updates in DNS, as described in RFC 2136.

Support for dynamic updates is recommended but not essential. Support for the SRV resource record is mandatory because it is required to provide basic DNS support to Active Directory. For example, a DNS server that does not support dynamic updates, like that provided with Windows NT Server 4.0 (updated to Service Pack 4 or later), supports the DNS requirements of Active Directory because SRV resource record support was added with Service Pack 4.

Additional manual administration of SRV resource records is needed for DNS configuration support of Active Directory to function properly on a DNS server that does not support dynamic updates. For more information, see "Service Location Resource Records" in this chapter.

INTEROPERATING WINDOWS DNS SERVERS WITH OTHER DNS SERVER IMPLEMENTATIONS • If you decide to use Windows DNS service and manage it with a split DNS configuration in which existing DNS servers for root zones are not to be upgraded or migrated to other DNS solutions. The DNS service and Windows 2000 Server are to be deployed and provide management of any DNS domain names required to register, update, and support for use with Active Directory.

You can modify your DNS namespace design plans in either of the following ways:

1. *Create a single new subdomain in your current DNS domain namespace to root your first Active Directory domain.* For example, if your organization has registered and is using a second-level domain name, such as *microsoft.com,* you can create a single subdomain, such as

example.microsoft.com, and use this domain to root the DNS domain namespace used by Active Directory. The DNS service is automatically configured to support Active Directory when you install the first domain controller.

Before you have created a zone for the new subdomain at a computer running the DNS Server service, you can delegate these subdomains away at the primary zone for your second-level domain, such as *microsoft.com.* In some cases, you might only need to notify another DNS or UNIX system administrator in your organization to make the delegation for you. For more information, see "Delegating Zones" in this chapter.

2. *Create multiple subdomains based on your DNS second-level domain to support registration of Active Directory in DNS.* For example, if your organization has a registered second-level DNS domain name already in use, such as *microsoft.com*, you can create additional subdomains that are delegated to Windows DNS servers and used only for registering DNS names related to Active Directory.

This method is more complex to implement, but enables less change to your currently deployed DNS infrastructure that is not Windows-based. With this namespace design, you create only those additional subdomains and appropriate zones needed to support your Active Directory deployment. For example, in this configuration, the domain name *microsoft.com* is both the root DNS and the root Active Directory domain name for your organization. For this configuration, you first need to create zones for the following subdomains using the DNS snap-in tool at a computer running DNS service and Windows 2000 Server:

_msdcs.microsoft.com
_ldap._tcp.microsoft.com

Before these zones are created, you can delegate these subdomains away at the primary zone for your parent or second-level domain name, or notify another DNS administrator who manages these zones for your organization to do so. For more information, see "Delegating Zones" in this chapter.

USING DNS ON THE INTERNET

To establish a presence on the Internet, an individual or business must first apply for and register a second-level domain name with an authorized DNS domain name registration authority. Your Internet service provider (ISP) can often perform this function and obtain a name on your behalf, usually for an additional fee.

To register your domain name, there are several required tasks, including:

- *Selecting and researching a second-level domain name that is not currently registered or in use.* This can easily be done if you have Internet access by using a WHOIS query engine provided at the Web site for your applicable Internet DNS domain name registrar. Be prepared to select an alternate name if your WHOIS query indicates that your preferred selection is already registered and in use.

- *Registering and obtaining at least one IP address valid for use on the Internet.* This address is needed for the DNS server on the Internet that you want to establish as the host for the primary copy of the zone based on your second-level domain name. In many cases, if you are using an ISP to register a domain name on your behalf, they can specify the IP addresses for one or two of their servers as primary and secondary for the Internet.

  As part of the registration process, an applicant must provide at least two currently active DNS servers that are used on the Internet as the primary and secondary servers designated for the new domain. This requirement is necessary to ensure proper Internet root server configuration and referral for others that query for your registered DNS domain name on the Internet.

  After one IP address has been obtained, you can sometimes arrange (or your ISP can do so on your behalf) to use another company or ISP's DNS server as a secondary server for the zone. If you still need to obtain an IP address directly for use in the United States, a valid IP address can be obtained through the American Registry for Internet Numbers (ARIN). In other countries, you might contact your local Internet service or telephone provider to find out how to register and acquire an IP address if one is needed.
- *Complete the registration application form and submit it with your registration fee to the appropriate Internet DNS domain name registration authority.* Registrations are typically in force for a finite period of time and must be periodically renewed.

For more information, here are some related Internet Web sites that might be useful to you when selecting and registering your Internet DNS name.

- Network Solutions, Inc. (NSI) Registry Web site

  www.nsiregistry.net/

- Internet Corporation for Assigned Names and Numbers (ICANN) Web site

  www.icann.org/

- Internet Assigned Numbers Authority (IANA) Web site

  www.iana.org/

In the past, the process of registering DNS domain names was managed solely by NSI. It is now transitioning to a shared registration system, the details of which are still being determined.

Refer to the NSI Registry Web site for updated information and related links to other organizations that might be involved in the new or proposed system for registering Internet DNS domain names.

INTEROPERABILITY PLANNING: CONFIGURING RELATED SERVICES

Windows 2000 Server provides several interoperability options when using the DNS service with other TCP/IP services. In many cases, you can use these features to reduce the amount of time you need to spend administering your DNS namespace and provide an improved naming service for your network.

These options most often include use of the following enhancements:

- *WINS forward and reverse lookups.* In Windows NT Server 4.0, Windows 2000, or later, the DNS service provides for the use of WINS lookup. This feature enables configured DNS zones to refer queries not answered from current zone information to a WINS server for further resolution. With this added search of the WINS namespace, both DNS and WINS are used to complete a full search of registered names for a matched response. WINS lookup is supported for both forward and reverse lookup zones and can be enabled on a per-zone basis or configured for selected zones. This feature should also be configured to prevent replication or zone transfer of WINS resource records to servers with other DNS implementations that do not recognize the WINS resource records.
- *Dynamic integration with DHCP servers.* In Windows 2000 Server, the DHCP service provides default support to register and update information for legacy DHCP clients in DNS zones. Legacy clients typically include other Microsoft TCP/IP client computers that were released prior to Windows 2000. The DNS-DHCP integration provided in Windows 2000 Server enables a DHCP client that is unable to dynamically update DNS resource records directly to have this information updated in DNS forward and reverse lookup zones by the DHCP server.

Dynamic integration with the DHCP service is only available with Windows 2000 Server. DHCP servers running under Windows NT Server 4.0 (and earlier versions) do not support DNS-DHCP integration.

Managing Servers

This section covers,

- Configuring a new primary server
- Updating existing servers
- Using secondary servers

- Using caching-only servers
- Managing the aging and scavenging of server data

Configuring a New Primary Server

There are several situations in which you might add and configure a new DNS server for your network:

- When you are adding a new DNS server to your network and configuring a new zone for first-time use.
- When you have already created a zone at another DNS server and are adding a new server that also needs to load and provide service for the zone.
- When you already have a DNS server configured with a zone or zones, but need to add a new zone for another domain name, such as a subdomain.

ADDING A PRIMARY SERVER FOR AN EXISTING ZONE

The primary server for a zone acts as the zone's point of update. Newly created zones are always this type. With Windows 2000 Server, you can use primary zones in one of two ways: as standard primary zones or as primary zones integrated with Active Directory.

For standard primary-type zones, only a single server can host and load the master copy of the zone. If you create a zone and keep it as a standard primary zone, no additional primary servers for the zone are permitted. Only one server is allowed to accept dynamic updates and process zone changes.

The standard primary model implies a single point of failure. For example, if for any reason the primary server for a zone is unavailable to the network, no dynamic updates to the zone can be made. Note that queries for names in the zone are not affected and can continue uninterrupted, as long as secondary servers for the zone are available to answer them.

In Windows 2000 Server, however, you can add more primary servers for a zone by using the directory-integrated storage and replication features of the DNS service. To do this, you need to change a zone and integrate it into Active Directory.

You can integrate an existing zone into Active Directory by changing the type of a zone at the originating primary server where it was first created. Once the zone type is changed from Standard primary to Active Directory-integrated, you can add the zone to other DNS servers by configuring them to use the Boot From DS option when they initialize DNS service.

When the Boot From DS option is selected, other DNS servers operating as part of the Active Directory domain namespace—such as domain controllers for the Active Directory domain—can query the directory and automatically load all directory-integrated zones, which are stored in the directory database. No other steps are necessary. With the Boot From DS option, any DNS servers operating as part of Active Directory are, by default, also primary servers for directory-integrated zones.

For more information on changing the zone type and changing the server boot method, see Chapter 10.

ADDING A NEW PRIMARY ZONE TO AN EXISTING SERVER

Adding a new primary zone to an existing server can be done whenever additional domains or subdomains are needed in your DNS domain namespace. For example, you might have a zone for a second-level domain, such as *microsoft.com,* and want to add a primary zone for the new subdomain, *example.microsoft.com.*

In this example, you can create the new zone for the subdomain using the DNS snap-in, by running the Configure New Zone wizard. When you are done, you need to create a delegation in the parent zone for the new subdomain (such as the *microsoft.com* zone) to complete the addition of the new subdomain and its primary zone.

Once the new primary zone is added, you can perform other zone configuration tasks as needed to fully configure the zone for use. For more information, see "Managing Zones" in this chapter.

Updating Existing Servers

Updating the configuration of your DNS servers can be necessary for various reasons, such as to:

- Change the computer (host) name of the server computer.
- Change the primary or parent DNS domain name of the server computer.
- Change the IP address for the server computer.
- Remove a DNS server from the network.
- Change the primary server for a zone (standard primary zones only).

Each of these is covered in the following sections.

CHANGING THE COMPUTER NAME OF THE SERVER

If you need to change the computer name (host name) of a DNS server (but not its parent or primary DNS domain name), make the following changes in the zone where the server is configured as an authoritative server for the zone:

1. Change the computer name for the server in System properties.
2. Restart the computer to initiate the following DNS dynamic updates:
    a. Add the new host (A) and pointer (PTR) resource records for the new name and IP address of the server.

   b. Remove the old A and PTR resource records for the old name and IP address of the server.

3. Update the name server (NS) resource record in zones where the server is configured as authoritative to point to the new A resource record added in step 2.
4. If the server is the primary server for a standard zone, revise the name in the owner field of the start of authority (SOA) resource record for the zone (if the zone is directory-integrated, this step is not needed).
5. Check in the zones to ensure that any delegation records—NS or A resource records—that are used are updated for the new name of the server.

CHANGING THE PRIMARY DNS DOMAIN NAME OF THE SERVER

When changing the DNS domain name of a computer, the ability to change the primary DNS domain name of the server can depend on whether or not you are using the computer as a domain controller.

If you are running the server computer as a domain controller, the primary DNS domain name of the server computer is set to be the same as the name of the Active Directory domain where the server was promoted to be a domain controller. To change this name, you must first demote the server so that it is no longer a domain controller. For a server changing its parent DNS domain name in this situation, the process of adding and deleting A and PTR resource records for the server is done automatically when joining and leaving an Active Directory domain. In this case, only manual updating of the NS resource records for the old and new DNS parent domains might be needed.

To change the DNS domain name for a DNS server computer not using Active Directory, such as a domain member server or a standalone server, some additional changes and manual administration might be necessary. For example, if the old and new DNS domain names are in two different zones, such as Zone A (the old zone) and Zone B (the new zone), you would need to make the following changes:

1. Change the Primary DNS suffix for this computer in System properties and restart the computer.
2. In Zone A, remove the A resource record for the server.
3. In Zone B, add the A resource record for the server.
4. Update all SOA and NS resource records in zones containing the name of the renamed DNS server.

CHANGING THE IP ADDRESS OF THE SERVER

To change the IP address for an existing DNS server, the process is the same as for any DNS host computer. Update the IP address in the server address (A) resource record. If the name of the server does not change, NS and SOA records are not affected.

A common configuration error that occurs when changing an IP address in the A resource record in a zone is that the same information used elsewhere in DNS is not updated. For example, if a DNS server that has a name or address change is used in a parent zone as part of a set of delegation records, the zone records might be updated but the delegation records left unchanged. For this reason, it is good to check the parent zone as well when changing or updating IP addresses for A resource records for DNS servers in a zone. Otherwise, zone delegation can fail.

Also, if you are using a multihomed server, be aware of the events and conditions under which Windows 2000 can initiate a dynamic update when connection-specific DNS domain naming is used. For more information, see "Configuring Multiple Names" in this chapter.

REMOVING A DNS SERVER FROM THE NETWORK

To remove a DNS server from the network, make the following changes in zones where the server is configured as an authoritative server for the zone:

1. Remove the A resource record for the server.
2. Update the NS records in zones where the server is configured as authoritative to no longer include the server by name (as it appeared in the A record deleted in step 1).
3. If the server is the primary server for a standard zone, revise the owner field of the SOA resource record for the zone to point to the new primary DNS server for the zone (if the zone is directory-integrated, this step is not needed).
4. Check the parent zone to ensure that any records (NS or A resource records) used for delegation to the zone are revised and no longer point to the removed server.

CHANGING THE PRIMARY SERVER FOR A ZONE (STANDARD PRIMARY ZONES ONLY)

For standard primary zones, it can sometimes be necessary to change the designated primary server for a zone. For example, suppose that the current primary server for a standard primary zone is Server A, and the new primary server for the zone is Server B.

To effect the changeover in status from Server A to Server B, make the following zone changes:

1. Add a new A resource record for Server B.
2. Update the NS resource record in the zone to remove Server A and include Server B as a configured server of authority that points to the new A resource record added in step 1.
3. Revise the name in the owner field of the SOA resource record for the zone from Server A to Server B.
4. Remove the old A resource record for Server A.
5. Check the parent zone to ensure that any delegation records (NS or A resource records) used are updated to refer to Server B.

Using Secondary Servers

DNS design specifications recommend that at least two DNS servers be used to host each zone. For standard primary-type zones, a secondary server is required to add and configure the zone to appear to other DNS servers in the network. For directory-integrated primary zones, secondary servers are supported but not required for this purpose. For example, two DNS severs operating as Windows 2000 domain controllers can be redundant primary servers for a zone, providing the same benefits of adding a secondary server while including additional advantages.

Secondary servers can provide a means to offload DNS query traffic in areas of the network where a zone is heavily queried and used. Additionally, if a primary server is down, a secondary server can provide some name resolution in the zone until the primary server is available.

If you add a secondary server, try to locate it as close as possible to clients that have a high demand for names used in the zone. Also, consider placing secondary servers across a router, either on other subnets (if you use a routed LAN) or across WAN links. This provides a good use of a secondary server as a local backup in cases where an intermediate network link becomes the point of failure between DNS servers and clients that use the zone.

Because a primary server always maintains the master copy of updates and changes to the zone, a secondary server relies on DNS zone transfer mechanisms to obtain its information and keep it current. Issues like zone transfer methods—either using full or incremental zone transfers—are more applicable when using secondary servers. For more information about zones and zone transfer, see Chapter 8.

In considering the impact of zone transfers caused by secondary servers, consider their advantage as a backup source of information and measure this against the added cost they impose on your network infrastructure. A simple rule is that for each secondary server you add, network usage (because of added zone replication traffic) increases, and so does the time required to synchronize the zone at all secondary servers.

Secondary servers are most heavily used for forward lookup zones. If you are using reverse lookup zones, you can assume that you do not need to add as many secondary servers for those zones. Typically, a secondary server for a reverse lookup zone is not used outside of the network and subnet that correspond to the reverse zone. For information about adding a secondary server for an existing zone, see Chapter 10.

Using Caching-only Servers

Although all DNS name servers cache queries that they have resolved, caching-only servers are DNS name servers that only perform queries, cache the answers, and return the results. They are not authoritative for any domains and the information that they contain is limited to what has been cached while resolving queries.

In determining when to use this kind of server, note that when this server is initially started, it has no cached information. This information is obtained over time as client requests are serviced. However, if you are dealing with a slow-speed WAN link between sites, this option might be ideal because once the cache is built, traffic decreases. In addition, the caching-only server does not perform zone transfers, which can also be network intensive in WAN environments.

For information about installing a caching-only DNS server, see Chapter 10.

Managing the Aging and Scavenging of Server Data

Aging and scavenging of stale resource records are features of Windows 2000 DNS available when deploying your server with primary zones.

Where aging and scavenging are available for use, you can use the DNS console to perform the following related tasks for your DNS servers and any directory-integrated zones that they load:

- Enable or disable the use of scavenging at a DNS server.
- Enable or disable the use of scavenging for selected zones at the DNS server.
- Modify the no-refresh interval, either as a server default or by specifying an overriding value at selected zones.
- Modify the refresh interval, either as a server default or by specifying an overriding value at selected zones.
- Specify whether periodic scavenging occurs automatically at the DNS server for any of its eligible zones, and how often these operations are repeated.
- Manually initiate a single scavenging operation for all eligible zones at the DNS server.
- View other related properties, such as the time stamp for individual resource records or the start scavenging time for a specified zone.

ENABLING SCAVENGING OF STALE RESOURCE RECORDS

By default, aging and scavenging features are disabled on all Windows 2000 DNS servers and any of their zones. Before using these features, you should configure these settings for the applicable server and its directory-integrated zones:

- **Server aging/scavenging properties** for determining the use of these features on a server-wide basis. First, you need to enable aging and scavenging of stale resource records for use at the server. These settings are used to determine the effect of zone-level properties for any directory-integrated zones loaded at the server. For more information, see Chapter 10.
- **Zone aging/scavenging properties** for determining the use of these features on a per-zone basis. When zone-specific properties are

set for a selected zone, these settings apply only to the applicable zone and its resource records. Unless these zone-level properties are otherwise configured, they inherit their defaults from comparable settings maintained in server aging/scavenging properties. For more information, see Chapter 10.

MODIFYING NO-REFRESH INTERVALS

When the no-refresh interval is in effect for a specific resource record, attempts to dynamically refresh its time stamp are suppressed by the DNS server. This aspect of the aging/scavenging mechanism prevents unnecessary refreshes from being processed by the server for aged resource records. These early refresh attempts, if not handled in this way, might otherwise increase Active Directory replication traffic related to processing DNS zone changes.

To ensure that records do not refresh prematurely, keep the **No-refresh interval** comparable in length to the current refresh interval for each resource record. For example, if you increase the **Refresh interval** to a higher value you can similarly increase the no-refresh interval. In most instances, the default interval of 7 days is sufficient and does not need to be changed.

MODIFYING REFRESH INTERVALS

When the refresh interval is in effect for a resource record, attempts to dynamically refresh its time stamp are accepted and processed by the DNS server. When setting this interval, it is important that the length of time used be greater than the maximum possible refresh period for any resource records contained within the zone. This period is equal to the maximum amount of time that it might take the record to be refreshed under normal network conditions, based on the specific source generating the record refresh.

Table 9.3 shows maximum refresh periods for various services known to dynamically refresh records in DNS.

TABLE 9.3 *Maximum Refresh Periods in DNS*

Service	Maximum refresh period
Net logon	60 minutes (1 hour)
Clustering	15–20 minutes
DHCP client	24 hours Note: By default, the DHCP Client service is used by all Windows 2000 computers to send refresh attempts once every 24 hours. This includes both computers that obtain a leased IP address using DHCP and those that are configured statically for TCP/IP.
DHCP server	4days Note: Refresh attempts are only made by Windows 2000 DHCP servers providing DHCP/DNS integration where the server provides proxied updates in DNS for its clients. The period is based on the frequency in which DHCP clients renew their IP address leases with the server. Typically, this occurs when 50 percent of the scope lease time has elapsed. If the Windows 2000 default scope lease duration of 8 days is used, then the maximum refresh period for records updated by DHCP servers on behalf of clients is 4 days.

By default, the refresh interval is 7 days. In most instances, this value is sufficient and does not need to be changed unless any resource records in the zone are refreshed less often than every 7 days.

AUTOMATED AND MANUALLY-INITIATED SCAVENGING

Although scavenging start time and other factors determine when zones and records are actually eligible for scavenging, you have the option to perform scavenging using either of two methods to initiate it:

- **Automatic scavenging** specifies that aging and scavenging of stale records is to be performed automatically by the server for any eligible zones at a recurring interval specified as the *scavenging period*. When using automatic scavenging, the default scavenging period is 1 day and the minimum allowed value you can use is 1 hour. For more information, see Chapter 10.
- **Manual scavenging** specifies that aging and scavenging of stale records is to be performed as a nonrecurring operation for any eligible zones at the server. For more information, see Chapter 10.

MODIFYING TIME STAMP VALUES

For resource records that are not dynamically added to DNS zone data, a record time stamp value of zero is applied, preventing these records from aging or removal during scavenging.

You can, however, manually reset record properties to enable any statically entered records to qualify for the aging/scavenging process. If you do this, the record will be deleted based upon the modified time stamp value, at which point, you might need to recreate a record if it is still needed. For more information, see Chapter 10.

Caution Enabling aging and scavenging for use with standard primary zones modifies the format of zone files. This change does not affect zone replication to secondary servers, but the modified file cannot be loaded by other DNS servers not running Windows 2000 DNS.

Before using information in this topic, be sure that you have reviewed the aging and scavenging process and use of its configurable properties and features. For more information, see Chapter 8.

For information on using Active Directory and Windows 2000 DNS, see Chapter 8.

Managing Clients

This section covers,

- Configuring client settings
- Configuring multiple names
- Updating client information

Configuring Client Settings

For Windows 2000 clients, DNS configuration involves the following tasks when configuring TCP/IP properties for each computer:

- Setting a DNS computer (host) name for each computer.
- Setting a primary DNS suffix for the computer, which is placed after the computer or host name to form the FQDN.
- Setting a list of DNS servers for clients to use when resolving DNS names, such as a preferred DNS server, and any alternate DNS servers to use if the preferred server is not available.
- Setting the DNS suffix search list or search method to be used by the client when it performs DNS query searches for short, unqualified domain names.

These tasks are discussed in more detail in each of the following sections.

SETTING COMPUTER NAMES

When setting computer names for DNS, it is useful to think of the name as the leftmost portion of an FQDN. For example, in *wkstn1.example.microsoft.com.*, the first part of the name that precedes the first period (.) in the FQDN *(wkstn1)* is the name of the computer.

You can configure all Windows DNS clients with a computer name based on any of the standard supported characters defined in RFC 1123 for Internet DNS use. These characters include the use of:

- Uppercase letters, A through Z
- Lowercase letters, a through z
- Numbers, 0 through 9
- Hyphens (-)

If you are supporting both NetBIOS and DNS namespaces on your network, you can use a different computer name within each namespace. It is recommended that wherever possible, however, you try to use computer names that are 15 characters or less and that you follow the RFC 1123 naming requirements outlined above.

By default, for Windows 2000, the leftmost label in the full DNS computer name for clients equals the NetBIOS computer name, unless this label is 16 or more octets. When these labels exceed the maximum length for NetBIOS, the NetBIOS computer name is truncated based on the full label that is specified.

Before configuring computers running Windows 2000 with varying DNS and NetBIOS names, consider the following implications and their related issues for your deployment:

- If WINS lookup is enabled for zones hosted by your Windows DNS servers, you need to use the same name for both NetBIOS and DNS computer naming. Otherwise, the results of clients attempting to query and resolve the names of these computers will be inconsistent.
- If computers joined to an Active Directory domain are to have the first label of the Full computer name be longer than 15 bytes, additional administration is needed. This is to ensure that access control entries (ACEs) for computer objects in the directory are modified to enable registration of DNS host names where the first label is 16 bytes or more in length. The reason for additional configuration changes is that DNS names longer than 15 characters are different from the Security Account Manager (SAM) account name, which is used by default when securely writing a change to the first label of a DNS host name to the directory. For this reason, you must update the ACE security properties for the computer object to permit a computer with a DNS computer name longer than 15 bytes to write to it.

Important Modifying the default access control for computer objects is vital to enable writing a longer DNS computer name not identical to the SAM account name. However, you should also realize that by modifying the default security for a computer object, an unintended computer might advertise itself under a name different from the SAM-based name. In this situation, the use of secure dynamic update can help to strengthen update security for DNS host names used with your computers. For more information, see Chapter 8.

If you have an investment in using NetBIOS names to support legacy Microsoft networking technology, it is recommended that you revise NetBIOS computer names used on your network to prepare for migration to a standard DNS-only environment. This prepares your network well for long term growth and interoperability with future naming requirements. For example, if you use the same computer name for both NetBIOS and DNS resolution, consider converting any special characters such as the underscore (_) in your current NetBIOS names that do not comply with DNS naming standards. While these characters are permitted in NetBIOS names, they are more often incompatible with traditional DNS host naming requirements and most existing DNS resolver client software.

Although the use of the underscore in DNS host names or in A resource records has been traditionally prohibited by DNS standards, the use of underscores in service-related names—such as those used for SRV resource records—has been proposed to avoid naming collisions in the Internet DNS namespace. For more information, see Appendix D.

In addition to DNS standard naming conventions, DNS service running in Windows 2000 Server supports the use of extended ASCII and Unicode characters. However, since most resolver software written for other platforms (such as UNIX) is based on the Internet DNS standards, this enhanced character support can be used only in private networks that are running a pure Windows 2000 environment.

For Windows 2000, the initial setup of DNS and TCP/IP displays a warning to suggest a standard DNS name if a nonstandard DNS name is entered.

By default, computers running Windows 2000 use DNS to resolve any name that is greater than 15 characters in length. If the name is less than or equal to 15 characters, both NetBIOS and DNS name resolution can be attempted and used to resolve the name.

SETTING DOMAIN NAMES

The domain name is used with the client computer name to form the FQDN, known also as the full computer name. In general, the DNS domain name is the remainder of the FQDN that is not used as the unique host name for the computer.

For example, the DNS domain name used for a client computer running Windows 2000 could be the following: If the FQDN (or Full computer name) configured is *wkstn1.example.microsoft.com,* the domain name is the example.microsoft.com portion of this name.

Windows 2000 domain names have two variations—a DNS name and a NetBIOS name. For Windows 2000 computers, the full computer name (a fully qualified DNS name) is used during querying and location of named resources on your network. For earlier version clients, the NetBIOS name is used to locate various types of NetBIOS services that are shared on your network.

An example that shows the need for both NetBIOS and DNS names is the Net Logon service. In Windows 2000 Server, the Net Logon service on a domain controller registers its SRV resource records on a DNS server. For Windows NT Server 4.0 and earlier versions, domain controllers register a *DomainName* [1C] entry in WINS to perform the same registration and to advertise their availability for providing authentication service to the network.

When a client computer running Windows 2000 is started on the network, it uses the Windows 2000 resolver to query a DNS server for SRV records for its configured domain name. This query is used to locate domain controllers and provide logon authentication for accessing network resources. If either a client or a domain controller on the network is running Windows

NT Server 4.0 or earlier, Windows 2000 optionally uses the NetBIOS resolver service to query WINS servers, attempting to locate *DomainName* [1C] entries to complete the logon process.

Your DNS domain names should follow the same standards and recommended practices that apply to DNS computer naming described in the previous section. In general, acceptable naming conventions for domain names include the use of letters A through Z, numerals 0 through 9, and the hyphen (-). The use of the period (.) in a domain name is always used to separate the discrete parts of a domain name, commonly known as *labels*. Each label corresponds to an additional level defined in the DNS namespace tree.

For most computers, the primary DNS suffix configured for the computer can be the same as its Active Directory domain name, although the two values can also be different. To allow member computers to use a different Full computer name based on a modified DNS suffix, additional steps must be performed for Active Directory configuration.

For example, if a computer is to have a different DNS primary suffix (that is, all other labels to the right of the first label of its Full computer name) from the name of the Active Directory domain where it is joined, you need to modify the default access control for the domain object. This can be done using the Active Directory Users and Computers console. This change is needed to ensure registration of the DNSHostName and Service Principal Name (SPN) attributes where they differ (based on the modified DNS primary suffix) from the Active Directory domain name.

Important Modifying the default access control for domain objects can be vital to enable writing a full DNS computer name based on a modified DNS primary suffix. Without these changes, computers are not able to successfully join or leave a domain.

However, you should also realize that by modifying the default security for a domain object, additional security could be useful. In this situation, the use of secure dynamic updates for DNS zones based on the modified DNS suffix can help to restore or strengthen update security for domain names used in your network. For more information, see Chapter 8.

CONFIGURING A DNS SERVERS LIST

For DNS clients to operate effectively, a prioritized list of DNS name servers must be configured for each computer to use when processing queries and resolving DNS names. In most cases, the client computer contacts and uses its preferred DNS server, which is the first DNS server on its locally configured list. Listed alternate DNS servers are contacted and used when the preferred server is not available. For this reason, it is important that the preferred DNS server be appropriate for continuous client use under normal conditions.

For computers running Windows 2000, clients use the DNS servers list only to resolve DNS names. When clients send dynamic updates, such as when they change their DNS domain name or a configured IP address, they might contact these servers or other DNS servers as needed to update their DNS resource records. For information about dynamic update, see Chapter 8.

When DNS clients are configured dynamically using a DHCP server, it is possible to have a larger list of provided DNS servers. To provide an IP address list of DNS servers to your DHCP clients, enable option code 6 on the configured options types provided by your DHCP server. For Windows DHCP servers, you can configure a list of up to 25 DNS servers for each client with this option.

To effectively share the load when multiple DNS servers are provided in a DHCP options-specified list, you can configure a separate DHCP scope that rotates the listed order of DNS and WINS servers provided to clients.

CONFIGURING A DNS SUFFIX SEARCH LIST

For Windows clients, you can configure a DNS domain suffix search list that extends or revises their DNS search capabilities. By adding additional suffixes to the list, you can search for short, unqualified computer names in more than one specified DNS domain. Then, if a DNS query fails, the DNS Client service can use this list to append other name suffix endings to your original name and repeat DNS queries to the DNS server for these alternate FQDNs.

For Windows 2000 computers, the following default DNS search behavior is predetermined and used when completing and resolving short, unqualified names:

- When the suffix search list is empty or unspecified, the primary DNS suffix of the computer is appended to short unqualified names and DNS query is used to resolve the resultant FQDN. If this query fails, the computer can try additional queries for alternate FQDNs by appending any connection-specific DNS suffix configured for network connections.
- If no connection-specific suffixes are configured, or queries for these resultant connection-specific FQDNs fail, the client can then begin to retry queries based on systematic reduction of the primary suffix (also known as *devolution*). For example, if the primary suffix were *example.microsoft.com,* the devolution process would be able to retry queries for the short name by searching for it in the *microsoft.com* and *com* domains.
- When the suffix search list is not empty and has at least one DNS suffix specified, attempts to qualify and resolve short DNS names is limited to searching only those FQDNs made possible by the specified suffix list. If queries for any FQDNs formed as a result of appending and trying each suffix in the list, the query process fails, producing a "name not found" result.

- If the domain suffix list is used, clients continue to send additional alternate queries based on different DNS domain names when a query is not answered or resolved. Once a name is resolved using an entry in the suffix list, unused list entries are not tried. For this reason, it is most efficient to order the list based on its priority for use.

Domain name suffix searches are used only when a DNS name entry is not fully qualified. To fully qualify a DNS name, a trailing period (.) is entered at the end of the name.

Configuring Multiple Names

In Windows 2000, computers are given DNS names by default. Each computer running Windows 2000 can have its DNS names configured using one of two possible methods:

- A primary DNS domain name, which applies as the default fully qualified DNS name for the computer and all of its configured network connections.
- A connection-specific DNS domain name, which can be configured as an alternate DNS domain name that applies only for a single network adapter installed and configured on the computer.

Although most computers do not need to support or use more than one name in DNS, support for configuring multiple connection-specific DNS names is sometimes useful. For example, by using multiple names, a user could specify which network connection to use when connecting to a multihomed computer.

USING CONNECTION-SPECIFIC NAMES

As shown in Figure 9-1, a multihomed server computer named *host-a* can be named according to both its primary and connection-specific DNS domain names.

In this example, the server computer *host-a* attaches to two separate subnets—Subnet 1 and Subnet 2—which are also linked at redundant points using two routers for additional paths between each subnet. Given this configuration, *host-a* provides access as follows through its separately named LAN connections:

- The name *host-a.public.example.microsoft.com* provides access using LAN connection 1 over Subnet 1, a lower-speed (10 megabit) Ethernet LAN, for normal access to users who have typical file and print service needs.
- The name *host-a.backup.example.microsoft.com* provides access using LAN connection 2 over Subnet 2, a higher-speed (100 megabit) Ethernet LAN, for reserved access by server applications and adminis-

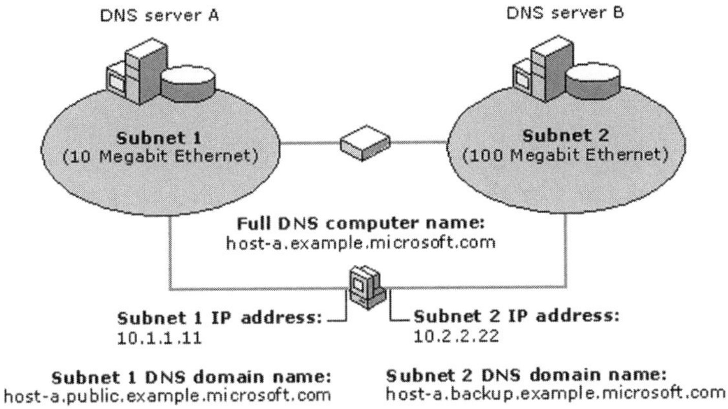

FIGURE 9–1 *A multihomed DNS computer configured with multiple names*

trators who have special needs, such as troubleshooting server networking problems, performing network-based backup, or replicating zone data between servers.

In addition to the connection-specific DNS names, the computer can also be accessible using either of the two LAN connections by specifying its primary DNS domain name, *host-a.example.microsoft.com*.

When configured as shown, Windows 2000 can register resource records in DNS according to its three distinct names and sets of IP addresses, as shown in Table 9.4.

TABLE 9.4 *Windows 2000 Resource Records Registration in DNS*

DNS name	IP addresses	Description
host-a.example.microsoft.com	10.1.1.11, 10.2.2.22	Primary DNS name for computer. The computer registers A and PTR resource records for all configured IP addresses under this name in the *example.microsoft.com* zone.
host-a.public.example.microsoft.com	10.1.1.11	Connection-specific DNS name for LAN connection 1, which registers A and PTR resource records for IP address 10.1.1.11 in the *public.example.microsoft.com* zone.
host-a.backup.example.microsoft.com	10.2.2.22	Connection-specific DNS name for LAN connection 2, which registers A and PTR resource records for IP address 10.2.2.22 in the *public.example.microsoft.com* zone.

DNS names can be set using remote administration and other remote configuration services, such as DHCP. For a Windows 2000 computer, the primary DNS domain name can be set using either remote administration or the unattended setup option.

For connection-specific naming, you can use TCP/IP configuration methods. You can manually configure the DNS domain name for each connection that appears in the Network and Dial-Up Connections folder or use a DHCP option type (option code 15).

Updating Client Information

Updating DNS client information on a computer is sometimes necessary—for example, if a computer is added or removed from an Active Directory domain. In most cases, clients perform dynamic updates for the following changes when entering or leaving a domain:

- When a computer is joined to a domain, it adds its A and PTR records to DNS.
- When a computer is removed from a domain, it deletes its A and PTR records from DNS.

If you have enabled dynamic update for zones, these changes occur automatically. For more information, see Chapter 8.

Managing Zones

This section covers,

- Managing general properties
- Managing authority records
- Managing resource records
- Delegating zones
- Configuring notify lists
- Using WINS lookup
- Managing reverse lookup zones

Managing General Properties

When you add a zone using the DNS console, you can manage these general properties for it.

- Pause or start the zone, to interrupt or restore service for it.
- Change or convert the type for the zone.
- Disable or enable dynamic updates for the zone.

For directory-integrated zones, you can enable the use of secure dynamic updates. This enables you to restrict updates to only a specific set of authorized users or systems. When a secure update policy is enabled for the zone, only users, systems, or groups authorized through Active Directory and included in the access control list (ACL) for each directory-integrated zone, are permitted to update the zone or specific resource records used in it.

In addition to these general zone properties, you can configure or manage the following zone properties using the DNS console:

- *SOA properties.* These include properties supported by the SOA resource record, which is used to initialize the zone and indicate zone authority for a DNS domain name (and any of its subdomains not delegated away to other servers) to others in the DNS namespace. This record affects how often the zone must be renewed and transferred by other servers that load the zone and how long clients can cache resource records when returned in answered queries for names in the zone. For more information on this record and configuring it, see "Managing Authority Records" in this chapter.
- *NS properties.* These include all fields supported by the NS resource record for the zone. The NS resource record is used for designating the names of DNS servers authoritative for the zone to others. For more information on this record and configuring it, see "Managing Authority Records."
- *Zone Transfer properties.* With this feature, you can configure how the zone permits transfers to be performed. You can choose to deny all requests to the server for transfer of this zone, to allow them only for other DNS servers configured on the Name Servers tab, or to transfer the zone only to DNS servers that you specify by IP address in a configured list. Using Notify located here, you can also enable and configure DNS notification for secondary servers of the zone. When notification is used, other servers (either those configured on the Name Servers tab or on a list that you specify) are notified of zone changes. These servers can then pull changes by initiating a zone transfer to update the zone. For more information, see "Configuring Notify Lists" in this chapter.
- *WINS lookup properties.* The WINS lookup feature can be used to provide an expanded DNS name resolution path for zones when a queried name is not found in the zone. If WINS lookup is enabled for the zone, a WINS server (or list of WINS servers) can be contacted to assist in resolving a host name in the WINS-managed NetBIOS namespace. Only *Microsoft DNS servers* support this feature. For more information, see "Using WINS Lookup" in this chapter.

Managing Authority Records

Zones are based on a concept of server authority. When a DNS server is configured to load a zone, it uses two types of resource records to determine the authoritative properties of the zone.

- First, the SOA resource record indicates the name of origin for the zone and contains the name of the server that is the primary source for information about the zone. It also indicates other basic properties of the zone.
- Next, the NS resource record is used to notate which DNS servers are designated as authoritative for the zone. By listing a server in the NS resource record, it becomes known to others as an authoritative server for the zone. This means that any server specified in the NS resource record is to be considered an authoritative source by others, and is able to answer with certainty any queries made for names included in the zone.

The SOA and NS resource records occupy a special role in zone configuration. They are required records for any zone and are typically the first resource records listed in files. By default, the Add New Zone wizard automatically creates these records when a new primary zone is added using the DNS snap-in.

THE START OF AUTHORITY RESOURCE RECORD

The SOA resource record is always first in any standard zone. It indicates the DNS server that either originally created it or is now the primary server for the zone. It is also used to store other properties such as version information and timings that affect zone renewal or expiration. These properties affect how often transfers of the zone are done between servers authoritative for the zone.

The SOA resource record contains the information shown in Table 9.5.

The following is an example of a default SOA resource record:

```
@ IN SOA ameserver.example.microsoft.com. postmaster.example.microsoft.com. (
                1              ; serial number
                3600           ; refresh    [1h]
                600            ; retry      [10m]
                86400          ; expire     [1d]
                3600 )         ; min TTL    [1h]
```

In the example SOA record shown above, the primary or originating server for the zone is shown as *nameserver.example.microsoft.com*. The e-mail address for the person to contact regarding questions about this zone is *postmaster.example.microsoft.com*.

TABLE 9.5 *The SOA Resource Record*

Field	Description
Primary server (owner)	The host name for the primary DNS server for the zone.
Responsible person	The e-mail address of the person responsible for administering the zone. A period (.) is used instead of an at sign (@) in this e-mail name.
Serial number	The revision number of the zone file. This number increases each time a resource record in the zone changes. It is important that this value increase each time the zone is changed, so that either partial zone changes or the fully revised zone can be replicated to other secondary servers during subsequent transfers.
Refresh interval	The time, in seconds, that a secondary DNS server waits before querying its source for the zone to attempt renewal of the zone. When the refresh interval expires, the secondary DNS server requests a copy of the current SOA record for the zone from its source, which answers this request. The secondary DNS server then compares the serial number of the source server's current SOA record (as indicated in the response) with the serial number in its own local SOA record. If they are different, the secondary DNS server requests a zone transfer from the primary DNS server. The default for this field is 900 seconds (15 minutes).
Retry interval	The time, in seconds, a secondary server waits before retrying a failed zone transfer. Normally, this time is less than the refresh interval. The default value is 600 seconds (10 minutes).
Expire interval	The time, in seconds, before a secondary server stops responding to queries after a lapsed refresh interval where the zone was not refreshed or updated. Expiration occurs because at this point in time, the secondary server must consider its local data unreliable. The default value is 86,400 seconds (24 hours).
Minimum (default) TTL	The minimum TTL value applied to all resource records in the zone with unspecified record-specific TTLs. This value is supplied in query responses by servers for the zone to inform others how long they should cache a resource record provided in an answer. The default value is 3,600 seconds (1 hour).

Periods are used to represent e-mail addresses when writing and storing DNS domain names in a zone. In an e-mail application, the previous example address would instead likely appear as *postmaster@example.microsoft.com*.

The parentheses used in the SOA resource record as it appears in a zone file are used to enable wrapping of the record over multiple lines of text.

If an individual TTL value is assigned and applied to a specified resource record used in the zone, it overrides the minimum (default) TTL set in the SOA record.

THE NS RESOURCE RECORD

Name server resource records can be used to assign authority to specified servers for a DNS domain name in two ways:

- By establishing a list of authoritative servers for the domain so that those servers can be made known to others that request information about this domain (zone).
- By indicating authoritative DNS servers for any subdomains that are delegated away from the zone.

In the case of assigning servers with host names in the same zone, corresponding A resource records are normally used in the zone to resolve the names of specified servers to their IP addresses. For servers that are specified using this resource record as part of a zone delegation to a subdomain, the NS resource record usually contains out-of-zone names. For the out-of-zone names to be resolved, A resource records for the specified out-of-zone servers might be needed. When these out-of-zone NS and A records are needed to provide delegation, they are known as *glue records*.

Description:	Used to map a DNS domain name as specified in owner to the name of hosts operating DNS servers specified in the *name_server_domain_name* field.
Syntax:	*owner ttl* IN NS *name_server_domain_name*
Example:	`example.microsoft.com.     IN NS nameserver1.example.microsoft.com`

Managing Resource Records

After you create a zone, additional resource records need to be added to it. The most common resource records to be added are:

- *Host (A)* for mapping a DNS domain name to an IP address used by a computer.
- *Alias (CNAME)* for mapping an alias DNS domain name to another primary or canonical name.
- *Mail Exchanger (MX)* for mapping a DNS domain name to the name of a computer that exchanges or forwards mail.
- *Pointer (PTR)* for mapping a reverse DNS domain name based on the IP address of a computer that points to the forward DNS domain name of that computer.
- *Service location (SRV)* for mapping a DNS domain name to a specified list of DNS host computers that offer a specific type of service, such as Active Directory domain controllers.
- Other resource records as needed.

HOST RESOURCE RECORDS

Host (A) resource records, also called *address resource records* or simply *A resource records,* are used in a zone to associate DNS domain names of computers (or hosts) to their IP addresses, and can be added to a zone in several ways:

- You can manually create an A resource record for a static TCP/IP client computer using the DNS console.
- Computers running Windows 2000 use the DHCP Client service to dynamically register and update their own A resource records in DNS when an IP configuration change occurs.
- DHCP-enabled client computers running earlier versions of Microsoft operating systems can have their A resource records registered and updated by proxy if they obtain their IP lease from a qualified DHCP server (only the DHCP service provided with Windows 2000 Server currently supports this feature).

The A resource record is not required for all computers, but is needed by computers that share resources on a network. Any computer that shares resources and needs to be identified by its DNS domain name needs to use A resource records to provide DNS name resolution to the IP address for the computer.

Most A resource records that are required in a zone can include other workstations or servers that share resources, other DNS servers, mail servers, and Web servers. These resource records comprise the majority of resource records in a zone database.

ALIAS RESOURCE RECORDS

Alias, or CNAME, resource records are also sometimes called canonical names. These records allow you to use more than one name to point to a single host, making it easy to do such things as host both an FTP server and a Web server on the same computer. For example, the well-known server names, such as *ftp* and *www,* are registered using CNAME resource records that map to the DNS host name, such as server-1, for the server computer that hosts these services.

CNAME resource records are recommended for use in the following scenarios:

- When a host specified in an A resource record in the same zone needs to be renamed.
- When a generic name for a well-known server such as *www* needs to resolve to a group of individual computers (each with individual A resource records) that provide the same service. For example, a group of redundant Web servers.

When renaming a computer with an existing A resource record in the zone, you can use a CNAME resource record temporarily to allow a grace period for users and programs to switch from specifying the old computer name to using the new one. To do this, you need the following:

- For the new DNS domain name of the computer, a new A resource record is added to the zone.

- For the old DNS domain name, a CNAME resource record is added that points to the new A resource record.
- The original A resource record for the old DNS domain name (and its associated PTR resource record if applicable) is removed from the zone.

When using a CNAME resource record for aliasing or renaming a computer, set a temporary limit on how long the record is used in the zone before removing it from DNS. If you forget to delete the CNAME resource record and later its associated A resource record is deleted, the CNAME resource record can waste server resources by trying to resolve queries for a name no longer used on the network.

The most common and most popular use of a CNAME resource record is to provide a permanent DNS aliased domain name for generic name resolution of a service-based name, such as *www.example.microsoft.com,* to more than one computer or one IP address used in a Web server. For example, the following shows the basic syntax of how a CNAME resource record is used.

alias_name IN CNAME primary_canonical_name

In this example, a computer named *host-a.example.microsoft.com* needs to function as both a Web server named *www.example.microsoft.com.* and an FTP server named *ftp.example.microsoft.com.* To achieve the intended use for naming this computer, you can add and use the following CNAME entries in the example.microsoft.com zone:

```
host-a     IN  A       10.0.0.20
ftp        IN  CNAME   host-a
www        IN  CNAME   host-a
```

If you later decide to move the FTP server to another computer, separate from the Web server on *host-a,* simply change the CNAME resource record in the zone for *ftp.example.microsoft.com* and add an additional A resource record to the zone for the new computer hosting the FTP server.

Based on the earlier example, if the new computer were named *host-b.example.microsoft.com,* the new and revised A and CNAME resource records would be as follows:

```
host-a     IN  A       10.0.0.20
host-b     IN  A       10.0.0.21
ftp        IN  CNAME   host-b
www        IN  CNAME   host-a
```

MAIL EXCHANGER RESOURCE RECORDS

The mail exchanger (MX) resource record is used by e-mail applications to locate a mail server based on a DNS domain name used in the destination address for the e-mail recipient of a message. For example, a DNS query for the name *example.microsoft.com* could be used to find an MX resource record, enabling an e-mail application to forward or exchange mail to a user with the e-mail address *user@example.microsoft.com.*

The MX resource record shows the DNS domain name for the computer or computers that process mail for a domain. If multiple MX resource records exist, the DNS Client service attempts to contact mail servers in the order of preference from lowest value (highest priority) to highest value (lowest priority). The following shows the basic syntax for use of an MX resource record:

mail_domain_name ***IN MX*** *preference mailserver_host*

By using the MX resource records shown below in the *example.microsoft.com* zone, mail addressed to *user@example.microsoft.com* is delivered to *user@mailserver0.example.microsoft.com* first, if possible. If this server is unavailable, the resolver client can then use *user@mailserver1.example.microsoft.com* instead.

```
@          IN   MX   1    mailserver0
@          IN   MX   2    mailserver1
```

Note that the use of the at sign (**@**) in the records indicates that the mailer DNS domain name is the same as the name of origin *(example.microsoft.com)* for the zone.

POINTER RESOURCE RECORDS

Pointer, or PTR, resource records are used to support the reverse lookup process, based on zones created and rooted in the *in-addr.arpa* domain. These records are used to locate a computer by its IP address and resolve this information to the DNS domain name for that computer.

PTR resource records can be added to a zone in several ways:

- You can manually create a PTR resource record for a static TCP/IP client computer using the DNS snap-in, either as a separate procedure or as part of the procedure for creating an A resource record.
- Computers running Windows 2000 can use the DHCP Client service to dynamically register and update their PTR resource record in DNS when an IP configuration change occurs.
- All other DHCP-enabled client computers can have their PTR resource records registered and updated by the DHCP server if they obtain their IP lease from a qualified server. The DHCP service provided with Windows 2000 Server provides this capability

The PTR resource record is used only in reverse lookup zones to support reverse lookup.

SERVICE LOCATION RESOURCE RECORDS

To locate Active Directory domain controllers in Windows 2000, SRV resource records are required. Typically, you can avoid manual administration of the SRV resource record when installing Active Directory.

By default, the Active Directory installation wizard attempts to locate a DNS server based on the list of preferred or alternate DNS servers, configured in any of its TCP/IP client properties, for any of its active network connections. If a DNS server that can accept dynamic update of the SRV resource record (and other resource records related to registering Active Directory as a service in DNS) is contacted, the configuration process is complete.

If, during the installation, a DNS server that can accept updates for the DNS domain name used to name your Active Directory is not found, a Windows 2000 DNS server can be installed locally and automatically configured with a zone that is based on the Active Directory domain.

For example, if the Active Directory domain that you chose for your first domain in the forest was *example.microsoft.com,* a zone rooted at the DNS domain name of *example.microsoft.com* would be added and configured to use with the DNS server running on the new domain controller.

If you do not install the DNS server provided with Windows 2000, a file *(Netlogon.dns)* is written and created during the Active Directory installation process that contains the SRV resource records and other resource records needed to support the use of Active Directory. This file is created in the *%SystemRoot%\System32\Config* folder.

If you are using a DNS server that fits one of the following descriptions, you should use the records in *Netlogon.dns* to manually configure the primary zone on that server to support Active Directory.

1. The computer operating your DNS server is running on another platform, such as UNIX, and cannot accept or recognize dynamic updates.
2. The DNS server at this computer is authoritative for the primary zone corresponding to the DNS domain name for your Active Directory domain.
3. The DNS server supports the SRV resource record, as defined in the Internet draft, "A DNS RR specifying the location of services (DNS SRV)," but does not support dynamic updates. For example, the DNS service provided with Windows NT Server 4.0, when updated to Service Pack 4 or later, fits this description.

In the future, the SRV resource record might also be used to register and lookup other well-known TCP/IP services on your network if applications implement and support DNS name queries that specify this record type.

OTHER RESOURCE RECORDS

Other resource records are supported by Windows 2000 DNS servers and are used less frequently in most zones. These additional types of resource records can be added as needed using the DNS console.

Delegating Zones

DNS provides the option of dividing up the namespace into one or more zones, which can then be stored, distributed, and replicated to other DNS servers. When deciding whether to divide your DNS namespace to make additional zones, consider the following reasons to use additional zones:

- A need to delegate management of part of your DNS namespace to another location or department within your organization.
- A need to divide one large zone into smaller zones to distribute traffic loads among multiple servers, improve DNS name resolution performance, or create a more fault-tolerant DNS environment.
- A need to extend the namespace by adding numerous subdomains at once, such as to accommodate the opening of a new branch or site.

If, for any of these reasons, you could benefit from delegating zones, it might make sense to restructure your namespace by adding additional zones. When choosing how to structure zones, you should use a plan that reflects the structure of your organization.

When delegating zones within your namespace, be aware that for each new zone you create, you will need delegation records in other zones that point to the authoritative DNS servers for the new zone. This is necessary both to transfer authority and to provide correct referral to other DNS servers and clients of the new servers being made authoritative for the new zone.

When a standard primary zone is first created, it is stored as a text file containing all resource record information on a single DNS server. This server acts as the primary master for the zone. Zone information can be replicated to other DNS servers to improve fault tolerance and server performance.

When structuring your zones, there are several good reasons to use additional DNS servers for zone replication:

1. Added DNS servers provide zone redundancy, enabling DNS names in the zone to be resolved for clients if a primary server for the zone stops responding.
2. Added DNS servers can be placed so as to reduce DNS network traffic. For example, adding a DNS server to the opposing side of a low-speed WAN link can be useful in managing and reducing network traffic.
3. Additional secondary servers can be used to reduce loads on a primary server for a zone.

DELEGATING A SUBDOMAIN TO A NEW ZONE

As shown in Figure 9-2, when a new zone for a subdomain *(example.microsoft.com)* is created, delegation from the parent zone *(microsoft.com)* is needed.

In this example, an authoritative DNS server computer for the newly delegated *example.microsoft.com* subdomain is named based on a derivative subdomain included in the new zone, *ns1.na.example.microsoft.com*. To make this server known to others outside of the new delegated zone, two resource records are needed in the *microsoft.com* zone to complete delegation to the new zone.

- An NS resource record to effect the delegation. This resource record is used to advertise that the server named *ns1.na.example.microsoft.com* is an authoritative server for the delegated subdomain.
- An A resource record (also known as a glue record) is needed to resolve the name of the server specified in the NS resource record to its IP address. The process of resolving the host name in this resource record to the delegated DNS server in the NS resource record is sometimes referred to as *glue chasing*.

When zone delegations are correctly configured, normal zone referral behavior can sometimes be circumvented if you are using a forwarders list in your DNS server configuration. For more information, see "Using Forwarders" in this chapter.

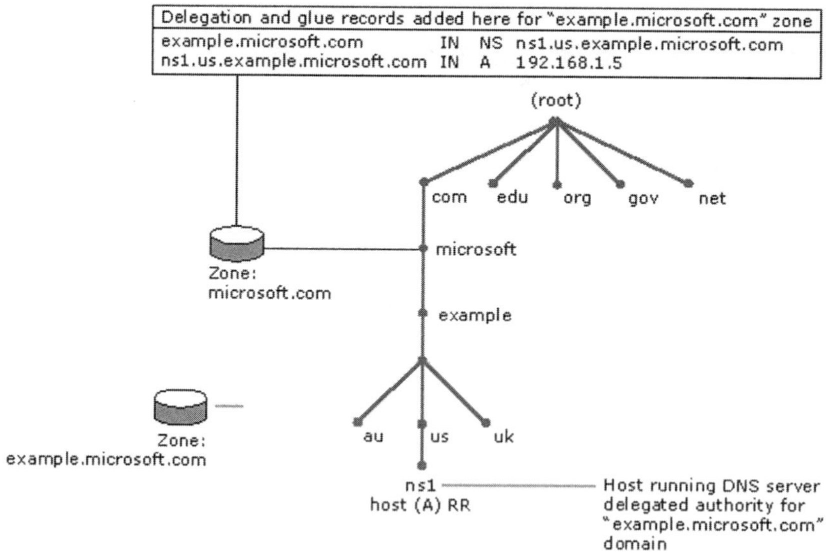

FIGURE 9–2 *How zone delegation works*

Configuring Notify Lists

Notify lists can be created and managed to provide a method for a master server for a zone (either the primary server or another secondary server) to push notify a list of secondary servers when the zone changes.

To create or manage a notify list, you can use the DNS console to add and remove servers by their IP addresses in the notify list for a zone. The list is created and managed for each zone, using the Notify tab in zone properties. By default, the notify list is based on the authoritative servers for the zone as listed on the Name Servers tab. For more information on how DNS notification works and on configuring and managing notify lists, see Chapter 8.

Using WINS Lookup

The DNS service provides the ability to use WINS servers to look up names not found in the DNS domain namespace by checking the NetBIOS namespace managed by WINS.

To use WINS lookup integration, two special resource record types—the WINS and WINS-R resource records—are enabled and added to a zone. When the WINS resource record is used, DNS queries that fail to find a matched A resource record in the zone are forwarded to WINS servers configured in the WINS resource record. For reverse lookup zones, the WINS-R resource record can be enabled and used to provide a similar benefit for further resolving a reverse query not answerable in the reverse *in-addr.arpa* domain. For information about WINS lookup integration, see Chapter 8.

A good example of when to use WINS lookup is when you are using a mixed-mode client environment consisting of UNIX clients that use only DNS name resolution and earlier-version Microsoft clients that require NetBIOS naming. In these environments, WINS lookup provides a method for permitting UNIX DNS clients to locate your WINS clients by extending DNS host name resolution into the WINS-managed NetBIOS namespace.

The WINS lookup integration feature is only supported by Windows DNS servers. If you use a mixture of Windows and other DNS servers to host a zone, you should enable the **Do not replicate this record** check box option for any primary zones when using the WINS lookup record. This prevents the WINS lookup record from being included in zone transfers to other DNS servers that do not support or recognize this record. If you do not enable the WINS lookup record to be used only on the local server, it can cause data errors or failed zone transfers at servers running other DNS server implementations that replicate the zone.

The following sections discuss WINS lookup interoperability considerations and explain:

- How the caching TTL and lookup time-out values are configured for use with the WINS and WINS-R records.
- The format of the WINS and WINS-R resource records as they are used in zone files created by the DNS service.

WINS LOOKUP INTEROPERABILITY

Typically, WINS lookup provides the best and most predictable results if only Windows DNS servers are used, and is only available directly for use at Windows DNS servers. There are ways, however, that you can use and benefit from WINS lookup as an interoperable solution when other DNS servers are deployed.

For example, consider adding a Windows DNS server that hosts a new WINS lookup-enabled zone. When creating and naming the zone, use a subdomain added to your existing DNS namespace that is used just for WINS-specific referrals added to your DNS domain namespace. For instance, in *example.microsoft.com,* call the zone *wins.example.microsoft.com* when you create it. You can then use this new WINS referral zone as the root zone for any of your WINS-aware computers with names that are not found in your other traditional DNS zones.

In order to use the WINS referral zone, you need to specify its domain name *(wins.example.microsoft.com)* in a DNS suffix search list for your clients. The suffix list is configurable as part of the TCP/IP properties for a client connection and can be updated either manually or using DHCP. As long as the name of the WINS referral zone is included in the domain suffix list, any DNS names not resolved in traditional zones can be resolved using the WINS referral subdomain.

Under normal conditions, this should result in recursion from your other DNS servers to the Windows DNS servers that host the WINS-enabled zone. If the queried host names match NetBIOS computer names found in the WINS database, the names are resolved to the IP addresses mapped in WINS data there.

Because the WINS-enabled zone is only used for WINS lookup, no additional resource records need to be added to it.

By using a specific subdomain just for WINS lookup and specifying a static DNS suffix list to be used in resolving and searching for names, you can prevent unusual situations in which DNS queries for different FQDNs resolve to the same WINS client name and IP address. This might easily occur if you add and configure many zones at each level of your namespace and enable each of them to use WINS lookup integration.

For example, suppose you have two zones both configured to use WINS lookup. The zones are rooted and originate at the following DNS domain names:

example1.microsoft.com.
example2.microsoft.com.

With this configuration, a WINS client named HOST-A could be unintentionally resolved using either of the following FQDNs:

host-a.example1.microsoft.com.
host-b.example2.microsoft.com.

WINS RESOURCE RECORD

WINS forward lookup resource records are used in a zone to provide further resolution of DNS queries for names not found in the zone by using a name query to WINS servers configured and listed with this record. If used, the WINS record only applies for the topmost level within a zone and not for subdomains used in the zone. The various fields that are used with the WINS resource record include the following:

- ***owner*** indicates the owner domain for this record should always be set to "@" to indicate that the current domain is the same as the zone origin.
- ***class*** indicates the class for this record should always be set to "IN" as the Internet class is the only supported class for Windows 2000 DNS servers.
- **LOCAL**, when used, indicates that the WINS resource record is to be used only locally at the DNS server and is not to be included during zone replication with other DNS servers. This field corresponds to whether the **Settings only affect local server** check box was selected when configuring WINS lookup at the DNS console. If this check box was cleared, this field will not be included when the record is written to the zone.
- ***lookup_timeout*** indicates the lookup time-out value to be applied for this record.
- ***cache_timeout*** indicates the cache time-out value to be applied for this record.
- ***wins_ip_addresses*** is used to specify one or more IP addresses of WINS servers. At least one IP address of a valid WINS server is required.

The syntax for the WINS resource record is:

owner class ***WINS*** *[LOCAL] [**L**<lookup_timeout>] [**C**<cache_timeout>] <wins_ip_addresses>*

An example of a WINS resource record is:

```
@   IN      WINS      10.0.0.1
@   IN      WINS      LOCAL L1 C10 10.10.10.1 10.10.10.2 10.10.10.3
```

Note that in the previous example, the zone root is assumed to be the current origin.

WINS-R RESOURCE RECORD

A WINS reverse lookup resource record isused in a reverse lookup zone to provide further resolving for reverse queries not found in the zone by using a NetBIOS adapter node status query in WINS for the queried IP addresses. When it is used, you need to specify the parent domain to be appended to a NetBIOS computer name when a successful WINS reverse lookup occurs for an IP address contained within the reverse lookup zone. Other fields used in the WINS-R record have similar description and purpose as described for their use in the WINS forward lookup record.

The syntax for the WINS reverse lookup resource record is:

owner class ***WINS*** *[LOCAL] [**L**<lookup_timeout>] [**C**<cache_timeout>] Domain_to_append_to_returned_NetBIOS_names*

An example of the WINS resource record is:

```
@   IN      WINS-R      LOCAL L1 C10 example.microsoft.com.
@   IN      WINS-R      wins.example.microsoft.com.
```

Note that in the previous example, the zone root is assumed to be the current origin.

ADVANCED PARAMETERS FOR WINS LOOKUPS

Two advanced timing parameters are used with the WINS and WINS-R records:

- The Cache timeout value, which indicates to a DNS server how long it should cache any of the information returned in a WINS lookup. By default, this value is set to 15 minutes.
- The Lookup timeout value, which specifies how long to wait before timing out and expiring a WINS lookup performed by the DNS Server service. By default, this value is set to 2 seconds.

These parameters are configured using the **Advanced** button in the zone properties dialog box when you configure the zone. This button appears on either the WINS or WINS-R tab, depending on whether the zone you are configuring is being used for forward lookup or reverse lookup.

If you are using either the WINS or WINS-R resource record, be aware that the minimum TTL set in the SOA record for the zone is not the default TTL used with these records. Instead, when either an IP address or a host name gets resolved with WINS lookup, the information is cached on the DNS server for the amount of time configured for the WINS cache time-out value. If this address is then ever forwarded to another DNS server, the WINS cache time-out value TTL is what is sent. If your WINS data rarely changes, you can increase the default TTL of 15 minutes.

If you have a zone configured for WINS lookup, then all DNS servers that are authoritative for that zone need to be capable of WINS lookup or you will have intermittent behavior.

Because you can select that the WINS and WIN-R resource records not be replicated to other DNS servers, you can selectively enable and configure WINS lookup at each of your secondary servers for zones where this feature is used. This is not a standard practice for other types of resource records that are only to be configured at the primary server for the zone.

Managing Reverse Lookup Zones

When adding reverse lookup zones, you can simplify the process of adding PTR resource records to these zones by,

- Using the **Update associated PTR record** option when manually adding A resource records to forward lookup zones.
- Deploying Windows 2000 DHCP servers and enabling DHCP-DNS integration features to help manage and update reverse lookup zones for legacy clients.
- Installing Windows 2000 Professional as the standard operating system in your organization for deploying new client hardware.

With Windows 2000 on your client computers, either the client or its Windows 2000 DHCP server can be enabled to perform PTR resource record registration for the client when its IP address is obtained and configured.

SUBNETTED REVERSE LOOKUP ZONES

Default subnet masks (which have a value of either 0 or 255 used in each of the four octets of the masked value) are assumed by the DNS snap-in when configuring a new reverse lookup zone. If necessary, you can use custom subnetting to adjust the subnet mask value to a non-default length.

Subnetted reverse lookup zones are supported when using the **Advanced view** setting available through Microsoft Management Console (MMC) and the DNS snap-in. This allows you to add and configure a reverse lookup for an IP network address that uses non-default subnet mask lengths, such as 255.255.248.0, which has a non-default subnet value of 248 in the third octet.

Subnetted reverse lookup zones are further described in RFC 2317, "Classless IN-ADDR.ARPA delegation." For more information on RFCs and how to obtain them, see Appendix A, "TCP/IP Resources."

Monitoring and Optimizing Servers

This section covers,

- Monitoring server performance
- Using server debug logging options
- Verifying server configuration
- Tuning advanced server parameters

Monitoring Server Performance

Because DNS servers are of critical importance in most environments, monitoring their performance can help in the following ways:

- By providing a useful benchmark for predicting, estimating, and optimizing DNS server performance.
- In troubleshooting DNS servers where server performance has degraded either over time or during periods of peak activity.

As you begin your DNS server monitoring, you can review sample test results for Windows 2000 DNS servers that were collected during product development and testing. You can use this information as a starting reference as you begin to monitor your DNS servers to measure and benchmark performance.

Windows 2000 Server also provides a set of DNS server performance counters that can be used with System Monitor to measure and monitor various aspects of server activity.

SAMPLE DNS SERVER PERFORMANCE TEST RESULTS

The DNS development and testing team compiled some statistics as a profile of DNS server performance during preliminary testing of Windows 2000 Server. In testing, two different DNS server hardware configurations were used and overall DNS query and dynamic update activity was measured, along with processor utilization.

The results of each of these tests are listed as follows:

Server configuration:	Intel P-II 400 MHz dual-processor
Queries/sec:	900
Dynamic updates/sec:	100
Processor utilization:	30%

During the collection of these measurements, the monitored DNS server was processing both queries and dynamic updates simultaneously. The numbers above reflect this.

For dynamic updates, standard primary type zones were used, not Active Directory-integrated zones. Where directory integration is used for zones, the rate at which dynamic updates can be processed decreases, since the DNS server must additionally write to and rely upon the Active Directory database.

In addition, if a zone is configured to accept only secure dynamic updates, the update rate can also decrease. Network performance might also be a factor in these cases, since the directory database may require network activity to process updates.

For additional background information about the two server hardware configurations used during these tests, see the following section.

Important These measurements are not intended to indicate maximum performance or server limitations for Windows 2000 DNS servers. The objective of the tests was to sample typical DNS server performance and obtain a working benchmark based on standard available hardware as a basis to begin server capacity planning.

Note that these numbers are approximate and can be influenced by the type of resource records entered in zones, the number of resource records with the same owner name, and the number of zones in use at a specific DNS server.

DNS SERVER PERFORMANCE COUNTERS

Table 9.6 lists the specific hardware that the Windows 2000 DNS development and test team used during the described testing.

TABLE 9.6 *Hardware Used by Windows 2000 DNS Development and Test Team*

Hardware components	*Sizing*
Number of processors	**Two**
Processor	**Intel Pentium II 400 MHz**
Amount of RAM	**256 MB**
Hard disk drive space	**4 GB**

These measurements were based on the server computer running a DNS server, with no additional services in use. Where other hardware specifications or software configurations are made when deploying Windows 2000 DNS servers, your performance results are likely to vary from those documented here. For more information on determining how to perform DNS server capacity planning, see "Server Planning for DNS" in this chapter.

Using Server Debug Logging Options

Windows 2000 Server provides a set of DNS server performance counters that can be used to measure and monitor various aspects of server activity, such as the following:

- Overall DNS server performance statistics, such as the number of overall queries and responses processed by a DNS server.
- User Datagram Protocol (UDP) or Transmission Control Protocol (TCP) counters, for measuring DNS queries and responses that are processed respectively using either of these transport protocols.
- Dynamic update and secure dynamic update counters, for measuring registration and update activity generated by dynamic clients.
- Memory usage counters, for measuring system memory usage and memory allocation patterns created by operating the server computer as a Windows 2000 DNS server.
- Recursive lookup counters, for measuring queries and responses when the DNS Server service uses recursion to look up and fully resolve DNS names on behalf of requesting clients.
- WINS lookup counters, for measuring queries and responses made to WINS servers when the WINS lookup integration features of the DNS Server service are used.
- Zone transfer counters, including specific counters for measuring: all zone transfer (AXFR), incremental zone transfer (IXFR), and DNS zone update notification activity.

Each of these DNS server performance counters is described in more detail in Tables 9.7 through 9.18.

TABLE 9.7 *All Zone Transfer Counters*

Field	Description
AXFR Request Received	The total number of full zone transfer requests received by the DNS Server service when operating as a master server for a zone.
AXFR Request Sent	The total number of full zone transfer requests sent by the DNS Server service when operating as a secondary server for a zone.
AXFR Response Received	The total number of full zone transfer requests received by the DNS Server service when operating as a secondary server for a zone.
AXFR Success Received	The total number of full zone transfers received by the DNS Server service when operating as a secondary server for a zone.
AXFR Success Sent	The total number of full zone transfers successfully sent by the DNS Server service when operating as a master server for a zone.

TABLE 9.8 *DNS Server Memory Counters*

Field	Description
Caching Memory	The total amount of system memory in use by the DNS Server service for caching.
Database Node Memory	The total amount of system memory in use by the DNS Server service for database nodes.
Nbtstat Memory	The total amount of system memory in use by the DNS Server service for Nbtstat.
Record Flow Memory	The total amount of system memory in use by the DNS Server service for record flow.

TABLE 9.9 *Dynamic Update Counters*

Field	Description
Dynamic Update NoOperation	The total number of No-operation/Empty dynamic update requests received by the DNS server.
Dynamic Update NoOperation/sec	The average number of No-operation/Empty dynamic update requests received by the DNS server in each second.
Dynamic Update Queued	The total number of dynamic updates queued by the DNS server.
Dynamic Update Received	The total number of dynamic update requests received by the DNS server.
Dynamic Update Received/sec	The average number of dynamic update requests received by the DNS server in each second.
Dynamic Update Rejected	The total number of dynamic updates rejected by the DNS server.
Dynamic Update TimeOuts	The total number of dynamic update time-outs of the DNS server.
Dynamic Update Written to Database	The total number of dynamic updates written to the database by the DNS server.
Dynamic Update Written to Database/sec	The average number of dynamic updates written to the database by the DNS server in each second.

TABLE 9.10 *Incremental Zone Transfer Counters*

Field	Description
IXFR Request Received	The total number of incremental zone transfer requests received by the master DNS server.
IXFR Request Sent	The total number of incremental zone transfer requests sent by the secondary DNS server.
IXFR Response Received	The total number of incremental zone transfer responses received by the secondary DNS server.
IXFR Success Received	The total number of successful incremental zone transfers received by the secondary DNS server.
IXFR Success Sent	The total number of successful incremental zone transfers of the master DNS server.
IXFR TCP Success Received	The total number of successful TCP incremental zone transfers received by the secondary DNS server.
IXFR UDP Success Received	The total number of successful UDP incremental zone transfers received by the secondary DNS server.

TABLE 9.11 *Notification Counters*

Field	Description
Notify Received	The total number of notifies received by the secondary DNS server.
Notify Sent	The total number of notifies sent by the master DNS server.

TABLE 9.12 *Recursion Counters*

Field	Description
Recursive Queries	The total number of recursive queries received by the DNS server.
Recursive Queries/sec	The average number of recursive queries received by the DNS server in each second.
Recursive Query Failure	The total number of recursive query failures.
Recursive Query Failure/sec	The average number of recursive query failures in each second.
Recursive TimeOuts	The total number of recursive query sending time-outs.
Recursive TimeOuts/sec	The average number of recursive query sending time-outs in each second.

TABLE 9.13 *Secure Dynamic Update Counters*

Field	Description
Secure Update Failure	The total number of secure updates failed on the DNS server.
Secure Update Received	The total number of secure update requests received by the DNS server.
Secure Update Received/sec	The average number of secure update requests received by the DNS server in each second.

TABLE 9.14 *TCP Counters*

Field	Description
TCP Message Memory	The total TCP message memory used by the DNS server.
TCP Query Received	The total number of TCP queries received by the DNS server.
TCP Query Received/sec	The average number of TCP queries received by the DNS server in each second.
TCP Response Sent	The total number of TCP responses sent by the DNS server.
TCP Response Sent/sec	The average number of TCP responses sent by the DNS server in each second.

TABLE 9.15 *Total Counters (Overall Performance)*

Field	Description
Total Query Received	The total number of queries received by the DNS server.
Total Query Received/sec	The average number of queries received by the DNS server in each second.
Total Response Sent	The total number of responses sent by the DNS server.
Total Response Sent/sec	The average number of responses sent by the DNS server in each second.

TABLE 9.16 *UDP Counters*

Field	Description
UDP Message Memory	The total UDP message memory used by the DNS server.
UDP Query Received	The total number of UDP queries received by the DNS server.
UDP Query Received/sec	The average number of UDP queries received by the DNS server in each second.
UDP Response Sent	The total number of UDP responses sent by the DNS server.
UDP Response Sent/sec	The average number of UDP responses sent by the DNS server in each second.

TABLE 9.17 *WINS Lookup Counters*

Field	Description
WINS Lookup Received	The total number of WINS lookup requests received by the server.
WINS Lookup Received/sec	The average number of WINS lookup requests received by the server in each second.
WINS Response Sent	The total number of WINS lookup responses sent by the server.
WINS Response Sent/sec	The average number of WINS lookup responses sent by the server in each second.
WINS Reverse Lookup Received	The total number of WINS reverse lookup requests received by the server.
WINS Reverse Lookup Received/sec	The average number of WINS reverse lookup requests received by the server in each second.
WINS Reverse Response Sent	The total number of WINS Reverse lookup responses sent by the server.
WINS Reverse Response Sent/sec	The average number of WINS Reverse lookup responses sent by the server in each second.

TABLE 9.18 *Zone Transfer Counters*

Field	Description
Zone Transfer Failure	The total number of failed zone transfers of the master DNS server.
Zone Transfer Request Received	The total number of zone transfer requests received by the master DNS server.
Zone Transfer SOA Request Sent	The total number of zone transfer SOA requests sent by the secondary DNS server.
Zone Transfer Success	The total number of successful zone transfers of the master DNS server.

Verifying Server Configuration

When using the DNS console, you can perform either manual or automated verification testing of your DNS servers to monitor their ability to process and resolve queries. This feature is accessed through the Monitoring tab in DNS server Properties.

When using this feature, two types of tests are available:

1. *A simple query against this DNS server.* This type of test specifies that the DNS server perform a simple or iterative query. This test is a localized query using the DNS resolver (client) on the server computer to query the local DNS server (also located on the same computer). For information about how iteration works, see Chapter 8.
2. *A recursive query to other DNS servers.* This type of test specifies that the DNS server perform a recursive query. This test is similar in its initial query processing to the previous test in that it uses the local DNS resolver (client) to query the local DNS server, also located on the same computer. In this test, however, the client asks the server to use recursion to resolve an NS-type query for the root of the DNS domain namespace, stated as a single dot (.). This type of query should typically require additional recursive processing and can be helpful in verifying that server root hints or zone delegations have been properly set. For information about how DNS query works, see Chapter 8.

Once you have selected the tests to be used, you can either click the **Test Now** button to manually perform the tests immediately, or you can perform automatic testing at a specified time interval.

Automated tests are performed periodically when the **Perform automatic testing at the following interval** check box is selected and are done according to the duration configured in Time interval.

Results of all selected tests, whether manually or automatically performed, are displayed in the Test results list box. Typically, this information includes:

- The date and time when each query was made.
- Additional status results of the specific test used, such as whether the simple or recursive query failed or succeeded.

Tuning Advanced Server Parameters

When initialized for service, Windows 2000 DNS servers use server configuration settings taken from the parameters stated in a boot information file, the Windows 2000 registry, or server defaults provided through Active Directory integration.

In most situations, the installation defaults are acceptable and should not require modification. However, when needed, you can use the DNS console to tune the advanced parameters listed in Table 9.19, accommodating special deployment needs and situations.

For making these adjustments, use the **Advanced** tab in DNS server **Properties**.

TABLE 9.19 *Tuning Advanced Server Parameters*

Value	Description
Disable recursion	Determines whether or not the DNS server uses recursion By default, Windows 2000 DNS servers are enabled to use recursion. For more information, see "Disabling Recursion" in this chapter.
BIND secondaries	Determines whether to use fast transfer format when transferring a zone to DNS servers running legacy BIND implementations. By default, all Windows-based DNS servers use a fast zone transfer format, which uses compression and can include multiple records per TCP message during a connected transfer. This format is also compatible with more recent BIND-based DNS servers that run versions 4.9.4 and later. For more information, see "Zone Transfer with BIND and Other DNS Server Implementations" in this chapter.
Fail on load if bad zone data	Sets the DNS server to parse files strictly. By default, Windows 2000 DNS servers log data errors, ignore any erred data in zone files, and continue to load a zone. This option can be reconfigured using the DNS console so that the DNS Server service logs errors and fails to load a zone file containing records data that is determined to have errors. For more information, see "Checking Names and Zone Data" in this chapter.
Enable round robin	Determines whether the DNS server uses round robin to rotate and reorder a list of multiple A resource records if a queried host name is for a computer configured with multiple IP addresses. By default, Windows 2000 DNS servers use round robin. For more information, see "Configuring Round Robin" in this chapter.
Enable netmask ordering	Determines whether the DNS server reorders a list of multiple A resource records based on local subnet priority if the queried host name is for a multihomed computer. By default, Windows 2000 DNS servers use local subnet priority. For more information, see "Prioritizing Local Subnets" in this chapter.
Secure cache against pollution	Determines whether the server attempts to clean up responses to avoid cache pollution. By default, Windows 2000 DNS servers use a secure response option that eliminates adding unrelated resource records included in a referral answer to their cache. In most cases, any names added in referral answers are typically cached and help expedite the speed of resolving subsequent DNS queries. With this feature, however, the server can determine that referred names are potentially polluting or unsecure and discard them. The server determines whether to cache the name offered in a referral on the basis of whether or not it is part of the exact related DNS domain name tree for which the original queried name was made. For example, if a query was originally made for *example.microsoft.com* and a referral answer provided a record for a name outside of the *microsoft.com* domain name tree, such as *msn.com,* then that name would not be cached where this feature is enabled for use.

Caution Incorrectly editing the registry may severely damage your system. Before making changes to the registry, you should back up any valued data on the computer.

When using the DNS console to configure these and other server parameter values, some settings can be modified, and in some cases, behavior can be dynamically changed without restarting the DNS server.

DNS server parameter key values are stored in the Windows 2000 registry. Each of these is a value stored under:

HKEY_LOCAL_MACHINE\System\CurrentControlSet\Services\DNS\Parameters

When using registry-based configuration, changes are applied to DNS servers only when the service is reinitialized. In these cases, if a value is manually changed directly in the registry, the DNS server must always be restarted for the new value to be used. For information aboutstarting or stopping a DNS server, see Chapter 10.

Advanced Server Configuration

This section covers,

- Updating root hints
- Using forwarders
- Configuring multihomed servers
- Checking names and zone data
- Modifying server defaults
- Configuring round robin
- Prioritizing local subnets
- Automating server administration using **Dnscmd**

Updating Root Hints

Root hints are used to prepare servers authoritative for non-root zones so that they can learn and discover authoritative servers that manage domains located at a higher level or in other subtrees of the DNS domain namespace. These hints are essential for servers authoritative at lower levels of the namespace when locating and finding servers under these conditions.

For example, suppose a DNS server (Server A) has a zone called *sub.example.microsoft.com*. In the process of answering a query for a higher-level domain, such as the *microsoft.com domain,* Server A needs some assistance to locate an authoritative server (such as Server B) for this domain.

In order for Server A to find Server B, or any other servers that are authoritative for the *microsoft.com* domain, it needs to be able to query the root servers for the DNS namespace. The root servers can then refer Server A to the authoritative servers for the *com* domain. The servers for the *com* domain can, in turn, offer referral to Server B or other servers that are authoritative for the *microsoft.com* domain.

The root hints used by Server A must have helpful hints to the root servers for this process to locate Server B (or another authoritative server) as intended.

To configure and use root hints correctly, first determine how the following applies to your DNS servers:

- Are you using DNS on the Internet or on a private network?
- Is the server used as a root server?

By default, the DNS service implements root hints using a file, *Cache.dns,* stored in the *%SystemRoot%\System32\Dns* folder on the server computer. This file normally contains the NS and A resource records for the Internet root servers. If, however, you are using the DNS service on a private network, you can edit or replace this file with similar records that point to your own internal root DNS servers.

Another server configuration in which root hints are treated differently is one in which a DNS server is configured to be used by other DNS servers in an internal namespace as a forwarder for any DNS queries of names managed externally (the Internet, for example). Even though the DNS server used as a forwarder can be located internally on the same network as servers using it as a forwarder, it needs hints for the Internet root servers to work properly and resolve external names.

If you are operating internal root servers, do not use root hints. Instead, delete the *Cache.dns* file entirely for any of your root servers.

If a DNS server is configured to know about other DNS servers, such as through a list of DNS servers configured in its client TCP/IP properties for an installed network connection, the DNS service is capable of gathering its own root hints during new server configuration. You can use the Configure New Server wizard provided with the DNS console to accomplish this.

Using Forwarders

DNS servers can be configured to send all recursive queries to a selected list of servers, known as forwarders. Servers used in the list of forwarders provide recursive lookup for any queries that a DNS server receives that it cannot answer based on its local zones. During the forwarding process, a DNS server configured to use forwarders (either one or more servers, based upon the forwarders list) essentially behaves as a DNS client to its forwarders.

BENEFITS OF USING FORWARDERS

Forwarders are often desirable when access to remote DNS servers requires use of a slow link, such as a fast-speed internal network linked to the Internet over a relatively low-speed connection. Using forwarders in this situation can cut down on expensive traffic over the low-speed link in two ways:

1. *Reduce the number of overall queries that get sent across the slow link.* For example, if your DNS server has a slow, expensive dial-up connection to an ISP. When the DNS server used as a forwarder for your internal network receives a query for a remote name on the Internet, it can directly contact remote servers on the Internet. It can repeat additional queries until it determines the authoritative server for the name. Once it finds the authoritative server, the forwarder contacts it and receives a complete response.

   Another option that can reduce traffic is using a DNS server on the Internet as a forwarder. Before deciding on this configuration, obtain permission to use an Internet DNS server as your designated forwarder, such as a server managed by your ISP. In this configuration, the DNS server at your ISP is forwarded all remote queries once and responds only when it has the complete answer. Each query represents a single round-trip across the slow link.
2. *Share remote results on your local network.* Forwarders provide a way to share information about remote names with a group of DNS servers located in the same area. For example, assume your organization has several DNS servers on a LAN. Rather than having each server send queries through a firewall and out to the Internet, all DNS servers are configured to forward queries to one DNS server (perhaps sitting on the firewall) that makes the necessary queries to the remote servers. In the process, the forwarder builds up a cache of Internet DNS names from the responses it receives. Over time, as local DNS servers continue to forward queries to it, the forwarder answers more queries from its cache because it begins to have an increasing number of answers based on previous queries for the same or similar names.

As shown in Figure 9-3, a forwarder is typically used in a barrier or firewall that exists between your network and the Internet. However, this is just one suggested configuration and not a requirement for using forwarders.

When a list of forwarders is configured, listed servers are identified by IP address. The first server listed should be preferred and used primarily to build a local cache. Generally speaking, however, more than one forwarder should be listed. Each server on the list is only tried once unless its IP address is repeated within the list.

If a DNS server is not configured to use forwarders, it uses the normal iterative query process to answer recursive queries for remote names.

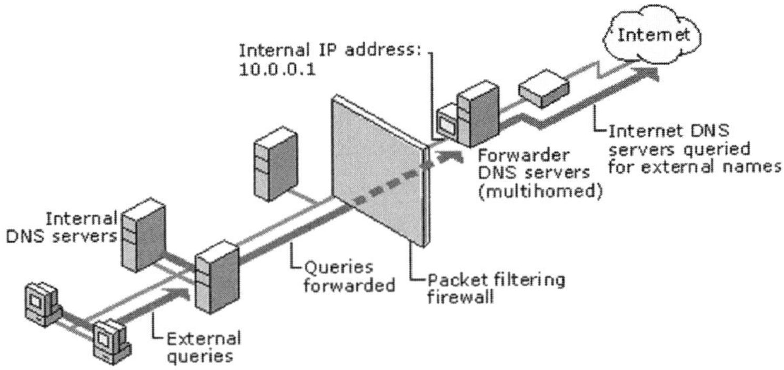

FIGURE 9–3 *Use of DNS forwarders*

USING FORWARDERS EXCLUSIVELY (NO RECURSION)

When a DNS server is configured to use forwarders, they are used before any other means of resolving a name is tried. If the list of forwarders fails to provide a positive answer, a DNS server can attempt to resolve the query itself using iterative queries and standard recursion.

A server can also be configured to not perform recursion after forwarders fail. In this configuration, the server does not attempt any further recursive queries itself to resolve the name. Instead, it fails the query if it does not get a successful query response from any of the forwarders.

This forces a DNS server to use its configured forwarders exclusively to perform final resolution when resolving a name query. In this mode of operation, a server configured to use forwarders can still check in its configured zones first to attempt to resolve a queried name. If it finds a match in its authoritative data there, it can answer the query based on that information.

To use this option, select the **Do not use recursion** option on the **Forwarders** tab when a server is configured to use forwarders.

When using forwarders, queries are sent to each forwarder in the list, which is given a time-out value, in seconds, within which it must respond before the next forwarder is tried.

Configuring Multihomed Servers

For multihomed DNS servers, you can configure the DNS service to selectively enable and bind only to IP addresses that you specify using the DNS console. By default, the DNS service binds to all IP interfaces configured for the computer.

This can include,

- Any additional IP addresses configured for a single network connection.
- Individual IP addresses configured for each separate connection where more than one network connection is installed on the server computer.

For multihomed DNS servers, you can restrict DNS service for selected IP addresses. When this feature is used, the DNS service only listens for and answers DNS requests that are sent to the IP addresses specified on the **Interface** tab in Server properties.

WHEN TO SPECIFY INTERFACES

By default, the DNS service listens on all IP addresses and accepts all client requests sent to its default service port (UDP 53 or TCP 53 for zone transfer requests). Some DNS resolvers (including original version Windows 95 clients) require that the source address of a DNS response be the same as the destination address that was used in the query. If these addresses differ, clients can reject the response. To accommodate these resolvers, you can specify the list of allowed interfaces for the DNS server. When a list is set, the DNS service binds sockets only to allowed IP addresses used on the computer.

In addition to providing support for clients that require explicit bindings to be used, specifying interfaces can be useful for other reasons.

1. If, for administrative reasons, you do not want to use some IP addresses or interfaces on a multihomed server computer.
2. If the server computer is configured to use a large number of IP addresses and you do not want the added expense of binding to all of them.

ADDITIONAL CONSIDERATIONS FOR MULTIHOMING DNS SERVERS

When configuring additional IP addresses and enabling them for use with the Windows 2000 DNS server, consider the following:

- Additional system resources are consumed at the server computer.
- DNS server performance overhead increases slightly, which can affect DNS query reception for the server.
- Although Windows 2000 provides the means to configure multiple IP addresses for use with any of your installed network adapters, there is no performance benefit for doing so.
- Even if the DNS server is handling multiple zones registered for Internet use, it is not necessary or required by Internet registration process to have different IP addresses registered for each zone.

Given these considerations,

- Recognize that when adding IP addresses for DNS server use, each additional address might only slightly increase server performance. In instances when a large overall number of IP addresses are enabled for use, server performance can be degraded noticeably.
- In general, when adding network adapter hardware to the server computer, assign only a single primary IP address for each network connection.
- Whenever possible, remove nonessential IP addresses from existing server TCP/IP configurations.

For more information on how to specify interfaces with the DNS service, see Chapter 10.

Checking Names and Zone Data

The name-checking methods listed in Table 9.20 can be used with the DNS service and managed using the DNS snap-in.

TABLE 9.20 *Name-Checking Methods*

Method	Description
Strict RFC (ANSI)	Uses strict checking of names according to RFC 1123 Internet host naming specifications.
Non RFC (ANSI)	Permits names that are nonstandard and that do not follow RFC 1123 Internet host naming specifications.
Multibyte (UTF8)	Permits recognition of characters other than ASCII, including Unicode, which is normally encoded as more than one octet (8 bits) in length. With this option, multibyte characters can be transformed and represented using Unicode Transformation Format (UTF-8) support provided with Windows 2000 Server.

For more information on when to use non-default settings for name checking with the DNS service, see Chapter 8.

CHECKING FOR BAD ZONE DATA

You can configure the DNS service to check for bad or unrecognized zone data when the service is started. To enable this option, see "Prevent Loading of a Zone when Bad Data Is Found" in Chapter 10.

DNS WILDCARDING

The DNS service can use wildcards to associate multiple possible DNS name destinations with a single computer acting as a gateway for all names based on a wildcarded name. The most common use of wildcards in DNS records is with the MX resource record, such as to configure DNS for an Internet mail gateway host routing mail between your private network and the Internet.

BASICS OF USING DNS WILDCARDS • When you are trying to determine where to use a wildcard in DNS, such as an MX resource record used to route and forward mail, note these guidelines:

- The asterisk (*) is the character reserved to indicate the wildcarded name.
- The asterisk is only used once as the leading (leftmost) character in a DNS name.
- If used, an asterisk must always match at least one or more whole label parts of a name that precede any exact labels specified by non-wildcarded (exact) characters in the remaining part of the name.
- Wildcards are not used when a query for an exact name produces an exact match.
- The contents of wildcarded resource records conform to normal DNS formats and rules for resource records.

Typically, wildcards are only used when the DNS name queried is an indeterminate name subordinate to a known name. In this case, the closest match to the wildcarded name is used. For example, if the following MX resource record is used in the example.microsoft.com zone,

**.example.microsoft.com. IN MX 10 mailserver1.example.microsoft.com.*

this record would allow mail destined for the following possible DNS domain names to be routed to the mail routing host *(mailserver1.example.microsoft.com.)* specified in the MX resource record:

haifa.example.microsoft.com.
seattle.us.example.microsoft.com.
santiago.sa.example.microsoft.com.

When wildcarding is used, the asterisk wildcard symbol must match at least one whole label beyond the specified part of the DNS name in which the wildcard is used.

For example, an e-mail message destined to *user@example.microsoft.com* could not use the previous example MX resource record to be forwarded to its destination. For the e-mail to be forwarded correctly, an additional explicit MX resource record needs to be added in the same zone, such as,

example.microsoft.com. IN MX 10 mailserver1.example.microsoft.com.

LOOSE RFC WILDCARDING • For Windows NT Server 4.0 (prior to Service Pack 4), the DNS service was not strictly compliant with the method for using wildcards in a DNS name lookup described in RFC 1034. It only stopped a wildcard lookup when it reached a node in the DNS domain namespace tree that had resource records of the type specified in a query.

For example, if in the *example.microsoft.com.* zone the following records were used:

*.example.microsoft.com.	IN	MX	10	mailserver1.example.microsoft.com.
example.microsoft.com.	IN	MX	10	mailserver2.example.microsoft.com.
host-a.example.microsoft.com.	IN	A		10.0.0.1
mailserver1.example.microsoft.com.	IN	A		10.0.0.2
mailserver2.example.microsoft.com.	IN	A		10.0.0.3

and a DNS query was made by a computer, Host B, as follows:

Queried name:	*host-a.example.microsoft.com.*
Queried type:	MX

With loose wildcarding in effect, the following sequence occurs between the DNS service and Host B:

1. Host B sends the example query to a DNS server configured to use loose RFC wildcarding, such as a DNS server running under Windows NT Server 4.0 prior to Service Pack 4.
2. No MX resource records match the specified name *(host-a.example.microsoft.com.)*.
3. An MX resource record—the type specified in the query—is included in the zone and uses a wildcarded name that is the parent of the queried name *(*.example.microsoft.com.)*.
4. The DNS service checks the wildcarded MX resource record name *(*.example.microsoft.com.)* for its mapped host names, finds a matching A resource record for the specified name *(mailserver1.example.microsoft.com.)* and uses this information to answer Host B.
5. The mail program on Host B can then send mail to *mailserver1.example.microsoft.com.* by using its IP address.

The loose RFC approach allows you to set up only two MX records and cover queries to the entire zone. However, the two MX resource records need to be added for both the zone root (the explicit name of the zone) and a wildcard node (*) directly below the zone root. However, if you have individual mail hosts that should receive their own mail directly, then add MX resource records for each of those hosts that refer directly to their own host name, as stated in their registered A resource record.

STRICT RFC WILDCARDING • With the strict wildcarding approach as described in RFC 1034, a revised sequence of events occurs when reviewing the previous example. Based on the same specified zone and query information provided, the revised sequence of steps would be used between the DNS service and Host B:

1. Host B sends the example query to a DNS server configured to use strict RFC wildcarding.
2. No MX resource records match the specified name *(host-a.example.microsoft.com.)*, but an A resource record of that name is found in the zone. Because the queried name was found, no wildcarding is done.

3. The DNS service responds to the query with an authoritative negative response that includes no errors or resource records in the answer section of the response.
4. The mail program on Host B then sends a new query for the same name, specifying that A resource records be used for the query type.
5. The DNS service answers the A query with an authoritative positive response, which includes the A resource record in the answer section of the response.
6. The mail program on Host B can then send mail to *mailserver1.example.microsoft.com.* by using its IP address.

The strict RFC approach to wildcarding is easier if your mail hosts are capable of receiving mail directly. The disadvantage to this approach is that you typically need to add more MX resource records to the zone. This can happen if you have mail hosts not capable of receiving mail directly or if you need to advertise any mail hosts that are not mail servers.

Modifying Server Defaults

The DNS snap-in provides the ability to reconfigure some types of DNS server defaults for instances when defaults are not appropriate for use with a specific DNS server. Some configurable non-default settings include:

- Selecting an alternate server configuration method to be used when initiating service.
- Disabling the use of recursion.

METHODS FOR INITIATING SERVICE

The methods listed in Table 9.21 are available to determine how the DNS service initializes and provides service when started.

TABLE 9.21 *Methods for Initiating DNS Service*

Method	Description
Boot from registry	Initializes the DNS Server service by reading parameters stored in the Windows registry.
Boot from file	Initializes the DNS Server service using an optional boot file, as used by BIND servers. To use this file, supply a copy of a boot file from another DNS server running a DNS server that is based on the BIND implementation. On BIND-based DNS servers, this file is typically called the *Named.boot* file. The format of this file must be the older BIND 4 format, not the more recent BIND 8 boot file format. If used, settings and directives in this file are used instead of comparable settings stored in the registry on the DNS server computer. For any parameters not configurable using boot file directives, registry defaults (or stored reconfigured server settings) are applied by the DNS Server service.
Boot from directory service and registry	Initializes the DNS Server service by reading parameters stored in the Active Directory database and the server registry. For Windows 2000 DNS servers, this is the default boot option.

For more information on how to change the method used to initiate the DNS service, see Chapter 10. For more information on Active Directory integration with the DNS service, see Chapter 8.

DISABLING RECURSION

By default, recursion is enabled for the DNS service, and clients typically request that the server use recursion to resolve a name when sending a query. If recursion is disabled, the DNS service always uses referral, regardless of the client request.

In general, DNS servers can answer queries for names outside of their authoritative zones in two ways:

- Servers can send referral answers, which are an immediate response to the requesting client with a list of resource records for other DNS servers it knows about that appear to be closer or more likely to be of help in resolving the queried name.
- Servers can use recursion to query other servers on behalf of the requesting client, attempting to fully resolve the name. Recursive lookups continue until the server receives an authoritative answer for the queried name. The server then forwards this answer in response to the original query from the requesting client.

In most cases, disabling recursion on a DNS server happens when DNS clients are to be limited to resolving names authoritatively managed on a specific server. For example, this is the case when a DNS server has only DNS names data for an internal network or when the DNS server is incapable of resolving external DNS names (such as Internet DNS names) and clients are expected to retry another DNS server to resolve these names. For more information on how to enable or disable the use of recursion with the DNS service, see Chapter 10.

Configuring Round Robin

Round robin is a local balancing mechanism used by DNS servers to share and distribute network resource loads. You can use it to rotate A resource records contained in a query answer if multiple A resource records for a host name are found.

By default, the DNS Server service uses round robin to order resource records returned in an answer of the host name resolved to more than one mapped resource record. This feature provides a simple method for load balancing client use of Web servers and other frequently queried multihomed computers.

For round robin to work, multiple A resource records for the queried name must first be registered in the zone. If round robin is disabled for a DNS server, the order of the response for these queries is based on a static ordering of resource records in the answer list as they are stored in the zone (either its zone file or Active Directory).

ROUND ROBIN ROTATION

A forward lookup-type query (for all A resource records that match a DNS domain name) is made for a multihomed computer *(multihomed.example.microsoft.com)* that has three IP addresses. Separate A resource records are used to map the host's name to each of these IP addresses in the zone. In the stored *example.microsoft.com* zone, the resource records appear in this fixed order:

multihomed IN A 10.0.0.1
multihomed IN A 10.0.0.2
multihomed IN A 10.0.0.3

The first DNS client that queries the server to resolve this host's name receives the list in default order. When a second client sends a subsequent query to resolve this name, the list is rotated as follows:

multihomed IN A 10.0.0.2
multihomed IN A 10.0.0.3
multihomed IN A 10.0.0.1

Local subnet priority supersedes the use of round robin rotation for multihomed names. When enabled, however, round robin continues to be a secondary method used to sort multiple resource records returned in a listed answer as part of an address query response.

Prioritizing Local Subnets

By default, the DNS service uses local subnet prioritizing as the method for giving preference to IP addresses on the same network when a client query resolves to a host name that is mapped to more than one IP address. This feature requires that the client application attempt to connect to the host using its closest (and typically fastest) IP address available for connection.

The DNS service uses local subnet priority as follows:

1. The DNS service determines if local subnet prioritization is needed to order the query response. If more than one A resource record matches the queried host name, the DNS service can reorder the records by their subnet location. If the queried host name matches only a single A resource record, or if the IP network address of the client does not match an IP network address for any of the mapped addresses in an answer list of multiple resource records, no prioritizing is necessary.

2. For each resource record in the matched answer list, the DNS service determines which records (if any) match the subnet location of the requesting client.
3. The DNS service reorders the answer list so that A resource records which match the local subnet of the requesting client are placed first in the answer list.
4. Prioritized by subnet order, the answer list is returned to the requesting client.

SIMPLE EXAMPLE: LOCAL NETWORK PRIORITIZING

A multihomed computer, *multihomed.example.microsoft.com,* has three A resource records for its three separate host IP addresses in the *example.microsoft.com* zone. A separate A resource record is used for each of the host's addresses, which appear in this order in the zone:

```
multihomed  IN  A  192.168.1.27
multihomed  IN  A  10.0.0.14
multihomed  IN  A  172.16.20.4
```

If a DNS client resolver at IP address 10.4.3.2 queries the server for the IP addresses of host *multihomed.example.microsoft.com,* the DNS service notes that the originating IP network address (10.0.0.0) of the client matches the network (class A) portion of the 10.0.0.4 address in the answer list of resource records. The DNS service then reorders the addresses in the response as follows:

```
multihomed  IN  A  10.0.0.14
multihomed  IN  A  192.168.1.27
multihomed  IN  A  172.16.20.4
```

If the IP address of the requesting client has no local network match with any of the resource records in the answer list, then the list is not prioritized.

COMPLEX EXAMPLE: LOCAL SUBNET PRIORITIZING

If you are working in a network that uses IP subnetting (non-default subnet masks), there are only a few minor differences. If more than one address matches in the network portion, then the matching addresses are further ordered and the resource record having the closest matching subnet address is placed first.

For example, a multihomed computer, *multihomed.example.microsoft.com,* has four A resource records for four separate host IP addresses in the *example.microsoft.com* zone. Two of these IP addresses are for non-local networks. The other two IP addresses share a common IP network address but, because IP subnetting is used, represent different physical subnetted network connections based on their custom (non-default) subnet mask value of 255.255.248.0. These example resource records appear in the following order in the zone:

```
multihomed  IN  A  192.168.1.27
multihomed  IN  A  172.16.22.4
multihomed  IN  A  10.0.0.14
multihomed  IN  A  172.16.31.5
```

If the IP address of the requesting client is 172.16.22.8, both of the IP addresses that match the same IP network as the client, the 172.16.0.0 network, are returned at the top of the answer list to the client. However, in this example, the 172.16.22.4 address is placed ahead of the 172.16.31.5 address because it matches the client IP address down through the 172.16.20.0 subnet address.

The reordered answer list returned by the DNS service would be:

```
multihomed  IN  A  172.16.22.4
multihomed  IN  A  172.16.31.5
multihomed  IN  A  192.168.1.27
multihomed  IN  A  10.0.0.14
```

Using a custom or non-default subnet mask value with all IP addresses on your network indicates the presence of IP subnetting. For more information about subnet masks, see Chapter 10.

Local subnet priority supersedes the use of round-robin rotation for multihomed names. When round robin is enabled, however, resource records continue to be rotated using round robin as the secondary method of sorting the response list. For more information on round robin, see "Configuring Round Robin" in this chapter

Automating Server Administration Using Dnscmd

For Windows 2000 Server, **dnscmd** is provided as a command-line interface for managing DNS servers. This tool can be used to script batch files, to help automate management and update of existing DNS server configurations, or to perform setup and configuration of new DNS servers on your network.

You can install the dnscmd command by copying it from the *\Support\Enterprise\Reskit* folder on the product compact disc. For help in using the command, type *dnscmd /?* at a command prompt. For complete documentation of the dnscmd command, see the Windows 2000 Server Resource Kit.

T E N

Installing and Maintaining DNS Servers

Install a DNS Server

There are three different types of DNS Zone configurations that can be installed. They are Active Directory Integrated, Standard Primary, and Standard Secondary. In the Active Directory Integrated model, the zone storage is done in the Active Directory database. In the Standard Primary and Standard Secondary model, the zone storage is done in text-based files on each server in the*%SystemRoot%\System32\DNS* folder.

Note To install the DNS service on a server, the server must have a static IP address. This example will show how to install a Standard Secondary DNS and how to change the IP address from a DHCP address to a static address dynamically.

1. To open the Windows Component wizard, from the desktop, click **Start**, point to **Settings**, and click **Control Panel**.
2. When Control Panel opens, double-click **Add/Remove Programs** and then click **Add/Remove Windows Components**.
3. Highlight **Networking Services** and click **Details** to view all the subcomponents of Networking Services. You will see a window similar to Figure 10-1.
4. Mark the box beside **Domain Name System (DNS)** and click **OK** to continue. You will see a window similar to Figure 10-2.

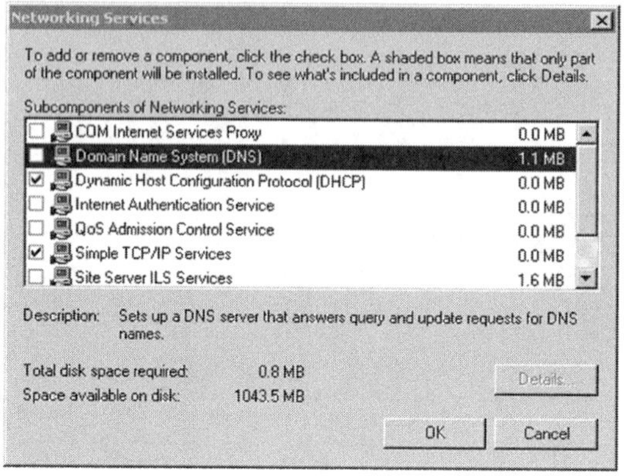

FIGURE 10–1 *Networking Services*

5. Click **OK** to continue. At this point, the wizard will configure a static IP address. You will see a window similar to Figure 10-3.
6. Highlight **Internet Protocol (TCP/IP)** and click **Properties.** You will see a window similar to Figure 10-4.
7. In the section **Use the following IP address**, type in the IP address, subnet mask, and default gateway. In the section **Use the following DNS server addresses**, type the preferred DNS server address. This address is the address of the Primary DNS Server. Click **OK** to continue. The IP address has been dynamically changed. Required files are copied to your hard disk, and server software can be used after restarting the system.

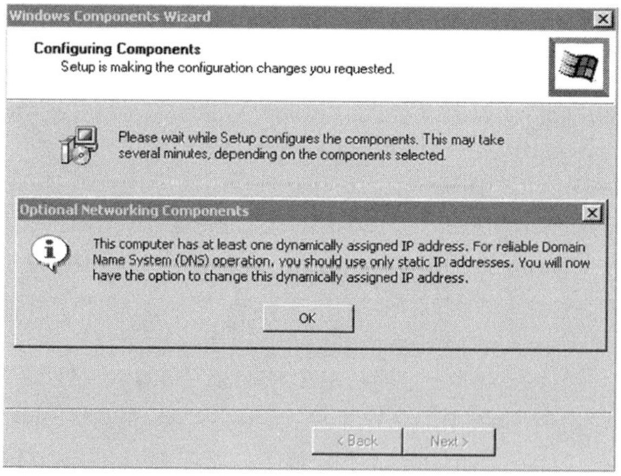

FIGURE 10–2 *Configuring Components window*

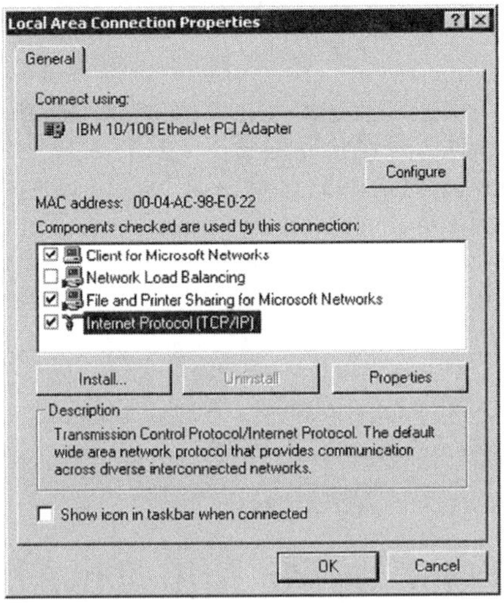

FIGURE 10–3 *Local Area Connection Properties*

Certain Windows components require configuration before they can be used. If you installed one or more of these components, but did not configure them, when you click **Add/Remove Windows Components**, a list of components that need to be configured is displayed. To start the Windows Components wizard, click **Components**.

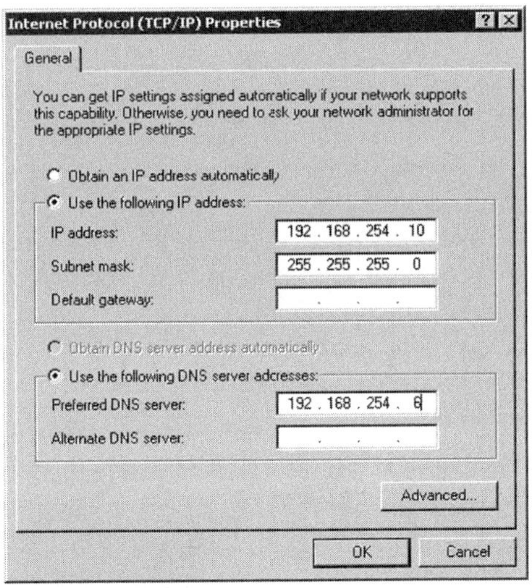

FIGURE 10–4 *Internet Protocol (TCP/IP) Properties*

It is strongly recommended that you manually configure the computer to use a static IP address.

After you install a DNS server, you can decide how to administer it and its zones. Although you can use a text editor to make changes to server boot and zone files, this method is not recommended. The DNS console simplifies maintenance of these files and should be used whenever possible. Once you begin using console-based management of these files, manually editing them is not recommended.

Where Active Directory-integrated zones are used, file-based zone management cannot be used.

When writing DNS server boot and zone data to text files, Windows 2000 DNS servers use the Berkeley Internet Name Domain (BIND) file format recognized by legacy BIND 4 servers, not the more recent BIND 8 format.

Configure a DNS Server for Use With Active Directory

When Active Directory is installed, the option to automatically install and configure a DNS server for use is provided. To install Active Directory on this computer, use the Active Directory Installation wizard.

This procedure only applies to server computers used as domain controllers. If member servers are used as DNS servers, they are not integrated with Active Directory. The *Windows 2000 Resource Kit* has more information about setting up DNS for Active Directory.

Configure a New DNS Server

To configure a new DNS server,

1. To open DNS, click **Start**, point to **Programs**, point to **Administrative Tools**, and then click **DNS**.
2. If needed, add and connect to the applicable server in the console.
3. In the console tree, click the applicable DNS server (console tree | DNS | *applicable DNS server*).
4. On the **Action** menu, click **Configure the server**.
5. Follow the instructions in the Configure DNS Server wizard.

As a best practice, use the checklist provided in the online help for installing a new DNS server.

When you finish configuring the server, you might need to complete additional tasks, such as enabling dynamic updates for its zones or adding resource records to its zones.

In step 2, you only need to add the DNS server to the console if it is not running locally on the same computer you are using to manage it.

Add a Secondary Server for an Existing Zone

To add a secondary server for an existing zone,

1. To open DNS, click **Start**, point to **Programs**, point to **Administrative Tools**, and then click **DNS**.
2. In the console tree, click the applicable DNS server (console tree | DNS | *applicable DNS server*).
3. On the **Action** menu, click **New Zone**.
4. Follow the instructions in the New Zone wizard. When adding the zone, select **Standard secondary** as the zone type.

In order to add a secondary server for an existing zone, you need to have network access to the server acting as the master server for this server and its use of the zone. The master server acts as the source for zone data. It is contacted periodically to assist in renewing the zone and to transfer zone updates whenever they are needed.

In step 2, you might need to add the applicable DNS server to the console first if it is not running locally on the same computer you are using to manage it.

Install a Caching-only DNS Server

To install a caching-only DNS server,

1. To install a caching-only DNS server, install a DNS server on the server computer.
2. Do not configure the DNS server (as you might normally) to load any zones.
3. Verify server root hints are configured or updated correctly.

Caching-only DNS servers do not host any zones and are not authoritative for a particular domain. They are DNS servers that build a local server cache of names learned while performing recursive queries on behalf of their clients. This information is then available from its cache when answering subsequent client queries.

A caching-only DNS server can be valuable at a site where DNS functionality is needed locally but it is not administratively desirable to create a separate domain or zone for that location.

It is strongly recommended that when operating the computer as a DNS server, you manually configure TCP/IP and use a static IP address.

Restrict a DNS Server to Listen Only on Selected Addresses

To restrict a DNS server to listen only on selected addresses,

1. To open DNS, click **Start**, point to **Programs**, point to **Administrative Tools**, and then click **DNS**.
2. In the console tree, click the applicable DNS server (console tree | DNS | *applicable DNS server*).
3. On the **Action** menu, click **Properties**.
4. On the **Interfaces** tab, click **Only the following IP addresses**.
5. In the **IP address** text box, type an IP address for the DNS server to be enabled for use and then click **Add**.
6. As needed, repeat step 5 to specify other server IP addresses to be enabled for use by this DNS server.

   If you need to remove an IP address from the list, click it and then click **Remove**.

By default, the DNS service listens for DNS message communications on all configured IP addresses for the server computer. If you choose to restrict interfaces at this server, at least one server IP address must be added to the list.

Server IP addresses that are added here need to be statically managed. If you later change or remove addresses specified here from TCP/IP configurations maintained at this server, update this list accordingly.

After you update or revise the list of restricted interfaces, you need to stop and restart the DNS server to apply the new list.

Have a DNS Server Use Forwarders

To have a DNS server use forwarders,

1. To open DNS, click **Start**, point to **Programs**, point to **Administrative Tools**, and then click **DNS**.
2. In the console tree, click the applicable DNS server (console tree | DNS | *applicable DNS server*).
3. On the **Action** menu, click **Properties**.
4. Click the **Forwarders** tab.
5. Select the **Enable forwarders** check box.
6. If you want this DNS server to only use forwarders, select the **Do not use recursion** check box.
7. Add IP addresses for other DNS servers that act as forwarders for this server.

8. As an option, you can change the **Forward time-out (seconds)** value, if the **Do not use recursion** check box is cleared.

Forwarders are DNS servers configured to provide recursive service for other DNS servers. When forwarders are specified, they are used to help resolve any DNS names not answered by this server.

Configure DNS for Static Clients

To configure DNS for static clients with statically configured IP addresses, you likely need to configure the following:

- DNS host name (or names) for the client computer.
- Primary and alternate DNS servers that the client uses to assist in resolving DNS domain names.
- A list of DNS suffixes to be appended for use in completing unqualified DNS names, which are used for searching and submitting DNS queries at the client for resolution.
- Connection-specific dynamic update and registration behavior, such as whether specific network adapters installed at the client dynamically register their configured IP addresses with a DNS server.

If you want to use static DNS, you can of course do so. The static configuration consists of a server and a client part. On the server, you are responsible for defining all hosts whose names should be resolved by the DNS server. Be very careful because it is very difficult to discover wrong DNS host entries.

The client configuration has to be done within its IP configuration by performing the following steps:

1. Right-click the object **My Network Places** and select **Properties**.
2. Then right-click **Local Area Connection** and select **Properties**.
3. The dialog box contains the TCP/IP protocols. It reads Internet Protocol (TCP/IP). You can either double-click the entry or select it and click the **Properties** button. The dialog box shown in Figure 10-5 appears:
4. The lower frame contains the static DNS server address. To change to static DNS, you must activate **Use the following DNS server addresses**.

   You can see in Figure 10-5 that we put in two DNS servers, the second working as the backup DNS server. Also, in this figure, the client machine still obtains its IP address from a DHCP server. Usually, static DNS combines with static IP. Since Windows 2000 offers dynamic DNS, a static configuration would only lead to superfluous work when coupled with DHCP.

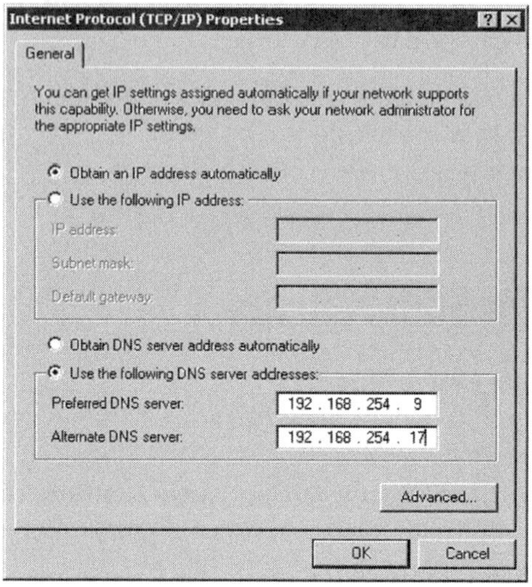

FIGURE 10–5 Internet Protocol (TCP/IP) Properties

5. Click **Advanced.** This brings up another dialog box that contains more details (see Figure 10-6).

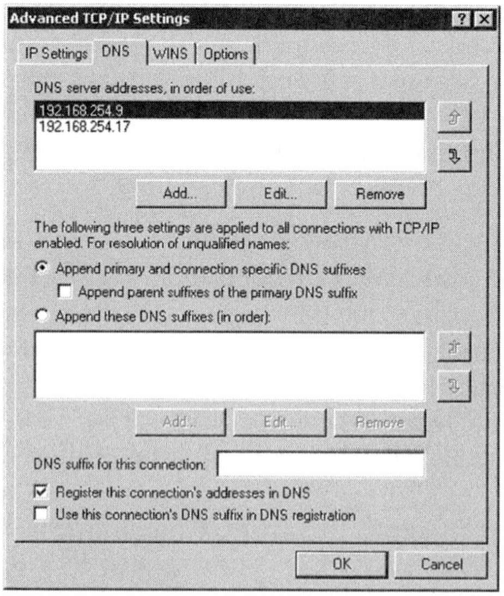

FIGURE 10–6 Advanced settings for static DNS

6. To change specific DNS configuration items, click the **DNS** tab.
7. Click **OK** in every dialog box that has to be confirmed.

For more information on how to configure DNS for static clients not running Windows 2000, see the applicable TCP/IP or DNS documentation provided by the appropriate vendor for these clients.

Enable DNS for DHCP-Enabled Clients

To configure DNS for clients with dynamically configured IP addresses provided by a DHCP server, you generally need to configure the following at either the DHCP server or applicable clients:

- *DNS host name (or names) for the client computer.* For Windows 2000 DHCP clients, this must be set at the client computer or assigned during unattended setup.
- *Primary and alternate DNS servers that the client uses to assist in resolving DNS domain names.* For Windows 2000 DHCP clients, this can be set by assigning the DNS Server service option (option 6) and providing a configured list of ordered IP addresses for DNS servers that the client is configured to use.
- *A list of DNS suffixes to be appended for use in completing unqualified DNS names used for searching and submitting DNS queries at the client for resolution.* For Windows 2000 DHCP clients, this can be set by assigning the DNS domain name option (option 15) and providing single DNS suffix for the client to append and use in searches. To configure additional DNS suffixes, configure TCP/IP manually for DNS configuration.
- *Connection-specific dynamic update and registration behavior, such as whether specific network adapters installed at the client dynamically register their configured IP addresses with a DNS server.* For Windows 2000 DHCP clients, the default is for client connections to register their configured IP addresses with a DNS server. To modify this behavior at the client, configure TCP/IP manually for DNS configuration.

For more information on how to configure DNS for DHCP clients not running Windows 2000, see the applicable TCP/IP or DNS documentation provided by the appropriate vendor.

Configure the Primary DNS Suffix for a Client Computer

To configure the primary DNS suffix for a client computer,

1. To open System, click **Start**, point to **Settings**, and then click **Control Panel**. In Control Panel, double-click **System**.
2. Click the **Network Identification** tab. This tab displays the computer name, the workgroup or domain to which it belongs, and a brief description of the computer.
3. Click **Properties**, and then click **More**.
4. In **DNS Suffix and NetBIOS Computer Name**, do the following:
5. For **Primary DNS suffix of this computer**, specify the DNS suffix to be appended to the name of this computer when completing its fully qualified domain name (FQDN).
6. After applying these changes, restart the computer to initialize it with its new DNS domain name
7. If the computer has been previously installed and configured as a Windows 2000 DNS server, verify that zone authority records are updated by the DNS Server service. These include the start of authority (SOA) and name server (NS) resource records, substituting the new FQDN to replace the single label name previously in use.

For more information on how to configure the DNS suffix for clients not running Windows 2000, see the applicable TCP/IP or DNS documentation provided by the appropriate vendor for your other clients.

If you are configuring a DNS primary suffix that is different than the name of the Active Directory domain where the computer is joined, you need to perform additional configuration steps.

Preload the Client Resolver Cache

To preload the client resolver cache,

1. To open Notepad, click **Start**, point to **Programs**, point to **Accessories**, then click **Notepad**.
2. Find the Host file and open in Notepad for editing.
3. Using the default entry in the file (a mapping for the local host to the loopback IP address, 127.0.0.1), add additional host name-to-address mappings on separate lines to be preloaded into the resolver cache of the client. For example, you might add *10.0.0.1 host-a host-a.example.microsoft.com*.
4. On the **File** menu, click **Save**, and then **Exit**.
5. As an option, you can verify that your changes have been updated in the resolver cache by viewing its contents.

Entries you add are always answered first from the local resolver cache and not sent to the DNS query when queries are made locally to resolve these names to host (A) resource records.

Every line in the Hosts file should contain an IP address followed by one or more host names. For example, you could add a line such as the following with an IP address (10.0.0.1) that maps to more than one DNS host name:

10.0.0.1host-a host-a.example.microsoft.com host-b.example2.microsoft.com

Likewise, a single DNS host name can correspond to more than one IP address if each of the addresses is mapped and used in separate lines. For example, you could add lines for the following multihomed or multi-addressable DNS host computer:

10.0.0.1 host-a.example.microsoft.com
10.0.0.2 host-a.example.microsoft.com
10.0.0.3 host-a.example.microsoft.com

When multiple names or IP addresses are used in the file, the DNS Client service must be running for all entries to be returned or used in answering queries. If the DNS Client service is not running, only the first entry in the file is used to resolve the query.

Open the DNS Console

To open DNS, click **Start**, point to **Programs**, point to **Administrative Tools**, and then click **DNS**. The DNS console is an administrative tool for managing Windows 2000 DNS servers only.

Start or Stop a DNS Server

To start or stop a DNS server,

1. To open DNS, click **Start**, point to **Programs**, point to **Administrative Tools**, and then click **DNS**.
2. In the console tree, click the applicable DNS server (console tree | DNS | *applicable DNS server*).
3. On the **Action** menu, point to **All Tasks** and then click one of the following:

   a. To start the service, click **Start**.
   b. To stop the service, click **Stop**.
   c. To interrupt the service, click **Pause**.
   d. To stop and then automatically restart the service, click **Restart**.

The DNS Server service is an optional server component provided with Windows 2000 Server. If, on the computer you are managing, this service was not previously installed, it does not appear in the listed services.

After you pause or stop the service, on the **Action** menu in **All Tasks**, you can click **Resume** to immediately resume service.

You can also perform most of these tasks at a command prompt by using the following commands:

- **net start dns**
- **net stop dns**
- **net pause dns**
- **net continue dns**

Add a Server to the DNS Console

To add a server to the DNS console,

1. To open DNS, click **Start**, point to **Programs**, point to **Administrative Tools**, and then click **DNS**.
2. On the **Action** menu, click **Connect To Computer**.
3. From **Select Target Computer**, select either:
   a. **This computer**, if the server you want to connect to and manage is located on the same computer you are using to manage it.
   b. **The following computer**, if the server you want to connect to and manage is located on a remote computer.

   If you choose to connect to a remote server, specify either its DNS computer name or its IP address.

4. Select the **Connect to the specified computer now** check box, and then click **OK**.

The DNS console is an administrative tool for managing Windows 2000 DNS servers only.

Remove a Server From the DNS Console

To remove a server from the DNS console,

1. To open DNS, click **Start**, point to **Programs**, point to **Administrative Tools**, and then click **DNS**.
2. In the console tree, click the applicable DNS server (console tree | DNS | *applicable DNS server*).

3. On the **Action** menu, click **Delete**.
4. When prompted to confirm you want to delete this server from the list, click **OK**.

Manually Update Server Data Files

To manually update server data files,

1. To open DNS, click **Start**, point to **Programs**, point to **Administrative Tools**, and then click **DNS**.
2. In the console tree, click the applicable DNS server (console tree | DNS | *applicable DNS server*).
3. On the **Action** menu, click **Update Server Data Files**.

For standard primary zones, this procedure causes the DNS server to immediately write its in-memory changes out to disk for storage with the zone file. Normally, these changes are only written at predefined update intervals and when the DNS server is shut down.

For Active Directory-integrated zones, this procedure does not apply, since most changes to directory-integrated zone data are written immediately back to the applicable directory-integrated zone database.

Change the Boot Method Used by the DNS Server

To change the boot method used by the DNS server,

1. To open DNS, click **Start**, point to **Programs**, point to **Administrative Tools**, and then click **DNS**.
2. In the console tree, click the applicable DNS server (console tree | DNS | *applicable DNS server*).
3. On the **Action** menu, click **Properties**.
4. Click the **Advanced** tab.
5. In the **Load zone data on startup** list, select **From registry**, **From file**, or **From Active Directory and registry**.

By default, Windows 2000 DNS servers use information stored in the Windows 2000 registry to initialize for service and load any zone data for use at the server. As added options, you can configure the DNS server to boot from a file or, in Active Directory environments, you can supplement local registry data with zone data retrieved for directory integrated zones stored in the Active Directory database. If you use the file method, the file used must be a text file named *Boot,* located on this computer in the *Winnt**System32**Dns* folder.

Change the Name-Checking Method Used by the DNS Server

To change the name-checking method used by the DNS server,

1. To open DNS, click **Start**, point to **Programs**, point to **Administrative Tools**, and then click **DNS**.
2. In the console tree, click the applicable DNS server (console tree | DNS | *applicable DNS server*).
3. On the **Action** menu, click **Properties**.
4. Click the **Advanced** tab.
5. In the **Name checking** list, select **Non RFC (ANSI)**, **Strict RFC (ANSI)**, or **Multibyte (UTF8)**.

Windows 2000 DNS servers support three possible methods for checking names it receives and processes during normal server operations:

- **Strict RFC (ANSI)** This method strictly enforces RFC-compliant naming rules for all DNS names that the server processes. Names that are not RFC-compliant are treated as erred data by the server.
- **Non RFC (ANSI)** This method allows names that are not RFC-compliant, such as names that use ASCII characters but are not compliant with RFC host naming requirements to be used with the DNS server.
- **Multibyte (UTF8)** This method allows names that use the Unicode 8-bit translation encoding scheme, which is a proposed RFC draft, to be used with the DNS server.

By default, the server uses Non RFC (ANSI) to check names. This option provides loose name checking and allows any DNS names that use standard ANSI or ASCII encoded characters to be received and processed by the server, providing the highest possible interoperability with other DNS servers and host systems.

Enable or Disable Fast Transfer Format During Zone Transfers

To enable or disable fast transfer format during zone transfers,

1. To open DNS, click **Start**, point to **Programs**, point to **Administrative Tools**, and then click **DNS**.
2. In the console tree, click the applicable DNS server (console tree | DNS | *applicable DNS server*).

3. On the **Action** menu, click **Properties**.
4. Click the **Advanced** tab.
5. In the **Server options** list, select the **BIND secondaries** check box, and then click **OK**.

This setting is to be used only for optimizing zone transfers between Windows 2000 DNS servers and other DNS server implementations. Zone transfers between Windows-based DNS servers always use the fast transfer format.

DNS servers running BIND server implementation prior to version 4.9.4 do not support the fast transfer format. You should enable this option only if you are transferring zones to BIND servers running version 4.9.4 or later.

Prevent Loading of a Zone When Bad Data Is Found

To prevent loading of a zone when bad data is found,

1. To open DNS, click **Start**, point to **Programs**, point to **Administrative Tools**, and then click **DNS**.
2. In the console tree, click the applicable DNS server (console tree | DNS | *applicable DNS server*).
3. On the **Action** menu, click **Properties**.
4. Click the **Advanced** tab.
5. In **Server options**, select the **Fail on load if bad zone data** check box, and then click **OK**.

Disable Round Robin Rotation for Multihomed Names

To disable round robin rotation for multihomed names,

1. To open DNS, click **Start**, point to **Programs**, point to **Administrative Tools**, and then click **DNS**.
2. In the console tree, click the applicable DNS server (console tree | DNS | *applicable DNS server*).
3. On the **Action** menu, click **Properties**.
4. In **Server options**, clear the **Enable round robin** check box, and then click **OK**.

Disable Local Subnet Prioritization for Multihomed Names

To disable local subnet prioritization for multihomed names,

1. To open DNS, click **Start**, point to **Programs**, point to **Administrative Tools**, and then click **DNS**.
2. In the console tree, click the applicable DNS server (console tree | DNS | *applicable DNS server*).
3. On the **Action** menu, click **Properties**.
4. Click the **Advanced** tab.
5. In **Server options**, clear the **Enable netmask ordering** check box, and then click **OK**.

Restore Server Default Preferences

To restore server default preferences,

1. To open DNS, click **Start**, point to **Programs**, point to **Administrative Tools**, and then click **DNS**.
2. In the console tree, click the applicable DNS server (console tree | DNS | *applicable DNS server*).
3. On the **Action** menu, click **Properties**.
4. Click the **Advanced** tab.
5. Click **Reset to Default**, and then click **OK**.

Disable Recursion on the DNS Server

To disable recursion on the DNS server,

1. To open DNS, click **Start**, point to **Programs**, point to **Administrative Tools**, and then click **DNS**.
2. In the console tree, click the applicable DNS server (console tree | DNS | *applicable DNS server*).
3. On the **Action** menu, click **Properties**.
4. Click the **Advanced** tab.
5. In **Server options**, select the **Disable recursion** check box, and then click **OK**.

Update Root Hints on the DNS Server

To update root hints on the DNS server,

1. To open DNS, click **Start**, point to **Programs**, point to **Administrative Tools**, and then click **DNS**.
2. In the console tree, click the applicable DNS server (console tree | DNS | *applicable DNS server*).
3. On the **Action** menu, click **Properties**.
4. Click the **Root Hints** tab.
5. Modify server root hints as follows:
    a. To add a root server to the list, click **Add**, then specify the name and IP address of the server to be added to the list.
    b. To modify a root server in the list, click **Edit**, then specify the name and IP address of the server to be modified in the list.
    c. To remove a root server from the list, select it in the list and click **Remove**.

Secure Server Cache Against Names Pollution

To secure server cache against names pollution,

1. To open DNS, click **Start**, point to **Programs**, point to **Administrative Tools**, and then click **DNS**.
2. In the console tree, click the applicable DNS server (console tree | DNS | *applicable DNS server*).
3. On the **Action** menu, click **Properties**.
4. Click the **Advanced** tab.
5. In **Server options**, select the **Secure cache against pollution** check box, and then click **OK**.

Clear the Server Names Cache

To clear the server names cache,

1. To open DNS, click **Start**, point to **Programs**, point to **Administrative Tools**, and then click **DNS**.
2. In the console tree, click the applicable DNS server (console tree | DNS | *applicable DNS server*).
3. On the **Action** menu, click **Clear cache**.

Select and Enable Debug Logging Options on the DNS Server

To select and enable debug logging options on the DNS server,

1. To open DNS, click **Start**, point to **Programs**, point to **Administrative Tools**, and then click **DNS**.
2. In the console tree, click the applicable DNS server (console tree | DNS | *applicable DNS server*).
3. On the **Action** menu, click **Properties**.
4. Click the **Logging** tab.
5. Select the events that you want the DNS server to record for debug logging, and then click **OK**.

Using debug logging options slows DNS server performance. For this reason, all debug logging options are disabled by default.

Disable Debug Logging Options on the DNS Server

To disable debug logging options on the DNS server,

1. To open DNS, click **Start**, point to **Programs**, point to **Administrative Tools**, and then click **DNS**.
2. In the console tree, click the applicable DNS server (console tree | DNS | *applicable DNS server*).
3. On the **Action** menu, click **Properties**.
4. Click the **Logging** tab.
5. Click **Reset To Default**, and then click **OK**.

Test a Simple Query on the DNS Server

To test a simple query on the DNS server,

1. To open DNS, click **Start**, point to **Programs**, point to **Administrative Tools**, and then click **DNS**.
2. In the console tree, click the applicable DNS server (console tree | DNS | *applicable DNS server*).
3. On the **Action** menu, click **Properties**.
4. Click the **Monitoring** tab.
5. Select the **A simple query against this DNS server** check box.

6. Click **Test Now**.

   Results of the query test appear in **Test results**.

Test a Recursive Query on the DNS Server

To test a recursive query on the DNS server,

1. To open DNS, click **Start**, point to **Programs**, point to **Administrative Tools**, and then click **DNS**.
2. In the console tree, click the applicable DNS server (console tree | DNS | *applicable DNS server*).
3. On the **Action** menu, click **Properties**.
4. Click the **Monitoring** tab.
5. Select the **A recursive query to other DNS servers** check box.
6. Click **Test Now**.

   Results of the query test appear in the Test results list box.

Enable Automatic Query Testing on the DNS Server

To enable automatic query testing on the DNS server,

1. To open DNS, click **Start**, point to **Programs**, point to **Administrative Tools**, and then click **DNS**.
2. In the console tree, click the applicable DNS server (console tree | DNS | *applicable DNS server*).
3. On the **Action** menu, click **Properties**.
4. Click the **Monitoring** tab.
5. Select the type of testing to be used during automatic query testing. You can select from the following:
   a. A simple query against this DNS server
   b. A recursive query to other DNS servers
   c. Both query test types
6. Select the **Perform automatic testing at the following interval** check box.
7. Set the **Test interval** to be used. The query tests that you select are performed at regular intervals based on the value of the interval you specify. The default-polling interval is 1 minute.

Results of automated query tests appear in Test results and are updated after each test interval.

View the DNS Server System Event Log

To view the DNS server system event log,

1. To open Event Viewer, click **Start**, point to **Programs**, point to **Administrative Tools**, and then click **Event Viewer**.
2. If the DNS server for which you want to view the log is located on another computer, do the following:
   a. On the Action menu, click **Connect to another computer**.
   b. Select **Another computer** and specify the name or IP address of the remote computer.
3. In console tree, click **DNS Server**.
4. In the details pane, you can view the listing of events the DNS Server service has logged.

   To view additional details for a specific event, double-click the event.

View a DNS Server Debug Log File

To view a DNS server debug log file,

1. Stop the DNS Server service.
2. To open WordPad, click **Start**, point to **Programs**, point to **Accessories**, and then click **WordPad**.
3. On the **File** menu, click **Open**.
4. In **Open**, for **File name**, specify the path to the DNS server debug log file.
5. By default, if the applicable DNS server is running locally, the file and path are *%SystemRoot%\System32\Dns\Dns.log*.
6. After you specify the correct path and file, click **Open** to view the log file.

By default, the *Dns.log* file is empty if you have not previously enabled debug-logging options.

Debug logging slows DNS server performance and should only be enabled for temporary use.

Add a Forward Lookup Zone

To add a forward lookup zone,

1. To open DNS, click **Start**, point to **Programs**, point to **Administrative Tools**, and then click **DNS**.

2. In the console tree, click **Forward Lookup Zones** (console tree | DNS | *applicable DNS server* | Forward Lookup Zones).
3. On the **Action** menu, click **New Zone**.
4. In the New Zone wizard, follow the instructions to create the new forward lookup zone.

Add a Reverse Lookup Zone

To add a reverse lookup zone,

1. To open DNS, click **Start**, point to **Programs**, point to **Administrative Tools**, and then click **DNS**
2. In the console tree, click **Reverse Lookup Zones** (console tree | DNS | *applicable DNS server* | Reverse Lookup Zones).
3. On the **Action** menu, click **New Zone**.
4. In the New Zone wizard, follow the instructions to create the new reverse lookup zone.

Delete a Zone

To delete a zone,

1. To open DNS, click **Start**, point to **Programs**, point to **Administrative Tools**, and then click **DNS**.
2. In the console tree, click the applicable zone (console tree | DNS | *applicable DNS server* | Forward (or Reverse) Lookup Zones | *applicable zone*).
3. On the **Action** menu, click **Delete**.
4. When asked to confirm that you want to delete the zone, click **OK**.

Caution Deleting an Active Directory-integrated zone effectively deletes the zone from use at all other Windows 2000 DNS servers that use the same directory store of zone data to load and update the zone locally.

This procedure is most often used to delete a secondary copy of a zone, although it can also be used to delete a primary zone.

Deleting a standard primary zone is usually unnecessary, unless you are redesigning your DNS namespace and the zone is no longer needed or used. In most cases, you can change the zone type if you only want to modify it.

Pause a Zone

To pause a zone,

1. To open DNS, click **Start**, point to **Programs**, point to **Administrative Tools**, and then click **DNS**.
2. In the console tree, click the applicable zone (console tree | DNS | *applicable DNS server* | Forward (or Reverse) Lookup Zones | *applicable zone*).
3. On the **Action** menu, click **Properties**.
4. In the *Applicable zone* **Properties**, on the **General** tab, click **Pause**, and then click **OK**.

By default, zones are started when created or loaded at the server. Once you use this procedure to pause a zone, you must restart the zone before it is available for servicing clients or zone updates.

Start a Zone

To start a zone,

1. To open DNS, click **Start**, point to **Programs**, point to **Administrative Tools**, and then click **DNS**.
2. In the console tree, click the applicable zone (console tree | DNS | *applicable DNS server* | Forward (or Reverse) Lookup Zones | *applicable zone*).
3. On the **Action** menu, click **Properties**.
4. In *Applicable zone* **Properties**, on the **General** tab, click **Start**, and then click **OK**.

By default, zones are started when created or loaded at the server. Only zones that have previously been paused need to be restarted.

Change the Zone Type

To change the zone type,

1. To open DNS, click **Start**, point to **Programs**, point to **Administrative Tools**, and then click **DNS**.
2. In the console tree, click the applicable zone (console tree | DNS | *applicable DNS server* | Forward (or Reverse) Lookup Zones | *applicable zone*).
3. On the **Action** menu, click **Properties**.

4. On the **General** tab, note the current zone type, then click **Change**.
5. In **Change Zone Type**, select a zone type other than the current one, and then click **OK**.

You can select from Standard primary or Standard secondary as appropriate for all zones. When selecting the Standard secondary zone type, you need to specify the IP address of another DNS server to be used as the source for obtaining updated information for the zone.

If the DNS server computer is operating as a domain controller, the option to change the zone type to Active Directory-integrated is available. This option is not otherwise available. When this zone type is selected for use, zone data is stored and replicated as part of the Active Directory database.

Changing a zone from secondary to primary type can affect other zone activities, including management of dynamic updates and zone transfers, and the use of DNS notify lists to notify other servers about changes in the zone.

Change a Zone File Name

To change a zone file name,

1. To open DNS, click **Start**, point to **Programs**, point to **Administrative Tools**, and then click **DNS**.
2. In the console tree, click the applicable zone (console tree | DNS | *applicable DNS server* | Forward (or Reverse) Lookup Zones | *applicable zone*).
3. On the **Action** menu, click **Properties**.
4. From the **General** tab, in the **Zone file name** text box, type the new file name for this zone.
5. Click **OK** when you have finished entering the new zone file name.

Caution If the zone file name is changed, be sure to update **Zone file name** on other DNS servers that maintain this zone. Otherwise, subsequent zone transfers and updates might fail. This can occur in the following situations:

1. The zone type is primary on this server.

2. The zone type is secondary on this server and this server acts as a source or master server for this zone to other DNS servers that host secondary copies of this zone.

The name of the zone file changes, not the name of the zone. You can use Windows Explorer to view or verify the new zone file name.

The zone file name is not used for Active Directory-integrated zones because these zones store zone data in the Active Directory database and not a text file on the DNS server computer.

Modify the Start of Authority Record for a Zone

To modify the SOA record for a zone,

1. To open DNS, click **Start**, point to **Programs**, point to **Administrative Tools**, and then click **DNS**.
2. In the console tree, click the applicable zone (console tree | DNS | *applicable DNS server* | Forward (or Reverse) Lookup Zones | *applicable zone*).
3. On the **Action** menu, click **Properties**.
4. Click the **Start of Authority (SOA)** tab.
5. As needed, modify properties for the SOA record. For more information about a dialog box item, click the **What's This?** button, point to the item, and then click on it.
6. Click **OK** when you have finished making changes.

The settings applied for the SOA record affect how zone transfers are made between servers.

Create and Manage a Notify List for a Zone

To create and manage a notify list for a zone,

1. To open DNS, click **Start**, point to **Programs**, point to **Administrative Tools**, and then click **DNS**.
2. In the console tree, click the applicable zone (console tree | DNS | *applicable DNS server* | Forward (or Reverse) Lookup Zones | *applicable zone*).
3. On the **Action** menu, click **Properties**.
4. Click the **Zone Transfers** tab.
5. Click **Notify**.
6. Verify that the **Automatically notify** check box is checked.
7. Select the method to be used for creating a list for notifying other DNS servers when changes to the zone occur. Your options are:
   a. Use the default, **Servers listed on the Name Servers** tab, to permit only those servers that appear by IP address on the **Name Servers** tab to be included in the notify list.

   b. Select **The following servers** if you want to specify a different notify list to be used instead.

8. If you selected **The following servers** in the previous step, add or remove server IP addresses to form the notify list as needed:
   a. To add a server to the notify list, type its IP address in the **IP address** field and click **Add**.
   b. To remove a server from the notify list, click the server IP address in the list box and click **Remove**.

Changes to the notify list properties are only available on primary zones. For secondary zones, these properties are read-only. DNS Notify is an RFC-compliant extension of the DNS standard defined in RFC 1996, "A Mechanism for Prompt Notification of Zone Changes."

Create a Zone Delegation

To create a zone delegation,

1. To open DNS, click **Start**, point to **Programs**, point to **Administrative Tools**, and then click **DNS**.
2. In the console tree, click the applicable subdomain (console tree | DNS | *applicable DNS server* | Forward (or Reverse) Lookup Zones | *applicable zone* | *applicable domain (if used)* | *applicable subdomain*).
3. On the **Action** menu, click **New Delegation**.
4. Follow the instructions provided in the New Delegation wizard to finish creating the new delegated domain.

All domains (or subdomains) that appear as part of the applicable zone delegation must be created in the current zone prior to performing delegation as described here. As necessary, use the DNS console to first add domains to the zone before completing this procedure.

Specify Other DNS Servers as Authoritative for a Zone

To specify other DNS servers as authoritative for a zone,

1. To open DNS, click **Start**, point to **Programs**, point to **Administrative Tools**, and then click **DNS**.
2. In the console tree, click the applicable zone (console tree | DNS | *applicable DNS server* | Forward (or Reverse) Lookup Zones | *applicable zone*).

3. On the **Action** menu, click **Properties**.
4. Click the **Name Servers** tab.
5. Click **Add**.
6. Specify additional DNS servers by their IP address, and then click **Add** to add them to the list.

You can add to the list of authoritative servers for the zone by either specifying server IP addresses or entering their DNS names. When entering names, click **Resolve** to resolve the name to its IP address prior to adding it to the list.

DNS servers specified using this procedure are added to those server IP addresses already present for the existing NS resource record for the zone. Typically, you might only need to perform this procedure at the primary zone when adding DNS servers to act as secondary servers and also to specify that these servers are known to be authoritative when answering queries for zone data.

Windows 2000 DNS servers automatically add and perform initial configuration of the NS resource record for each new primary type zone added to the server.

Update the Master Server for a Secondary Zone

To update the master server for a secondary zone,

1. To open DNS, click **Start**, point to **Programs**, point to **Administrative Tools**, and then click **DNS**.
2. In the console tree, click the applicable secondary zone (console tree | DNS | *applicable DNS server* | Forward (or Reverse) Lookup Zones | *applicable zone*).
3. On the **Action** menu, click **Properties**.
4. On the **General** tab, in **IP address**, specify the IP address for a new master server and click **Add** to update it in the list. For more information about a dialog box item, click the **What's This?** button, point to the item, and then click on it.

Enable DNS to Use WINS Resolution

To enable DNS to use WINS resolution,

1. To open DNS, click **Start**, point to **Programs**, point to **Administrative Tools**, and then click **DNS**.

2. In the console tree, click the applicable zone (console tree | DNS | *applicable DNS server* | Forward (or Reverse) Lookup Zones | *applicable zone*).
3. On the **Action** menu, click **Properties**.
4. Click the applicable tab:
   a. The **WINS** tab, if the applicable zone is a forward lookup zone.
   b. The **WINS-R** tab, if the applicable zone is a reverse lookup zone.
5. Select the applicable check box to enable the use of WINS resolution:
   a. The **Use WINS forward lookup** check box, if the applicable zone is a forward lookup zone.
   b. The **Use WINS-R lookup** check box, if the applicable zone is a reverse lookup zone.
6. Type the IP address of a WINS server to be used for further resolution of names not found in DNS. (Or, in the case of a reverse lookup zone, type a name in **Domain to append to returned name**).
7. Click **Add** to add the server IP address to the list.
8. If additional WINS server addresses should be used for a forward lookup zone during WINS lookup referral, repeat steps 6 and 7 as needed to add them to the list.
9. Select the **Do not replicate this record** check box for this WINS record if applicable. If you are replicating this zone between other DNS servers that do not recognize the WINS or WINS-R resource records, click this check box. This prevents these records from being replicated to these other servers during zone transfers.
10. Optionally, click **Advanced** to adjust advanced WINS lookup parameters. For more information about a dialog box item, click the **What's This?** button, point to the item, and then click on it.

When this option is used, specified WINS servers configured in this procedure are used for final referral of names not found in the applicable zone.

Allow Dynamic Updates

To allow dynamic updates,

1. To open DNS, click **Start**, point to **Programs**, point to **Administrative Tools**, and then click **DNS**.
2. In the console tree, click the applicable zone (console tree | DNS | *applicable DNS server* | Forward (or Reverse) Lookup Zones | *applicable zone*).
3. On the **Action** menu, click **Properties**.

4. On the **General** property tab, verify that the zone type is either **Primary** or **Active Directory-integrated**.
5. In the **Allow dynamic updates?** list, click **Yes**.

Dynamic update is an RFC-compliant extension to the DNS standard. The DNS update process is defined in RFC 2136, "Dynamic Updates in the Domain Name System (DNS UPDATES)."

Allow Only Secure Dynamic Updates

To allow only secure dynamic updates,

1. To open DNS, click **Start**, point to **Programs**, point to **Administrative Tools**, and then click **DNS**.
2. In the console tree, click the applicable zone (console tree | DNS | *applicable DNS server* | Forward (or Reverse) Lookup Zones | *applicable zone*).
3. On the **Action** menu, click **Properties**.
4. On the **General** tab, verify that the zone type is **Active Directory-integrated**.
5. In the **Allow dynamic updates?** drop-down list, click **Only secure updates**.

Caution For Windows 2000, the use of secure dynamic updates can be compromised by running a DHCP server on a domain controller when a Windows 2000 DHCP server is configured to perform registration of DNS records on behalf of its clients. To avoid this issue, deploy DHCP servers and domain controllers on separate computers. If you are not concerned about the security of reverse lookup (PTR) records, this precaution is only advisable if the DHCP server is configured to perform registration of host records on behalf of its clients (which is not a default behavior).

Secure dynamic update is supported only for Active Directory-integrated zones. If the zone type is configured differently, you must change the zone type and directory-integrate the zone prior to securing it for DNS dynamic updates.

Dynamic update is an RFC-compliant extension to the DNS standard. The DNS update process is defined in RFC 2136, "Dynamic Updates in the Domain Name System (DNS UPDATES)."

Initiate a Zone Transfer at a Secondary Server

To initiate a zone transfer at a secondary server,

1. To open DNS, click **Start**, point to **Programs**, point to **Administrative Tools**, and then click **DNS**
2. In the console tree, click the applicable zone (console tree | DNS | *applicable DNS server* | Forward (or Reverse) Lookup Zones | *applicable zone*).
3. On the **Action** menu, click **Transfer from master**.

Adjust the Refresh Interval for a Zone

To adjust the refresh interval for a zone,

1. To open DNS, click **Start**, point to **Programs**, point to **Administrative Tools**, and then click **DNS**.
2. In the console tree, click the applicable zone (console tree | DNS | *applicable DNS server* | Forward (or Reverse) Lookup Zones | *applicable zone*).
3. On the **Action** menu, click **Properties**.
4. On the **General** tab, verify that the zone type is either **Primary** or **Active Directory-integrated**.
5. Click the **Start of Authority (SOA)** tab.
6. To adjust the **Refresh interval**, select from the drop-down list a time period in minutes, hours, or days, and type a number in the text box.
7. Click **OK** to save the adjusted interval.

By default, the refresh interval for each zone is set to 1 hour. The refresh interval is used to determine how often other DNS servers that load and host the zone must attempt to renew the zone.

Adjust the Retry Interval for a Zone

To adjust the retry interval for a zone,

1. To open DNS, click **Start**, point to **Programs**, point to **Administrative Tools**, and then click **DNS**.
2. In the console tree, click the applicable zone (console tree | DNS | *applicable DNS server* | Forward (or Reverse) Lookup Zones | *applicable zone*).

3. On the **Action** menu, click **Properties**.
4. On the **General** tab, verify that the zone type is either **Primary** or **Active Directory-integrated**.
5. Click the **SOA** tab.
6. To adjust the **Retry interval**, select from the drop-down list an interval in minutes, hours, or days, and type a number in the text box.
7. Click **OK** to save the adjusted interval.

By default, the retry interval for each zone is set at 10 minutes. The retry interval is used to determine how often other DNS servers that load and host the zone are to retry an update request for the zone each time the refresh interval occurs.

Adjust the Expire Interval for a Zone

To adjust the expire interval for a zone,

1. To open DNS, click **Start**, point to **Programs**, point to **Administrative Tools**, and then click **DNS**.
2. In the console tree, click the applicable zone (console tree | DNS | *applicable DNS server* | Forward (or Reverse) Lookup Zones | *applicable zone*).
3. On the **Action** menu, click **Properties**.
4. On the **General** tab, verify that the zone type is either **Primary** or **Active Directory-integrated**.
5. Click the **SOA** tab.
6. For **Expires after**, select from the drop-down list an interval in either minutes, hours, or days, and then type a number in the text box.
7. Click **OK** to save the adjusted interval.

By default, the expire interval for each zone is set to 1 day. The expire interval is used by other DNS servers configured to load and host the zone to determine when zone data expires if not renewed.

Modify Security for a Directory Integrated Zone

To modify security for a directory integrated zone,

1. To open DNS, click **Start**, point to **Programs**, point to **Administrative Tools**, and then click **DNS**.

2. In the console tree, click the applicable zone (console tree | DNS | *applicable DNS server* | Forward (or Reverse) Lookup Zones | *applicable zone*).
3. On the **Action** menu, click **Properties**.
4. On the **General** tab, verify that the zone type is **Active Directory-integrated**.
5. On the **Security** tab, modify the list of member users or groups that are allowed to securely update the applicable zone and reset their permissions as needed. For more information about a dialog box item, click the **What's This?** button, point to the item, and then click it.

Secure dynamic updates are only supported for Active Directory-integrated zones.

Add a Host Resource Record to a Zone

To add a host resource record to a zone,

1. To open DNS, click **Start**, point to **Programs**, point to **Administrative Tools**, and then click **DNS**.
2. In the console tree, click the applicable forward lookup zone (console tree | DNS | *applicable DNS server* | Forward Lookup Zones | *applicable zone*).
3. On the **Action** menu, click **New Host**.
4. In the **Name** text box, type the DNS computer name for the new host.
5. In the **IP address** text box, type the IP address for the new host.
6. As an option, select the **Create associated pointer (PTR) record** check box to create an additional pointer record in a reverse zone for this host, based on the information you entered in **Name** and **IP address**.
7. Click **Add Host** to add the new host record to the zone.

Add a Mail Exchanger Resource Record to a Zone

To add a mail exchanger (MX) resource record to a zone,

1. To open DNS, click **Start**, point to **Programs**, point to **Administrative Tools**, and then click **DNS**.
2. In the console tree, click the applicable forward lookup zone (console tree | DNS | *applicable DNS server* | Forward Lookup Zones | *applicable zone*).
3. On the **Action** menu, click **New Mail Exchanger**.
4. In the **Host or domain** text box, type the domain name for which this record is to be used to deliver mail.

5. In the **Mail server** text box, type the DNS host computer name of the mail exchanger or mail server host that delivers mail for the specified domain name.

   As an option, you can click **Browse** to view the DNS namespace for mail exchanger hosts in this domain that have host records already defined.
6. Adjust the **Mail server priority** as needed for this zone.
7. Click **OK** to add the new record to the zone.

Add an Alias Resource Record to a Zone

To add an alias (CNAME) resource record to a zone,

1. To open DNS, click **Start**, point to **Programs**, point to **Administrative Tools**, and then click **DNS**.
2. In the console tree, click the applicable forward lookup zone (console tree | DNS | *applicable DNS server* | Forward Lookup Zones | *applicable zone*).
3. On the **Action** menu, click **New Alias**.
4. In the **Alias name** text box, type the alias name.
5. In the **Fully qualified name for target host** text box, type the fully qualified domain name of the DNS host computer for which this alias is to be used.

   As an option, you can click **Browse** to search the DNS namespace for hosts in this domain that have host records already defined.
6. Click **OK** to add the new record to the zone.

Add a New Domain to a Zone

To add a new domain to a zone,

1. To open DNS, click **Start**, point to **Programs**, point to **Administrative Tools**, and then click **DNS**.
2. In the console tree, click the applicable zone (console tree | DNS | *applicable DNS server* | Forward (or Reverse) Lookup Zones | *applicable zone*).
3. On the **Action** menu, click **New Domain**.
4. In **New Domain**, type the name of the new domain without using periods.
5. Click **OK** to add the new domain to the zone.

Add a Pointer Resource Record to a Reverse Zone

To add a pointer (PTR) resource record to a reverse zone,

1. To open DNS, click **Start**, point to **Programs**, point to **Administrative Tools**, and then click **DNS**.

2. In the console tree, click the applicable reverse lookup zone (console tree | DNS | *applicable DNS server* | Reverse Lookup Zones | *applicable zone*).
3. On the **Action** menu, click **New Pointer**.
4. In the **Host IP number** text box, type the host IP address octet number.
5. In the **Host name** text box, type the fully qualified domain name for the DNS host computer for which this pointer record is to be used to provide reverse lookup (address-to-name resolution).

   As an option, you can click **Browse** to search the DNS namespace for hosts in this domain that have host (A) records already defined.
6. Click **OK** to add the new record to the zone.

Add a Resource Record to a Zone

To add a resource record to a zone,

1. To open DNS, click **Start**, point to **Programs**, point to **Administrative Tools**, and then click **DNS**.
2. In the console tree, click the applicable zone (console tree | DNS | *applicable DNS server* | Forward (or Reverse) Lookup Zones | *applicable zone*). On the **Action** menu, click **Other New Records**.
3. In **Select a resource record type** list box, scroll to and select the type of resource record you want to add.
4. Click **Create Record**.
5. In **New Resource Record**, enter the information needed to complete the resource record.
6. After you specify all of the necessary information for the resource record, click **OK** to add the new record to the zone.

Modify an Existing Resource Record in a Zone

To modify an existing resource record in a zone,

1. To open DNS, click **Start**, point to **Programs**, point to **Administrative Tools**, and then click **DNS**.
2. In the console tree, click the applicable zone (console tree | DNS | *applicable DNS server* | Forward (or Reverse) Lookup Zones | *applicable zone*).
3. In the details pane, click the resource record you want to modify.
4. On the **Action** menu, click **Properties**.
5. In **Properties**, edit any properties available to be modified. If necessary, you can view and modify advanced resource record properties for the DNS console. To display advanced properties, on the **View** menu, click **Advanced**.
6. Click **OK** when you have finished modifying the record.

When **Advanced** view options are enabled, you can modify additional settings for an existing resource record, such as its record-specific Time-to-Live (TTL), or set a record-specific time stamp to be used where aging and scavenging are available.

Delete a Resource Record From a Zone

To delete a resource record from a zone,

1. To open DNS, click **Start**, point to **Programs**, point to **Administrative Tools**, and then click **DNS**.
2. In the console tree, click the applicable zone (console tree | DNS | *applicable DNS server* | Forward (or Reverse) Lookup Zones | *applicable zone*).
3. In the details pane, click the resource record you want to delete.
4. On the **Action** menu, click **Delete**.
5. When you are asked to confirm that you want to delete the selected resource record, click **OK**.

View Unsupported Resource Records in a Zone

To view unsupported resource records in a zone,

1. To open DNS, click **Start**, point to **Programs**, point to **Administrative Tools**, and then click **DNS**.
2. In the console tree, click the applicable zone (console tree | DNS | *applicable DNS server* | Forward (or Reverse) Lookup Zones | *applicable zone*).
3. In the details pane, click the record you want to view.
4. On the **Action** menu, click **Properties**.
5. In **Properties**, view properties specific to this record.
6. When you have finished viewing the record, click **OK**.

The DNS console allows you to view unsupported resource records in secondary zones that are obtained from other DNS server implementations, such as DNS servers running versions of BIND. These records are not used by Windows 2000 DNS servers and cannot be managed through the DNS console. These include the following types of records:

- Legacy records, such as mail forwarder (MF) and mail domain (MD) resource records.
- Secure or encrypting DNS records, such as signature (SIG) or next (NXT) resource records.

Modify Security for a Resource Record

To modify security for a resource record,

1. To open DNS, click **Start**, point to **Programs**, point to **Administrative Tools**, and then click **DNS**.
2. In the console tree, click the applicable zone (console tree | DNS | *applicable DNS server* | Forward (or Reverse) Lookup Zones | *applicable zone*).
3. In the details pane, click the record you want to view.
4. On the **Action** menu, click **Properties**.
5. On the **Security** tab, modify the list of member users or groups that are allowed to securely update the applicable record and reset their permissions as needed. For more information about a dialog box item, click the **What's This?** button, point to the item, and then click it.

Secure dynamic updates are only supported or configurable for resource records stored with Active Directory-integrated zones.

Set Aging and Scavenging Properties for the DNS Server

To set aging and scavenging properties for the DNS server,

1. To open DNS, click **Start**, point to **Programs**, point to **Administrative Tools**, and then click **DNS**.
2. In the console tree, click the applicable DNS server (console tree | DNS | *applicable DNS server*).
3. On the **Action** menu, click **Set Aging/Scavenging for all zones**.
4. Select the **Scavenge stale resource records** check box.
5. Modify other aging and scavenging properties as needed. For more information about a dialog box item, click the **What's This?** button, point to the item, and then click on it.

Aging and scavenging properties configured by this procedure act as server defaults that apply only toward Active Directory-integrated zones. For standard primary zones, you must set the appropriate properties at the applicable zone.

Once you apply changes for server aging/scavenging settings, the DNS console prompts you to confirm. You then have the option to apply your changes to new Active Directory-integrated zones only. If needed, you can also apply your changes to existing Active Directory-integrated zones.

Regardless of whether the Scavenge stale resource records check box is selected as described in step 4, for standard primary zones, this feature is disabled unless manually enabled at the applicable zone.

Set Aging and Scavenging Properties for a Selected Zone

To set aging and scavenging properties for a selected zone,

1. To open DNS, click **Start**, point to **Programs**, point to **Administrative Tools**, and then click **DNS**.
2. In the console tree, click the applicable zone (console tree | DNS | *applicable DNS server* | Forward (or Reverse) Lookup Zones | *applicable zone*).
3. On the **Action** menu, click **Properties**.
4. On the **General** tab, click **Aging**.
5. Select the **Scavenge stale resource records** check box.
6. Modify other aging and scavenging properties as needed. For more information about a dialog box item, click the **What's This?** button, point to the item, and then click it.

Enable Automatic Scavenging of Stale Resource Records

To enable automatic scavenging of stale resource records,

1. To open DNS, click **Start**, point to **Programs**, point to **Administrative Tools**, and then click **DNS**.
2. In the console tree, click the applicable DNS server (console tree | DNS | *applicable DNS server*).
3. On the **Action** menu, click **Properties**.
4. Click the **Advanced** tab.
5. Select the **Enable automatic scavenging of stale records** check box.
6. To adjust the **Scavenging period**, select from the drop-down list an interval in either hours or days, and then type a number in the text box.

Start Immediate Scavenging of Stale Resource Records

To start immediate scavenging of stale resource records,

1. To open DNS, click **Start**, point to **Programs**, point to **Administrative Tools**, and then click **DNS**.
2. In the console tree, click the applicable DNS server (console tree | DNS | *applicable DNS server*).
3. On the **Action** menu, click **Scavenge stale resource records**.

View When a Zone Can Start Scavenging Stale Records

To view when a zone can start scavenging stale records,

1. To open DNS, click **Start**, point to **Programs**, point to **Administrative Tools**, and then click **DNS**.
2. In the console tree, click the applicable zone (console tree | DNS | *applicable DNS server* | Forward (or Reverse) Lookup Zones | *applicable zone*).
3. On the **View** menu, click **Advanced**.
4. On the **Action** menu, click **Properties**.
5. On the **General** tab, click **Aging**.
6. In the **Zone Aging/Scavenging Properties** dialog box, view the value in **Date and time** to see when the zone is first eligible to be scavenged for stale resource records.

The start scavenging date and time stamp are used to determine when zone scavenging starts. After the start scavenging date and time stamp are reached, scavenging can occur only if the Scavenge stale resource records check box is selected. If the check box is cleared, scavenging for the zone cannot be performed.

Reset Scavenging and Aging Properties for a Specified Resource Record

To reset scavenging and aging properties for a specified resource record,

1. To open DNS, click **Start**, point to **Programs**, point to **Administrative Tools**, and then click **DNS**.
2. In the console tree, click the applicable zone (console tree | DNS | *applicable DNS server* | Forward (or Reverse) Lookup Zones | *applicable zone*).
3. In the details pane, double-click the resource record for which you want to reset scavenging and aging properties. The properties for the selected resource record appears.
4. Depending on the how the resource record was originally added to the zone, do the following as appropriate to reset the **Delete this record when it becomes stale** check box:
   a. If the record was added dynamically using the DNS dynamic update protocol, you can clear the check box to prevent its aging or potential removal during the scavenging process.

b. If you added the record statically, you can select the check box to permit its aging or potential removal during the scavenging process.

This procedure is only necessary for resource records that are dynamically registered. For records that you manually add to a zone, a time stamp value of zero always applies to the record, excluding it from the scavenging process.

Display and View a Client Resolver Cache Using the ipconfig Command

To display and view a client resolver cache using the ipconfig command, at a command prompt, type: *ipconfig /displaydns*. Or, type *ipconfig /displaydns | more* to pause the display of the command output to one screen at a time.

To open a command prompt, click **Start**, point to **Programs**, point to **Accessories**, and then click **Command Prompt**.

The ipconfig /displaydns command provides you with a means to view the contents of the DNS client resolver cache, which includes entries preloaded from the local Hosts file, as well as any recently obtained resource records for name queries resolved by the system. This information is used by the DNS Client service to quickly resolve frequently queried names before it queries its configured DNS servers.

When the ipconfig /displaydns command is used to display current resolver cache contents, the resultant output generally includes the local host and loopback IP address (127.0.0.1) mappings. This is because these mappings typically exist in the default (unmodified) contents of the local Hosts file.

After you add host mapping entries to the local Hosts file and save the file, these entries are added to the displayed output of this command.

The resolver cache can also support negative caching of unresolved or nonvalid DNS names. These entries are added by the DNS Client service when it receives a negative answer from a DNS server for a queried name. The negative result is cached for a short period of time so that it is not again queried, which could cause query performance problems.

During DNS troubleshooting, you can flush and reset the cache to discard negative entries from the cache and any other dynamically added entries that were not preloaded.

Although the ipconfig command is provided for earlier versions of Windows, the /displaydns option is only available for use at computers running Windows 2000 where the DNS Client service is started.

Flush and Reset a Client Resolver Cache Using the ipconfig Command

To flush and reset a client resolver cache using the ipconfig command at a command prompt, type: *ipconfig /flushdns.*

The ipconfig /flushdns command provides you with a means to flush and reset the contents of the DNS client resolver cache. During DNS troubleshooting, if necessary, you can use this procedure to discard negative cache entries from the cache, as well as any other dynamically added entries.

Resetting the cache does not eliminate entries that are preloaded from the local Hosts file. To eliminate those entries from the cache, remove them from this file.

Although the ipconfig command is provided for earlier versions of Windows, the /flushdns option is only available for use at computers running Windows 2000. The DNS Client service must also be started.

Renew DNS Client Registration Using the ipconfig Command

To renew DNS client registration using the ipconfig command at a command prompt, type: *ipconfig /registerdns.* Or, type *ipconfig /registerdns [adapter],* where *adapter* is the name of a specific network adapter installed on the computer for which you want to renew or update registrations.

The ipconfig /registerdns command provides you with a means to manually initiate dynamic registration for the DNS names and IP addresses configured at a computer. This option can assist in troubleshooting a failed DNS name registration or in resolving a dynamic update problem between a client and the DNS server without requiring a client reboot.

By default, the ipconfig /registerdns command refreshes all DHCP address leases and registers related DNS names configured and used by the client computer.

To learn the names of adapters that you can optionally specify with this command, first type the ipconfig command by itself (that is, do not specify any additional parameters). The command output displays all adapters by name that are available for use at the computer.

Although the ipconfig command is provided for earlier versions of Windows, the /registerdns option is only available for use at computers running Windows 2000 with the DHCP Client service started.

For Windows 2000, the DHCP Client service is used to perform dynamic registrations and updates, regardless of whether the computer uses a DHCP server or static configuration to obtain its IP address.

If you are troubleshooting a failed DNS dynamic registration for a client computer and its DNS names, it might help to verify that the cause is not related to one of the following commonly known causes for such failures:

- The zone where the client requires update or registration is not able to accept dynamic updates.
- The DNS servers that the client is configured to use do not support or recognize the DNS dynamic update protocol.
- The primary (or directory-integrated) DNS server for the zone refused the update request. This can most likely occur because the client is not permitted under current zone or resource records security sufficient access rights to update its own name.
- The server or zone is not available because of other problems, such as a network or server failure.

Verify DNS Server Responsiveness Using the nslookup Command

To verify DNS server responsiveness using the nslookup command,

1. At a command prompt, type:

   nslookup server_ip_address 127.0.0.1

   where *server_ip_address* is the IP address of the DNS server at which you are verifying its responsiveness. For example, if the IP address of your DNS server is 10.0.0.1, you would type:

   nslookup 10.0.0.1 127.0.0.1

2. If the server is responding, the name "localhost" is returned. If the server does not respond, continue troubleshooting the DNS server.

Verify a Zone Delegation Using the nslookup Command

To verify a zone delegation using the nslookup command,

1. At a command prompt, type:

   nslookup root_server_ip_address

   where *root_server_ip_address* is the IP address of a valid root server for your network.
2. At the nslookup command prompt, type:

   set norecursion

3. After the previous command completes, type:

   set q=rr_type

   where *rr_type* is the type of resource record for the failed name for which you are attempting to verify (or troubleshoot) a zone delegation. For example, type *set q=a* if the type of resource record used by the failed name is an A resource record.
4. Type the FQDN for the failed name. Use the trailing period (.) when entering the name. If zone delegations are set correctly, a list of NS resource records for delegated servers should be returned in the response.
5. If the NS query response contains no names or IP addresses for delegated servers, type *q=ns* and query again using the FQDN for the parent zone of the failed name. For example, if the failed name you used in the previous step was *example.microsoft.com,* query for *microsoft.com.*
6. If the response contains NS resource records, but no A resource records, type *set recursion* and query individually for any of the A resource records of servers listed in the NS resource records. If, for each NS resource record you encounter in a zone, you do not find at least one valid IP address in an A resource record, you have a broken delegation.
7. Either fix the broken delegation or retry the delegation test described in the previous step using a different IP address.

If more than one A resource record or IP address is found, use it to repeat the delegation test described in step 7. To fix a delegation, add or update an A resource record in the parent zone with a valid IP address for a correct DNS server for the delegated zone.

Verify DNS Registration for Domain Controllers Using the nslookup Command

To verify DNS registration for domain controllers using the nslookup command,

1. At a command prompt, type: *nslookup*
2. After the previous command completes, at the nslookup (>) prompt type:

   set q=rr_type

   where *rr_type* is the resource record (RR) type to apply as a filter for subsequent lookups. For example, in this instance, because you want to limit subsequent name queries to filter and return only service location (SRV) RRs that use a specified name, type:

   set q=srv.

3. After the previous command completes, type:

   _ldap._tcp.dc._msdcs.Active_Directory_domain_name

   where *Active_Directory_domain_name* is the DNS name configured for use with your Active Directory domain and any of its associated domain controllers. For example, if the DNS domain name of your Active Directory domain is *example.microsoft.com,* type:

   _ldap._tcp.dc._msdcs.example.microsoft.com.

4. Review the output of the previous SRV query and determine if further action is needed based on whether the previous query succeeded or failed:

   a. If the query succeeded, review the registered SRV resource records returned in the query to determine if all domain controllers for your Active Directory domain are included and registered using valid IP addresses.

   b. If the query failed, continue troubleshooting dynamic update or DNS server related issues to determine the exact cause of the problem.

In some cases, when performing the above procedure, you might see several time-outs reported. This happens when reverse lookup is not configured for DNS servers servicing the same DNS domain as your Active Directory domain.

The following is an example of command-line output for an Nslookup session, used to verify SRV resource records that are registered by Windows 2000 domain controllers. In this example, the two domain controllers are dc1 and dc2, and are registered for the *example.microsoft.com* domain.

```
C:\>nslookup
Default Server:  dc1.example.microsoft.com
Address:  10.0.0.14
> set type=srv
> _ldap._tcp.dc._msdcs.example.microsoft.com
Server:  dc1.example.microsoft.com
Address:  10.0.0.14
_ldap._tcp.dc._msdcs.example.microsoft.com   SRV service location:
          priority       = 0
          weight         = 0
          port           = 389
          svr hostname   = dc1.example.microsoft.com
_ldap._tcp.dc._msdcs.example.microsoft.com   SRV service location:
          priority       = 0
          weight         = 0
          port           = 389
          svr hostname   = dc2.example.microsoft.com
dc1.example.microsoft.com     internet address = 10.0.0.14
dc2.example.microsoft.com     internet address = 10.0.0.15
```

The nslookup command is a standard command-line utility provided in most DNS service implementations, including Windows 2000. It offers the ability to perform query testing of DNS servers and obtain detailed responses as the command output. This information is useful in troubleshooting name resolution problems, verifying that resource records are added or updated correctly in a zone, and debugging other server-related problems.

Verify that resource records used to register services and critical hosts, such as domain controllers, are correctly added to zones. In some cases, you might need to manually add or verify registration of the SRV resource records used to support Windows 2000 domain controllers. To add the SRV resource records that have been created for a domain controller, open and view the *Netlogon.dns* file, created by the Active Directory Installation wizard when a server computer is promoted to a domain controller. It can be found at *systemroot\System32\Config\Netlogon.dns.*

The resource records used in this file are listed in RFC-compliant text-file format. When verifying these records, look for the following records:

_ldap._tcp.*Active_Directory_domain_name* IN SRV 0 0 389 *ldap_server_name*
_ldap._tcp.dc._msdcs.*Active_Directory_domain_name* IN SRV 0 0 389 *domain_controller_name*

In some cases, you might need to modify the Lightweight Directory Access Protocol (LDAP) server name if you are using a non-domain controller as an LDAP server for your network.

The Net Logon service on each Windows 2000 domain controller registers, as appropriate, a number of different DNS resource records with DNS servers. To learn more about these records and how Net Logon updates DNS, obtain additional technical information on Windows 2000 DNS, available from the Microsoft Web site.

Verify WINS as the Source for Answering a DNS Query

To verify WINS as the source for answering a DNS query,

1. At a command prompt, type: *nslookup*
2. After the previous command completes, at the nslookup (>) prompt type:

   set debug

   to enable the nslookup command to operate in debug mode, providing extended information in the command output. This mode is required to view query response information about whether the source for a query answer is:

a. *authoritative* (from a DNS zone or WINS server database).
b. *non-authoritative* (cached data from previous queries made by the DNS server or loaded from root hints).

3. Next, either type:

   set qtype=a

   if you are testing for a WINS forward lookup, or

   set qtype=ptr

   if you are testing for a WINS-R reverse lookup.

   Respectively, these two commands can be used to set the query type to filter either by A or PTR resource records as appropriate for researching either a forward or reverse lookup.
4. Based on whether you are verifying possible WINS sourcing for either a forward or reverse lookup, type the appropriate FQDN.

   For example, if the forward lookup you are tracing is for a domain name *host-a.example.microsoft.com,* type:

   host-a.example.microsoft.com.

   If the reverse lookup you are tracing is for an IP address 10.0.0.1, type:

   1.0.0.10.in-addr.arpa.

5. In the response, note whether the server answered authoritatively or non-authoritatively, and note the TTL value.
6. If the server answered authoritatively, repeat the same query you performed in step 4.
7. In the response, note whether the TTL value decreased with the second query answer or if it remained consistent with the TTL value specified in the first query answer.
8. To leave debug mode and return to the command prompt, type: *exit*

Normally, when a Windows 2000 DNS server answers a query from its authoritative zone data, it uses the set minimum or default TTL for the zone or the record-specific TTL value (if one is configured). In so doing, TTLs are decreased in answers the server returns if based on non-authoritative data, such as a cached record at the server.

WINS lookups present an exceptional case, where an answer received back from a WINS server is cached by the DNS server but is also considered to be authoritative data. In this case, the WINS sourced data is returned to clients as authoritative but ages while in the DNS server names cache, causing the TTL used by the server to decrease over time.

APPENDIX A

TCP/IP Resources

This appendix covers

- TCP/IP RFCs
- TCP/IP references
- Converting binary to decimal
- TCP/IP utilities
- TCP/IP database files
- Using Performance Logs and Alerts

TCP/IP RFCs

The standards for TCP/IP are published in a series of documents called Requests for Comments (RFCs). RFCs are an evolving series of reports, proposals for protocols, and protocol standards that describe the internal workings of TCP/IP and the Internet.

Although TCP/IP standards are always published as RFCs, not all RFCs specify standards. RFCs are authored by individuals who voluntarily write and submit a draft proposal for a new protocol or specification to the Internet Engineering Task Force (IETF) and other working groups. Submitted drafts are first reviewed by a technical expert, a task force, or an RFC editor, and then assigned a status.

If a draft passes this initial review stage, it is circulated to the larger Internet community for a period of further comment and review, and assigned an RFC number. This RFC number remains constant.

If changes are made to the proposed specification, drafts that are revised or updated are circulated by using a new RFC (a number higher than the original RFC number) to identify more recent documents.

There are six status assignments for RFCs in the standards process, as shown in Table A.1.

TABLE A.1 *RFC Status Assignments*

Status	Description
Standard protocol	An official standard protocol of the Internet.
Draft standard protocol	Under active consideration and review to become a standard protocol.
Proposed standard protocol	A protocol that in the future may become a standard protocol.
Experimental protocol	A protocol designed for experimental purposes. An experimental protocol is not intended for operational use.
Informational protocol	A protocol developed by another standards organization that is included for the convenience of the Internet community.
Historic protocol	Protocols that have been superceded or made obsolete by other protocols.

RFCs for TCP/IP for Windows 2000

Table A.2 shows the RFCs supported by the TCP/IP protocol in Windows 2000.

TABLE A.2 *RFCs Supported by Windows 2000 TCP/IP*

RFC number	Title
768	User Datagram Protocol (UDP)
783	Trivial File Transfer Protocol (TFTP)
791	Internet Protocol (IP)
792	Internet Control Message Protocol (ICMP)
793	Transmission Control Protocol (TCP)
816	Fault Isolation and Recovery
826	Address Resolution Protocol (ARP)
854	Telnet Protocol (TELNET)
862	Echo Protocol (ECHO)
863	Discard Protocol (DISCARD)
864	Character Generator Protocol (CHARGEN)
865	Quote of the Day Protocol (QUOTE)
867	Daytime Protocol (DAYTIME)
894	IP over Ethernet
919	Broadcasting Internet Datagrams
922	Broadcasting Internet Datagrams in the Presence of Subnets
950	Internet Standard Subnetting Procedure

(continued)

TABLE A.2 *RFCs Supported by Windows 2000 TCP/IP (Continued)*

RFC number	Title
959	File Transfer Protocol (FTP)
1001	Protocol Standard for a NetBIOS Service on a TCP/UDP Transport: Concepts and Methods
1002	Protocol Standard for a NetBIOS Service on a TCP/UDP Transport: Detailed Specifications
1009	Requirements for Internet Gateways
1034	Domain Names – Concepts and Facilities
1035	Domain Names – Implementation and Specification
1042	IP over Token Ring
1112	Internet Group Management Protocol (IGMP)
1122	Requirements for Internet Hosts – Communication Layers
1123	Requirements for Internet Hosts – Application and Support
1157	Simple Network Management Protocol (SNMP)
1179	Line Printer Daemon Protocol (LPDP)
1188	IP over FDDI
1191	Path MTU Discovery
1201	IP over ARCNET
1256	ICMP Router Discovery Messages
1323	TCP Extensions for High Performance
1518	An Architecture for IP Address Allocation with CIDR
1519	Classless Inter-Domain Routing (CIDR): An Address Assignment and Aggregation Strategy
1812	Requirements for IPVersion 4 Routers
1878	Variable Length Subnet Table For IPv4
2018	TCP Selective Acknowledgment Options
2131	Dynamic Host Configuration Protocol (DHCP)
2136	Dynamic Updates in the Domain Name System (DNS UPDATE)
2236	Internet Group Management Protocol, Version 2

Obtaining RFCs

You can obtain RFCs from the Request for Comments Web site, *www.rfc-editor.org/*. This Web site is currently maintained by members of the Information Sciences Institute (ISI), who publish a classified listing of all RFCs. RFCs are classified as one of the following: approved Internet standard, proposed Internet standard (circulated in draft form for review), Internet best practices, or For Your Information (FYI) document.

TCP/IP References

For more information about the TCP/IP protocol suite, consult the following references:

Comer, D., *Internetworking with TCP/IP, Volume I: Principles, Protocols, and Architecture*. Third edition. Englewood Cliffs, NJ: Prentice Hall, 1995.

Comer, D., and D. Stevens. *Internetworking with TCP/IP, Volume II: Design, Implementation, and Internals*. Englewood Cliffs, NJ: Prentice Hall, 1991.

Lee, T., and J. Davies. *Microsoft Windows 2000 TCP/IP Protocols and Services Technical Reference*. Redmond, WA: Microsoft Press, 1999.

Stevens, W.R. *TCP/IP Illustrated, Volume 1: The Protocols*. Reading, MA: Addison-Wesley, 1994.

Converting Binary to Decimal

Because all IP addresses and subnet mask values are composed of a standard-length 32-bit data field, they are viewed and interpreted by computers as a single binary numeric string, such as

10001010 00111001 00000111 00011011

Obviously, binary notation is not well suited for use by people, who prefer to express the same number in a simpler way, such as 138.57.7.27. To communicate IP addresses and enter them in configurations quickly, you can use *dotted decimal notation* to convert IP address numbers from binary format.

With dotted decimal notation, each 32-bit address number is viewed as four distinct groupings of 8 bits. Each of the four groupings of 8 consecutive bits is referred to as an *octet*.

The first octet uses the first 8 bits (bit places 1–8), the second octet uses the next 8 bits (bit places 9–16), followed by the third octet (bit places 17–24), and fourth octet (bit places 25–32). Periods are used to separate the four octets that are described as separate decimal number values in the IP address.

Table A.3 shows the scientific notation for each bit place in an individual octet and the equivalent decimal value.

For example, if the first bit place is filled with a bit value of 1, the equivalent decimal value is 128. Where the bit value is 0, the equivalent decimal value is 0 as well.

TABLE A.3 *Equivalent Decimal Values for Bit Places in a Single IP Address Octet*

Octet	First bit	Second bit	Third bit	Fourth bit	Fifth bit	Sixth bit	Seventh bit	Eighth bit
Scientific notation	2^7	2^6	2^5	2^4	2^3	2^2	2^1	2^0
Decimal notation	128	64	32	16	8	4	2	1

If all the bit places in an octet are filled with ones (1), the highest equivalent decimal value is 255. If all the bit places are filled with zeros (0), the lowest equivalent decimal value is 0.

To see how each octet in an IP address is converted from an 8-digit binary number to an equivalent decimal number from 0 through 255, a brief example follows.

The following binary string shows the first octet in an IP address:

10001010

In this 8-digit binary number the first, fifth, and seventh bit places are filled with ones. All other bit places are filled with zeroes. By using Table A.3 as a reference, you can perform simple addition of each bit place's decimal equivalent value to find the decimal sum for this octet string, as follows:

First bit (128) + Fifth bit (8) + Seventh bit (2) = octet total (138)

Because the sum is 138, the first octet of the example IP address is 138. After using this method on the other octets, the final result of the conversion is the dotted decimal equivalent, 138.57.7.27.

TCP/IP Utilities

This section covers,

- Windows 2000 utilities
- Command-line utilities

Windows 2000 Utilities

Table A.4 lists the TCP/IP diagnostic utilities that are included with Windows 2000. You can use these utilities to help identify or resolve TCP/IP networking problems. Further information about these utilities is included in Appendix E, "TCP/IP Utilities."

Table A.5 lists additional Windows 2000 administrative utilities you can use for TCP/IP troubleshooting:

TABLE A.4 *Windows 2000 TCP/IP Diagnostic Utilities*

Utility	Description
ARP	Allows viewing and editing of the ARP cache. The ARP cache contains software-to-hardware address mappings used by Windows 2000 for sending data on the local network.
Hostname	Displays the host name of the computer as used for authentication by the Rcp, Rsh, and Rexec utilities.
Ipconfig	Displays current TCP/IP configuration values. Also used to manually release and renew a TCP/IP configuration lease assigned by a DHCP server and to reset DNS name registrations.
LPQ	Displays print queue status information on computers running Line Printer Daemon (LPD) print server software.
Nbtstat	Checks the state of current NetBIOS over TCP/IP connections, updates the Lmhosts cache, and determines the registered names and scope ID.
Netstat	Displays protocol statistics and information on current TCP/IP connections.
Nslookup	Checks records, domain host aliases, domain host services, and operating system information by querying DNS server.
Ping	Verifies whether TCP/IP is configured correctly and tests connectivity to other host systems.
Route	Allows viewing and editing of the local IP routing table.
Tracert	Traces the network route taken by an IP datagram to its destination.
Pathping	Traces the route a packet takes to a destination and displays information on packet losses for each router in the path. Pathping can also be used to troubleshoot Quality of Service (QoS) connectivity.

TABLE A.5 *Windows 2000 Administrative Utilities for TCP/IP Troubleshooting*

Administrative tool	Description
SNMP service	Provides statistical information to SNMP management systems.
Event Viewer	Tracks errors and events.
Performance Logs and Alerts	Analyzes TCP/IP core protocol performance when the SNMP service is installed.
Network Monitor	Captures and analyzes TCP/IP to and from a computer running Windows 2000 Server.
Registry Editor	Allows viewing and editing of registry settings.

Command-line Utilities

This section covers,

- Viewing configuration by using ipconfig /all
- Refreshing configuration by using ipconfig /renew
- Managing DNS and DHCP class IDs by using ipconfig
- Testing connections by using ping
- Troubleshooting hardware addresses by using arp

- Troubleshooting NetBIOS names by using nbtstat
- Displaying connection statistics by using netstat
- Tracing network connections by using tracert
- Testing routers by using pathping

VIEWING CONFIGURATION BY USING IPCONFIG /ALL

When you troubleshoot a TCP/IP networking problem, begin by checking the TCP/IP configuration on the computer that is experiencing the problem. You can use the ipconfig command to get host computer configuration information, including the IP address, subnet mask, and default gateway.

Note For Windows 95 and Windows 98 clients, use the winipcfg command instead of ipconfig.

When you use the ipconfig command with the /all option, a detailed configuration report is produced for all interfaces, including any configured serial ports. With ipconfig /all, you can redirect command output to a file and paste the output into other documents. You can also use this output to confirm the TCP/IP configuration of each computer on the network or to further investigate TCP/IP network problems. For example, if a computer is configured with an IP address that is a duplicate of an existing IP address, the subnet mask appears as 0.0.0.0.

The following example shows the output of the ipconfig /all command on a computer that is configured to use the DHCP server for automatic TCP/IP configuration, and WINS and DNS servers for name resolution.

```
Windows 2000 IP Configuration

        Node Type . . . . . . . . . : Hybrid
        IP Routing Enabled. . . . . : No
        WINS Proxy Enabled. . . . . : No

Ethernet adapter Local Area Connection:

        Host Name . . . . . . . . . : corp1.microsoft.com
        DNS Servers . . . . . . . . : 10.1.0.200
        Description . . . . . . . . : 3Com 3C90x Ethernet Adapter
        Physical Address. . . . . . : 00-60-08-3E-46-07
        DHCP Enabled. . . . . . . . : Yes
        Autoconfiguration Enabled . : Yes
        IP Address. . . . . . . . . : 192.168.0.112
        Subnet Mask . . . . . . . . : 255.255.0.0
        Default Gateway . . . . . . : 192.168.0.1
        DHCP Server . . . . . . . . : 10.1.0.50
        Primary WINS Server . . . . : 10.1.0.101
        Secondary WINS Server . . . : 10.1.0.102
        Lease Obtained. . . . . . . : Wednesday, September 02, 1998 10:32:13 AM
        Lease Expires . . . . . . . : Friday, September 18, 1998 10:32:13 AM
```

If no problems appear in the TCP/IP configuration, the next step is testing the ability to connect to other host computers on the TCP/IP network.

REFRESHING CONFIGURATION BY USING IPCONFIG /RENEW

When you troubleshoot a TCP/IP networking problem, begin by checking the TCP/IP configuration on the computer that is experiencing the problem. If the computer is DHCP-enabled and is using a DHCP server to obtain configuration, you can initiate a refresh of the lease by using the ipconfig /renew command.

When you use ipconfig /renew, all network adapters on the computer that uses DHCP (except those that are manually configured) try to contact a DHCP server and renew their existing configuration or obtain a new configuration.

You can also use the ipconfig command with the /release option to immediately release the current DHCP configuration for a host. For more information about DHCP and the lease process, see Chapter 3, "DHCP Overview."

Note For Windows 95 and Windows 98 DHCP-enabled clients, use the release and renew options of the winipcfg command instead of ipconfig /release and ipconfig /renew to perform manual release or renewal of the IP configuration lease for a client.

MANAGING DNS AND DHCP CLASS IDS BY USING IPCONFIG

You can also use the ipconfig command to

- *Display or reset the DNS cache.* For more information, see Chapter 10, "Installing and Maintaining DNS Servers."
- *Refresh registered DNS names.* For more information, see Chapter 10.
- *Display the DHCP class IDs for an adapter.* For more information, see Chapter 5, "Installation and Administration of DHCP Servers and Clients."
- *Set the DHCP class IDs for an adapter.* For more information, see Chapter 5.

TESTING CONNECTIONS BY USING PING

The ping command helps to verify IP-level connectivity. When troubleshooting, you can use ping to send an ICMP echo request to a target host name or IP address. Use ping whenever you need to verify that a host computer can connect to the TCP/IP network and network resources. You can also use ping to isolate network hardware problems and incompatible configurations

It is usually best to verify that a route exists between the local computer and a network host by first using the ping command and the IP address of the network host to which you want to connect. Try pinging the IP address of the target host to see if it responds, as follows:

ping *IP_address*

You should perform the following steps when using ping:

1. Ping the loopback address to verify that TCP/IP is installed and configured correctly on the local computer.

   ping 127.0.0.1

2. Ping the IP address of the local computer to verify that it was added to the network correctly.

   ping *IP_address_of_local_host*

3. Ping the IP address of the default gateway to verify that the default gateway is functioning and that you can communicate with a local host on the local network.

   ping *IP_address_of_default_gateway*

4. Ping the IP address of a remote host to verify that you can communicate through a router.

   ping *IP_address_of_remote_host*

The ping command uses Windows Sockets-style name resolution to resolve a computer name to an IP address, so if pinging by address succeeds, but pinging by name fails, then the problem lies in address or name resolution, not network connectivity. For more information, see "Troubleshooting Hardware Addresses by Using ARP" in this appendix.

If you cannot use ping successfully at any point, confirm that

- The computer was restarted after TCP/IP was installed and configured.
- The IP address of the local computer is valid and appears correctly on the **General** tab of the **Internet Protocol (TCP/IP) Properties** dialog box.
- IP routing is enabled and the link between routers is operational.

You can use different options with the ping command to specify the size of packets to use, how many packets to send, whether to record the route used, what Time-to-Live (TTL) value to use, and whether to set the "don't fragment" flag. You can type *ping -?* to see these options.

The following example illustrates how to send two pings, each 1,450 bytes in size, to IP address 172.16.48.10:

```
C:\>ping -n 2 -l 1450 172.16.48.10
Pinging 172.16.48.10 with 1450 bytes of data:

Reply from 172.16.48.10: bytes=1450 time<10ms TTL=32
Reply from 172.16.48.10: bytes=1450 time<10ms TTL=32

Ping statistics for 157.59.8.1:
Packets: Sent = 2, Received = 2, Lost = 0 (0% loss),
Approximate roundtrip times in milli-seconds:
Minimum = 0ms, Maximum = 10ms, Average = 2ms
```

By default, ping waits 1,000 ms (1 second) for each response to be returned before displaying the "Request Timed Out" message. If the remote system being pinged is across a high-delay link, such as a satellite link, responses may take longer to be returned. You can use the -w (wait) option to specify a longer time-out

TROUBLESHOOTING HARDWARE ADDRESSES BY USING ARP

The Address Resolution Protocol allows a host to find the media access control address of a host on the same physical network, given the IP address of the host. To make ARP efficient, each computer caches IP-to-media access control address mappings to eliminate repetitive ARP broadcast requests.

You can use the arp command to view and modify the ARP table entries on the local computer. The arp command is useful for viewing the ARP cache and resolving address resolution problems. For more information, see Chapter 2, "Installing, Managing, and Diagnosing TCP/IP."

TROUBLESHOOTING NETBIOS NAMES BY USING NBTSTAT

NetBIOS over TCP/IP (NetBT) resolves NetBIOS names to IP addresses. TCP/IP provides many options for NetBIOS name resolution, including local cache lookup, WINS server query, broadcast, DNS server query, and lmhosts and Hosts file lookup.

- Nbtstat is a useful tool for troubleshooting NetBIOS name resolution problems. You can use the **nbtstat** command to remove or correct preloaded entries.
- **nbtstat -n** displays the names that were registered locally on the system by programs such as the server and redirector.
- **nbtstat -c** shows the NetBIOS name cache, which contains name-to-address mappings for other computers.
- **nbtstat -R** purges the name cache and reloads it from the Lmhosts file.
- **nbtstat -RR** releases NetBIOS names registered with a WINS server and then renews their registration.
- **nbtstat -a** *name* performs a NetBIOS adapter status command against the computer specified by *name*. The adapter status command

returns the local NetBIOS name table for that computer plus the media access control address of the adapter.

- **nbtstat -S** lists the current NetBIOS sessions and their status, including statistics, as shown in the following example:

```
NetBIOS connection table
Local name State     In/out Remote Host    Input Output
-----------------------------------------------------------
CORP1 <00> Connected Out    CORPSUP1<20>   6MB   5MB
CORP1 <00> Connected Out    CORPPRINT<20>  108KB 116KB
CORP1 <00> Connected Out    CORPSRC1<20>   299KB 19KB
CORP1 <00> Connected Out    CORPEMAIL1<20> 324KB 19KB
CORP1 <03> Listening
```

DISPLAYING CONNECTION STATISTICS BY USING NETSTAT

You can use the netstat command to display protocol statistics and current TCP/IP connections. The netstat -a command displays all connections, and netstat -r displays the route table plus active connections. The netstat -e command displays Ethernet statistics, and netstat -s displays per-protocol statistics. If you use netstat -n, addresses and port numbers are not converted to names. The following shows sample output for netstat:

```
C:\>netstat -e
Interface Statistics

                       Received       Sent
Bytes                  3995837940     47224622
Unicast packets        120099         131015
Non-unicast packets    7579544        3823
Discards               0              0
Errors                 0              0
Unknown protocols      363054211

C:\>netstat -a

Active Connections

 Proto Local Address    Foreign Address              State
 TCP   CORP1:1572       172.16.48.10:nbsession       ESTABLISHED
 TCP   CORP1:1589       172.16.48.10:nbsession       ESTABLISHED
 TCP   CORP1:1606       172.16.105.245:nbsession     ESTABLISHED
 TCP   CORP1:1632       172.16.48.213:nbsession      ESTABLISHED
 TCP   CORP1:1659       172.16.48.169:nbsession      ESTABLISHED
 TCP   CORP1:1714       172.16.48.203:nbsession      ESTABLISHED
 TCP   CORP1:1719       172.16.48.36:nbsession       ESTABLISHED
 TCP   CORP1:1241       172.16.48.101:nbsession      ESTABLISHED
 UDP   CORP1:1025       *:*
 UDP   CORP1:snmp       *:*
 UDP   CORP1:nbname     *:*
 UDP   CORP1:nbdatagram *:*
 UDP   CORP1:nbname     *:*
 UDP   CORP1:nbdatagram *:*
```

```
C:\>netstat -s
IP Statistics

 Packets Received                   = 5378528
 Received Header Errors             = 738854
 Received Address Errors            = 23150
 Datagrams Forwarded                = 0
 Unknown Protocols Received         = 0
 Received Packets Discarded         = 0
 Received Packets Delivered         = 4616524
 Output Requests                    = 132702
 Routing Discards                   = 157
 Discarded Output Packets           = 0
 Output Packet No Route             = 0
 Reassembly Required                = 0
 Reassembly Successful                   = 0
 Reassembly Failures                     = 0
 Datagrams Successfully Fragmented = 0
 Datagrams Failing Fragmentation         = 0
 Fragments Created                       = 0

ICMP Statistics
                          Received  Sent
 Messages                 693       4
 Errors                   0         0
 Destination Unreachable  685       0
 Time Exceeded            0         0
 Parameter Problems       0         0
 Source Quenches          0         0
 Redirects                0         0
 Echoes                   4         0
 Echo Replies             0         4
 Timestamps               0         0
 Timestamp Replies        0         0
 Address Masks            0         0
 Address Mask Replies     0         0

TCP Statistics

 Active Opens                       = 597
 Passive Opens                      = 135
 Failed Connection Attempts         = 107
 Reset Connections                  = 91
 Current Connections                = 8
 Segments Received                  = 106770
 Segments Sent                      = 118431
 Segments Retransmitted             = 461

 UDP Statistics

 Datagrams Received     = 4157136
 No Ports               = 351928
 Receive Errors         = 2
 Datagrams Sent         = 13809
```

TRACING NETWORK CONNECTIONS BY USING TRACERT

Tracert (Trace Route) is a route-tracing utility that is used to determine the path that an IP datagram takes to reach a destination. The tracert command uses the IP TTL field and ICMP error messages to determine the route from one host to another through a network.

HOW TRACERT WORKS • The Tracert diagnostic utility determines the route taken to a destination by sending ICMP echo packets with varying IP TTL values to the destination. Each router along the path is required to decrement the TTL on a packet by at least 1 before forwarding it. When the TTL on a packet reaches 0, the router should send an "ICMP Time Exceeded" message back to the source computer.

Tracert determines the route by sending the first echo packet with a TTL of 1 and incrementing the TTL by 1 on each subsequent transmission until the target responds or the maximum TTL is reached. The route is determined by examining the "ICMP Time Exceeded" messages sent back by intermediate routers. Some routers silently drop packets with expired TTLs and are invisible to the Tracert utility.

The tracert command prints out an ordered list of the near-side interface of the routers in the path that returned the "ICMP Time Exceeded" message. If the -d option is used, the Tracert utility does not perform a DNS lookup on each IP address.

In the following example, the packet must travel through two routers (10.0.0.1 and 192.168.0.1) to get to host 172.16.0.99. The default gateway of the host is 10.0.0.1 and the IP address of the router on the 192.168.0.0 network is 192.168.0.1.

```
C:\>tracert 172.16.0.99 -d
Tracing route to 172.16.0.99 over a maximum of 30 hops
1  2 ms  3 ms  2 ms 10.0.0.1
2 75 ms 83 ms 88 ms 192.168.0.1
3 73 ms 79 ms 93 ms 172.16.0.99 Trace complete.
```

TROUBLESHOOTING WITH TRACERT • You can use the tracert command to determine where a packet stopped on the network. In the following example, the default gateway has determined that there is not a valid path for the host on 192.168.10.99. There is probably a router configuration problem or the 192.168.10.0 network does not exist (a bad IP address).

```
C:\>tracert 192.168.10.99

Tracing route to 192.168.10.99 over a maximum of 30 hops

1 10.0.0.1 reports: Destination net unreachable.

Trace complete.
```

The Tracert utility is useful for troubleshooting large networks where several paths can be taken to arrive at the same point.

TRACERT COMMAND-LINE OPTIONS • The **tracert** command supports several options, as shown in Table A.6.

TABLE A.6 *tracert [-d] [-h maximum_hops] [-j host-list] [-w timeout] target_name*

Option	Description
-d	Specifies that IP addresses are not resolved to host names.
-h maximum_hops	Specifies the number of hops to allow in tracing a route to the host named in *target_name*.
-j host-list	Specifies the list of router interfaces in the path taken by the Tracert utility packets.
-w timeout	Waits the number of milliseconds specified by timeout for each reply.
target_name	Name or IP address of the target host.

For more information about tracing a path using the tracert command, see Chapter 2.

TESTING ROUTERS BY USING PATHPING

The pathping command is a route-tracing tool that combines features of the ping and tracert commands with additional information that neither of those tools provides. The pathping command sends packets to each router on the way to a final destination over a period of time, and then computes results based on the packets returned from each hop. Since the command shows the degree of packet loss at any given router or link, it is easy to determine which routers or links might be causing network problems. A number of options are available, as shown in Table A.7.

TABLE A.7 *pathping Command Options*

Option	Name	Function
-n	Hostnames	Does not resolve addresses to host names.
-h	Maximum hops	Maximum number of hops to search for target.
-g	Host-list	Loose source route along host list.
-p	Period	Number of milliseconds to wait between pings.
-q	Num_queries	Number of queries per hop.
-w	Time-out	Waits this many milliseconds for each reply.
-T	Layer 2 tag	Attaches a layer-2 priority tag (for example, for IEEE 802.1p) to the packets and sends it to each of the network devices in the path. This helps in identifying the network devices that do not have layer-2 priority configured properly. The -T switch is used to test for QoS connectivity.
-R	RSVP test	Checks to determine whether each router in the path supports the RSVP, which allows the host computer to reserve a certain amount of bandwidth for a data stream. The -R switch is used to test for QoS connectivity.

The default number of hops is 30, and the default wait time before a time-out is 3 seconds. The default period is 250 milliseconds, and the default number of queries to each router along the path is 100.

The following is a typical pathping report. The compiled statistics that follow the hop list indicate packet loss at each individual router.

```
D:\>pathping -n msw

Tracing route to msw [7.54.1.196]
over a maximum of 30 hops:
  0  172.16.87.35
  1  172.16.87.218
  2  192.68.52.1
  3  192.68.80.1
  4  7.54.247.14
  5  7.54.1.196

Computing statistics for 125 seconds...
            Source to Here   This Node/Link
Hop RTT     Lost/Sent = Pct  Lost/Sent = Pct  Address
  0                                           172.16.87.35
                                0/ 100 =  0%   |
  1 41ms       0/ 100 =  0%     0/ 100 =  0%  172.16.87.218
                               13/ 100 = 13%   |
  2 22ms      16/ 100 = 16%     3/ 100 =  3%  192.68.52.1
                                0/ 100 =  0%   |
  3 24ms      13/ 100 = 13%     0/ 100 =  0%  192.68.80.1
                                0/ 100 =  0%   |
  4 21ms      14/ 100 = 14%     1/ 100 =  1%  10.54.247.14
                                0/ 100 =  0%   |
  5 24ms      13/ 100 = 13%     0/ 100 =  0%  10.54.1.196

Trace complete.
```

When pathping is run, you first see the results for the route as it is tested for problems. This is the same path that is shown by the tracert command. The pathping command then displays a busy message for the next 125 seconds (this time varies by the hop count). During this time, pathping gathers information from all the routers previously listed and from the links between them. At the end of this period, it displays the test results.

The two rightmost columns—This Node/Link Lost/Sent=Pct and Address—contain the most useful information. The link between 172.16.87.218 (hop 1) and 192.68.52.1 (hop 2) is dropping 13 percent of the packets. All other links are working normally. The routers at hops 2 and 4 also drop packets addressed to them (as shown in the This Node/Link column), but this loss does not affect their forwarding path.

The loss rates displayed for the links (marked as a | in the rightmost column) indicate losses of packets being forwarded along the path. This loss indicates link congestion. The loss rates displayed for routers (indicated by their IP addresses in the rightmost column) indicate that those routers' CPUs might be overloaded. These congested routers might also be a factor in end-to-end problems, especially if packets are forwarded by software routers.

TCP/IP Database Files

Table A.8 lists the UNIX-style database files that are stored in the *systemroot\System32\Drivers\Etc* folder when you install TCP/IP for Windows 2000.

TABLE A.8 *UNIX-style Database Files in TCP/IP for Windows 2000*

File name	Use
Hosts	Provides host name-to-IP address resolution for Windows Sockets programs.
Lmhosts	Provides NetBIOS name-to-IP address resolution for Windows-based networking.
Networks	Provides network name-to-network ID resolution for Windows Sockets programs.
Protocols	Provides protocol name-to-protocol ID resolution for Windows Sockets programs.
Services	Provides service name-to-port ID resolution for Windows Sockets programs.

To troubleshoot any of these files on a local computer, do the following:

1. Make sure the format of entries in each file matches the format defined in the sample file originally installed with TCP/IP for Windows 2000.
2. Check for spelling errors.
3. Check for invalid IP addresses and identifiers.

Note By default, the Lmhosts file does not exist. There is an Lmhosts.sam sample file that you can use as a basis for creating an Lmhosts file.

Using Performance Logs and Alerts

You can use the Windows 2000 Performance Logs and Alerts to view many different TCP/IP-related counters. Because the Performance Logs and Alerts access statistics that are gathered by the SNMP service, the SNMP service must be installed on computers running Windows 2000 where TCP/IP statistics are to be monitored. Counters for Performance Logs and Alerts are available for network adapters, IP, ICMP, UDP, and TCP.

With Performance Logs and Alerts, you can monitor counters from various systems from a single management window. You can also set alert levels for the counters being monitored.

Troubleshooting

1. Host name resolution is failing.

Cause: Host name resolution techniques are failing to resolve a host name to its IP address.

Solution: Windows 2000 includes several basic TCP/IP tools that you can use to troubleshoot address and name resolution problems, including the ping command. If you receive the correct response when you use the ping command with an IP address but an incorrect response when you use ping with the host name or NetBIOS name, there is a name resolution problem.

When you use TCP/IP tools such as the ping command, the Hosts file or a DNS server is used for name resolution. You can find the Hosts file in the *systemroot\System32\Drivers\Etc* folder. This file is *not* dynamic; you must manually add entries. The format of the file is as follows:

IP address	Friendly name	
`172.16.48.10`	`jsmith`	`# Remarks are denoted with a #.`

When you use a Hosts file for name resolution, the following steps occur:

a. A user at Computer A enters a command by using the host name of Computer B.

b. The Hosts file on Computer A (in the *systemroot\System32\Drivers\Etc* folder) is parsed. When the host name of Computer B is found, it is resolved to an IP address.

The following problems can occur because of errors related to the Hosts file:

- The Hosts file or the DNS server does not contain the particular host name.
- The host name in the Hosts file or in the command is misspelled.
- An invalid IP address is entered for the host name in the Hosts file.
- The Hosts file contains multiple entries for the same host on separate lines; if so, the first entry from the top of the file is used.
- A mapping for a computer name-to-IP address was mistakenly added to the Hosts file, rather than to the Lmhosts file.

For DNS server host name resolution, verify that the correct DNS servers are configured and in the proper order. You can use the ipconfig /all command to check the current TCP/IP configuration and the ping command to check connectivity with your DNS servers. You can use the nslookup command to send DNS name queries to your primary DNS server.

If you use a DNS server for host name resolution, the name resolution steps are similar. Computer A sends a DNS name query to its configured DNS server. The DNS server resolves the host name of Computer B to an IP address and sends the results back to Computer A.

2. Unable to add a default gateway.

   Cause: The IP address of the default gateway is not on the same IP network ID as your IP address.

   Solution: Find out whether the default gateway is located on the same logical network as the network adapter of the computer by comparing the IP address of the default gateway with the network IDs of any of the network adapters of the computer. For example, a computer with a single network adapter that is configured with an IP address of 192.168.0.33 and a subnet mask of 255.255.0.0 requires that the default gateway be in the form 192.168.y.z because the network ID portion of the IP interface is 192.168.0.0.

3. System error 53 occurred.

   Cause: System error 53 is returned if name resolution fails for a particular computer name when the net use command is used.

   Solution: If the computer is on the local subnet, confirm that the name is spelled correctly and that the target computer is running TCP/IP as well. If the computer is not on the local subnet, be sure that its name and IP address mapping are available in the Lmhosts file or the WINS database. If all TCP/IP elements appear to be installed properly, use the ping command with the remote computer to verify that its TCP/IP software is working.

4. Cannot connect to a specific server.

   Cause: Either NetBIOS name resolution is failing to resolve the name or the wrong IP address is being resolved.

   Solution: Use the nbtstat -n command on the server to determine what names the server registered on the network. The computer name of the computer you are trying to connect to should be on the displayed list. If the name is not listed, try one of the other unique computer names displayed by nbtstat. If the name being used by a remote computer is the same as the name displayed by the nbtstat -n command, then make sure that the remote computer has an entry for the server name on the WINS server or in its Lmhosts file.

5. Long connect times when using Lmhosts for name resolution.

   Cause: The Lmhosts file is parsed sequentially to locate entries without the #PRE option.

   Solution: Place frequently used entries near the top of the file and place the #PRE entries near the bottom. If an entry is added to the end of a large Lmhosts file, mark the entry in Lmhosts as a preloaded entry by using the #PRE option. Then use the nbtstat -R command to update the local name cache immediately.

6. **TCP/IP connection to a host appears to be hung.**

   Cause: Either data is blocked in TCP and UDP queues or there are network or application delay problems.

   Solution: Use the netstat -a command to show the status of all activity on TCP and UDP ports on the local computer. The state of a good TCP connection is usually established with 0 bytes in the send and receive queues. If data is blocked in either queue, or if the state is irregular, there is probably a problem with the connection. If not, you are probably experiencing a network or application delay.

7. Cannot ping across a local router when using a dial-up connection.

   Cause: This problem occurs if the **Use default gateway on remote network** check box is selected on the **General** tab in the **Advanced TCP/IP Settings** dialog box (in the **Internet Protocol (TCP/IP)** dialog box on the **General** or **Networking** tab for the properties of the dial-up connection). This feature adds a default route to the IP routing table that is used instead of the current default route for the duration of the connection. The new default route causes network traffic for IP addresses that are not resolved by other entries in the routing table to be sent across the dial-up connection. This new default route is needed when you dial an Internet service provider and use Internet utilities, such as a Web browser or FTP, to access Internet resources.

   Solution: If you want to ping or otherwise connect to computers in a remote network segment across a local router while you are connected as a dial-up client to an ISP, then use the route add command to add the route of the network segment you are attempting to reach by specifying the destination network and subnet mask of the remote network segment and the IP address of the local router.

8. A "The registry subkey already exists" message is displayed.

   Cause: The registry keys for a component being installed already exist.

   Solution: Ensure that all the components of a given TCP/IP service are properly removed, and then remove the appropriate registry subkeys by using the Windows 2000 Registry Editor.

   If you removed TCP/IP and its related service components, you must also remove the following registry subkeys:

   - HKEY_LOCAL_MACHINE\SYSTEM\CurrentControlSet\Services\NetBT
   - HKEY_LOCAL_MACHINE\SYSTEM\CurrentControlSet\Services\Tcpip
   - HKEY_LOCAL_MACHINE\SYSTEM\CurrentControlSet\Services\TcpipCU
   - HKEY_LOCAL_MACHINE\SYSTEM\CurrentControlSet\Services\Dhcp

- HKEY_LOCAL_MACHINE\SYSTEM\CurrentControlSet\Services\Lmhosts
- HKEY_LOCAL_MACHINE\SYSTEM\CurrentControlSet\Services*AdapterName*\Parameters\Tcpip

If you removed the SNMP service components, you must also remove the following registry subkeys:

- HKEY_LOCAL_MACHINE\SOFTWARE\Microsoft\RFC1156Agent
- HKEY_LOCAL_MACHINE\SOFTWARE\Microsoft\Snmp
- HKEY_LOCAL_MACHINE\SYSTEM\CurrentControlSet\Services\Snmp

If you removed the TCP/IP Printing service components, you must also remove the following registry subkeys:

- HKEY_LOCAL_MACHINE\SOFTWARE\Microsoft\Lpdsvc
- HKEY_LOCAL_MACHINE\SOFTWARE\Microsoft\TcpPrint
- HKEY_LOCAL_MACHINE\SYSTEM\CurrentControlSet\Services\LpdsvcSimple TCP/IP Services

If you removed the Simple TCP/IP Services components, you must also remove the following registry subkeys:

- HKEY_LOCAL_MACHINE\SOFTWARE\Microsoft\SimpTcp
- HKEY_LOCAL_MACHINE\SYSTEM\CurrentControlSet\Services\SimpTcp

If you removed the DHCP service components, you must also remove the following registry subkeys:

- HKEY_LOCAL_MACHINE\SOFTWARE\Microsoft\DhcpMibAgent
- HKEY_LOCAL_MACHINE\SOFTWARE\Microsoft\DhcpServer
- HKEY_LOCAL_MACHINE\SYSTEM\CurrentControlSet\Services\DhcpServer

If you removed the WINS service components, you must also remove the following registry subkeys:

- HKEY_LOCAL_MACHINE\SOFTWARE\Microsoft\Wins
- HKEY_LOCAL_MACHINE\SOFTWARE\Microsoft\WinsMibAgent
- HKEY_LOCAL_MACHINE\SYSTEM\CurrentControlSet\Services\Wins

If you removed the DNS service components, you must also remove the following registry subkeys:

- HKEY_LOCAL_MACHINE\SOFTWARE\Microsoft\Dns
- HKEY_LOCAL_MACHINE\SYSTEM\CurrentControlSet\Services\Dns

APPENDIX B

DHCP Resources and Troubleshooting

This appendix covers,

- DHCP options reference
- DHCP RFCs
- DHCP database files
- Netshell commands for DHCP
- DHCP performance monitoring reference
- DHCP updated technical information
- DHCP bibliography
- Troubleshooting

DHCP Options Reference

This section covers,

- Standard DHCP and BOOTP options
- Advanced and new options
- Microsoft options

Standard DHCP and BOOTP Options

The following topics provide descriptions of all predefined options available for use with Windows 2000 DHCP and all earlier versions of Microsoft-based DHCP servers. These options are defined according to the updated standards reference for DHCP options (RFC 2132, "DHCP Options and BOOTP Vendor Extensions").

- Basic options (RFC 1497)
- IP host options

- IP interface options
- Link layer options
- TCP options
- Application layer options
- NetBIOS over TCP/IP options

BASIC OPTIONS (RFC 1497)

Tables B.1–B.20 describe the basic DHCP option types originally defined in RFC 1497 for use with DHCP and BOOTP service. In BOOTP service, these option types are referred to as vendor extensions.

TABLE B.1 *Pad*

Code:	0
Length:	(Not used)
Value:	(Not used)
Description:	This option type is a single octet of zero (00) used for padding. This option differs from most DHCP option types in that it does not use a length or value field. Where used, this option causes subsequent DHCP option types as they appear in the DHCP packet to align on word boundaries. This option does not require configuration.
Structure:	(see below)

```
Code
+-----+
|  0  |
+-----+
```

TABLE B.2 *End*

Code:	255
Length:	(Not used)
Value:	(Not used)
Description:	This option is a single octet of decimal 255 (FF) used to indicate the end of a DHCP options area in DHCP message packets. This option differs from most DHCP option types because it does not use a length or value field. Typically, it is used at the end of the options field to indicate that there is no more options data in a DHCP message packet. It can also be used within the message, in connection with the vendor specific information (option 43), to indicate the end of an encapsulated vendor specific options subfield. This option does not require configuration.
Structure:	(see below)

```
Code
+-----+
| 255 |
+-----+
```

TABLE B.3 *Subnet Mask*

Code:	1
Length:	Fixed, 4 octets.
Value:	Signed 32-bit integer representing the subnet mask for an IP address provided in a DHCP message.
Description:	Specifies the subnet mask of the client subnet, as described in RFC 950, "Internet Standard Subnetting Procedure." The value for this option type is taken from the **Subnet Mask** field, as defined in a DHCP scope **Properties** dialog box in the DHCP console.
Structure:	see below

```
 Code   Len         Subnet mask
+-----+-----+-----+-----+-----+-----+
|  1  |  4  | m1  | m2  | m3  | m4  |
+-----+-----+-----+-----+-----+-----+
```

TABLE B.4 *Time Offset*

Code:	2
Length:	Fixed, 4 octets.
Value:	Signed 32-bit integer used for offset of UCT time.
Description:	Specifies an offset value (in seconds) from the Universal Coordinated Time (UCT) that applies to the client subnet. This value is configured as a signed 32-bit integer. Positive offset values indicate a subnet location east of the zero meridian. Negative offset values indicate a subnet location west of the zero meridian.
Structure:	see below

```
 Code   Len         Time offset
+-----+-----+-----+-----+-----+-----+
|  2  |  4  | n1  | n2  | n3  | n4  |
+-----+-----+-----+-----+-----+-----+
```

TABLE B.5 *Router*

Code:	3
Length:	Variable, minimum length of 4 octets. Octet length increases in multiples of 4 for each router address listed.
Value:	Signed 32-bit integer representing IP address of each assigned router.
Description:	Specifies a list of IP addresses for routers on the subnet of the client. When more than one router is assigned, the client interprets and uses the addresses in the specified order.
Structure:	see below

```
 Code   Len         Address 1                     Address 2
+-----+-----+-----+-----+-----+-----+-----+-----+--
|  3  |  n  | a1  | a2  | a3  | a4  | a1  | a2  |  ...
+-----+-----+-----+-----+-----+-----+-----+-----+--
```

TABLE B.6 *Time Server*

Code:	4
Length:	Variable, minimum length of 4 octets. Octet length increases in multiples of 4 for each RFC 868 time server address listed.
Value:	Signed 32-bit integer representing IP address of each assigned RFC 868 time server.
Description:	Specifies a list of IP addresses for RFC 868 time servers that are available to the client. When more than one time server is assigned, the client interprets and uses the addresses in the specified order.
Structure:	(see below)

```
 Code   Len        Address 1              Address 2
+-----+-----+-----+-----+-----+-----+-----+-----+--
|  4  |  n  | a1  | a2  | a3  | a4  | a1  | a2  |  ...
+-----+-----+-----+-----+-----+-----+-----+-----+--
```

TABLE B.7 *IEN Name Server*

Code:	5
Length:	Variable, minimum length of 4 octets. Octet length increases in multiples of 4 for each IEN name server address listed.
Value:	Signed 32-bit integer representing IP address of each assigned IEN name server.
Description:	Specifies a list of IP addresses for Internet Engineering Note (IEN) name servers available to the client. When more than one server is assigned, the client interprets and uses the addresses in the specified order.
Structure:	(see below)

```
 Code   Len        Address 1              Address 2
+-----+-----+-----+-----+-----+-----+-----+-----+--
|  5  |  n  | a1  | a2  | a3  | a4  | a1  | a2  |  ...
+-----+-----+-----+-----+-----+-----+-----+-----+--
```

TABLE B.8 *DNS Server*

Code:	6
Length:	Variable, minimum length of 4 octets. Octet length increases in multiples of 4 for each DNS server address listed.
Value:	Signed 32-bit integer representing the IP address of each assigned DNS server.
Description:	Specifies a list of IP addresses for Domain Name System (DNS) name servers available to the client. When more than one server is assigned, the client interprets and uses the addresses in the specified order. DHCP client computers that are multihomed and obtain multiple DHCP leases can have only one DNS server list per host computer, not per adapter interface.
Structure:	(see below)

```
 Code   Len        Address 1              Address 2
+-----+-----+-----+-----+-----+-----+-----+-----+--
|  6  |  n  | a1  | a2  | a3  | a4  | a1  | a2  |  ...
+-----+-----+-----+-----+-----+-----+-----+-----+--
```

TABLE B.9 *Log Server*

Code:	7
Length:	Variable, minimum length of 4 octets. Octet length increases in multiples of 4 for each log server address listed.
Value:	Signed 32-bit integer representing the IP address of each assigned log server.
Description:	Specifies a list of IP addresses for MIT-LCS UDP log servers available to the client. When more than one server is assigned, the client interprets and uses the addresses in the specified order.

Structure:

```
 Code   Len          Address 1                  Address 2
+-----+-----+-----+-----+-----+-----+-----+-----+--
|  7  |  n  | a1  | a2  | a3  | a4  | a1  | a2  |  ...
+-----+-----+-----+-----+-----+-----+-----+-----+--
```

TABLE B.10 *Cookie Server*

Code:	8
Length:	Variable, minimum length of 4 octets. Octet length increases in multiples of 4 for each cookie server address listed.
Value:	Signed 32-bit integer representing the IP address of each assigned cookie server.
Description:	Specifies a list of IP addresses for RFC 865 cookie servers available to the client. When more than one server is assigned, the client interprets and uses the addresses in the specified order.

Structure:

```
 Code   Len          Address 1                  Address 2
+-----+-----+-----+-----+-----+-----+-----+-----+--
|  8  |  n  | a1  | a2  | a3  | a4  | a1  | a2  |  ...
+-----+-----+-----+-----+-----+-----+-----+-----+--
```

TABLE B.11 *LPR Server*

Code:	9
Length:	Variable, minimum length of 4 octets. Octet length increases in multiples of 4 for each LPR server address listed.
Value:	Signed 32-bit integer representing the IP address of each assigned LPR server.
Description:	Specifies a list of IP addresses for RFC 1179 line printer servers available to the client. When more than one server is assigned, the client interprets and uses the addresses in the specified order.

Structure:

```
 Code   Len          Address 1                  Address 2
+-----+-----+-----+-----+-----+-----+-----+-----+--
|  9  |  n  | a1  | a2  | a3  | a4  | a1  | a2  |  ...
+-----+-----+-----+-----+-----+-----+-----+-----+--
```

TABLE B.12 *Impress Server*

Code:	10
Length:	Variable, minimum length of 4 octets. Octet length increases in multiples of 4 for each Impress server address listed.
Value:	Signed 32-bit integer representing IP address of each assigned Impress server.
Description:	Specifies a list of IP addresses for Imagen Impress servers available to the client. When more than one server is assigned, the client interprets and uses the addresses in the specified order.
Structure:	see below

```
 Code   Len         Address 1                Address 2
+-----+-----+-----+-----+-----+-----+-----+-----+--
|  10 |  n  | a1  | a2  | a3  | a4  | a1  | a2  |  ...
+-----+-----+-----+-----+-----+-----+-----+-----+--
```

TABLE B.13 *Resource Location Server*

Code:	11
Length:	Variable, minimum length of 4 octets. Octet length increases in multiples of 4 for each resource location server address listed.
Value:	Signed 32-bit integer representing the IP address of each assigned resource location server.
Description:	Specifies a list of IP addresses for RFC 887 resource location servers available to the client. When more than one server is assigned, the client interprets and uses the addresses in the specified order.
Structure:	see below

```
 Code   Len         Address 1                Address 2
+-----+-----+-----+-----+-----+-----+-----+-----+--
|  11 |  n  | a1  | a2  | a3  | a4  | a1  | a2  |  ...
+-----+-----+-----+-----+-----+-----+-----+-----+--
```

TABLE B.14 *Host Name*

Code:	12
Length:	Length varies depending on data in value. Minimum length is 1 octet. Maximum length is limited to 63 characters, or one octet for each character used in the host name configured for use with this option.
Value:	ASCII character text.
Description:	Specifies a host name for the client of up to 63 characters in length. (See RFC 1035 for possible character set restrictions.) In some cases, this name can also be fully qualified by appending the name value provided here with the DNS domain name, as specified in option 15. For Windows clients, this option is not supported for use when configuring the host name of the client, which is set in **Computer Name** in the **Network Identification Properties** dialog box on the client computer.
Structure:	see below

```
 Code   Len               Host name
+-----+-----+-----+-----+-----+-----+-----+-----+--
|  12 |  n  | h1  | h2  | h3  | h4  | h5  | h6  |  ...
+-----+-----+-----+-----+-----+-----+-----+-----+--
```

Table B.15 *Boot File Size*

Code: 13

Length: Fixed, 2 octets.

Value: Unsigned 16-bit integer to indicate the number of 512-octet blocks needed to make up the boot file.

Description: Specifies the size of the default boot image file for the client.

Structure:

```
 Code  Len   File size
+-----+-----+-----+-----+
| 13  | 02  | 11  | 12  |
+-----+-----+-----+-----+
```

Table B.16 *Merit Dump File*

Code: 14

Length: Length varies depending on data in value. Minimum length is 1 octet.

Value: ASCII character text.

Description: Specifies a path name of a file to which the core memory image of the client should be dumped in the event that the client fails. For this option type, data used for a value is ASCII character text. The length of the value field depends on the number of characters used in the file path name specified here. For example, if the path name entered has 20 characters, the value field for this option should also be 20 octets in length.

Structure:

```
 Code   Len      Dump file pathname
+-----+-----+-----+-----+-----+-----+---
| 14  |  n  | n1  | n2  | n3  | n4  | ...
+-----+-----+-----+-----+-----+-----+---
```

Table B.17 *DNS Domain Name*

Code: 15

Length: Length varies depending on data in value. Minimum length is 1 octet.

Value: ASCII character text.

Description: Specifies the domain name that the DHCP client should use when resolving host names using DNS. For this option type, ASCII character text is used for the data value. The length of the value field depends on the number of characters used in the DNS domain name specified here. For example, if the domain name has 20 characters, the value field for this option should also be 20 octets in length.

Structure:

```
 Code   Len        Domain name
+-----+-----+-----+-----+-----+-----+--
| 15  |  n  | d1  | d2  | d3  | d4  |  ...
+-----+-----+-----+-----+-----+-----+--
```

TABLE B.18 *Swap Server*

Code:	16
Length:	Length is fixed at 4 octets.
Value:	A single IP address for the swap server of the client (unsigned 32-bit integer).
Description:	Specifies the IP address of the swap server.
Structure:	(see below)

```
 Code   Len    Swap server address
+-----+-----+-----+-----+-----+-----+
| 16  |  n  | a1  | a2  | a3  | a4  |
+-----+-----+-----+-----+-----+-----+
```

TABLE B.19 *Root Path*

Code:	17
Length:	Length varies depending on data in value. Minimum length is 1 octet.
Value:	A single IP address for the swap server of the client (unsigned 32-bit integer).
Description:	Specifies the path name that contains the root disk of the client. The path is formatted as ASCII text. For this option type, data used for a value is ASCII character text. The length of the value field depends on the number of characters used in the root path name specified here. For example, if the root path name entered has 20 characters, the value field for this option should also be 20 octets in length.
Structure:	(see below)

```
 Code   Len      Root disk pathname
+-----+-----+-----+-----+-----+-----+---
| 17  |  n  | n1  | n2  | n3  | n4  | ...
+-----+-----+-----+-----+-----+-----+---
```

TABLE B.20 *Extensions Path*

Code:	18
Length:	Length varies depending on data in value. Minimum length is 1 octet.
Value:	ASCII character text.
Description:	Specifies a file that can be retrieved using Trivial File Transfer Protocol (TFTP) containing information to be interpreted in the same way as the 64-octet vendor-extension field within a BOOTP response. To allow more than 64 octets of BOOTP vendor extension information, this option can be used. When used, the length of the specified extension path file is not limited in size and all references in the extensions file to Tag 18 (such as instances of the BOOTP Extensions Path field) are ignored.
Structure:	(see below)

```
 Code   Len      Extensions pathname
+-----+-----+-----+-----+-----+-----+---
| 18  |  n  | n1  | n2  | n3  | n4  | ...
+-----+-----+-----+-----+-----+-----+---
```

Note For all option types provided here that use a list of IP addresses as the valued options data, IP addresses are always used in order of preference by the DHCP client. The first address in the list is used first.

Windows 2000 DHCP servers support configuration and distribution of any of these options that are assigned using the DHCP console. By default, Microsoft DHCP-enabled clients require and provide storage and interpretation only for options 1, 3, 6, and 15 of the option types listed in this section for default client configuration. Other options are predefined for assignment and distribution by Windows 2000 DHCP servers, but are recognized only when clients use other DHCP software supporting these other options.

IP HOST OPTIONS

Tables B.21–B.27 describe the DHCP options that affect operation of the IP layer on a per-host basis.

TABLE B.21 *IP Forwarding Enable/Disable*

Code: 19

Length: Fixed, 1 octet.

Value: 1 = enable IP forwarding, 0 = disable IP forwarding.

Description: Used to determine whether the DHCP client enables or disables forwarding of datagrams at the IP layer.

Structure:

```
 Code   Len  Value
+-----+-----+-----+
| 19  |  1  | 0/1 |
+-----+-----+-----+
```

TABLE B.22 *Non-Local Source Routing Enable/Disable*

Code: 20

Length: Fixed, 1 octet.

Value: 1 = enable forwarding of datagrams from non-local sources, 0 = disable forwarding of datagrams from non-local sources.

Description: Used to determine whether the DHCP client enables or disables forwarding of datagrams at the IP layer, based on whether a received datagram is from a local or non-local source.

Structure:

```
 Code   Len  Value
+-----+-----+-----+
| 20  |  1  | 0/1 |
+-----+-----+-----+
```

TABLE B.23 *Policy Filter*

Code:	21
Length:	Variable. Minimum length is 8 octets for a single destination-and-mask pairing. Length increases in multiples of 8 octets for each additional pairing used.
Value:	Two, consecutive, unsigned 32-bit integers indicating a paired value, consisting of an IP address followed by a subnet mask.
Description:	Specifies policy filters for non-local source routing on the client. The filters consist of a list of paired IP addresses specifying destination-and-mask pairs for which to filter source routes of any incoming datagrams. The client discards any source routed datagram with a next-hop address that does not match one of the filters. For further information about policy filtering as it applies to this option type, see RFC 1122.
Structure:	

```
 Code   Len         Address 1                 Mask 1
+-----+-----+-----+-----+-----+-----+-----+-----+-----+-----+
|  21 |  n  |  a1 |  a2 |  a3 |  a4 |  m1 |  m2 |  m3 |  m4 |
+-----+-----+-----+-----+-----+-----+-----+-----+-----+-----+
       Address 2               Mask 2
+-----+-----+-----+-----+-----+-----+-----+-----+---
|  a1 |  a2 |  a3 |  a4 |  m1 |  m2 |  m3 |  m4 | ...
+-----+-----+-----+-----+-----+-----+-----+-----+---
```

TABLE B.24 *Maximum Datagram Reassembly Size*

Code:	22
Length:	Fixed, 2 octets.
Value:	A 16-integer specifying the maximum datagram size for reassembly. The minimum size for a datagram is 576.
Description:	Specifies the maximum size datagram that the client can reassemble.
Structure:	

```
 Code   Len      Size
+-----+-----+-----+-----+
|  22 |  2  |  s1 |  s2 |
+-----+-----+-----+-----+
```

TABLE B.25 *Default IP Time-to-Live*

Code:	23
Length:	Fixed, 1 octet.
Value:	A number (in seconds) between 1 and 255.
Description:	Specifies the default Time-to-Live (TTL) that the client uses on outgoing datagrams.
Structure:	

```
 Code   Len   TTL
+-----+-----+-----+
|  23 |  1  | ttl |
+-----+-----+-----+
```

Table B.26 *Path MTU Aging Timeout*

Code:	24
Length:	Fixed, 4 octets.
Value:	A 32-bit unsigned integer that specifies a time-out value (in seconds).
Description:	Specifies the time-out for aging Path Maximum Transmission Unit (MTU) values. (Values are discovered by the mechanism defined in RFC 1191.)
Structure:	

```
 Code   Len              Timeout
+-----+-----+-----+-----+-----+-----+
|  24 |  4  |  t1 |  t2 |  t3 |  t4 |
+-----+-----+-----+-----+-----+-----+
```

Table B.27 *Path MTU Plateau Table*

Code:	25
Length:	Variable, minimum length of 2 octets. Where length is more than 2, it increases in multiples of 2.
Value:	A table formatted as a list of 16-bit unsigned integers, ordered from smallest to largest. The minimum tabled MTU value cannot be smaller than 68.
Description:	Specifies a table of MTU sizes to use when performing Path MTU Discovered, as defined in RFC 1191.
Structure:	

```
 Code   Len     Size 1       Size 2
+-----+-----+-----+-----+-----+-----+---
|  25 |  n  |  s1 |  s2 |  s1 |  s2 | ...
+-----+-----+-----+-----+-----+-----+---
```

IP INTERFACE OPTIONS

Tables B.28–B3.35 describe the DHCP options that affect the operation of the IP layer on a per-interface basis.

Table B.28 *Interface MTU*

Code:	26
Length:	Fixed, 2 octets.
Value:	A 16-bit, unsigned integer specifying the interface MTU. The minimum legal value for the MTU is 68.
Description:	Specifies the MTU size that can be used on a specified host adapter interface.
Structure:	

```
 Code   Len       MTU
+-----+-----+-----+-----+
|  26 |  2  |  m1 |  m2 |
+-----+-----+-----+-----+
```

TABLE B.29 *All Subnets Are Local*

Code:	27
Length:	Fixed, 1 octet.
Value:	1 = client assumes all subnets are local and share the same MTU size; 0 = client assumes some subnets are not local and that smaller MTU sizes might be in use on remote subnets.
Description:	Specifies whether the client assumes that all subnets of Internetwork use are the same MTU as the local subnet on which the client is connected.
Structure:	

```
  Code   Len  Value
+-----+-----+-----+
|  27 |  1  | 0/1 |
+-----+-----+-----+
```

TABLE B.30 *Broadcast Address*

Code:	28
Length:	Fixed, 4 octets.
Value:	Typically, the limited broadcast IP address (255.255.255.255), but can be modified using legal values for broadcast addresses, as specified in section 3.2.1.3 of RFC 1122, "Requirements for Internet Hosts—Communication Layers."
Description:	Specifies the broadcast address used on the subnet of the client.
Structure:	

```
  Code   Len     Broadcast address
+-----+-----+-----+-----+-----+-----+
|  28 |  4  | b1  | b2  | b3  | b4  |
+-----+-----+-----+-----+-----+-----+
```

TABLE B.31 *Perform Mask Discovery*

Code:	29
Length:	Fixed, 1 octet.
Value:	1 = client performs subnet mask discovery; 0 = client does not perform subnet mask discovery.
Description:	Specifies whether the client uses Internet Control Message Protocol (ICMP) for subnet mask discovery.
Structure:	

```
  Code   Len  Value
+-----+-----+-----+
|  29 |  1  | 0/1 |
+-----+-----+-----+
```

Table B.32 *Mask Supplier*

Code:	30
Length:	Fixed, 1 octet.
Value:	1 = client responds to subnet mask requests; 0 = client does not respond to subnet mask requests.
Description:	Specifies whether the client responds to subnet mask requests using ICMP.
Structure:	

```
 Code   Len  Value
+-----+-----+-----+
|  30 |  1  | 0/1 |
+-----+-----+-----+
```

Table B.33 *Perform Router Discovery*

Code:	31
Length:	Fixed, 1 octet.
Value:	1 = client performs router discovery; 0 = client does not perform router discovery.
Description:	Specifies whether the client solicits routers using the router discovery method in RFC 1256.
Structure:	

```
 Code   Len  Value
+-----+-----+-----+
|  31 |  1  | 0/1 |
+-----+-----+-----+
```

Table B.34 *Router Solicitation Address*

Code:	32
Length:	Fixed, 4 octets.
Value:	An IP address (unsigned 32-bit integer).
Description:	Specifies the IP address to which the client submits router solicitation requests.
Structure:	

```
 Code   Len           Address
+-----+-----+-----+-----+-----+-----+
|  32 |  4  | a1  | a2  | a3  | a4  |
+-----+-----+-----+-----+-----+-----+
```

TABLE B.35 *Static Router*

Code:	33
Length:	Variable, minimum length of 8 octets. Octet length increases in multiples of 8 for each additional static route provided with this option.
Value:	A list of IP address pairs. Each 8 octets provides two consecutive IP addresses, pairing the destination and router addresses used for each route. The first 4 octets specifies the destination address, and the second 4 octets specifies the router for the destination address.
Description:	Specifies a list of static routes the client installs in its routing cache. Any multiple routes to the same destination are listed in descending order of priority. The default route of 0.0.0.0 is an illegal destination for a static route.
Structure:	

```
 Code   Len          Destination 1             Router 1
+-----+-----+-----+-----+-----+-----+-----+-----+-----+-----+
| 33  |  n  | d1  | d2  | d3  | d4  | r1  | r2  | r3  | r4  |
+-----+-----+-----+-----+-----+-----+-----+-----+-----+-----+
       Destination 2           Router 2
+-----+-----+-----+-----+-----+-----+-----+-----+---
| d1  | d2  | d3  | d4  | r1  | r2  | r3  | r4  | ...
+-----+-----+-----+-----+-----+-----+-----+-----+---
```

LINK LAYER OPTIONS

Tables B.36–B.38 describe the DHCP options that affect the operation of the datalink layer on a per-interface basis.

TABLE B.36 *Trailer Encapsulation*

Code:	34
Length:	Fixed, 1 octet.
Value:	1 = client attempts to use trailer; 0 = client does not attempt to use trailers.
Description:	Specifies whether the client negotiates the use of trailers, as described in RFC 983, when using Address Resolution Protocol (ARP).
Structure:	

```
 Code   Len  Value
+-----+-----+-----+
| 34  |  1  | 0/1 |
+-----+-----+-----+
```

TABLE B.37 *ARP Cache Timeout*

Code: 35

Length: Fixed, 4 octets.

Value: An unsigned 32-bit integer specifying a time-out value (in seconds).

Description: Specifies the time-out for ARP cache entries.

Structure:

```
  Code   Len             Time
+-----+-----+-----+-----+-----+-----+
|  35 |  4  |  t1 |  t2 |  t3 |  t4 |
+-----+-----+-----+-----+-----+-----+
```

TABLE B.38 *Ethernet Encapsulation*

Code: 36

Length: Fixed, 1 octet.

Value: 1 = client uses RFC 1042 encapsulation; 0 = client uses RFC 894 encapsulation.

Description: Specifies whether the client uses Ethernet v. 2 (RFC 894) or IEEE 802.3 (RFC 1042) encapsulation if the interface is Ethernet.

Structure:

```
  Code   Len  Value
+-----+-----+-----+
|  36 |  1  | 0/1 |
+-----+-----+-----+
```

TCP OPTIONS

Tables B.39–B41 describe the DHCP options that affect the operation of the TCP session layer on a per-interface basis.

TABLE B.39 *TCP Default TTL*

Code: 37

Length: Fixed, 1 octet.

Value: An unsigned 8-bit integer specifying a TTL value (in seconds). The minimum TTL value is 1.

Description: Specifies the default TTL the client uses when sending TCP segments.

Structure:

```
  Code   Len   TTL
+-----+-----+-----+
|  37 |  1  |  n  |
+-----+-----+-----+
```

TABLE B.40 *TCP Keepalive Interval*

Code: 38

Length: Fixed, 4 octets.

Value: An unsigned 32-bit integer that specifies a keepalive interval (in seconds).

Description: Specifies the interval the client waits before sending a keepalive message on a TCP connection. A value of 0 indicates that the client does not send keepalive messages on connections unless specifically requested by an application.

Structure:

```
 Code   Len            Time
+-----+-----+-----+-----+-----+-----+
|  38 |  4  |  t1 |  t2 |  t3 |  t4 |
+-----+-----+-----+-----+-----+-----+
```

TABLE B.41 *TCP Keepalive Garbage*

Code: 39

Length: Fixed, 1 octet.

Value: 1 = client sends keepalive garbage octet; 0 = client does not send keepalive garbage octet.

Description: Specifies whether the client sends TCP keepalive messages with an octet of garbage data for compatibility with older implementations.

Structure:

```
 Code   Len  Value
+-----+-----+-----+
|  39 |  1  | 0/1 |
+-----+-----+-----+
```

APPLICATION LAYER OPTIONS

Tables B.42–B.49 describe the DHCP options that affect the operation of the application layer on a per-interface basis. These are miscellaneous options you can use to configure programs and services.

For these options, you can dynamically configure DHCP clients that have more than one interface on a per-interface basis using additional DHCP leases (one per interface) for any of these option types.

TABLE B.42 *NIS Domain Name*

Code: 40

Length: Length varies depending on data in value. Minimum length is 1 octet.

Value: ASCII character text.

Description: Specifies the Network Information Service (NIS) domain name as an ASCII string.

Structure:

```
 Code   Len      NIS domain name
+-----+-----+-----+-----+-----+-----+---
|  40 |  n  |  n1 |  n2 |  n3 |  n4 | ...
+-----+-----+-----+-----+-----+-----+---
```

TABLE B.43 *NIS Servers*

Code:	41
Length:	Variable, minimum length is 4 octets. Octet length increases in multiples of 4 for each server address listed.
Value:	Signed 32-bit integer representing IP address of NIS server.
Description:	Lists the IP addresses in the order of preference for NIS servers available to the client.
Structure:	

```
 Code   Len         Address 1                 Address 2
+-----+-----+-----+-----+-----+-----+-----+-----+--
| 41  |  n  | a1  | a2  | a3  | a4  | a1  | a2  |  ...
+-----+-----+-----+-----+-----+-----+-----+-----+--
```

TABLE B.44 *NTP Servers*

Code:	42
Length:	Variable, minimum length is 4 octets. Octet length increases in multiples of 4 for each server address listed.
Value:	Signed 32-bit integer representing IP address of NTP server.
Description:	Lists the IP addresses in the order of preference for Network Time Protocol (NTP) servers available to the client.
Structure:	

```
 Code   Len         Address 1                 Address 2
+-----+-----+-----+-----+-----+-----+-----+-----+--
| 42  |  n  | a1  | a2  | a3  | a4  | a1  | a2  |  ...
+-----+-----+-----+-----+-----+-----+-----+-----+--
```

TABLE B.45 *X Window System Font Servers*

Code:	48
Length:	Variable, minimum length is 4 octets. Octet length increases in multiples of 4 for each server address listed.
Value:	Signed 32-bit integer representing each server IP address.
Description:	Lists the IP addresses in the order of preference for X Window System font servers available to the client.
Structure:	

```
 Code   Len         Address 1                 Address 2
+-----+-----+-----+-----+-----+-----+-----+-----+--
| 48  |  n  | a1  | a2  | a3  | a4  | a1  | a2  |  ...
+-----+-----+-----+-----+-----+-----+-----+-----+--
```

TABLE B.46 *X Window System Display Manager Servers*

Code:	49
Length:	Variable, minimum length is 4 octets. Octet length increases in multiples of 4 for each server address listed.
Value:	Signed 32-bit integer representing each server IP address.
Description:	Lists the IP addresses in the order of preference for X Window System display manager servers available to the client.
Structure:	see below

```
 Code   Len         Address 1               Address 2
+-----+-----+-----+-----+-----+-----+-----+-----+--
| 49  |  n  | a1  | a2  | a3  | a4  | a1  | a2  |  ...
+-----+-----+-----+-----+-----+-----+-----+-----+--
```

TABLE B.47 *NIS+ Domain Name*

Code:	64
Length:	Length varies depending on data in value. Minimum length is 1 octet.
Value:	ASCII character text.
Description:	Specifies the name of the Network Information Service Plus (NIS+) domain name of the client as an ASCII string.
Structure:	see below

```
 Code   Len     NIS+ domain name
+-----+-----+-----+-----+-----+-----+---
| 64  |  n  | n1  | n2  | n3  | n4  | ...
+-----+-----+-----+-----+-----+-----+---
```

TABLE B.48 *NIS+ Servers*

Code:	65
Length:	Variable, minimum length is 4 octets. Octet length increases in multiples of 4 for each server address listed.
Value:	Signed 32-bit integer representing IP address of NTP servers.
Description:	Lists the IP addresses in the order of preference for NIS+ servers available to the client.
Structure:	see below

```
 Code   Len         Address 1               Address 2
+-----+-----+-----+-----+-----+-----+-----+-----+--
| 65  |  n  | a1  | a2  | a3  | a4  | a1  | a2  |  ...
+-----+-----+-----+-----+-----+-----+-----+-----+--
```

TABLE B.49 *Mobile IP Home Agents*

Code:	68
Length:	Variable, minimum length is 4 octets. Octet length increases in multiples of 4 for each mobile IP home agent address listed.
Value:	Signed 32-bit integer representing IP address of a mobile IP home agent.
Description:	Lists the IP addresses in the order of preference for mobile IP home agents available to the client.
Structure:	See diagram below

```
 Code   Len        Address 1             Address 2
+-----+-----+-----+-----+-----+-----+-----+-----+--
| 68  |  n  | a1  | a2  | a3  | a4  | a1  | a2  | ...
+-----+-----+-----+-----+-----+-----+-----+-----+--
```

NETBIOS OVER TCP/IP OPTIONS

Tables B.50–B.53 describe the uses for NetBIOS over TCP/IP support. All Microsoft-based DHCP clients and DHCP servers can recognize and support the use of these option types.

TABLE B.50 *WINS Server*

Code:	44
Length:	Variable, minimum length is 4 octets. Length can be increased only by multiples of 4 for each address listed.
Value:	Each 4 octets in this field contain a listed WINS server IP address, specified as an unsigned 32-bit integer.
Description:	Lists the IP addresses for Windows Internet Name Service (WINS) servers or NetBIOS name servers (NBNS).
Structure:	See diagram below

```
 Code  Len        Address 1          Address 2
+----+----+----+----+----+----+----+----+----+----+--
| 44 |  n | a1 | a2 | a3 | a4 | b1 | b2 | b3 | b4 | ...
+----+----+----+----+----+----+----+----+----+----+--
```

TABLE B.51 *NetBIOS Datagram Distribution Server*

Code:	45
Length:	Variable, minimum length is 4 octets. Length can be increased only by multiples of 4.
Value:	Each 4 octets in this field contain a listed NetBIOS datagram distribution (NBDD) server IP address, specified as an unsigned 32-bit integer.
Description:	Lists the IP addresses for NetBIOS datagram distribution (NBDD) servers.
Structure:	See diagram below

```
 Code  Len        Address 1          Address 2
+----+----+----+----+----+----+----+----+----+----+---
| 45 |  n | a1 | a2 | a3 | a4 | b1 | b2 | b3 | b4 | ...
+----+----+----+----+----+----+----+----+----+----+---
```

TABLE B.52 *NetBIOS Node Type*

Code:	46
Length:	Fixed, 1 octet.
Value:	1 = b-node, 2 = p-node, 4 = m-node, and 8 = h-node.
Description:	Configures the client node type for NetBIOS over TCP/IP (NetBT) clients, as described in RFC 1001/1002. On multihomed computers, the node type is assigned for the computer, not to individual network adapters.
Structure:	see below

```
 Code   Len  Node type
+-----+-----+-----------+
|  46 |  1  | see above |
+-----+-----+-----------+
```

TABLE B.53 *NetBIOS Scope ID*

Code:	47
Length:	Variable, octet length is equal to the number of characters used in NetBIOS scope ID.
Value:	Specifies the NetBIOS over TCP/IP scope identifier used by the client. The format used for these scope IDs is further described in RFCs 1001/1002. See the RFCs for character-set restrictions.
Description:	Specifies a string that is the NetBIOS over TCP/IP scope ID for the client, as specified in RFC 1001/1002. On multihomed computers, the node type is assigned for the computer, not to individual network adapters.
Structure:	see below

```
 Code   Len       NetBIOS scope
+-----+-----+-----+-----+-----+-----+----
|  47 |  n  |  s1 |  s2 |  s3 |  s4 | ...
+-----+-----+-----+-----+-----+-----+----
```

Advanced and New Options

The following topics provide descriptions of recent, advanced options available for use with Windows 2000 DHCP service. Some new advancements include class-related options and the support for options classes that are recent additions to the DHCP standard.

For recently added options, the DHCP console includes some additional predefined option types that are defined according to the updated DHCP options standard reference, RFC 2132, "DHCP Options and BOOTP Vendor Extensions."

- Vendor specific options
- User class options
- DHCP extensions
- Recently added options (RFC 2132)

VENDOR SPECIFIC OPTIONS

Tables B.54 and B.55 describe reserved DHCP option types for assigning vendor-specific information and vendor class use, as specified in RFC 2132. Vendor classes can be added and used by the DHCP Server service to classify supporting vendor-specific DHCP clients that identify themselves using a common vendor class ID when they use DHCP service on your network.

In addition, the DHCP console provides a single default vendor class, the *DHCP Standard options* class, that can be used to group and classify clients that do not identify a vendor class to the DHCP service.

TABLE B.54 *Vendor Specific Information*

Code: 43

Length: Variable, minimum length of 1 octet.

Value: An opaque object of *n* octets (where *n* is equal to the length specified with this option). The definition of values stored for this option type are vendor specific, and values provided here are presumed to be interpreted by a vendor-specific code on DHCP clients and the DHCP server.

Description: This option is used by clients and servers to exchange vendor-specific information. Servers that are not equipped to interpret the information ignore it. Clients that expect but do not receive the information attempt to operate without it.

In some cases, a vendor uses this option type to send more than one information item, in which case, this option can serve as a subfield for encapsulating vendor-specific options. When encapsulating options, DHCP servers maintain the same syntax (that is, the same code, length, and value fields sequence) for each encapsulated option type as it would normally appear in the full standard options field, with the following exceptions for the encapsulated vendor-specific subfield:

- "Magic cookies" cannot be used.
- All standard option codes—other than the padding option (0) or the end option (255) may be redefined.

If present, the end option (255) signifies the end of the encapsulated vendor options, but not the end of the encapsulated vendor-specific subfield. If no end option is present, the end for the encapsulated vendor-specific subfield is taken from its stated length.

Structure:

```
 Code   Len   Vendor-specific information
+-----+-----+-----+-----+---
|  43 |  n  |  i1 |  i2 | ...
+-----+-----+-----+-----+---
```

When this option type uses an encapsulated vendor-specific subfield, the information bytes 1-*n* have the following format:

```
 Code  Len Data item      Code Len  Data item     Code
+----+----+----+----+----+----+----+----+----+----+-----+
| T1 | n  | d1 | d2 |... | T2 | n  | D1 | D2 |... |... |
+----+----+----+----+----+----+----+----+----+----+-----+
```

TABLE B.55 *Vendor Class Identifier*

Code:	60
Length:	Minimum of 1 octet. Length varies according to *n* (that is, the number of octets used as an identifier).
Value:	A value of *n* octets interpreted by DHCP servers that can support vendor classification of clients.
Description:	Can be used by DHCP clients to identify their vendor type and configuration. When using this option, vendors can define their own specific identifier values, such as to convey a particular hardware or operating system configuration or other identifying information. For Windows 2000, all computers that function as either DHCP servers or clients can use and support this option type. Where vendor classes are used, the DHCP server responds to identifying clients using option code 43 (described above), the reserved option type for returning vendor-specific information to the client. DHCP servers that do not interpret this option type are expected to ignore it when it is specified by clients. For earlier Windows-based clients and other clients that do not support this option type, the DHCP service classifies these clients as part of the default vendor class, the DHCP Standard options class that is predefined for Microsoft-based DHCP servers.
Structure:	See below

```
Code   Len   Vendor class identifier
+-----+-----+-----+-----+---
|  60 |  n  |  i1 |  i2 | ...
+-----+-----+-----+-----+---
```

USER CLASS OPTIONS

The User Class option for supporting user classes in DHCP is described in Table B.56. This option is described in the proposed Internet RFC draft, "The User Class Option for DHCP," currently under review for possible approval as an Internet TCP/IP standard by the Internet Engineering Task Force (IETF).

TABLE B.56 *User Class Information*

Code:	77
Length:	Variable, minimum is 2 octets.
Value:	ASCII character text.

(continued)

TABLE B.56 *User Class Information (Continued)*

Description:	A DHCP client can use this option to identify the type or category of user or applications it represents. The information contained in this option is an NVT ASCII text object that represents the user class of which the client is a member. You can use the DHCP console to define specific user classes. When user classes are created, each class sets an identifying string of information to be used by the DHCP Server service to classify identifying clients. Also, default user classes can be created for classifying clients that are unable to support a user class ID. User classes can be helpful in separating client computers that have a shared or common need for similar software configuration or user preferences. For example, an identifier can specify that a particular DHCP client is a member of the class "accounting auditors," which have special service needs, such as a particular database server. For Microsoft DHCP clients, only computers running under Windows 2000 support sending or use of this option type. Other legacy DHCP clients do not send a class ID or have the ability to recognize a user class. Therefore, these clients are assigned as members to the *Default user class,* which is a user class predefined for immediate use in the DHCP console. Other user classes must be manually created.
Structure:	(see below)

```
 Code   Len       User class information
+-----+-----+-----+-----+-----+-----+---
|  77 |  n  | c1  | c2  | c3  | c4  | ...
+-----+-----+-----+-----+-----+-----+---
```

DHCP EXTENSIONS

Tables B.57–B.60 describe option types that are specific to DHCP and that are used to implement default protocol interaction and system behavior between servers and clients. Some of these options are implicitly set when you configure server and scope properties at the DHCP console.

TABLE B.57 *Requested IP Address*

Code:	50
Length:	Fixed, 4 octets.
Value:	Single signed 32-bit integer indicating a requested IP address.
Description:	Can be used by clients when sending a DHCP discovery message to request that a specific IP address be assigned by the server.
Structure:	(see below)

```
 Code   Len   Requested IP address
+-----+-----+-----+-----+-----+-----+
|  50 |  n  | a1  | a2  | a3  | a4  |
+-----+-----+-----+-----+-----+-----+
```

TABLE B.58 *IP Address Lease Time*

Code: 51

Length: Fixed, 4 octets.

Value: Single signed 32-bit integer representing a client lease time in seconds.

Description: This option type is used to negotiate and exchange lease-time information between DHCP clients and servers in either of two ways:

- Can be used in a DHCP discovery or DHCP request message sent by a client to request a lease time for its IP address.
- Can be used in a DHCP offer message server reply sent by a server to specify a lease time the server can offer to the client.

Structure:

```
 Code   Len          Lease time
+-----+-----+-----+-----+-----+-----+
|  51 |  4  | t1  |  t2 |  t3 |  t4 |
+-----+-----+-----+-----+-----+-----+
```

TABLE B.59 *Option Overload*

Code: 52

Length: Fixed, 1 octet.

Value: Predefined, accepted values for this option type include:
1 = "file" field is overloaded.
2 = "sname" field is overloaded.
3 = both "file" and "sname" fields are overloaded.

Description: Used in messages sent by the DHCP server to indicate that either of the standard message fields in a DHCP packet for *SERVER HOST NAME* ("sname") and *BOOT FILE NAME* ("file") are to be overloaded (used to hold options).

Where this option is used, it extends the options area in each packet by indicating that unused space for one or both of these two standard fields should be allocated to the area used to carry DHCP options.

Structure:

```
 Code   Len  Value
+-----+-----+-----+
|  52 |  1  |1/2/3|
+-----+-----+-----+
```

TABLE B.60 *DHCP Message Type*

Code: 53

Length: Fixed, 1 octet.

Value: Predefined, accepted values for this option type are:
1 = DHCP discovery message (DHCPDISCOVER).
2 = DHCP offer message (DHCPOFFER)
3 = To select and request a lease from a specific DHCP server when lease offers were made simultaneously from several different servers. To confirm a previously leased IP address after the client system is restarted. To extend the current IP address lease for the client.

The DHCP request message name is DHCPREQUEST. DHCP request message (DHCPREQUEST).
4 = DHCP decline message (DHCPDECLINE)
5 = DHCP positive acknowledgment message (DHCPACK)
6 = DHCP negative acknowledgment message (DHCPNAK)
7 = DHCP release message (DHCPRELEASE)
8 = DHCP informational message (DHCPINFORM)

Description: This option is required for use in all DHCP messages to convey the type of message.

Structure:

```
 Code   Len   Type
+-----+-----+-----+
|  53 |  1  | 1-8 |
+-----+-----+-----+
```

TABLE B.61 *Server Identifier*

Code: 54

Length: Fixed, 4 octets.

Value: A single, signed 32-bit IP address that identifies the DHCP server.

Description: This option is used in DHCP offer and DHCP request messages and sometimes appears in DHCP acknowledgment messages (that is DHCPACK, DHCPNAK). The server identifier is the IP address of a selected DHCP server. This option type is used in two possible ways:

- Servers include this option type in DHCP lease offer messages so that clients can distinguish between multiple lease offers.
- In turn, clients include this option type in DHCP lease request messages to select a lease and indicate between multiple lease offers, which offer is being accepted. Also, clients can use the contents of this field for unicast sending of request messages to specific DHCP servers to renew a current lease.

Structure:

```
 Code   Len            Address
+-----+-----+-----+-----+-----+-----+
|  54 |  4  |  a1 |  a2 |  a3 |  a4 |
+-----+-----+-----+-----+-----+-----+
```

TABLE B.62	*Parameter Request List*
Code:	55
Length:	Minimum of 1 octet. Length increases by 1 octet for each additional option code included in the request list.
Value:	List of 8-bit values each representing an option type code between 0 and 255.
Description:	Used by a DHCP client to request specific option type values from the DHCP server. Each option type is requested and listed by a single octet value containing a valid or recognized DHCP option code for the server. For clients that use this option type, the list may be ordered by preference, although the DHCP server is not required to return options in the order they are requested. However, the DHCP server attempts to insert the requested options in the order requested by the client.
Structure:	(see below)

```
 Code   Len   Option codes
+-----+-----+-----+-----+---
| 55  |  n  | c1  | c2  | ...
+-----+-----+-----+-----+---
```

TABLE B.63	*Optional Message*
Code:	56
Length:	Minimum of 1 octet. Length depends on the length of the sent message.
Value:	ASCII character text.
Description:	Can be used by both the DHCP server and DHCP clients in the following ways: ● Servers can use this option type to provide and embed an error message in a DHCP negative acknowledgment message in the event of a failure. ● Clients can use this option type in a DHCP decline message to indicate why it declined offered parameters. ● The message consists of a variable length ASCII text string, which the receiving computer can then either log or display.
Structure:	(see below)

```
 Code   Len      Text
+-----+-----+-----+-----+---
| 56  |  n  | c1  | c2  | ...
+-----+-----+-----+-----+---
```

TABLE B.64	*Maximum Message Size*
Code:	57
Length:	Fixed, 2 octets.
Value:	A 16-bit integer indicating the maximum size in bytes/octets for a DHCP message packet. The maximum legal value for this option type is 576.
Description:	Used by the client to specify the maximum length for a DHCP message packet that it can accept. A client can include this option type in DHCP discovery or DHCP request messages; however, it does not include this option type in DHCP decline messages.

Structure:

```
 Code   Len      Length
+-----+-----+-----+-----+
|  57 |  2  |  11 |  12 |
+-----+-----+-----+-----+
```

TABLE B.65	*Lease Renewal Time*
Code:	58
Length:	Fixed, 4 octets.
Value:	A 32-bit unsigned integer indicating the number of seconds before the client begins to renew its address lease with the DHCP server.
Description:	This time is a function typically 50 percent of the full configured duration (or lease time) for a client lease. To adjust this timer, you should change the length of the client lease in the properties for the client scope on the DHCP server.

Structure:

```
 Code   Len           T1 interval
+-----+-----+-----+-----+-----+-----+
|  58 |  4  |  t1 |  t2 |  t3 |  t4 |
+-----+-----+-----+-----+-----+-----+
```

TABLE B.66	*Lease Rebinding Time*
Code:	59
Length:	Fixed, 4 octets.
Value:	A 32-bit unsigned integer indicating the number of seconds before the client enters the rebinding state if it has not renewed its current address lease with the DHCP server.
Description:	This time is a function (typically, 87.5 percent) of the full configured duration (or lease time) for a client lease. To adjust this timer you should change the length of client lease in the properties for the client scope on the DHCP server.

Structure:

```
 Code   Len           T2 interval
+-----+-----+-----+-----+-----+-----+
|  59 |  4  |  t1 |  t2 |  t3 |  t4 |
+-----+-----+-----+-----+-----+-----+
```

TABLE B.67 *Client Unique Identifier*

Code:	61
Length:	Variable length, minimum length is 2 octets.
Value:	A series of 2 or more octets that is treated as an opaque object by the DHCP server. Servers can interpret and use this value to uniquely identify clients.
Description:	Used by clients to specify their unique identifier to the server. This option type is most useful for reserved clients. When a reserved client contacts the DHCP server, it can check and match the client identifier value here to a corresponding identifier used to configure an address reservation in the server database. Where a matching reservation is found, the DHCP server returns the reserved address and its related parameters to the correct client. For this reason, the identifier of each client must be unique among all other client identifiers used on the effective DHCP network to which the client is attached (that is, the local subnet of the client and any remote subnets reachable by DHCP relay). Vendors and system administrators are responsible for choosing client identifiers that meet this requirement. One common approach to ensuring uniqueness is to configure client reservations at the DHCP server based on the client Media Access Control (MAC) address as the client identifier value. MAC addresses are encoded in the network adapter hardware of each client and are assigned to hardware manufacturers in such a way as to ensure that they are unique for each device.
Structure:	see below

```
Code   Len   Type  Client-identifier
+-----+-----+-----+-----+-----+---
| 61  |  n  | t1  | i1  | i2  | ...
+-----+-----+-----+-----+-----+---
```

TABLE B.68 *TFTP Server Name*

Code:	66
Length:	Length varies depending on data in value. Minimum length is 1 octet.
Value:	ASCII character text.
Description:	In most other DHCP implementations, this option specifies the host name of the TFTP server (the "sname" field) in a DHCP message packet, when it is overloaded and used for carrying additional DHCP options. In Windows-based DHCP server implementations, this option can be used to fill in the TFTP server IP address field, "siaddr"—and not the "sname" field, "sname"—in DHCP protocol messages. This option can also be configured as either an IP address or a fully qualified domain name (FQDN). If an FQDN is used, the DHCP server will resolve the name to an IP address before including and sending the option to clients in DHCP offer messages and DHCP acknowledgment messages. When this option is used for support of BOOTP clients, such as by adding and configuring entries in the BOOTP table at the DHCP server, the name or IP address of the TFTP server is used to provide the boot image file required to complete the second phase of the bootstrap process.
Structure:	see below

```
Code  Len   TFTP server
+-----+-----+-----+-----+-----+---
| 66  |  n  | c1  | c2  | c3  | ...
+-----+-----+-----+-----+-----+---
```

TABLE B.69 *Boot File Name*

Code:	67
Length:	Length varies depending on data in value. Minimum length is 1 octet.
Value:	ASCII character text.
Description:	Specifies the name of a boot image file on the TFTP server in the boot file name ("file") field of a DHCP message packet, when the message is overloaded and used for carrying additional DHCP options. In Windows-based DHCP server implementations, this option can be used to fill in the boot file name ("file") field in DHCP offer messages. For this behavior, add and configure entries in the BOOTP table at the DHCP server. For more information, see Chapter 4, "Using DHCP." When this option is used for support of BOOTP clients, the boot image file must be located at a validly specified TFTP server for use in downloading the boot image file named here to complete the final phase of the BOOTP client initialization process. Microsoft does not provide TFTP servers.
Structure:	see below

```
 Code  Len   Bootfile name
+-----+-----+-----+-----+-----+---
| 67  |  n  | c1  | c2  | c3  | ...
+-----+-----+-----+-----+-----+---
```

TABLE B.70 *Client FQDN*

Code:	81
Length:	Variable, minimum of 4 octets.
Value:	Specifies at least four (4) single-octet subfield values, which are always included: • **Length**. This field is standard for most DHCP options and is used to indicate the number of octets specifying the length of the data of this option within the large DHCP standard options field used, reserved for included use in protocol messaging. (1 octet) • **Flag**. This 1-octet field is used by the client to specify the way in which it requests its DNS records—host (A) and pointer (PTR) resource records—to be updated. It can also be used by the DHCP server to indicate that it is overriding the request to update according to client request. Values: 0 = client requests to update its own A resource record; 1 = client requests that the DHCP server bear responsibility for updating its A resource record; 3 = the DHCP server notifies the client it has assumed responsibility for updating the A resource record of the client. (1 octet) • **Result code fields (RCODE1, RCODE2)**. These two fields can be used by the DHCP server to indicate to the client responses related to any DNS dynamic updates it performed on behalf of the client. (2 octets) If present, additional octets are used to store a text string value corresponding to the client FQDN. If null (not present), the client is either not configured with an FQDN or did not specify one with this option.

(continued)

TABLE B.70	Client FQDN (Continued)
Description:	Used by supporting clients to indicate their FQDN to the server and to request the manner in which the server processes dynamic updates of client DNS name-to-address mappings. Also used by supporting DHCP servers to return response information back to the client, indicating whether the requested update policy was accepted. The server can also use this option to return response information about the result of any DNS updates it attempted to perform on behalf of the client. This option is based on the Internet RFC draft, "Interaction between DHCP and DNS," under review by the IETF working group for DHCP. For current information, you can find the latest draft at the Request for Comments Web site, *www.rfc-editor.org/*.
Structure:	See diagram below

```
 Code    Len     Flags   RCODE1 RCODE2    Client FQDN
+------+------+------+------+------+------+--
|  81  |   n  |      |      |      |      ...
+------+------+------+------+------+------+--
```

RECENTLY ADDED OPTIONS (RFC 2132)

Tables B.71–B.78 describe the DHCP option types that are reserved and specified for use in RFC 2132, but are not predefined for use in DHCP Manager. These option types can be added to support other DHCP clients that recognize these options. For more information on adding these options types, see Chapter 5, "Installation and Administration of DHCP Servers and Clients."

TABLE B.71	Simple Mail Transport Protocol (SMTP) Server
Code:	69
Length:	Variable, minimum length is 4 octets. Octet length increases in multiples of 4 for each server IP address listed.
Value:	Signed 32-bit integers representing IP addresses of servers.
Description:	Lists the IP addresses in the order of preference for SMTP servers available to the client.
Structure:	See diagram below

```
 Code   Len          Address 1                 Address 2
+-----+-----+-----+-----+-----+-----+-----+-----+--
| 69  |  n  | a1  | a2  | a3  | a4  | a1  | a2  |  ...
+-----+-----+-----+-----+-----+-----+-----+-----+--
```

TABLE B.72 *Post Office Protocol (POP3) Server*

Code: 70

Length: Variable, minimum length is 4 octets. Octet length increases in multiples of 4 for each server IP address listed.

Value: Signed 32-bit integers representing IP addresses of servers.

Description: Lists the IP addresses in the order of preference for POP3 servers available to the client.

Structure:

```
 Code   Len          Address 1                Address 2
+-----+-----+-----+-----+-----+-----+-----+-----+--
| 70  |  n  | a1  | a2  | a3  | a4  | a1  | a2  |  ...
+-----+-----+-----+-----+-----+-----+-----+-----+--
```

TABLE B.73 *Network News Transport Protocol Server*

Code: 71

Length: Variable, minimum length is 4 octets. Octet length increases in multiples of 4 for each server IP address listed.

Value: Signed 32-bit integers representing IP addresses of servers.

Description: Lists the IP addresses in the order of preference for Network News Transport Protocol (NNTP) servers available to the client.

Structure:

```
 Code   Len          Address 1                Address 2
+-----+-----+-----+-----+-----+-----+-----+-----+--
| 71  |  n  | a1  | a2  | a3  | a4  | a1  | a2  |  ...
+-----+-----+-----+-----+-----+-----+-----+-----+--
```

TABLE B.74 *Default World Wide Web Server*

Code: 72

Length: Variable, minimum length is 4 octets. Octet length increases in multiples of 4 for each server IP address listed.

Value: Signed 32-bit integers representing IP addresses of servers.

Description: Lists the IP addresses in the order of preference for default Web servers available to the client.

Structure:

```
 Code   Len          Address 1                Address 2
+-----+-----+-----+-----+-----+-----+-----+-----+--
| 72  |  n  | a1  | a2  | a3  | a4  | a1  | a2  |  ...
+-----+-----+-----+-----+-----+-----+-----+-----+--
```

TABLE B.75 *Default Finger Server*

Code:	73
Length:	Variable, minimum length is 4 octets. Octet length increases in multiples of 4 for each server IP address listed.
Value:	Signed 32-bit integers representing IP addresses of servers.
Description:	Lists the IP addresses in the order of preference for default Finger servers available to the client.
Structure:	

```
 Code   Len        Address 1              Address 2
+-----+-----+-----+-----+-----+-----+-----+-----+--
| 73  |  n  | a1  | a2  | a3  | a4  | a1  | a2  |  ...
+-----+-----+-----+-----+-----+-----+-----+-----+--
```

TABLE B.76 *Default Internet Relay Chat Server*

Code:	74
Length:	Variable, minimum length is 4 octets. Octet length increases in multiples of 4 for each server IP address listed.
Value:	Signed 32-bit integers representing IP addresses of servers.
Description:	Lists the IP addresses in the order of preference for default Internet Relay Chat (IRC) servers available to the client.
Structure:	

```
 Code   Len        Address 1              Address 2
+-----+-----+-----+-----+-----+-----+-----+-----+--
| 74  |  n  | a1  | a2  | a3  | a4  | a1  | a2  |  ...
+-----+-----+-----+-----+-----+-----+-----+-----+--
```

TABLE B.77 *StreetTalk Server*

Code:	75
Length:	Variable, minimum length is 4 octets. Octet length increases in multiples of 4 for each server IP address listed.
Value:	Signed 32-bit integers representing IP addresses of servers.
Description:	Lists the IP addresses in the order of preference for StreetTalk servers available to the client.
Structure:	

```
 Code   Len        Address 1              Address 2
+-----+-----+-----+-----+-----+-----+-----+-----+--
| 75  |  n  | a1  | a2  | a3  | a4  | a1  | a2  |  ...
+-----+-----+-----+-----+-----+-----+-----+-----+--
```

TABLE B.78	*StreetTalk Directory Assistance Server*
Code:	76
Length:	Variable, minimum length is 4 octets. Octet length increases in multiples of 4 for each server IP address listed.
Value:	Signed 32-bit integers representing IP addresses of servers.
Description:	Lists the IP addresses in the order of preference for StreetTalk Directory Assistance (STDA) servers available to the client.
Structure:	see below

```
  Code   Len         Address 1               Address 2
+-----+-----+-----+-----+-----+-----+-----+-----+--
| 76  |  n  | a1  | a2  | a3  | a4  | a1  | a2  |  ...
+-----+-----+-----+-----+-----+-----+-----+-----+--
```

Microsoft Options

The following topics provide descriptions of all options and option classes that are predefined in Windows 2000 Server and provided by Microsoft as vendor-specific additions. These options and classes are only supported for Windows 2000 DHCP servers and clients.

- Microsoft vendor-specific options
- Microsoft vendor classes
- Microsoft predefined user classes

MICROSOFT VENDOR-SPECIFIC OPTIONS

Reserved DHCP option types, defined by Microsoft for use, are described in Tables B.79–B.81. These options are only available for use with supporting Microsoft DHCP clients, such as computers running Windows 2000.

TABLE B.79	*Disable NetBIOS over TCP/IP*
Code:	1
Length:	1 octet, accepted values are either 0 or 1.
Value:	2 = Disable NetBIOS over TCP/IP (NetBT) for Windows 2000 DHCP clients. If any other value is specified, NetBT remains enabled.
Description:	This option can be used to selectively enable or disable NetBT for DHCP-enabled computers running Windows 2000 only. By installation default, if this option is not present Windows 2000 enables the use of NetBT for network connections that are configured to use TCP/IP. Earlier Windows clients require NetBT and do not support this option.
Structure:	see below

```
  Code     NetBT on/off
+--------+--------+--
|  001   |   n    |
+--------+--------+--
```

TABLE B.80 *Release DHCP Lease on Shutdown*

Code:	2
Length:	1 octet, currently accepted values are 0–2.
Value:	0 = Windows 2000 DHCP clients do not send an **ipconfig /release** command at a command prompt. The DHCP release message name is DHCPRELEASE. DHCP release message (DHCPRELEASE) on proper shutdown. 1 = Windows 2000 DHCP clients send DHCP release (DHCPRELEASE) message on proper shutdown.
Description:	This option can be used to control whether DHCP-enabled computers running Windows 2000 send a release for their current DHCP lease to the DHCP server when shutdown occurs. It is actually implemented and interpreted as a bitmasked value by the DHCP Client service. In most cases, the default (that is, the functional equivalent to this option value not being used or present in DHCP messages) is that Windows 2000 clients do not send DHCP release messages on proper shutdown.
Structure:	(see below)

```
  Code     Release on/off
+--------+--------+--
|  002   |   n    |
+--------+--------+--
```

TABLE B.81 *Default Router Metric Base*

Code:	3
Length:	Variable.
Value:	This value is a specified router metric base to be used for all default gateway routes used at Windows 2000 DHCP-enabled client computers.
Description:	This option can be used to set the default base metric for Windows 2000 DHCP clients. When this option is set, the DHCP Client service uses the value configured here as the base metric for its default gateways. This value can be assigned as an integer cost metric ranging from 1 through 9,999. It is used in calculating the fastest, most reliable, and least expensive routes. If a value is not specified, a default of either one (1) or the currently set interface-specific metric is used.
Structure:	(see below)

```
  Code     Rt. metric
+--------+--------+--
|  003   |   n    |
+--------+--------+--
```

OTHER MICROSOFT OPTIONS SUPPORTED

The following are other DHCP options that are not predefined but can be added to support features for other Microsoft released products.

TABLE B.82 *Proxy Autodiscovery (Internet Explorer 5 Only)*

Code:	252
Length:	Variable, depending upon the length of the specified string.
Value:	A URL that points to the configuration file that the client should use for automatic configuration of Internet Explorer 5. The file this URL points to can be a *.pac, .jvs, .js,* or *.ins* configuration file created by your system or Web administrator when deploying Internet Explorer 5 on your intranet. It might include settings for other Internet Explorer 5 configurable options, such as which home page to use, or settings for locating and using a proxy server.
Description:	This option is used to set the location of the Internet Explorer 5 automatic configuration file.
Notes:	This option is communicated between Internet Explorer 5 client computers and the DHCP server using the DHCP information message (DHCPINFORM), which is currently only supported for Windows 2000 DHCP server and clients. The use of additional DHCP configuration is only supported by Internet Explorer 5, not earlier versions that use different methods for automatic detection and configuration of proxy server settings. You can also add and configure an alias (CNAME) resource record at the DNS server to support Internet Explorer 5 proxy server autodiscovery and configuration features. For more information, see Resource records reference: CNAME. For further details, refer to the Internet Explorer 5 Resource Kit.

Note These options are provided as encapsulated vendor-specific data fields within the vendor-specific information option. Currently, these options are only assignable in the DHCP console through the following vendor classes: Microsoft options and Microsoft Windows 2000 options. For more information, see Chapter 4.

MICROSOFT VENDOR CLASSES

For Windows 2000 Server, Microsoft has predefined several DHCP vendor classes for use when assigning DHCP options on the basis of identifying the vendor information, such as the version of Microsoft Windows that the DHCP client computer is running. Each of these classes is described in Table B.83.

TABLE B.83 *Microsoft Predefined DHCP Vendor Classes*

Class name	Class data	Description
Microsoft Windows 2000 options	MSFT 5.0	Used to classify all DHCP clients that are running Windows 2000. By default, each Windows 2000 DHCP client computer sends this as its vendor class. Options assigned for this class are only applied for Windows 2000 client computers and are not provided to clients running other versions of Windows or other operating systems.

(continued)

Table B.83 *Microsoft Predefined DHCP Vendor Classes (Continued)*

Class name	Class data	Description
Microsoft Windows 98 options	MSFT 98	Used to classify all DHCP clients that are running Windows 98. By default, each Windows 98 DHCP client computer sends this as its vendor class. Options assigned for this class are only applied for Windows 98 client computers and are not provided to clients running other versions of Windows or other operating systems. Currently, vendor-specific options for Windows 98 are not defined.
Microsoft options	MSFT	Used to classify all DHCP clients that are running either Windows 98 or Windows 2000. By design, DHCP clients do not specifically identify themselves to this class, but the DHCP server can use this class to apply options for any of its clients identified as running these versions of Windows. Options assigned for this class are only applied for Windows 98 or Windows 2000 client computers and are not provided to clients running other versions of Windows or other operating systems.
DHCP standard options	(Unspecified)	This class is used to classify all other DHCP clients that are not running either Windows 98 or Windows 2000 or identified as members of another vendor class. Note that for this class, options are not distributed using the reserved vendor subfield of option 43, the Vendor specific information. Instead, options in this class are communicated as part of the larger nonvendor-specific "options" field, which is always used in any of the following DHCP client/server messaging events: ● When DHCP offer messages (DHCPOFFERs) are sent by servers. ● When to select and request a lease from a specific DHCP server when lease offers were made simultaneously from several servers. ● To confirm a previously leased IP address after the client system is restarted. ● To extend the current IP address lease for the client. The DHCP request message name is DHCPREQUEST. DHCP request messages (DHCPREQUESTs) are sent by clients.

Important For computers running Windows 2000 DHCP Server service, you can create additional vendor classes at the DHCP server.

When working with vendor classes, be sure that the class data used or set at the client matches identically the ASCII data value as it is set at the server for applicable vendor class. Also, character data used to identify the class is case sensitive and must be entered in matching case for both server and client configurations. For more information, see Chapter 5. For information about other DHCP vendor classes supported for other types of DHCP clients, refer to the applicable vendor-provided documentation.

Note For more information about using option classes, see Chapter 4.

MICROSOFT PREDEFINED USER CLASSES

For Windows 2000 Server, Microsoft has predefined several DHCP user classes for use when assigning DHCP options to clients on the basis of identifying whether the client is a member of one of the specified user classes. Each of these classes is described in Table B.84.

TABLE B.84 *Microsoft Predefined DHCP User Classes*

Class name	Class data	Description
Default user class	(unspecified)	Used to classify clients that do not explicitly identify themselves as members of a user class defined at the DHCP server. By default, this options class is typically used where most DHCP clients are grouped and included. Clients are assigned to this class under the following conditions: • DHCP clients that have no concept of a DHCP user class or a DHCP class ID. This is true for most legacy and older DHCP clients prior to Windows 2000. • Windows 2000 clients configured with a DHCP class ID unknown to the DHCP server. For example, the user class that the client identifies itself for has not been defined at the DHCP server.
Default remote access class	RRAS.Microsoft	Used to classify clients making a PPP-type connection through a Routing and Remote Access server. Typically, this class includes most remote access clients that use DHCP to obtain a lease. Routing and Remote Access clients are assigned to this class under the following conditions: • Routing and Remote Access clients that have no concept of this user class or its associated reserved class ID string ("RRAS.Microsoft"). Most remote access clients released prior to Windows 2000 fit this description. • Windows 2000 clients that are operating as Routing and Remote Access clients. Options assigned for distribution with this class are only in effect for Routing and Remote Access clients.
Default BOOTP class	BOOTP.Microsoft	Used to classify any clients recognized as BOOTP-type clients, including dynamic and nondynamic (static) BOOTP cleints. Options assigned for distribution with this class are only in effect for BOOTP clients.

Important For computers running Windows 2000, you can create additional user classes at the DHCP server and set or show the DHCP class data used as matching ID strings at your DHCP clients.

When working with user classes, be sure that the class data set at the client identically matches the ASCII data value as it is set at the server for applicable user class. Also, character data used to identify the class is case-sensitive and must be entered in matching case for both server and client configurations. For more information, see Chapter 5.

Note For more information about using option classes, see Chapter 4.

DHCP RFCs

RFCs are an evolving series of reports, proposals for protocols, and protocol standards used by the Internet community. Dynamic Host Configuration Protocol (DHCP) specifications are defined in RFCs published by the IETF and other working groups.

The following RFCs specify the core DHCP standards:

- RFC 2131: Dynamic Host Configuration Protocol (obsoletes RFC 1541)
- RFC 2132: DHCP Options and BOOTP Vendor Extensions

The following RFCs might also be helpful for understanding how DHCP is used with other services on your network:

- RFC 951: The Bootstrap Protocol (BOOTP)
- RFC 1534: Interoperation Between DHCP and BOOTP
- RFC 1542: Clarifications and Extensions for the Bootstrap Protocol
- RFC 2136: Dynamic Updates in the Domain Name System (DNS UPDATE)
- RFC 2241: DHCP Options for Novell Directory Services
- RFC 2242: Netware/IP Domain Name and Information

Obtaining RFCs

You can obtain RFCs from the Request for Comments Web site, *www.rfc-editor.org/*. This Web site is currently maintained by members of the Information Sciences Institute (ISI) who publish a classified listing of all RFCs. RFCs are classified as one of the following: approved Internet standards, proposed Internet standards (circulated in draft form for review), Internet best practices, or For Your Information (FYI) documents.

Note To see the most current RFCs related to DHCP, see the Active IETF Working Groups Web site www.ietf.org/html.charters/dhc-charter.html.

DHCP Database Files

The DHCP server database in Windows 2000 Server uses the performance-enhanced Exchange Server storage engine. When you install DHCP service, the files shown in Table B.85 are automatically created in the *Winnt\System32\Dhcp* directory.

TABLE B.85 *DHCP Service Database Files*

File	Description
Dhcp.mdb	The DHCP server database file.
Dhcp.tmp	A temporary file used by the DHCP database as a swap file during database index maintenance operations. This file sometimes remains in the *WINNT\System32\Dhcp* directory after a system failure.
J50.log and J50#####.log	A log of all database transactions. This file is used by the DHCP database to recover data when necessary.
J50.chk	A checkpoint file.

Important The J50.log file, J50#####.log file, Dhcp.mdb file, and Dhcp.tmp file should not be removed or altered.

The DHCP server database is a dynamic database that is updated as DHCP clients are assigned or as they release their TCP/IP configuration parameters. Because the DHCP database is not a distributed database like the WINS server database, maintaining the DHCP server database is less complex.

The DHCP database and related registry entries are automatically backed up at a specific interval (15 minutes by installation default). You can change this installation default by changing the value of BackupInterval in the following registry key:

HKEY_LOCAL_MACHINE\SYSTEM\CurrentControlSet\Services\DHCPServer \Parameters.

Netshell Commands for DHCP

The Netshell commands for DHCP offer a fully equivalent command-line helper tool, *Dhcpmon.dll,* for use in administering DHCP servers that can be used as an alternative to console-based management. This can be useful for the following situations:

- When managing DHCP servers in wide area networks (WANs), commands can be used in interactive mode at the Netshell command prompt to better manage across slow-speed network links.
- When managing a large number of DHCP servers, commands can be used in batch mode to help script and automate recurring administrative tasks that need to be performed for all DHCP servers.

The following tables list commands that can be used at the Netshell command prompt (which is not the same as the Windows 2000 command prompt) to manage DHCP servers. For more information on how to use Netshell commands provided for DHCP, see Chapter 5.

Netshell Commands for Use with DHCP

The Netshell commands in Table B.86 are available for use in DHCP command-based server administration.

TABLE B.86 *Netshell Commands for DHCP Command-based Server Administration*

Command	Description
list	Lists all available DHCP commands.
dump	Dumps DHCP server configuration to command output or a text file.
?	Displays help.

Note The list command is available at all supported contexts within the DHCP command-line environment. To redirect output of the dump command to a text file, type the command at a Windows command prompt and use the standard MS-DOS redirection operator (>).

For example, you might type *netsh dump dhcp server > dhcpsrv.dmp* to dump the current configuration for the local DHCP server on the same computer to a text file called *Dhcpsrv.dmp*. This file can then be copied to another new DHCP server and used to recreate the same configuration by using the exec subcommand to execute the dumped configuration as a command script.

You could copy the file created by the previous command to a folder on the destination computer. You could then type *netsh exec dhcpsrv.dmp* to load and execute the saved configuration for the new DHCP server installed there.

DHCP First-Level Commands

The commands in Table B.87 are available to be run from the dhcp>/? prompt within the Netshell command environment.

Table B.87 *Commands Run from the dhcp>/? Prompt*

Command	Description
add server	Adds a DHCP server to the DHCP console. For more information, type ***add server /?***
delete server	Deletes a DHCP server from the DHCP console. For more information, type ***delete server/?***
show server	Displays all DHCP servers currently added under the DHCP console. For more information, type ***show server /?***
server [name/ address]	Shifts the current DHCP command-line context to the server specified by either its name or IP address. For more information, type ***help /?***

DHCP Server Commands

The commands in Table B.88 are available to be run from the dhcp server>/? prompt, which is rooted within the Netshell command environment.

Table B.88 *Commands Run from the dhcp server>/? Pr o m p t*

Command	Description
add class	Adds a class to the currently specified DHCP server. For more information, type ***add class /?***
add mscope	Adds a multicast scope to the currently specified DHCP server. For more information, type ***add mscope /?***
add optiondef	Adds a new option type definition to the currently specified DHCP server. For more information, type ***add optiondef /?***
add scope	Adds a new scope to the currently specified DHCP server. For more information, type ***add scope /?***
delete class	Deletes a class from the currently specified DHCP server. For more information, type ***delete class /?***
delete mscope	Deletes a multicast scope from the currently specified DHCP server. For more information, type ***delete mscope /?***
delete optiondef	Deletes a new option type definition from the currently specified DHCP server. For more information, type ***delete optiondef /?***
delete optionvalue	Deletes a new option type definition from the currently specified DHCP server. For more information, type ***delete optionvalue /?***
delete scope	Deletes a new scope from the currently specified DHCP server. For more information, type ***delete scope /?***
delete superscope	Deletes a new scope from the currently specified DHCP server. For more information, type ***delete superscope /?***
initiate auth	Initiates or retries authorization of the currently specified DHCP server in Active Directory. For more information, type ***initiate auth /?***

(continued)

TABLE B.88 *Commands Run from the dhcp server>/? Prompt (Continued)*

Command	Description
scope [scope_ip_address]	Switches the command context to DHCP scope specified by its IP network address, such as 169.254.1.0. For more information, see "DHCP Scope Commands" in this appendix.
mscope [mscope_name]	Switches the command context to DHCP multicast scope specified by name (case-sensitive), such as 239.239.254.0. For more information, see "DHCP Multicast Scope Commands" in this appendix.
set auditlog	Sets the audit log path parameters for the currently specified DHCP server. For more information, type *set auditlog /?*
set backupinterval	Sets the backup interval of the currently specified DHCP server. For more information, type *set backupinterval /?*
set backupdatabasepath	Sets the database backup path to be used by the currently specified DHCP server. For more information, type *set backupdatabasepath /?*
set databasecleanupinterval	Sets the database cleanup interval of the currently specified DHCP server. For more information, type *set databasecleanupinterval /?*
set databaseloggingflag	Sets/resets database logging flag for the currently specified DHCP server. For more information, type *set databaseloggingflag /?*
set databasename	Sets the name of the DHCP server database file for the currently specified DHCP server. For more information, type *set databasename /?*
set databasepath	Sets the path of the DHCP server database file for the currently specified DHCP server. For more information, type *set databasepath /?*
set databaserestoreflag	Sets/resets the database restore flag for the currently specified DHCP server. For more information, type *set databaserestoreflag /?*
set detectconflictretry	Sets the number of conflict detection attempts made by the currently specified DHCP server. For more information, type *set detectconflictretry /?*
set dnsconfig	Sets the DNS dynamic update configuration for the currently specified DHCP server. For more information, type *set dnsconfig /?*
set optionvalue	Sets a server option value, which will be applied for all scopes defined at the currently specified server. For more information, type *set optionvalue /?*
set server	Sets the current server in the Server mode. For more information, type *set server /?*
set userclass	Sets the userclass name for use in subsequent command operations. For more information, type *set userclass /?*
set vendorclass	Sets the vendor class name for use in subsequent command operations. For more information, type *set vendorclass /?*
show all	Displays all information for the currently specified DHCP server. For more information, type *show all /?*

(continued)

TABLE B.88 *Commands Run from the dhcp server>/? Prompt (Continued)*

Command	Description
show auditlog	Displays audit log path parameters for the currently specified DHCP server. For more information, type *show auditlog /?*
show bindings	Displays bindings information for the currently specified DHCP server. For more information, type *show bindings /?*
show class	Displays all class information for the currently specified DHCP server. For more information, type *show class /?*
show detectconflictretry	Displays the number of conflict detection settings for the currently specified DHCP server. For more information, type *show detectconflictretry /?*
show dnsconfig	Displays the DNS dynamic update configuration for the currently specified DHCP server. For more information, type *show dnsconfig /?*
show mibinfo	Displays Management Information Base (MIB) information for the currently specified DHCP server. For more information, type *show mibinfo /?*
show mscope	Displays all information about multicast scopes for the currently specified DHCP server. For more information, type *show mscope /?*
show optiondef	Displays all defined and available options for the currently specified DHCP server. For more information, type *show optiondef /?*
show optionvalue	Displays all available option values currently set for the specified DHCP server. For more information, type *show optionvalue /?*
show scope	Displays all information about scopes for the currently specified DHCP server. For more information, type *show scope /?*
show server	Displays information about the currently specified DHCP server. For more information, type *show server /?*
show dbproperties	Displays server database configuration information for the currently specified DHCP server. For more information, type *show dbproperties /?*
show serverstatus	Displays status information for the currently specified DHCP server. For more information, type *show serverstatus /?*
show userclass	Displays the current user class setting at the specified DHCP server. For more information, type *show userclass /?*
show vendorclass	Displays the current vendor class setting at the specified DHCP server. For more information, type *show vendorclass /?*
show version	Displays current version information for the specified DHCP server. For more information, type *show version /?*

B.4.4 DHCP scope commands

The commands in Table B.89 are available to be run from the dhcp server scope>/?, which is rooted at the DHCP server context within the Netshell command environment.

TABLE B.89 *Commands Run from the dhcp server scope>/? Prompt*

Command	Description
add excluderange	Adds a range of excluded addresses to the current scope. For more information, type add *excluderange /?*
add iprange	Adds a range of IP addresses to the current scope. For more information, type *add iprange /?*
add reservedip	Reserves an IP address for use by a specified MAC address in the current scope. For more information, type *add reservedip /?*
delete excluderange	Deletes an exclusion range of previously excluded IP addresses in the current scope. For more information, type *delete excluderange /?*
delete iprange	Deletes a range of IP addresses from the current scope. For more information, type *delete iprange /?*
delete optionvalue	Removes or clears an assigned scope option value from the current scope. For more information, type *delete optionvalue /?*
delete reservedip	Deletes a reservation for an IP address in the current scope. For more information, type *delete reservedip /?*
delete reservedoptionvalue	Removes an option value assigned for a reserved client in the current scope. For more information, type *delete reservedoptionvalue /?*
initiate reconcile	Checks and reconciles the current scope. For more information, type *initiate reconcile /?*
set comment	Sets the comment for the current scope. For more information, type *set comment /?*
set name	Sets the name of the current scope. For more information, type*set name /?*
set optionvalue	Sets an option value for the current scope. For more information, type *set optionvalue /?*
set reservedoptionvalue	Sets the comments for the current scope. For more information, type *set reservedoptionvalue /?*
set scope	Sets the scope to be used in subsequent operations. For more information, type *set scope /?*
set state	Sets/resets the state of the current scope to either an active or inactive state. For more information, type *set state /?*
set superscope	Sets the superscope to be used in subsequent operations. For more information, type *set superscope /?*
show clients	Displays all available version 4 clients for the current scope. For more information, type *show clients /?*
show clientsv5	Displays all available version 5 clients for the current scope. For more information, type *show clientsv5 /?*
show excluderange	Displays all currently excluded ranges of IP addresses for the current scope. For more information, type *show excluderange /?*

(continued)

TABLE B.89 *Commands Run from the dhcp server scope>/? Prompt (Continued)*

Command	Description
show iprange	Displays all available address ranges for the current scope. For more information, type *show iprange /?*
show optionvalue	Displays all option values that are set for the current scope. For more information, type *show optionvalue /?*
show reservedip	Displays all currently reserved IP addresses for the current scope. For more information, type *show reservedip /?*
show reservedoptionvalue	Displays all currently set option values for a reserved client IP address in the current scope. For more information, type *show reservedoptionvalue /?*
show scope	Displays information for the current scope. For more information, type *show scope /?*
show state	Displays the state of the current scope, indicating whether it is active or inactive. For more information, type *show state /?*

DHCP Multicast Scope Commands

The commands in Table B.90 can be run from the dhcp server mscope>/? prompt, which is rooted at the DHCP server context within the Netshell command environment.

TABLE B.90 *Commands Run from the dhcp server mscope>/? Prompt*

Command	Description
add excluderange	Adds a range of excluded addresses to the current multicast scope. For more information, type *add excluderange /?*
add iprange	Adds a range of IP addresses to the current multicast scope. For more information, type *add iprange /?*
delete excluderange	Deletes an exclusion range of previously excluded IP addresses in the current multicast scope. For more information, type *delete excluderange /?*
delete iprange	Deletes a range of IP addresses from the current multicast scope. For more information, type *delete iprange /?*
initiate reconcile	Checks and reconciles the current multicast scope. For more information, type *initiate reconcile /?*
set comment	Sets the comment for the current multicast scope. For more information, type *set comment /?*
set lease	Sets the lease duration for multicast scope IP addresses. For more information, type *set lease /?*
set mscope	Sets the multicast scope to be used in subsequent operations. For more information, type *set mscope /?*

(continued)

TABLE B.90 *Commands Run from the dhcp server mscope>/? Prompt (Continued)*

Command	Description
set name	Sets the name of the current multicast scope. For more information, type *set name /?*
set state	Sets/resets the state of the current multicast scope to either an active or inactive state. For more information, type *set state /?*
set ttl	Sets the TTL value for the current multicast scope. For more information, type *set ttl /?*
show clients	Displays all available clients for the current multicast scope. For more information, type *show clients /?*
show excluderange	Displays all currently excluded ranges of IP addresses for the current multicast scope. For more information, type *show excluderange /?*
show iprange	Displays all available IP address ranges for the current multicast scope. For more information, type *show iprange /?*
show lease	Displays the current lease duration settings for the multicast scope. For more information, type *show lease /?*
show mibinfo	Displays Management Information Base (MIB) information for the current multicast scope. For more information, type *show mibinfo /?*
show mscope	Displays information for the current multicast scope. For more information, type *show mscope /?*
show state	Displays the state of the current multicast scope, indicating whether it is active or inactive. For more information, type *show state /?*
show ttl	Displays the TTL value for the current multicast scope. For more information, type *show ttl /?*

Note When working within the DHCP command-line context and any of its subcontexts, you can type any of the following to list commands currently available for use: *help/?, /?/?, -?/?, ?/?*

DHCP Performance Monitoring Reference

For Windows 2000 Server, the DHCP Server service includes a set of performance counters that can be used to monitor various types of server activity. To access these counters, you must use System Monitor.

By default, performance monitoring of DHCP servers is available for use after the DHCP service component is installed. DHCP performance is measured using the metrics and counters listed in Table B.91.

TABLE B.91 *DHCP Performance Metrics and Counters*

Name	Description
Packets Received/sec	The number of message packets received per second by the DHCP server. A large number indicates heavy DHCP-related message traffic to the server.
Duplicates Dropped/sec	The number of duplicated packets per second dropped by the DHCP server. This number can be affected by multiple DHCP relay agents or network interfaces forwarding the same packet to the server. A large number here indicates that either clients are probably timing out too fast or the server is not responding fast enough.
Packets Expired/sec	The number of packets per second that expire and are dropped by the DHCP server. When a DHCP-related message packet is internally queued for 30 seconds or more, it is determined to be stale and expired by the server. A large number here indicates that the server is either taking too long to process some packets while other packets are queued and becoming stale, or traffic on the network is too high for the server to manage.
Milliseconds per packet (Avg.)	The average time in milliseconds used by the DHCP server to process each packet it receives. This number can vary depending on the server hardware and its I/O subsystem. A sudden or unusual increase might indicate a problem, either with the I/O subsystem becoming slower or because of an intrinsic processing overhead on the server computer.
Active Queue Length	The current length of the internal message queue of the DHCP server. This number equals the number of unprocessed messages received by the server. A large number might indicate heavy server traffic.
Conflict Check Queue Length	The current length of the conflict check queue for the DHCP server. This queue holds messages without responses while the DHCP server performs address conflict detection. A large value here might indicate that Conflict Detection Attempts has been set too high or that there is unusually heavy lease traffic at the server.
Discovers/sec	The number of DHCP discover messages (DHCPDISCOVERs) received per second by the server. These messages are sent by clients when they start on the network and obtain a new address lease. A sudden or unusual increase indicates a large number of clients are attempting to initialize and obtain an IP address lease from the server, such as when a number of client computers are started at any given time.
Offers/sec	The number of DHCP offer messages (DHCPOFFERs) sent per second by the DHCP server to clients. A sudden or unusual increase in this number indicates heavy traffic on the server.
Requests/sec	The number of DHCP request messages (DHCPREQUESTs) received per second by the DHCP server from clients. A sudden or unusual increase in this number indicates a large number of clients trying to renew their leases with the DHCP server. This might indicate that scope lease durations are too short.

TABLE B.91 *DHCP Performance Metrics and Counters (Continued)*

Name	Description
Informs/sec	The number of DHCP inform messages (DHCPINFORMs) received per second by the DHCP server. DHCP inform messages are used when the DHCP server queries for the directory service for the enterprise root and when dynamic updates are being done on behalf of clients by the server.
Acks/sec	The number of DHCP acknowledgment messages (DHCPACKs) sent per second by the DHCP server to clients. A sudden or unusual increase in this number indicates that a large number of clients are being renewed by the DHCP server. This might indicate that scope lease durations are too short.
Nacks/sec	The number of DHCP negative acknowledgment messages (DHCPNAKs) sent per second by the DHCP server to clients. A very high value might indicate potential network trouble in the form of misconfiguration of either the server or clients. When servers are misconfigured, one possible cause is a deactivated scope. For clients, a very high value could be caused by computers moving between subnets, such as laptop portables or other mobile devices.
Declines/sec	The number of DHCP decline messages (DHCPDECLINEs) received per second by the DHCP server from clients. A high value indicates that several clients have found their address to be in conflict, possibly indicating network trouble. In this situation, it can help to enable conflict detection on the DHCP server. This should only be used temporarily. Once the situation returns to normal, it should be turned off.
Releases/sec	The number of ipconfig /release commands at a command prompt. The DHCP release message name is DHCPRELEASE. DHCP release messages (DHCPRELEASEs) received per second by the DHCP server from clients. This number only exists if a DHCP client sends a release to the server. This can occur manually, such as when the ipconfig command is used at the client computer. Release messages can also be sent by the client if it is configured with the Release DHCP lease on shutdown option. Because clients rarely release their address, the value of this counter remains low for many DHCP network configurations.

Note Values for the following registry key can be used by a member of the local Administrators group:

HKEY_LOCAL_MACHINE\System\CurrentControlSet\Services\DHCPServer \Performance

By changing values stored at this registry path location, you can deny or modify permissions that determine who can view System Monitor counters used for the DHCP server on the server computer. Values under this key are used by the System Monitor DLL (*Perfctrs.dll*) to identify each of the counters described.

DHCP Updated Technical Information

Updated technical information for DHCP can be obtained by searching technical articles available from the Personal Support Center at the Microsoft Web site *support.microsoft.com*.

You can also obtain additional in-depth information on DHCP in the Windows 2000 Server Resource Kit. For more information, see Windows 2000 Resource Kit.

DHCP Bibliography

For detailed technical information about using DHCP, refer to the following texts and articles:

Comer, D. *Internetworking with TCP/IP, Volume I: Principles, Protocols, and Architecture*. Third edition. Englewood Cliffs, NJ: Prentice Hall, 1995.

Hunt, C., and R. B. Thompson. *Windows NT TCP/IP Network Administration*. Sebastopol, CA: O'Reilly and Associates, 1998.

Microsoft Corporation. *Managing a Microsoft Windows NT Network*. Redmond, WA: Microsoft Press, 1999.

Microsoft Corporation. *Optimizing Network Traffic*. Redmond, WA: Microsoft Press, 1999.

Minasi, M., T. Lammle, and M. Lammle. *Mastering TCP/IP for NT Server*. Alameda, CA: Sybex, 1997.

Parker, T. *TCP/IP Unleashed*. Indianapolis, IN: Sams Publishing, 1996.

Stevens, W. R. *TCP/IP Illustrated, Volume 1: The Protocols*. Reading, MA: Addison-Wesley, 1994.

Troubleshooting

Troubleshooting DHCP Clients

1. The DHCP client does not have an IP address configured or indicates that its IP address is 0.0.0.0.

Cause: The client was not able to contact a DHCP server and obtain an IP address lease, either because of a network hardware failure or because the DHCP server is unavailable.

Solution: Verify that the client computer has a valid functioning network connection. First, check that related client hardware (cables and network adapters) are working properly at the client, using basic network and hardware troubleshooting steps.

If the client hardware appears to be prepared and functioning properly, check that the DHCP server is available on the network by pinging it from another computer on the same network as the affected DHCP client.

2. The DHCP client appears to have automatically assigned itself an IP address that is incorrect for the current network.

   Cause: The Windows 2000 or Windows 98 DHCP client could not find a DHCP server and has used the Automatic Private IP Addressing (APIPA) feature to configure its IP address. In some larger networks, disabling APIPA might be desirable for network administration.

   Solution: First, use the **ping** command to test connectivity from the client to the server. Your next step would be to either verify or manually attempt to renew the client lease. Depending on your network requirements, it might be necessary to disable APIPA at the client. You can learn more about APIPA and how it works prior to making this decision.

3. The DHCP client appears to be missing some network configuration details or is unable to perform related tasks, such as resolving names.

   Cause: The client might be missing DHCP options in its leased configuration, either because the DHCP server is not configured to distribute them or the client does not support the options distributed by the server.

   Solution: For Microsoft DHCP clients, verify that the most commonly used and supported options have been configured at the server, scope, client, or class level of options assignment.

4. The DHCP client appears to have incorrect or incomplete options, such as an incorrect or missing router (default gateway) configured for the subnet on which it is located.

   Cause: The client has the full and correct set of DHCP options assigned but its network configuration does not appear to be working correctly.

   If the DHCP server is configured with an incorrect DHCP router option (option code 3) for the default gateway address of the client, clients running Windows NT or Windows 2000 do not use the incorrect address. However, DHCP clients running Windows 95 do use the incorrect address.

   Solution: Change the IP address list for the router option at the applicable DHCP scope and server. If you are configuring the router option as a Server Option at the affected DHCP server, remove it there and set the correct value in the Scope Options node for the applicable DHCP scope that services the client.

In rare instances, you might have to configure the DHCP client to use a specialized list of routers different from other scope clients. In such cases, you can add a reservation and configure the router option list specifically for the reserved client.

5. Many DHCP clients are unable to get IP addresses from the DHCP server.

Cause: The IP address of the DHCP server was changed and now DHCP clients cannot get IP addresses.

Solution: A DHCP server can only service requests for a scope that has a network ID that is the same as the network ID of its IP address. Make sure that the DHCP server IP address falls in the same network range as the scope it is servicing. For example, a server with an IP address in the 192.168.0.0 network cannot assign addresses from scope 10.0.0.0 unless superscopes are used.

Cause: The DHCP clients are located across a router from the subnet where the DHCP server resides and are unable to receive an address from the server.

Solution: A DHCP server can provide IP addresses to client computers on remote multiple subnets only if the router that separates them can act as a DHCP relay agent. Completing the following steps might correct this problem:

- Configure a BOOTP/DHCP Relay Agent on the client subnet (that is, the same physical network segment). The relay agent can be located on the router itself or on a Windows NT Servercomputer running the DHCP Relay service component.
- At the DHCP server, do the following:
  - **a.** Configure a scope to match the network address on the other side of the router where the affected clients are located.
  - **b.** In the scope, make sure that the subnet mask is correct for the remote subnet.
  - **c.** Use a default gateway on the network connection of the DHCP server in such a way that it is not using the same IP address as the router that supports the remote subnet where the clients are located.
  - **d.** Do not include this scope (that is, the one for the remote subnet) in superscopes configured for use on the same local subnet or segment where the DHCP server resides.
- Make sure there is only one logical route between the DHCP server and the remote subnet clients.

Cause: Multiple DHCP servers exist on the same local area network (LAN).

Solution: Make sure that you do not configure multiple DHCP servers on the same LAN with overlapping scopes.

You might want to rule out the possibility that one of the DHCP servers in question is a Small Business Server (SBS) computer. By design, the DHCP Server service, when running under SBS, automatically stops when it detects another DHCP server on the LAN.

6. The DHCP client appears to be affected by another problem not described above.

   Cause: My problem is not described above.

   Solution: Search the Microsoft Web site for updated technical information that might relate to the problem you have observed. If necessary, you can obtain information and instructions that pertain to your current problem or issue.

   If you are connected to the Internet, the latest updates for Windows 2000 Server are available at the Microsoft Web site. For obtaining the latest Service Pack updates for Windows NT Server, see the Microsoft Web site.

   Familiarize yourself with other useful documentation and resources for DHCP, such as the DHCP Troubleshooter.

Troubleshooting DHCP Servers

1. The DHCP server is stopped.

   Cause: The DHCP server has not been authorized to operate on the network.

   Solution: Authorize the DHCP server in the enterprise where it is being used.

   Cause: Configuration details might be incorrect or missing at the server.

   Solution: Because many DHCP failures are first detected as client-side errors, you might want to start by investigating the problem there.

   Cause: The DHCP server has been stopped.

   Solution: Check the system event log and DHCP server audit log files for details.

   When the DHCP Server service either stops or cannot start, useful explanatory information about the source of the service failure or shutdown can generally be found in these logs.

2. The DHCP server is unable to provide service to clients.

   Cause: The server is a multihomed computer and is not providing service on one or more of its network connections.

Solution: Review Windows 2000 DHCP server binding defaults for network connections based on whether you have elected to either statically or dynamically configure TCP/IP for any or all installed connections on the server computer. Also, review an example of multihomed DHCP server configuration to see if you have missed any critical details.

Cause: Scopes or superscopes on the DHCP server have not been either configured or activated for use.

Solution: Add scopes and make sure that they are correctly configured along with any DHCP scope options that need to be assigned for client use.

Cause: The server is located on a different subnet as some of its clients and is not providing service to clients on remote subnets.

Solution: If you are using a DHCP server in a routed network, you might want to review issues related to DHCP relay agents and the appropriate use of superscopes.

Cause: The scope in use is full and can no longer lease addresses to requesting clients.

Solution: If the DHCP server does not have IP addresses available to provide to its clients, it returns DHCP negative acknowledgment messages (DHCPNAKs) to them. When this occurs, consider the following possible solutions:

- Expand the address range by increasing the End IP address for the current scope.
- Create a new additional scope and a superscope, then add the current scope and the new scope to the superscope.
- Create a new scope or extend the range. Optimally, you could renumber your current IP network. Deactivate the old scope as needed, and then configure and activate the new one.
- Reduce the lease duration. This can help to expedite the reclaiming of lapsed scope addresses.

Other DHCP-related procedures and techniques might also help to accelerate or ease the transition from an existing scope being retired to a new scope created to take its place at the server. These include deleting client leases from the scope being retired, excluding addresses from that scope, and then deactivating it once the new scope has been activated. This ensures that the DHCP client obtains leasing from the new scope.

Cause: The range of IP addresses being offered by the DHCP server is in conflict with the range of addresses being offered by another DHCP server on the network.

You can confirm that this is the likely cause if DHCP server logs still indicate that DHCP negative acknowledgment messages (DHCPNAKs) are being returned to requesting clients or if you have tried unsuccessfully at the client to renew its lease manually.

Solution: Modify the scope address pool for the scopes at each DHCP server to ensure that scope IP addresses do not overlap. You can add exclusions to the scopes as necessary, delete client leases, and temporarily enable server-side conflict detection to assist in solving the problem.

3. The DHCP server appears to have suffered some data corruption or loss.

   Cause: The DHCP server database has become corrupted or is missing server data, possibly reporting Jet database errors.

   Solution: Use DHCP server data recovery options to restore the database and correct any of the reported errors. You can also use the Reconcile feature in the DHCP console to verify and reconcile any database inconsistencies that the server is able to find.

4. The server appears to be affected by another problem not described above.

   Cause: My problem is not described above.

   Solution: Search the Microsoft Web site for updated technical information that might relate to the problem you have observed. You can obtain information and instructions that pertain to your current problem or issue.

   If you have connection to the Internet, the latest updates for Windows 2000 Server are available at the Microsoft Web site. For obtaining the latest Service Pack updates for Windows NT Server, see the Microsoft Web site.

   Familiarize yourself with other useful documentation and resources for DHCP, such as the DHCP Troubleshooter.

APPENDIX C

WINS Resources and Troubleshooting

NetBIOS Names Reference

For all Microsoft operating systems that support and use NetBIOS names, the first 15 characters of a name can be specified by a user. However, the sixteenth character of the name (00FF hex) always indicates a resource type.

This section contains additional information and examples of NetBIOS names used by Microsoft networking components.

NetBIOS Name Types: An Overview

Tables C.1 through C.3 list the most common types of NetBIOS names that can be used in the WINS database. When creating static mappings, these general types are available for selected use.

Table C.1 *Common Types of NetBIOS Names for Use in WINS Database*

Type	Description
Unique	Used to associate the computer specified by name in **Computer name** and a single IP address in **IP address** for this static mapped entry. When this type is selected, three types of records are statically added to the WINS database for the specified computer name. These are the [00h]WorkStation, [03h]Messenger, and [20h] File Server types.
Group	Also referred to as a normal group. This type is used to add a static entry for the computer, specified by name in a static mapping, to a workgroup used on your network. If this type is used, the IP address for the computer is not stored in WINS, but is resolved through local subnet broadcasts.
Domain Name	Indicates a *domain name* [1C] mapped entry for locating Windows NT domain controllers. For information about locating domain controllers using NetBT, see Chapter 6, "WINS Overview."
Internet Group	Used for special user-defined administrative groups. You can use this to group resources. For example, you can indicate a group of file or print servers for organizing shared resources that are visible when browsing your network places. Each Internet group is represented by a shared group name of [20h] type in the WINS database.
Multihomed	Used to register a unique name for a computer that has more than one IP address (either multiple adapters, each using a single address, or one network adapter configured with multiple IP addresses).

Table C.2 *NetBIOS Unique Names*

Format	Description
computer_name[00h]	Registered by the Workstation Service on the WINS client. In general, this name is called the NetBIOS computer name.
computer_name[03h]	Registered by the Messenger Service on the WINS client. This service is used by the client when sending and receiving messages. This name is usually appended to both the NetBIOS computer name for the WINS client computer and the name of the user currently logged on to that computer when sending messages on the network.
computer_name[06h]	Registered by the Routing and Remote Access service on the WINS client (when the service is started).
domain_name[1Bh]	Registered by each Windows NT Server 4.0 domain controller running as the domain master browser. This name record is used to allow remote browsing of domains. When a WINS server is queried for this name, a WINS server returns the IP address of the computer that registered this name.
computer_name[1Fh]	Registered by the Network Dynamic Data Exchange (NetDDE) services. This appears only if the NetDDE services are started on the computer.
computer_name[20h]	Registered by the Server service on the WINS client. This service is used to provide points of service to the WINS client to provide sharing of its files on the network.
computer_name[21h]	Registered by the Remote Access Server (RAS). Client service on the WINS client (when the RAS Client is started).

(continued)

TABLE C.2 *NetBIOS Unique Names (Continued)*

Format	Description
computer_name[BEh]	Registered by the Network Monitoring Agent Service and appearing only if the service is started on the WINS client computer. If the computer name has fewer than 15 characters, the remaining character spaces are padded with plus (+) symbols.
computer_name[BFh]	Registered by the Network Monitoring Utility (included with Microsoft Systems Management Server). If the computer name has fewer than 15 characters, the remaining character spaces are padded with plus (+) symbols.
username[03h]	User names for currently logged-on users are registered in the WINS database. Each user name is registered by the Server service component so that users can receive any net send commands sent to the user name. If more than one user logs on with the same user name, only the first computer logged on with that name registers the name.

TABLE C.3 *NetBIOS Group Names*

Format	Description
domain_name[00h]	Registered by the Workstation Service so that it can receive browser broadcasts from LAN Manager-based computers.
domain_name[1Ch]	Registered for use by the domain controllers within the domain. These contain up to 25 IP addresses.
domain_name[1Dh]	Registered for use by master browsers, of which there is only one per subnet. Backup browsers use this name to communicate with the master browser, retrieving the list of available servers from the master browser. WINS servers always return a positive registration response for domain_name[1D], even though the WINS server does not register this name in its database. Therefore, when a WINS server is queried for the domain_name[1D], the WINS server returns a negative response, which forces the client to broadcast for name resolution.
group_name[1Eh]	A normal group name. Any computers configured to be network browsers can broadcast to this name and listen for broadcasts to this name to elect a master browser. A statically mapped group name uses this name to register itself on the network. When a WINS server receives a name query for a name ending with [1E], the WINS server always returns the network broadcast address for the local network of the requesting client. The client can then use this address to broadcast to the group members. These broadcasts are for the local subnet and should not cross routers.
group_name[20h]	A special group name called the Internet Group is registered with WINS servers to identify groups of computers for administrative purposes. For example, "printersg" could be a registered group name used to identify an administrative group of print servers.
__MSBROWSE__[01h]	Registered by the master browser for each subnet. When a WINS server receives a name query for this name, the WINS server always returns the network broadcast address for local network of the requesting client.

Netshell Commands for WINS

The NetShell commands for WINS offer a fully equivalent command-line tool for administering WINS servers that can be used as an alternative to console-based management. This is useful in the following situations:

- When managing WINS servers in WANs, commands can be used in interactive mode at the NetShell command prompt to better manage over slow-speed network links.
- When managing a large number of WINS servers, commands can be used in batch mode to script and automate recurring administrative tasks that need to be performed for all WINS servers.

Table C.4 lists commands available at the NetShell command prompt (as distinguished from the Windows 2000 command prompt) to manage WINS servers.

TABLE C.4 *NetShell Commands for Managing WINS Servers*

Command	Description
List	Lists all available WINS commands.
Dump	Dumps WINS server configuration to command output.
add name	Registers a name to the server. For more information, type *add name /?*
add partner	Adds a replication partner to the server. For more information, type *add partner /?*
add pngserver	Adds a list of Persona Non Grata servers for the current server. For more information, type *add pngserver /?*
check database	Checks the consistency of the database. For more information, type *check database /?*
check name	Checks a list of name records against a set of WINS servers. For more information, type *check name /?*
check version	Checks the consistency of the version number. For more information, type *check version /?*
delete name	Deletes a registered name from the server database. For more information, type *delete name /?*
delete partner	Deletes a replication partner from the list of replication partners. For more information, type *delete partner /?*
delete records	Deletes or tombstones all or a set of records from the server. For more information, type *delete records /?*
delete owners	Deletes a list of owners and their records. For more information, type *delete owners /?*

(continued)

TABLE C.4 *NetShell Commands for Managing WINS Servers (Continued)*

Command	Description
delete pngserver	Deletes all or selected Persona Non Grata servers from the list. For more information, type *delete pngserver /?*
init backup	Initiates backup of the WINS database. For more information, type *init backup /?*
init import	Initiates import from an Lmhosts file. For more information, type *init import /?*
init pull	Initiates and sends a pull trigger to another WINS server. For more information, type *init pull /?*
init pullrange	Initiates and pulls a range of records from another WINS server. For more information, type *init pullrange /?*
init push	Initiates and sends a push trigger to another WINS server. For more information, type *init push /?*
init replicate	Initiates replication of the database with replication partners. For more information, type *init replicate /?*
init restore	Initiates restoring of the database from a file. For more information, type *init restore /?*
init scavenge	Initiates scavenging of the WINS database for the server. For more information, type *init scavenge /?*
init search	Initiates search on the WINS database for the server. For more information, type *init search /?*
reset statistics	Resets the server statistics. For more information, type *reset statistics /?*
set autopartnerconfig	Sets the automatic replication partner configuration information for the server. For more information, type *set autopartnerconfig /?*
set backuppath	Sets the backup parameters for the server. For more information, type *set backuppath /?*
set burstparam	Sets the burst handling parameters for the server. For more information, type *set autopartnerconfig /?*
set logparam	Sets the database and event logging options. For more information, type *set logparam /?*
set migrateflag	Sets the migration flag for the server. For more information, type *set migrateflag /?*
set namerecord	Sets Interval and Timeout values for the server. For more information, type *set namerecord /?*
Set periodicdbchecking	Sets periodic database checking parameters for the server. For more information, type *set periodicdbchecking /?*
Set pullpartnerconfig	Sets the configuration parameters for the specified pull partner. For more information, type *set pullpartnerconfig /?*
Set pushpartnerconfig	Sets the configuration parameters for the specified push partner. For more information, type *set pushpartnerconfig /?*

(continued)

TABLE C.4 *NetShell Commands for Managing WINS Servers (Continued)*

Command	Description
set pullparam	Sets the default pull parameters for the server. For more information, type *set pullparam /?*
set pushparam	Sets the default push parameters for the server. For more information, type *set pushparam /?*
set replicateflag	Sets the replication flag for the server. For more information, type *set replicateflag /?*
set startversion	Sets the start version ID for the database. For more information, type *set startversion /?*
show browser	Displays all active domain master browser [1Bh] records. For more information, type *show browser /?*
show database	Displays the database and records for the specified server. For more information, type *show database /?*
show info	Displays configuration information. For more information, type *show info /?*
show name	Displays detailed information for a particular record in the server. For more information, type *show name /?*
show partner	Displays pull or push (or both) partners for the server. For more information, type *show partner /?*
Show partnerproperties	Displays default partner configuration. For more information, type *show partnerproperties /?*
Show pullpartnerconfig	Displays configuration information for a pull partner. For more information, type *show pullpartnerconfig /?*
Show pushpartnerconfig	Displays configuration information for a push partner. For more information, type *show pushpartnerconfig /?*
show reccount	Displays number of records owned by a specific server. For more information, type *show reccount /?*
show recbyversion	Displays records owned by a specific server. For more information, type *show recbyversion /?*
show server	Displays the currently selected server. For more information, type *show server /?*
show statistics	Displays the statistics for the WINS server. For more information, type *show statistics /?*
show version	Displays the current version counter value for the WINS server. For more information, type *show version /?*
show versionmap	Displays the owner ID to Maximum Version Number mappings. For more information, type *show versionmap /?*

WINS RFCs

Requests for Comments (RFCs) are an evolving series of reports, proposals for protocols, and protocol standards used by the Internet community. Although TCP/IP standards are always published as RFCs, not all RFCs specify standards.

RFCs are authored by individuals who voluntarily write and submit a draft proposal for a new protocol or specification to the Internet Engineering Task Force (IETF) and other working groups. Submitted drafts are first reviewed by a technical expert, a task force, or an RFC editor, and then assigned a status.

WINS is based on the standard RFCs for designing and implementing NetBIOS over TCP/IP, and are published by the IETF and other working groups.

RFCs for WINS in Windows 2000

The RFCs supported by WINS in Windows 2000 are listed in Table C.5.

TABLE C.5 *RFCs Supported by WINS in Windows 2000*

RFC	Title
1001	Protocol Standard for a NetBIOS Service on a TCP/UDP Transport: Concepts and Methods
1002	Protocol Standard for a NetBIOS Service on a TCP/UDP Transport: Detailed Specifications

Obtaining RFCs

You can obtain RFCs from the Request for Comments Web site, *http://www.rfc-editor.org/*. This Web site is currently maintained by members of the Information Sciences Institute (ISI), who publish a classified listing of all RFCs. RFCs are classified as one of the following: approved Internet standards, proposed Internet standards (circulated in draft form for review), Internet best practices, or For Your Information (FYI) documents.

Note RFCs 1001 and 1002 define a standard protocol to support NetBIOS services in a TCP/IP environment. These RFCs describe NetBIOS over TCP (NetBT) protocols in a general manner, emphasizing the underlying ideas and techniques used by all NetBT implementations.

WINS complies with these RFCs and provides an open and standards-based interoperability as a NetBIOS name service. However, because Windows 2000 has added enhancements beyond those specified in the RFCs, WINS servers are more accurately described as enhanced NetBIOS name servers.

WINS Performance Monitoring Reference

For Windows 2000 Server, the WINS Server service includes a set of performance counters that can be used to monitor various types of server activity. To access these counters, you must use System Monitor.

By default, after WINS is installed on Windows 2000 Server, the WINS performance counters listed in Table C.6 are available for use in monitoring server activity:

TABLE C.6 *WINS Performance Counters*

Name	Description
Queries/sec	The rate, in seconds, at which NetBIOS name queries are received by the WINS server. A large number indicates heavy WINS-related message traffic to the server.
Releases/sec	The rate, in seconds, at which NetBIOS release messages are received by the WINS server.
Successful Queries/sec	The rate, in seconds, at which NetBIOS name queries are successfully processed when received by the WINS server.
Successful Releases/sec	The rate, in seconds, at which NetBIOS release messages are successfully processed when received by the WINS server.
Total Number of Conflicts/sec	The rate, in seconds, at which all name conflicts are detected by WINS. This total is determined by averaging the sum of all unique and group name conflicts.
Total Number of Registrations/sec	The rate, in seconds, at which all name registrations are detected by WINS. This total is determined by averaging the sum of all unique and group name registrations.
Total Number of Renewals/sec	The rate, in seconds, at which all name renewals are detected by WINS. This total is determined by averaging the sum of all unique and group name renewals.
Unique Conflicts/sec	The rate, in seconds, at which unique name conflicts are detected by the WINS server. This total is determined by averaging conflicts for unique names only.
Unique Registrations/sec	The rate, in seconds, at which unique name registrations are detected by the WINS server. This total is determined by averaging registrations for unique names only.
Unique Renewals/sec	The rate, in seconds, at which unique name renewals are detected by the WINS server. This total is determined by averaging renewals for unique names only.

Note Values for the following registry key can be used by a member of the local Administrators group:

HKEY_LOCAL_MACHINE\System\CurrentControlSet\Services\WINS\Performance

By changing values stored at this registry path location, you can deny or modify permissions, determining who can view the System Monitor counters used for WINS on the server computer. Values under this key are used by the System Monitor dynamic-link library (*Perfctrs.dll*) to identify each counter described.

WINS Updated Technical Information

Updated technical information for WINS can be obtained by searching technical articles available from the Personal Support Center at the Microsoft Web site, *support.microsoft.com*.

You can also obtain additional in-depth information on WINS in the Windows 2000 Server Resource Kit. For more information, see Windows 2000 Resource Kit.

WINS Bibliography

For detailed technical information about using WINS, refer to the following texts:

Hunt, C., and R. B. Thompson. *Windows NT TCP/IP Network Administration*. Sebastopol, CA: O'Reilly and Associates, 1998.

Microsoft Corporation. *Managing a Microsoft Windows NT Network*. Redmond, WA: Microsoft Press, 1999.

Microsoft Corporation. *Optimizing Network Traffic*. Redmond, WA: Microsoft Press, 1999.

Minasi, M., T. Lammle, and M. Lammle. *Mastering TCP/IP for NT Server*. Alameda, CA: Sybex, 1997.

Parker, T. *TCP/IP Unleashed*. Indianapolis, IN: Sams Publishing, 1996.

Troubleshooting

Troubleshooting WINS Clients

1. Name resolution failed at client computer.

   Cause: The type of name resolution used is not appropriate. Determine whether WINS or DNS is being used for name resolution and if the name failure is occurring for a NetBIOS or fully qualified domain name (FQDN).

Solution: NetBIOS names are 15 characters or less and are typically used to provide named access to NetBIOS services based on a computer or group name, such as Messenger, Server, or Workstation. For example, the short NetBIOS name "PRINT-SRV1" might refer to a computer used for print and file sharing. It might also be known by a full DNS computer name, *print-srv1.example.microsoft.com,* when referring to this same computer as a Windows 2000 shared or published printer resource.

For the DNS example name used above, Winsock-based host name resolution is used to associate an IP address to a named computer and further identify it in a system of domains, either on an intranet or the Internet. This is needed for an entirely different set of applications, such as to access Web, SMTP mail, FTP, or LDAP servers.

The key point is that each of these name schemes, WINS or DNS, requires name resolution for different names used in different applications and for locating different types of network services. NetBIOS has its own set of applications that demand NetBIOS name resolution, the absence of which can cause network failures. These can be repaired or detected through an Lmhosts file used temporarily to troubleshoot or correct the name resolution failure.

DNS and FQDNs use Winsock-style host name resolution and are primarily used in Windows 2000 and for Active Directory and Internet use. For this type of name resolution, you can also repair or detect most problems through a Hosts file used temporarily to troubleshoot or correct the name resolution failure.

Verify the exact form of the name that has failed during resolution and determine whether the correct type of name resolution was involved.

Cause: The client could be using an application or version of Windows that requires the use of WINS to resolve names.

Solution: Not all Windows computers or applications require WINS or NetBT. For example, if the failed name resolution occurred as part of a URL entered in a Web browser or FTP program or as part of an address in an Internet e-mail program, the problem is more likely related to DNS.

In a pure Windows 2000 environment, DNS can be used instead of WINS as a naming service. For a pure environment to exist, both the client and the resource server (the computer the client has targeted for locating by name) must be running Windows 2000. For other cases where either the client or resource server is running an earlier version of Windows or MS-DOS, a mixed environment exists.

In mixed environments, name resolution could fail when any clients need access to shared resources not published through Active Directory. For example, resources such as these could include legacy file and print servers, or domain controllers or member servers used to complete logon or browsing of Windows NT domains. Some examples of applications that a client might use and need WINS to assist in name resolution include My Network Places, the Map Network Drive feature in Windows Explorer, or the net command *(Net.exe)* and any of its supported options, such as net use or net view.

Cause: The client computer may not be correctly configured, or may not be able to use WINS.

Solution: First, determine whether the client is configured or enabled to use both TCP/IP and WINS. Client configuration of WINS-related settings can be done in one of the two following ways:

Manually, by an administrator setting the client TCP/IP configuration.

Dynamically, by a DHCP server providing the client with TCP/IP configuration.

In most cases, computers running earlier versions of Microsoft operating systems are already able to use WINS once TCP/IP is installed and configured for the client. For Windows 2000, administrators can optionally disable NetBT for each client. By disabling NetBT, WINS cannot be used at the client.

In addition, determine whether the client has a valid IP configuration. To check a client IP configuration, use the ipconfig /all command. You can use ipconfig /all|more as a way to slow or pause viewing of the output of this command for screen-by-screen review.

In the command output, verify that the client computer has the following configured for the network where it is connected:

A valid IP address

A valid subnet mask

A default gateway

Primary and secondary WINS servers

If the client does not have a valid configuration, you can either use the ipconfig /renew command to force the client to obtain a renewal of its IP configuration with the DHCP server or you can update the TCP/IP configuration for the client manually.

Cause: The client may not have basic connectivity with its configured WINS servers.

Solution: To verify whether a client has basic TCP/IP access to the WINS server, first try pinging the WINS server by its IP address.

For example, if the client uses a primary WINS server of 10.0.0.1, type ping 10.0.0.1 at the command prompt on the client computer. If you are not sure what the IP address is for the WINS server, you can usually learn it by repeating the previous command, using ipconfig /all|more if necessary to pause the displayed command output so you can read the WINS server information.

If the WINS server responds to a direct ping of its IP address, try using the nbtstat -RR command at both the client and also at the resource server that the client is attempting to locate by name. This command forces the WINS client services on each computer to send name release and refresh requests to the WINS server and reregister their names.

If the WINS server does not respond to direct pinging of its IP address, this indicates that the source of the problem more likely stems from network connectivity issues between the client and WINS server. If this is the case, follow basic TCP/IP network troubleshooting steps to fix the problem.

Cause: The primary or secondary WINS server may not be able to service the client.

Solution: At the primary or secondary WINS server for the client, use either Event Viewer or the WINS console to see if WINS is started and currently running. If WINS is running on the server, search for the name previously requested by the client to see if it is in the WINS server database. If the name does not appear in the server database, check whether replication is configured correctly and is operational between your WINS servers.

2. Clients do not use load balancing when connecting to a multihomed server.

   Cause: The WINS server providing name resolution for the multihomed server name to network clients is running an earlier version of Windows NT Server that has not been updated.

   For all versions of Windows that support NetBT, network clients configured to use WINS attempt to resolve any NetBIOS-based name for a computer to its IP address or addresses. To perform this resolution, clients query the WINS server for the address of the multihomed server and receive a list of addresses that are always in the same order. NetBT then takes and sorts the list, arranging multiple IP addresses according to the following three categories:

   Any IP addresses located on the same subnet as the client are given first priority in the list.

   Next, IP addresses located within the same network class are listed.

   Finally, any remaining addresses are listed.

Then, NetBT starts at the top of this list and pings the first address to make sure it is valid. If it gets a reply, it uses the address. If there is no reply, it goes on to the next address.

The problem is that for earlier versions of WINS, within these three categories, the order of addresses is left unchanged from the list provided by the WINS server. This means that, as long as the first address in the list is online, it will be the one that is always used by every WINS client. This does not provide load balancing or round-robin rotation, as DNS servers can perform when more than one name-to-address mapping is available.

Solution: Upgrade WINS servers to Windows 2000 Server or update those running earlier versions of Windows NT Server to the most current Service Pack.

3. Clients appear to be affected by another problem not described above.

   Cause: My problem is not described above.

   Solution: Search the Microsoft Web site for updated technical information that might relate to the problem you have observed. If necessary, you can obtain information and instructions that pertain to your current problem or issue.

   If you have connection to the Internet, you can obtain the latest updates for Windows 2000 Server at the Microsoft Web site. For obtaining the latest Service Pack updates for Windows NT Server, see the Microsoft Web site.

   Familiarize yourself with other useful documentation and resources for WINS, such as the Windows Internet Name Service (WINS) Troubleshooter.

Troubleshooting WINS Servers

1. The server cannot resolve names for clients.

   Cause: Configuration details might be incorrect or missing.

   Solution: To help prevent the most common types of problems, review WINS best practices for deploying and managing your WINS servers. Most WINS-related problems start as failed queries at a client, so it is best to start there.

   Cause: The WINS server might not be able to service the client.

   Solution: At the primary or secondary WINS server for the client that cannot locate a name, use **Event Viewer** or the WINS console to see if WINS is started and currently running. If WINS is running on the server, search for the name previously requested by the client to see if it is in the WINS server database.

Cause: WINS server is failing or registering database corruption errors.

Solution: Use WINS database recovery techniques to help restore WINS operations.

Cause: The name does not appear in the server database.

Solution: Check whether replication is configured correctly and is operational between your WINS servers.

Cause: The WINS server answering clients might be returning stale or incorrect information to clients. The WINS server might be affected by a static mapping blocking the dynamic registration of a valid name-to-address mapping for the computer hosting the service or resource in question.

Solution: In general, static mappings are not recommended for clients that can dynamically use WINS to update their name and address information. If the information returned to a client during name resolution is incorrect or stale, check to see if the name entry in the WINS server database was entered statically. If the name was entered using a static type entry, you can choose from the following options to update WINS:

- Enable Migrate (Overwrite unique static record with dynamic record) in Replication Partners Properties.
- Edit the static mapping to update the mapped address information.
- Delete the static entry from WINS.

Cause: Replication might not be occurring between all WINS servers.

Solution: In some WINS designs, the use of one-way replication partnerships, such as push-only or pull-only partners, can create situations where WINS names data is not regularly replicated to all network servers.

2. The server intermittently loses its ability to resolve names.

   Cause: There might be a split registration problem, where the WINS server is registering its names in WINS at two servers on the network. This is possible when the WINS server settings configured in TCP/IP properties at the server computer are pointing to IP addresses of remote WINS servers and are not configured to use the IP address of the local WINS server.

   Solution: Reconfigure client TCP/IP properties at the WINS server to have its primary and secondary WINS servers point to the IP address of the local server computer.

3. The server appears to be affected by another problem not described above.

   Cause: My problem is not described above.

Solution: Search the Microsoft Web site for updated technical information that might relate to the problem you have observed. If necessary, you can obtain information and instructions that pertain to your current problem or issue.

If you have connection to the Internet, you can obtain the latest updates for Windows 2000 Server at the Microsoft Web site. For obtaining the latest Service Pack updates for Windows NT Server, see the Microsoft Web site.

Familiarize yourself with other useful documentation and resources for WINS, such as the Windows Internet Name Service (WINS) Troubleshooter.

Troubleshooting WINS Databases

1. WINS backups are failing consistently.

   Cause: The specified WINS backup directory might be a remote drive.

   Solution: Make sure that the path for the WINS backup directory is on a local disk on the WINS server. WINS cannot back up its database files to a remote drive.

2. My WINS database might be corrupt.

   Cause: The WINS database might need to be deleted, either fully or partially, so its contents can be replaced from another WINS server to restore consistency and data integrity between WINS servers on your network.

   Solution: Depending upon the extent of the corruption and whether the corrupted records are at an owner or replica WINS server, you can rebuild the local WINS database through replication with another WINS server.

   To remove corrupted data at a replica (nonowner) server, use the Delete Owner command option in the WINS console. When using this feature, you can delete the owner and any of its associated records in question from local WINS data.

   For an owner WINS server, you can restore data integrity by starting WINS with a fresh database and then initiating replication with a configured replication partner. At the local WINS server that has ownership of corrupted records, perform the following steps:

   - Stop WINS.
   - Delete all current WINS database files. These files are located at the path currently set in **Database path** on the **Advanced** tab in ***WINS server*** **Properties** for the local WINS server.
   - Restart WINS.

When WINS is started with a blank database, it will replicate back all records (including those for which it is the registered owner) that are contained in data stored at other servers. This is because it starts with a fresh version ID that is lower than the highest version ID in use for data at any of the other WINS servers on your network.

WINS servers use record version IDs to keep track of which records are new and which need to be replicated to other WINS servers. Every record in a WINS database has an owner associated with it. This owner is generally the server with which the WINS client originally registered.

Normally, the owner (in this case, the local WINS server) does not receive its own records from its replication partners. For this reason, if records are lost from the local WINS database, it can typically be difficult to replace these records, even if they exist at other partners. In this solution, this difficulty is solved because records that exist on other WINS servers are certain to have higher version IDs than the local server after you delete the local database and restart WINS.

On a WINS network with many records, two registry entries affect the ability of WINS to perform local database replacement as described in earlier steps. The first value, InitTimeReplication, keeps the server from accepting queries or registrations until the database is reconstructed. The second, InitTimePause, causes WINS to pause while the replication takes place. The location and configurable settings for these keys are discussed more in the following tables.

Caution Incorrectly editing the registry may severely damage your system. Before making changes to the registry, you should back up any valued data on the computer.

TABLE C.7 *InitTimeReplication*

Location:	HKEY_LOCAL_MACHINES\System\CurrentControlSet\Services\WINS\Partners
Type:	REG_DWORD
Default:	1
Values:	1 = The WINS server pulls replicas of new WINS database entries from its partners when the system is initialized or when a replication-related parameter changes. 0 = Replication occurs only as often as specified in the value of **TimeInterval**.

TABLE C.8 *InitTimePause*

Location:	HKEY_LOCAL_MACHINES\System\CurrentControlSet\Services\WINS\Parameters
Type:	REG_DWORD
Default:	0
Values:	0 = WINS does not start in paused state. 1 = WINS starts in paused state. The value set determines whether WINS starts in a paused state and remains in that state until its first replication is completed. In the paused state, WINS does not accept any name registrations, releases, or queries. WINS remains in the paused state until it has replicated with its partners or until its first replication attempt has failed. If the value of InitTimePause is set to 1, then InitTimeReplication (in the Pull partners subkey) should either be set to 1 or deleted from the registry.

Additional information about these and other WINS server registry parameters is available in the Windows 2000 Server Resource Kit.

3. I am still having WINS database problems, different from the ones that are described above.

   Cause: My WINS database problem was not described above.

   Solution: Search the Microsoft Web site for updated technical information that might relate to the problem you have observed. If necessary, you can obtain information and instructions that pertain to your current problem or issue.

   If you have connection to the Internet, you can obtain the latest updates for Windows 2000 Server at the Microsoft Web site. For obtaining the latest Service Pack updates for Windows NT Server, see the Microsoft Web site.

   Familiarize yourself with other useful documentation and resources for WINS, such as the Windows Internet Name Service (WINS) Troubleshooter.

Troubleshooting WINS Replication

1. I can't locate the source of "duplicate name" error messages.

   Cause: You might need to manually remove static records, or enable static mappings to be overwritten during replication.

Solution: If the duplicate name exists already as a static mapping, you can tombstone or delete the entry. If possible, this should be done at the WINS server that owns the static mapping for the duplicate name record. As a preventive measure, in cases where a static mapping needs to be replaced and updated by a dynamic mapping, you can also enable Overwrite unique static mappings at this server (migrate on) in Replication Partners Properties.

2. I need to locate the source of "network path not found" error messages on a WINS client.

   Cause: The network path might contain the name of a server computer configured as a p-node, m-node, or h-node and its IP address is different from the one in the WINS database. In this case, the IP address for this computer might have changed recently and the new address has not yet replicated to the local server.

   Solution: Check the WINS database for the name and IP address mapping information. If they are not current, you can start replication at the WINS server that owns the name record requiring an update at other servers.

   Cause: If the computer name is configured as b-node, its name might be missing in the WINS database.

   Solution: Check the WINS database for the name. If the name is not present in WINS and clients on other subnets need to locate the b-node computer by name, you can add a static mapping in WINS for the computer name and IP address.

3. The WINS server cannot pull or push replications to another WINS server.

   Cause: If the other WINS server is located across a router, there might be a failed router or other network problem.

   Solution: Check for network connectivity to the server. Ping the other WINS server and troubleshoot any network or TCP/IP-related problems.

   Cause: If the other WINS server is located on the same network or can be successfully pinged, the server might not be configured correctly as either a push or pull partner of the other server.

   For example, suppose the two WINS servers are called WINS-A and WINS-B. If WINS-A needs to perform pull replications with WINS-B, make sure it is a push partner of WINS-B. Likewise, if WINS-A should push replications to WINS-B, it should be a pull partner of WINS-B.

   Solution: Determine the current configuration of replication partners between the servers. If partnerships are missing at either server, add the missing partner IP addresses as needed for the appropriate server. If needed, you can also change the replication partner type, such as from either **Pull only** or **Push only**, to **Push/Pull**.

4. I am having intermittent problems with WINS not replicating between servers on my network.

    Cause: The replication pattern in use on your network might not be correct or appropriate to use.

    Solution: In general, deployments of more than 20 WINS servers are strongly discouraged. Also, for best results and simpler administration, follow a hub-and-spoke replication topology when designing your replicated WINS network that utilizes push/pull partnerships between each WINS hub server and its member spoke servers.

    If a single hub-and-spoke exceeds the recommended total of 20 WINS servers for a single enterprise, you should contact Microsoft Consulting Services or Microsoft Product Support Services about how to better revise or reduce your current WINS installation. For larger or enterprise installations, multiple hub-and-spoke designs are acceptable to use.

    In rare cases, the limited use of push-only and pull-only partner relationships might be needed. You should, however, carefully review added WINS administration issues when these configurations are deployed. At a minimum, establish reliable support procedures for occasions when you might need to manually trigger replication between WINS servers configured to operate using these types of limited replication partnering.

    Cause: The version ID might not be incrementing for WINS entries when replicating on all servers.

    Solution: The version ID is incremented in the WINS database by each server that owns and registers a name record. This identifier is a hexadecimal value stored with each name record in the database and is used for version tracking when the record is replicated to other servers.

    Version IDs are only incremented for certain types of record changes. For example, a typical refresh of a name in WINS does not increment the version ID, but other changes, such as an updated IP address, can cause the version ID to increment in most cases.

    When the version ID is not consistently incrementing for a name record at all servers in the replicated WINS network, you can use either the WINS console or command-line options to administratively increase the starting version count for the server and correct the problem.

5. I still have a problem with WINS replication not described above.

    Cause: My problem is not described above.

    Solution: Search the Microsoft Web site for updated technical information that might relate to the problem you have observed. If necessary, you can obtain information and instructions that pertain to your current problem or issue there.

If you have connection to the Internet, you can obtain the latest updates for Windows 2000 Server at the Microsoft Web site. For obtaining the latest Service Pack updates for Windows NT Server, see the Microsoft Web site.

Familiarize yourself with other useful documentation and resources for WINS, such as the Windows Internet Name Service (WINS) Troubleshooter.

APPENDIX D

DNS Resources and Troubleshooting

Resource Records Reference

A DNS database consists of one or more zone files used by the DNS server. Each zone holds a collection of structured resource records, the following of which are supported by the DNS service running in Windows 2000 Server.

Format of DNS Resource Records

All resource records have a defined format that uses the same top-level fields, as described in Table D.1.

TABLE D.1 *Format of DNS Resource Records*

Field	Description
Owner	Indicates the DNS domain name that owns a resource record. This name is the same as that of the console tree node where a resource record is located.
Time-to-Live (TTL)	For most resource records, this field is optional. It indicates a length of time used by other DNS servers to determine how long to cache information for a record before expiring and discarding it. For example, most resource records created by the DNS Server service inherit the minimum (default) TTL of 1 hour from the start of authority (SOA) record, which prevents overlong caching by other DNS servers. For an individual resource record, you can specify a record-specific TTL that overrides the minimum TTL inherited from the SOA resource record. TTL values of zero (0) can also be used for resource records that contain volatile data not to be cached for later use after the current DNS query in progress is completed.
Class	Contains standard mnemonic text indicating the class of the resource record. For example, a setting of "IN" indicates that the resource record belongs to the Internet class, which is the only class supported by Windows 2000 DNS servers. This field is required.

(continued)

TABLE D.1 *Format of DNS Resource Records (Continued)*

Field	Description
Type	Contains standard mnemonic text indicating the type of resource record. For example, a mnemonic of "A" indicates that the resource record stores host address information. This field is required.
Record-specific data	A required, variable-length field that contains information describing the resource. The format of this information varies according to the type and class of the resource record.

A

Description: Host address (A) resource record. Maps a DNS domain name to an Internet Protocol (IP) version 4 32-bit address. For more information, see RFC 1035.

Syntax:

owner class ttl ***A*** *IP_v4_address*

Example:

host1.example.microsoft.com. IN A 127.0.0.1

AAAA

Description: IPv6 host address (AAAA) resource record. Maps a DNS domain name to an IP version 6 128-bit address. For more information, see RFC 1886.

Syntax:

owner class ttl ***AAAA*** *IP_v6_address*

Example:

ipv6_host1.example.microsoft.com. IN AAAA 4321:0:1:2:3:4:567:89ab

AFSDB

Description: Andrew File System Database (AFSDB) resource record. Maps a DNS domain name in the *server_host_name* field to the host name for a server computer of a server subtype. The **subtype** field can have either of the following recognized and supported values:

- A value of **1** to indicate that the server is an AFS version 3.0 volume location server for the named AFS cell.

- A value of **2** to indicate that the server is an authenticated name server holding the cell-root directory node for the server that uses either Open Software Foundation's (OSF) DCE authenticated cell-naming system or HP/Apollo's Network Computing Architecture (NCA).

For more information, see RFC 1183.

Syntax:

*owner ttl class **AFSDB** subtype server_host_name*

Example:

example.microsoft.com.   AFSDB   1 afs-server1.example.microsoft.com.

ATMA

Description: Asynchronous Transfer Mode address (ATMA) resource record. Maps a DNS domain name in the *owner* field to an ATM address referenced in the *atm_address* field.

For more information, refer to the technical specification entitled "ATM Name System Specification Version 1.0" published by the ATM Forum. To obtain this specification, download it from the ATM Forum FTP site, ftp://ftp.atmforum.com/.

When downloading, specify the name of the file to transfer as either:

- **af-saa-0069.000.doc** for a copy of the document formatted using Microsoft Word
- **af-saa-0069.000.rtf** for a rich text formatted (RTF) version of the document, which can be opened using WordPad

Note: Web addresses can change, so you might be unable to connect to the Web site or sites mentioned here.

Syntax:

*owner ttl class **ATMA** atm_address*

Example:

atm-host   ATMA   47.0079.00010200000000000000.00a03e000002.00

CNAME

Description: Canonical name (CNAME) resource record. Maps an aliased or alternate DNS domain name in the **owner** field to a canonical or primary DNS domain name specified in the *canonical_name* field. The canonical or primary DNS domain name used in the data is required and must resolve to a valid DNS domain name in the namespace.

Syntax:

owner ttl class ***CNAME*** *canonical_name*

Example:

aliasname.example.microsoft.com. CNAME 1 truename.example.microsoft.com.

HINFO

Description: Host information (HINFO) resource record. Specifies the type of CPU and operating system in the *cpu_type* and *os_type* fields, respectively, for the host DNS domain name in the **owner** field. Well-known CPU and operating system types that are most often used are noted in RFC 1700. This information can be used by application protocols such as FTP, which use special procedures when communicating with computers of a known CPU and operating system type.

Syntax:

owner ttl class ***HINFO*** *cpu_type os_type*

Example:

my-computer-name.example.microsoft.com. HINFO INTEL-386 WIN32

ISDN

Description: Integrated Services Digital Network (ISDN) resource record. Maps a DNS domain name to an ISDN telephone number. Telephone numbers used with this record should follow ITU-T E.163/E.164 international telephone numbering standards, which are compatible with current international phone numbering plans. For more information, see RFC 1183.

Syntax:

owner ttl class ***ISDN*** *isdn_address sub_address*

Example:

my-isdn-host.example.microsoft.com. ISDN 141555555539699 002

MB

Description: Mailbox (MB) resource record. Maps a specified domain mailbox name in the **owner** field to a mailbox host name in *mailbox_hostname*. The mailbox host name must be the same as a valid A resource record already used by a host in the same zone. Additionally, the specified host must have a domain mailbox that accepts mail for the specified owner. For more information, see RFC 1035.

Syntax:

owner ttl class ***MB*** *mailbox_hostname*

Example:

mailbox.example.microsoft.com. MB mailhost1.example.microsoft.com

MG

Description: Mail group (MG) resource record. Used to add domain mailboxes, each specified by an MB resource record in the current zone, to the domain mailing group identified by **owner** in this resource record. Names used in the *mailbox_name* field must be identical to valid MB resource records already present in the current zone. For more information, see RFC 1035.

Syntax:

owner ttl class ***MG*** *mailbox_name*

Example:

administrator.example.microsoft.com. MG mailbox1.example.microsoft.com
mailbox2.example.microsoft.com

MINFO

Description: Mailbox mail list information (MINFO) resource record. Specifies (in *responsible_mailbox*) a domain mailbox name for a responsible person who maintains a mailing list or mailbox specified in the **owner** field. The *error_mailbox* field can also be used to specify a domain mailbox that receives error messages related to this mailing list or mailbox. Mailboxes specified for responsible contacts and error forwarding must be the same as valid MB records that already exist in the current zone. For more information, see RFC 1035.

Syntax:

owner ttl class ***MINFO*** *responsible_mailbox error_mailbox*

Example:

administrator.example.microsoft.com. MINFO resp-mbox.example.
microsoft.com err-mbox.example.microsoft.com

MR

Description: Mailbox renamed (MR) resource record. Specifies a domain mailbox name in *new_renamed_mailbox*, the proper rename of an existing mailbox specified in the **owner** field. An MR resource record is often used as a forwarding entry for a user who has moved to a different mailbox. MR records do not cause additional section processing. For more information, see RFC 1035.

Syntax:

owner ttl class ***MR*** *new_renamed_mailbox*

Example:

old-mbox.example.microsoft.com. MR new-renamed-mbox.
example.microsoft.com

MX

Description: Mail exchanger (MX) resource record. Provides message routing to a mail exchanger host, as specified in *mail_exchanger_host*, for mail sent to the domain name specified in the **owner** field. A 2-digit preference value indicates preferred ordering if multiple exchanger hosts are specified. Each exchanger host must have a corresponding A resource record in a valid zone. For more information, see RFC 1035.

Syntax:

owner ttl class ***MX*** *preference mail_exchanger_host*

Example:

example.microsoft.com. MX 10 mailserver1.example.microsoft.com

PTR

Description: Pointer (PTR) resource record. Points from the name in **owner** to another location in the DNS namespace as specified by *targeted_domain_name*. Often used in special domains, such as the *in-addr.arpa* domain tree, to provide reverse lookups of address-to-name mappings. In most cases, each record provides information that points to another DNS domain name location, such as a corresponding A resource record in a forward lookup zone. For more information, see RFC 1035.

Syntax:

owner ttl class ***PTR*** *targeted_domain_name*

Example:

1.0.0.10.in-addr.arpa. PTR host.example.microsoft.com.

RP

Description: Responsible person (RP) resource record. Specifies the domain mailbox name for a responsible person in *mailbox_name*. This name is then mapped to a domain name in *text_record_name* for which text resource records exist in the same zone. When RP records are used in DNS queries, subsequent queries are used to retrieve associated text resource record information. For more information, see RFC 1183.

Syntax:

owner ttl class ***RP*** *mailbox_name text_record_name*

Example:

example.microsoft.com. RP admin.example.microsoft.com. admin-info.
example.microsoft.com.
admin-info.example.microsoft.com. TXT "Joe Administrator, (555) 555-0110"

RT

Description: Route through (RT) resource record. Provides an intermediate host binding for internal hosts that do not have a direct WAN or external network connection. The RT record is similar to the MX record in that any communication from an internal host is routed through the *intermediate_host* for the destination DNS domain name specified in the **owner** field. A 2-digit preference value is used to set priority if multiple intermediate routing hosts are specified. For each intermediate host specified, a corresponding A resource record is needed in the current zone. For more information, see RFC 1183.

Syntax:

owner ttl class ***RT*** *preference intermediate_host*

Example:

example.microsoft.com. RT 2 lan-router.example.microsoft.com
RT 10 wan-router.example.microsoft.com

SRV

Description: Service locator (SRV) resource record. Allows multiple servers providing a similar TCP/IP-based service to be located using a single DNS query operation. This record enables you to maintain a list of servers for a well-known server port and transport protocol type ordered by preference for a DNS domain name. For example, in Windows 2000 Server, it provides the means to locate domain controllers that use Lightweight Directory Access Protocol (LDAP) service over TCP port 389.

The purposes of each of the specialized fields used in an SRV resource record are as follows:

- **service** – A symbolic name for the desired service. For well-known services, a reserved universal symbolic name such as *_telnet* or *_smtp* is defined in RFC 1700. If a well-known service name is not defined in RFC 1700, a local or user-preferred name can be used instead. Some widely used TCP/IP services, notably the Post Office Protocol (POP), do not have a single universal symbolic name. If RFC 1700 assigns a name for a service indicated in this field, the RFC-defined name is the only name that is legal to use. Only locally defined services can be named locally.
- **protocol** – Indicates the transport protocol type. Typically, this is either TCP or UDP, although any transport protocol named in RFC 1700 can be used.
- **name** – The DNS domain name referred to by this resource record. The SRV resource record is unique among other DNS record types in that it is not used to perform the search or query.
- **priority** – Sets the preference for a host specified in the **target** field. DNS clients that query for SRV resource records attempt to contact the first reachable host of the lowest numbered preference listed here. Although target hosts have the same stated preference value, they can be tried in random order. The range of preference values is 0 to 65535.
- **weight** – Can be used in addition to *preference* to provide a load-balancing mechanism where multiple servers are specified in the **target** field and are all set to the same level of preference. When selecting a target server host among those of equal preference, this value can be used to set an added level of preference that can be used to determine the exact order or balancing of selection for the target hosts used in an answered SRV query. When a nonzero value is used, servers of equal preference are tried in proportion to the weight of this value. The range of values is 1 to 65535. If load balancing is not needed, use a value of 0 in this field to make the record easier to read.
- **port** – The server port on the target host that provides the service indicated in the **service** field. The range of port numbers is 0 to 65535, although the number is often a well-known assigned service port number, as specified in RFC 1700. Unassigned ports can be used as needed.

- **target** – Specifies the DNS domain name of the host that provides the type of service being requested. For each host name used, a corresponding A resource record in the DNS namespace is required. A single period (.) can be used in this field to indicate authoritatively that the requested service specified in this SRV resource record is not available at this DNS domain name.

For more information, see the Internet draft "A DNS RR for specifying the location of services (DNS SRV)."

Syntax:

service.protocol.name ttl class ***SRV*** *preference weight port target*

Example:

```
_ldap._tcp.ms-dcs    SRV   0 0  389 dc1.example.microsoft.com
                     SRV 10 0  389 dc2.example.microsoft.com
```

TXT

Description: Text (TXT) resource record. Maps a DNS domain name specified in the **owner** field to a string of characters in *text_string* serving as descriptive text. For more information, see RFC 1035.

Syntax:

owner ttl class ***TXT*** *text_string*

Example:

example.microsoft.com. TXT "This is an example of additional domain name information."

WKS

Description: Well-known service (WKS) resource record. Describes the well-known TCP/IP services supported by a particular protocol on a specific IP address. WKS records provide TCP and UDP availability information for TCP/IP servers. If a server either supports both TCP and UDP for a well-known service or has multiple IP addresses that support a service, then multiple WKS records are used. For more information, see RFC 1035.

Syntax:

owner ttl class ***WKS*** *address protocol service_list*

Example:

example.microsoft.com.   WKS 10.0.0.1 TCP (telnet smtp ftp)

X25

Description: X.25 (X25) resource record. Maps a DNS domain name in the **owner** field to a Public Switched Data Network (PSDN) address number specified in *psdn_number*. PSDN numbers used with this record should follow the X.121 international numbering plan. For more information, see RFC 1183.

Syntax:

owner ttl class ***X25*** *psdn_number*

Example:

example.microsoft.com.   X25   52204455506

DNS Server Log Reference

Table D.2 provides a partial listing of events recorded in the DNS server log. You can view this log by using Event Viewer after Windows 2000 DNS server is installed on the server computer. For information about viewing the DNS server system event log, see Chapter 10, "Installing and Maintaining DNS Servers."

TABLE D.2 *Some Events Recorded in DNS Server Log*

Event ID	Description
2	The DNS server has started. This message generally appears at startup when either the server computer is started or the DNS Server service is manually started. For information about starting and stopping a DNS server, see Chapter 10.
3	The DNS server has shut down. This message generally appears when either the server computer is shut down or the DNS Server service is stopped manually.
408	The DNS server could not open socket for address [*IPaddress*]. Verify that this is a valid IP address for the server computer. To correct the problem, you can do the following: • If the specified IP address is not valid, remove it from the list of restricted interfaces for the server and restart the server. For information about restricting a DNS server to listen only on selected addresses, see Chapter 10. • If the specified IP address is no longer valid, and was the only address enabled for the DNS server to use, the server might not have started as a result of this configuration error. To correct this problem, delete the following value from the Windows 2000 registry and restart the DNS server: *HKEY_LOCAL_MACHINE\System\CurrentControlSet\Services\DNS\Parameters \ListenAddress* • If this is a valid IP address for the server computer, verify that no other application that would attempt to use the same DNS server port (such as another DNS server application) is running. By default, the Windows 2000 server uses TCP port 53.

(continued)

TABLE D.2 *Some Events Recorded in DNS Server Log (Continued)*

Event ID	Description
413	The DNS server will send requests to other DNS servers on a port other than its default port (TCP port 53). This DNS server is multihomed and has been configured to restrict DNS service to only some of its configured IP addresses. For this reason, there is no assurance that DNS queries made by this server to other remote DNS servers will be sent using one of the IP addresses enabled for the DNS server. This might prevent query answer responses returned by these servers from being received on the DNS port that the server is currently configured to use. To avoid this problem, the DNS server sends queries to other DNS servers using an arbitrary non-DNS port, and the response is received regardless of the IP address used. If you want to limit the DNS server to using only its configured DNS port for sending queries to other DNS servers, use the DNS console to perform one of the following changes in server properties configuration on the **Interfaces** tab: 1. Either select **All IP addresses** to enable the DNS server to listen on all configured server IP addresses 2. Or, if you continue to select and use **Only the following IP addresses**, limit the **IP address** list to a single server IP address. For more information, see Chapter 10.
414	The server computer currently has no primary DNS suffix configured. Its DNS name is currently a single label host name. For example, its currently configured name is *host* rather than *host.example.microsoft.com* or another fully qualified name. While the DNS server has only a single label name, default resource records created for its configured zones use only this single label name when mapping the host name for this DNS server. This can lead to incorrect and failed referrals when clients and other DNS servers use these records to locate this server by name. In general, the DNS server should be reconfigured with a full DNS computer name appropriate for its domain or workgroup use on your network. For information about configuring the primary DNS suffix for a client computer, see Chapter 10.
708	The DNS server did not detect any zones of either primary or secondary type. It will run as a caching-only server but will not be authoritative for any zones. For information about using caching-only servers, see Chapter 9, "Using DNS."
3150	The DNS server wrote a new version of zone [*zonename*] to file [*filename*]. You can view the new version number by clicking the **Record Data** tab. This event should only appear if the DNS server is configured to operate as a root server. For more information, see "DNS-related Files" in this appendix.

(continued)

TABLE D.2 *Some Events Recorded in DNS Server Log (Continued)*

<table>
<tr><th>Event ID</th><th>Description</th></tr>
<tr><td>6527</td><td>Zone [zonename] expired before it could obtain a successful zone transfer or update from a master server acting as its source for the zone. The zone has been shut down.

This event ID might appear when the DNS server is configured to host a secondary copy of the zone from another DNS server acting as its source or master server. Verify that this server has network connectivity to its configured master server.

If the problem continues, consider one or more of the following options:

1. Delete the zone and recreate it, specifying either a different master server, or an updated and corrected IP address for the same master server. For information on adding and removing zones, see Chapter 10.

2. If zone expiration continues, consider adjusting the expire interval. For information on adjusting the expire interval for a zone, see Chapter 10, and for information about understanding zones and zone transfer, see Chapter 8, "DNS Overview."</td></tr>
</table>

For more information about all other messages not described in this topic, refer directly to the message text itself as it appears in the DNS server event log.

Caution Incorrectly editing the registry may severely damage your system. Before making changes to the registry, you should back up any valued data on the computer.

Note Event messages logged by the DNS Client service are logged in System log and can also be viewed using Event Viewer at the applicable client computer.

If needed to troubleshoot persistent problems, you can also enable for use advanced debugging options at the DNS server for obtaining a more detailed log of server activity. For information about using server debug logging options, see Chapter 9, and for viewing a DNS server debug log file, see Chapter 10.

DNS-related Files

The files listed in Table D.3 relate to using and configuring DNS servers and clients for use under Windows 2000.

TABLE D.3 *Files Related to Using and Configuring DNS Servers and Clients*

File	Description
Boot	BIND boot configuration file. This file is not created by the DNS console. However, as an optional configuration for the DNS Server service, it can be copied from another DNS server running the Berkeley Internet Name Domain (BIND) server implementation of DNS. To use this file with the DNS Server service, you need to click the **Boot From File** option in Server properties. On BIND servers, this file is often called the *named.boot* file.
Cache.dns	Used to preload resource records into the DNS server names cache. Windows 2000 DNS servers use this file to help locate root servers on either your network or the Internet. By default, this file contains DNS resource records that prime the local cache of the server with the addresses of authoritative root servers for the Internet. If you are setting up a DNS server to resolve Internet DNS names, the information in this file is required unless you enable the use of another DNS server as a forwarder to resolve these names. Traffic to the Internet root servers is heavy, but because host names are not usually resolved at this level, the load can be reasonably handled. Instead, the root hints file provides referral information that can be useful during DNS name resolution to redirect a query to other servers that are authoritative for names located beneath the root. For DNS servers operating privately on your internal network, the DNS console can learn and replace the contents of this file with internal root servers on your network, provided they are reachable through the network when you are setting up and configuring new DNS servers. It can be updated using the DNS console from the **Root Hints** tab located under the applicable server properties. This file preloads the server names cache when it is started.
Root.dns	Root zone file. This file can appear at a computer running as a Windows 2000 DNS server if it is configured as a root server for your network.
zone_name.dns	Used when a standard zone (either primary or secondary) is added and configured for the server. Files of this type are not created or used for primary type zones that are directory-integrated, which are stored in the Active Directory database.

These files can be found in the *%SystemRoot%\System32\Dns* folder on the server computer.

Note

For more information on operating a DNS server as a root server, hosting your own DNS presence on the Internet, and configuring DNS servers on your network to use forwarders, see Chapter 9.

If you are migrating server files from a BIND server to use with a Windows DNS server, you need to rename these files and copy them to the folder used by the DNS service. Information about migrating servers can also be found in Chapter 9.

DNS Updated Technical Information

Updated technical information for DNS can be obtained by searching technical articles available from the Personal Support Center at the Microsoft Web site.

You can also obtain additional in-depth information on DNS in the Windows 2000 Server Resource Kit. For more information, see Windows 2000 Resource Kit.

DNS RFCs

Requests for Comments (RFCs) are an evolving series of reports, proposals for protocols, and protocol standards used by the Internet community. Domain Name System specifications are based on approved RFCs published by the Internet Engineering Task Force (IETF) and other working groups.

RFCs for Windows 2000 DNS

The RFCs listed in Table D.4 contain specifications used to design and implement DNS service for Windows 2000.

TABLE D.4 *RFCs for Windows 2000 DNS Service*

RFC	Title
1034	Domain Names—Concepts and Facilities
1035	Domain Names—Implementation and Specification
1123	Requirements for Internet Hosts—Application and Support
1886	DNS Extensions to Support IP Version 6
1995	Incremental Zone Transfer in DNS
1996	A Mechanism for Prompt DNS Notification of Zone Changes
2136	Dynamic Updates in the Domain Name System (DNS UPDATE)
2181	Clarifications to the DNS Specification
2308	Negative Caching of DNS Queries (DNS NCACHE)

Internet Drafts for Windows 2000 DNS

The Internet drafts listed in Table D.5 contain specifications used to design and implement DNS service for Windows 2000.

TABLE D.5 *Internet Drafts for Windows 2000 DNS Service*

Filename	Title
Draft-ietf-dnsind-rfc2052bis-02.txt	A DNS RR for Specifying the Location of Services (DNS SRV)
Draft-skwan-utf8-dns-02.txt	Using the UTF-8 Character Set in the Domain Name System
Draft-ietf-dhc-dhcp-dns-08.txt	Interaction between DHCP and DNS
Draft-ietf-dnsind-tsig-11.txt	Secret Key Transaction Signatures for DNS (TSIG)
Draft-ietf-dnsind-tkey-00.txt	Secret Key Establishment for DNS (TKEY RR)
Draft-skwan-gss-tsig-04.txt	GSS Algorithm for TSIG (GSS-TSIG)

Other Specifications for Windows 2000 DNS

The additional specifications listed in Table D.6 are used to design and implement DNS service for Windows 2000.

TABLE D.6 *Additional Specifications for Windows 2000 DNS Service*

Filename	Title
af-saa-0069.000.doc	ATM Name System Specification version 1.0 This specification is published by the ATM Forum. For more information, you can obtain this specification by downloading it from the ATM Forum FTP site, ftp://ftp.atmforum.com/.

Obtaining DNS RFCs and Other Internet Draft Specifications

You can obtain RFCs and other Internet drafts from the Request for Comments Web site, *www.rfc-editor.org/*. RFCs are classified as one of the following: approved Internet standards, proposed Internet standards (circulated in draft form for review), Internet best practices, or For Your Information (FYI) documents. Internet drafts are not assigned an RFC number but are specifications currently in the proposal stage and generally published by one of the IETF working groups, of which several groups focus on discussion of DNS-related topics.

Note RFCs 1034 and 1035 define the original DNS standard protocol to support domain name services in a TCP/IP environment. These RFCs describe the protocols in a detailed manner, emphasizing the underlying ideas and techniques used in all DNS implementations.

Top-Level Domains

Table D.7 lists the eight top-level domains most often used on the Internet to classify organizations by type when they register a second-level domain name for use. For example, *microsoft.com* (the second-level domain name registered to Microsoft) is registered in the *com* domain, because this is the top-level domain provided for organizations that do business (commerce) on the Internet

TABLE D.7 *Top-Level Domains*

Top-level name	Description	Used by
arpa	Owned by Advanced Research Project Agency (ARPA). Used to register reverse mapping of Internet Protocol version 4 (IPv4) addresses assigned by the Internet Assigned Number Authority (IANA) to DNS domain names for computers that use those addresses on the Internet.	The *in-addr.arpa* domain
com	For business and commercial use.	Businesses and corporations
edu	For educational use.	Public and private schools, colleges, and universities
gov	For use by governmental institutions.	Local, state, and federal government agencies
int	Reserved for international use. Currently planned for use in RFC 1886 to register reverse mapping of Internet Protocol version 6 (IPv6) addresses assigned by IANA to DNS domain names in the *ip6.int* domain for computers that use those addresses on the Internet.	The *ip6.int* domain
mil	For use by military agencies.	Department of Defense, U.S. Navy, U.S. Army, U.S. Air Force, and other military agencies
net	For use by organizations that provide large-scale Internet or telephony-based service.	InterNIC, AT&T, and other large-scale Internet and telephone service providers
org	For use by noncommercial, nonprofit organizations.	Churches and charitable institutions

Note In addition to these top-level domains, which are all three letters in length, the use of two-letter country/region codes (such as "uk" for United Kingdom) are reserved for use. These country/region codes can also be used in conjunction with the three-letter codes listed above to further specify the country or region of origin for organizations that register names in the Internet DNS namespace.

DNS Bibliography

For more information on the Domain Name System or other DNS server implementations, you can consult the following references:

Albitz, P., M. Loukides, and C. Liu. 1998. *DNS and BIND, Third Edition*. Sebastopol, California: O'Reilly and Associates, Inc.

Albitz, P., M. Larson, and C. Liu. 1998. *DNS on Windows NT*. Sebastopol, California: O'Reilly and Associates, Inc.

Comer, D. 1995. *Internetworking with TCP/IP, Vol. 1, Third Edition*. Englewood Cliffs, New Jersey: Prentice Hall.

Masterson, M., H. Knief, S. Vinick, and E. Roul. 1998. *Windows NT DNS*. Indianapolis, Indiana: New Rider Publishing.

Troubleshooting

This section covers

- Troubleshoot DNS clients
- Troubleshoot DNS servers
- Troubleshoot dynamic updates
- Troubleshoot zone problems

Troubleshoot DNS Clients

1. The DNS client received a "Name not found" error message.

   Cause: The DNS client computer does not have a valid IP configuration for the network.

   Solution: Verify that TCP/IP configuration settings for the client computer are correct, particularly those used for DNS name resolution.

   To verify a client IP configuration, use the **ipconfig** command. In the command output, verify that the client has a valid IP address, subnet mask, and default gateway for the network where it is attached and being used.

If the client does not have a valid TCP/IP configuration, you can either:

a. For dynamically configured clients, use the **ipconfig /renew** command to manually force the client to renew its IP address configuration with the DHCP server.

b. For statically configured clients, modify the client TCP/IP properties to use valid configuration settings or complete its DNS configuration for the network.

Cause: The client was not able to contact a DNS server because of a network or hardware related failure.

Solution: Verify that the client computer has a valid and functioning network connection. First, check that related client hardware (cables and network adapters) is working properly at the client, using basic network and hardware troubleshooting steps. If the client hardware appears to be prepared and functioning properly, verify that it can ping other computers on the same network.

Cause: The DNS client cannot contact its configured DNS servers.

Solution: If the DNS client has basic connectivity to the network, verify that it can contact a preferred (or alternate) DNS server.

To verify whether a client has basic TCP/IP access to the DNS server, first try pinging the preferred DNS server by its IP address. For example, if the client uses a preferred DNS server of 10.0.0.1, type **ping 10.0.0.1** at the command prompt on the client computer. If you are not sure what the IP address is for the preferred DNS server, you can observe it by using the **ipconfig** command.

For example, at the client computer, type **ipconfig /all|more** if necessary to pause the display so you can read and note any IP addresses listed in **DNS servers** for the command output.

If no configured DNS servers respond to a direct pinging of their IP address, it indicates that the source of the problem is more likely a network connectivity problem between the client and the DNS servers. If that is the case, follow basic TCP/IP network troubleshooting steps to fix the problem.

Cause: The DNS server is not running or responding to queries.

Solution: If the DNS client can ping the DNS server computer, ver ify that the DNS server is started and able to listen for and respond to client requests. Try using the **nslookup** command to test whether the server can respond to DNS clients.

Cause: The DNS server the client is using does not have authority for the failed name and cannot locate the authoritative server for this name.

Solution: Confirm whether the DNS domain name the client is trying to resolve is one for which its configured DNS servers are authoritative. For example, if the client is attempting to resolve the name *host.example.microsoft.com,* verify that the preferred (or an alternate, if one is being used) DNS server queried by the client loads the authoritative zone where an A resource record for the failed name should exist.

If the preferred server is authoritative for the failed name and loads the applicable zone, determine whether the zone is missing the appropriate resource records. If needed, add the resource records to the zone.

If the preferred server is not authoritative for the failed name, it indicates that configuration errors at the DNS server are the likely cause. As needed, further troubleshoot the problem at the DNS server.

2. The DNS client appears to have received a response with stale or incorrect information in it.

   Cause: The DNS server the client is using does not have authority for the failed name and is using stale information from its local DNS database.

   Solution: Determine whether the DNS server is authoritative for the name and proceed accordingly. For example, if the client is attempting to resolve the name *host.example.microsoft.com,* verify that the preferred (or an alternate, if one is being used) DNS server queried by the client loads the authoritative zone where an A resource record for the failed name should exist.

   If the preferred server is authoritative for the name and answered using incorrect data, it indicates that the applicable zone might have outdated or stale information in the applicable resource record data. If that is the case, you can add and remove the appropriate resource records in the zone.

   Another option, where dynamic updates are enabled, is to force registration and update at the computer targeted by the query. If the target computer is running Windows 2000, you can force it to update the registration of its resource records by typing the **ipconfig /registerdns** command at a command prompt.

   If the preferred server is not a direct authority for the queried name, it likely answered the query based on information obtained and cached during an earlier recursive lookup. In this case, you might consider clearing the server names cache. This compels the server to use new recursive queries for this resource record data and rebuild its cache contents based on current information.

   Cause: The preferred DNS server is a secondary server for the zone containing the targeted name and has outdated information.

Solution: If the server that answered the client is a secondary server for the zone, the version of the zone in use at that server might be stale and need to be updated more often. As an immediate solution, you can initiate a zone transfer at the secondary server to its master server to update the zone. You might also consider using any of the following to improve the freshness of secondary zone data in the future:

a. Specify additional master servers for the secondary server to use when refreshing the zone.

b. Adjust the refresh interval on the zone slightly to decrease the length of time that all authoritative servers for the zone can use the zone before they are required to refresh it.

c. Configure a notify list at a master server that acts as the zone source for the secondary server and enable it to notify this server when the zone changes.

Cause: The name queried was specified in error, either through user input or in a stored client configuration.

Solution: Verify that the name was correctly specified in the application where the name query originated.

In most cases, incorrect data in a positive query response indicates one of three possibilities:

- An incorrect DNS name was entered at the client by a user.
- A short unqualified name was used at the client and completed by the local resolver, using an unintended DNS suffix.
- Resource records specified in the query were not updated correctly at the DNS server.

Confirm that the name was not entered in error by the user. Verify the exact set of characters entered by the user when the original DNS query was made or check in application settings, such as for any Internet mail or Web browser configurations that were made.

If the name used in the initial query was unqualified, and not the fully qualified domain name (FQDN), try using the FQDN instead in the client application and repeating the query. If you do, be sure to include the trailing dot (.) at the end of the name to indicate that the name entered is an exact FQDN.

If the FQDN query succeeds and returns correct data in the response, the most likely cause of the problem is a misconfigured DNS domain suffix search list used in the client resolver settings.

If you are using DNS in an environment that does not support dynamic updates, or if you generally administer zone data manually, you might also want to verify that the resource records involved in answering the query were not entered incorrectly. View them to ensure the record data stored in the zone is correct, or modify it accordingly.

Cause: The primary zone might have missing or errored data.

Solution: Verify that the primary server for the zone has complete and accurate data.

The most likely cause for a primary DNS server for a zone to have missing or incomplete data is because of a failed update request. It is possible that support for dynamic update has not been fully implemented or configured. To resolve the problem, review the DNS dynamic update protocol and any requirements it has for DNS servers and clients that use it.

For directory-integrated zones, it is also possible that the affected records for the errored query have been updated in Active Directory but not replicated to all DNS servers loading the zone. By default, all DNS servers that load zones from Active Directory poll it at a set interval (typically, every 15 minutes), and update the zone for any incremental changes to it. In most cases, a DNS update takes no more than 20 minutes to replicate to all DNS servers used in an Active Directory domain environment using default replication settings and reliable high-speed links.

If you have specifically configured your zones to disable dynamic update, keep in mind that you need to manually add and update most types of resource records used in a zone. If this is the case, use the DNS console to view and update the affected records.

Another possibility for the errored data is in whether WINS lookup integration is enabled and used with the zone. If you are using WINS lookup with your zones, verify that WINS is not the source of the errored data.

3. The DNS client appears to be affected by another problem not described above.

   Cause: My problem is not described above.

   Solution: Search the Microsoft Web site for updated technical information that might relate to the problem you have observed. If necessary, you can obtain information and instructions that pertain to your current problem or issue.

   If you are connected to the Internet, the latest updates for Windows 2000 Server are available at the Microsoft Web site. For obtaining the latest Service Pack updates for Windows NT Server, see the Microsoft Web site.

   Familiarize yourself with other useful documentation and resources for DNS, such as the DNS Troubleshooter.

Troubleshoot DNS Servers

1. The DNS server is not responding to clients.

   Cause: The DNS server is affected by a network failure.

Solution: Verify that the server computer has a valid functioning network connection. First, check that related client hardware (cables and network adapters) is working properly at the client, using basic network and hardware troubleshooting steps.

If the server hardware appears to be prepared and functioning properly, check that it has network connectivity by pinging other computers or routers (such as its default gateway) that are used and available on the same network as the affected DNS servers.

Cause: The DNS server is reachable through basic network testing but is not responding to DNS queries from clients.

Solution: If the DNS client can ping the DNS server computer, verify that the DNS server is started and able to listen to and respond to client requests. Try using the **nslookup** command to test whether the server can respond to DNS clients.

Cause: The DNS server has been configured to limit service to a specific list of its configured IP addresses. The IP address originally used in testing its responsiveness is not included in this list.

Solution: If the server was previously configured to restrict the IP addresses for which it responds to queries, it is possible that the IP address being used by clients to contact it is not in the list of restricted IP addresses permitted to provide service to clients.

Try testing the server for a response again, but specify a different IP address known to be in the restricted interfaces list for the server. If the DNS server responds for that address, add the missing server IP address to the list.

Cause: The DNS server has been configured to disable the use of its automatically created default reverse lookup zones.

Solution: Verify that automatically created reverse lookup zones have been created for the server or that advanced configuration changes have not been previously made to the server.

By default, Windows 2000 DNS servers automatically create three standard reverse lookup zones, based on RFC recommendations.

These zones are created with common IP addresses covered by these zones that are not useful in a reverse lookup search (0.0.0.0, 127.0.0.1, and 255.255.255.255). By being authoritative for the zones corresponding to these addresses, the DNS service avoids unnecessary recursion to root servers in order to perform reverse lookups on these types of IP addresses.

It is possible, although unlikely, that these automatic zones are not created. This is because disabling the creation of these zones involves advanced manual configuration of the server registry by a user. To verify that these zones have been created at a Windows 2000 DNS server, do the following:

a. Open the DNS console.
b. From the **View** menu, click **Advanced**.
   - In the console tree, click **Reverse Lookup Zones**. (console tree | DNS | *applicable DNS server* | Reverse Lookup Zones)
c. In the details pane, verify that the following reverse lookup zones are present:
   - 0.in-addr.arpa
   - 127.in-addr.arpa
   - 255.in-addr.arpa

Cause: The DNS server is configured to use a nondefault service port, such as in an advanced security or firewall configuration.

Solution: Verify that the DNS server is not using a nonstandard configuration.

This is a rare but possible cause. By default, the **nslookup** command sends queries to targeted DNS servers using UDP port 53. If the DNS server is located on another network only reachable through an intermediate host (such as a packet-filtering router or proxy server), the DNS server might use a nonstandard port to listen for and receive client requests.

If this situation applies, determine whether any intermediate firewall or proxy server configuration is intentionally used to block traffic on well-known service ports used for DNS. If not, you might be able to add such a packet filter onto these configurations to permit traffic to standard DNS ports.

Also, check the DNS server event log to see if Event ID 414 or other critical service-related events have occurred, which might indicate why the DNS server is not responding.

2. The DNS server does not resolve names correctly.

Cause: The DNS server provides incorrect data for queries it successfully answers.

Solution: Determine the cause of the incorrect data for the DNS server. Some of the most likely causes include the following:

- Resource records were not dynamically updated in a zone.
- An error was made when manually adding or modifying static resource records in the zone.
- Stale resource records, left from cached lookups or from zone records not updated with current information or removed when no longer needed, are in the DNS server database.

To help prevent the most common types of problems, be sure to first review best practices for tips and suggestions on deploying and managing your DNS servers. Also, follow and use the checklists appropriate for installing and configuring DNS servers and clients based on your deployment needs.

If you are deploying DNS for Active Directory, note new directory integration features. When the DNS database is directory-integrated, these features can cause some differences for Windows 2000 DNS server defaults that differ from those used with traditional file-based storage.

Many DNS server problems start with failed queries at a client, so it is often good to start there and troubleshoot the DNS client first.

Cause: The DNS server does not resolve names for computers or services outside of your immediate network, such as those located on external networks or the Internet.

Solution: The server has a problem based on its ability to correctly perform recursion. Recursion is used in most DNS configurations to resolve names that are not located within the configured DNS domain name used by the DNS servers and clients.

If a DNS server fails to resolve a name for which it is not authoritative, the cause is usually a failed recursive query. Recursive queries are used frequently by DNS servers to resolve remote names delegated to other DNS zones and servers.

For recursion to work successfully, all DNS servers used in the path of a recursive query must be able to respond to and forward correct data. If not, a recursive query can fail for any of the following reasons:

- The recursive query times out before it can be completed.
- A remote DNS server fails to respond.
- A remote DNS server provides incorrect data.

If a server fails a recursive query for a remote name, review the remaining possible causes to troubleshoot the problem. If you do not understand recursion or the DNS query process, review conceptual topics in Help to better understand the issues involved.

Cause: The DNS server is not configured to use other DNS servers to assist it in resolving queries.

Solution: Check whether the DNS server can use both forwarders and recursion. By default, all Windows 2000 DNS servers are enabled to use recursion, although the option to disable its use is configurable using the DNS console to modify advanced server options. The other possibility where recursion might be disabled is if the server is configured to use forwarders and recursion has been specifically disabled for that configuration.

Cause: Current root hints for the DNS server are not valid.

Solution: Check whether server root hints are valid.

If configured and used correctly, root hints always should point to DNS servers authoritative for the zone containing the domain root and top-level domains.

By default, Windows 2000 DNS servers are configured or updated to use root hints appropriate to your deployment, based on the following available choices when using the DNS console to configure a server:

a. If the DNS server is installed as the first DNS server for your network, it is configured as a root server. For this configuration, root hints are disabled at the server because the server is authoritative for the root zone.

b. If the installed server is an additional DNS server for your network, you can direct the Configure DNS Server wizard to update its root hints from an existing DNS server on the network.

c. If you do not have other DNS servers on your network but still need to resolve Internet DNS names, you can use the default root hints file, which includes a list of Internet root servers authoritative for the Internet DNS namespace.

Cause: The DNS server does not have network connectivity to the root servers.

Solution: Test for connectivity to the root servers.

If root hints appear to be configured correctly, verify that the DNS server used in a failed query can ping its root servers by IP address.

If a ping attempt to one root server fails, it might indicate that an IP address for that root server has changed. Reconfiguration of root servers, however, is uncommon.

A more likely cause is a full loss of network connectivity or, in some cases, poor network performance on the intermediate network links between the DNS server and its configured root servers. Follow basic TCP/IP network troubleshooting steps to diagnose connections and determine whether this is the problem.

By default, the DNS service uses a recursive time-out of 15 seconds before failing a recursive query. Under normal network conditions, this time-out does not need to be changed. If performance warrants it, however, you can increase this value.

To review additional performance related information on DNS queries, you can enable and use the DNS server debug log file, *Dns.log,* which can provide extensive information about some types of service-related events.

Cause: Other problems exist with updating DNS server data, such as an issue related to zones or dynamic updates.

Solution: Determine whether the problem is related to zones. As needed, troubleshoot any issues in this area, such as possible failure of zone transfer.

3. The DNS server appears to be affected by a problem for reasons not described above.

Cause: My problem is not described above.

Solution: Search the Microsoft Web site for updated technical information that might relate to the problem you have observed. If necessary, you can obtain information and instructions that pertain to your current problem or issue.

If you are connected to the Internet, the latest updates for Windows 2000 Server are available at the Microsoft Web site.

For obtaining the latest Service Pack updates for Windows NT Server, see the Microsoft Web site.

Familiarize yourself with other useful documentation and resources for DNS, such as the DNS Troubleshooter.

Troubleshoot Dynamic Updates

1. The DNS client is not performing dynamic updates.

   Cause: The client (or its DHCP server) does not support the use of the DNS dynamic update protocol.

   Solution: Verify that your clients or servers support the DNS dynamic update protocol, using the options for dynamic update support provided in Windows 2000.

   In order for client computers to be registered and updated dynamically with a DNS server, either:

   a. Install or upgrade client computers to Windows 2000.
   b. Install and use a Windows 2000 DHCP server on your network to lease client computers.

   By default, computers running any version of Windows 2000 attempt to register and perform dynamic update of their DNS names and IP addresses with a DNS server.

   For computers not running Windows 2000, you can deploy Windows 2000 DHCP servers, which can perform proxied registrations and updates as needed for nondynamic clients.

   Cause: The client was not able to register with the DNS server because of intermittent problems with either the DNS server or the network.

   Solution: At the client computer, use the **ipconfig** command as appropriate to retry registration or renewal and update client information with the DNS server.

   For computers running Windows 2000, use the **ipconfig /registerdns** command option to manually force a retry of its dynamic registration.

   For computers running earlier versions of Windows, you can use the options of the **ipconfig** command to verify, view, or renew the client TCP/IP configuration details, as appropriate. For example, if the client computer obtains its IP address lease from a Windows 2000 DHCP server, you might use the **ipconfig /renew** command to force it to renew its lease with the DHCP server. This action would then cause the DHCP server to proxy an update request to its configured DNS server on behalf of the client.

If the DHCP server succeeds in performing the proxied update with the DNS server, the result would be updated DNS host name and IP address information for the client computer in the DNS database.

Cause: The client was not able to register and update with the DNS server because of missing or incomplete DNS configuration.

Solution: Verify that the client is fully and correctly configured for DNS, and update its configuration as needed.

One common cause of the client failing to update with the DNS server is that it does not have a DNS suffix (either a primary suffix or connection-specific suffix) configured. This might result in the client attempting to register an incorrect or unintended DNS domain name. For example, the client could be attempting to register its short or unqualified computer or host name as a top-level domain name in the root zone. This happens because without a DNS suffix configured for the client computer, Windows 2000 determines the configured short name of a computer (such as host-a) is its FQDN. This only occurs because the computer name does not have a DNS suffix to append to it and qualify the computer name when registering it for the client in DNS.

To update the DNS configuration for a client, either:

a. Configure a primary DNS suffix at the client computer for static TCP/IP clients.

b. Configure a connection-specific DNS suffix for use at one of the installed network connections at the client computer.

Cause: The DNS client attempted to update its information with the DNS server but failed because of a problem related to the server.

Solution: If a client can reach its preferred and alternate DNS servers as configured, it is likely that the cause of its failed updates can be found elsewhere.

At Windows 2000 client computers, you can use Event Viewer to check the System log for any event messages that explain why attempts by the client to dynamically update its A or PTR resource records failed.

When reviewing messages in the System log, filter or order the display of all messages to view those that specify *DnsApi* as the source for the message. Typically, these messages are related to the performance of DNS activities, such as DNS queries or dynamic updates.

A common reason updates might fail for a mobile client is that the DNS server required to accept and perform the update does not respond when the client starts at a remote location on the network. This could be due to network performance issues or might indicate a problem in the underlying design of your network. Where these issues persist or seem likely, you should review your DNS deployment and modify it accordingly.

2. The DNS server is not performing dynamic updates.

    Cause: The DNS server does not support dynamic updates.

    Solution: Verify that the DNS server used by the client can support the DNS dynamic update protocol, as described in RFC 2136.

    For Windows DNS servers, only Windows 2000 DNS servers support dynamic updates. The DNS server provided with Windows NT Server 4.0 does not.

    If you are using other DNS servers on your network, verify that they are running a DNS server implementation that supports dynamic updates.

    Cause: The DNS server supports dynamic updates but is not configured to accept them.

    Solution: Verify that the primary zone where clients require updates is configured to allow dynamic updates. For Windows 2000 DNS servers, the default for a new primary zone is to not accept dynamic updates. At the DNS server that loads the applicable primary zone, modify zone properties to allow updates.

    Cause: The zone database is not available.

    Solution: Verify that the zone is available for update.

    If necessary, verify that the zone exists. For a standard primary zone, verify that the zone file exists at the server and that the zone is not paused. If you are using Active Directory-integrated zones, verify that the DNS server is running as a domain controller and has access to the Active Directory database where zone data is stored.

    Secondary zones do not support dynamic updates. If you are trying to determine which server is the primary server for a standard zone, review zone authority records to determine which server is referenced in both the SOA and NS resource records for the zone. This is the primary server for the zone, which can accept dynamic updates to it.

    If you need to, you can use the DNS console to change a secondary zone to become a primary zone so that it can accommodate dynamic updates. However, because standard primary zones use a single-master update model, you can only configure one server to accept dynamic updates for the zone.

    If you change the zone type at a secondary server so that it becomes the primary server for that zone, you need to either remove the zone or convert it to another zone type (such as a secondary zone) at the original primary server. Otherwise, zone data would become inconsistent and cause additional problems.

    If you want to have more than one DNS server be able to update a zone, it is recommended that you change the zone type so that it becomes Active Directory-integrated. To be able to use this zone type, Active Directory must be installed and the server computer must be promoted to a domain controller.

Once the zone is integrated and stored in the directory, other domain controllers can load the zone automatically and be allowed to update it when they are installed as Windows 2000 DNS servers. This is because Active Directory supports a multiple (or floating) master update model in which more than one computer can process updates to the directory database.

Cause: The DNS server is configured to allow only secure dynamic updates and has a security-related problem.

Solution: Verify that zone or resource record security, which might block or prevent dynamic updates at the server, is not in effect.

Secure update can be enabled for directory-integrated zones. If secure dynamic update is in effect, current zone or resource record security might block or prevent a DNS client (or its DHCP server) from performing an update of its A and PTR resource records.

In most cases, secure dynamic update does not prevent new records from being created or added to a zone, but it does restrict who is given default permissions to update or modify records. Where necessary, you can use the access control list (ACL) editing features available for directory-integrated zones to modify security permissions on a zone or its resource records and enable update by another user, group, or computer.

This typically is only needed if the computer requesting update is different from the one that owns the client records and originally created them.

Cause: The DNS server required to perform the updates is not available on the network.

Solution: Verify that the DNS server is available on the network or troubleshoot any further issues as necessary.

3. I am having a different problem related to dynamic updates than those described above.

Cause: My problem is not described above.

Solution: Search the Microsoft Web site for updated technical information that might relate to the problem you have observed. If necessary, you can obtain information and instructions that pertain to your current problem or issue.

If you are connected to the Internet, the latest updates for Windows 2000 Server are available at the Microsoft Web site. For obtaining the latest Service Pack updates for Windows NT Server, see the Microsoft Web site.

Familiarize yourself with other useful documentation and resources for DNS, such as the DNS Troubleshooter.

Troubleshoot Zone Problems

1. I am having\ a problem related to zone transfers.

Cause: The DNS Server service is stopped or the zone is paused.

Solution: Verify that the master (source) and secondary (destination) DNS servers involved in completing transfer of the zone are both started and that the zone is not paused at either server.

Cause: The DNS servers used during a transfer do not have network connectivity with each other.

Solution: Eliminate the possibility of a basic network connectivity problem between the two servers.

Using the **ping** command, ping each DNS server by its IP address from its remote counterpart.

For example, at the source server, use the **ping** command to test IP connectivity with the destination server. At the destination server, repeat the ping test, substituting the IP address for the source server.

Both ping tests should succeed. If not, investigate and resolve intermediate network connectivity issues.

Cause: The serial number is the same at both the source and destination servers. Because the value is the same at both servers, no zone transfer occurs between the servers.

Solution: Using the DNS console, perform the following tasks:

   a. Increase the value of the serial number for the zone at the master server (source) to a number greater than the value at the applicable secondary server (destination).
   b. Once you have increased the serial number at the master server to a higher value than is used currently at the secondary server, initiate zone transfer at the secondary server.

When working within the DNS console, the zone serial number can be viewed from the **Start of Authority (SOA)** tab in the applicable zone properties. To increase this number in the zone, click **Increment**.

Cause: The master server (source) and its targeted secondary server (destination) are having interoperability-related problems.

Solution: Investigate possible causes for any problems related to interoperability between Windows 2000 DNS servers and other DNS servers running different implementations, such as an older version of the BIND distribution.

Older BIND servers use an uncompressed zone transfer format. By default, Windows 2000 servers (and later version BIND servers) use a faster compressed format during zone transfers. To accommodate zone transfer with older BIND servers, you need to change advanced server options at your Windows 2000 DNS servers.

Another possible interoperability issue is the use and inclusion of WINS forward lookup (WINS) resource records in a zone or their counterpart, the WINS reverse lookup (WINS-R) resource record used for reverse lookup zoncs. BIND servers do not recognize these records when they are included in zone data being transferred and can flag these records as bad data, possibly failing the zone transfer.

To prevent these records from being used or included in zone transfers to BIND-based servers and other servers that do not recognize them, select **Do not replicate this record** when configuring WINS properties at the applicable zone.

Cause: The zone has resource records or other data that cannot be interpreted by the DNS server.

Solution: Verify that the zone does not contain incompatible data, such as unsupported resource records types or data errors.

In most cases, the DNS Server service supports all resource record types that are approved and required for Internet standard DNS usage.

Also, verify that the server has not been configured in advance to prevent loading a zone when bad data is found and investigate its method for checking names. These settings can be configured using DNS console.

Cause: Authoritative zone data is incorrect.

Solution: If a zone transfer continues to fail, ensure that the zone does not contain nonstandard data.

If you manually edit zone files, be aware that records need to be formatted and used according to standard record usage and formatting guidelines, as specified in the RFCs for DNS. In most cases, user input and data errors can be avoided if records are added and managed using the DNS console.

To determine if errored zone data is a likely source for a failed zone transfer, look in the DNS server event log for messages. You can also use the **nslookup** command with the -ls option to simulate and test a zone transfer.

2. I am trying to use a zone delegation but it appears to be broken.

   Cause: Zone delegations are not configured correctly.

   Solution: Review how zone delegations are used and revise your zone configurations as needed.

   Zones contain information about DNS domains and subdomains. For each new zone you create, the zone originally begins as a single-node database for one DNS domain. As needed, new subdomain nodes can be added directly below the original (parent) domain and stored as a single zone. Sometimes when new subdomains remain part of the same zone, they are called *subzones*.

If used as subzones, new subdomains are retained as part of the zone and replicated and updated along with it as a single entity. You can, however, delegate subdomains away and manage them in their own zones. For each subdomain delegated to its own zone, the parent zone needs to have delegation records added to it.

With Windows 2000 DNS servers, you can use the New Delegation wizard provided in the DNS console to simplify adding these records.

3. I am having a different zone problem than the ones described above.

Cause: My problem is not described above.

Solution: Search the Microsoft Web site for updated technical information that might relate to the problem you have observed. If necessary, you can obtain information and instructions that pertain to your current problem or issue.

If you are connected to the Internet, the latest updates for Windows 2000 Server are available at the Microsoft Web site. For obtaining the latest Service Pack updates for Windows NT Server, see the Microsoft Web site.

Familiarize yourself with other useful documentation and resources for DNS, such as the DNS Troubleshooter.

APPENDIX E

TCP/IP Utilities

Arp

Displays and modifies the IP-to-Ethernet or token-ring physical address translation tables used by the Address Resolution Protocol (ARP). This command is available only if the TCP/IP protocol has been installed.

arp -a [*inet_addr*] [**-N** [*if_addr*]]

arp -d *inet_addr* [*if_addr*]

arp -s *inet_addr ether_addr* [*if_addr*]

PARAMETERS

-a	Displays current ARP entries by querying TCP/IP. If *inet_addr* is specified, only the IP and physical addresses for the specified computer are displayed.
-g	Identical to -a.
inet_addr	Specifies an IP address in dotted decimal notation.
-N	Displays the ARP entries for the network interface specified by *if_addr*.
if_addr	Specifies, if present, the IP address of the interface whose address translation table should be modified. If not present, the first applicable interface is used.
-d	Deletes the entry specified by *inet_addr*.
-s	Adds an entry in the ARP cache to associate the IP address *inet_addr* with the physical address *ether_addr*. The physical address is given as 6 hexadecimal bytes separated by hyphens. The IP address is specified using dotted decimal notation. The entry is permanent, that is, it is automatically removed from the cache after the time-out expires.
ether_addr	Specifies a physical address.

Finger

Displays information about a user on a specified system running the Finger service. Output varies based on the remote system. This command is available only if the TCP/IP protocol has been installed.

finger [**-l**] [*user*]@*computer* [...]

PARAMETERS

-l	Displays information in long list format.
user	Specifies the user you want information about. Omit the user parameter to display information about all users on the specified computer.
@computer	Specifies computer.

Ftp and Commands

Transfers files to and from a computer running an FTP server service (sometimes called a daemon). Ftp can be used interactively. Click **ftp commands** in the Related Topics list for a description of available ftp subcommands. This command is available only if the TCP/IP protocol has been installed. Ftp is a service that, once started, creates a subenvironment in which you can use ftp commands and from which you can return to the Windows 2000 command prompt by typing the *quit* subcommand. When the ftp subenvironment is running, it is indicated by the ftp command prompt.

ftp [-v] [-n] [-i] [-d] [-g] [-s:*filename***] [-a] [-w:***windowsize***] [***computer***]**

PARAMETERS

-v	Suppresses display of remote server responses.
-n	Suppresses autologin upon initial connection.
-I	Turns off interactive prompting during multiple file transfers.
-d	Enables debugging, displaying all ftp commands passed between the client and server.
-g	Disables file name globbing, which permits the use of wildcard characters (* and ?) in local file and path names. (See the glob command in the online Command Reference.)

-s:*filename*	**Specifies a text file containing ftp commands; the commands automatically run after ftp starts. No spaces are allowed in this parameter. Use this switch instead of redirection (>).**
-a	**Use any local interface when binding data connection.**
-w:*windowsize*	**Overrides the default transfer buffer size of 4096.**
computer	**Specifies the computer name or IP address of the remote computer to connect to. The computer, if specified, must be the last parameter on the line.**

Ftp: !

Escape from the ftp subsystem to the shell.

!

Note This command is used without parameters. Use it when you are finished using ftp commands and want to return to the Windows 2000 command shell.

Ftp: ?

Displays descriptions for ftp commands. ? is identical to help.

? [*command*]

PARAMETER

command	**Specifies the name of the command about which you want a description. If** *command* **is not specified, ftp displays a list of all commands.**

Ftp: append

Appends a local file to a file on the remote computer using the current file type setting.

append *local-file* [*remote-file*]

PARAMETERS

local-file	**Specifies the local file to add.**
remote-file	**Specifies the file on the remote computer to which** *local-file* **will be added. If** *remote-file* **is omitted, the local file name is used for the remote file name.**

Ftp: ascii

Sets the file transfer type to ASCII, the default.

ascii

Note

FTP supports two file transfer types, ASCII and binary image. You should use ASCII when transferring text files. For more information on binary file transfer, see "Ftp: binary" in this appendix.

In ASCII mode, character conversions to and from the network standard character set are performed. For example, end-of-line characters are converted as necessary, based on the target operating system.

Ftp: bell

Toggles a bell to ring after each file transfer command is completed. By default, the bell is off.

bell

Ftp: binary

Sets the file transfer type to binary.

binary

Note

Ftp supports two file transfer types, ASCII and binary image. You should use binary when transferring executable files. In binary mode, the file is moved byte by byte. For more information on ASCII file transfer, see "Ftp: ascii" in this appendix.

Ftp: bye

Ends the FTP session with the remote computer and exits ftp.

bye

Ftp: cd

Changes the working directory on the remote computer.

cd *remote-directory*

PARAMETER

remote-directory	Specifies the directory on the remote computer to change to.

Ftp: close

Ends the FTP session with the remote server and returns to the command interpreter.

close

Ftp: debug

Toggles debugging. When debugging is on, each command sent to the remote computer is printed, preceded by the string >. By default, debugging is off.

debug

Ftp: delete

Deletes files on remote computers.

delete *remote-file*

PARAMETER

remote-file	Specifies the file to delete.

Ftp: dir

Displays a list of a remote directory's files and subdirectories.

dir [*remote-directory*] [*local-file*]

PARAMETERS

remote-directory	Specifies the directory for which you want to see a listing. If no directory is specified, the current working directory on the remote computer is used.
local-file	Specifies a local file to store the listing. If not specified, output is displayed on the screen.

Ftp: disconnect

Disconnects from the remote computer, retaining the ftp prompt.

disconnect

Ftp: get

Copies a remote file to the local computer using the current file transfer type.

get *remote-file* [*local-file*]

Parameters

remote-file	Specifies the remote file to copy.
local-file	Specifies the name to use on the local computer. If not specified, the file is given the *remote-file* name.

Ftp: glob

Toggles file name globbing. Globbing permits use of wildcard characters (* and ?) in local file or path names. By default, globbing is on.

glob

Ftp: hash

Toggles number-sign (#) printing for each data block transferred. The size of a data block is 2048 bytes. By default, hash mark printing is off.

hash

Ftp: help

Displays descriptions for ftp commands.

help [*command*]

PARAMETER

command	Specifies the name of the command about which you want a description. If *command* is not specified, ftp displays a list of all commands.

Ftp: lcd

Changes the working directory on the local computer. By default, the working directory is the directory in which ftp was started.

lcd [*directory*]

PARAMETER

directory	Specifies the directory on the local computer to change to. If *directory* is not specified, the current working directory on the local computer is displayed.

Ftp: literal

Sends arguments, verbatim, to the remote FTP server. A single FTP reply code is expected in return.

literal *argument* [...]

PARAMETER

argument	Specifies the argument to send to the FTP server.

Ftp: ls

Displays an abbreviated list of a remote directory's files and subdirectories.

ls [*remote-directory*] [*local-file*]

PARAMETERS

remote-directory	Specifies the directory for which you want to see a listing. If no directory is specified, the current working directory on the remote computer is used.
local-file	Specifies a local file to store the listing. If not specified, output is displayed on the screen.

Ftp: mdelete

Deletes files on remote computers.

mdelete *remote-files* [...]

PARAMETER

remote-files	Specifies the remote files to delete.

Ftp: mdir

Displays a list of a remote directory's files and subdirectories. You can use mdir to specify multiple files.

mdir *remote-files* [...] *local-file*

PARAMETERS

remote-files	Specifies the directory for which you want to see a listing. You must specify *remote-files*. Type — to use the current working directory on the remote computer.
local-file	Specifies a local file to store the listing. Type — to display the listing on the screen.

Ftp: mget

Copies remote files to the local computer using the current file transfer type.

mget *remote-files* [...]

PARAMETER

remote-files	Specifies the remote files to copy to the local computer.

Ftp: mkdir

Creates a remote directory.

mkdir *directory*

PARAMETER

directory	Specifies the name of the new remote directory.

Ftp: mls

Displays an abbreviated list of a remote directory's files and subdirectories.

mls *remote-files* [...] *local-file*

PARAMETERS

remote-files	Specifies the files for which you want to see a listing. You must specify *remote-files*; type — to use the current working directory on the remote computer.
local-file	Specifies a local file to store the listing. Type — to display the listing on the screen.

Ftp: mput

Copies local files to the remote computer, using the current file transfer type.

mput *local-files* [...]

PARAMETER

local-files	Specifies the local files to copy to the remote computer.

Ftp: open

Connects to the specified FTP server.

open *computer* [*port*]

PARAMETERS

computer	Specifies the remote computer to connect to. Computer can be specified by IP address or computer name (a DNS or Hosts file must be available). If auto-login is on (default), ftp also attempts to automatically log the user in to the FTP server.
port	Specifies a port number to use to contact an FTP server.

Ftp: prompt

Toggles prompting. Ftp prompts during multiple file transfers to allow you to selectively retrieve or store files, while mget and mput transfer all files if prompting is turned off. By default, prompting is on.

prompt

Ftp: put

Copies a local file to the remote computer using the current file transfer type.

put *local-file* [*remote-file*]

PARAMETERS

local-file	Specifies the local file to copy.
remote-file	Specifies the name to use on the remote computer. If not specified, the file is given the *local-file* name.

Ftp: pwd

Displays the current directory on the remote computer.

pwd

Ftp: quit

Ends the FTP session with the remote computer and exits ftp.

quit

Ftp: quote

Sends arguments, verbatim, to the remote FTP server. A single FTP reply code is expected in return. Quote is identical to literal.

quote *argument* [...]

PARAMETER

argument	Specifies the argument to send to the FTP server.

Ftp: recv

Copies a remote file to the local computer using the current file transfer type. Recv is identical to get.

recv *remote-file* [*local-file*]

PARAMETERS

remote-file	Specifies the remote file to copy.
local-file	Specifies the name to use on the local computer. If not specified, the file is given the *remote-file* name.

Ftp: remotehelp

Displays help for remote commands.

remotehelp [*command*]

PARAMETER

command	Specifies the name of the command about which you want help. If *command* is not specified, ftp displays a list of all remote commands.

Ftp: rename

Renames remote files.

rename *filename newfilename*

PARAMETERS

filename	Specifies the file you want to rename.
newfilename	Specifies the new file name.

Ftp: rmdir

Deletes a remote directory.

rmdir *directory*

PARAMETER

directory	Specifies the name of the remote directory to delete.

Ftp: send

Copies a local file to the remote computer using the current file transfer type. Send is identical to put.

send *local-file* [*remote-file*]

PARAMETERS

local-file	Specifies the local file to copy.
remote-file	Specifies the name to use on the remote computer. If not specified, the file is given the *local-file* name.

Ftp: status

Displays the current status of FTP connections and toggles.

status

Ftp: trace

Toggles packet tracing. Trace displays the route of each packet when running an ftp command.

trace

Ftp: type

Sets or displays the file transfer type.

type [*type-name*]

PARAMETER

type-name	Specifies the file transfer type. The default is ascii. If *type-name* is not specified, the current type is displayed.

Note

Ftp supports two file transfer types, ASCII and binary image.

ASCII should be used when transferring text files. In ASCII mode, character conversions to and from the network standard character set are performed. For example, end-of-line characters are converted as necessary, based on the destination's operating system.

Binary should be used when transferring executable files. In binary mode, the file is moved byte by byte.

Ftp: user

Specifies a user to the remote computer.

user *user-name* [*password*] [*account*]

PARAMETERS

user-name	Specifies a user name with which to log on to the remote computer.
password	Specifies the password for *user-name*. If not specified, but required, ftp prompts for the password.
account	Specifies an account with which to log on to the remote computer. If *account* is not specified, but required, ftp prompts for the account.

Ftp: verbose

Toggles verbose mode. If on, all ftp responses are displayed. When a file transfer completes, statistics regarding the efficiency of the transfer are also displayed. By default, verbose is on.

verbose

Hostname

Prints the name of the current computer (host). This command is available only if the TCP/IP protocol has been installed.

hostname

Ipconfig

This diagnostic command displays all current TCP/IP network configuration values. This command is of particular use on systems running DHCP, allowing users to determine which TCP/IP configuration values have been configured by DHCP.

ipconfig [/all | **/renew** [*adapter*] | **/release** [*adapter*]]

PARAMETERS

all	Produces a full display. Without this switch, **ipconfig** displays only the IP address, subnet mask, and default gateway values for each network card.
/renew [*adapter*]	Renews DHCP configuration parameters. This option is available only on systems running the DHCP Client service. To specify an adapter name, type the adapter name that appears when you use **ipconfig** without parameters.
/release [*adapter*]	Releases the current DHCP configuration. This option disables TCP/IP on the local system and is available only on DHCP clients. To specify an adapter name, type the adapter name that appears when you use **ipconfig** without parameters.

With no parameters, the **ipconfig** utility presents all of the current TCP/IP configuration values to the user, including IP address and subnet mask.

Lpr

This connectivity utility is used to print a file to a computer running an LPD server.

lpr -**S***Server* -**P***Printer* [-**C***Class*] [-**J***Jobname*] [-**O** *option*] *filename*

PARAMETERS

-S*Server*	Specifies the name or IP address of the computer that has the printer attached to it.
-P*Printer*	Specifies the name of the printer for the desired queue.
-C*Class*	Specifies the content of the banner page for the class.
-J*Jobname*	Specifies the name of this job.
-O *option*	Indicates the type of file. The default is a text file. Use -Ol (lowercase *L*) for a binary file (for example, PostScript).
filename	The name of the file to be printed.

Lpq

This diagnostic utility is used to obtain status of a print queue on a computer running the LPD server.

lpq -**S***Server* -**P***Printer* [-**l**]

PARAMETERS

-S*Server*	Specifies the name of the computer that has the printer attached to it.
-P*Printer*	Specifies the name of the printer for the desired queue.
-l	Specifies that a detailed status should be given.

Nbtstat

This diagnostic command displays protocol statistics and current TCP/IP connections using NetBT (NetBIOS over TCP/IP). This command is available only if the TCP/IP protocol has been installed.

nbtstat [-**a** *remotename*] [-**A** *IP address*] [-**c**] [-**n**] [-**R**] [-**r**] [-**S**] [-**s**] [*interval*]

PARAMETERS

-a *remotename*	Lists the remote computer's name table using its name.
-A *IP address*	Lists the remote computer's name table using its IP address.
-c	Lists the contents of the NetBIOS name cache giving the IP address of each name.
-n	Lists local NetBIOS names. Registered indicates that the name is registered by broadcast (b-node) or WINS (other node types).
-R	Reloads the Lmhosts file after purging all names from the NetBIOS name cache.
-r	Lists name resolution statistics for Windows networking name resolution. On a Windows 2000 computer configured to use WINS, this option returns the number of names resolved and registered via broadcast or via WINS.
-S	Displays both client and server sessions, listing the remote computers by IP address only.
-s	Displays both client and server sessions. It attempts to convert the remote computer IP address to a name using the Hosts file.
interval	Redisplays selected statistics, pausing *interval* seconds between each display. Press CTRL+C to stop redisplaying statistics. If this parameter is omitted, nbtstat prints the current configuration information once.

Net: Command Options

Many Windows 2000 networking commands begin with the word **net**. These net commands have some common properties:

- You can see a list of all available net commands by typing *net /?*.
- You can get syntax help at the command line for a net command by typing *net help command*. For example, for help with the net accounts command, type *net help accounts*.
- All net commands accept /yes and /no options (can be abbreviated /y and /n). The /y option automatically answers yes to any interactive prompt that the command generates, while /n answers no. For example, net stop server usually prompts you to confirm that you want to stop all services that depend on the Server service, while net stop server /y automatically answers yes to the prompt and the Server service shuts down.

Net accounts

Updates the user accounts database and modifies password and logon requirements for all accounts. The Net Logon service must be running on the computer for which you want to change account parameters.

net accounts [**/forcelogoff:**{*minutes* | **no**}] [**/minpwlen:***length*] [**/maxpwage:**{*days* | **unlimited**}] [**/minpwage:***days*] [**/uniquepw:***number*] [**/domain**]

net accounts [**/sync**] [**/domain**]

PARAMETERS

none	Type *net accounts* without parameters to display the current settings for password, logon limitations, and domain information.
/forcelogoff:{*minutes* | **no**}	Sets the number of minutes to wait before ending a user's session with a server when the user account or valid logon time expires. The no option prevents forced logoff. The default is no. When the /forcelogoff:*minutes* option is specified, Windows 2000 sends a warning minutes before it forces the user off from the network. If any files are open, Windows 2000 warns the user. If *minutes* is less than two, Windows 2000 warns the user to log off from the network immediately.
/minpwlen:*length*	Sets the minimum number of characters for a user account password. The range is 0 to 127 characters, and the default is 6 characters.
/maxpwage:{*days* | **unlimited**}	Sets the maximum number of days that a user account's password is valid. A value of unlimited sets no maximum time. The /maxpwage option must be greater than /minpwage. The range is 1 to 49,710 days (unlimited), and the default is 90 days.
/minpwage:*days*	Sets the minimum number of days before a user can change a new password. A value of 0 sets no minimum time. The range is 0 to 49,710 days, and the default is 0 days.
/uniquepw:*number*	Requires that a user not repeat the same password for *number* password changes. The range is 0 to 24 password changes, and the default is 5 password changes.
/domain	Performs the operation on the primary domain controller of the current domain. Otherwise, the operation is performed on the local computer. This parameter applies only to Windows 2000 Workstation computers that are members of a Windows 2000 Server domain. By default, Windows 2000 Server computers perform operations on the primary domain controller.

/sync	When used on the primary domain controller, causes all backup domain controllers in the domain to synchronize. When used on a backup domain controller, causes that backup domain controller only to synchronize with the primary domain controller. This command applies only to computers that are members of a Windows 2000 Server domain.

Net computer

Adds or deletes computers from a domain database. All additions and deletions are forwarded to the primary domain controller. This command is available only on computers running Windows 2000 Server.

net computer *computername* {**/add** | **/del**}

PARAMETERS

computername	Specifies the computer to add or delete from the domain.
/add	Adds the specified computer to the domain.
/del	Removes the specified computer from the domain.

Net config

Displays the configurable services that are running, or displays and changes settings for a service.

net config [*service* [*options*]]

PARAMETERS

none	Type *net config* without parameters to display a list of configurable services.
service	Specifies a service (server or workstation) that can be configured with the net config command.
options	Are specific to the service. See net config server or net config workstation for more information on the complete syntax.

Note Use the net config *service* command to change configurable Server or Workstation service parameters. The changes take effect immediately and are permanent.

Net config server

Displays or changes settings for the Server service while the service is running.

net config server [/autodisconnect:*time*] [**/srvcomment:***"text"*]
[**/hidden:**{**yes** | **no**}]

PARAMETERS

none	Type *net config server* to display the current configuration for the Server service.
/autodisconnect:*time*	Sets the maximum number of minutes a user's session can be inactive before it is disconnected. You can specify -1 to never disconnect. The range extends from -1 to 65535 minutes, and the default is 15.
/srvcomment:*"text"*	Adds a comment for the server that is displayed in Windows 2000 screens and with the net view command. The comment can have as many as 48 characters. Enclose the text in quotation marks.
/hidden:{yes | no}	Specifies whether the computer name of the server appears on display listings of servers. Note that hiding a server does not alter the permissions on that server. The default is **no**.

Note Use the net config server command to change configurable Server service parameters. The changes take effect immediately and are permanent.

Not all Server service parameters can be changed using the net config server command; however, the net config server display includes additional information about the server:

- The computer name of the server, a descriptive comment, and the software version.
- The network description.
- The hidden setting of the server.
- The maximum number of users who can use the shared resources of the server.
- The maximum number of server files that can be open.
- The Idle session time setting.

Net config workstation

Displays or changes settings for the Workstation service while the service is running.

net config workstation [**/charcount:***bytes*] [**/chartime:***msec*]
[**/charwait:***sec*]

PARAMETERS

none	Type *net config workstation* to display the current configuration for the local computer.
/charcount:*bytes*	Specifies the amount of data Windows 2000 collects before sending the data to a communication device. If /chartime:*msec* is also set, Windows 2000 acts on whichever option is satisfied first. The range extends from 0 to -65535 bytes, and the default is 16 bytes.
/chartime:*msec*	Sets the number of milliseconds Windows 2000 collects data before sending the data to a communication device. If / charcount:*bytes* is also set, Windows 2000 acts on whichever option is satisfied first. The range extends from 0 to 65535000 milliseconds, and the default is 250 milliseconds.
/charwait:*sec*	Sets the number of seconds Windows 2000 waits for a communication device to become available. The range extends from 0 to 65535 seconds, and the default is 3600 seconds.

Note Use the net config workstation command to change configurable Workstation service parameters. The changes take effect immediately and are permanent.

Not all Workstation service parameters can be changed using the net config workstation command. Other parameters can be changed in the configuration registry.

Net continue

Reactivates suspended services.

net continue *service*

PARAMETER

service	Services that can be continued are file server for macintosh (Windows 2000 Server only), ftppublishing service, lpdsvc, net logon, network dde, network dde dsdm, nt lm security support provider, remote access server, schedule, server, simple tcp/ip services, and workstation.

Note Use the net continue command to reactivate a service that has been paused. Pause a service before stopping the service to let users complete jobs or disconnect from resources. To make a minor correction to a resource, pausing the service or printer might be sufficient. Then use the net continue command to reactivate the service or printer, without canceling users' connections.

The effect of pausing and continuing a service can vary with each service.

Net file

Displays the names of all open shared files on a server and the number of file locks, if any, on each file. This command also closes individual shared files and removes file locks.

net file [*id* [**/close**]]

PARAMETERS

none	Type *net file* without parameters to get a list of the open files on a server.
id	Specifies the identification number of the file.
/close	Closes an open file and releases locked records. Type this command from the server where the file is shared.

Note This command can also be typed net files.

Use the net file command to view and control files shared on the network. Shared files are sometimes left open and locked by mistake. When this happens, the locked portions of a file cannot be accessed by other computers on the network. Use the net file command's /close option to remove the lock and close the file.

The display for the net file command is similar to the following:

```
File        Path              Username     #locks
-----------------------------------------------------------
0           C:\A_FILE.TXT     MARYSL        0
1           C:\DATABASE       DEBBIET       2
```

Net group

Adds, displays, or modifies global groups on Windows 2000 Server domains. This command is available for use only on Windows 2000 Server Domain Controllers.

net group [*groupname* [**/comment:** *"text"*]] [**/domain**]

net group *groupname* {**/add** [**/comment**: *"text"*] | **/delete**} [**/domain**]

net group *groupname username*[...] {**/add** | **/delete**} [**/domain**]

PARAMETERS

none	Type *net group* without parameters to display the name of a server and the names of groups on the server.
groupname	Specifies the name of the group to add, expand, or delete. Supply only a group name to view a list of users in a group.
/comment: *"text"*	Adds a comment for a new or existing group. The comment can have as many as 48 characters. Enclose the text in quotation marks.
/domain	Performs the operation on the primary domain controller of the current domain. Otherwise, the operation is performed on the local computer. This parameter applies only to Windows 2000 Professional computers that are members of a Windows 2000 Server domain. By default, Windows 2000 Server computers perform operations on the primary domain controller.
username[...]	Lists one or more user names to add to or remove from a group. Separate multiple user name entries with a space.
/add	Adds a group, or adds a user name to a group. An account must be established for users added to a group with this command.
/delete	Removes a group, or removes a user name from a group.

Note This command can also be typed net groups.

Use the net group command to group users who use the network in the same or similar ways. When you assign rights to a group, each member of the group automatically has those rights.

A display of groups on the server is similar to the following:

Group Accounts for `\\PRODUCTION`

Net help

Provides a list of network commands and topics you can get help with, or provides help with a specific command or topic. The available net commands are also listed in the Commands window of the Command Reference under N. Click Windows 2000 Command Reference in the Related Topics list.

net help [*command*]

net *command* {/help | /?}

PARAMETERS

none	Type *net help* without parameters to display a list of commands and topics for which you can get help.
command	The command that you need help with. Don't type net as part of *command*.
{**/help** | /?}	Displays the correct syntax for the command. /help provides an alternate way to display the help text.

Net helpmsg

Provides help with Windows 2000 error messages.

net helpmsg *message#*

PARAMETER

message#	Specifies the four-digit number of the Windows 2000 message you need help with.

Net localgroup

Adds, displays, or modifies local groups.

net localgroup [*groupname* [/**comment:**"*text*"]] [/**domain**]
net localgroup *groupname* {/add [/comment:"*text*"] | /delete} [/domain]
net localgroup *groupname name* [...] {/add | /delete} [/domain]

PARAMETERS

none	Type *net localgroup* without parameters to display the name of the server and the names of local groups on the computer.
groupname	Specifies the name of the local group to add, expand, or delete. Supply only a *groupname* to view a list of users or global groups in a local group.
/comment:"*text*"	Adds a comment for a new or existing group. The comment can have as many as 48 characters. Enclose the text in quotation marks.
/domain	Performs the operation on the primary domain controller of the current domain. Otherwise, the operation is performed on the local computer. This parameter applies only to Windows 2000 Professional computers that are members of a Windows 2000 Server domain. By default, Windows 2000 Server computers perform operations on the primary domain controller.

name [...]	Lists one or more user names or group names to add or remove from a local group. Separate multiple entries with a space. Names may be local users, users on other domains, or global groups, but not other local groups. If a user is from another domain, preface the user name with the domain name (for example, SALES\RALPHR).
/add	Adds a global group name or user name to a local group. An account must first be established for users or global groups before it is added to a local group with this command.
/delete	Removes a group name or user name from a local group.

Net name

Adds or deletes a messaging name (sometimes called an *alias*), or displays the list of names the computer will accept messages for. The Messenger service must be running to use **net name**.

net name [*name* **[/add | /delete]]**

PARAMETERS

none	Type *net name* without parameters to display a list of names currently in use.
name	Specifies the name to receive messages. The name can have as many as 15 characters.
/add	Adds a name to a computer. Typing */add* is optional. Typing net *name name* works the same way as typing *net name name /add.*
/delete	Removes a name from a computer.

Note

Use the net name command to specify a name for receiving messages. The Messenger service must be started to use the net name command. Each messaging name must be unique on the network. Names created with net name are strictly for messaging, and names are not groups.

Windows 2000 uses three kinds of names:

- Any name for messaging, which is added with net name.
- The computer's machine name, which is added when the Workstation service starts.
- Your user name, which is added when you log on, provided your user name is not in use as a message name elsewhere on the network.

The computer's machine name cannot be deleted. The user name can be deleted.

Net pause

Pauses running services.

net pause *service*

PARAMETER

service	Includes: file service for macintosh (Windows 2000 Server only), ftp publishing service, lpdsvc, net logon, network dde, network dde dsdm, nt lm security support provider, remote access server, schedule, server, simple tcp/ip services, and workstation.

Note

On a server, use the net pause command before stopping a service to let users complete jobs or disconnect from resources. Pausing a service puts it on hold but doesn't remove the software from memory. Users who already have a connection to the resource are able to finish their tasks, but new connections to the resource are prevented.

If you plan to stop a service that affects shared resources, first pause the service. Then, using the net send command, broadcast a message that the service will be stopped. After sufficient time for people to finish using the resource, stop the service using the net stop command.

To reactivate a service that has been paused, use the net continue command.

Not all services can be paused.

Pausing affects the Windows 2000 services in the following ways:

- Pausing the Net Logon service prevents the computer from processing logon requests. If the domain has other logon servers, users can still log on to the network.
- Pausing the Server service prevents users from making new connections to the shared resources of the server and, if there are no other logon servers on the network, from logging on to the network. An existing connection is unaffected. Administrators can make connections to the server even if it is paused.
- Pausing the Workstation service keeps the user name, password, and connections defined, but directs requests for print devices to printers attached to the computer rather than to printers connected to the network.

Net print

Displays or controls print jobs and printer queues.

net print *computername**sharename*

net print [*computername*] *job#* [/hold | /release | /delete]

PARAMETERS

computername	Specifies the name of the computer sharing the printer queue(s).
sharename	Specifies the name of the printer queue. When including the *sharename* with the *computername,* use a backslash (\) to separate the names.
job#	Specifies the identification number assigned to a print job in a printer queue. A computer with one or more printer queues assigns each print job a unique number. If a job number is being used in one printer queue shared by a computer, that number is not assigned to any other job on that computer, not even to jobs in other printer queues on that computer.
/hold	When used with *job#,* holds a print job waiting in the printer queue. The print job stays in the printer queue, and other print jobs bypass it until it is released.
/release	Releases a print job that has been held.
/delete	Removes a print job from a printer queue.

Net send

Sends messages to other users, computers, or messaging names on the network. The Messenger service must be running to receive messages.

net send {*name* | * | /**domain**[:*name*] | /**users**} *message*

PARAMETERS

name	Specifies the user name, computer name, or messaging name to send the message to. If the name is a computer name that contains blank characters, enclose the alias in quotation marks. Long user names may lead to problems when used as NetBIOS names. NetBIOS names are limited to 16 characters, and Windows 2000 reserves the sixteenth character.
*	Sends the message to all the names in your domain or workgroup.
/domain[:*name*]	Sends the message to all the names in the computer's domain. If *name* is specified, the message is sent to all the names in the specified domain or workgroup.
/users	Sends the message to all users connected to the server.
message	Specifies text to be sent as a message.

Note You can send a message only to a name that is active on the network. If the message is sent to a user name, that user must be logged on and running the Messenger service to receive the message.

Windows 2000 provides several ways to broadcast a message to multiple users. You can broadcast a message to all the names in your computer's domain (use * or /**domain**) or in a different domain (/**domain**:domainname). Broadcast messages can have as many as 128 characters.

The /**users** option lets you send a message to all users who have sessions with the server. Parameters that send to multiple users should be used with discretion.

Net session

Lists or disconnects the sessions between a local computer and the clients connected to it.

net session [*computername*] [/**delete**]

PARAMETERS

none	Type *net session* without parameters to display information about all sessions with the local computer.
computername	Identifies the computer for which to list or disconnect sessions.
/delete	Ends the computer's session with *computername* and closes all open files on the computer for the session. If *computername* is omitted, all sessions on the local computer are canceled.

Note The net session command can also be typed *net sessions* or *net sess*.

Use the net session command to display the computer names and user names of users accessing a server, whether they have files open, and how long each user's session has been idle.

The display is similar to the following:

```
Computer      User name        Client type  Opens  Idle time
-------------------------------------------------------------
\\BASSETT     CHRISDR          NT              1    00:00:13
\\SHARONCA    Administrator    DOS LM 2.1      0    01:05:13
```

To display one user's session, include *computername* with the command. A single user's display includes a list of shared resources to which the user has connections.

A session is recorded when a user at a client successfully contacts a server. A successful session occurs when the two systems are on the same network and the user has a user name and password that are accepted by the server. A user at a client has to have a session with a server before being able to use the resources of the server, and a session is not established until a user at a client connects to a resource. A client and a server have only one session, but they can have many entry points, or connections, to resources.

To set how long a session can remain idle before being automatically disconnected, set the autodisconnect feature using the /autodisconnect option of the net config server command. An automatic disconnection is transparent to the user because Windows 2000 automatically reconnects the session when the user uses the resource again.

To end a session with the server, use the /delete option along with *computername*.

Net share

Creates, deletes, or displays shared resources.

net share *sharename*

net share *sharename=drive:path* [/**users**:*number* | /**unlimited**][/**remark**:*"text"*]

net share *sharename* [/**users**:*number* | **unlimited**] [/**remark**: *"text"*]

net share {*sharename* | *drive:path*} /**delete**

PARAMETERS

none	Type *net share* without parameters to display information about all resources being shared on the local computer.
sharename	Is the network name of the shared resource. Type *net share* with a *sharename* only to display information about that share.
drive:path	Specifies the absolute path of the directory to be shared.
/users:*number*	Sets the maximum number of users who can simultaneously access the shared resource.
/unlimited	Specifies an unlimited number of users who can simultaneously access the shared resource.
/remark: *"text"*	Adds a descriptive comment about the resource. Enclose the text in quotation marks.
/delete	Stops sharing the resource.

Note Use the net share command to share resources.

To share a directory with a path that contains a blank character, enclose the drive and the path of the directory in quotation marks.

When you display all the shared resources on a computer, Windows 2000 reports the sharename of the resource, the devicename(s) or path associated with the resource, and a descriptive comment about the resource.

The display is similar to the following:

```
Sharename  Resource          Remark
----------------------------------------------------------
ADMIN$     C:\WINNT          Remote Admin
C$         C:\               Default Share for Internal Use
print$     C:\WINNT\SYSTEM\SPOOL
IPC$                         Remote IPC
LASER      LPT1 Spooled      Laser printer
```

As you create shares on a server, they are saved. When you stop the Server service, all shares are disconnected, but they are reconnected automatically the next time the Server service is started or the computer is restarted.

Net start

Starts a service, or displays a list of started services. Service names of two or more words, such as Net Logon or Computer Browser, must be enclosed in quotation marks.

net start [*service*]

PARAMETERS

none	Type *net start* without parameters to display a list of running services.
service	Includes: alerter, client service for netware, clipbook server, content index, computer browser, dhcp client, directory replicator, eventlog, ftp publishing service, hypermedia object manager, logical disk manager, lpdsvc, media services management, messenger, Fax Service, Microsoft install server, net logon, network dde, network dde dsdm, nt lm security support provider, ole, plug and play, remote access connection manager, remote access isnsap service, remote access server, remote procedure call (rpc) locator, remote procedure call (rpc) service, schedule, server, simple tcp/ip services, site server ldap service, smartcard resource manager, snmp, spooler, task scheduler, tcp/ip netbios helper, telephony service, tracking service, tracking (server) service, ups, Windows time service, and workstation. These services are available only on Windows 2000 Server: file service for macintosh, gateway service for netware, microsoft dhcp service, print service for macintosh, and windows Internet name service.

Note Use the net start *service* command to start Windows 2000 services. Some services are dependent on other services.

You can also use the Services snap-in to configure services to stop and start automatically. Use this snap-in also to manually stop, start, pause, and continue network services.

This command will also start network services that are not provided with Windows 2000.

Net start Alerter

Starts the Alerter service. The Alerter service sends alert messages.

net start alerter

Net start Client Service for NetWare

Starts the Client Service for NetWare service. This command is available only on Windows 2000 Professional if Client Service for NetWare has been installed.

net start "client service for netware"

Net start ClipBook Server

Starts the ClipBook Server service. Service names with two words, such as ClipBook Server, must be enclosed in quotation marks.

net start "clipbook server"

Net start Computer Browser

Starts the Computer Browser service.

net start "computer browser"

Net start DHCP Client

Starts the DHCP Client service. This command is available only if the TCP/IP protocol has been installed.

net start "dhcp client"

Net start Directory Replicator

Starts the Directory Replicator service. The Directory Replicator service copies designated files to specified servers. Service names with two words, such as Directory Replicator, must be enclosed in quotation marks. You can also start this service with the command net start replicator.

net start "directory replicator"

Note

Start the Directory Replicator service to ensure that designated files are exactly the same on all specified servers. The Directory Replicator must be configured prior to starting the Directory Replicator service.

Net start Eventlog

Starts the event logging service, which logs events on the local computer. This service must be started prior to using Event Viewer to view the logged events.

net start eventlog

Note

The Eventlog service logs any significant system, security, and application occurrences that require users to be notified. For more information on Event Viewer and configuring log maintenance information, see the online Help for Event Viewer.

You cannot stop or pause the Eventlog service.

Net start File Server for Macintosh

Starts the File Service for Macintosh service, permitting the sharing of files with Macintosh computers. This command is available only on computers running Windows 2000 Server.

net start "file service for macintosh"

Net start FTP Publishing Service

Starts the FTP Publishing Service. This command is available only if Internet Information Services has been installed.

net start "ftp publishing service"

Net start Gateway Service for NetWare

Starts the Gateway Service for NetWare service. This command is available only on Windows 2000 Server if Gateway Service for NetWare has been installed.

net start "gateway service for netware"

Net start Lpdsvc

Starts the TCP/IP Print Server service. This command is available only if Print Services for UNIX, as well as the TCP/IP protocol, have been installed.

net start lpdsvc

Note The TCP/IP Print Server service is the server side of TCP/IP printing for UNIX clients. If any UNIX clients on the network want to print to a printer connected to a Windows 2000 computer, this service needs to be running on the Windows 2000 computer so it can accept requests from the UNIX clients. The TCP/IP Print Server service supports any print format, including plain text.

The TCP/IP Print Server service is independent of LPR ports. LPR ports allow a Windows 2000 computer (and all clients who can access this computer) to print to a printer connected to a UNIX computer.

Net start Messenger

Starts the Messenger service. The Messenger service enables a computer to receive messages.

net start messenger

Note Starts the Messenger service so that a computer can receive messages. A message is sent to a computer using the names assigned to the computer as identification.

Net start Microsoft DHCP Service

Starts the Microsoft DHCP Service. This command is available only on computers running Windows 2000 Server and where the TCP/IP protocol and DHCP service have been installed.

net start "microsoft dhcp service"

Note The Microsoft DHCP Service supplies network clients with IP addresses. Service names with two words must be enclosed in quotation marks. This service can also be started with the command net start dhcpservice.

Net start Net Logon

Starts the Net Logon service. The Net Logon service verifies logon requests and controls replication of the user accounts database domainwide. Service names with two words, such as Net Logon, must be enclosed in quotation marks. This service can also be started with the command net start netlogon.

net start "net logon"

Note Start the Net Logon service on all the servers in a domain that use a copy of the domain's user accounts database.

When starting services at the command prompt, service names with two words, such as Net Logon, must be enclosed in quotation marks. This service can also be started by typing *net start netlogon*.

Primary domain controllers in Windows 2000 and LAN Manager 2.x mixed domains

If you are using Windows 2000 Server domains, the primary domain controller must be a Windows 2000 Server computer. Backup domain controllers in the domain can be either Windows 2000 Servers or LAN Manager 2.x computers.

All Windows 2000 computers must log on to a Windows 2000 Server primary domain controller. LAN Manager 2.x computers can log on to LAN Manager 2.x or Windows 2000 Server primary domain controllers.

Net start Network DDE

Starts the Network DDE service.

net start "network dde"

Net start NT LM Security Support Provider

Starts the NT LM Security Support Provider service. This command is available only if the NT LM Security Support Provider has been installed.

net start "nt lm security support provider"

Net start OLE

Starts the object linking and embedding service.

net start ole

Net start Print Server for Macintosh

Starts the Print Server for Macintosh service, permitting printing from Macintosh computers. This command is available only on computers running Windows 2000 Server.

net start "print server for macintosh"

Net start Remote Access Connection Manager

Starts the Remote Access Connection Manager service. This command is available only if the Remote Access Service has been installed.

net start "remote access connection manager"

Net start Remote Access ISNSAP Service

Starts the Remote Access ISNSAP Service. This command is available only if the Remote Access Service has been installed.

net start "remote access isnsap service"

Net start Remote Procedure Call (RPC) Locator

Starts the RPC Locator service. The Locator service is the RPC name service for Microsoft Windows 2000.

net start "remote procedure call (rpc) locator"

Net start Remote Procedure Call (RPC) Service

Starts the Remote Procedure Call (RPC) Service. The Remote Procedure Call (RPC) Service is the RPC subsystem for Microsoft Windows 2000. The RPC subsystem includes the endpoint mapper and other miscellaneous RPC services.

net start "remote procedure call (rpc) service"

Note Start the Remote Procedure Call (RPC) Service *service* to allow distributed applications to use dynamic endpoints. The Remote Procedure Call (RPC) Service service manages the endpoint map database

The server side of the distributed application registers its endpoints with the Remote Procedure Call (RPC) Service. The client run-time library, on behalf of the client side of the distributed application, queries the Remote Procedure Call (RPC) Service service to obtain the endpoint information.

To determine whether a distributed application uses the endpoint mapper service, see the documentation for that distributed application.

Service names with two words must be enclosed in quotation marks. You can also start this service with the command net start rpcss.

Net start Schedule

Starts the Schedule service. The Schedule service enables a computer to start programs at a specified time with the at command.

net start schedule

Note The Schedule service must be started to use the at command. Scheduled commands may require that other services be running for the command to successfully run.

The Schedule service is initially configured to run in the System account on the local computer. When the Schedule service runs using this account, there are no restrictions on the jobs that can be executed by Schedule service. However, these jobs will have limited network access, because the System account on a local computer is not recognized by other computers.

To overcome network access limitations, you can configure the Schedule service to run in a user's account. Then, jobs executed by the Schedule service will be governed by network access of the user's account. However, because Schedule service is not using the local System account in this case, only jobs that do not require presence of a window can be run successfully.

Net start Server

Starts the Server service. The Server service enables a computer to share resources on the network.

net start server

Note Start the Server service to share a server's resources with users on the network.

Net start Simple TCP/IP Services

Starts the Simple TCP/IP Services service. This command is available only if TCP/IP and the Simple TCP/IP Services have been installed.

net start "simple tcp/ip services"

Note The Simple TCP/IP Services service supports the TCP/IP services Character Generator, Daytime, Discard, Echo, and Quote of the Day. When started, the computer can respond to requests from other computers that support these protocols.

Service names with two words must be enclosed in quotation marks.

Net start Site Server LDAP Service

Starts the Site Server LDAP Service. The Site Server LDAP Service publishes IP multicast conferences in the Windows 2000 Active Directory. This command is available only if Site Server LDAP Service has been installed.

net start "site server ldap service"

Net start SNMP

Starts the SNMP service. The SNMP service allows a server to report its current status to an SNMP management system on a TCP/IP network. This command is available only if TCP/IP and SNMP have been installed.

net start snmp

Net start Spooler

Starts the Spooler service.

net start spooler

Net start TCP/IP NetBIOS Helper

Enables the Netbios Helper over TCP service. This command is available only if TCP/IP has been installed.

net start "tcp/ip netbios helper"

Net start UPS

Starts the Uninterruptible Power Supply (UPS) service.

net start ups

Net start Windows Internet Name Service

Starts the Windows Internet Name Service. This command is available only on Windows 2000 Servers if TCP/IP and the Windows Internet Name Service have been installed.

net start "windows internet name service"

Note The Windows Internet Name Service maps computer names to TCP/IP addresses for client computers on the network.

Service names with two or more words, such as Windows Internet Name or Uninterruptible Power Supply, must be enclosed in quotation marks. This service can also be started with the command net start wins.

Net start Workstation

Starts the Workstation service. The Workstation service enables a computer to connect to and use network resources.

net start workstation

Note Start the Workstation service so that your computer can use information and equipment on the network.

Net statistics

Displays the statistics log for the local Workstation or Server service, or the running services for which statistics are available.

net statistics [workstation | server]

PARAMETERS

none	Type *net statistics* without parameters to list the running services for which statistics are available.
workstation	Displays statistics for the local Workstation service.
server	Displays statistics for the local Server service.

Note This command can also be typed *net stats.*

Use the net statistics command to display performance information for the specified service.

The Server service

Windows 2000 reports the computer's name, the date and time when the statistics were last updated, and the following information:

- The number of sessions that were started, disconnected automatically, and disconnected because of an error.
- The number of kilobytes sent and received, and the average server-response time.
- The number of errors and violations of password and permission limits.
- The number of times the shared files, printers, and communication devices were used.
- The number of times the size of the memory buffer was exceeded.

The Workstation service

Windows 2000 reports the computer's name, the date and time when the statistics were last updated, and the following information:

- The number of bytes and Server Message Blocks (SMBs) received and transmitted.
- The number of read-and-write operations that succeeded or failed.
- The number of network errors.
- The number of sessions that failed, were disconnected, or were reconnected.
- The number of connections to shared resources that succeeded or failed.

Net stop

Stops a Windows 2000 network service.

net stop *service*

PARAMETERS

service	Includes the following services: alerter, network dde dsdm, simple tcp/ip services, client service for netware, nt lm security support provider, site server LDAP service, clipbook server, ole, snmp, computer browser, remote access connection manager, spooler, directory replicator, remote access isnsap service, tcp/ip netbios helper, ftp publishing service, remote access server, ups, lpdsvc, remote procedure call (rpc) locator, workstation, messenger, remote procedure call (rpc) service, net logon, schedule, network dde, server. The following services are available only on Windows 2000 Server: File Service for Macintosh, Gateway Service for NetWare, Microsoft DHCP Service, Print Service for Macintosh, Windows Internet Name Service.

Note

Use net stop to stop a service, halt the function it performs, and remove the software from memory. Stopping the Server service prevents users from accessing the computer's shared resources. If you stop the Server service when users are accessing resources, Windows 2000 displays a warning message, requesting confirmation that you want to cancel the connections. A y (for yes) response cancels all connections to the computer.

Before stopping the Server service, you can do the following:

- Pause the service (to disallow new connections).
- Send a message advising users to disconnect from the server's resources.

The net stop command can also stop network services not provided with Windows 2000.

Net time

Synchronizes the computer's clock with that of another computer or domain. Used without the **/set** option, displays the time for another computer or domain.

net time [*computername* | /**domain**[:*domainname*] | /**rtsdomain** [:*domainname*]] [/**set**]

net time [*computername*] [/**querysntp**] | [/**setsntp**[:*ntp server list*]]

PARAMETERS

none	Displays the current date and time at the computer designated as the time server for the local computer's Windows Server domain
computername	Specifies the name of a server you want to check or with which you want to synchronize.
/domain[:*domainname*]	Specifies the domain with which to synchronize time.
/rtsdomain[:*domainname*]	Specifies the domain of the Reliable Time Server with which to synchronize time.
/set	Synchronizes the computer's clock with the time on the specified computer or domain.
/querysntp	Displays the name of the Network Time Protocol (NTP) server currently configured for the local computer or the one specified in *computername*.
/setsntp[:*ntp server list*]	Specifies a list of NTP timeservers to be used by the local computer. The list may contain IP addresses or ping remotehost rather than ping 1.2.3.4 if the mapping for the system named *remotehost* was contained in the DNS database. DNS domains should not be confused with Windows 2000 networking domains. See also *DNS name; domain; IP address; service; TCP/IP."DNS names,* separated by spaces. If multiple timeservers are used, the list must be surrounded by quotes.

Net use

Connects a computer to or disconnects a computer from a shared resource, or displays information about computer connections. The command also controls persistent net connections.

net use [*devicename* | *] [*computername**sharename*[*volume*]] [*password* | *]] [/**user**:[*domainname*\]*username*] [[/**delete**] | [/**persistent**:{**yes** | **no**}]]

net use *devicename* [/**home**[*password* | *]] [/**delete**:{**yes** | **no**}]

net use [/**persistent**:{**yes** | **no**}]

PARAMETERS

none	Used without parameters, net use retrieves a list of network connections.
devicename	Assigns a name to connect to the resource or specifies the device to be disconnected. There are two kinds of device names: disk drives (D: through Z:) and printers (LPT1: through LPT3:). Type an asterisk instead of a specific device name to assign the next available device name.
*computername**sharename*	Specifies the name of the server and the shared resource. If *computername* contains blank characters, enclose the entire computer name from the double backslash (\\) to the end of the computer name in quotation marks. The computer name may be from 1 to 15 characters long.
\volume	Specifies a NetWare volume on the server. You must have Client Service for NetWare (Windows 2000 Professional) or Gateway Service for NetWare (Windows 2000 Server) installed and running to connect to NetWare servers.
password	Specifies the password needed to access the shared resource.
*	Produces a prompt for the password. The password is not displayed when you type it at the password prompt.
/user	Specifies a different user name with which the connection is made.
domainname	Specifies another domain. For example, net use *d:\\server\share /user:admin\mariel* connects the user identifier *mariel* as if the connection were made from the *admin* domain. If *domainname* is omitted, the current logged on domain is used.
username	Specifies the user name with which to log on.

/delete	Cancels the specified network connection. If the user specifies the connection with an asterisk, all network connections are canceled.
/home	Connects a user to the home directory.
/persistent	Controls the use of persistent network connections. The default is the setting used last. Deviceless connections are not persistent.
yes	Saves all connections as they are made, and restores them at next logon.
no	Does not save the connection being made or subsequent connections. Existing connections are restored at the next logon. Use the /delete switch to remove persistent connections.

Note

Use the net use command to connect to and disconnect from a network resource, and to view your current connections to network resources. You cannot disconnect from a shared directory if it is used as your current drive or is being used by an active process.

Getting information about a connection

To get information about a connection, you can do either of the following:

- Type *net use devicename* to get information about a specific connection.
- Type *net use* to get a list of all the computer's connections.

Deviceless connections

Deviceless connections are not persistent.

Connecting to NetWare servers

After the Client or Gateway Service for NetWare software is installed and running, you can connect to a NetWare server on a Novell network. You use the same syntax as when connecting to a Windows Networking server, except you must include the volume you want to connect to.

Net user

Adds or modifies user accounts or displays user account information.

net user [*username* [*password* | *] [*options*]] [/**domain**]

net user *username* {*password* | *} /**add** [*options*] [/**domain**]

net user *username* [/**delete**] [/**domain**]

PARAMETERS

none	Used without parameters, net user displays a list of the user accounts on the computer.
username	Specifies the name of the user account to add, delete, modify, or view. The name of the user account can have as many as 20 characters.
password	Assigns or changes a password for the user's account. A password must satisfy the minimum length set with the /minpwlen option of the net accounts command. It can have as many as 127 characters. However, if you're using Windows 2000 on a network that also has computers using Windows 95 or Windows 98, consider using passwords not longer than 14 characters. Windows 95 and Windows 98 support passwords of up to 14 characters. If your password is longer, you may not be able to log on to your network from those computers.
*	Produces a prompt for the password. The password is not displayed when you type it at a password prompt.
/domain	Performs the operation on the primary domain controller of the computer's primary domain. This parameter applies only to Windows 2000 Professional computers that are members of a Windows 2000 Server domain. By default, Windows 2000 Server computers perform operations on the primary domain controller. *Note: This action is taken on the primary domain controller of the computer's primary domain. This may not be the logged-on domain.*
/add	Adds a user account to the user accounts database.
/delete	Removes a user account from the user accounts database.
options	Specifies the remaining net user parameters:
/active:{**no** | **yes**}	Enables or disables the user account. If the user account is not active, the user cannot access resources on the computer. The default is yes (active).
/comment: *"text"*	Provides a descriptive comment about the user's account. This comment can have as many as 48 characters. Enclose the text in quotation marks.
/countrycode:*nnn*	Uses the operating-system Country/Region codes to implement the specified language files for a user's Help and error messages. A value of 0 signifies the default Country /Region code.

/expires:{*date* | **never**}	Causes the user account to expire if *date* is set; does not ever set a time limit on the user account. Expiration dates can be in *mm/dd/yy, dd/mm/yy,* or *mmm,dd,yy* format, depending on the Country/Region code. Note that the account expires at the beginning of the date specified. Months can be a number, spelled out, or abbreviated with three letters. Years can be two or four numbers. Use commas or slashes to separate parts of the date (no spaces). If *yy* is omitted, the next occurrence of the date (according to your computer's date and time) is assumed. For example, the following *date* entries are equivalent if entered between Jan. 10, 1994, and Jan. 8, 1995: jan,9 1/9/95 january,9,1995 1/9
/fullname: *"name"*	Specifies a user's full name rather than a user name. Enclose the name in quotation marks.
/homedir:*path*	Sets the path for the user's home directory. The path must exist.
/passwordchg:{**yes** | **no**}	Specifies whether users can change their own password. The default is **yes**.
/passwordreq:{**yes** | **no**}	Specifies whether a user account must have a password. The default is **yes**.
/profilepath:[*path*]	Sets a path for the user's logon profile. This path points to a registry profile.
/scriptpath:path	Sets a path for the user's logon script. The *path* value cannot be an absolute path; *path* is relative to *%systemroot%\System32\Repl\Import\Scripts.*
/times:{*times* | **all**}	Specifies the times the user is allowed to use the computer. The *times* value is expressed as *day*[*-day*][,*day*[*-day*]], *time*[*-time*][,*time*[*-time*]], limited to 1-hour time increments. Days can be spelled out or abbreviated (M,T,W,Th,F,Sa,Su). Hours can be 12- or 24-hour notation. For 12-hour notation, use AM, PM, or A.M., P.M. The value all means a user can always log on. A null value (blank) means a user can never log on. Separate day and time with commas, and units of day and time with semicolons (for example, M,4AM-5PM;T,1PM-3PM). Do not use spaces when designating times.
/usercomment:*"text"*	Specifies that an administrator add or change the "User comment" for the account. Enclose the text in quotation marks.
/workstations:{*computer name*[,...] | *}	Lists as many as eight workstations from which a user can log on to the network. Separate multiple entries in the list with commas. If /workstations has no list, or if the list is *, the user can log on from any computer.

Note This command can also be typed net users.

Use the net user command to create and control user accounts for users in a domain. User account information is stored in the user accounts database.

When you type the net user command at a computer running Windows 2000 Server, changes to the user accounts database automatically occur on the primary domain controller and then are replicated to backup domain controllers. This applies only to Windows 2000 Server domains.

Net view

Displays a list of domains, a list of computers, or the resources being shared by the specified computer.

net view [*computername* | /**domain**[:*domainname*]]

net view /**network:nw** [*computername*]

PARAMETERS

none	Used without parameters, net view displays a list of computers in your current domain.
computername	Specifies the computer whose shared resources you want to view.
/domain[:*domainname*]	Specifies the domain for which you want to view the available computers. If *domainname* is omitted, displays all domains in the network.
/network:nw	Displays all available servers on a NetWare network. If a computer name is specified, the resources available on that computer in the NetWare network are displayed. Other networks that are added to the system can also be specified with this switch.

Note Use the net view command to display a list of computers. The display is similar to the following:

```
Server Name              Remark
---------------------------------------------------
\\Production             Production file server
\\Print1                 Printer room, first floor
\\Print2                 Printer room, second floor
```

NetSh

The NetShell utility (netsh) is a command-line, scripting interface for configuring and monitoring Windows 2000. The configuration tool provides an interactive shell interface to the user. The front end is the command shell that accepts your commands, and the back end is a helper that corresponds to a system component or utility. A helper is a Dynamic Link Library file (.dll) that extends the functionality of netsh. A helper provides configuration and/or monitoring support for one or more services, utilities, or protocols, but helpers can also be used to extend other helpers. The command shell directs the command to the appropriate helper, and the helper carries out the command.

The netsh command allows you to run the NetShell utility to display or modify the configuration of a currently running computer. It also provides a scripting feature that you can use to run a collection of commands in batch mode against a specified computer.

Contexts

The command shell provides for *contexts,* which are groupings of netsh commands for specific networking components. A context is identified by a string that is appended to commands. Commands entered in a given context are passed to an associated helper. The contexts available depend on the Windows 2000 components installed. For example, typing *routing* at the netsh command changes to the routing context. Typing *ras* at the netsh command changes to the *ras* (remote access portion of the Routing and Remote Access service) context.

Subcontexts may exist within each context. For example, within the routing context, you can change to the *ip* and *ipx* subcontexts.

netsh [**-r** *RemoteComputer*] [**-a** *AliasFile*] [**-c** *Context*] [**Command** | **-f** *ScriptFile*]

To display a list of subcontexts and commands that can be used in a context, at the netsh prompt, type the context name, followed by a space and ?. For example, to display a list of subcontexts and commands that can be used in the *routing* context, at the netsh prompt, type the following: *netsh>routing ?*

Netsh Commands

As well as the context commands shown above, the additional commands listed in Table E.1 can be used with Netsh. Optional parameters are shown in brackets ([ ]). Alternative entries are shown with a pipe (|) between them.

TABLE E.1 *Additional Netsh Commands*

Command	Result
?	Displays help.
abort	Discards any changes made in offline mode. No effect in online mode.
add helper *DLL-name*	Installs the helper DLL in netsh.
alias [*alias-name*] [*string1*] [*string2 ...*]	If alias, lists all aliases. If alias *alias-name*, displays the equivalent string. If alias *alias-name string1 string2 ...*, sets alias-name to the specified strings.
bye	Exits the program.
commit	Commits any changes made in the offline mode to the router. No effect in the online mode.
delete helper *DLL-name*	Removes the helper DLL from netsh.
dump *-file-name*	Dumps or appends configuration to a text file.
exec *Script-file-name*	Loads the script file and executes commands from it.
exit	Exits the program.
h	Displays help.
help	Displays help.
offline	Sets the current mode to offline. Any changes made in this mode will be saved, but require a commit or online command to be set in the router.
online	Sets the current mode to online. Any changes in this mode will be immediately reflected in the router.
popd	Pops a context from the stack.
pushd	Pushes current context onto the stack.
quit	Exits the program.
set mode [mode =] online | offline	Sets the current mode to online or offline.
show alias | helper | mode	If **show alias**, lists all defined aliases. If **show helper**, lists all top-level helpers. If **show mode**, shows the current mode.
unalias *alias-name*	Deletes the specified alias.

Netstat

Displays protocol statistics and current TCP/IP network connections. This command is available only if the TCP/IP protocol has been installed.

netstat [**-a**] [**-e**] [**-n**] [**-s**] [**-p** *protocol*] [**-r**] [*interval*]

PARAMETERS

-a	Displays all connections and listening ports. Server connections are normally not shown.
-e	Displays Ethernet statistics. This may be combined with the **-s** option.
-n	Displays addresses and port numbers in numerical form (rather than attempting name look-ups).
-s	Displays per-protocol statistics. By default, statistics are shown for TCP, UDP, ICMP, and IP. The -p option can be used to specify a subset of the default.
-p *protocol*	Shows connections for the protocol specified by *protocol*; *protocol* can be tcp or udp. If used with the -s option to display per-protocol statistics, *protocol* can be tcp, udp, icmp, or ip.
-r	Displays the contents of the routing table.
interval	Redisplays selected statistics, pausing *interval* seconds between each display. Press CTRL+B to stop redisplaying statistics. If this parameter is omitted, netstat prints the current configuration information once.

Netstat Notes

The **Netstat** utility provides statistics on the following network components:

- **Foreign Address** – The IP address and port number of the remote computer to which the socket is connected. The name corresponding to the IP address is shown instead of the number if the Hostsfile contains an entry for the IP address. In cases where the port is not yet established, the port number is shown as an asterisk (*).
- **Local Address** – The IP address of the local computer, and the port number the connection is using. The name corresponding to the IP address is shown instead of the number if the Hostsfile contains an entry for the IP address. In cases where the port is not yet established, the port number is shown as an asterisk (*).
- **Proto** – The name of the protocol used by the connection.
- **(state)** – Indicates the state of TCP connections only. The possible states are as follows:
- CLOSED
- FIN_WAIT_2

- SYN_RECEIVED
- CLOSE_WAIT
- LAST_ACK
- SYN_SEND
- ESTABLISHED
- LISTEN
- TIMED_WAIT
- FIN_WAIT_1

Nslookup

This diagnostic tool displays information from DNS name servers. Before using this tool, you should be familiar with how DNS works. Nslookup is available only if the TCP/IP protocol has been installed.

Modes

Nslookup has two modes: interactive and noninteractive.

If you need to look up only a single piece of data, use noninteractive mode. For the first argument, type the name or IP address of the computer to be looked up. For the second argument, type the name or IP address of a DNS name server. If you omit the second argument, the default DNS name server is used.

If you need to look up more than one piece of data, you can use interactive mode. Type a hyphen (-) for the first argument and the name or IP address of a DNS name server for the second argument. Or, omit both arguments and the default DNS name server is used.

nslookup [-*option* ...] [*computer-to-find* | - [*server*]]

PARAMETERS

-*option* ...	Specifies one or more nslookup commands as a command-line option. For a list of commands, see "Nslookup Subcommands" in this appendix. Each option consists of a hyphen (-) followed immediately by the command name and, in some cases, an equal sign (=) and then a value. For example, to change the default query type to host (computer) information and the initial time-out to 10 seconds, you would type: **nslookup -querytype**=*hinfo* **-timeout**=*10* The command line length must be less than 256 characters.

computer-to-find	Looks up information for *computer-to-find* using the current default server or using *server* if specified. If *computer-to-find* is an IP address and the query type is A or PTR, the name of the computer is returned. If *computer-to-find* is a name and does not have a trailing period, the default DNS domain name is appended to the name. This behavior depends on the state of the set options: domains, srchlist, defname, and search. To look up a computer not in the current DNS domain, append a period to the name. If you type a hyphen (-) instead of *computer-to-find*, the command prompt changes to nslookup interactive mode.
server	Specifies to use this server as the DNS name server. If you omit *server*, the default DNS name server is used.

Note

Interactive commands

1. To interrupt interactive commands at any time, type CTRL+B.
2. To exit, type *exit*.
3. The command line length must be less than 256 characters.
4. To treat a built-in command as a computer name, precede it with the escape character (\).
5. An unrecognized command is interpreted as a computer name.

Diagnostics

If the lookup request fails, an error message prints. Possible errors include the following:

```
* Timed out
```

The server did not respond to a request after a certain amount of time (changed with set timeout=value) and a certain number of retries (changed with set retry=value).

```
* No response from server
```

No DNS name server is running on the server computer.

```
* No records
```

The DNS name server does not have resource records of the current query type for the computer, although the computer name is valid. The query type is specified with the set querytypc command.

```
* Nonexistent domain
```

The computer or DNS domain name does not exist.

```
* Connection refused
```

-or-

```
Network is unreachable
```

The connection to the DNS name server or finger server could not be made. This error commonly occurs with ls and finger requests.

```
* Server failure
```

The DNS name server found an internal inconsistency in its database and could not return a valid answer.

```
* Refused
```

The DNS name server refused to service the request.

```
* Format error
```

The DNS name server found that the request packet was not in the proper format. It may indicate an error in nslookup.

References

For in-depth coverage of nslookup, see *DNS* and *BIND* by Paul Albitz and Cricket Liu, published by O'Reilly and Associates.

Nslookup Subcommands

- **Nslookup: help**

Displays a brief summary of nslookup subcommands. The ? is a synonym for the help command.

help | **?**

- **Nslookup: exit**

Exits **nslookup**.

exit

- **Nslookup: finger**

Connects with the finger server on the current computer. The current computer is defined when a previous lookup for a computer was successful and returned address information. See the set querytype=A command in the Related Topics list.

finger [*username*] [> *filename*] | [>> *filename*]

PARAMETERS

username	Specifies the name of the user to look up.
filename	Specifies a file name in which to save the output. You can use the greater than (>) and double greater than (>>) characters to redirect the output in the usual manner.

• Nslookup: ls

Lists information for a DNS domain. The default output contains computer names and their IP addresses. When output is directed to a file, hash marks are printed for every 50 records received from the server.

ls [*option*] *dnsdomain* [> *filename*] | [>> *filename*]

PARAMETERS

option	
-t *querytype*	Lists all records of the specified type. For a description of *querytype*, see the set querytype topic.
-a	Lists aliases of computers in the DNS domain. This parameter is a synonym for -t CNAME.
-d	Lists all records for the DNS domain. This parameter is a synonym for -t ANY.
-h	Lists CPU and operating system information for the DNS domain. This parameter is a synonym for -t HINFO.
-s	Lists well-known services of computers in the DNS domain. This parameter is a synonym for -t WKS.
dnsdomain	Specifies the DNS domain for which you want information.
filename	Specifies a file name in which to save the output. You can use the greater-than (>) and double greater-than (>>) characters to redirect the output in the usual manner.

• Nslookup: lserver

Changes the default server to the specified DNS domain. The lserver command uses the initial server to look up the information about the specified DNS domain. This is in contrast to the server command, which uses the current default server.

lserver *dnsdomain*

PARAMETER

dnsdomain	Specifies the new DNS domain for the default server.

• Nslookup: root

Changes the default server to the server for the root of the DNS domain name space. Currently, the computer ns.nic.ddn.mil is used. This command is a synonym for lserver ns.nic.ddn.mil. You can change the name of the root server with the set root command.

root

• Nslookup: server

Changes the default server to the specified DNS domain. The server command uses the current default server to look up the information about the specified DNS domain. This is in contrast to the lserver command, which uses the initial server.

dnsdomain

PARAMETER

dnsdomain	Specifies the new DNS domain for the default server.

• Nslookup: set

Changes configuration settings that affect how lookups function.

set *keyword*[=*value*]

PARAMETER

keyword	The keywords are listed under individual Help topics. See set *keyword*. Use set all to see a listing of the current settings.

• Nslookup: set all

Prints the current values of the configuration settings. Also prints information about the default server and computer (host).

set all

• Nslookup: set cl[ass]

Changes the query class. The class specifies the protocol group of the information.

set cl[**ass**]=*value*

Default = **IN**

PARAMETERS

value

IN	Specifies the Internet class.
CHAOS	Specifies the Chaos class.
HESIOD	Specifies the MIT Athena Hesiod class.
ANY	Specifies the any of the previously listed wildcards ().

● Nslookup: set [no]deb[ug]

Turns debugging mode on or off. With debugging on, more information is printed about the packet sent to the server and the resulting answer.

set [no]deb[ug]

Default = **nodebug**

● Nslookup: set [no]d2

Turns exhaustive debugging mode on or off. All fields of every packet are printed.

set [no]d2

Default = **nod2**

● Nslookup: set [no]def[name]

Appends the default DNS domain name to a single component lookup request. A single component is a component that contains no periods.

set [no]def[name]

Default = **defname**

● Nslookup: set do[main]

Changes the default DNS domain to the name specified. The default DNS domain name is appended to a lookup request depending on the state of the defname and search options. The DNS domain search list contains the parents of the default DNS domain if it has at least two components in its name. For example, if the default DNS domain is *mfg.widgets.com,* the search list is named both *mfg.widgets.com* and *widgets.com*. Use the set srchlist command to specify a different list. Use the set all command to display the list.

set do[main]=*name*

Default = value from hostname

PARAMETER

name	Specifies a new name for the default DNS domain.

- **Nslookup: set [no]ig[nore]**

Ignores packet truncation errors.

set [no]ig[nore]

Default = **noignore**

- **Nslookup: set po[rt]**

Changes the default TCP/UDP DNS name server port to the value specified.

set po[rt]=*value*

Default = 53

PARAMETER

value	Specifies the new value for the default TCP/UDP DNS name server port.

- **Nslookup: set q[uerytype]**

Changes the type of information query. More information about types can be found in Request For Comment (RFC) 1035. The set type command is a synonym for set querytype

set q[uerytype]=*value*

Default = A

PARAMETERS

value

A	Computer's IP address.
ANY	All types of data.
CNAME	Canonical name for an alias.
GID	Group identifier of a group name.
HINFO	Computer's CPU and operating system type.
MB	Mailbox domain name.
MG	Mail group member.
MINFO	Mailbox or mail list information.
MR	Mail rename domain name.
MX	Mail exchanger.
NS	DNS name server for the named zone.
PTR	Computer name if the query is an IP address; otherwise, is the pointer to other information.
SOA	DNS domain's start-of-authority record.

TXT	Text information.
UID	User identifier.
UINFO	User information.
WKS	Well-known service description.

• Nslookup: set [no]rec[urse]

Tells the DNS name server to query other servers if it does not have the information.

set [no]rec[urse]

Default = **recurse**

• Nslookup: set ret[ry]

Sets the number of retries. When a reply to a request is not received within a certain amount of time (changed with set time-out), the time-out period is doubled and the request is resent. The retry value controls how many times a request is resent before giving up.

set ret[ry]=*number*

Default = 4

PARAMETER

number	Specifies the new value for the number of retries.

• Nslookup: set ro[ot]

Changes the name of the root server. This affects the root command.

set ro[**ot**]=*computerr*

Default = ns.nic.ddn.mil

PARAMETER

computer	Specifies the new name for the root server.

• Nslookup: set [no]sea[rch]

If set and the lookup request contains at least one period but does not end with a trailing period, append the DNS domain names in the DNS domain search list to the request until an answer is received.

set [no]sea[rch]

Default = **search**

- **Nslookup: set srchl[ist]**

Changes the default DNS domain name and search list. You can specify a maximum of six names separated by slashes (/). This command overrides the default DNS domain name and search list of the set domain command. Use the set all command to display the list.

Set srchl[ist] *name1/name2/...*

Default = value based on hostname

PARAMETER

name1/ name2/...	Specifies new names for the default DNS domain and search list. For example, the following code sets the DNS domain to *mfg.widgets.com* and the search list to the three names: set srchlist=mfg.widgets.com/mrp2.widgets.com/widgets.com

- **Nslookup: set ti[meout]**

Changes the initial number of seconds to wait for a reply to a request. When a reply to a request is not received within this time period, the time-out is doubled and the request is resent. The number of retries is controlled with the set retry option.

set ti[meout]=*number*

Default = 5

PARAMETER

number	Specifies the new value for the number of seconds to wait for a reply.

- **Nslookup: set ty[pe]**

Changes the type of information query. More information about types can be found in Request For Comment (RFC) 1035. The set type command is a synonym for set querytype.

set ty[pe]=*value*

Default = A

- **Nslookup: set [no]v[c]**

Indicates to always use a virtual circuit when sending requests to the server.

set [no]v[c]

Default = **novc**

- **Nslookup: view**

Sorts and lists the output of previous ls command or commands.

view *filename*

PARAMETER

filename	Specifies the name of the file containing output from the previous ls command or commands.

Pathping

A route tracing tool that combines features of the ping and tracert commands with additional information that neither of those commands provides. The pathping command sends packets to each router on the way to a final destination over a period of time, and then computes results based on the packets returned from each hop. Since pathping shows the degree of packet loss at any given router or link, you can determine which routers or links might be causing network problems.

pathping [**-n**] [**-h** *maximum_hops*] [**-g** *host-list*] [**-p** *period*] [**-q** *num_queries* [**-w** *timeout*] [**-T**] [**-R**] *target_name*

PARAMETERS

-n	Does not resolve addresses to host names.
-h *maximum_hops*	Specifies maximum number of hops to search for the target. Default is 30 hops.
-g *host-list*	Allows consecutive computers to be separated by intermediate gateways (loose source route) along *host-list*.
-p *period*	Specifies number of milliseconds to wait between consecutive pings. Default is 250 milliseconds (1/4 second).
-q *num_queries*	Specifies number of queries to each computer along the route. Default is 100.
-w *timeout*	Specifies number of milliseconds to wait for each reply. Default is 3000 milliseconds (3 seconds).
-T	Attaches a layer-2 priority tag (for example, 802.1p) to the ping packets that it sends to each of the network devices along the route. This helps identify network devices that do not have layer-2 priority configured. This parameter must be capitalized.

-R	Checks to see if each network device along the route supports the Resource Reservation Setup Protocol (RSVP), which allows the host computer to reserve a certain amount of bandwidth for a data stream. This parameter must be capitalized.
target_name	Specifies the destination endpoint, identified either by IP address or host name.

Note The pathping command performs the equivalent of a traceroute to identify which routers are on the path. It then sends pings periodically to all of the routers over a given time period and computes statistics based on the number returned from each.

To avoid congestion, pings should be sent at a sufficiently slow interval.

To minimize the effects of burst losses, do not send pings too close together.

-p period parameter

Pings are sent to each intermediate hop, one at a time. Therefore, the interval between two pings sent to the same hop is (*period*) x (number of hops).

-w timeout parameter

Multiple pings can be done in parallel, so the amount of time specified in the timeout parameter is not bounded by the amount of time specified for the period parameter for waiting between pings.

-T parameter

Enabling layer-2 priority on the host computer allows packets to be sent with a layer-2 priority tag, which can be used by layer-2 devices to assign a priority to the packet. Legacy devices that do not understand layer-2 priority will toss tagged packets, since they will appear as malformed packets. Therefore, a switch that connects to a legacy network should be configured to strip the tag before forwarding the packets. This option helps identify the network elements that are tossing the tagged packets.

The pathping command is case-sensitive. This parameter must be capitalized.

-R parameter

An RSVP reservation message for a nonexistent session is sent to each network device along the route. If the device is not configured to support RSVP, it returns an Internet Control Message Protocol (ICMP) unreachable message. If it is configured to do RSVP, it returns a Reservation Error. Some devices may not return either of these messages. If this happens, pathping returns a time-out message.

The pathping command is case-sensitive. This parameter must be capitalized.

The following example shows output for pathping:

```
D:\>pathping -n msw

Tracing route to msw [7.54.1.196]
over a maximum of 30 hops:
  0  172.16.87.35
  1  172.16.87.218
  2  192.68.52.1
  3  192.68.80.1
  4  7.54.247.14
  5  7.54.1.196

Computing statistics for 125 seconds...
            Source to Here   This Node/Link
Hop  RTT    Lost/Sent = Pct  Lost/Sent = Pct  Address
  0                                           172.16.87.35
                                0/ 100 =  0%   |
  1   41ms     0/ 100 =  0%     0/ 100 =  0%  172.16.87.218
                               13/ 100 = 13%   |
  2   22ms    16/ 100 = 16%     3/ 100 =  3%  192.68.52.1
                                0/ 100 =  0%   |
  3   24ms    13/ 100 = 13%     0/ 100 =  0%  192.68.80.1
                                0/ 100 =  0%   |
  4   21ms    14/ 100 = 14%     1/ 100 =  1%  7.54.247.14
                                0/ 100 =  0%   |
  5   24ms    13/ 100 = 13%     0/ 100 =  0%  7.54.1.196

Trace complete.
```

When pathping is run, the first results list the route. This is the same path that is shown using tracert. Next, pathping displays a busy message for approximately the next minute and a half (the exact time varies by the hop count). During this time, pathping gathers information from all the routers previously listed and from the links between them. At the end of this period, it displays the test results.

In the sample report above, the This Node/Link Lost/Sent = Pct and Address columns show that the link between 172.16.87.218 and 192.68.52.1 is dropping 13 percent of the packets. The routers at hops 2 and 4 also are dropping packets addressed to them, but this loss does not affect their forwarding path.

The loss rates displayed for the links (identified as | in the Address column) indicate link congestion causing the loss of packets being forwarded along the path. The loss rates displayed for routers (identified by their IP addresses) indicate that the CPUs or local packet buffers of those routers might be overloaded.

Ping

Verifies connections to a remote computer or computers. This command is available only if the TCP/IP protocol has been installed.

ping [**-t**] [**-a**] [**-n** *count*] [**-l** *length*] [**-f**] [**-i** *ttl*] [**-v** *tos*] [**-r** *count*] [**-s** *count*] [[**-j** *computer-list*] | [**-k** *computer-list*]] [**-w** *timeout*] *destination-list*

PARAMETERS

-t	Pings the specified computer until interrupted.
-a	Resolves addresses to computer names.
-n *count*	Sends the number of ECHO packets specified by *count*. The default is 4.
-l *length*	Sends ECHO packets containing the amount of data specified by *length*. The default is 32 bytes; the maximum is 65,527.
-f	Sends a Do not Fragment flag in the packet. The packet will not be fragmented by gateways on the route.
-I *ttl*	Sets the Time-to-Live field to the value specified by *ttl*.
-v *tos*	Sets the Type-of-Service field to the value specified by *tos*.
-r *count*	Records the route of the outgoing packet and the returning packet in the Record Route field. A minimum of 1 and a maximum of 9 computers can be specified by *count*.
-s *count*	Specifies the timestamp for the number of hops specified by *count*.
-j *computer-list*	Routes packets by way of the list of computers specified by *computer-list*. Consecutive computers can be separated by intermediate gateways (loose source routed). The maximum number allowed by IP is 9.
-k *computer-list*	Routes packets by way of the list of computers specified by *computer-list*. Consecutive computers cannot be separated by intermediate gateways (strict source routed). The maximum number allowed by IP is 9.
-w *timeout*	Specifies a time-out interval in milliseconds.
destination-list	Specifies the remote computers to ping.

Note

The ping command does the following:

- Verifies connections to one or more remote computers by sending ICMP echo packets to the computer and listening for echo reply packets.
- Waits for up to one second for each packet sent.
- Prints the number of packets transmitted and received.

Each received packet is validated against the transmitted message. By default, four echo packets containing 32 bytes of data (a periodic uppercase sequence of alphabetic characters) are transmitted.

You can use ping to test both the computer name and the IP address of the computer. If the IP address is verified but the computer name is not, you may have a name resolution problem. In this case, be sure that the computer name you are querying is in either the local Hosts file or in the DNS database.

The following example shows output for ping:

```
C:\>ping ds.internic.net
Pinging ds.internic.net [192.20.239.132] with 32 bytes of data:
Reply from 192.20.239.132: bytes=32 time=101ms TTL=243
Reply from 192.20.239.132: bytes=32 time=100ms TTL=243
Reply from 192.20.239.132: bytes=32 time=120ms TTL=243
Reply from 192.20.239.132: bytes=32 time=120ms TTL=243
```

Rcp

Copies files between a Windows 2000 computer and a system running rshd, the remote shell daemon. The rcp command, a connectivity command, can also be used for other transfers to copy files between two computers running rshd when the command is issued from a Windows 2000 computer. The rshd daemon is available on UNIX computers, but not on Windows 2000, so the Windows 2000 computer can only participate as the system from which the commands are issued. The remote computer must also provide the rcp utility by running rshd.

rcp [**-a** | **-b**] [**-h**] [**-r**] *source1 source2 ... sourceN destination*

PARAMETERS

-a	Specifies ASCII transfer mode. This mode converts the carriage return/line feed characters to carriage returns on outgoing files and line feed characters to carriage return/line feed characters for incoming files. This is the default transfer mode.
-b	Specifies binary image transfer mode. No carriage return/line feed conversion is performed.
-h	Transfers source files marked with the hidden attribute on the Windows 2000 computer. Without this option, specifying a hidden file on the rcp command line has the same effect as if the file did not exist.
-r	Recursively copies the contents of all subdirectories of the source to the destination. Both the *source* and *destination* must be directories, although using **-r** works even if the source is not a directory. There just will be no recursion.

source and *destination*	Must be of the form [*computer*[.*user*]:]*filename*. If the [*computer*[.*user*]:] portion is omitted, the computer is assumed to be the local computer. If the [.*user*] portion is omitted, the currently logged on Windows 2000 user name is used. If a fully qualified computer name is used, which contains the period (.) separators, then the [.*user*] must be included. Otherwise, the last part of the computer name will be interpreted as the user name. If multiple source files are specified, the *destination* must be a directory. If the file name does not begin with a forward slash (/) for UNIX or a backward slash (\) for Windows 2000 systems, it is assumed to be relative to the current working directory. On Windows 2000, this is the directory from which the command is issued. On the remote system, it is the logon directory for the remote user. A period (.) means the current directory. Use the escape characters (\ , ", or ') in remote paths to use wildcard characters on the remote computer.

Rexec

Runs commands on remote computers running the REXEC service. The rexec command authenticates the user name on the remote computer before executing the specified command, and is available only if the TCP/IP protocol has been installed.

rexec *computer* [**-l** *username*] [**-n**] *command*

PARAMETERS

computer	Specifies the remote computer on which to run *command*.
-l *username*	Specifies the user name on the remote computer.
-n	Redirects the input of rexec to NULL.
command	Specifies the command to run.

Note Standard operation

The **rexec** command prompts the user for a password and authenticates the given password on the remote computer. If the authentication succeeds, the command is executed.

The **rexec** command copies standard input to the remote command, standard output of the remote *command* to its standard output, and the standard error of the remote command to its standard error. The **rexec** normally terminates when the remote command does.

Using redirection symbols

Use quotation marks around redirection symbols to redirect onto the remote computer. If quotation marks are not used, redirection occurs on the local computer. For example, the following command appends the remote file *remotefile* to the local file *localfile*:

```
rexec othercomputer cat remotefile >> localfile
```

The following command appends the remote file *remotefile* to the remote file *otherremotefile*:

```
rexec othercomputer cat remotefile ">>" otherremotefile
```

Using interactive commands

You cannot run most interactive commands. For example, **vi** or **emacs** cannot be run using **rexec**. Use **telnet** instead.

Route

Manipulates network routing tables. This command is available only if the TCP/IP protocol has been installed.

route [-f] [**-p**] [*command* [*destination*] [**mask** *subnetmask*] [*gateway*] [**metric** *costmetric*]]

PARAMETERS

-f	Clears the routing tables of all gateway entries. If this is used in conjunction with one of the commands, the tables are cleared prior to running the command.
-p	When used with the add command, makes a route persistent across boots of the system. By default, routes are not preserved when the system is restarted. When used with the print command, displays the list of registered persistent routes. Ignored for all other commands, which always affect the appropriate persistent routes.
command	Specifies one of the following commands: Print: Prints a route Add: Adds a route Delete: Deletes a route Change: Modifies an existing route

destination	Specifies the computer to send command.
mask *subnetmask*	Specifies a subnet mask to be associated with this route entry. If not specified, 255.255.255.255 is used.
gateway	Specifies gateway. All symbolic names used for destination or gateway are referenced in both the network database file called Networks, and the computer name database file called *Hosts*. If the command is print or delete, wildcards may be used for the destination and gateway, or the gateway argument may be omitted.
metric *costmetric*	Assigns an integer cost metric (ranging from 1 to 9999) to be used in calculating the fastest, most reliable, and/or least expensive routes.

Rsh

Runs commands on remote computers running the RSH service. This command is available only if the TCP/IP protocol has been installed.

rsh *computer* [**-l** *username*] [**-n**] *command*

PARAMETERS

computer	Specifies the remote computer on which to run *command*.
-l *username*	Specifies the user name to use on the remote computer. If omitted, the logged on user name is used.
-n	Redirects the input of rsh to NULL.
command	Specifies the command to run.

Note

Standard operation

The **rsh** command copies standard input to the remote *command*, standard output of the remote *command* to its standard output, and the standard error of the remote *command* to its standard error. **Rsh** normally terminates when the remote command does.

Using redirection symbols

Use quotation marks around redirection symbols to redirect onto the remote computer. If quotation marks are not used, redirection occurs on the local computer. For example, the following command appends the remote file *remotefile* to the local file *localfile*:

```
rsh othercomputer cat remotefile >> localfile
```

The following command appends the remote file *remotefile* to the remote file *otherremotefile*:

```
rsh othercomputer cat remotefile ">>" otherremotefile
```

Using rsh

When using a computer running Windows 2000 Server, the primary domain controller for the logged on domain must be available to verify the user name or the rsh command will fail.

The .rhosts file

The *.rhosts* file generally permits network access rights on UNIX systems. The *.rhosts* file lists computer names and associated logon names that have access to remote computers. When issuing **rcp**, **rexec**, or **rsh** commands to a remote system with a properly configured *.rhosts* file, you do not need to provide logon and password information for the remote computer.

The *.rhosts* file is a text file in which each line is an entry. An entry consists of the local computer name, the local user name, and any comments about the entry. Each entry is separated by a tab or space, and comments begin with a hash mark (#), for example:

```
computer5marie#This computer is in room 31A
```

The *.rhosts* file must be in the user's home directory on the remote computer. For further information about a remote computer's specific implementation of the *.rhosts* file, see the remote system's documentation.

Tftp

Transfers files to and from a remote computer running the TFTP service. This command is available only if the TCP/IP protocol has been installed.

tftp [-i] *computer* [**get** | **put**] *source* [*destination*]

PARAMETERS

-i	Specifies binary image transfer mode (also called octet). In binary image mode, the file is moved literally, byte by byte. Use this mode when transferring binary files. If -i is omitted, the file is transferred in ASCII mode. This is the default transfer mode. This mode converts the EOL characters to a carriage return for UNIX and a carriage return/line feed for personal computers. This mode should be used when transferring text files. If a file transfer is successful, the data transfer rate is displayed.
computer	Specifies the local or remote computer.

put	Transfers the file *destination* on the local computer to the file *source* on the remote computer.
get	Transfers the file *destination* on the remote computer to the file *source* on the local computer.
	Specify put if transferring file *file-two* on the local computer to file *file-one* on remote computer. Specify get if transferring file *file-two* on the remote computer to file *file-one* on the remote computer.
	Since TFTP does not support user authentication, the user must be logged on, and the files must be writable on the remote computer.
source	Specifies the file to transfer. If the local file is specified as -, the remote file is printed out on *stdout* (if getting), or is read from *stdin* (if putting).
destination	Specifies where to transfer the file. If *destination* is omitted, it is assumed to have the same name as *source*.

Tracert

This diagnostic utility determines the route taken to a destination by sending ICMP echo packets with varying TTL values to the destination. Each router along the path is required to decrement the TTL on a packet by at least 1 before forwarding it, so the TTL is effectively a hop count. When the TTL on a packet reaches 0, the router is supposed to send back an ICMP Time Exceeded message to the source system. Tracert determines the route by sending the first echo packet with a TTL of 1 and incrementing the TTL by 1 on each subsequent transmission until the target responds or the maximum TTL is reached. The route is determined by examining the ICMP Time Exceeded messages sent back by intermediate routers. However, some routers silently drop packets with expired TTL values and are invisible to tracert.

tracert [**-d**] [**-h** *maximum_hops*] [**-j** *computer-list*] [**-w** *timeout*] *target_name*

PARAMETERS

-d	Specifies not to resolve addresses to computer names.
-h *maximum_hops*	Specifies maximum number of hops to search for target.
-j *computer-list*	Specifies loose source route along *computer-list*.
-w *timeout*	Waits the number of milliseconds specified by *timeout* for each reply.
target_name	Name of the target computer.

INDEX

A

B

E

F